DATE DUE

A FINE WILL BE CHARGED
FOR EACH OVERDUE BOOK

Constantine and the Bishops

Ancient Society and History

Constantine

H. A. DRAKE

and the Bishops
The Politics
of Intolerance

The Johns Hopkins University Press
Baltimore and London

© 2000 The Johns Hopkins University Press
All rights reserved. Published 2000
Printed in the United States of America on acid-free paper
9 8 7 6 5 4 3 2 1

The Johns Hopkins University Press
2715 North Charles Street
Baltimore, Maryland 21218-4363
www.press.jhu.edu

Frontispiece: Constantine sits among bishops at the Council of Nicaea in this sixteenth-century fresco from the refectory of the Lavra monastery on Mount Athos (photothèque G. Millet, EPHE Paris).

Library of Congress Cataloging-in-Publication Data will be found at the end of this book.

A catalog record for this book is available from the British Library.

ISBN 0-8018-6218-3

For Susan and Kate

It is a bitter thought, how different a thing the Christianity of the world might have been, if the Christian faith had been adopted as the religion of the empire under the auspices of Marcus Aurelius instead of those of Constantine.

John Stuart Mill, *On Liberty* (1859)

Revolutionary upheavals may change how the world looks but seldom change the way the world works.

Richard M. Nixon, *Seize the Moment* (1992)

Contents

Contents

Illustrations

Preface

This is a book about politics. It seeks to bring into sharp relief two aspects of the fourth century which have been obscured by other concerns. The first is the extraordinary political skills exhibited by Constantine the Great (306–337), an emperor who has been venerated as an instrument of God and dismissed as a credulous buffoon, but whose greatest achievement—his ability to create a stable consensus of Christians and pagans in favor of a religiously neutral public space—has been buried by time. The second is a struggle within Christian ranks over the propriety of using the coercive powers of the state in support of their beliefs. The records of this struggle have long been known, but since they have little to say about the more celebrated struggles with heresy and paganism, their importance has rarely been grasped.

Much of my subject is one that, by longstanding scholarly convention, has been declared unsuitable for political inquiry. Constantine's conversion to the unconventional religion of Christianity, traditionally as the result of a miraculous vision in the year 312, has been a source of endless fascination, for believers and skeptics alike. But it has been a hindrance to understanding one of the most important transfers of power in Western history. Constantine's conversion is merely one stage in a process whereby members of a previously scorned and outcast faith moved into the centers of power and, in the course of the fourth century, undertook to use the coercive force of the state to compel attachment to their unique set of beliefs. The train of events culminating in that militant posture should be of consuming interest to students of politics and political behavior, as well as to all persons concerned with moderating those violent tempers that are ever present in our midst.

That it has not been so is due in large part to the credence scholars continue to place in the notion that religious coercion is somehow unique to Christian circumstances, or at any rate a natural and inevitable result of Christianity's inherent "intolerance." But while "intolerance" may be a theological problem, "coercion" is a political one. If there has been one paramount error in the study of Christianity in the fourth century, that error has been to use theological tools to understand political problems. The result is serious misdiagnosis of the causes, origins, and nature of Christian coercion. The thesis of this book is simply that the explanation lies in social processes, not theology.

It is because those scholars who have been most vociferous in asserting Constantine's political ambitions have been the same ones to question his religious sincerity that others with a more balanced view have formed such a low opinion of political approaches to this reign. The taboo is well intentioned but ultimately misfounded. What both sides of this debate have failed to realize is that politics as a distinct field of inquiry is the study of a process; it has nothing to say about a given individual's religious sincerity or lack of same. Politics is, quite simply, the art of getting things done. It is the art of winning agreement, of mobilizing support, of gaining consensus. At some level, everything has a political dimension; every act of decision making requires political skills. Theology, like all ideas, certainly can be studied in a domain of its own. But once an idea, any idea, is put into practice, it falls subject to the rules of politics.

Practical people—politicians and journalists—grasp this difference more readily than those of us in the theory-driven world of academia. A veteran observer of California politics summarized the difference succinctly when he wrote, "Good ideas are a dime a dozen. . . . What really matters in Sacramento are 54 votes in the Assembly, plus another 27 in the Senate and the governor's signature."[1] Or, as another writer put it, without command of the political process, "you don't have a policy—you have a hypothesis."[2]

But can insights gained from observation of political bodies apply to the decision-making process of religious bodies? Of course. Theoretically, Christians believe that the Holy Spirit guides their leaders to decisions, in accordance with Jesus' promise "Where two or three are gathered in my name, there am I in the midst of them."[3] But in practice, the Spirit must work through Edward Gibbon's "weak and degenerate race of beings," with its "inevitable mixture of error and corruption."[4] The councils of the early church may have been subject to the Spirit in their content, but as blasphemous as it may sound, in getting things done even the Spirit had to bow to the rules of politics. In practice, church councils are as subject as any other human gathering to dissention, to compromise, to threat, to petty bickering—hence the truth behind the old saw "Whenever there is a council of the church, there is rejoicing in Hell." The motives and goals of saints and sinners may vary widely, but to convince or lead others, they both must use the political process—a process with its own rules, its own dynamics, its own universals.

Some words of caution, and self-defense. Much of what has become the apparatus of classical scholarship—prosopography, inscriptions, close analysis of texts for chronological clues—is prominent in these pages only by its absence. I do not wish to seem indifferent to those painstaking labors that have provided a much surer footing for the events of this period, but it would be misleading to pretend that they are my chief interest here. Rather, this book is, thus, quite deliberately a sketch. It participates in the vices of such works, but I hope it will also offer some of the virtues—chief among which is that of keeping the important questions in the foreground. This task is far more important than the resolution of questions that by their nature defy scientific certitude. I do not expect to persuade many readers to discard an interpretation of this period which has worn so comfortably for so many years. If the sole effect of this book is to prompt more skilled and learned specialists to enter the field, or to provoke the insight that is often achieved by looking at familiar material from an unusual perspective, I will count myself satisfied.

There are fingerprints all over this book. Skilled detectives will have no difficulty discerning the hand of Peter Brown; indeed, any topic of late antiquity which has not been touched by this prodigious scholar would have to be exceptional. Mine being an unusual approach for an ancient historian, I have also had to look in fields usually not worked by toilers in my trade. Informed readers will recognize my debt to several individuals whom I have met only through their writings. Hedrick Smith's *The Power Game: How Washington Works* (1988) is a readable and informative account of decision making in the nation's capital which allowed me to enter vicariously the world of practical politics. Less obvious will be my debt to a classic of policy study, Graham Allison's *Essence of Decision: Explaining the Cuban Missile Crisis* (1971). Initially, I was inspired to look at the Age of Constantine through the same series of "cuts" which Allison had used to study that famous Cold War confrontation. Ultimately, I was forced to concede that the records for this type of analysis do not exist for my period; but Allison's goal of creating a dialogue between policymakers and historians continued to inspire my efforts, and I like to think that in some way his spirit hovers over the results. Rodney Stark's *Rise of Christianity* (1996) did not appear until this book was already well in hand, but his earlier studies helped me to frame questions and, even more, convinced me I was on a useful track.

This book also reflects the character of the two research institutes where it took shape. The core of Chapter 9 is based on work undertaken when I held a National Endowment for the Humanities Fellowship at the Institute for Advanced Study in Princeton in 1976–77, at a time when I envisioned a much different book, one that would be primarily legal and administrative in content. The faculty, staff, and visiting scholars of that year are largely to blame for the very different turn this book has taken, for there is nothing quite so stimulating, or so seductive, as the combination of leisure, resources, and intellectual stimulation provided by that unique institution. Fifteen years later, in 1991–92, this book took its present shape in the equally congenial setting of the Annenberg Research Institute in Philadelphia, where a lively and heterodox seminar encouraged me to explore theoretical and interdisciplinary aspects of my topic. I will never be able fully to express my gratitude and appreciation to these two institutions, or to the individuals who made these stays so meaningful.

I am equally grateful to the Senate Research Committee and Inter-disciplinary Humanities Center at my home university, the University of California, Santa Barbara, for providing the ongoing support that was crucial to completion of this project.

The ideas in Chapter 11, which I first expressed at the Annenberg Institute, were developed with the aid of respondents to papers on this topic which I was allowed to deliver at the annual meeting of the American Historical Association's Pacific Coast Branch in 1992, Macquarie University in 1993, and the University of Southern California in 1995. A draft of Chapter 10 was first vetted in the congenial setting of PENATES, the Southern California reading group in late antiquity, in 1997, and a portion of it was read at the annual meeting of the North American Patristics Society in 1998.

Although I alone am responsible for this book's many defects, I can honestly say that it would not have turned out the way it did had I not had the benefit of serving in a department with unique conditions for dialogue between old and new and ancient and modern, and for encouraging risk. Were it not for the kind and cheerful confidence of Jeffrey Burton Russell, this project might have been abandoned long ago. In subtler ways, the book also reflects the influence of Jack Talbott—one of the most original historians I know, and certainly one of the most fun to talk with.

I am deeply grateful to friends and colleagues who read all or part of this manuscript in various stages. Naphtali Lewis was unstinting in his advice and criticism; Brian Warmington was characteristically supportive and challenging; and Guy Stroumsa helped familiarize me with important concepts. David Tipton, Laura Wertheimer, and Elizabeth De Palma Digeser never tired of commenting on successive versions, and Justin Stephens, Jim Emmons, and Mike Proulx all cheerfully took time from their own labors to provide much-needed assistance. I owe a special debt to Neil McLynn for vetting a late draft with an expertise and verve that few could match, and to my editors at the Johns Hopkins University Press, especially Grace Buonocore, for handling an author's lapses and panics with far more care and understanding than the rigors of modern publishing normally allow.

My friend and helpmate Kathleen, who scorns gratuitous acknowledgments, will perhaps allow me to commemorate our thirty years together with these words.

Books, like children, take on lives of their own. It seems fitting, therefore, to dedicate this newest offspring to my two other children, who for so long have had to make room for a jealous and demanding sibling. May its life be as rich, interesting, and full of pleasure for them as theirs have been for me.

PART I

PRELIMINARIES

> Merely to classify governments as monarchies,
> aristocracies, and democracies is, as we all know,
> to omit a tremendous amount of what is
> politically interesting.
> R. E. Dowling (1972)

One

Constantinople, A.D. 335

E arly in November of the year 335, a remarkable meeting took place in Constantinople, the glittering new capital built by Constantine on the shores of the European Bosphorus. There, in the Great Palace, the emperor himself met with a delegation of Christian bishops who were determined to get rid of Athanasius, the fiery young patriarch of Alexandria in Egypt. Athanasius faced serious charges—not only that he had illegally seized the bishopric of one of the empire's largest and most important cities but also that he maintained his position through violence and corruption. In his zeal to eliminate all dissident voices, as his opponents charged, he had beaten and imprisoned rival clergy and desecrated church property. In one incident that would haunt him for decades, opponents claimed Athanasius's goons had thrown over an altar and broken a holy chalice.

Athanasius had made his own plea to the emperor some days earlier. In his eyes, and in those of his followers, it was he who was the injured party. His "crime" was to support the orthodox faith as it had been defined just ten years earlier at the great Council of Nicaea, called by Constantine himself and attended by some three hundred bishops, coming from throughout the empire and even beyond. Athanasius, only a deacon at the time, had been a chief strategist—some said *the*

3

chief strategist—of the movement to condemn as heretical the teachings of an Alexandrian priest named Arius. For this, he believed, he was now being persecuted by Arius's discredited friends and allies, heretics all. Only months earlier, they had succeeded in dragging him from the safety of his Egyptian base to a council at Tyre, on the coast of modern-day Lebanon. Fleeing from there, Athanasius had come to Constantinople to seek sanctuary at the emperor's knees.

Three years after the great council, Athanasius had succeeded to the powerful See of Alexandria, after barely reaching the canonical age of thirty. Passionate, eloquent, and ruthless, he combined the skills of a tough infighter and street politician with an unyielding devotion to Nicene orthodoxy and the Egyptian church. Drawn, like so many of his contemporaries, to the ascetic ideals of the fledgling monastic movement (his name traditionally is associated with the Life of Anthony, the archetypal desert saint, which launched the genre of hagiography), Athanasius early on formed an unshakable bond with these spiritual warriors, whose feats could both inspire and terrify their neighbors. Athanasius would rule the Christians of his native land off and on for almost fifty years, under five very different emperors, and he would fight with all but the most ephemeral of them.

In 335, Constantine was, by the best estimates, about sixty-three years old. Less than two years from his grave, he had entered the thirtieth year of his reign, the longest of any emperor since the forty-five years of Augustus, who had created the imperial system almost four centuries earlier. For twenty-three of those years, according to a standard reckoning, Constantine had ruled as a Christian, the first ever to sit in Augustus's place. Increasingly exasperated by the squabbling he had hoped to bury at Nicaea, Constantine complained to the bishops at Tyre, "Even the barbarians now through me, the true servant of God, know God and have learned to reverence him, . . . [while the bishops] do nothing but that which encourages discord and hatred and, to speak frankly, which leads to the destruction of the human race."[1] The year earlier, 334, he had ordered Athanasius to appear at a similar council scheduled to meet at Caesarea in Palestine, but the bishop had balked at the last moment and failed to appear. This time, Constantine wrote, "Should any one, though I deem it most improbable, venture on this occasion to violate my command, and refuse his attendance, a messenger shall be despatched forthwith to banish that person by virtue of an imperial edict, and to teach him that it does not become him to resist an emperor's decrees when issued in defense of truth."[2]

The Council of Tyre was a tawdry affair, a circus even by the turbulent standards of that era. Athanasius arrived with some fifty Egyptian bishops in his train, all of them prepared to react on cue at the slightest provocation. One of the charges against their bishop had been that he had personally ordered the execution of Arsenius of Hypsele, a bishop of the breakaway Meletian sect. That charge had been withdrawn when Athanasius's agents managed to track down the missing bishop. But there was a further charge—that Athanasius had cut off Arsenius's hand—and grisly evidence had been shown around, a box containing what purported to be the very article. Specialists now believe Athanasius actually disposed of this charge prior to the conference at Tyre, but by the fifth century Christian accounts had moved the exposé to the council, where Athanasius could refute his accusers in spectacular fashion:

> He caused Arsenius to be introduced, having his hands covered by his cloak. Then he again asked them, "Is this the person who has lost a hand?" All were astonished at the unexpectedness of this procedure, except those who knew whence the hand had been cut off; for the rest thought that Arsenius was really deficient of a hand, and expected that the accused would make his defense in some other way. But Athanasius turning back the cloak of Arsenius on one side showed one of the man's hands; again, while some were supposing that the other hand was wanting, permitting them to remain a short time in doubt, afterward he turned back the cloak on the other side and exposed the other hand. Then, addressing himself to those present, he said, "Arsenius, as you see, is found to have two hands: let my accusers show the place whence the third was cut off."[3]

As is often the case in partisan narratives, the function of this change of venue seems to have been to help the reader get past some uncomfortable details by establishing the protagonist's innocence in a dramatically conclusive fashion. Despite this supposed triumph, and over the strenuous objections of the Egyptian delegation, the Council of Tyre proceeded to deputize a commission of inquiry to travel to

Egypt and take depositions about the other accusations. Athanasius was despondent. Convinced that the commission was not friendly to his cause and fearing for his safety, he slipped away from Tyre in a small local craft, eluding harbor patrols that had been posted for just such an eventuality. This was in early September. Athanasius did not resurface for almost two months, by which time he had somehow made his way to Constantinople. There, dressed in suppliant rags to beg relief from his persecutors, he accosted the emperor as he rode in state through the streets. Constantine described the scene in a letter he wrote to the bishops at Tyre:

> As I was going into our eponymous and all-blessed city of Constantinople (as it happened, I was on horseback at the time), suddenly the bishop Athanasius came into the middle of the street with certain others whom he had with him, so unexpectedly as even to give cause for alarm. For as God who sees all is my witness, I neither recognized him nor was I able to tell at first sight who he was, until certain of our companions, when we asked to be informed, as was fitting, reported to us both who he was and the injustice he had suffered.

Athanasius was fortunate to have been recognized, for disrupting imperial processions was a risky gambit. Just one overzealous guard, and the voice of Nicene orthodoxy might have been stilled forever. That it worked indicates Athanasius had been able to coordinate his action with palace insiders sympathetic to his plight—the companions who were able to soothe the alarm raised in the emperor's entourage. Constantine himself was sufficiently moved to call on the bishops to come to Constantinople and give an accounting of themselves. His words are testy:

> I do not know what has been decided amid the tumult and fury of your synod, but it seems somehow the truth has been distorted by a certain turbulent disorder, clearly through that squabbling with your neighbors which you want to prevail, not taking into account what is pleasing to God. But it will be an act of divine Providence both to dissipate the evils of this love of strife that has come into the open and to disclose whether those who met in that place paid any attention to the truth and if you judged the issues without any favor or enmity. Therefore I wish all of you to assemble before

my Piety with all haste, so that you yourselves may present a precise account of your activities.

Shortly thereafter, the other bishops, delegates from the council who, according to the more fanciful accounts, were riding in hot pursuit of their fugitive colleague, themselves arrived with tales of Athanasius's brigandage and the decision of the council to depose him.[4]

Thus had the stage been set for this November meeting in Constantine's chambers. We know little of its proceedings. Decades later, Athanasius claimed that his opponents were so desperate to secure his conviction that they trumped up a charge of meddling with the Alexandrian grain fleet—Constantinople's lifeline. According to one account, the meeting provoked a blistering exchange between emperor and bishop, during which Athanasius forgot both imperial protocol and basic common sense. "Angry as the emperor was, Pope Athanasius spoke painful words to him: 'The Lord will judge between me and you, since you yourself agree with those who calumniate your humble servant.'"[5] We do know the meeting's outcome: following this tirade, Constantine ordered Athanasius to exile at Trier in Gaul, at almost the opposite end of the empire from his Egyptian base. With unusual dispatch, he was bundled aboard a freighter and sailed the very next day. It would be almost three years before he saw Alexandria again.

What makes this meeting remarkable is not the fireworks between emperor and bishop, much less the confrontation that preceded it. Western history is strewn with the debris of such conflict between what we have now come to call church and state, and this was neither the first nor the most significant. What is remarkable about the meeting, ironically, is that it seems so utterly unremarkable to those who speak of it, then or now. Yet for the three previous centuries, the Christian faith had had to contend with a government that was, in the best of times, mildly resentful of its existence. It had come to define itself by the persecutions it periodically suffered and the threat of a new one that always existed. Indeed, within the lifetime of every person at this meeting, Rome had launched the most bitter persecution of all, unprecedented in its severity and duration. Scars from that ordeal were yet visible on some of the petitioners who now were suing the Roman

7

state, in the person of Constantine, to take action against one of their own. The casual acceptance of this dramatic reversal is testimony to the extraordinary impact of this emperor's reign, during which relations between church and state had not only changed from cold to warm but indeed had become intertwined in ways that are not yet fully untangled. Here begins a process that leads to the institution of caesaropapism in the East and, in the West, to a less easy alliance, the traces of which lie but thinly beneath the contours of modern Europe.

The frontispiece to this book provides a clue to the ease with which this transition occurred. It depicts Constantine sitting in the midst of key figures at the first of these councils, which he summoned to meet in Nicaea in 325 and which produced the forerunner of the Christian profession of faith still recited today. The dominating position of this council in Christian thought is one reason why it was so easy for Christian bishops ten years later to turn to the emperor responsible for summoning it and enforcing its decision. This particular rendition dates from the sixteenth century, but its arrangement of this scene can be traced to representations that were being made as early as the eighth century and that continue to be made today. The collection of saints flanking Constantine is not always the same, but the place of honor almost always is assigned to Constantine himself. Just as the protocols established by Constantine set the pattern for future ecumenical councils, so too did this representation become the prototype for depicting emperors in meetings with bishops. The arrangement sometimes varies, with emperors sitting to one side and the bishops another, or emperor and bishops sitting en banc rather than, as here, the emperor seated amid bishops arrayed like imperial counselors, but always the emperor is depicted in fellowship with the saints and ranged against the adversaries of the church, typified here by Arius groveling in the foreground.[6]

The scene is a tribute to the charismatic authority that Constantine assumed, but even more it is testimony to the political skills of this emperor, which were considerable. For reasons discussed below, this is a topic that has been shunned by modern scholarship, with the curious result that the effort involved in coaxing Christians stunned by a decade of persecution into partnership with their former adversaries has gone unnoticed and unappreciated. This is perhaps the most remarkable aspect of the meeting of 335, the assumption that it could have happened without any of the stroking and soothing, wheeling and dealing, promises and compromises that are universal aspects of the political process. Though failure to appreciate the political skills of the long-dead ruler of an empire that ceased to exist centuries ago may by itself be no great loss, as a symptom of a more widespread misreading of the age it pertains directly to a central question in the story of early Christianity: Did the success of Christianity inevitably lead to the forcible suppression of that set of traditional beliefs we now label "paganism"? To this question modern scholarship gives an overwhelming and resounding yes: Christianity excludes other gods; the reason Rome persecuted Christians is because they would not acknowledge the gods of Rome; therefore, there is no reason to ask further why Christians did the same thing to the old gods, as soon as Constantine gave them the power to do so.

All of this argument, however, follows from failure to pay as much attention to this humdrum meeting in 335 as to its celebrated predecessor in Nicaea, to the agendas of the participants, and to the way problems were defined and resolved in that era—in short, to the world of politics. Because of this indifference, the question of Constantine's relationship to Christianity has been misformulated and the goals of his policy misread, and all this in turn has skewed our understanding of one of the most important half centuries in Western history, during which a religion based on love and charity adopted the instruments of its former persecutors. This meeting in Constantinople opens the way to remove the religious barriers by which this subject has been hedged, and it shows how the question of Christian coercion can both inform and be informed by treating it as a phenomenon of mass movements rather than a trait that is peculiar to Christian belief.

The "First Christian Emperor"

One of the bishops present at that November meeting was the elderly Eusebius of Caesarea, author of the first history of the church and widely regarded as the most learned churchman of his day. Shortly after Constantine's death in 337, and before his own no later than 339,

Eusebius would compose *De vita Constantini,* an essay on the life of Constantine which remains a starting point for study of the monumental developments of this reign. Here, Eusebius tells a story that helps explain this casual acceptance of the events of 335. It is a story so incredible that, Eusebius tells us, he himself would not have believed it had he not heard it from Constantine's own lips. "He said that about noon, when the day was already beginning to decline, he saw with his own eyes the trophy of a cross of light in the heavens, above the sun, and bearing the inscription, CONQUER BY THIS. At this sight he himself was struck with amazement, and his whole army also, which followed him on this expedition, and witnessed this miracle."[7]

This event, the famous "Vision of the Cross," occurred sometime before October 28, 312, on which date Constantine defeated his rival Maxentius outside Rome and became master of the Western half of the Roman Empire. Eusebius is unclear about when, exactly, the vision occurred—before Constantine had left his base in Gaul or while he was already on the march. But he leaves no doubt that it was connected with this event, coming in response to Constantine's fervent belief "that he needed some more powerful aid than his military forces could afford him, on account of the wicked and magical enchantments which were so diligently practiced by the tyrant" in control of Rome. Subsequently, Eusebius continues, Christ himself appeared to the emperor in a dream, commanding him to make a likeness of the sign he had seen and to use it "as a safeguard in all engagements with his enemies." Thus was born the fabulous labarum, a golden standard surmounted by a jewel-encrusted wreath within which were displayed a monogram composed of the Greek letters *chi* and *rho*, the first two letters of the appellation Χριστός. Miraculous stories of survival were told by soldiers who carried this emblem into battle, Eusebius says, and were protected by it from the spears and arrows that felled comrades all around them.

It was this victory in 312, according to Eusebius, which led Constantine to adopt "the salutary sign" and attach himself with all the fervor of a new convert to the faith of the apostles. But even more than victory, it was the miraculous vision, endowing him with charisma of biblical proportions, which gave Constantine special standing in Christian eyes, marking him, as it did, with the sign of God's favor.

Within a year, he was working with the bishop of Rome to settle a church dispute, the Donatist controversy, and little more than a decade later he would take the unprecedented step of calling a worldwide assembly of bishops, the historic Council of Nicaea. As he discusses these events in the *vita Constantini,* Eusebius also describes the emperor's constant progress in the faith, his devoted study of Scripture, and his care for the souls of his subjects, all of which made him a vigorous champion of orthodoxy and enemy of polytheism and idolatry. Turning the imperial palace into a virtual house of worship, he spent his time with priests and theologians and suppressed the wicked practices of paganism.[8]

The record appears abundantly to confirm Eusebius's account. In the quarter century between 312 and 337, Constantine not only convened the first ecumenical council of the church, but he also inaugurated his new capital and filled the empire with important new churches, including St. Peter's in Rome, the Holy Sepulchre in Jerusalem, and Hagia Sophia in Constantinople. Also in Constantinople, he built a cruciform church to the Twelve Apostles, where his own remains were deposited after his death, thereby ensuring that he would become in fact as well as name *Isapostolos,* "the equal of the apostles." Such actions guaranteed that the city that would be the capital for a millennium of Eastern history remained solidly grounded in the new faith. In addition to these physical monuments, Constantine undertook a massive diversion of state resources into the control of Christian bishops, on a scale to make credible the thought that Athanasius might indeed have tampered with Constantinople's grain supply. At the same time, Constantine endowed the bishops with unprecedented legal and juridical privileges. By one simple act—ordering that Sunday be observed as a day of rest and prayer—he gave a new rhythm and feel to the pace of ancient life.[9]

Thanks to Eusebius's *vita Constantini,* Constantine stood for centuries as a model for all future Christian emperors, who could wish for no greater praise than to be hailed as "a new Constantine." The story of his vision was burnished for a thousand years, by as many hands. Along with the discovery of the wood of the cross (attributed to his mother, Helena), Constantine's vision became the centerpiece of the great archetypal myth of Christian Europe: the "Legend of the Cross," which traced the precious wood all the way back to the Garden of Eden. Variants of the legend show the influence of a major forgery of later ages, the so-called Donations of Constantine, according to which the emperor ceded secular control over Western lands to the bishop of Rome when he left the West for his new city on the Bosphorus. This version involves more than legend, for popes of the Middle Ages based their claim to jurisdiction on this document.[10]

Amid such monumental events, it is easy to see why the little dustup with Athanasius in 335 rates no more than a footnote. Unlike Nicaea, no great decision hung in the balance at this meeting, and it made no lasting mark on the careers of any of those present. In contrast to those earlier events, moreover, nobody comes out of this meeting looking very good, the motives of both Athanasius and his accusers and the jurisdiction of Constantine unclear and to this day fiercely debated.[11] Just because it is so messy and unsatisfactory, however, the meeting in 335 is the right place to begin this study, for what really makes it so remarkable is that it occurs in a situation that is patently and undisguisedly political. *Political* is a word that does not occur much in scholarship on this period. In many a hallowed library, its mere mention is enough to make Constantine scholars roll their eyes and inquire politely after the sherry. The reason lies in a book that is now some 150 years old. In the middle of the nineteenth century, the great Swiss cultural historian Jacob Burckhardt turned his attention to the subject of Constantine. Here he found a record that was not quite as unambiguous as the traditional account makes out. At the same time that Constantine was lavishing favor on the Christian Church, Burckhardt found, the emperor continued to support pagan rites and officials and even to advertise them on his coins. Moreover, as pontifex maximus he remained official head of the Roman state religion and in fact did not accept the sacrament of baptism until he was on his deathbed. More important, Burckhardt thought the relentless pursuit of power which characterizes Constantine's career ill suited the godly monarch who marches through Eusebius's pious pages.

Although such anomalies had begun to tarnish Constantine's reputation as early as the Reformation, in Burckhardt's day his image remained much as his episcopal biographer had crafted it. This was the image that Burckhardt set out to remake. In 1853, seven years before his epochal *Die Kultur der Renaissance in Italien* defined a new period in European art and culture, Burckhardt published in Basel *Die Zeit Konstantins des Grossen (The Age of Constantine the Great)*. Its thesis was simple and admirably suited in its self-confidence to both the new profession of history and the age of ruthless state building in which he lived. Burckhardt, who came to loathe the amorality soon to be idealized by his younger contemporary Nietzsche, decided that Constantine, like the state builders of his own day, was driven by only one ambition—a consuming lust for power. That drive, Burckhardt thought, gave Constantine the insight to grasp the enormous potential of the Christian Church, with its well-organized cadres distributed throughout the empire. Constantine thus forged an alliance with the church not because of faith or miracle but to further his personal ambitions. "Attempts have often been made," Burckhardt warned, "to penetrate into the religious consciousness of Constantine and to construct a hypothetical picture of changes in his religious convictions. Such efforts are futile. In a genius driven without surcease by ambition and lust for power there can be no question of Christianity and paganism, of conscious religiosity or irreligiosity; such a man is essentially unreligious, even if he pictures himself standing in the midst of a churchly community." In Burckhardt's majestic summary, Constantine became "a calculating politician who shrewdly employed all available physical resources and spiritual powers to the one end of maintaining himself and his rule without surrendering himself wholly to any party."[12]

The Age of Constantine the Great is still in print; but it is less important now for its thesis than for being one of those rare books that frames a question in a way that sets the terms for future work. Powerful as it was, Burckhardt's thesis was decisively overturned by the simplest of historical arguments. Whereas his picture of Constantine was well suited to his own nineteenth-century world, it simply did not conform to the heightened religiosity that—as we soon shall see—characterized Constantine's own age. Thus, Burckhardt's thesis ignored the first rule of historians, which is to fashion an explanation for distant events in a way that makes sense to their own age but which is also sensitive to the beliefs and conditions of the period under study. Although it took the scholarly world by storm, Burckhardt's portrait of

Constantine simply failed this test. Half a century later, the great Otto Seeck dryly observed in his own study, "Oddly enough, no one has thought it necessary to offer any evidence for believing that such an orientation was at all possible in [Constantine's] age." Seeck then laid down a ringing challenge: "Show me a single individual in the fourth century who was not completely superstitious," he offered, "and I will gladly subscribe to the prevailing opinion."[13] Seeck was as extreme in his characterization of Constantinian "superstition" as was Burckhardt with his cynical rationalism, but his retort nonetheless effectively exposed the anachronism in the Swiss scholar's thinking.

Seeck's demand has been sufficient to silence all but the most foolhardy contenders. It has been so decisive, in fact, that an obvious question has gone unasked: Was Burckhardt's approach really "political"? True, Burckhardt questioned the sincerity of Constantine's conversion; but he did so on the premise that the political and spiritual realms are not only separate but also mutually exclusive and fundamentally incompatible. That might be true in the modern world, but was it so for the ancient one?

It might be useful to look again at Eusebius's account of Constantine's conversion, for the miracle story was repeated at the start of this chapter (as it usually is) without the context in which it occurs. In building up to it, Eusebius explains that Constantine felt obliged to free the city of Rome from the tyrant Maxentius, who had so far defeated every army sent against him. "He said," Eusebius reports, "that life was without enjoyment to him as long as he saw the imperial city thus afflicted, and prepared himself for the overthrowal of the tyranny." His account continues,

> Being convinced, however, that he needed some more powerful aid than his military forces could afford him, on account of the wicked and magical enchantments which were so diligently practiced by the tyrant, he sought Divine assistance, deeming the possession of arms and a numerous soldiery of secondary importance, but believing the co-operating power of Deity invincible, and not to be shaken. He considered, therefore, on what God he might rely for protection and assistance.

Of the other emperors, Eusebius writes, Constantine noted that those who worshiped many gods ended their careers in disgrace and failure; conversely, his own father, the emperor Constantius I, had "honored the one Supreme God during his whole life" and ruled with both honor and success. Thus, he realized that this One God had been "the Savior and Protector of his empire, and the Giver of every good thing."

> Reflecting on this, and well weighing the fact that they who had trusted in many gods had also fallen by manifold forms of death, without leaving behind them either family or offspring, stock, name, or memorial among men: while the God of his father had given to him, on the other hand, manifestations of his power and very many tokens: and considering farther that those who had already taken arms against the tyrant, and had marched to the battle-field under the protection of a multitude of gods, had met with a dishonorable end (for one of them had shamefully retreated from the contest without a blow, and the other, being slain in the midst of his own troops, became, as it were, the mere sport of death); reviewing, I say, all these considerations, he judged it to be folly indeed to join in the idle worship of those who were no gods, and, after such convincing evidence, to err from the truth; and therefore felt it incumbent on him to honor his father's God alone.[14]

The narrative raises many intriguing questions that cannot delay us here. What is important at the moment is the obviously political reasoning that Eusebius says went into Constantine's decision: he wanted to find a god who would not only protect him from magical arts but also give him a secure and successful reign. Entirely missing from the story are those spiritual concerns that, to a modern reader at least, are the prime components of a conversion experience: concerns for immortality and ethical conduct, the afterlife and the fate of one's soul. The passage, Burckhardt concluded, is one of many in Eusebius's pages which show not only the overwhelming primacy of power politics in Constantine's calculations but also the bishop's utter duplicity in putting a pious veneer over such raw ambition—"the first thoroughly dishonest historian of antiquity," Burckhardt called him.[15]

This is one of the many judgments that led scholars to discount the Swiss scholar's work. But it is important to be clear about what the mistake was. Burckhardt was not wrong in seeing that Constantine's conversion took place in conditions that, according to the standards of his own day, were inappropriate for such a deeply personal and spiritual experience.[16] His error lay in assuming that those standards were the only ones that should apply. As we shall see (Chapter 5), as a measure of sincerity the standards Burckhardt assumed are both arbitrary and incomplete.

It is, in fact, the polemics in Burckhardt's account, not the politics, that should have been repudiated. Although Burckhardt based his argument on assumptions about the emperor's political motives, he continued to ask the same question that had been in play at least since the Reformation—was the emperor's conversion sincere? Or, as the Reformers argued, was it but part of a process that corrupted the church with earthly wealth and power? Essentially, this is a religious question. If Burckhardt had genuinely intended a political approach, he would have paid far less attention to the question of belief and instead looked at the political process of Constantine's age. How, he would have asked, did this age define problems in the public sphere? How did it formulate options and implement—or attempt to implement—solutions?

The first thing he should have noticed was not Eusebius's "duplicity" but the fact that a bishop who was widely regarded as the most learned Christian of his day, while writing an account in which he obviously, almost embarrassingly, dotes on his subject, sees no contradiction, much less shame, in Constantine's behavior at the moment of his conversion. On the contrary, Eusebius's account is so matter-of-fact that, on first reading at least, nothing in it seems in the least abnormal. Why is that? Pursuing this question reveals what is in many ways the biggest gap dividing our world and the world of the fourth century. In our world, the separation of church and state, and even more, of religion and politics, is a pervasive reality; even in those increasingly rare instances in which the two continue to function in tandem, they do so as two separate and distinct entities. The separation spills over into the way we identify and classify varieties of behavior, and it makes it difficult for us even to conceive of a world not only where the two were united but where no conceptual category existed for their separation. In ancient thinking, the state itself was, at least theoretically, a religious institution, intended first and foremost to maintain the goodwill of the gods. Public officials whom we think of as secular simply because they were not priests all had duties that we would categorize as religious. The emperor, in particular, was a figure with strong religious associations that even Christians recognized. This inability to separate secular from religious functions, not any wish to be deceptive, is what accounts for the ease with which Eusebius relates Constantine's conversion to events that, to us, are patently political. Whether his account is true or not, what is important is that it was in accord with the sentiment of the time, which expected rulers to demonstrate a charismatic association with deity. This was one of many points on which Christians and pagans would have agreed. But if the ancient world was one in which religion and politics could not easily be separated, it was even more one in which deity was not a distant and abstract force, a "master clockmaker" who set up a universe to run on its own mechanism. No, all sides, Christian and pagan alike, believed that deity intervened in human affairs on a regular basis. In such a world spiritual power is also secular power—adding yet further meaning to Constantine's miracle. It is difficult, if not impossible, for the modern mind to grasp these differences; yet ignoring them only leads to wrongheaded conclusions.

Burckhardt's real flaw, thus, was not in seeing that there were political implications to Constantine's actions; it was something subtler, something that might be called conceptual anachronism. Anachronisms—things that are placed outside their proper times—are well known and fun to spot. Conceptual anachronisms are more dangerous, and harder to identify, because they are unconscious and rarely questioned. They project modern assumptions about values and behavior onto periods in which such standards may not apply. Saying "Brutus pulled out a revolver and shot Caesar to death" is an obvious anachronism that few would miss. But a text that said Brutus killed Caesar in order to promote class struggle, or because of repressed sexual urges, might well win serious consideration in some quarters, even though anyone familiar with the ruling class of which Brutus was a part would find the revolver easier to accept than these so-called explanations. Burckhardt's particular conceptual anachronism was that he failed to consider differences between Constantine's world and his own, assuming instead that the disdain for established institutions which he saw all around him prevailed in the fourth century as well.

Such anachronisms are particularly common in the study of Christian history. One that can be found in a great many studies of Rome and Christianity is the assumption that the Romans knew they were killing a god, or at least a very great and distinguished person, when they put Jesus of Nazareth on the cross. It is hard to avoid, if you live in a Western culture. The calendar, which divides time into the years before and after the year traditionally assigned to Jesus' birth, by itself conditions Western minds to think of Jesus as a central event in human history, and we live in a culture so imbued with a monotheistic outlook that even atheists think in terms of a single god whose existence they choose to deny. Unconsciously, it is easy to assume that the Romans also knew they were participating in a significant event, thereby incidentally proving that polytheists are morally and spiritually inferior to monotheists—a proposition never put more charmingly than by an actor in the television series "I, Claudius" who breathlessly told her interviewer, "It is almost impossible for us to understand people like the Romans who had no restraints, no checks at all, no sense of right and wrong, of good and evil, no guilts."[17]

Laughable as this premise is to anyone who has read Seneca or Epictetus, it points to another, even deeper and more sinister assumption that pervades *The Age of Constantine*. Burckhardt's evidence for the emperor's insincerity consisted in actions which were favorable to other beliefs. In Burckhardt's eyes, a sincere Christian would never have done such things; in other words, to Burckhardt, a sincere Christian was by definition an intolerant one. Ironically, although his critics lampoon Burckhardt's conclusions about Constantine, virtually all of them share this assumption about Christianity. The work that is best to read in tandem with Burckhardt's *Age of Constantine* is Norman Baynes' magisterial Raleigh Lecture of 1929, *Constantine the Great and the Christian Church,* which is also still the best starting place for study of this question.[18] Taking deliberate aim at the thesis that Constantine allied himself with the church for political profit, Baynes drew a picture of an emperor whose initial conversion may have amounted to little more than a primitive test of gods in battle but which was a conversion nonetheless. Ever afterward, Baynes held, Constantine devoted himself to the triumph of Christianity and the suppression of paganism; whatever deviations from and inconsistencies with this policy which the record holds can only be due to the political reality of introducing these measures in a polity that was still overwhelmingly pagan. Therefore, any evidence of toleration is merely tactical and temporary. "The important fact to realize," Baynes argued, "is that this alteration in policy entailed no change of spirit, only a change of method. What Constantine would have recommended in 323 he later felt free to proclaim as the imperial will."[19]

Baynes' thesis, which can be found underlying virtually every significant work on Constantine written since, actually uses a more genuinely political analysis to condemn Burckhardt than Burckhardt himself used to attack Constantine. Burckhardt used Constantine's continued favor to pagans and Jews to cast doubt on the sincerity of his conversion and commitment to Christianity. Since Baynes, Burckhardt's critics instead have postulated a series of stages in Constantine's religious policy to explain this apparent contradiction, holding that, while Constantine consistently desired the triumph of the Christian Church, he was initially forced by political realities—his need to deal with a pagan Senate in Rome and to share power until 324 with a pagan colleague in the East—to make tactical concessions.[20] Although, as we shall see, there are grounds for doubting the conclusions, this line of reasoning at least has the advantage of looking for answers in the political process. The problem is that it does not do so systematically, or even intentionally, its aim really being to explain how Constantine might have acted in ways contrary to what the miracle account would lead one to expect, in order to keep the traditional conversion story intact. And so this line of argument winds up being both inconsistent and incomplete. If Constantine truly rose to power—or truly believed he rose to power—by the direct intervention of deity in his personal life, it makes no sense to say that he would put that experience aside when deciding how to deal with such mundane obstacles as senatorial opinion. Two questions, one political, the other theological, have become carelessly intermingled in an effort to have it both ways—to maintain the priority of a religious calling and deny the existence of political motives, yet using what is essentially a political argument to do so. In the process, conversion in any meaningful sense ceases to exist.

Christian Intolerance

Thus, although these two titans could not be more different in either the conclusions they reached or the spirit with which they approached their studies, Burckhardt and Baynes share a similarity that has proved crucial to all subsequent scholarship: though neither would wish to state it so baldly, both start from the premise that the key to this age lies in the sincerity of the emperor's belief and that intolerance is the best proof of that sincerity. Accordingly, both seek first and foremost to reconcile the record with their interpretation of the emperor's personal faith (or lack of same). Here Burckhardt had the simpler argument: since the record is contradictory, Constantine's conversion must have been insincere. Baynes seemingly broke the connection by claiming that the inconsistencies were not a matter of belief but of tactics. Yet by the mere act of using this premise to resolve differences between what Constantine said and what he did, Baynes actually bound even more tightly the two separate questions of policy and belief. It has been incumbent on scholars ever since to reconcile, one way or another, Constantine's deeds with his beliefs. For all their differences, then, both Baynes and Burckhardt have had this similar effect on subsequent scholarship: together, they bonded belief and policy, following a framework that derives, ultimately, from the religious controversies of the Reformation.

More important still is the premise that normative Christianity is intolerant. The premise is understandable, for over the course of the fourth century a growing Christian intolerance of other forms of belief came to be expressed in acts of imperial legislation and popular violence. Arguably, no development in the ancient world has had a more profound effect on subsequent Western history than the ideological intolerance that became institutionalized during this period. So closely linked are these two phenomena—the triumph of Christianity and the suppression of paganism—that for at least the past two centuries it has seemed axiomatic that the one was the inevitable product of the other. In an analysis that still forms the basis of all modern studies, Edward Gibbon listed what he called "intolerant zeal" first among five factors that he identified in the *Decline and Fall* as contributing to Christianity's success.[21] No less important was Gibbon's complementary picture of a paganism that was inherently tolerant and therefore doomed to succumb before this Christian onslaught. "Such was the mild spirit of antiquity," he wrote, "that the nations were less attentive to the difference than to the resemblance of their religious worship."[22] Indeed, at least one modern scholar has proposed a definition of Christianity and paganism in which the one is virtually equated with intolerance, the other with toleration, and another has clothed Gibbon's insight in the trappings of a law of social science.[23]

The prominence Gibbon gave to intolerance puts him squarely in the center of Enlightenment thought. To the *philosophes,* led by the passionate and eloquent Voltaire, religion was antithetical to Reason, and they ranged themselves solidly against a clerical influence over government and culture which, in their own day, had led to wasting wars and suppression of freedom of belief. Accordingly, the *philosophes* fought to remove every restraint on freedom of thought and belief. Given the legacy of religious strife and bigotry that had divided Europe since the Reformation and the resistance of the church to their call for looser controls, it is understandable that they saw intolerance as a quality inherent to Christian belief, a conclusion that seemed proven by the history of the church in the Roman Empire. Gibbon shared these views, and they clearly influenced his conclusion that the fall of Rome was caused by "barbarism and religion."[24] That intolerance was inherent to Christianity seemed beyond dispute. Not only were converts obliged to renounce belief in all other gods—an immediate contrast to the inclusive spirit of polytheism, as Gibbon so aptly noted—but also within decades of Constantine's conversion Christian emperors began a violent suppression of variant beliefs that had continued seemingly unabated to his own day.

This correlation gave the hypothesis of inherent Christian intolerance a semblance of scientific objectivity, making it a powerful paradigm that continues to be used right down to the present—so powerful, in fact, that it masks what should be an obvious flaw: for three centuries prior to Constantine, the only persecutions known to the Roman world were those that Christians suffered and pagans sponsored. Enlightenment ideology was predisposed to discount this situation, and it must be admitted that a millennium of pious embroidering—of both the numbers of the martyrs and the cruelty of their tormentors—made the task an easy one. In one of his most impassioned broadsides, "On Toleration," provoked by the execution of the Toulouse merchant Jean Calas, wrongfully accused because of his Huguenot faith of killing his own son, Voltaire cast scorn on the image of Romans as persecutors. Using formal reasoning to refute the record, Voltaire asked how the church had been able to hold so many councils if the Romans were so intent on persecution, and he concluded with the triumphant, if somewhat shaky, Q.E.D., "There were persecutions; but if they were as violent as we are told, it is probable that Tertullian, who wrote so vigorously against the established cult, would not have died in his bed."[25]

Gibbon, who often found occasion to disparage the French sage's historical skills, was not above dismissing evidence that contradicted his preconceptions. Accounts of vicious treatment by Roman judges, he ruled, showed a "total disregard of truth and probability" which could be ascribed to "a very natural mistake. The ecclesiastical writers of the fourth and fifth centuries ascribed to the magistrates of Rome the same degree of implacable and unrelenting zeal which filled their own breasts."[26] In general, however, Gibbon was far less cavalier than Voltaire. But the result was, if anything, even more devastating. Rather than deny the obvious, Gibbon simply finessed the question of persecution by transforming his Roman magistrates into models of Enlightenment rulers—reluctant persecutors, too sophisticated to be themselves victims of religious zeal but nonetheless thwarted by Christian intransigence. He set the tone early, remarking during a survey of conditions in the second century that "the various modes of worship which prevailed in the Roman world were all considered by the people as equally true; by the philosopher as equally false; and by the magistrate as equally useful." Later, he applied this premise to the specific topic of persecution, contrasting the "inflexible obstinacy" of Christians and "the furious zeal of bigots" with Roman magistrates whom he was pleased to see as "strangers to those principles." Implicitly, Gibbon thereby suggested that the cause for such persecutions as did take place was none other than the Christians themselves. "As they were actuated, not by the furious zeal of bigots, but by the temperate policy of legislators," Gibbon wrote of the Roman authorities, "contempt must often have relaxed, and humanity must frequently have suspended, the execution of those laws which they enacted against the humble and obscure followers of Christ."[27]

Undoubtedly, there were instances of the reluctance and distaste that Gibbon described. More than one surviving record of martyr trials show magistrates eagerly trying to dissuade detainees from condemnation, even to the point of being willing to bend rules and look the other way in return for token concessions. But Gibbon ignored at least as many surviving indications of cruel and zealous judges, including one that must be a candidate for the title of World's Shortest Trial: "You are a bishop?" "Yes, I am." "You were!"[28] The question is not whether some judges were reluctant and some Christians zealous but whether there was anything inherent in the one or the other to make them so.

While "intolerant zeal" certainly is an aspect of Christian behavior, it skews the picture to concentrate on it as a prime factor in the success of that faith. Christians were, indeed, "exclusive" both in their concept of divinity and in their relations with the pagan community, many of whose ceremonies thoughtlessly jeopardized the Christian's chances for immortality. But "intolerance" can at best be thought of as a theoretical position: the fact is, in these centuries Christians were rarely, if ever, in a position to impose their beliefs on others; indeed, Christians were themselves the objects of persecution by communities that did not tolerate their threatening concepts of divinity. Gibbon's successful finagling of this issue is one more proof of how powerful a grip the Enlightenment paradigm of Christian intolerance has held on modern scholarship, for there is good reason to wonder whether "toleration," in the sense in which it has been used in modern times as an officially legislated act of restraint, even applies to the ancient world. To the extent that it does, the only voices up to the time of Constantine which can be found raised in favor of freedom of belief as a universal principle (rather than a political expedient) are those of Christian authors.[29]

The premise that intolerance was inherent to Christianity begs a very large question: How did a religion whose central tenet is to suffer, rather than do, harm—to "turn the other cheek"—come to accept the coercive power of the state as its reasonable due? This is, indeed, the core of the Constantinian question, which really concerns not so much Constantine's belief as a decision to involve the Christian hierarchy in the maintenance of the Roman state. The two actions—to become a

Christian and to involve Christianity in the working of government—
are not identical, although scholarship has made them so. The one
question is essentially ideological and theological, the other political.
Yet the combined effect of Burckhardt and Baynes has been to discredit
a political approach to the Constantinian question—Burckhardt by
ignoring evidence that went against his preconceptions, Baynes by
pointing out that flaw so effectively. The few exceptions continue to
use "politics" in polemical terms, as antithetical to "belief" and therefore a test of the emperor's spiritual nature.[30]

In one other way, Baynes and Burckhardt reinforce each other. Both
see the alignment of church and state which began during this period
as primarily the result of one man's interests, needs, and decisions. In
both works, everything turns on Constantine; the church is no more
than a passive recipient of his decisions, a blank tablet on which he
writes the future of Western history. Constantine, to Baynes, was one
of those "personalities which resist rationalization and remain unexpected and embarrassing." Mustering all his considerable eloquence,
Baynes wrote, "The more closely Constantine's life and achievement
are studied, the more inevitably is one driven to see in them an erratic
block which has diverted the stream of human history."[31] This is a
well-known method of analysis, to which scholars in other fields have
given a name. They call it the Rational Actor, or sometimes the Central
Actor or Classical method.[32] In its purest form, the Rational Actor
approach presumes that such a figure has complete freedom of action
to achieve goals that he or she has articulated through a careful process
of rational analysis involving full and objective study of all pertinent
information and alternatives. At the same time, it presumes that this
central actor is so fully in control of the apparatus of government that a
decision once made is as good as implemented. There are no staffs on
which to rely, no constituencies to placate, no generals or governors to
cajole. By attributing all decision making to one central figure who is
always fully in control and who acts only after carefully weighing all
options, the Rational Actor method allows scholars to filter out extraneous details and focus attention on central issues. It is particularly
useful for periods like classical antiquity, where little of the documentation for more sophisticated analysis of decision making, such as
personal diaries or the minutes of meetings, survives. In the hands of a

skilled practitioner, it is a powerful tool. Baynes' classic study shows the strengths of the Rational Actor approach. By making such assumptions about Constantine, he was able to cut through the fog that enshrouds this great historical issue and, in a relatively few sharply focused and skillfully written pages, argue a viable thesis for the growth of church-state relations.

The problem arises when the method comes to be taken as fact. There is no need to agree with Ronald Syme's famous judgment that "whatever the form and name of government, be it monarchy, republic, or democracy, an oligarchy lurks behind the façade" in order to realize that no ruler of any polity in any period has had such complete and effective exercise of power.[33] To the extent that they are leaders, rulers must have followers—followers who enforce their orders, other followers who obey them. These followers constitute a constituency. The nature of this constituency will vary from one type of polity to another, as will the restraints they impose on leaders by the standards, values, and expectations that they share. But the need to keep this constituency satisfied in order to rule effectively remains a constant of political life.

The best historians—and Baynes surely ranks among them—have always known that they are merely using a kind of shorthand when they condense all the complicated processes of governmental decision making into the person of a single central character. Were he still alive, Baynes might not hesitate to reply that doing so makes more sense than positing alternative positions put forth by officials whose views, and even names, are now lost to history. Indeed it does. The problem is that when studies as powerful as those by Baynes and Burckhardt frame an issue, it is easy for those who follow to mistake the shorthand for the complete record.

One dangerous side effect of the Rational Actor method is that it encourages practitioners to think in terms of rational outcomes, dulling the senses, so to speak, to the possibility of unintended consequences. To modify the premise of Fergus Millar's monumental study *The Emperor in the Roman World*—that "the emperor 'was' what the emperor did"[34]—it is simply too easy in a Rational Actor study to conclude that "what the emperor did must be what the emperor intended." Yet even when decisions have been made through a rational process of deliberating alternatives, the result can be something other than what was intended.

It is not just in terms of the central figure that the Rational Actor approach oversimplifies decision making. Consider, for instance, the title of Baynes' study: *Constantine the Great and the Christian Church*. This is, in fact, a typical title for works on this topic. On one side is the Rational Actor, Constantine, and on the other "Christianity" or "the church," a faceless institution that is the subject of the Actor's attention. Again, it is a framework that simplifies the job of analysis. But here even more the product can be dangerously misleading, for by framing the question in this way, the student is encouraged to think in terms of a single Christianity, a monolithic church, and to ignore the variety of options from which the Actor, in this case Constantine, was able to choose. The process becomes completely one sided: all initiative is on the emperor's end. The Actor acts, and the church reacts. What the model does, in effect, is remove from consideration the possibility of the church, or various churchmen, actively pursuing their own agendas. In this scheme, there is only one agenda, the emperor's, and the church's primary role is to become the beneficiary of the central character's considerable largesse. The possibility that Christians might have taken an active role in formulating the emperor's policy, or even on occasion have seized the initiative and prodded a reluctant or even truculent emperor into action, never arises, much less the possibility that Christians might have been as much divided among themselves over the question of imperial policy as they were over questions of theology and doctrine.

These theoretical problems may seem a small price to pay in order to make the sense out of a turbulent era which the Rational Actor method allows. But, in fact, ignoring the possibility of unintended consequences and multiple agendas leads to misperceptions that in turn produce misdiagnoses. The difference is crucial when attempting to understand the growth of Christian intolerance. If there was only one kind of Christian and that Christian was invariably intolerant, then it can be assumed that the Christian use of coercion which becomes pronounced by the end of the fourth century was an inevitable product of Constantine's conversion, just as it can be assumed that a sincerely converted Constantine must have undertaken repressive measures.

The intolerance that is such a pronounced feature of Christian history can confidently be attributed to some characteristic or internal logic peculiar to that faith. But if there was more than one type of Christian in the early fourth century, then it becomes premature to speak of Constantine's desire for a "triumph of the church" without first asking what kind of church, and what kind of triumph, he sought. In the same way, a search for answers to the growth of Christian intolerance which limits itself to the terrain of faith without considering the influence of external factors on that development risks serious misdiagnosis.

It is the premise of this study that Christian use of coercion to enforce belief in the latter part of the fourth century was not the inevitable product of inherent Christian intolerance; rather, it can be explained by attention to the nature of Christianity as an organization and the dynamics of Christian-pagan relations in the fourth century. Accordingly, to search for coercive measures as proof of the sincerity of Constantine's conversion is both misguided and misleading. The real brilliance of this emperor's achievement lies in precisely the opposite direction: his ability to soothe the rightful fears of wary parties and bring them to work together in the name of a higher purpose.

More recent scholars have greatly enriched our understanding of this pivotal period in Western history by enlarging the scope of their study. The effect is visible in two of the most important recent studies of Constantine in English, T. D. Barnes' *Constantine and Eusebius* and *Pagans and Christians* by Robin Lane Fox.[35] Polar opposites in other respects (Barnes sees Constantine as the product of a fully evolved and vigorous Christian movement, while Lane Fox pictures the religion at a standstill until it was rescued from oblivion by the imperial conversion), the two works are important for the same reason. Both attempt to set the Constantinian period in a broader context—Barnes by looking at Christianity as a rapidly evolving social and intellectual force, Lane Fox by bringing to the fore a pagan tradition that was anything but moribund by the fourth century. Other studies—of priesthood, the civic nature of ancient religion, and the evolving character of Roman belief, to name but a few—have served to make the important developments of Constantine's reign less unique, less dependent on the whim of a single individual.[36]

By broadening the scope, it is possible to envision a more active role for the church and to see instances of a conflict in goals between emperor and church, as well as divisions among Christians themselves which concerned not only those theological matters that have been the focus of most studies but also the topic of how Christians were to go about the process of winning new converts and coexisting with other beliefs. Using this criterion, it becomes far less certain that the Christian in the first half of the fourth century who favored coercion as the answer to these questions should be considered normative. If this is so, then an entirely new question must be asked: If Christianity was not inherently intolerant, then why did Christians turn to coercion? Put another way, the question is not why did Christianity win, but why did a particular type of Christianity win?

For all these reasons, the title of this study is emphatically plural. Constantine did not encounter a church but a number of churches, loosely bound together by a common tradition and, even more, by the willingness of their local leaders, the bishops, to cooperate with one another. There was, at this time, no universally recognized authority above that of the bishop to enforce conformity, much less unity—only subsequent to Constantine's reign, and in large part as a reaction to it, do such mechanisms come into being.

In the plural lies a purpose. By assuming that intolerance is something unique to Christian belief, scholars have limited, and to a certain degree privileged, the question. Certainly the requirement in Judaeo-Christian monotheism not merely to shun but explicitly to deny the existence of other gods added an exclusivism that is lacking in other faiths. But intolerance, that is, the active use of the coercive powers of the state to compel conformity to a given set of beliefs, is a phenomenon that extends far beyond the particular problem of Christian-pagan relations in antiquity, or the normal boundaries of religion and theology. Intolerance exists, at least in a latent state, in every human group and organization, and in every group there are individuals who are inclined to favor repression and coercion over other methods of social interaction as a means to promote their views. The need to achieve a firm understanding of the conditions under which this latent characteristic can be triggered in a community so as to put control in the hands of such individuals is one of the most important challenges facing students of the human condition. If this is so, then it is a mistake to assume that the answer to this particular manifestation of intolerance in late antiquity must lie in theological, rather than more broadly political, conditions. At the very least, it denies an opportunity for the advancement of understanding which frequently results from comparative study. Neither inherent nor peculiar to Christianity, coercive intolerance is the result of a process that is essentially social and political in character. To understand what happened in the fourth century, therefore, our study must go beyond those unique aspects of Christian belief which have preoccupied most other studies and consider what Christianity, as a social movement, has in common with all other social movements. Here, in the dynamics of groups and organizations, is where the explanation for Christian intolerance can be found.

Saul Alinsky was a radical activist and grassroots organizer in the middle years of the twentieth century. His specialty was teaching low-income and minority groups how to use political pressure to solve their problems, and for more than three decades he was a massive pain in the collective backside of the American Establishment. His name will come up again in these pages. Near the end of his career, Alinsky put down the principles that he had learned in a small book entitled *Rules for Radicals.* The prose is homely and there are no footnotes, but it is a book that shows up time and again in the bibliographies of high-powered academic consultants. One of his central observations was the following: "Power is the reason for being of organizations. When people agree on certain religious ideas and want the power to propagate their faith, they organize and call it a church. When people agree on certain political ideas and want the power to put them into practice, they organize and call it a political party. The same reason holds across the board. Power and organization are one and the same."[37]

Alinsky was making a basic point—every type of human organization has one thing in common with every other type. At some basic level, all organizations operate as organizations; they are all subject to the same rules and the same limitations. Organized movements, whether their purpose is to promote radios or religion, free trade or free love, fall subject to certain rules of political behavior. At this level, what matters is not whether the Christian organization was secular or religious but that it was an organization and, as such, subject to certain routines that can be first discovered and then used to analyze and explain the actions of its members.

It is altogether too easy, however, for scholars engaged in the pursuit of this question to lose sight of the fact that the part being studied does not constitute the whole, and more than one scholar has protested against church histories that are nothing more than stories of "power struggles, manipulations, negotiations, lobbyings, trade-offs, compromises, revolutions."[38] The Christian message of a personal savior and a blessed afterlife may well have had more to do with the success of Christianity than anything discussed in these pages. But that message is by definition a personal and spiritual one; it would have been the same whether or not Christianity became an established and powerful institution of Western government. More harm can be done by failing to separate spiritual and secular success. Historians increasingly are aware of the dangers that ensue from failing to recognize what one has called "the perennial tendency to apply theological categories to disagreements over political power within the church." Here, too, Alinsky had a rule. "To operate on a good-will rather than on a power basis," he decided after a lifetime of experience and reflection, "would be to attempt something that the world has not yet experienced."[39]

The conclusion remains the same: the fact that the organization involved in this case is a religious one does not prevent the use of political tools to analyze the problem, for once a question—any question—enters the public arena, it becomes subject to certain principles of political behavior. If, as this study contends, intolerance is not a religious but a political issue, then progress toward its understanding and control will only come about by attention to the political factors that contribute to its rise.

In this process, the bishops were pivotal characters. The bishops. Not "Christianity," an ideology; not "the church," an abstract monolith, but a collection of leaders with local power bases who over the course of three centuries had developed mechanisms for working with, and against, one another, to promote mutual concerns and to present a collective authority that usually was capable of controlling the peculiarly volatile and anarchistic potential of their movement. What those few studies that have looked at specific instances of coercion in the late fourth century indicate is that the most significant single factor in determining whether or not a community would condone the use of violence against non-Christians was the attitude of its bishop[40]— hence the focus of this study, and the reason for beginning with the events of 335. In these events it is obvious that there was not just one, monolithic church but a church that spoke with many voices, through the mouths of bishops who had much more than theology to scream about.

The events of 335 also give us a very different Constantine to consider. In his relations with the church Constantine has been characterized as everything from a white knight to a robber baron. But whether seen as the saint who laid Rome at the feet of the church or the predator who perverted Christianity to his own secular ends, as creator of the "Reichskirche," or lawgiver who clearly defined rules of church and state, it is Constantine the Rational Actor who has been at the center of scholarly attention, and "the church," a faceless monolith unified in purpose and methods, with which he has dealt. There is no way, however, to look at the events of 335 and conclude that Constantine was in control. Instead of the Man of God who sat calmly debating points of theology at Nicaea, the events of 335 show us a Constantine employing all his considerable skill to keep the lid on an increasingly volatile situation that had, in fact, been deteriorating for some years. The marks of this Constantine are all over the letter that he sent from Constantinople to the bishops at Tyre. It is evidence, one piece among many, of separate agendas and priorities that clouded relations between Constantine and the bishops.

This is what makes the year 335 so fascinating and also potentially so much more valuable than the better-known dates of 312 or 325. The former, the year of the vision, focuses attention entirely on Constantine, while the latter, the year of the Nicene Council and Creed, inevitably raises issues fraught with consequence for the church. By contrast, the events of 335 force both to share the spotlight and thus shed light on the dynamics of a relationship that was very much a two-way process. And they bring to the fore divisions in a church that might not have been ready to triumph, whether the emperor wanted it to or not.

In fact, the incident shows a very different Constantine than the clear-eyed and fiercely committed ruler of Eusebius's pages. Or of Burckhardt's or Baynes'. Here is a Constantine who rants and wheedles, and, yes, who blusters, too, if that will get him what he wants. It is a Constantine who does not preside impartially but who takes sides, and shifts sides, with an ease that alarms later theologians. One who wheels and deals, to the dismay of those scholars who would like to tie up his arrangement between church and state in pretty little constitutional ribbons. This is the reality of the first decades of church and state under Constantine: there were no rules, and no ruler, but a scramble for position. These events show us not the single, unified "Christianity" with which Constantine usually is thought to have dealt but a number of different Christian constituencies, each represented by a leader, the bishop. These bishops, in turn, show themselves to be no strangers to the game of political hardball. This sort of rough-and-tumble is more characteristic of modern politics than of the autocratic and stately Roman Empire, at least as it usually is depicted. Indeed, none of the traditions or ideology that had grown up around the person of the Roman emperor would have prepared Constantine to deal with this kind of behavior. He had to feel his way, and this, too, is what makes the events of 335 so alluring. They reveal that the relationship between Constantine and the bishops still was being worked out in the very last months of his reign, a quarter century after, traditionally, everything had been settled at the moment of his conversion. They show an ongoing process of negotiation in which the bishops were not mere appendages to Constantine's will but significant forces with which he had to deal in unprecedented ways. They raise questions about the extent to which Constantine controlled the new movement and the types of pressures which might have been brought to bear on his decision making.

The events of 335, thus, show how dangerous it is to assume that Constantine and the bishops shared exactly the same agenda, or even that all the bishops did so with one another. Ultimately, the importance of this meeting in Constantine's chambers is that it points our attention to the real significance of his reign, which is not the quality of the emperor's faith or even the nature of his conversion but the relationship he worked out with the Christian leadership on an official level, the relationship between church and state which developed during this period.

There are more layers to this situation. Why was Constantine willing to allow charges against Athanasius to be revived after he himself had said they were settled? What does it mean that there were members of Constantine's entourage who recognized Athanasius when he himself did not, and who convinced the emperor that he should talk to him? But this story is running ahead of itself. The road to Constantinople is a twisted one. It must begin with the empire itself and the political realities of the system created by the first of the emperors, Augustus. Next, the bishops. They have been called "a major political novelty of the fourth century."[41] Who were these imperious individuals, and whence did their powers derive? This groundwork laid in Chapters 2 and 3, a thornier issue may be tackled in Chapter 4: the grounds for Constantine's own powers, and the conditions that brought him and the bishops into one another's arms.

After we pause in Chapter 5 to look at the question of what Constantine believed—not so much for the religious significance of the question as to get a sense of the man—the political and organizational problems he faced subsequent to his victory at the Milvian Bridge take center stage in Chapters 6 and 7. His involvement in these years in major church controversies—the Donatist schism and Arian heresy— has made it easy for historians to posit an identical agenda for emperor and bishops. Too easy. Chapter 8 offers a new appreciation of Constantine's seemingly endless recourse to church councils and his almost obsessive concern for speech making. Objects of endless speculation and even derision in the past, these activities now appear as part of a highly successful effort to articulate his own agenda and to isolate those very Christians whose desire to coerce belief other studies have taken as normative. With Constantine's own agenda in mind, Chapter 9 uses one of this emperor's most controversial laws to disentangle his goals from those of the bishops and to show how misleading it can be to assume religious motives behind every favorable action he took toward the clergy.

A very different Constantine, and thus an urgent question: What happened? How did those Christians who had been neutralized by Constantine come to gain the upper hand? Now the bishops return, in a study of unintended consequences. In Chapter 10, a quieter but in many ways more profound change is revealed by looking at one of the most unassuming of their number, Eusebius of Caesarea. Chapter 11 looks inside the Christian community of the fourth century for factors that help explain the increased used of coercion during that period, one of the most volatile of the ancient world.

Another confrontation between an emperor and a bishop, this one a good deal more famous, is the subject of Chapter 12. This facedown, between Ambrose of Milan and Theodosius the Great, occurred little more than half a century after Constantine tangled with Athanasius, and its outcome was decidedly different. It provides an opportunity to reflect on the changed relationship between emperor and bishop during the course of the fourth century and the part this change played in the development of Christian coercion.

Two

The Game of Empire

When Constantine met with the bishops in 335, both he and they were making use of centuries of established procedure to find their bearings in a relationship that was, in many ways, unprecedented. Rome had never known a priesthood that was both organized and independent in a way that Christian bishops had become over the course of three centuries. There were organized priesthoods in Rome, to be sure—the pontiffs and augurs are two obvious examples—but these were limited by ancient custom in both the range and scope of their activities, and neither commanded the extensive and loyal clientele that now was part of the apparatus of every bishop. Moreover, Roman priesthoods were held by the same elites that monopolized all public office, and thus were tied to the same criteria of wealth and status which distinguished citizens in every other field of activity.[1] Although by the fourth century Christian bishops could be extremely well educated and powerful individuals, the criteria for their office, the signs and markers that identified a bishop as a bishop, were distinctly different, based on personal qualities of faith and spirit rather than the external standards of class and culture. The Roman ruling apparatus had no say in the selection of a bishop, but now the Roman emperor had to establish a working relationship with an organization over which he had no formal control whatsoever.

Despite the newness of their relationship, however, both sides had almost three centuries of experience on which to rely for guidance as to how they should behave with each other. When we look back on that period today, we do so with full knowledge of the predominant role Christian prelates would play in the subsequent history of Europe. The participants necessarily saw things differently; they had to act on the basis of a known past, not an unknown or dimly seen future. In Constantine's case, more than three centuries of precedent, summed up in the titles that adorned his name—Augustus, Imperator, Victor— governed his behavior and assumptions. The view of Constantine would have been that he, as emperor, was the final decision-making authority for anything that happened in his empire. This is the view that has been mistakenly translated in the modern imagination as raw military power, which the emperor exercised with complete scorn for rights and traditions—the type of arbitrary authority personified by a Nero or a Caligula. It is a misleading view, reinforced by both political and religious ideologies, and a treacherous one that has provided the shaky foundation for a surprisingly large number of otherwise admirable academic studies. Only slightly less misleading is the concept of *caesaropapism*, the term coined in modern ages to characterize, from a Christian perspective, the power that the Roman emperor, or "Caesar," came to exercise over the ordained clergy, acting as if he were "pope." The ancient world did not make such distinctions, for the state was itself a religious institution, and the emperor of Rome was in fact, literally and figuratively, pope—pontifex maximus, head of the Roman state religion.[2]

The military was, indeed, an indispensable tool of the emperor's power, shaped in the civil wars of the last century of the republic. But ruling Rome was a more complicated matter than winning the support of the military, because of the elaborate steps that the first of the emperors, Caesar's heir Octavian, took to convince others (if not himself) that he had restored the republic. The political world into which Constantine was born, probably sometime in the 270s,[3] had changed dramatically since that time, but enough of its premises remained the same that, just as knowledge of an eighteenth-century Constitution is necessary to understand the United States government in the late twentieth century, so a student of the Roman empire in the fourth century must be aware of rules, written and unwritten, which were laid down at the empire's start.

The most important of these rules came about as a result of Octavian's decision, once he had eliminated his rival Mark Antony in 31 B.C., not to rule merely with the consent of his legions. As a result of the civil wars, the armies pledged their loyalty directly to the young Caesar, who also commanded the devotion of Rome's volatile masses— hence the meaning of the title *Imperator,* from which our term *emperor* derives. Its origins lie in the military. In the old republic, a winning commander would be hailed on the field of battle by his troops as Imperator, an honorific title signifying one who had successfully exercised his *imperium,* or power of office. Octavian restricted the title to himself, and his successors did likewise; thus did it pass into our vocabulary as the name for the ruler of Rome. The origins of the title betray an important truth about the Roman Empire: the power of any incumbent emperor resided ultimately on the loyalty of the armies.

Instead of continuing to rely so visibly on the armies, however, in 27 B.C. Octavian went before the Senate and modestly laid down the emergency powers with which he had ruled for the previous fifteen years. The senators reacted with appropriate noises of horror and indignation, compelling Octavian to keep his post at the helm of state. When, reluctantly, he agreed to do so, for the good of the republic, the Senate endowed him with the novel title *Augustus*—a word with vaguely religious connotations, signifying at once both Octavian's moral supremacy and the pleasure the gods took in his rule. Modern scholars have dubbed this exercise Octavian's *beau geste,* a fine phrase for what otherwise would be called a cynical, but brilliant, propaganda ploy. It seems perfectly clear that Octavian had no intention actually to relinquish power, for he did not make the offer until he had carefully purged the Senate of all members whose loyalty was in any way suspect.

Why did he bother? A standard answer is that he wanted to avoid the fate of his uncle, who had gotten himself assassinated by failing to make just such a ritual bow. The answer is correct but incomplete. Octavian might have continued to rule with the emergency powers he had been granted, or with a few of the elementary precautions (such as a bodyguard) that Caesar had spurned, or he might have continued his uncle's experiment with the office of "dictator for life," confident that the senators most offended by such an arrangement, along with their objections, had now been laid to rest. But this solution had its own pitfalls. Whatever his title, no one person can rule a state effectively without competent lieutenants. As David Hume observed long ago, "The Soldan of Egypt, or the Emperor of Rome, might drive his harmless subjects, like brute beasts, against their sentiments and inclinations; but he must, at least, have led his mamelukes, or praetorian bands, like men, by their opinion."[4] The force of Hume's dictum, that even an emperor needs subordinates whose allegiance he cannot coerce, was what drove Octavian to dress his powers in clothes acceptable to senatorial interest. Hume limited his observation to military subordinates, but it applies equally to civil administrators. While skilled individuals, such as Octavian's brilliant commander Agrippa, could always be found, only the Senate was able to provide a pool of competent administrators in the numbers required to run an empire. Senators with the power to carry out Octavian's wishes would also have the power, at least potentially, of thwarting them. If force were the only reason for their loyalty, they might even turn their thoughts to ruling in Octavian's place should circumstances allow. Like it or not, Octavian would have had to devise a form of rule which was sensitive to senatorial opinion.

He had further incentive. Whatever Octavian's theoretical powers during the years of civil war, his real ability to rule had rested all too obviously on the loyalty of his armies. To no one had this been more obvious than to the soldiers themselves. Decades of civil war had taught them their importance to the designs of their commanders. Even Caesar, whose sway was legendary, had had uncomfortable moments. His heir was forced several times during the years of rivalry with Mark Antony to negotiate for the favor, and even bend to the will, of his troops. Octavian's efforts to restore a sense of continuity with republican government soothed the constitutional spirits of the Senate, but they also dampened the revolutionary bravado of the legions, who had come to think of themselves as kingmakers. It is not always sufficiently appreciated that the gesture of 27 B.C. was made for the benefit of the army as much as the Senate. To convince the soldiery that they were *not* the core of his power was an important reason for the charade. The gesture had the effect of transferring Octavian's title, so to speak, from the armies to the Senate, for in giving him the name *Augustus,* the Senate also gave Octavian an alternative sanction for his rule, one that was stronger and more stable than the armies could provide.[5]

Finally, beyond the needs of either of these two powerful constituencies, Octavian was responding to a deeper, if more generalized, need to restore stability. Given Rome's culture and traditions, there was simply no way to do so without involving the Senate. Individual senators had done much to discredit the institution during the last century of the republic, but however much Romans of the lower orders might criticize and even scorn the blatant self-interest of particular senators, the Senate itself still stood, more than any other institution, as the symbol of five centuries of republican rule. It was the Senate that had expelled the kings, the Senate that held Rome together during the dark days of the war with Hannibal and then guided Rome to mastery over the great kingdoms of the Greek East. Its members were recruited, at least theoretically, on the basis of service to the state, and its enormous moral authority was summed up by another name used for senators, "conscript fathers." In a paternalistic society like Rome's where a sense of duty was celebrated as the finest virtue a citizen could possess, such a title was doubly significant, indicating leaders who were not just playing the role in the state which the father did in the household but more than that, fathers who had put aside their own interests in response to this call. To bring an end to the period of troubles without restoring the dignity of the Senate was inconceivable. Although individual members had disgraced themselves by putting faction or self-interest before the public good, the prestige of the institution itself continued to hold a special place at the core of the nation's identity, its self-definition, summed up in the well-known acronym *SPQR, Senatus PopulusQue Romanus*—"Senate and People of Rome."

The act of 27 B.C. thus purged Octavian of the taint of ambition which had proved so ruinous to Julius Caesar. Eventually, Augustus ceased to hold any elected office except for brief, ceremonial periods. "After this time," he wrote years later in an autobiographical account set up on inscribed columns around the empire, "I excelled all in influence [*auctoritas*], although I possessed no more official power [*potestas*] than others who were my colleagues in the several magistracies."[6] The words *potestas* and *auctoritas,* roughly signifying "coercive force" and "prestige," make a potent juxtaposition. Centuries later, another Roman ruler—this one wearing the shoes of the fisherman— would use them to contrast the powers of state and church.[7] With his indefinite powers and a consistent policy of deference to the Senate, Augustus thus created a façade of constitutional government which modern scholars have labeled the Principate, after *princeps,* Latin for "first man" or "leader" and basis for the English word *prince.* In the republic, this was an honorary title given to the most distinguished member of the Senate, much as a modern assembly might call one of its members the "dean" or "doyen." Its use to characterize Augustan government reflects once again the emperor's contention that his advice was followed because of his *auctoritas,* not because of his control of the legions. In effect, Augustus reassured the Senate by such acts that the emperor was one of their own, a member of their body who shared their values and interests. In doing so, he showed that he would be different from Caesar, whose greatest crime in the eyes of fellow senators may well have been that he sought to establish distance between himself and that body.

The most significant part of Octavian's gesture in 27 B.C. lies in what he did not do. He did not assume any new offices. Instead, he ruled through a series of vague powers conferred on him by the Senate and People. Symbolically, the most important of these was the one that was in fact the most limited, tribunician power, the right to bring any action in the city of Rome to a halt. But the symbolic importance of this power went far beyond its actual use. Tribunes were the representatives of the plebeian order, and their powers went back almost to the beginning of the republic, when the then disenfranchised plebs won the right for their representatives to protect them from abuse by the ruling patrician class. Tribunes were, thus, champions of "the people" against the established order, and it was this role that the grant of tribunician power symbolized. In the future, emperors would date their reigns from the time they received it. With this sense of people's champion, combined with the oath of the legions, the moral authority connoted by his new name of Augustus, and the title that he eventually picked up of pontifex maximus, head of the Roman state religion, the first of the emperors wove into his new position a host of associations that were both emotive and pragmatic.

On this completely Roman peg the peoples of the Greek East were able to hang the ancient theories of kingship by which they had been accustomed to judge and venerate their rulers. Gradually, Eastern theories of kingship supplied a loss that Octavian's *beau geste* could not restore. In the republic, law had been the product of the various assemblies. Under the new government, these assemblies met less and less frequently and finally ceased to meet altogether. The change put legal purists in a quandary. If no assemblies met, how could emperors legislate? Hellenistic kingship theorists had devised a solution: the emperor, as image of the divine order on earth, ruled as "living law," the embodiment of perfect justice. The Principate could not incorporate wholesale a theory that ran so blatantly counter to its presumptions, but in its fading moments, the jurist Ulpian devised a solution. "A decision given by the emperor has the force of a statute," he ruled. "This is because the populace commits to him and into him its own entire authority and power, doing this by the *lex regia* which is passed anent his authority." In other words, Ulpian postulated a final legislative act of the people delegating to the emperor their rights—a theory that established the ultimate basis of the emperor's legislative authority in the popular will.[8]

Augustus's aim was to gain legitimacy for his personal rule. But why did the senators cooperate? Beyond his gesture, Augustus took practical steps to gain senatorial support, giving those members who played along with him unprecedented guarantees. Senators in the republic— at least the important ones—were always millionaires, but only incidentally so. Theoretically, service, not wealth, was what qualified one for membership. Now, for the first time, Augustus established a formal property qualification of approximately one million sesterces for members of the senatorial class. To sweeten the deal, he also made membership hereditary. This change did not exactly close the order, because the emperor could still adlect new members, but it did guarantee stability, not only for incumbent senators but also for their offspring. Having looked into the abyss opened by revolutionary upheavals, the senators gratefully accepted.

Undoubtedly, what was even more important to the senators' calculations was the opportunity Octavian gave them to share in the perquisites of power. During the republic progress up the ladder could be controlled by a variety of competing groups, led by the great consular families who functioned as the heads of huge patronage networks. These included humble retainers or "clients" whose loyalty earned them the equivalent of a social security net, as well as lesser politicians who brought with them their own, smaller client networks. Large or small, the distinction of a patron consisted in his ability to provide access to desirable commodities; his ability to do so, in turn, depended as much on his own prestige as on his other resources. Prestige and patronage thus went hand in hand, one reason that the quest for the consulship often became, literally, a matter of life or death. Patronage was the glue of the republican system, the point at which social and political networks intersected. For this reason, it has been called *the* singularly Roman institution, as characteristic for its society—and as elusive in its operation—as was feudalism for the Middle Ages.[9]

The system survived the end of the republic, with the difference that now advancement was the sole gift of the emperor, whose vast resources made him the person with the most prestige and also the greatest patron. An earlier model cast the change in terms of a conflict from which the emperor emerged as "universal patron," supplanting the republican nobles here just as he did elsewhere in the political system. More nuanced approaches now see the system as providing the same glue for the empire as it had for the republic, uniting, rather than dividing, the interests of emperor and senatorial elite, for the empire, even though its bureaucracy was skeletal by modern standards, required staff in larger numbers, and junior administrators with lower prestige, than the Senate by itself could supply. While senators supplied the governors for provinces, therefore, emperors filled lesser positions with candidates recommended by their senatorial allies. Meanwhile, emperors also confirmed the traditional authority of the provincial elites over local affairs in return for maintaining order and collecting taxes and adlected them to the Senate in increasingly greater numbers, thereby gradually making that body the representative of a truly imperial elite. This division of labor and identity of interests underlies the efficient administration for which the high empire is so frequently praised, since it allowed a vast territory to be run by what today would barely suffice for a single city of moderate size.[10]

By allowing senators to act as brokers of his patronage, as he did when he accepted their protégés for imperial appointments, the emperor simultaneously reinforced their prestige and bound their interests to his own. In other words, the act of conferring prestige augmented, rather than diminished, the prestige of the giver.[11] So understood, patronage becomes the key ingredient of the game of empire, surviving all the other changes that will occur between Augustus and Constantine and allowing a more satisfactory explanation of the ties between church and state forged during the latter's reign. With everyone watching to see what kind of behavior won the ruler's favor, the emperor was able to use access as a form of leverage, influencing attitudes by his choice of whom to hear and to promote.

As the political scientist R. E. Dowling once observed, "Merely to classify governments as monarchies, aristocracies, and democracies is, as we all know, to omit a tremendous amount of what is politically interesting." Rather, what is important to know is "whether group A has affected group B by argument or trickery or physical force," or in other words, how power is distributed and exercised.[12] The point certainly holds for Rome. To understand how and why Constantine behaved with the bishops, it is better to think of the empire not as an autocratic despotism but as a game with many players. What, exactly, are "players"? In any political game, players are the people who influence events—the ones who need to be informed, because their support will be needed either to secure approval or to implement the decision effectively. They are the ones who decide which things are important enough to require attention in the first place. They are the policymakers. As a veteran observer of the twentieth-century American political game once put it, "To be a player is to have power or influence on some issue. Not to be a player is to be out of the policy loop and without influence."[13] The resources that each player brings to the table are his or her constituencies—blocs or groups whose assent the player guarantees to deliver. The game consists of each player trying to get maximum value for the interests of his or her constituency while paying the minimum for those of any other player.

Rules of the Game

By tying his legitimacy to the Senate, Augustus also tied the hands of his successors in significant ways, making it incumbent on them to treat the Senate, however minimally, as a valued partner, hearkening to its advice, refraining from exercise of the various powers by which they ruled until they were formally conferred by that body, and glorying in the honor of being recognized as the Senate's leading member. The result was an elaborate ritual, a dance conducted with all the delicate steps and intricate courtesies of a stately pavan, a game with fanciful and intricate rules—a strange game, and sometimes a lethal one, with formal rules that could easily be ignored and unwritten ones that were sacrosanct. To follow it, a modern observer needs to keep alive to the importance of appearances—the constitutional issues—without ignoring the underlying reality of the army; or, in other words, to remember that the Augustus was also the Imperator. Both titles represent facets of the game. What at first appeared to be a simple case of one-man rule becomes on closer inspection a delicate balancing act in which the emperor played off Senate against army, *auctoritas* against *potestas.*

Two centuries after Augustus, Dio Cassius, a senator from the city of Nicaea in the Roman province of Bithynia, imagined a debate between two of Octavian's key advisers on the eve of his *beau geste.* The topic was what shape the new regime should take. In the exchange, Agrippa, the general who was architect of Octavian's greatest victories, speaks in favor of democracy, for "equality before the law has an auspicious name and is most just in its workings."[14] Dio assigns the argument for monarchy to the worldly Maecenas, Octavian's chief negotiator and head of a sort of informal arts council that brought into the imperial orbit such luminaries as Horace and Vergil. Leaving little doubt as to the outcome, Dio not only allows Maecenas to dispose of the case for democracy in a few scornful sentences as the equivalent of "putting a sword in the hands of a child or a madman" but also gives him the lion's share of the discussion, more than four times the space allotted Agrippa.[15] Maecenas's advice goes well beyond theoretical considerations, extending to details of administration, finance, budget, and public relations. His speech is, in fact, an elaborate, if idealized, rationale for a government that Dio's readers would, of course, have recognized as that of their own time.

Although the debate is utterly fictitious, it is nonetheless useful for establishing the rules of the game of empire. Dio worked at the highest levels of government, achieving the consulship—by now an honorific office, but nonetheless a recognition of successful service and imperial favor—not just once but twice, the second time sharing it with the emperor himself, a signal honor. We must assume, therefore, that he knew how the game was played. For this reason, one quirk in Maecenas's argument deserves attention: although he speaks firmly for monarchy, Maecenas advises caution with regard to the title itself. If, he says,

> you prefer the monarchy in fact but fear the title of "king" as being accursed, you have but to decline this title and still be sole ruler under the appellation of "Caesar." And if you require still other epithets, your people will give you that of "*imperator*" as they gave it to your father; and they will pay reverence to your august position by still another term of address, so that you will enjoy fully the reality of the kingship without the odium which attaches to the name of "king."[16]

Writing two centuries after the fact, it was, of course, easy for Dio to know what advice to put in Maecenas's mouth, and Dio's contemporaries must have enjoyed as much as we do Maecenas's prescient use of the three key terms on which the Principate rested: *imperator* signifying control of the military, *Caesar* the hereditary relationship, and *Augustus* (here cleverly introduced through wordplay, the actual title itself not having yet been devised by the dramatic date of this discussion) the religious and senatorial tie.

The real significance of the passage lies not in its premise of Maecenas's astuteness but in Dio's choice of this setting for his rationale of the Principate. Dio wrote in the twilight of the Principate. Yet his use of a debate between Agrippa and Maecenas to discuss Octavian's options is modeled on one that the Athenian Xenophon inserted into an account of Cyrus, the founder of the Persian Empire, which he wrote early in the fourth century B.C. Ostensibly a biography of the great Persian king, Xenophon's Life of Cyrus is in fact a highly idealized treatise on leadership in which a very prescient and highly articulate Cyrus learns and explains the secrets to successful rule. Right after the first of his many victories, for instance, Cyrus learns that "the one who is overcome by strength sometimes conceives the idea that, if he trains his body, he may renew the combat. Even cities too, when captured, think that by taking on new allies they might renew the fight. But if people are convinced that others are superior to themselves, they are often ready even without compulsion to submit to them."[17] This, Xenophon explains, is the secret: Cyrus succeeded because "all [were] willing to be his subjects."[18]

Cyrus's debate occurs in the aftermath of his great victory over Babylon, when, Xenophon says, Cyrus had to make formal arrangements for ruling a great empire.[19] Six centuries separate Xenophon from Dio; the latter's use of Xenophon as a model for his own discussion is a reminder that the rules for judging rulers like Augustus and his successors were well established long before Octavian's grand gesture in 27 B.C. Thus it comes as no surprise to hear Maecenas counsel his master to show goodwill to all, to be generous with benefits, and in general to rule justly and set a good example. Such advice also shows up in Xenophon's pages, showing that these were already the marks of the good king. More significant, Dio's choice of setting reveals a continuity in classical culture which the shifting political landscape—from Greece to Rome, from republic to empire—often obscures.

The political world of the Roman Empire was, by modern standards, extremely restricted. Some fifty to sixty million people lived in it, and of these the senatorial class that was the prime constituency of the Principate composed the tiniest fraction, some two-tenths of 1 percent.[20] Throw in the other major constituency, the legions, which with noncitizen auxiliaries numbered about half a million, and all the other classes from local elites to merchants and traders which might be expected to have some political role, and the total percentage still would not reach double digits. Among this highly restricted and privileged political elite, the path to prominence began at the same place, with a thorough grounding in the classical authors from Homer to Vergil and mastery of the principles of philosophy, public speaking, and forensic oratory. More and more, scholars have come to see this training as a kind of code, communicated through gesture, dress, and deportment as much as speech. The classical curriculum equipped its beneficiaries with the ability to read this code and to pick out fellow recipients at a glance from a crowd of unwashed and untutored faces.[21] More important, just as the major training grounds for public life in the modern world—law schools and schools of public administration and policy—train students to perceive issues, to define problems and devise solutions according to certain sets of criteria and methods which are agreed to be "sound," so this classical curriculum equipped its students not just with a language but even more with habits of thought and behavior which governed their political judgment. Because the premises of classical scholarship remained unbroken for so long, Xenophon's Life of Cyrus could serve Dio as a guidebook to the political terrain of the Roman Empire, even though it was written centuries earlier in a vastly different political climate.

Given the weight of this tradition, the most significant thing of all about Maecenas's advice is that it deviates from the most visible aspect of the tradition. Cyrus, once he becomes the Great King, devotes his energy, and advice, to putting distance between himself and his subjects. He surrounds himself with pomp and ceremony and takes to using platform shoes and cosmetics as well as dazzling finery whenever he appears in public. Such steps were necessary, Xenophon explains, because, although Cyrus firmly "believed that no one had any right to rule who was not better than his subjects," he also recognized the importance of appearing to be better, so as "to cast a sort of spell upon them."[22] Yet despite this precedent, Maecenas advises Augustus to avoid display and honors: "So far as you yourself are concerned, permit no exceptional or prodigal distinction to be given you, through word or deed, either by the Senate or by any one else. For whereas the honour which you confer upon others lends glory to them, yet nothing can be given you that is greater than what you already possess and, besides, no little suspicion of insincerity would attach to its giving."[23] In Augustus's case, this modesty extended as well to his personal habits, and he became celebrated for the simplicity of his clothing and diet. But the crucial part is the conscious refusal, signaled by the act of 27 B.C., to rule by sheer force. "I counsel you," Maecenas says, "never to make full use of your power against your subjects as a body, nor to consider it any curtailment of your power if you do not actually put into effect all the measures you are in a position to enforce; but the greater your ability to do all you desire, the more eager you should be to desire in all things only what it is fitting you should desire."²⁴

As one acute observer has remarked, this act of denial is what truly sets off the Principate.²⁵ It is the key to the entire system, making the emperor—as another successful player, Pliny the Younger, put it in his panegyric to Trajan a century before Dio wrote—"one of us." Never, Pliny wrote, "should we flatter him as a divinity and a god; we are talking of a fellow-citizen, not a tyrant. . . . He is one of us—and his special virtue lies in his thinking so."²⁶ Everything else—the emperor's cultivation of senatorial friendships, his commitment to seek and heed the advice of the Senate, to promote culture and the arts, to reward merit and punish evil, the very security of his rule—hinges on this public demonstration of restraint. Act thus, Dio's Maecenas tells Octavian,

> and in consequence you will find your life most happy and utterly free from danger. For how can men help regarding you with affection as father and saviour, when they see that you are orderly and upright in your life, successful in war though inclined to peace; when you refrain from insolence and greed; when you meet them on a footing of equality, do not grow rich yourself while levying tribute on them, do not live in luxury yourself while imposing hardships upon them, are not licentious yourself while reproving licentiousness in them,—when, instead of all this, your life is in every way and manner precisely like theirs.²⁷

Within this key lies a key: not only is the restraint voluntary, but it must also be known to be voluntary, that the emperor is capable of a force that he chooses not to use. The emperor was expected not simply to be modest but to be ostentatiously so. It was a pose, and here, for all the difference in posture, it finds common ground with the showmanship advocated by Xenophon's Cyrus. Augustus's showmanship was of the homespun variety, but the point is that it was showmanship nonetheless; despite the contrast, attention to appearances remained the same. The difference amounted to a commitment to senatorial values—

courtesy, consultation, moderation. Despite all the distance opened between them, the rules required the emperor to act as if he were still just a member of their club. This was the first, and greatest, rule of the game of empire, continuing in force when the Principate itself was nothing but a memory. The general principle still held when Constantine met with the bishops in 335, although (as events will show) the nature of the club had changed considerably.

A second rule followed from the first but did not outlast the Principate: because there was no office of emperor, there could be no formally established criteria for selecting a successor. Indeed, since the emperor was theoretically simply an extraordinary magistrate selected to deal with a crisis that just never went away, officially there was no way even to recognize the need for a successor. The soldiers, who pledged their allegiance directly to the emperor, had a distinct preference for dynastic succession, but such a mechanism bared more of the body politic than suitable for senatorial modesty. Thus, when the emperor Vespasian (69–79) insisted that his son succeed him, there was not a murmur from the army. But Pliny the Elder slipped the following criticism into his *Natural History*, published at this very time. As part of an ethnography of Taprobane (Sri Lanka), he wrote that "their buildings were of only moderate height; the price of corn was never inflated; there were no lawcourts and no litigation, the deity worshipped was Hercules; the king was elected by the people on the grounds of age and gentleness of disposition, and as having no children, and if he afterwards had a child, he was deposed, to prevent the monarchy from becoming hereditary."[28] Coming as it does amid so idyllic a tale, Pliny's claim that kings in this faraway land must be barren is a pointed reminder of the strength of senatorial opposition to dynasties.

For this reason, the death of an incumbent emperor was the tender spot of the Principate. Augustus was able to finesse this problem by the fact that he had no direct male heir. Indeed, by the time he died in A.D. 14, only Tiberius, his wife Livia's son by a former marriage to Tiberius Claudius Nero, remained to succeed him. This set a workable precedent. So long as a Julio-Claudian, a descendant of one of the two great lines of the First Family, was available to succeed, the potential for conflict between Senate and army could be avoided. Since the senatorial concept of merit was still based on the old republican notion of cumulative family prestige, scions of this dynasty satisfied the senatorial criterion as well as the military's.

A third rule involved the military. It was the unwritten rule. Officially, the military played no role in the constitution of the empire, which was an agreement between the Senate and the emperor. So the role of the army could never be acknowledged. The army was the silent partner of the Principate, the man who was not there. Posted to distant frontiers, the soldiers were for the most part intermittently involved in the game of empire, able to assert themselves only under extraordinary conditions. In the first two centuries, such interventions, while spectacular and violent, were brief. It took organization and leadership for the legions to pose a coordinated threat. When the game was running properly—when the emperor held the loyalty and affection of the troops and kept his more skilled and ambitious commanders on a short leash—the legions did not intervene in day-to-day play.

There was a single, flamboyant exception. When Augustus stripped Italy of armed men, he left one military force intact. This was the Praetorian Guard, named after the unit that policed the commander's quarters—the Praetorium—in a Roman military camp. With no other units stationed in Italy, the guard stood as the only well-trained military force readily available, and the emperors jealously nurtured this asset. Under Augustus, the guard was scattered around Rome. But his successor, Tiberius, allowed it to bivouac in a single camp, thereby immeasurably increasing its political effectiveness and giving it an institutional focus and identity comparable to that which made the Senate such an effective representative of the interests of its members. The guard would be a major player, particularly in the selection of a new emperor, for the next three centuries.

Roughly a century after Augustus, the senator Tacitus, a brooding genius and the empire's greatest historian, alluded to these military reforms in the *Germania,* a fascinating mix of ethnography and veiled attack on the social and political ills of the empire. Coming to the tribe of the Suiones, he wrote,

> Among these peoples, further, respect is paid to wealth, and one man is
> accordingly supreme, with no restrictions and with an unchallenged right

to obedience; nor is there any general carrying of arms here, as among the other Germans: rather arms are locked up in charge of a warder, and that warder a slave. The ocean prevents sudden inroads from enemies; and, besides, the hands of armed men, with nothing to do, easily become riotous; and indeed, it is not to a king's interest to put a noble or a freeman or even a freedman in charge of the arms.[29]

In his allusive manner, Tacitus here exhibited a keen appreciation of the tactical benefits that control over weaponry can give an unscrupulous ruler. His equation of this tactic with tyranny, along with his juxtaposition of the "general carrying of arms" with freedom, was a thinly veiled allusion to the command of the Praetorian Guard, a post too sensitive to be turned over to someone of senatorial rank who might harbor unhealthy ambitions. For this reason, emperors limited it to men of equestrian rank—not exactly slaves as in Tacitus's analogy, but in the first century a rank deemed too low to aspire to independent power or to establish the kind of independent network of which a senator was capable. Therein lies the force of Tacitus's remark, which cuts with surgical precision through the Augustan façade to the military base on which it rested.

One proof, if proof were needed, of the accuracy of Tacitus's judgment lies in Maecenas's advice to Augustus, offered in Dio's imaginative conference, to limit military training instead of making it universal. Involuntarily (and probably unwittingly) confirming Tacitus's comment in the *Germania* about the nature of monarchy, Dio has Maecenas say, "If, on the other hand, we permit all the men of military age to have arms and to practise warfare, they will always be the source of seditions and civil wars."[30] The one unwritten, but never to be violated, rule of the game of empire was this: although the Senate could be alienated with impunity so long as the loyalty of the troops was secure, it was impossible to alienate both Senate and military and still survive. In 67, this is precisely what the infamous Nero did. Vengeance was swift. Alienated from both Senate and army, Nero took his own life in June 68.

Nero's death triggered a constitutional crisis, for he was also the last surviving Julio-Claudian. With no obvious successor available, senatorial and military criteria clashed head-on. On this occasion it was the armies, ever lurking behind the façade, which prevailed. In the course of a single year, A.D. 69, four different men, each backed by a different army, held the title of emperor. Tacitus later said that this "Year of the Four Emperors," as it was thereafter known, revealed the "secret of empire." As he defined it, the "secret" was that "emperors could be made elsewhere than at Rome."[31] The answer is elusive, as is much of Tacitus's prose. A senator who rose to the consulship in A.D. 98, Tacitus wrote for a highly sophisticated audience that he expected to be sufficiently adept to notice what he had left unsaid. The unspoken question in this case was, "If not at Rome, then where? And by whom?" The chilling answer—on the frontiers, and by the armies— lay bare the heart of the Augustan settlement. The revolt of the frontier armies revealed just how few cards the Senate actually held.

Although this passage is often cited as the quintessential proof of the military despotism that underlay the empire, it also stands as testimony to just how effectively the Augustan façade had worked.

The question of who was entitled to rule was never fully resolved, and the death of an incumbent emperor without a clearly designated successor in place always brought the Augustan house of cards to the point of collapse. But after the "Year of Four Emperors," everyone knew better than to take the frontier armies for granted. When the line of Vespasian ran out, thirty years later, in A.D. 98, the Senate tried a subtler approach, appointing the aged and childless Nerva, for whom, like Pliny's Indian ruler, it was physically impossible to harbor dynastic pretensions. The armies, not consulted, began to grumble, and Nerva quickly adopted as his heir and successor a popular military commander, Trajan, who turned out to be a skillful senatorial player as well. This tacit compromise between Senate and army seemed to hold for a century, leading later historians—of whom Edward Gibbon was the most enthusiastic—to identify this as the age of the "five good emperors," each of whom adopted a competent successor and thereby satisfied both the senatorial criterion of meritocracy and the military longing for a dynasty. Thus, in the opening words of the *Decline and Fall,* "The image of a free constitution was preserved with decent reverence."[32]

Tacitus knew better. Writing at the outset of Gibbon's Golden Age, he tried to alert his contemporaries to the instability lying just beneath the surface of their world. One clear message of his gloomy, brilliant *Annals* is that any system that depends on the whim of a single man is inherently unstable, no less so if his whim is to play by the rules than if it is not. His message fell on deaf ears, drowned out by a chorus of praise for the "good emperors." But subsequent generations came to understand it only too well.

The Rules Change

In the third century, the empire was battered by a series of invasions that led to a new set of rules. The armies, which bore the brunt of this attack, abandoned the passive role they had been assigned under the Principate and asserted the right to choose their own commanders. The result was half a century of domestic chaos. Stability returned with a vengeance in 284 with the accession of the emperor Diocletian, who ruled for twenty decisive years before making the unprecedented decision to retire voluntarily from office. Of obscure birth—his name originally was Diocles, according to one source, and only Romanized when he assumed the purple—Diocletian rose to power through the rough-and-tumble of military politics which made, and destroyed, so many emperors in this century. According to one anecdote, his version of the *beau geste* was not a graceful speech before the Senate but a spear that he personally drove through the chest of his chief rival.[33]

True or not, the story of Diocletian and the spear confirms that a major shift in the power relationship of the players in the Principate occurred well before the reorganization that he initiated after becoming emperor, and that its effect was to reduce the influence of the Senate. For a long time, scholars saw this transition through the eyes of senatorial sources. Their evaluations—larded with contrasts between "good emperors" of the second century and "barracks emperors" of the third, between peace and prosperity versus war and inflation, high culture and a laissez-faire government versus low culture and a totalitarian one—conformed to the model of "decline and fall," but they did so in such a way as to imply that little more than individual abilities were at fault, good emperors being succeeded by ones who were not so good. There is a bit of truth to this suggestion, but the biggest reason for the changes had nothing to do with the personal priorities or talents of individual emperors. An important premise of the Augustan settlement was relative stability on the frontiers. The lack of serious aggression allowed Augustus to diminish the size as well as influence of the armed forces, to demilitarize the heartland of the empire and reduce the cost of imperial government. In other words, the situation on the frontiers was a happy coincidence, not the product of superior skills on the part of second-century emperors, and certainly not dependent on the wisdom of senatorial government. With the third-century invasions, the free ride was over.

With reason, Diocletian has been called the second founder of the Roman Empire, for he oversaw the most extensive reorganization of the imperial game since Augustus first wrote the rules three centuries earlier. His changes, particularly a change in the rules for succession, directly affect Constantine, whose rise to power begins in the aftermath of Diocletian's reign; they are analyzed in Chapter 4. Here, it is important to take note only of the way Diocletian changed relations between emperor and Senate. The most obvious one was in the role of the emperor himself. Isolated and exalted as never before, the emperor now became surrounded by the trappings of elaborate court ceremonial, fitted out with costly garments and rare jewels, a sacred figure. Gone was the pretense of emperor as "first citizen." Self-consciously a remote and sacrosanct ruler, Diocletian surrounded himself with ceremony. Nothing could be more different from the simple, homespun fashion set by Augustus. Because *Dominus,* "lord," long an unofficial title, now became the standard form of address, scholars have named this new regime the Dominate, as opposed to the supposedly more open Principate.

Although the contrast between the two is usually what catches the eye, more may be learned by looking at the similarities between Augustus and his distant heir. Chief among these is that both men emerged in periods when a consensus about the rules of government had shattered into civil war. With this insight, another similarity becomes apparent. Although their style is different, their substance is the same: both men were problem solvers whose goal was to achieve stability and legitimacy. The circumstances, not the character of the individuals, were what had changed. It is worth asking whether even the astute Augustus would have gone to the lengths he did to respond to the sensitivities of its members had the Senate not been the obvious institution to legitimize his new and ambiguous position, or if he had not needed the pool of expertise it provided. Put that way, the answer seems self-evident. Augustus turned to the Senate not because of an inherent regard he had for that institution but because it was useful to him; had a more useful alternative been available, there is no reason to believe he would have preferred the Senate anyway. More fundamental, though harder to isolate, is to ask what gave the Senate the ability to provide such cover, for this is what it lost during the course of the Principate.[34]

The answer lies in that nexus of interest and responsibility which binds ruler and ruled. The republican Senate, as we saw, was made up of "fathers" who, tradition said, were committed to the long-run welfare of the state and its citizens. Bonds of common interest and theoretically equal standing—demonstrated annually when the great men canvassed for votes—contributed to senatorial prestige, while reminding the latter that at least in some distant and tenuous way their standing and greatness rested on the support of their lessers. When Augustus stabilized the senatorial order by making it hereditary, he also broke this psychological bond. To senators, fame and fortune now flowed all too obviously downward rather than upward, from the emperor rather than the people. They reoriented themselves accordingly. To the people, the Senate became in theory as well as in fact a different class. The consequences were profound for both sides, being somewhat akin to what Tocqueville had in mind when he placed even above the need for talent and virtue in rulers the need "that the interests of those men should not differ from the interests of the community at large." The result was, in Ramsay MacMullen's trenchant prose, rulers unable to "imagine themselves ever having to suffer what they inflicted on their inferiors."[35] In the fewest words, it is the difference between the republic and the empire.

This distance opened by the Augustan settlement widened as the Senate came to be drawn more and more from an empirewide base. This imperial scope—one of Rome's undeniable achievements—had the effect of integrating local elites into a single polity in a way that drew the admiration of contemporaries and has continued to draw praise from theorists of multicultural unions. Yet as the republican

Senate became an imperial Senate, it lacked a raison d'être. What gave the Augustan Senate the ability to legitimate imperial rule was not just the independent authority it exercised in the republic but also the nexus of invisible ties to a wider constituency which at least in theory led senators to the offices that qualified them for membership and prestige. The republic had defined itself as "the Senate and People of Rome" to indicate a mutual bond between the Senate and the popular assemblies. Now, two centuries after Augustus, it was the emperor who provided legitimacy to the Senate.

In this sense, the Principate was a victim of its own success. The Senate continued to be a vigorous institution in many respects; indeed, during the second century its membership had been strengthened by inclusion of ruling elites from the Greek East.[36] But what made the Senate central to the Augustan system was not the power of its members but its ability to confer legitimacy on the emperor. This role, so fundamental to the Principate, it no longer was able to play. Ultimately, the Senate could never be an effective check on the power of the emperor, because as an institution it lacked any means other than the whim of the emperor to enforce its will. As Edward Gibbon put it in the *Decline and Fall,* "The ideal restraints of the senate and the laws might serve to display the virtues, but could never correct the vices, of the emperor."[37] It could thus be said that by giving the senatorial class stability at the cost of its emotive bond with the Roman people, Augustus had given the Senate a Faustian bargain. If so, the trick backfired on Augustus's successors, who were left with an ever thinner mantle of legitimacy in which to wrap themselves.

From this standpoint, the most critical need of the third century was for a new basis of legitimacy. While the thought is difficult to entertain for citizens of modern, civilian states with an abhorrence of military involvement in government, the army in the ancient world was at least theoretically a viable alternative. In ancient thinking the military's claim to a role in approving rulers and providing them with legitimate authority was as strong as that of a body like the Senate, for the soldiers were heirs of that primitive assembly that modern scholars call "the folk in arms."[38] Especially was this so in Rome, where tradition said plebeians had first won political rights through military necessity, and where the Centuriate Assembly, entitled to elect senior magistrates and decide issues of war and peace, had grown out of a military muster. For the Romans' own attitude, one need look no further than the *Commentaries* of Julius Caesar: whenever the dictator-to-be is about to commit a particularly outrageous affront to Roman etiquette or international law, he is careful to show he acted with the support, or even at the insistence, of his soldiery. On coins, emperors were pleased to depict themselves in *adlocutio* with their troops, and the reason was not that it made people think they were being ruled by a military despot. The scene was meant to remind Romans of the *contio*, the republican assembly in which magistrates justified their decisions to the people and attempted to win public opinion over to their side. It showed that their emperor cared about the common people, here represented by their comrades in arms.

In calmer days, direct military participation in government might have made for an interesting constitutional experiment. Amid the pressures of the third century, however, the military's direct involvement was merely destabilizing. Whatever legitimacy military selection of the emperor might theoretically have provided was more than negated in practice by the lack of any means to prevent ambitious commanders from using their troops as a base from which to challenge imperial authority. As in the late republic, a counterbalance again was needed. In the late empire, religion came to provide that balance.

Playing the Game

In many ways, the change between Principate and Dominate was more apparent than real. The Senate of the late empire, for instance, should not be dismissed as merely a dim shadow of its republican ancestor, though this is admittedly a charge easy to substantiate. The minutes of a meeting of the Senate in Constantinople in 438, convened to ratify the Theodosian Code, precede the first book of that great compilation of late Roman law. They begin with an account of the preparation of the code by the praetorian prefect, Anicius Glabrio, which is interspersed with senatorial reaction. "The assembly shouted: 'Thou art newly eloquent! Truly eloquent,'" it reads at one point, and at another, "The assembly shouted: 'It is right! So be it! So be it!'" The minutes conclude with a full page of acclamations, including,

"Augustuses of Augustuses, the greatest of Augustuses!" (Repeated eight times.)

"For the good of the human race, for the good of the Senate, for the good of the State, for the good of all!" (Repeated twenty-four times.)

"Suppressors of informers, suppressors of chicanery!" (Repeated twenty-eight times.)

"Hail! Paulus!" (Repeated twelve times.)

"A consulship for you!" (Repeated eleven times.)

"We ask that no laws be promulgated in reply to supplications!" (Repeated twenty-one times.)

"Hail! Aetius!" (Repeated fifteen times.)

"A third term for you in the consulship!" (Repeated thirteen times.)

"All the rights of landholders are thrown into confusion by such surreptitious actions!" (Repeated seventeen times.)[39]

At first reading, the Senate in these pages appears reduced from its role of arbiter and architect of grand policy in the republic to little more than a cheering section. But like so much of the record of late antiquity, these minutes call for an ear attuned to phrasing and nuance to be understood correctly. Modern political discourse, with its broad and blatant tones, is no place to learn how to read this record; rather, it requires the kind of antennae used to negotiate more delicate settings—a board meeting, say, or an upscale cocktail party. Amid all the "three cheers" and "hip, hip, hoorays," it is undeniably strange to read, "We ask that no laws be promulgated in reply to supplications!" or "All the rights of landholders are thrown into confusion by such surreptitious actions!" In addition to raising the very real question of how these jawbreakers ever could have been chanted fifteen or twenty times (if, indeed, that is what these annotations signify), their presence suggests something more than gratuitous flattery, for they, and others such as "In order that the established laws may not be falsified, let all copies be written out in letters!" (that one was repeated eighteen times), speak to sensitive problems of late Roman government. Opinions, in other words, which might have been delivered in orations or debates in an earlier period were in the late empire conveyed through acclamations. Strange as they sound, they show that the Senate continued to serve, as it always had, as the institutional springboard for the expression of elite concerns.[40]

Perhaps a better way to understand these minutes is to think of the way media commentators will count the number of times a State of the Union speech in the United States is interrupted by applause, or time the length of a demonstration for a particular candidate at a nominating convention. Both events are largely ceremonial and ritualized. But the places in a speech at which Congress chooses to applaud can signal success or failure for a policy, and the size of a demonstration can indicate how much effort loyalists will put into a candidate's campaign back home. Indeed, it was "back home," rather than in Constantinople, that senators, increasingly drawn from provincial circles as well as high levels of the bureaucracy and military, demonstrated their power and influence, using their connections at court to make a closed and distant imperial government accessible to the local elites who ran the cities, and to make or break the careers of imperial governors sent out to run the provinces.[41]

There were real changes in the late empire and many differences from the Principate. But it is necessary to stay focused on underlying continuities in order not to be distracted by superficial differences. No matter what the period of Roman history, access to the corridors of power, along with the patronage that access brought, was the driving force. In both periods, emperors and aristocrats were driven into each other's arms by their need for legitimacy and administrators on the one hand, patronage and access on the other. In both periods, access was a marketable commodity. Perhaps the oldest principle of politics is that providing highly visible access can, therefore, be a means to confer prestige. Xenophon's omniscient Cyrus, once he became Great King, reinforced his own standing by conferring signs of favor on his friends. "And if he wished to have any one of his friends courted by the multitude [Xenophon observes], to such a one he would send presents from his table. And that device proved effective; for even to this day everybody pays more diligent court to those to whom they see things sent from the royal table; for they think that such persons must be in high favour and in a position to secure for them anything they may want."[42] It is not the table scraps that were important but what they symbolized: tight resources in general or, in particular, the favor of the holder of those resources, which of course was Xenophon's point. The nature of the "perks" changes, but the principle remains the same.

In a more complex society—Rome's or ours—information is the scrap more likely to be sought after. In a widely cited passage, Dio Cassius complained of the difficulty he faced uncovering information once his history reached the end of the republic: "Formerly, as we know, all matters were reported to the Senate and to the people, even if they happened at a distance; hence all learned of them and many recorded them, and consequently the truth regarding them. . . . But after this time most things that happened began to be kept secret and concealed, and even though some things are perchance made public they are distrusted just because they can not be verified."[43] Information and access were the vital ingredients of influence, conveying prestige to their recipients but also providing a valuable service to the emperor. To the extent that they strove to recommend reasonably qualified candidates (if for no other reason than to maintain their own credibility), senatorial brokers served as useful talent scouts for the emperor. They also shielded him, at least at the lower levels, from the resentment that being passed over generates. Disappointment was an inevitable product of a system that produced too many candidates for too few positions—no more than one hundred a year, according to one estimate. Thus Dio's Agrippa noted in his argument for democracy: "This being so, greater hostility will inevitably be felt toward the monarch by those who fail to get what they want, than friendliness by those who obtain their desires. For the latter take what they receive as due them and think there is no particular reason for being grateful to the giver, since they are getting no more than they expected."[44]

An American president, William H. Taft, put the same sentiment more pungently. "An appointment," he wrote, "not infrequently creates for the Congressman who secures it one ingrate and ten enemies."[45] As President Taft's comment suggests, patrons of disappointed candidates serve to deflect resentment from the source of patronage, be it a president or an emperor; this was their great value to Augustus and his successors. In return for access and influence, they could be expected to soothe the feelings of disappointed office seekers, at one and the same time keeping intact their hopes for a future appointment, their allegiance to the emperor, and their belief in the usefulness of the game.

In the late empire, imperial prestige was redefined yet again, with the emperor required to demonstrate access to an even higher patron, a divine *comes*, or companion, whose favor, negotiated by the emperor, protected the empire from its increasingly powerful enemies. Later ages fine-tuned this theory, but in the early fourth century there was a simple rule of thumb for demonstrating this connection: winning battles. Late Roman emperors, therefore, were extremely careful not to commit their prestige except in situations in which a positive outcome was assured. Constantine himself was a great one for threat and bluster—a tactic by which he tried to resolve the first Christian dispute to come his way—and at the end of this story Bishop Ambrose of Milan will play on precisely this fear during a dispute with the emperor Theodosius, with consequences that pertain directly to the question of Christian coercion. But this concern was in no way new with the Dominate; from the very start, skillful emperors knew the fine line that divided *auctoritas* from *potestas*. A story in Tacitus illustrates the careful steps an emperor needed to take to maintain his illusion of supremacy, as well as the consequences of failing to do so.

The situation, predictably, involved the military. The troops in Gaul had been unhappy about harsh treatment and low salaries, but Augustus's prestige was so immense that they dared not act. On his death in A.D. 14, however, they mutinied, thereby posing a mortal threat to the regime of his successor. Tiberius dealt with the situation through a series of moves designed to keep off balance both the troops on the frontier and any senators who might have been inclined to take advantage of the emperor's absence. Threatening his personal intervention, Tiberius would constantly order preparations for an imminent departure and then postpone the trip to deal with other issues. He was criticized for timidity and indecision; but Tacitus knew better:

> To all this criticism Tiberius opposed an immutable and rooted determination not to endanger himself and the empire by leaving the centre of affairs. . . . In the persons of his sons he could approach both at once, without hazarding the imperial majesty, always most venerable from a

distance. Further, it was excusable in the young princes to refer certain questions to their father, and it was in his power to pacify or crush resistance offered to Germanicus or Drusus; but let the emperor be scorned, and what resource was left?—However, as though any moment might see his departure, he chose his escort, provided his equipage, and fitted out vessels. Then with a variety of pleas, based on the wintry season or the pressure of affairs, he deceived at first the shrewdest; the populace, longer; the provinces, longest of all.[46]

Less prudent was Tiberius's nephew Germanicus, who confronted the rebels and tried to shame them into submission. Crying that he would sooner die than turn traitor, he attempted to fall on his sword, only to be restrained by conveniently placed well-wishers. Some, no doubt, were impressed. But Tacitus, who reports this incident as well, tells us of a soldier, "by the name of Calusidius, [who] drew his own blade and offered it with the commendation that 'it was sharper.'"[47] Germanicus's rash act resulted in his being briefly held hostage by the mutineers.

Such moments did more than humiliate the person who acted so foolishly; they also put the whole system at risk. Had Tiberius misstepped as badly as Germanicus, acting with too much haste or not enough, the façade that Augustus had worked so carefully to erect would have come tumbling down, bringing with it not only the emperor but also those senators and bureaucrats whose positions by now depended on the prestige of this individual. Awareness of their own liability in such situations no doubt is what kept senators like Tacitus playing the game.

The Good King

Peter Brown has called attention once again to this forbidden truth of the game of empire: nothing in either Principate or Dominate could prevent a determined emperor from ruling through terror.[48] It was a short-term game, for without the cooperation of the Senate and the local elites the emperor would be forced to rely on less skilled administrators on the one hand while increasing his vigilance against plots and conspiracies on the other. This, more than the virtue or vice of any particular emperor, is what drove the system to ever greater exaltation of the role and person of the emperor. Marcus Aurelius, the philosopher-emperor of the empire at its height, felt it every bit as much as Diocletian, who finally formalized the relationship. Both sides, therefore, danced around this dirty secret. The tune they used was culture, or *paideia,* as the Greeks called it—a light tune, airy and meaningless, yet subtle and capable of great complexity. In its simplest form, the emperor or governor showed his appreciation for, and willingness to respond to, the appeal of that culture to a life of balance and moderation. He did so by listening to speeches of all kinds, but in particular speeches in praise of the virtues of good rulers. By showing themselves attentive to such lessons, and willing to reward those who could present them with some art, emperors signaled to the ruling elites that the baser instincts of human nature and the terrors they provoked had been curbed; in moments of stress, their anger could, and would, be soothed.

Through this route the emperors tapped into a rich vein of political advice to "the good king," the echoes of which have been heard in Xenophon's Life of Cyrus. The tradition was already old when Xenophon adapted it for Greek use in the fourth century B.C.; parts can be found governing Near Eastern rulers as different as Hammurabi and King David. In the ensuing centuries, theorists in the great Hellenistic kingdoms of Alexander's successors combined these age-old maxims into weighty academic protocols. The responsibilities of the Good King were summed up succinctly in a tract entitled *On Kingship,* attributed to one Diotogenes, which may have been written as early as the third century B.C. "The functions of the King," Diotogenes writes, "are threefold: military command, the dispensation of justice, and the cult of the gods."[49] The Roman equivalent was summed up in a set of virtues that emperors took pains to show they possessed: everything from such predictable traits as courage, benevolence, wisdom, a sense of justice, and duty to the gods to the more mundane "speed" (*celeritas*) or more exalted "foresight" (*Providentia*) and fortune (*Fortuna*), these last two being signs of the qualities and favor of deities. The nature of these virtues was fluid, but the goal was always the same, as summed up by Cyrus, to rule over "willing subjects."[50]

Then as now, public works were a key means of satisfying this goal. Here, too, Augustus set a standard for his successors, with an extensive building program that, if it did not quite justify his boast to have "found Rome brick and left it marble," nevertheless remade Rome into an imperial city. The use of public space, scholars now realize, says as much about the goals and ambitions of a regime as the constitutional niceties that monopolized the attentions of an earlier generation of Roman historians.[51] Coins, on the other hand, have long been recognized as a means by which emperors signaled their intentions, goals, and priorities. During the empire, a rich iconography developed, as well as an extensive shorthand. With these two developments, coins became effective means of communication, able to carry in their restricted space, if not a full-blown speech, at least the ancient equivalent of a "sound bite." For example, after his victory over Antony and Cleopatra, Octavian issued a silver coin with the image of a crocodile and the legend *Aegypto Capta* ("Egypt Captured"). In periods of civil war, emperors were fond of issuing coins showing clasped hands and the hopeful motto *Fides Exercitum* ("Loyalty of the Armies"). A popular phrase on coins of the late empire is *Fel Temp Reparatio,* short for *Felicitas temporum reparatio,* nicely translated as "Happy Days Are Here Again!" It shows up on the coins of Romulus Augustulus, who has the unhappy distinction of being the last emperor in the West.

Although scholars still debate the importance and effectiveness of this means of communication, and even though they are more aware than earlier generations that propaganda is not a simple one-way process in which rulers freely manipulate their subjects,[52] there is nevertheless no reason to doubt one feature of the coins about which the Romans themselves were fully aware. For most periods, the high quality of the coins themselves projected an image of Roman power and trustworthiness. In the first century A.D., Pliny the Elder tells the story of a shipwrecked sailor whose coins convinced the king of Taprobane—that island of infertile kings—to send an embassy to Rome: "The king among all that he heard was remarkably struck with admiration for Roman honesty, on the ground that among the money found on the captive the denarii were all equal in weight, although the various figures on them showed that they had been coined by several emperors."[53] The story may be no more literally true than others Pliny told of this state, but at the very least it reflects the pride Romans like Pliny took in their coinage. Five centuries later, a Byzantine trader bested a Persian counterpart in a debate over the relative grandeur of their sovereigns before another Taprobanese king with the simple advice to compare the coins of each.[54]

Beyond a general idea of doing good, emperors did not as a rule come to power with a specific agenda or mandates to initiate new programs. They did not think of themselves as legislators but as conservators whose primary function was to adhere to policies and practices that had been laid down since time immemorial. In fact, despite their modern stereotype as power-hungry despots, Roman emperors were surprisingly passive by modern standards. Rather than ruling through legislation, emperors typically expressed their will through responses to a steady stream of petitions from subjects, referrals from friends, and inquiries from subordinates—an activity characterized as "petition-and-response."[55]

Because of this self-image, Roman emperors were much more susceptible than their modern counterparts to arguments about the nature of their rule, and in particular about what being a "good king" entailed. This situation created an opening for another kind of player in the game of empire—the writers, theorists, and intellectuals on whom emperors depended to demonstrate that they were fulfilling their time-honored obligations. In particular, however, it made players of orators, for this was a culture that placed the highest value on the spoken word. In Rome, eloquence and verbal dexterity were highly prized not just for ceremonial occasions or the courtroom but also for embassies and negotiations. Indeed, orators played roles that today would fall somewhere between political consultants and movie stars. Cities depended on such men to charm emperors into granting their requests; emperors, in turn, counted on such voices to celebrate their virtues and accomplishments.

There were plenty of occasions for celebrating the emperor's reign. Every embassy or appeal included set speeches in which the litigants quite naturally took the opportunity to recall in the most extravagant way possible their gratitude for benefactions previously received, as a way of demonstrating that a favorable decision in the present case would not be wasted on ingrates. Imperial anniversaries called for a speech, as did the annual installation of new consuls. Indeed, so many and varied were the occasions that one study of the imperial agenda asks in head-wagging wonder if the emperor did not spend all of his time listening to one speech or another.[56] Each occasion and type of speech had its own format and set of rules, taught in the schools and laid out in handbooks. For convenience, all these variations may here be summed up under the generic heading of panegyric, because all celebrated in one way or another the virtues of the emperor.[57]

The maestro, if the number of his orations to survive is any indication, was Dio of Prusa, whose eloquence earned him the surname Chrysostom ("golden tongued"). Early in the second century, Dio won the honor of celebrating the emperor Trajan's anniversary on no fewer than four separate occasions. He did so with a series of speeches on kingship, using a genre in which an ostensibly objective discussion of the duties of the ruler provided an artful alternative to outright praise of the emperor's virtues. "In plain and simple language," Dio says in the first of his discourses, "I have described the good king. If any of his attributes seem to belong to you, happy are you in your gracious and excellent nature, and happy are we who share its blessings with you."[58]

Chrysostom's counterpart in the late empire was unquestionably the philosopher-orator Themistius, who led ten embassies from the Senate in Constantinople to various emperors and delivered thirty-six political orations during a remarkable career that spanned almost forty years. Although he was speaking before Christian emperors, Themistius drew on the same themes as Dio two centuries earlier, praising emperors for their commitment to philosophy and civic virtues, holding them up as examples of justice and moderation.[59] His inaugural lecture, so to speak, was delivered before Constantine's son and successor, Constantius II, in 350, but its distinction of legitimate rule from rule by force could just as easily have been made by Dio more than two centuries earlier, or Xenophon five centuries before then. That man "alone makes no false pretence to kingship," Themistius points out, who "leads men who wish to follow him, not men who are in terror of him, and his rule is voluntary and not forced."[60]

Criticism in these speeches was limited to pointing out the failings of predecessors in the immediate or far-distant past. In the time-honored rules of the genre, such failings included ways in which they fell short of the present subject. Such criticism, therefore, became another way of indirect praise. Dio took this means of indirection to new heights in his *Second Discourse* by casting the whole discussion as a dialogue between Alexander the Great and his father, Philip II. Here it becomes Alexander, not Dio, who uses the unjust king as a counterexample of virtue. Such a man, Alexander argues,

> proves himself a violent, unjust and lawless ruler, visiting his strength, not upon the enemy, but upon his subjects and friends; . . . he is insatiate of pleasures, insatiate of wealth, quick to suspect, implacable in anger, keen for slander, deaf to reason, knavish, treacherous, degraded, willful, exalting the wicked, envious of his superiors, too stupid for education, regarding no man as friend nor having one, as though such a possession were beneath him.[61]

The genre also permitted the orator to attribute his praises to a special knowledge he possessed, a gambit that tempered praise that might have seemed extravagant coming from a less well informed source, and one that also did no harm to his own reputation as a man of influence. By the time of the *Third Discourse,* Dio could take this route with somewhat greater plausibility than normal, and it is one more mark of his skill that he turned it into yet another means of flattering the emperor: "Now Socrates thought that because he did not know the Persian king's inner life, he did not know his state of happiness either. I, however, most noble Prince, have been in your company and am perhaps as well acquainted with your character as anyone, and know that you delight in truth and frankness rather than in flattery and guile."[62] Indeed, the only innovation in these speeches sometimes seems to be in inventing ways to deny that their praises were mere flattery. Emperors are compared to gods and their word made the equivalent of law; their right to rule is bestowed by the gods, and their greatest obligation to their subjects is to appear as a god in their midst. Such adulation easily creates the impression that the emperors had succeeded in making the intelligentsia captives of their will. But the interaction was subtler than such abject language makes it appear. The symbols themselves were banal—virtues associated with the traditional duties of kingship, such as justice, courage, piety, philanthropy. But a skillful orator would juggle these symbols as the occasion demanded, emphasizing one, ignoring another. A knowledgeable audience would thereby know not only their sovereign's strengths but also, by omission, his weaknesses.

Lavish praise, when obviously not deserved, could signal an attempt to modify the ruler's behavior. Here, to be sure, the orator would have to tread lightly, tempering his advice to accord with what he thought the emperor wanted to hear, putting it in a way that he would be willing to receive. But as every parent knows, praise can also be a means of control. In the same way, these panegyrics could be a means of indicating the actions that would delegitimize an emperor. Attention to the unusual, therefore, can tease a policy even out of these achingly dull and seemingly insubstantial set pieces.

In Dio's *Second Discourse* quoted above, for instance, Alexander's catalogue of the vices of an unjust king serves also as a succinct counterindicator of the actions that were expected of a good king. Significantly, he ends his catalogue of the vices of an unjust king with the ominous words "such a one Zeus thrusts aside and deposes." Celebration of the benefits of an emperor's rule and his relation to gods thus cuts both ways: it could be a means also to assert the standards by which he would be judged, and remind him of his duties. In his *First Discourse,* Dio puts conditions on the adoration and love that emperors sought: it comes to the king who "understands how to repay kindness with gratitude," who is "kindly and humane," who "displays a soul benignant and gentle towards all." And in the *Second Discourse* he uses the figure of Alexander the Great to remind Trajan that a good king "forces the unrighteous to mend their ways and lends a helping hand to the weak."[63]

Above all, it was the panegyrists who asserted the ultimate means of control: memory. In ways subtle and direct, panegyrists reminded the emperor that this power of ultimate judgment, the judgment of posterity, was one that lay beyond even his vast power. Only good acts, in conformity with the lessons they taught, could ensure its award. How much better is it for the ruler, Dio asks, "to win credit rather than censure for his acts, to have the love of men and gods instead of their hate?"[64] The formal right of the Senate to perform *damnatio memoriae,* erasing the deeds of a hated emperor after his death, was asserted baldly by Pliny the Younger in a speech that is all the more important for having served as a model of the type for centuries. "Alongside all your other benefits and above many of them," he tells Trajan, "I set our freedom to avenge ourselves daily on the evil emperors of the past, and to warn by example all future ones that there will be neither time nor place for the shades of disastrous rulers to rest in peace from the execrations of posterity."[65] In a way, speakers like Dio and theorists like Diotogenes were the wild cards of the game of empire. What made them so was that, in the course of praising the emperor and celebrating his virtues, they wrote the rules of the game. In the fourth century, to the surprise of everybody except, perhaps, themselves, Christian bishops came to fill both these roles, providing the stability once the role of the Senate and writing the rules for the good king.

The Christian Card

Toward the end of the fourth century, another Chrysostom wrote a tract in this genre of imperial values. Evaluating good and bad kings, the speech describes a good king as "a king who truly rules over anger and envy and pleasure," a bad one as "one who seems to rule over men, but who is enslaved to anger and to the love of power and pleasures." How, this Chrysostom asks, can a person who is unable to rule himself guide others rightly by the laws? He then goes on to compare the good ruler to a person of exemplary virtue, one who had renounced public life and material values to concentrate on the search for truth. In all these judgments, the treatise would be completely unexceptional, except that in this case the author was not a rhetor like the other Chrysostom but a young man training to be a Christian priest, John Chrysostom, who subsequently became bishop of Constantinople, and his example of higher values is not, as it would have been earlier, a philosopher but a monk, the Christian solitary who begins to populate the landscape of late antiquity in this century. But there is a further, startling passage in this work which leaps out from all the stock phrases. Even a philosopher-king, Chrysostom concludes, cannot compare to a monk:

> For when he is vanquished, he fills his subjects with his own misfortunes, but when he conquers he becomes unbearable, adorning himself with trophies, becoming haughty, allowing his soldiers license to plunder, de-

spoil, and injure wayfarers, to besiege idle cities, to ruin the households of the poor, to exact each day from those who have received him what no law allows, on the pretext of some ancient custom, illegal and unjust. And the king does no harm to the wealthy with such evils, but he injures the poor, as if he were actually ashamed before the wealthy.

In contrast, Chrysostom continues, the monk "wins the favor of rich and poor alike; he approaches them each in the same way, using one cloak the whole year long, drinking water with greater pleasure than others drink marvellous wine, asking of the wealthy no favor for himself, neither great nor small, but for those in need he continually seeks many favors."[66]

In classical orations, rulers might be compared unfavorably to philosophers, and by replacing the philosopher with a monk Chrysostom had made only a minor change. But such comparisons were always made in a hortatory way, with the implicit assumption that nothing could be better than a ruler who did follow the dictates of philosophy, a philosopher-king. Only in Cynic diatribes could one find the probing of classical assumptions about class and the worth of the poor which tumbles out of this speech, and Cynics neither developed nor showed any interest in developing the institutional strength necessary to make their words effective. By the time John Chrysostom spoke, Christianity had. This youthful essay, therefore, from the pen of a man who will rise to one of the most powerful posts in the Christian empire, is an important demonstration of the fundamental changes in ancient values which Constantine's conversion helped bring about. At the same time, the continuities between it and the speeches of the earlier Chrysostom serve as a reminder that in equally fundamental ways nothing was changed by that conversion.

Constantine came to power in the aftermath, and partly as a result, of Diocletian's reforms. He ruled over an empire that was more structured, more militaristic, and more overtly religious than the one set up centuries earlier, but ruling remained a matter of maintaining a delicate balance of constituencies, of an emperor who needed to be endorsed by both military and civil authority, to rule with both *potestas* and *auctoritas*. It was natural for Constantine to think of Christians, once he decided to deal with them, as a new constituency and to seek leaders with whom he could deal on the analogy of the Senate. In an oft-quoted remark, Constantine is said to have spoken of himself to a company of bishops as "bishop of those outside" (*episcopos ton ektos*), a phrase that has generated endless controversy: Did Constantine mean "the things outside" or "the people outside" the church? Was he articulating the idea of a separation of powers, a theory of church and state?[67]

As usual, the inquiry has been framed in primarily religious terms. The first, small dividend from this lengthy excursion into the mechanics of empire is that a simpler and more obvious meaning can be suggested: Constantine was trying to establish a common ground with this new constituency, a collegial relationship that would make him *primus inter pares* with this group just as his predecessors had been with the Senate. The meeting between Constantine and the bishops in 335 with which this book began was one more step in that process.

Three

The Church Becomes a Player

lthough they had been around nearly as long as the emperors, the bishops were undoubtedly the novelty in the meeting of 335. Christians were using the term *bishop* (*episcopos*) within a generation of the Crucifixion, but at that time the bishop's duties were fairly limited and completely internal: he was, as the name implies, an "overseer," perhaps a "bookkeeper." During the course of the next three centuries, however, the bishop took on a variety of new functions and was recognized both by other Christians and by the non-Christian world as the leader and spokesperson for his community. In many ways, bishops could be equated with the traditional patrons and elites of the ancient world, protecting their perquisites and their flocks as great magnates always had. Bishops could be, and by the fourth century frequently were, as cultured and well born as traditional elites, as skilled in oratory, governance, and administration. But in one important way bishops differed radically from traditional elites. Where these achieved distinction by virtue of ascribed values—of class or inheritance, material worth or excellence in all the elite skills summed up by the word *paideia*—bishops derived their legitimacy on the basis of achieved values, of which spiritual worth was preeminent.

At least theoretically, Christians rejected all the traditional status markers: "If there come unto your assembly a man with a gold ring, in goodly apparel, and there come in also a poor man in vile raiment; and ye have respect to him that weareth the gay clothing, and say unto him, Sit thou here in a good place; and say to the poor, Stand thou there, or sit here under my footstool: Are ye not then partial in yourselves, and are become judges of evil thoughts?" So said one of the first of their bishops, James.[1] The one among them who demonstrated the fullest commitment to Christian values, even should he be mean and illiterate in the eyes of the world, was great in the community of faith. Bishops do not by themselves explain the success of Christianity, but they are crucial to the way the Christian community managed its success. Nowhere did that community display more flexibility and versatility than in the person of its bishops. Over the centuries, bishops displayed a remarkable ability to absorb every kind of distinction into their corporate identity. It was the bishops who prevented the Christian community from splintering into ever more diverse and independent traditions. Bishops were the carriers of continuity; they were the glue that held the movement together.

By 335, Constantine obviously saw bishops as players in the game of empire. They filled this role as representatives of a community that may have numbered as many as six million members by this date, upwards of 10 percent of the entire population of the empire.[2] This community knew itself as part of a single corporate body, the church, and as we shall see, this sense of unity and common identity helps account for their influence despite being what was still only a fraction of the total population. Important as the concept of the church is to Christian history, however, it can be misleading when trying to understand Christian intolerance, for constant use of the term leads to the assumption that there was a single Christianity, a single church, with which Constantine negotiated all the fateful arrangements that occurred during his reign. The game at Tyre and Constantinople in 335 was not played between Constantine and some abstract entity called "the church" but between Constantine and various individuals who claimed to represent that entity, the bishops. It was the bishops who made the church a player.

It is important to understand this distinction, because one of the consequences of the relationship worked out during Constantine's reign was that the Roman state became increasingly hostile to non-Christian forms of religious belief. The reason for this hostility, at least since the time that Edward Gibbon wrote *The Decline and Fall of the Roman Empire* two centuries ago, has seemed self-evident: it was an inevitable consequence of Christianity's inherently intolerant nature. But this conclusion flows from the religious context in which this question has traditionally been studied. Virulent intolerance has manifested itself in too many situations that have nothing to do with their belief for Christian refusal to worship other gods to be the only reason for this turn. The search for an explanation must be broadened.

Much of the issue is a matter of definition. When authors write of "Christian intolerance," they usually are thinking of instances of coercion—that is, violent measures undertaken in the aftermath of Constantine's reign to generate conformity to the true faith. This activity they then tie to exclusivism, a trait that undeniably inheres in Christianity and which, as Gibbon saw, leads Christians and Jews not just to reject worship of other gods but also to refuse to admit the legitimacy of or to associate with variant beliefs. It is via this link that intolerance then becomes identified as something inherent to Christianity. In one sense, the two concepts are similar, in that both would deny the right of such variant beliefs even to exist. Thus Gibbon could with some justification substitute "exclusive" for "intolerant" when at the end of his lengthy chapter he recapitulated the reasons for Christian success.[3] But both differ from "coercion" in being passive, or at best theoretical, positions. That is, one can be both exclusive and intolerant without actually doing anything to prevent the existence of variant beliefs. Persecution, which actively attempts to prevent variant belief from existing, and coercion, which seeks to compel conformity of belief, are both instruments, means of implementing intolerance; they are not identical to intolerance. Indeed, as Peter Brown has observed, an exclusive community can be even less inclined to persecute, simply because it removes the occasion for intermingling out of which persecution arises.[4]

The difference might seem negligible. But it permits two important distinctions. First, whereas exclusivism might be more typical of monotheistic than polytheistic belief, intolerance may be found in both systems. Second, to the extent that persecution and coercion

differ from either exclusivism or intolerance as being active manifestations of these attitudes, to that same extent they differ in being subject
to political analysis. The ability to tolerate differences is an individual
trait: some people just seem able to put up with much more diversity
than others.[5] This observation holds true for pagans as well as Christians. In every community or group, there will be both tolerant and
intolerant individuals, and among the intolerant individuals will be
some who are militantly so, individuals who would coerce others to
conform to their definition of right belief or right behavior. If tolerance
is a trait of personality, not theology, and thus equally observable in
pagans and Christians, then any search for an explanation of Christian
intolerance which limits itself to topics of Christian belief is fundamentally misguided.

As we shall see, there are as many tenets of Christianity which favor
tolerance and pacifism as there are those that would justify a more
militant and aggressive posture. The real challenge, then, is to identify
conditions that allow the views of those individuals who favor coercion, whether Christian or pagan, to prevail in their communities. The
tools needed are not those of theology but those of public policy and
the political process.

Christian organization, then, not Christian theology, is the place to
look for the answer to intolerance. Organization or, as he phrased it,
"the union and discipline of the Christian republic," was, indeed,
among the "secondary" causes that Gibbon put forth for the success of
the Christian faith. In recognizing the importance of its method of
organization to the success of the new faith, Gibbon was remarkably
prescient. He understood the significance of a tradition of regular
communication between local churches and the way regional meetings
contributed to the power and prestige of the bishops. Although his
judgment on these officials was typically jaundiced—to demonstrate
the zeal of the early Christians, for instance, he quotes Sulpicius Severus to the effect that they "desired martyrdom with more eagerness
than his own contemporaries solicited a bishopric"—Gibbon's appreciation of the tactical importance of organization was highly sophisticated. Even today, it is hard to improve on his observation that Christian organization "united their courage, directed their arms, and gave
their efforts that irresistible weight which even a small band of well-

trained and intrepid volunteers has so often possessed over an undisciplined multitude, ignorant of the subject, and careless of the event of the war."[6] But thanks to the growth of the social sciences since Gibbon's day, it is possible to go a great deal further than the historian-philosopher in identifying the type of organization which Christianity represents and the significance of that type of organization for understanding not only Christian success but also the phenomenon of intolerance.

Organizationally, Christianity was a "movement," that is, an organization devoted to effecting change in the public sphere. Because there is something that movements want to change, they are driven by a sense of purpose; they have an agenda. But a further distinction may be made: Christianity clearly was a social movement, not a protest movement. The distinction is crucial to the question of coercion, for protest movements are the type associated with violence and revolutionary change. They seek to win by means of a direct frontal assault on the political system. Social movements, by contrast, are in it for the long haul. They advance their goals by building their own alternative institutions, coexisting with the current political order rather than seeking to dismantle it. Moreover, social movements differ from protest movements in that they are broadly based; they are the type that can develop mass support and become a "mass movement," as clearly Christianity did.[7] When people speak of the "success" of Christianity, it is success in this way which is meant (spiritual salvation is an individual matter; it does not require large numbers in order to be "successful"). Mass movements have a number of traits that they share and requirements that they must meet in order to be successful. Chief among these, obviously, is size. While the largest mass movement is not necessarily the most successful one, a critical mass of members is certainly a distinguishing characteristic of the type. Durability, or stability, is only a shade less significant. Many movements achieve critical mass for a time but prove unable to hold on to members or attract new ones in sufficient quantity to endure. Mass movements that achieve both size and stability are those that manage to balance two necessary but contradictory requirements. First, they must find a way to maintain a separate identity, the special characteristics that set them apart from the dominant group or culture in which they developed and which give their members a way to distinguish themselves from nonmembers. Second, despite this separate identity, they must have enough in common with the dominant culture to be able to attract the new members from it which are needed for both renewal and growth.[8] In other words, the movement needs to have boundaries rigid enough to set its members apart yet porous enough to provide for growth. The threshold for membership can be a significant determinant of size. Just as a "millionaires' club," signaling a high threshold for membership, is likely to be smaller and more exclusive than a "worker's party" open to all and sundry, so fewer numbers will qualify for membership in a movement that insists on a high admissions standard than in one that sets relatively low standards.

Two other traits follow from these conditions. First, because of their relatively low threshold, successful movements are likely to be highly heterogeneous, with members of very different backgrounds drawn from all walks of life who have only their commitment to the movement's central belief or goal in common. It is essential, therefore, for the movement to identify and articulate clearly those central beliefs and goals and to impress on its members that differences in any ways other than these are unimportant. To do so, it has to develop an internal authority, a decision-making apparatus to whose jurisdiction the members are willing to submit. A successful mass organization, in other words, creates an atmosphere favorable to the heterogeneity that follows from a relatively low threshold for members, and it also creates mechanisms to resolve amicably the differences that inevitably come with such heterogeneity.

Jesus of Nazareth saw to it that his followers would maintain a separate identity. Over and over in the Gospels, he insists that those who would follow him had to develop a new frame of reference for their lives, a new social network. "If any man come to me," he says in the Gospel of Luke (14:26), "and hate not his father, and mother, and wife, and children, and brethren, and sisters, yea, and his own life also, he cannot be my disciple." In theological terms, these familiar words represent the new faith's demand for a total commitment. But they take on an entirely new meaning when looking for the principles under which the new community would organize and define itself. In the world in which Jesus lived, religious beliefs were as hereditary as family ties; in this world, his redefinition of family relationships on the basis of faith rather than blood lines turned this traditional connection upside down. "While he was still speaking to the people," Matthew writes (12:46–50), "behold, his mother and his brothers stood outside, asking to speak to him. But he replied to the man who told him, 'Who is my mother, and who are my brothers?' And stretching out his hand toward his disciples, he said, 'Here are my mother and my brothers! For whoever does the will of my Father in heaven is my brother, and sister, and mother.'" This consciousness of being a new people, a "nation apart," was evident a century later, when the author of the *Letter to Diognetus* wrote, "They live in their own countries, but only as aliens. They have a share in everything as citizens, and endure everything as foreigners. Every foreign land is their homeland, and yet for them every homeland is a foreign land." Its effect was to establish a different standard for membership in the new organization.[9]

Paradoxically, this demand for a new identity also facilitated the second goal of outreach, for it meant that by definition Christians were going to be heterogeneous. Groups that define themselves along kinship lines grow slowly, if at all, since (with only modest exceptions such as adoption) their membership requirements are limited to childbirth, which in the ancient world carried high mortality rates for both mothers and infants.[10] More important, kinship groups tend to organize along family and ethnic lines that restrict opportunities to grow through combination and merger. To the contrary, kinship organizations are more likely to view other groups with hostility and suspicion. But groups whose membership requirements, however strict, can be met by individuals from a host of different backgrounds can contact potential newcomers more readily because their members bring with them ties that cut across lines of kinship or residence or occupation. They are "cross-cutting groups," or "open networks."[11]

Heterogeneity helps create mass, but it also creates problems, chief among which is internal division, of which Christianity has always had plenty. Origen, a Christian theologian of the third century, responded to a pagan critic who mocked Christians of his day for their constant internal strife by pointing out that such divisions had been evident from the start.[12] To hold a heterogeneous movement together, leaders must be skilled in the use of tact and ambiguity. If the gospel record is any guide, Jesus had no lack of the verbal skills needed by those who would lead mass movements, the ability to offer something to everybody and to deflect potentially explosive issues through artful ambiguity. Indeed, the Gospel of Matthew contains one of the finest exhibitions of verbal footwork ever known in Jesus' reply to Pharisees who, Matthew says, were trying to "entangle him in his talk." The topic was taxation, ever the object of popular resentment. "Give us your ruling on this," they asked: "are we or are we not permitted to pay taxes to the Roman Emperor?" The question was a land mine: a "yes" answer would alienate those looking for a political messiah; a "no" would convict Jesus of sedition. "But Jesus perceived their wickedness, and said, . . . Show me the tribute money. And they brought unto him a penny. And he saith unto them, Whose is this image and superscription? They say unto him, Caesar's. Then saith he unto them, Render therefore unto Caesar the things which are Caesar's, and unto God the things that are God's." To be sure, this response communicated Jesus' indifference to the things of this world and lifted the petty concerns of his interrogators into an entirely different sphere. On a more mundane level, however, it was as nice a piece of political footwork as one could want, disarming the question and leaving his interrogators, as Matthew says, dumbfounded.[13]

This particular remark created a new field of theology and launched a thousand dissertations. But in other places the same skill also led to a record cluttered with two-sided and even contradictory statements. Even on the important principle of setting a threshold for inclusion in the Christian community, Jesus appears to give conflicting advice. In one passage, for instance, he rebukes the disciples for complaining that others were using his name to perform miracles. "John said to him, 'Teacher, we saw a man casting out demons in your name, and we forbade him, because he was not following us.' But Jesus said, 'Do not forbid him; for no one who does a mighty work in my name will be able soon after to speak evil of me. For he that is not against us is for us.'"[14] The passage shows Jesus' appreciation for an inclusive approach that would, in effect, "co-opt the middle" by counting as "in" those who had not explicitly opted out. It suggests a minimal threshold for inclusion in the Christian movement. Yet in another passage, Jesus takes the opposite tack, telling an admirer who had already met many of the criteria for inclusion that he must abandon all his worldly possessions and responsibilities before he could become a follower.[15] Such conflicting advice set the stage for significant tensions in later ages between those Christians who emphasized outreach in their approach to Christian mission and those others who decried the lowering of standards which seemed to come with an increase in numbers.

The Christian message is, indeed, a bundle of opposing statements, of which the pure god who is also pure man is only the beginning. Its earliest records reveal a community that was deeply divided over its purpose, its mission, even its origins: Should it be a small, pure church of the elect, untouched by contact with the outside world and the compromises that come with it, or should the message be preached throughout the known world? Should that world be seen as friendly or hostile? Would love conquer all, or would things end in a great confrontation between Good and Evil? These questions never have been fully resolved, even in the present day. It has been traditional to lament the internal squabbles such differences provoke, to yearn for the lost innocence of a pure and unified church. The theme is already present in the earliest church history, written by Eusebius of Caesarea at the turn of the fourth century.[16] Although it has been commonplace at least since the time of Eusebius to deplore these conflicts in the faith, without them Christianity might never have become a mass movement, or a player on the political scene. The effect was to add dimension to the message, giving the movement a flexibility to adapt to changing circumstances in a way that a one-dimensional, clearly stated and categorical set of rules could never have done.

Except in very rare circumstances, small, isolated, and homogeneous sects do not play such a role, nor do they want to. A successful mass movement needs to find a way to accommodate a variety of needs and interests, and this means it must learn to live with tension and ambiguity. Christians had to find a balance between exclusivism, the urge to ignore or despise outsiders, and ecumenicism, the desire to bring the whole world together in one faith. They needed to find a way to interact with the dominant culture while maintaining their own identity and the loyalty of their adherents. In modern parlance, this is known as keeping "dense but open social networks,"[17] and it is but one of the many contradictory goals and internal conflicts that movements must somehow reconcile in order to achieve the type of success required of political players. Nothing was lost by squabbling. On the contrary, the need to defend positions, to rethink them, to argue and persuade, led Christians to place a premium on the rational skills needed to articulate the theology of a world faith.[18]

Differences by themselves do not make a mass movement. Differences create the inner tensions that keep a movement alert and mentally active, but they do not provide a reason for the movement to stay together, rather than break up into separate, competing groups. Some overarching common objective whose achievement is so important to all members of the group that they are willing to abide others with whom they disagree on lesser matters also needs to be present. In the case of Christianity, this common objective obviously is eternal salvation. But why was it necessary to put up with others in order to achieve it? Ancient religious thinking held that the gods dealt with communities, not individuals. It might seem, therefore, that somehow the belief in communal salvation held Christians together. But, in another startling break with ancient thinking, Jesus insisted that his followers would be judged on the basis of their own actions.

The principle of individual judgment is, indeed, such a commonplace of modern thinking that it is difficult to grasp the ramifications of this difference. But as commonplace as it is now, the idea took a long time to take hold even in Judaeo-Christian thinking. The story of the destruction of Sodom and Gomorrah in the Book of Genesis is a snapshot of the evolution of Judaism toward the concept of individual responsibility before God. The idea of cities being laid waste because of divine wrath needed no explanation in the ancient world. But by the time this account was written down, the author obviously felt the need to reassure readers that only wicked people had been punished in this way—hence the following exchange between Abraham and his Lord: "And Abraham drew near, and said, Wilt thou also destroy the righteous with the wicked? Peradventure there be fifty righteous within the city: wilt thou also destroy and not spare the place for the fifty righteous that are therein? That be far from thee to do after this manner, to slay the righteous with the wicked; and that the righteous should be as the wicked, that be far from thee: Shall not the judge of all the earth do right?"[19] With such blandishments, Abraham progressively reduces the number of righteous from fifty to ten, extracting commitments by using on his God the same techniques Roman orators used on their emperor.

Although the bargaining ostensibly takes place between Abraham and his Lord, it is the reader who is reassured by Jehovah's reluctance to punish the innocent along with the guilty. From here, it is a relatively small step to the conclusion that divine judgment will be exercised on individuals, not communities. Yet so ingrained was the idea of a community judgment in the ancient world that centuries after Genesis was written Jesus of Nazareth had repeatedly and graphically to instruct his followers that Judgment Day would be an individual trial: "For as in those days before the flood they were eating and drinking, marrying and giving in marriage, until the day when Noah entered the ark and they did not know until the flood came and swept them all away; so will be the coming of the Son of man. Then two men will be in the field; one is taken and one is left. Two women will be grinding at the mill; one is taken and one is left."[20] Here, Jesus compares the flood and the Second Coming as both being sudden and unexpected; but deliberately or not, he contrasts the flood that swept over all with a judgment that will select between two people standing or working side by side.

Not communal salvation but the commandment to "love one another" was what provided the bond to reinforce the tie to a common goal of salvation. Love is the strongest ethical demand that Jesus laid on his followers. Asked to name the greatest commandment, Jesus replied, "Love." Love was the trait by which they were distinguished, at least in their own thinking, from nonbelievers. "A new commandment I give to you, that you love one another," Jesus told the disciples. "By this all men will know that you are my disciples, that you have love for one another."[21] But it was not enough, Jesus said, merely to love those who loved back.

> If you love those who love you, what credit is that to you? For even sinners do the same. And if you do good to those who do good to you, what credit is that to you? For even sinners do the same. And if you lend to those from whom you hope to receive, what credit is that to you? Even sinners lend to sinners, to receive as much again. But love your enemies, and do good, and lend, expecting nothing in return; and your reward will be great, and you

will be sons of the Most High; for he is kind to the ungrateful and the selfish. Be merciful, even as your Father is merciful.[22]

These words from the Sermon on the Mount lie at the core of Christian teaching. They provide the motive for Christians to reach out to the community of nonbelievers.

The lion's share of credit for Christianity's outreach usually goes to Paul, the apostle to the gentiles, who opened the new faith to non-Jews. As an organizer, Paul's great gifts included not just the ability to establish enduring communities wherever he went but also a rare combination of charismatic zeal and common sense. He grasped immediately, for instance, the self-defeating nature of speaking in tongues—"For one who speaks in a tongue speaks not to men but to God; for no one understands him"—and advised his missionaries, "If you in a tongue utter speech that is not intelligible, how will any one know what is said? For you will be speaking into the air."[23]

The critical moment in the growth of the new movement occurred around the end of the first century. The earliest Christians concentrated on living a pure life, in anticipation of a Second Coming that they believed would occur during their lifetime.[24] As that generation succumbed to age and mortality without any sign of Return, significant soul searching occurred which led, in turn, to a new understanding of their role on earth, according to which Judgment Day had been postponed so that as many souls as possible might be brought aboard the Ark of the Church. In this newly defined mission, Christians, while still thinking of themselves as pilgrims, now had to reconcile themselves to a residence of undetermined length on this foreign soil. Their experience may at least superficially be compared to that of immigrants who want both to maintain their identity and at the same time to "fit in" as best they can, with the difference that Christians first had to agree among themselves on what that identity was. A product of this effort was creation out of the numerous texts and variants then in circulation of a relatively compact corpus of literature regarded as authoritative by most Christian communities—the literature eventually known to Christians as the "New" Testament, to distinguish it from the Hebrew Bible, or "Old" Testament. The process was important and fundamental, for in choosing among the various stories then in circulation, Christians had to give conscious thought to what was, and was not, proper belief. They had to define themselves, and in the course of doing so, they created a history and a canon.

If the commandment to love neighbor and enemy alike was the incentive for Christians to reach out to the world, an equally strong injunction to worship no god but the True God ensured that Christians would keep their own identity as they did so. This central tension between love and resistance is the dynamic that fueled the Christian movement. Two early Christian symbols have traditionally been used to illustrate this tension—"the beacon" and "the ark." The two images symbolize differences over qualifications for membership and whether the community should be generally exclusive, with narrow and difficult criteria for admission, or generally inclusive, with criteria that are relatively few and easy to satisfy. The beacon, which is reflected in such sayings as "let your light shine on the mountaintop," characterizes those Christians who wanted to set a high standard for identity, insisting that their mission was to maintain exemplary purity and moral standards in relation to the outside world, to serve as a small but exceptionally bright light, shining the way to a better life. The ark, which derives from the image of Noah's ark, represents Christians who thought of the church as the vessel that would carry the bulk of humanity to salvation. Drawing on Jesus' parable of "the tares and the wheat," this wing interpreted their mission as one to save souls, not judge them—a task that would be performed on Judgment Day by Christ himself. It is the conflict between an inclusive and an exclusive interpretation of the faith, and in the guise of "puritan" and "catholic" (here taken in its original and broad sense of "universal"), the two strands can be seen at work throughout Christian history.

The way this dynamic played out in the early church can also be illustrated by the roles of two central and characteristic figures of that era, the apologist and the martyr. The martyr has captured the bulk of attention, and appropriately so. The heroism of the martyrs (the word means "witness" in Greek) in testifying to the truth of Christ's message by reliving his suffering and death kept alive the hopes of their co-religionists in the darkest periods of suffering and anguish while at the same time shining forth as a beacon of faith to the unbeliever. The martyrs kept Christian identity intact. They became the paradigmatic

Christians, setting the standard for achievement and virtue. Next to these sharply delineated figures, the apologists cast a dim shadow, easily overlooked. But without them—or at least without the effort they represent—Christianity would never have become the player that it did. Where martyrs defended the faith in the arena, the apologists (derived from another Greek legal term, *apologia,* or "defense") took the battle to the marketplace of ideas. Their defenses could be conciliatory or combative, but what marks all of them is an impulse to make their faith seem less foreign, more familiar to the dominant culture. What identifies apologists as a group is the search for points of contact between Christianity and paganism. Ignoring their role skews the study of Christian-pagan relations to the side of conflict and distorts our understanding of the results. While the two are not mutually exclusive—martyrs could be apologists, and apologists martyrs—they represent different impulses, the martyr standing for rigor and exclusion, the apologist for cooperation and inclusion. Thus they also represent an internal tension in Christianity which at all times has been an important dynamic for the movement. Together, they explain the success Christianity achieved in the Roman empire.

Persecution

The conflict between Christianity and Rome in the first three centuries is what draws most attention. Persecution had an important, and rarely appreciated, effect on the development of the church. It is conceivable that, without persecution, the power of the bishop would never have developed so rapidly or become so extensive. Even more important, scars on the Christian psyche which play an important role in the question of intolerance might never have developed.

The first question to ask is why persecution occurred. Thanks to the medium of motion pictures and the limited imagination of those who produce them, the image of righteous Christians surrounded by a sea of pagan orgies has become even more deeply embedded in the modern consciousness than it was in those of earlier generations raised on saints' lives and martyrologies. In the modern version, however, it is not God but democracy that accounts for the success of Christianity. As it is typically told, only the upper classes now appear as incurable degenerates; the common people, stunned by the virtue of the martyrs, convert in massive numbers to the new faith, which in turn gives them the courage to rise against their oppressors and establish both Christianity and democracy in a single, economical revolt.

There is something important in the notion that Christian ideology empowered common people in a radically new way. But to say this is quite different from saying that common people immediately flocked to the new faith, causing it to prevail over elite-controlled traditional beliefs. And in its central point—the contest of virtuous Christians and depraved pagans—the popular stereotype is most certainly wrong. Rather, there is every indication that, for the better part of two centuries, common people wholeheartedly supported, and usually instigated, persecution of Christian believers and that they did so, at least in part, out of a belief that Christians, not pagans, bore the taint of immoral behavior.

Others indicate disgust. Later in the second century, a pagan critic named Celsus wrote,

> Those who summon people to the other mysteries make this preliminary proclamation: Whosoever has pure hands and a wise tongue. And again, others say: Whosoever is pure from all defilement, and whose soul knows nothing of evil, and who has lived well and righteously. Such are the preliminary exhortations of those who promise purification from sins. But let us hear what folk these Christians call. Whosoever is a sinner, they say, whosoever is unwise, whosoever is a child, and, in a word, whosoever is a wretch, the kingdom of God will receive him.[25]

With similar scorn the satirist Lucian wrote, "Their first lawgiver persuaded them that they are all brothers of one another after they have transgressed once for all by denying the Greek gods and by worshipping that crucified sophist himself and living under his laws."[26] Even in the third century, Christians continued to be tarred with the taint of illegality. In *Octavius*, a dialogue on Christianity, one of the participants voices concern about a form of worship which took place outside the public eye: "They know one another by secret marks and insignia," he says of the Christians, adding, "Certainly suspicion is applicable to secret and nocturnal rites."[27]

The taint already was present at the time of the first major confrontation between Rome and Christianity, provoked by the Great Fire that swept through Rome during the reign of the emperor Nero in A.D. 64, destroying some of the city's most populous districts. Although minimal standards for construction and fire prevention made fire a constant threat, the extent of this blaze soon touched off rumors of arson, some of which implicated the emperor himself. The historian Tacitus, writing some fifty years later, says it was to deflect these rumors that Nero placed blame on the Christians, touching off a persecution in which tradition says the apostles Peter and Paul both were martyred.[28] Tacitus had no love for Nero—his pages on the fire stand as a primer on the use of invective and innuendo, by the use of which he maligns what even today seem farsighted efforts that Nero undertook to provide disaster relief and prevent recurrence of such a tragedy. It suits Tacitus's purpose, therefore, to cast the Christians as victims; even so, he scarcely portrays them as virtuous innocents, calling them instead "notoriously depraved" and concluding that they were convicted as much by their "anti-social tendencies" as by the evidence.[29]

A similar picture emerges from the writings of Pliny the Younger, whom we met in the last chapter. A contemporary of Tacitus, Pliny was a model of the "new style" senator produced by the empire's need for administrators. On just such a task, he wrote from the province of Bithynia in Asia Minor, where he had been sent by the emperor Trajan, probably around 111, to straighten out municipal finances. In the course of these duties, Pliny was forced to deal with some local Christians who had been denounced to him in anonymous accusations, and he wrote Trajan for instructions and advice.[30]

> In investigations of Christians I have never taken part [he explains]; hence I do not know what is the crime usually punished or investigated, or what allowances are made. So I have had no little uncertainty whether there is any distinction of age, or whether the very weakest offenders are treated exactly like the stronger; whether pardon is given to those who repent, or whether a man who has once been a Christian gains nothing by having ceased to be such; whether punishment attaches to the mere name apart from secret crimes, or to the secret crimes connected with the name.

With vintage Roman reasoning, Pliny explains why, pending Trajan's response, he has ordered those who continued to confess their faith put to death: "I have asked them themselves if they were Christians; if they admitted it, I asked the question again, and then a third time, having threatened them with execution; if they still persisted, I ordered them to be taken away and put to death. For I had no doubt that whatever it was that they were confessing to they assuredly deserved to be punished for their stubbornness and unbending obstinacy."

To some extent, Pliny's letter corroborates the stereotype of Roman-Christian relations: Christians here are clearly members of the lower orders—Pliny speaks of serving maids holding the office of deaconess—and it shows a Roman official in the act of torturing and executing Christians. In other ways, however, it comes closer to Gibbon's image of restrained and cultivated distaste. Although his letter makes plain that Pliny will execute Christians if he must, it makes equally plain the lack of what Gibbon would have called "furious zeal" in his prosecution, the death sentence being imposed not so much for belief as for bad manners. The victims, of course, are unlikely to have been subtle enough to appreciate such nuances, but it was surely administrators such as Pliny whom Gibbon had in mind when he thought of Roman magistrates who carried out their weary tasks with enlightened forbearance.

Pliny's judgment about "obstinacy" was brought on by Christian refusal to perform a ritual act with strong political implications. "Sacrifice" involved offering a few grains of incense to the "genius" of the emperor, his tutelary deity, what today we might call a patron saint. To Romans it was a harmless means of demonstrating loyalty. Refusal to perform this act was tantamount to treason. But to a Christian, it meant paying homage to false gods and thereby jeopardizing one's immortal soul. The source of confusion is obvious in a society like ours, long accustomed to separate categories for "political" and "religious" activities. In an ancient state, even one as sophisticated as Rome, it was much more difficult to think separately about activities that always had been regarded as one and the same.

Other sections of Pliny's report hint at further reasons Christians could incur the wrath of their neighbors. In one part, for instance, he writes of some suspects who admitted that they had once been Christians but since had abandoned the faith.

They asserted, however, that this was the sum of their guilt or error: that they had been in the habit of coming together on a fixed day before dawn and joining in singing a hymn to Christ as if to a god, and binding themselves to a vow, not to commit any crime, but to abstain from theft and robbery and adultery, not to bear false witness, not to refuse to give up anything entrusted to them when called upon for it. This done, they would break up and then reassemble for a meal, but a meal of an ordinary and harmless kind.

Pliny's last comment about the "harmless" nature of the Christian meal indicates he had heard the stories that were circulating about the Christian liturgy, in which the sharing of bread and wine, ritually identified as the body and blood of their sacrificed savior, was turned into an act of cannibalism—eating the "flesh" and drinking the "blood" of a sacrificed victim. This type of story undoubtedly is what Pliny had in mind when he described the food served at these meetings as "ordinary and harmless." Minucius Felix shows that the libel was still circulating a century later, when he wrote his Christian dialogue *Octavius*. Here the pagan speaker, Caecilianus, refers to the Christian liturgy as "a profane conspiracy," tainted by the consumption of "inhuman meats":

> Now the story about the initiation of young novices is as much to be detested as it is well known. An infant covered over with meal, that it may deceive the unwary, is placed before him who is to be stained with their rites: this infant is slain by the young pupil, who has been urged on as if to harmless blows on the surface of the meal, with dark and secret wounds. Thirstily—O horror! they lick up its blood; eagerly they divide its limbs. By this victim they are pledged together; with this consciousness of wickedness they are covenanted to mutual silence.[31]

In the same way, the Christian practice of referring to one another as "brother" and "sister" and their profession of love for one another as Jesus taught—the reason these early gatherings were called "love feasts" (*agape* in Greek)—gave rise to rumors of incest. In the *Octavius*, Caecilianus, professing shock at a people who "love one another almost before they know one another," provides a particularly lurid version:

> Their form of banqueting is notorious; everywhere all talk of it. . . . On an appointed day they assemble at a feast with all their children, sisters, and mothers, people of both sexes and every age. There, after much feasting,

when the banquet has become heated and intoxication has inflamed the drunken passions of incestuous lust, a dog which has been tied to a lamp is incited to rush and leap forward after a morsel thrown beyond the range of the cord by which it was tied. The telltale light is upset and extinguished, and in the shameless dark they exchange embraces indiscriminately, and all, if not actually, yet by complicity are equally involved in incest.[32]

Such rumors are the likely reason that Pliny pursued an investigation into the nature of Christian practice, and why he reported his findings to Trajan at such length. Pliny's report breathes with the no-nonsense approach that characterizes the best Roman administrators; he knew how to evaluate evidence and how to tell when a witness was lying, even under torture, and it is clear that he found the Christians' description of their activities credible. To say this is not to say that Pliny was won over to their cause or that he found Christianity particularly admirable. It is, he sniffs, "a depraved and immoderate superstition." But the letter does show that the impetus for Christian persecution did not always come from above. In this case, it came precisely from the area where our modern ideology has taught us not to look—the common people who we like to think were waiting for the Good News to free them from their wretched existence.

Such a conclusion is fully consistent with the other evidence that survives of persecution in this period. The Acts of the Apostles describes several riots that were touched off by Christian preachers, in all of which the public authorities can be seen trying to save the apostles from the wrath of a hostile crowd. The implication that the new teaching was not uniformly popular is obscured by the tendency of Christian sources to blame this opposition on moral depravity or economic self-interest—on anything, in fact, but sincere religious belief. A riot of the people of Ephesus, for instance, is presented as the work of the silversmiths who feared for the loss of their profitable trade making souvenir statues of the deity. Although the great temple of Artemis in that city was one of the wonders of the ancient world, the author of Acts never even considers the possibility that an excited crowd that sat hours in the local stadium chanting "Great is Artemis of the Ephesians!" was moved by anything other than greed and fear.[33] The thought that they might have caused genuine offense to religious sensibilities seems never to have crossed the minds of these apostles. But in fact, they offended much more than religious pride.

In the theory that underlies modern thinking about the state, government is a rational creation, the product of a social contract by which—at least ideally—all citizens have voluntarily surrendered some of their rights and abilities in return for the protection and security offered by membership in a group composed of others who have done likewise. The ancient state was something different. To be sure, ancient theorists posited a variety of rational and political reasons for its existence, but first and foremost it was a religious institution, whose primary purpose was to please the gods. This was, accordingly, the primary purpose of public officials—whether elected, appointed, or installed by force. The idea of a religious institution separate from the state not only would have made no sense; it would have been as difficult to conceive as it is for someone in the modern age to think of a "church" that was not only tied to but even lacked an identity separate from that of the "state." In the ancient world, the vocabulary for such a separate institution did not even exist.[34] There were priests, to be sure, but not a separate priestly class—at least, not for the traditional rites associated with the state; these priesthoods were held by the same people who held public office, sometimes simultaneously. In the Roman republic, elected officials had the last word even here, with the right to accept or reject the opinion of those specialists who consulted the gods' will through divination or augury (probably the best-known example being Julius Caesar's refusal to heed the advice of a soothsayer to "Beware the Ides of March"). In the empire, rulers after Augustus inherited with all their other powers the office of pontifex maximus, head of the Roman state religion.[35]

As a result of this basis in religion, virtually all the public activities and celebrations of the ancient state which Christians in a modern state would not hesitate to join were taboo to ancient Christians—holidays and festivals, obviously, but also such seemingly innocuous procedures as suing in court, where justice was administered in the name of the gods, or buying meat from the butcher, who was likely to have gotten it from a temple that had just performed a sacrifice. Doubtless it was this tendency to stand aloof from so many activities and public celebrations which earned Christians the reputation for "antisocial tendencies" with which Tacitus branded them.

By itself, this aloofness would not have been a cause of persecution. But ancient religion also considered such behavior a public danger. In ancient belief, as we saw above, the gods dealt with mortals as a community—not on a one-to-one basis as in the Judaeo-Christian tradition. In ancient thinking, judgment was communal, and it was not reserved until the last days. The gods moved against offending communities not with moral judgment but with physical ruin. In a prescientific age, those misfortunes that we call "natural" disasters—plague, famine, flood, earthquake—were sure signs of divine wrath, just as bountiful harvests proved the gods' pleasure. In the aftermath of such events, communities naturally would want to know what they had done to anger their gods. Christians were an all-too-obvious target of such an inquiry: here they were, residing in the gods' cities yet denying them their due, perhaps even mocking their worship. How could communities that had tolerated such conduct not conclude that this was the reason for their misfortunes? "If the Tiber rises as high as the city walls," the Christian Tertullian moaned toward the end of the second century, "if the Nile does not send its waters up over the fields, if the heavens give no rain, if there is an earthquake, if there is famine or pestilence, straightway the cry is, 'Away with the Christians to the lion!'"[36]

It is noteworthy that Pliny used the rite of sacrifice not to entrap Christians but as a means of absolving those who had been falsely accused. According to the stereotype of Christian-pagan relations, Christians were not supposed to be afforded any protections of the law, as here they clearly were. There are other divergences. Pliny did not come to Bithynia with the purpose of hunting Christians, nor does the problem seem to have occupied much of his attention. Of the more than one hundred letters that he exchanged with Trajan and subsequently published, this is one of only two in which the renegade sect appears at all. And in other ways this letter contains as many surprises. Other passages show that Pliny was not initiating these actions—the problem was thrust upon him by common people, some of them former Christians, denouncing suspects before his tribunal. And in one respect the letter is decidedly at odds with the traditional story. If the trial of Christians was as commonplace as the stereotype would have it, then it is odd that a man of Pliny's training and experience had to write Trajan for advice on how to deal with the problem.

The traditional stereotypes cannot explain Christianity's ultimate success, which was neither the product of intolerance nor the result of an instinctive appeal to Roman masses. To his eternal credit, Edward Gibbon put the lie to the self-congratulating stereotype of moral Christians hounded by ravening pagans which had been a staple of church history, banishing it forever from respectable academic circles to the more compatible confines of pulp fiction. His insistence on empirical reasons put the study of Christianity's eventual success on a firm footing; although they are now more than two centuries old, Gibbon's five "secondary" causes continue to be a convenient starting place for discussing the success of the Christian movement.[37] But taken as a whole, his list has a decidedly archaic cast to it, picturing Christianity as an alien and hostile substance residing "in the heart of the Roman empire," and taking for granted the question that most needs asking— not "how did Christianity 'conquer' an alien and hostile tradition?" but "how did Christianity come to be accepted by that tradition?" In other words, what is missing is an appreciation of the dynamics of Christian-pagan relations—the many positive ways in which the two traditions interacted with each other and learned from each other and the way both responded to new stimuli and new needs. Such an approach is necessary, also, to avoid the mistake of assuming that Christianity caused all of these changes.

The Marketplace

The tension between "the beacon" and "the ark," symbolized here by the figures of the martyr and the apologist, was a matter not just of balancing internal goals but also of balancing the urge to spread the Good News as broadly as possible, to make it acceptable to the widest possible audience, with the equally important need to maintain the identity and internal discipline of the community. As a result of this tension and the different ways in which different Christian communities resolved it, it is a mistake to think of Christianity in this period as a single, monolithic unit. Although certainly more identical and cohesive than the multiplicity of local traditions that are usually, and misleadingly, lumped together under the single heading "paganism," Christians at this time were more of a loose confederation of independent communities than a single entity, each community with only the most basic elements of belief in common with the others, and each fiercely protective of its local traditions and creeds.

As misleading as it is to think of a monolithic Christianity facing an equally monolithic paganism, it is even worse to think of the relationship between the two traditions as static and unchanging. Both were constantly evolving, and part of that evolution came not just from periods of conflict but also from longer periods of peaceful interaction and mutual learning from which each tradition profited. The apologists represent this dynamic side to Christian-pagan relations. As such, they must be considered an important factor in Christianity's ultimate success.

Monty Python's *Life of Brian* includes a scene in which various visionaries pitch their ideas in a sort of religious marketplace. Scandalous as it seems, it is useful for two reasons to think of Christians as having a product to sell, if not in a literal marketplace, at least in a marketplace of Roman ideas. First, doing so serves as a reminder that apologists, like salespeople, had an interest in making their product palatable to the market of potential consumers, of putting their message into the most attractive package. Second, it serves as a reminder that consumers are an important part of the equation of Christian success: no matter what Christians had to sell, there had to be somebody ready to buy it. As one scholar has put it, there had to be "a favorable ecology" for the new movement to succeed.[38] By itself, the idea of Christians bringing their message to a pagan marketplace is not new. But for a long time this effort was cast in terms of Christian mission to a jaded and weary world. Intentionally or not, this approach undervalued traditional pagan beliefs, which were presented as ossified and outdated, unable to respond to the needs of a world that longed for an afterlife and a personal deity. Or, if you were Edward Gibbon, you told the same story in reverse—as evidence of decline from the heights of rational and enlightened inquiry achieved in his favored second century, a descent into superstition brought on by the advances of Christianity. Either way, paganism by the time of Christianity's success in the fourth century was presented as a dead faith, kept alive merely by the antiquarian interests of aristocratic dilettantes and the darkling desires of increasingly arcane philosophers.

It is better to realize that, just as Christianity was not a single, static body of unchanging belief, neither was that body of ideas and practices which collectively we label paganism.[39] Traditional religions were fully capable of responding to the market for a more universal and personal deity such as Christianity offered, and they did so in a variety of ways. As we shall see in Chapter 4, one general result of all this ferment was broader attention paid than ever before to the idea of a Highest God, or Supreme God, who was simply known by different names in different places. This trend toward what might be called, for want of a better word, "pagan monotheism" obviously made the work of the apologists easier in some ways.[40] But the proposition that Jesus of Nazareth was a god was never the real sticking point, the ancient world being thoroughly familiar with the idea of gods that took human form, and even of gods who died and then returned from the dead. Nor were they unfamiliar with the idea of a Supreme God who was responsible for all creation. The difficulty lay in the unique way in which Christians combined the two types of deity in the person of Christ. The idea that the creator god of the philosophers could ever condescend to take human form—much less the form of a humble carpenter in a backwater province—and suffer a humiliating form of death at human hands was, to put it mildly, simply beneath contempt. Witness this exchange, which took place during a martyr trial of the mid-third century:

> Lepidus said: "Pionius, why do you and your people not sacrifice?"
>
> The group around Pionius said, "Because we are Christians."
>
> "Which god do you worship?" asked Lepidus.
>
> Pionius answered: "The God who made heaven and earth and the sea and all that is in them."
>
> Lepidus said: "You mean, then, the one who was crucified?"
>
> "Yes," said Pionius, "him whom God sent for the redemption of the world."
>
> At this the officials gave a loud guffaw and Lepidus cursed Christ.[41]

Christians were scandalized by the attitude of pagans like Lepidus, who in their eyes committed sacrilege when they refused to recognize the deep spiritual truth of the Incarnation. But railing at this problem would not make it go away. To address it effectively, the apologists had to show that they understood the philosophical objections on which it was based and then pose a solution that would be intellectually satisfying.[42] The need to find common ground, to begin with thoughts that are already familiar, sets up a dynamic well known to everyone who has ever tried to teach—to teach effectively, it is important to understand the thinking of the group to whom the message is directed. It is the same impulse that in later centuries led one bishop of Rome to encourage his missionary to the Anglo-Saxons to seek common ground with the natives by using sites and symbols already familiar to them, and another centuries later to find similarities between apostolic tradition and the ancestor worship of voodoo priests.[43] The dynamics meant that the apologists needed to study pagan thought and pagan methods of communication (rhetoric) in order to put their message in terms pagans could understand, and which they would most readily receive.

As an illustration: the proposition that the Supreme God of the universe might suffer the particularly demeaning punishment of crucifixion posed an obvious difficulty to thoughtful pagans who might otherwise have been attracted to the Christian message. But pagan philosophy has long postulated the principle that the logos—a Greek term usually translated as "word" but having the more basic meaning of "rational faculty"—served as a bridge between god and man, allowing imperfect and fallible mortals to conceive of a perfect and eternal One. The principle had long ago become personified into the Logos, a philosophical intermediary between infinite perfection and the limited senses of humans. Christian apologists speaking in this medium could readily identify Jesus with this philosophical Logos, and to do so on no less authority than the Gospel of John, which opens with the words, "In the beginning was the Logos, and the Logos was with God and the Logos was God." Here, then, was an obvious common ground on which an apologist could begin to overcome pagan objections without deviating from the gospel message. Similar links could be drawn between the pagan sun god—Sol or Helios—and references to god in the

Old Testament as the "Sun of Righteousness" and "Sun of Salvation." It was a powerful message, particularly because of the great deference shown in antiquity to any writing that came with an ancient pedigree.[44]

The apologist who relied on such parallels used them as a bridge. But how exactly did the convert receive them? The opportunity for distortion and misunderstanding in such a situation is obvious. For one thing, the person of Jesus, his suffering, the Crucifixion itself, all the elements that usually are thought of as central to the Christian message, could be—not ignored, and certainly not denied—perhaps finessed. There was nothing sinister or devious in this process. It is a natural product of communication itself. But one result was that Christians and pagans in the late second and third centuries developed a large vocabulary of shared symbolism, a language that we hear now only from the surviving side. Unless their origins in a common context are remembered, words like *Logos* and *Supreme God,* or even *Father* and *Savior,* can signal a more Christian message to a modern reader than their ancient author ever intended.

It is hard to say for how many converts the apologists directly were responsible. Their chief significance is that they represent a factor in the relationship between Christians and pagans which otherwise is easily overlooked: three centuries of development prior to Constantine, during which time it was not just pagans who came to understand the Christian message but also Christians who developed and refined their own thinking and interpretive skills, and in so doing moved closer to the pagan world.

This interchange posed a problem. Since the tools of discourse were all pagan, there was always the risk that putting the Christian message into this framework would also somehow alter the message itself. In Christianity, a correct understanding of the god-man Jesus has always been deemed essential for salvation, and the effort to find common ground ran the risk of accommodating too much, at the cost of misrepresenting the central message and thereby threatening correct belief, or orthodoxy. Many of the early heresies can be fruitfully studied as efforts at apologetics gone awry. In the second century, for instance, Basilides taught that Christ had not suffered and died on the cross but had instead magically changed places with Simon of Cyrene—the volunteer who carried the cross to Calvary when Jesus' strength gave out—and then stood by laughing at the great trick he had played. A monstrous distortion of the core message of Christianity, the thought clearly was meant to satisfy pagan doubts about the propriety of a suffering god.

Heresy was an enduring problem; it plays an important part in the explanation of Christian coercion (Chapter 11). For now, it is sufficient to notice that Jesus' most unforgiving statements in the Gospels are directed at heretics. "As for the man who is a cause of stumbling to one of these little ones who have faith, it would be better for him to be thrown into the sea with a millstone round his neck. If your hand is your undoing, cut it off; it is better for you to enter into life maimed than to keep both hands and go to hell and the unquenchable fire."[45] In later centuries, philosophy would come to be despised as the mother of heresy. But without the apologists' effort in these early centuries to reconcile contradictory elements in their faith with the tenets of pagan philosophy, it is highly doubtful that Christianity ever would have developed the capacity for abstract, intellectual discourse that made it a world religion.[46]

The Arena

Important as the apologists were to the future of Christian fortunes, they never became heroes to inspire awe in future generations. Negotiators rarely do. Instead, this honor went to another group, made up of ordinary people who showed extraordinary endurance when confronted with the demand to deny Christ, the martyrs. It was these who, by their fortitude and refusal to compromise, confirmed Christian principles in a way that the apologists, for all their eloquence, could never match. The martyrs played another important role: if the apologists stood for reconciliation with at least some aspects of existing belief, then the more successful they were, the more risk they created that the Christian community would lose its particular identity and be swallowed up by the dominant culture. The martyrs were the ones who drew the line when the dominant culture demanded too much; they kept Christian identity intact. They were "witnesses" not just to the existence of Christianity but also to the depth of Christian belief and commitment. In a more profound sense, they gave body to Christian arguments, witnessing to the truth of Christ's sacrifice by their willingness to endure the same fate themselves—"Christ suffering in him," as the Lyons congregation described the death of one of their martyrs.[47] Eventually, the martyrs won through such endurance a respect on the popular level which the apologists could never have hoped to achieve.

That the martyrs came to be so esteemed does not mean they were objects of universal praise. The gentle Pliny clearly did not admire the people he executed for their obstinate stubbornness. More than a century later, another Roman official, the proconsul Quintillianus, echoed Pliny when he told the martyr Pionius right before sentencing him to be burned at the stake, "You accomplish very little hastening towards your death. For those who enlist to fight the beasts for a trifling bit of money despise death."[48] In the same spirit, the emperor Marcus Aurelius dismissed Christian martyrs as practicing "stage-heroics." As his Meditations makes clear, for this philosopher-king, dying was the easy way out.[49] Lesser thinkers had a more traditional reason for mocking the martyrs. In a world that considered protection from life's dangers the primary proof of a deity's worth, the martyrs easily appeared as witnesses not to the power of their god but to his impotence. So the critic Celsus wrote, "Do you not see, my excellent man, that anyone who stands by your daemon and not only blasphemes him, but proclaims his banishment from every land and sea, and after binding you who have been dedicated to him like an image takes you away and crucifies you; but the daemon or, as you say, the son of God, takes no vengeance on him?"[50]

Numerous accounts from these early centuries confirm this picture of crowds reacting with ridicule and contempt to the martyrs' suffering. One of the most chilling is contained in a letter written in the aftermath of a persecution in Lyons late in the second century, roughly the same time that Celsus was writing his more theoretical attack. Its authors were Christians of the Lyons community, writing to describe the ordeal of their martyrs to friends and relations in Smyrna:

> They [the martyrs] endured again the customary running of the gauntlet and the violence of the wild beasts, and everything which the furious

people called for or desired, and at last, the iron chair in which their bodies being roasted, tormented them with the fumes. And not with this did the persecutors cease, but were yet more mad against them, determined to overcome their patience. . . . And some raged and "gnashed with their teeth" against them [the bodies of the martyrs], desiring to execute more severe vengeance upon them; but others laughed and mocked at them, magnifying their own idols, and imputed to them the punishment of the Christians.

For all the sickening violence it contains, this detailed account also reveals how pagans came to see the martyrs, and through them Christians in general, in a more positive light, for it ends by reporting that "the more reasonable [pagans] and those who had seemed to sympathize somewhat, reproached them often, saying: 'Where is their God, and what has their religion, which they have chosen rather than life, profited them?'"[51]

The question, though still reflecting the ancient belief in a deity who provides comfort and protection in this life, reflects less puzzlement at the seeming failure of the Christian god than at the willingness of his adherents to endure such tortures on his behalf. At the start of the Lyons persecution, the old charges of incest and cannibalism had been used to arouse the mob. It did not seem right that such monsters should be set free merely by denying their faith, as Christians at least since the time of Trajan were allowed to be. But it made even less sense for such people to prefer torture and death when such an escape hatch existed. Something more had to be involved. Could it be that they really believed this foolishness about a god who had broken all the rules to bring eternal life?

The great hero of pagan philosophy was Socrates. Every educated person had read Plato's moving account of his trial early in the fourth century B.C. and had learned the message that anything worth living for must be worth dying for. It did not take extraordinary imagination to connect Socrates' willingness to die for his beliefs with the actions of the martyrs. For those who needed help doing so, there were always Christians ready to remind them. In another part of the account of the martyr Pionius which was cited above for the laughter it provoked, this exchange is recorded:

At this a bystander named Rufinus, one of those who had a reputation for superiority in rhetoric, said to him, "Cease, Pionius; do not be a fool!"

And Pionius answered him: "Is this your rhetoric? Is this your literature? Even Socrates did not suffer thus from the Athenians. But now everyone is an Anytus and a Meletus [the accusers of Socrates]. Were Socrates and Aristides and Anaxarchus and all the rest fools in your view because they practiced philosophy and justice and courage?"

And Rufinus when he heard this merely kept quiet.[52]

Here also is an example of a martyr using the tools of the apologists. Pionius did not rebuke Rufinus by appealing to Scripture, a document that the rhetorician would not have found persuasive, even if he had known of its contents. What made the rebuke effective was that Pionius drew on an example from Rufinus's own intellectual tradition.

Martyrdom is actually a two-stage process: the action of the individual, and the reaction of the community to that act. Being willing to suffer and die is not enough to make one a martyr, if the community decides that in this or that particular instance the individual was foolhardy or, worse, behaved in a way that threatened established values. But when instead the community decides that the individual acted in defense of those values, then the self-sacrifice makes the perpetrator into a hero. These changes in what might be called the climate of opinion are hard to gauge or predict. Wartime is the most obvious one, wherein national security condones and even celebrates acts that in time of peace are regarded as heinous offenses. Pionius's success in silencing a distinguished opponent by invoking the image of a cultural icon like Socrates—whether it actually happened or was embroidered into the account at a later date—shows that at some point Christians no longer seemed so alien to classical culture that such a comparison would have seemed ridiculous or offensive. That it served instead to silence a trained rhetorician like Rufinus is a tribute as much to the thoughtful groundwork of the apologists as it is to the valor of the martyrs.

Although surviving martyr accounts—both the handful of genuine ones and the far larger number of pious frauds—show martyrs engaged in spirited defenses of their faith, often with a style and skill worthy of the finest apologists, still they differ from the latter in one critical point. Their defenses hardly sought common ground. Indeed, frequently they seem to be at pains to bring out differences between themselves and their antagonists, even when these were trying to find enough common ground to grant them release. Once again, the account of the martyr Pionius:

> The proconsul [Quintillianus] said, "Offer sacrifice."
>
> "No," he [Pionius] answered. "My prayers must be offered to God."
>
> But he said: "We reverence all the gods, we reverence the heavens and all the gods that are in heaven. What then, do you attend to the air? Then sacrifice to the air."
>
> "I do not attend to the air," answered Pionius, "but to him who made the air, the heavens, and all that is in them."
>
> The proconsul said: "Tell me, who did make them?"
>
> Pionius answered: "I cannot tell you."
>
> The proconsul said: "Surely it was the god, that is Zeus, who is in heaven; for he is the ruler of all the gods."

An apologist would not have responded to the proconsul's overtures with the wariness that is obvious in Pionius's guarded answers, nor would he ever have passed up the opportunity afforded by a pagan official asking for enlightenment, even if for the sake of disputation. This belligerence undoubtedly is what established the image of early Christians in general as death-seeking zealots that Gibbon, and others before and since, have found so distasteful. It is a stigma with serious repercussions. The martyrs became the icons of Christian faith. But they are ambiguous icons. Like the central teachings themselves, martyrs can stand for the ultimate sacrifice made out of overwhelming love, or they can stand for rigor and unyielding opposition. This ambiguity makes them, for us, bellwethers as well as icons, for the particular lesson a given individual draws from the martyrs can be a strong indicator of that person's position on a range of other issues.

Too much can be made of the distinction between apologist and martyr, for the two functions were not mutually exclusive. One of the first apologists, Justin, was also a martyr, and the martyr Pionius showed himself no mean apologist. But as symbols, the two stand for diametrically opposite impulses, accommodation versus resistance.

Despite this tension, they have at least one trait in common: both depended on qualities that were essentially personal and charismatic. Neither could be the rock on which a church might be built.

The Bishops

The martyr and the apologist illustrate tensions in Christianity which will play an important part in explaining the role of Christian intolerance. Both, as we shall see, heavily influenced Constantine's understanding of the faith. But neither by themselves nor together do they account for the success of Christianity in organizational terms. That answer lies with another figure, the bishop. It is easy to underestimate the centrifugal forces that might well have kept Christians from being anything but highly diversified local sects with little more than a common point of origin by which to identify one another. The bishop is the figure who gave the movement cohesion and stability. If one thing made Christianity a player, that one thing would be the capacity Christians showed for organizing and maintaining their membership, creating in the person of the bishop a leader who, by means of frequent communication and a habit of assembling with other bishops to deal with common needs and problems, eventually was capable of defining a common message, establishing criteria for identifying a canon of sacred texts, and coordinating their activities to a degree unprecedented for a nongovernmental body in the ancient world. As Gibbon saw, organization was a major advantage of the new faith over the diffuse and localized traditional religions. Just because this asset is now so widely recognized, the odds against it ever having occurred are easily overlooked.

A passage in the Acts of the Apostles illustrates the potential problem. "And suddenly a sound came from heaven like the rush of a mighty wind, and it filled the house where they were sitting. And there appeared to them tongues as of fire, distributed and resting on each one of them." With these words, the book of Acts records the arrival of the Holy Spirit at Pentecost, fulfilling Jesus' promise to send those who obey his commands "even the Spirit of truth, whom the world cannot receive, because it neither sees him nor knows him; you know him, for he dwells with you, and will be in you."[53] In dramatic testimony to the arrival of this Spirit, the disciples poured out of the upper room in which they were staying—traditionally identified as "the Mother of Churches" on Mount Zion—and began proclaiming the gospel in a wide variety of tongues, known and unknown. From the standpoint of faith, the arrival of the Holy Spirit is of incalculable importance to the success of the church. It was the Spirit that stood by the martyrs and gave them their fortitude. It was the Spirit that filled the minds and pens of the apologists with words of vision and persuasion. But from the standpoint of organization, the arrival of the Spirit is absolutely appalling.

The Spirit is, without doubt, the revolutionary member of the Trinity. Unlike the Father, so distant as to be almost beyond human comprehension, or the Son, a model of perfect obedience, the Spirit works in ways that are neither predictable nor always desirable, bringing with it a criterion of inner worth to measure those who would rule and a knowledge that respects neither person nor process, a capacity for defiance always ready to take on state or church. It is as likely to settle on a milkmaid as on an apostle. The Spirit brings what the sociologist Max Weber called charismatic authority, authority that derives from a talent or power that people can see is extraordinary, a gift of God. For that reason, the charismatic leader's authority is an entirely personal one, resting on no institution or office; we obey such a leader because of an instinctive response he or she can evoke by means of this gift. As Weber well knew, such authority is inherently threatening to the more customary authority of law or tradition on which institutions depend. Because the Spirit dwells within, it ever threatens to burst forth with new revelations, new interpretations, new meanings in contradiction to established thought. The Spirit is anarchy.

Given the counterorganizing principle embodied by the Spirit, there was every likelihood that Christianity would splinter into what anthropologist Robert Hefner has called "babble," a message so cluttered with the specific concerns of individual constituencies that its overarching central meaning dissipates into increasingly narrow and localized channels.[54] Such, in fact, has been the fate of the vast majority of new religious movements. That this was not Christianity's fate is obvious, and the bishops are the reason. It was they who held the movement together and gave it coherence. But where did the bishops come from? The way Christianity spread in the first generation, recorded in the Acts of the Apostles, holds much of the answer. Paul and the other missionaries were constantly on the move, staying in one location only long enough to get a new community started. This meant that in each new community a local core group that was itself newly converted had to be left in control of the message. As each of these franchises expanded, newer members naturally looked to older ones for guidance (the Greek word *presbuteros,* from which the English word *priest* derives, means "elder"). But where did these older members turn when questions arose which they could not answer? In the first generation, they could contact the apostle who had first brought the word to them, as the Corinthians and others did with Paul. Afterward, emigrants who carried the faith with them to their new homes kept ties with their original communities which were maintained by subsequent generations. Thus when the church at Lyons experienced persecution late in the second century, it sent an account of the ordeal not to Marseilles or even to Rome but to its parent community in distant Smyrna on the Asia Minor coast. Although this sketch greatly simplifies the actual process, the result was that by the end of the second century the empire was crossed by a vast network of Christian communities in regular contact with one another.

By this time, too, each community had developed the practice of appointing a particular individual to serve as the point of contact to the larger Christian network, not just for letters but for periodic meetings at which common problems could be discussed and resolved. This was the bishop. He maintained order in the local community, while also representing it to other communities.

Although the bishop's original duties might have been primarily bureaucratic, he rapidly began to accrue extraordinary powers, eventually becoming virtual monarch of his community, with a combination of power and experience to match that of all but the most established civic officials. At that time, congregations played a significant role in the selection of their bishop, and this popular participation in their selection gave bishops a power base among the citizenry which few civic officials could match. As Christian communities grew larger and wealthier, the patronage flowing from the bishop's supervision of charity and distribution of alms added significantly to his powers. But what turned him into the leader he might otherwise never have become were the two ongoing crises of early Christian life: heresy and persecution. Heresy was a constant threat not just to the stability of the Christian community but to the individual Christian's hopes for an afterlife of eternal bliss. The severity of the threat prompted a constant and ongoing effort to define and clarify orthodox thought and to recognize a canon of orthodox literature. As modern scholars increasingly appreciate, constant thinking, constant debate, and constant meetings not only solidified Christian identity but also led to a more abstract and intellectualized understanding of the faith, one that increasingly required mastery of the tools of classical philosophy. Simply by being the one who attended these meetings, participated in the debates, and wrote or approved key documents, the bishop naturally took on a special role as the link between the local community and the worldwide body of the church. Language picturing him as the "shepherd" who cared for his "flock" enhanced the prestige and authority of his office.

With regular meetings, a superstructure took place. The framework already existed in Roman provincial organization, and for convenience, if nothing else, the capital city of a province became in ordinary circumstances the site of these synods, or councils, thereby enhancing the role of the bishop of that site, who gradually became thought of as the leading bishop, the *archiepiscopos*, or "archbishop" (also sometimes as the "metropolitan," by virtue of presiding in the *metropolis*). Together, the bishops came to exercise a collective authority that reinforced the powers each already wielded in his home community.

The degree of organization should not be exaggerated. Decrees of synods could not be enforced and could be contradicted by synods elsewhere. The only criteria for adjudicating between councils that reached contradictory conclusions were informal, with certain sees being accorded wider prestige than others because of the fame or antiquity of their community, as Antioch, or for their ties to the apostles, as Alexandria (traditionally founded by Saint Mark) and Rome (Peter and Paul). But in these early centuries there was simply no generally recognized mechanism for imposing conformity on recalcitrant bishops, especially if they enjoyed the support of their local communities. In the decades following Constantine, this lack of clear criteria for precedence and jurisdiction will become a cause of frequent turmoil. Still, for what was a private and relatively new society, Christian episcopal administration by the end of the third century was impressive and unprecedented. And it created an environment for Christians to resolve disputes by means (assembly), and with skills (debate), that were quintessentially political.

In one important way, Christian priests differed dramatically from those known to traditional religion. Theoretically, the people who filled priestly offices in the Greco-Roman world did so because of some personal worth. But in that world "personal worth" pretty much was defined as a matter of station, or of birth, or both. This meant that in practice traditional priests came from the same elites who ran everything else in the ancient state. To Christians, it was not birth or station that mattered, or even that other prize commodity of the ancient world, eloquence. What mattered was the extent to which a leader embodied Christ's teachings, "men of good repute, full of the Spirit and of wisdom," as the apostles specified in the first selection of new leaders.[55] Spiritual qualities completely displaced traditional criteria of nobility or fortune, opening the leadership to classes disenfranchised by the "civic compromise," as the traditional religion of the cities has been dubbed.[56] To Gibbon, such a criterion brought with it an unseemly contrast to men chosen by the old order, in whom "zeal and devotion were seldom animated by a sense of interest, or by the habits of an ecclesiastical character."[57] But the potential conflict was even greater. This criterion opened the way for a leadership drawn from entirely different sectors than the relatively homogeneous ruling elite. It posed a different set of standards for excellence and judgment, and even for wisdom. Wealthy converts who were used to receiving the credit due to patrons in the classical world had to be taught that Christ was the sole patron of their new community; to be effective, benefactions had first to be consecrated at his altar, an act that could only be performed by their bishop.[58]

Spiritual excellence, however, and the more pragmatic talents of political leadership do not often occur in the same individual. Whom was a Christian to obey when they did not—when, for instance, a martyr who had already borne witness to his or her spiritual fortitude and was awaiting the final test issued pardons that the bishop had refused to grant? Or when the apologist turned his skills against the hierarchy? Both the martyr and the apologist were capable of operating as independent sources of authority, and as such both could pose a threat to a given bishop, martyrs by virtue of greater spirituality, apologists greater eloquence. Bishops had to deal with these alternate sources of authority. What they had to offer was stability through an alternate principle of authority, according to which personal traits counted for less than the cumulative powers that each bishop acquired upon accession to the office. In Christian terms, this became known as the principle of "apostolic succession," which held that each bishop belonged to a line that, through the "laying on of hands" by other bishops which took place at the time of his accession, traced back to the apostles, who had received their commission directly from Christ. Looked at more broadly, "apostolic succession" played the same role in the Christian community which dynastic succession plays in a monarchy: it defined legitimacy as a matter of descent rather than personal worth. More than monarchs, however, bishops increasingly had, by means of their practice of meeting together to make decisions that affected a much larger community than any individual bishopric, a corporate authority and sense of identity which no individual, no matter how brilliant or charismatic, could easily match.

Of course, these qualities are not mutually exclusive, and at least in theory the person chosen to be bishop would also be the one who had lived the most exemplary Christian life. Indeed, bishops could also be martyrs and frequently were. Peter and Paul were both martyrs as well as apostles, and in the immediate postapostolic period, the bishop of Antioch, Ignatius, suffered an eloquent martyrdom, as did Bishop Cyprian of Carthage a century later. Ignatius, Cyprian, and others were equally steadfast in their support of the primacy of the bishop, paradoxically asserting the role of the Spirit to do so. Their prestige spread over the entire corps of bishops, excusing the shortcomings of their lesser members, just as the Senate in the old republic had developed a corporate prestige that overshadowed, and if necessary compensated for, the shortcomings of particular senators. However much the martyrs deserve the spotlight history has given them for their role in the persecutions, a case can be made that it was the resilience of the episcopal organization and the leadership skills of the bishops which kept whole communities from cracking. Constant communication, such as the report from Lyons, prepared individual Christians for the ordeal they might face and incidentally provided bishops with an intelligence network that often functioned more efficiently than the government's. It was bishops who dealt with the local authorities, who set the example for their flocks to follow, and most important, ultimately it was the bishops who decided rewards and penalties.[59]

In the end, it was the bishops who came to judge the martyrs and to decide which apologists were orthodox, and not vice versa. Bishops even took it upon themselves to define the meaning of martyrdom, as when Dionysius of Alexandria, writing in the mid-third century of Christians who died ministering to the sick during a plague, ruled that "death in this form, the result of great piety and strong faith, seems in every way the equal of martyrdom."[60] Their effect on Christian faith can be debated, but bishops were absolutely crucial to the strength of Christianity as a movement. They grew in importance precisely because of the ease with which the Christian message could be distorted and contaminated. By defining the Christian canon and the criteria for sainthood, appropriating to themselves the prestige of the martyrs and the skills of the apologists, they made the church a fact as well as a theory, representing their local traditions to the universal body and universal traditions to their localities, serving in their own persons as the hinge that united the one to the other. Though rarely as charismatic as martyrs or as eloquent as apologists, bishops were more significant than either, because they constituted the effective power of the church. The bishops were the players.

Passing the Test

The Christians whom Constantine knew were no little group of transplanted fishermen. Possibly influenced by the example of the bishops with whom he had to work, Constantine himself characterized the apostles not as men drawn from humble stations but as "the wisest among men" and "the best men of their age."[61] Nobody knows how many Christians there were in the empire by the beginning of Constantine's reign. Estimates range from 15 percent of the population—which most people think is too high—to 5 percent, which seems a little low. But the whole point of thinking in terms of players is to show how misleading this debate over numbers can be. The importance of Senate and armies did not lie in their numbers—even combined they did not add up to even the smallest estimate of the Christian population at the start of the fourth century[62]—but in their role as critical constituencies of the emperor. What matters to a player is the amount of influence he can exert at the highest levels of government, whether he is or is not "in the loop." Persecutions of the third century, originating with imperial decrees, indicate that Christianity had achieved at least notoriety by Constantine's time, and the failure of those persecutions left Christians a force to be reckoned with. What is more important is that by the end of the third century Christianity had negotiated several of the pitfalls into which new sects usually step. Thanks to the impulse represented by the apologists to engage the dominant culture, they had avoided becoming a small, inward-looking and isolationist group of the elect. Thanks to the martyrs, they had done so without losing either identity or commitment. While the martyrs kept the Christian message from being absorbed beyond recognition by that culture, the apologists prevented it from becoming completely alienated. Between them, they created the balance of strong internal ties to hold members together and the flexibility to form and maintain ties with the outside community which was needed to attract converts.

But without a stable organization providing continuity in leadership, Christianity never would have accomplished the leap from splinter group to mass movement. The bishops, appropriating to themselves the authority of the martyr and the duties of the apologist, gave the movement an effective organization. In the third century, the empire would experience an unprecedented series of disasters, both natural and civic. If playing the game of empire meant commanding sufficient resources to ensure that one's interests could not be ignored, then the disasters of that century made clear that the church was ready to become a player, and the bishops to serve as an alternative to the traditional ruling elites.

PART II

OPPORTUNITIES

To one who understands the structure of the situation
and the face of the issue—both determined by the
organizational outputs—the formal choice of the
leaders is frequently anticlimactic.

Graham Allison (1971)

Four

The Old Guard Changes

However blustery the meeting between Constantine and the bishops in November 335, it was nothing like the confrontation that had ended a mere quarter century earlier. Yet without the decision by Constantine's predecessor, Diocletian, to launch a brutal and systematic persecution in the waning years of his long reign (284–305), it is unlikely that such a meeting ever would have occurred—or if it had, that Constantine would have been a participant. Diocletian's "Great Persecution," as it came to be known, set in force a train of events that were little short of revolutionary in their impact. But in this as in so many other revolutionary actions during his reign, Diocletian was not so much innovating as acting on well-established precedent. By the middle of the third century, Roman leaders had clearly come to see Christianity as an anomaly in their empire but were less clear on the means to resolve that anomaly. Like a bad tooth, this policy question created a dull ache for more than half a century, with moments of intense anguish interrupting long periods of relative calm. The third century produced the first empirewide persecutions, differing from the localized outbreaks of the second century not just in scope but also in origin. Unlike those earlier ones, which tended to be produced from below, by popular clamor, these came from above, on orders of the emperor. The first two—by Decius in 250 and Valerian in 258—were short lived, ended by the death of the former in battle and the capture of the latter by the Persian king Shapur I. The third was the most severe. In the winter of 302–3, little more than two years before he was to retire, Diocletian issued the first of what would be four edicts of increasing severity aimed at forcing Christians to renounce their faith. Diocletian's edicts of persecution continued in force until 311, and persecution itself did not cease entirely for another two years.

This shift in policy defies easy explanation. The answer that comes most readily to modern readers—that Christianity had simply become too powerful to be ignored—assumes that there was no alternative, no middle ground between persecution and surrender. The written record, as we shall see, certainly supports this assumption; but that record consists on both sides of writings by people most likely to see the world in these terms, philosophers and theologians who were able to perceive the strong theoretical gap that separated Christian thinking from traditional practice and who were inclined by both nature and training to define problems into strong, polar opposites. Other voices, though more muted, are also there, the voices of people who do not fret overmuch about theoretical consequences, voices expressing the deep-seated human urge to make do, to get along and go along. The record also contains evidence that a policy of mutual toleration was viable; in 260 Valerian's son Gallienus reversed his father's policy, ending the persecution and recognizing the corporate status of the church, a crucial decision that made possible direct ownership of cemeteries, churches, and other properties.[1]

Gallienus's policy inaugurated a period of peaceful coexistence which endured for almost half a century. Christian sources remember this as a period when the fortunes of their faith flourished, a memory abundantly confirmed in other ways. "It is beyond our ability to describe in a suitable manner the extent and nature of the glory and freedom with which the word of piety toward the God of the universe, proclaimed to the world through Christ, was honored among all men, both Greeks and barbarians, before the persecution in our day," writes Eusebius of Caesarea, who came of age during this period.[2] Diocletian's persecution brought this "Little Peace of the Church," as it has been called, to a crashing halt, raising yet another set of questions, the loudest and most insistent of which must be, "Why?"

In the aftermath of these events, Christians developed an explanation based on a concept of divine retribution. Shortly after Constantine's victory at the Milvian Bridge in 312, Lactantius, a Christian rhetorician hired to tutor Constantine's oldest son, produced a pamphlet entitled On the Deaths of the Persecutors which had the clear polemical aim of showing that, despite pagan claims to the contrary, God did indeed protect his chosen people from their adversaries. There is nothing subtle about this thesis. As if the title were not sufficient indication, in the opening chapter Lactantius explains that his purpose is to "relate who were the persecutors of the Church from the time of its first constitution, and what were the punishments by which the divine Judge, in His severity, took vengeance on them." He then narrates the deaths of Nero and Domitian before coming to the third-century persecutors Decius and Valerian. Pointing out that Decius, the first emperor to undertake an empirewide persecution, was also the first emperor to die in battle, and that Valerian, the first to attack the corporate body of the church, was also the first to be captured alive by an enemy, Lactantius draws a direct cause-and-effect relationship between the policies of these emperors and the fates they encountered.[3] Naturally, in a work such as this, Diocletian, as the author of the Great Persecution, must also be an archvillain. Evil and bloodthirsty, the Diocletian of these pages is a grasping monster who increased the size of government to the point that there were "more people collecting taxes than paying them." Even a thing so trifling, in Lactantius's eyes, as the cost of a loaf of bread could be a means to inflict new bloodshed. The persecution was but another manifestation of Diocletian's violent and superstitious nature, triggered when priests told him that Christians were interfering with his attempts to divine the will of the gods.[4]

Few specialists now would be content with this explanation of Diocletian's motives for either the persecution or any of his other reforms. Cumulatively the sum of his changes is staggering, particularly in retrospect, but Diocletian himself was no revolutionary. His aim was stability, and most of his changes merely formalized practices that had gradually evolved, some of them having been followed informally for centuries. Indeed, it is entirely likely that for the most part Diocletian thought he was restoring traditional practice, not destroying it. Like Christianity itself, Diocletian was as much a product as a cause of the changed environment. There is something to what Lactantius says about the immediate cause for the Great Persecution, but Diocletian's decision, fraught as it is with so many consequences for the fate of Christianity and the empire, must be set in the broader context of changes in the makeup and function of government, the role of the emperor, religious thought, and Christianity.

The empirewide persecutions of the third century are best seen as the result of a series of changes, including a general extension of imperial government into areas that previously had been left to local control and the rise of a new set of players along with new rules for playing the game

Soldier-Emperors

Diocletian's reorganization involved a reduction in the size and increase in the number of the provinces, which ultimately came to almost ninety, double the number they had reached by the second century. Over them he added a new layer of government, the diocese. There were twelve of these, corresponding in number and (roughly) area to the provinces of the old republic. The dioceses stood between the province and the imperial court, whose chief officer was the old praetorian prefect—the same title as the Augustan guard commander but with a vastly different set of responsibilities, now primarily judicial and administrative. The changes led to a corresponding increase in the number of imperial personnel. Whereas the provinces in the second century were run by about 150 top administrators, by the end of the fourth century that number had grown twentyfold to an estimated 3,000 "very good jobs" in the Eastern half of the empire alone.[5]

This increase in central government, which drew the wrath of Lactantius, is one of the most obvious hallmarks of the late empire, as this period of Roman history is called, and it has been a favorite target of critics of government abuse and political moralists who, cheerfully following Lactantius's lead, paint a picture of power-hungry emperors invading the liberties of senators and provinces. In fact, emperors rarely needed to make such exertions, for inertia accounts for most of the extension of imperial power: there was no need to take the initiative and risk being wrong when keeping one's head down and leaving difficult decisions to others was such a safe alternative. What drew provincial authorities to the emperor like a magnet was the lure of resources, constitutional niceties yielding to cold cash and the easy solution of an imperial bailout. The process was well under way in the peaceful days of the Principate. The problem that brought Pliny the Younger to Bithynia was not Christianity but the mess created by overspending municipalities, and the steady stream of his letters, which he published to let us see both his graceful style and the ready access he enjoyed with Trajan, now witnesses as well to the transformation of the senatorial class from independent-minded executives to career-minded administrators.[6]

Despite Lactantius's grumbling, it is not so much the size of the increase in late imperial administration—well below China in the twelfth century, not to mention that of any modern bureaucracy—as other effects that caused him the greatest chagrin, primarily the fact that this great extension of direct imperial activity, along with a similarly large increase in the military, was to create a new career class.[7] Lactantius scoffs at these new functionaries as "rude and illiterate men," a phrase that in the Roman political vocabulary often means no more than that they were not among the author's friends. The full comment however, points in this case to a more substantive change. "Eloquence was extinguished," Lactantius wails, "pleaders were removed [and] legal experts either exiled or executed." It mattered little, he continued, "that literature was regarded as an evil activity, and that those versed in it were crushed and vilified as enemies of both the emperor and the state. The laws were set aside; licence to act arbitrarily in everything was assumed by the emperor and granted to his judges. Military judges devoid of any humanity or culture were sent into the provinces without any assessors at their side."[8] Stripped of the histrionics, what this passage shows is Lactantius's anguish over the government's lack of respect for class and culture. This was not playing by the rules. Lactantius's complaint is echoed by others. Aurelius Victor, a pagan writing toward the end of the fourth century, was broad minded enough to concede that Diocletian and his colleagues, "although they were deficient in culture," had been "sufficiently schooled by the hardships of the countryside and of military service to be the best men for the state." But he concluded that "it is indisputable that learning, refinement and courtesy are essential, particularly in emperors, since without these qualities natural talents are despised as if they are unfinished or even crude."[9]

What accounts for the change in personnel? Warfare as usual was a crucible, and success no respecter of privilege or tradition. To win, emperors as early as Marcus Aurelius, the second century's revered "philosopher-king" and last of Gibbon's "good" emperors, began to circumvent senatorial standards and reach into lower ranks for talented officer material. Septimius Severus, victor in the round of civil wars that followed the assassination of Marcus's unstable son Commodus in 193, is supposed to have advised his own sons on his deathbed in 211 to take care of the army and ignore all else. The advice, reported by Dio, reflects the cavalier manner his dynasty adopted to senatorial prerogatives, and it is hardly surprising to witness the constitutional tailspin into which the Principate fell on the death of the last of his line, Severus Alexander, despite that ruler's concerted effort to restore senatorial dignities.[10] Alexander's death, in 235, came at the hands of his own troops, an ominous sign, more than confirmed by events of the next half century. Gallienus, the emperor who decided to end the persecution of Christians, broke with tradition as well with regard to imperial appointments. Cutting military command loose from senatorial privilege, he based promotion to the highest levels on merit rather than birth. His reward was twofold: a pool of superb rulers who pulled the empire back together in the final decades of the century, and vilification by the senators who lost the privileges but wrote the histories. Digging into an arsenal of invective stocked with a millennium of practice, they gave him everything they had: Gallienus was effete, self-indulgent, a tyrant and party giver, degenerate, a bibliophile, unfit for office. It is up to modern scholars to fill in the record: Gallienus ruled for almost twenty years, found time in an age of crisis and scarcity to patronize the most brilliant philosopher of the century, and addressed real problems.[11]

The new players who came onto the imperial stage were drawn from a lower and ruder class than that encompassed by the Principate.

They brought with them a different set of values, which also helps account for the greater extension of government, for if the record of complaints about abuse of privilege which fills the legal codes of the period is any guide, rulers of the late empire insisted on a more level playing field than had their predecessors. This goal should be kept in mind when reading descriptions of the late empire as an "intrusive and totalitarian state"; too often, that description has been repeated without much thought about the perspective on which it is based. With spokesmen as eloquent as Cicero and Pliny the Younger it is easy to forget just how narrowly self-centered senatorial values were. A "good" emperor, to the Senate, was one who shared senatorial values, the rights and privileges of senators—one who was, in other words, good to the Senate. If the rest of the empire suffered, if the armies were poorly fed and led, if the frontiers collapsed, such an emperor nonetheless showed he knew and appreciated the rules of the game and was accordingly judged a good emperor.

The comfortable nexus of courtesy and patronage on which the Principate was based required the emperor to put friendship ahead of justice, and Lactantius's complaint only indicates that the new ruling class of the late empire had standards and attitudes that differed significantly from those of the senatorial and provincial elites who ran the empire under the Principate. But his reference to "the soldiery" points to a more fundamental change, involving more aggressive play by the lower ranks of the military The soldiery, broadly defined, certainly was the big winner of the Dominate, and senatorial values the loser.

Diocletian's own concern for the welfare of the military is well known, thanks to the survival of a quirky document, the Edict on Prices of A.D. 301. Here, he attempted to deal with the galloping inflation that accompanied all the other disasters of the third century by setting a maximum price on every conceivable commodity for sale in the Roman Empire. A gold mine for social historians, and an object lesson for economists in the futility of price controls, the edict is important here primarily for its prefatory remarks, where Diocletian asks,

> Who does not know that wherever the common safety requires our armies
> to be sent, the profiteers insolently and covertly . . . charge extortionate

prices for merchandise, not just fourfold or eightfold, but on such a scale
that human speech cannot find words to characterize their profit and their
practices. Indeed, sometimes in a single retail sale a soldier is stripped of his
donative and pay . . . , and our soldiers appear to bestow with their own
hands the rewards of their military service and their veterans' bonuses upon
the profiteers.[12]

Such sentiments certainly confirm the paramount importance of the
soldiery in Diocletian's thinking, and various changes, including a
requirement that all government officials wear uniforms, give an undoubtedly military aura to his reforms. But to say this is not to say that
his concerns were solely military. The Edict on Prices conveys a strong
sense of outrage not just against exploitation of the soldiers but in
general against individuals who have put their private gain above the
general good—"uncontrolled madmen" who "have no thought for the
common need," as he puts it. Among such individuals, Diocletian
complains, the right to plunder "is considered almost a creed." Who,
Diocletian asks, "is so insensitive and so devoid of human feeling that
he can be unaware or has not perceived that uncontrolled prices are
widespread in the sales taking place in the markets and in the daily life
of the cities?" Remarks such as these show that Diocletian's interests
were by no means limited to the military. More important, they provide
a key to understanding many of the changes that characterize the late
empire, for the "uncontrolled madmen" against whom he rails likely
are the very same city elites entrusted with the governance of the
empire under the Principate. The edict thus shows what really changed
between Principate and Dominate: in the latter, the central government no longer trusted the local elites, or, better, no longer saw its
goals as identical with those of the local elites. Late Roman emperors
elaborated administration in order to maintain greater control. The
new layers of government—palatines (officials sent directly from the
court to supervise local affairs), *agentes in rebus* (the secret service),
new governors and their staffs—can easily be presented as a stark
contrast to the efficiency of the Principate, which made free use of the
local elites to perform the same services; on the other hand, the Principate could just as easily be described as putting the fox in charge of the
henhouse.

The Tetrarchy

Less than two years after assuming the purple, Diocletian elevated another general, Maximian, to equal status, assigning him to be Augustus of the Western half of the empire while he himself stayed in the East. Collegial authority was not unprecedented in the empire, but in 293 Diocletian took the further step of selecting junior colleagues for himself and Maximian, each of whom would bear the title *Caesar.* This group became known as the Tetrarchy, and it has been a source of endless fascination for scholars. What was its purpose? No official rationale survives (if one was ever offered). Lactantius has a typically bilious explanation: "He appointed three men to share his rule, dividing the world into four parts and multiplying the armies, since each of the four strove to have a far larger number of troops than previous emperors had had when they were governing the state alone. The number of recipients began to exceed the number of contributors."[13]

Fear and avarice, however, seem less likely explanations for Diocletian's "militarization" of government than his desire for order and stability. It is, indeed, to his credit that he did not hesitate to share power in order to achieve that goal. There was ample precedent. For one thing, military organization was efficient, at least in comparison with the alternatives, and could be held up as a model for organizing rule in ways that would never be gleaned from reading sources like Lactantius. When Xenophon's idealized Cyrus turns to the problem of organizing his new empire, the model he comes up with is military organization, because of the better supervision its chain of command provides:

> the sergeants care for the ten men under them, the lieutenants for the sergeants, the colonels for the lieutenants, the generals for the colonels, and thus no one is uncared for, even though there be many brigades; and when the commander-in-chief wishes to do anything with his army, it is sufficient for him to issue his commands only to his brigadier-generals. On this same model, then, Cyrus centralized the administrative functions also. And so it was possible for him, by communicating with only a few officers, to have no part of his administration uncared for.[14]

Even more, Diocletian sought to deal with the multiple-front conflicts from which the armies of the Principate had been spared and with which they had not been designed to deal. Contemporary authors, trained to define problems in moral terms, tended to explain the upheavals of the third century as the result of a lust for absolute power on the part of the pretenders. But the issue was structural, not moral. In an age of instant communication such as our own, it is easy to forget Fernand Braudel's observation that, in premodern times, distance was "the first enemy."[15] These days, it takes a natural disaster to be reminded of the importance of having the highest executive authority at the scene of action. Without it, other priorities—everything from a supply clerk's insistence on signed paperwork to the prospect of a major budget shortfall—inevitably crowd in. In Rome, where by the third century the self-protective impulse to refer every decision to higher authority had developed into a form of high art, there was simply no way for imperial authority to respond in time to the constant brushfires that now characterized life on the frontiers. Frustration, as much as ambition, propelled frontier commanders to seize the purple.

In other words, the crises of the third century exposed weaknesses in a system of imperial administration which relied too heavily on the authority of a single individual. How to keep the empire intact and yet decentralize his authority? That was the great dilemma confronting Diocletian. His solution was the Tetrarchy, and by multiplying the resources available at the imperial level he succeeded brilliantly in finally bringing an end to the crises of the third century.

Did he intend to do more? After ruling for twenty decisive years, Diocletian made the unprecedented decision to retire voluntarily from office. Why? What really intrigues scholars is the thought that Diocletian might have intended the Tetrarchy to resolve constitutional as well as military weaknesses of the Principate. Chief among these was the issue of succession, the most destabilizing side effect of Augustus's artful compromise with the Senate. As a result of that compromise, the office of emperor never became clearly enough defined for a clear line of succession to emerge. The turmoil of the third century made the cost of this oversight painfully apparent.

Did Diocletian intend to have a trained successor for each Augustus in place and ready to succeed him, thereby closing that window of instability which opened whenever an incumbent died? Certainly the Tetrarchy gave pause to potential usurpers, simply by confronting them with four incumbents, rather than just one. Two actions, however, point in the direction of a more elaborate plan. First, when Diocletian opted to retire in 305, he persuaded Maximian to do so as well. Unless something like a regular succession was intended, there was no inherent reason why the abdication of one Augustus required the other to follow suit—events would prove that Maximian in fact did so unwillingly. Second, two grown sons of ruling emperors were passed over in the selection of new Caesars. Both of these men proved to be well trained, imaginative, and highly competent. The most likely explanation for their exclusion, therefore, is that Diocletian intended to use some criterion other than birth to select successors. To drive the point home, and thereby prevent heirs from even hoping to succeed, blood ties that formerly ensured the choice of a Caligula or a Nero now automatically disqualified even a competent candidate. If this was Diocletian's intention, it was stillborn, with the system falling apart virtually in the aftermath of his retirement. A key figure in its failure is none other than Constantine, one of the natural sons excluded by the arrangement.

Although it was a failure, the Tetrarchy cannot be forgotten, because it is central to the political dynamics of the succeeding era. Success in restabilizing the empire had won enormous prestige for Diocletian, and by extension for the collegial system he introduced. Like Caesar and Augustus before him, Diocletian was now in a position to legitimize a new form of rule. His system did not last long, but while it lasted, being designated a junior member of the Tetrarchy was the surest route to success.

Pomp and Circumstance

More enduring than the Tetrarchy was a change in the ideology of the emperor which characterizes the late empire, the simple "first citizen" metastasizing into "lord and god" (*dominus et deus*), a swollen, vainglorious figure to modern eyes, captured for all time in the description by the late Roman historian Ammianus Marcellinus of the emperor Constantius II's entry into Rome in A.D. 357:

> Accordingly, being saluted as Augustus with favouring shouts, while hills and shores thundered out the roar, he never stirred, but showed himself as

calm and imperturbable, as he was commonly seen in his provinces. For he both stooped when passing through lofty gates (although he was very short), and as if his neck were in a vice, he kept the gaze of his eyes straight ahead, and turned his face neither to right nor to left, but (as if he were a clay figure) neither did he nod when the wheel jolted nor was he ever seen to spit, or to wipe and rub his face or nose, or move his hands about. And although this was affectation on his part, yet these and various other features of his more intimate life were tokens of no slight endurance, granted to him alone, as was given to be understood.[16]

As part of the glorification that took place under the Dominate, the office took on the trappings of religious ceremonial, with such terminology as "divine" and "sacred" routinely attached to the emperor and all that surrounded him. Diocletian gave the Tetrarchy supernatural ties, naming his dynasty "Jovian" after Jupiter, the head of the Roman pantheon, and that of Maximian "Herculian," after the heroic laborer who became a god for doing his father's bidding. Imperial ideology emphasized these divine ties, and panegyrists frequently spoke of Diocletian and Maximian as if they were personifications of Jupiter and Hercules.

As is so often true of the late empire, this is a change that usually has been negatively compared with the Principate, at the price of misunderstanding its function and purpose. Yet, as much as he hated Constantius II, Ammianus shows a certain admiration for the emperor's demeanor; this alone should indicate that it meant something more to contemporaries than empty strutting. Once again, that role model for ancient kingship, Xenophon's Cyrus, indicates how to understand such behavior: "He [Cyrus] trained his associates also not to spit or to wipe the nose in public, and not to turn round to look at anything, as being men who wondered at nothing. All this he thought contributed, in some measure, to their appearing to their subjects men who could not lightly be despised."[17] The similarity between Constantius II's memorable entry into Rome and Cyrus's advice suggests that something older and deeper than individual megalomania was involved in this new style of imperial deportment. Underlying these changes in fashion were more fundamental changes in the relationship of the emperor to the Senate, the role of the military, and assumptions about the role of government.

The place to begin is with Diocletian himself, an emperor who gives every indication of having been both level headed and down to earth. These traits are indicated not just by his willingness to surrender power but also by his conduct in retirement—contentedly growing cabbages in his palace at Spalato, the modern Split on the Adriatic's Dalmatian coast. If such a person surrounded himself with pomp and circumstance, the reason must lie elsewhere. One obvious reason surely was pragmatic: layers of ceremony made the task of the potential assassin more difficult. But there was a deeper level to this ceremonial, for it gave expression to the aspirations and values of the age as surely as did Augustus's republican pose. In both cases, style was tied to the need to demonstrate legitimacy.

With the distance of centuries, it is easy to see that the problem emperors faced in the third century was to find an alternative source of legitimacy, now that the Senate could no longer keep the armies in check. Although they are unlikely to have defined the problem in these terms, emperors found the answer to it by natural means. Harking back to principles established millennia earlier, they abandoned the comfortable nexus with a senatorial elite that was the heart of the Principate and based their power more overtly on popular support and acclaim. The problem was that lower orders lacked an institution that could focus their sentiments as clearly as the Senate had done for the aristocracy. To supply the loss, emperors increasingly substituted ceremonies and acclamations for more substantive methods of interaction. Late imperial ceremonial was thus the result of a combination of practical and ideological needs. No longer *princeps,* or first among equals, the emperor now was a figure for all to adore and venerate. Hence the pose: serenity was a characteristic of the gods, and the person who displayed it was therefore thought to possess divine virtue.[18]

What made this ceremonial deportment such a natural alternative was that it was not a new or sudden change. Like so much of late imperial behavior, it had grown up gradually during the Principate. Thus Trajan's orator, Dio Chrysostom, personified "Tyranny" and "Lady Royalty" in his *First Discourse on Kingship,* distinguishing between true monarchy and its opposite on the basis of demeanor:

Furthermore, in her zeal to imitate the character of the other woman [Lady Royalty], instead of the friendly smile Tyranny wore a leer of false humility, and instead of a glance of dignity she had an ugly and forbidding scowl. But in order to assume the appearance of pride, she would not glance at those who came into her presence but looked over their heads disdainfully. And so everybody hated her, and she herself ignored everybody. She was unable to sit with composure, but would cast her eyes incessantly in every direction, frequently springing up from her throne.[19]

Dio's lampoon shows that even in the early second century dignity and serenity were associated with the look of a true king. The one big change between the demeanor of his ideal ruler and that of a late Roman emperor lies in the royal gaze: the rigid posture that Ammianus admired in Constantius II was to Dio a sign of hauteur out of keeping with the collegiality of the Principate.

The difference is not due to the vainglory of late Roman emperors but rather is one more effect of the heightened religiosity that separates the Dominate from the Principate. Fragments from the Hellenistic political tract attributed to Diotogenes (Chapter 2) reflect this idea of a divine tie that separates true from false kings. This author lists "solemn majesty" as one of the three attributes that a king must cultivate (the other two being "a gracious behavior" and "capacity to inspire awe" through punishment of wrongdoers). Merely to look upon a good king, he writes, "ought to affect the souls of those who watch him no less than a flute or harmony could do."[20] In so writing, Diotogenes reveals the deep ideological purpose that underlay the late empire's regal display. According to this thinking, it was the ruler's chief duty to improve the moral worth of his subjects. He did this by making himself a reflection—a likeness or icon (from the Greek *eikōn,* "image")—of deity. Another of these pseudonymous tracts, this one attributed to "Ecphantus," explained that "only the king can bring about this blessing [of spontaneous loyalty] in men's nature, and make them able—through imitation of himself, their superior—to follow in the path of duty." Or, as an orator who may have spoken in front of Diocletian himself put it, "We must practice ourselves by praising earthly kings, and so habituate and train ourselves for adoration of the deity." The emperor's tie to the divine is so great, Ecphantus suggests, that it should be visible in the radiance of his office; he should appear "as it were in a blaze of light."[21]

So strong was this concept of the kingly icon that it continued to be applied even to Christian emperors. "He makes manifest the august title of monarchical authority in the remarkable fabric of his robes, since he alone deserves to wear the royal purple which so becomes him," Bishop Eusebius of Caesarea says of Constantine in an oration delivered near the end of the emperor's reign. As a sop to Christian modesty, Eusebius adds that this emperor "laughs at his raiment, interwoven with gold, finished with intricate blossoms," wearing it merely "out of regard for his subjects' sense of proper style."[22] The disclaimer did not stop Constantine's renegade nephew, the emperor Julian, from later mocking with republican sarcasm his uncle's love of finery. Ironically, in this case it was Julian who was out of step. Although modern scholars frequently write with admiration of Julian's efforts to restore the simpler behavior of the Principate, contemporaries found it demeaning; while Christian writers scorned the man they called "the Apostate" for turning away from the faith, even their pagan counterparts conceded that he had failed to achieve the dignity of his office.[23]

The king's iconic qualities help explain an aspect of this political theory which has been a source of endless misunderstanding: the practice of ruler worship. Paying divine honors to rulers was nothing new to the ancient world; in the Greek East, kings had routinely received such honors since the time of Alexander the Great. But the association of kingship with the gods goes back much further. In one of history's first law codes, issued in Babylon around 1800 B.C., Hammurabi claims that the gods

> named me
> to promote the welfare of the people,
> me, Hammurabi, the devout, god-fearing prince,
> to cause justice to prevail in the land,
> to destroy the wicked and the evil,
> that the strong might not oppress the weak.[24]

From the moment Octavian became Augustus, the Roman emperor was never simply a secular figure. Like Livy's Romulus, Julius Caesar had been declared a god to soothe an aroused populace. Augustus, as his adopted son, was officially "son of the divine one" (*divi filius*), adding another layer of legitimacy to his mantle and abetting the growth of a religious cult around the person of the emperor. Augustus accepted such cult in the provinces and eventually assumed the office of pontifex maximus, official head of the Roman state religion, as did all of his successors for the next four hundred years. Burning incense on an altar to the emperor's "genius"—a tutelary deity in Roman belief, something akin to a "patron saint" but more personal and unique— became a standard way of expressing loyalty to the regime. Later ages scorned this practice as "emperor worship," but a polytheistic world was capable of subtler distinctions than is a monotheistic one. Following Caesar's precedent, the Senate did declare "good" emperors gods after their death; but, with the exception of those deranged few on whom, unfortunately, Hollywood loves to dwell, no emperor thought himself a god during his lifetime.[25] A tract that survives from a body of documents attributed to the Egyptian god Thoth, known to the Greeks as Hermes Trismegistus, makes the distinction clear. Here, in response to a question from her son Horus about "kingly souls," the goddess Isis explains:

> There are in the universe four regions . . . namely, heaven, the aether, the air, and the earth. Above, my son, in heaven, dwell gods, over whom, as over all else likewise, rules the Maker of the universe; . . . and upon earth dwell men, over whom rules he who is king for the time being; for the gods, my son, cause to be born at the right time a man that is worthy to govern upon earth. . . . He who is king on earth is the last of the four rulers, but the first of men. As long as he is on earth, he has no part in true deity; but as compared with other men, he has in him something exceptional, which is like to God.[26]

Last of the gods, first among men: such was the religious sanction that Augustus bequeathed to his heirs.

In this thought world, religious terminology readily attached itself to the ruler, and the Roman emperor was no exception. The process was sufficiently well advanced under Augustus that the more tradition-minded Tiberius already had to fight efforts to sanctify the person and acts of the emperor;[27] by the third century it had become entirely commonplace. Sacralization of Diocletian's rule was thus not a sudden and startling change, nor was his choice of Roman gods as eponymous ancestors inspired by megalomaniac delusions. Earlier in the third century, emperors had begun to assert a connection with a divine counterpart, a comrade, or *comes,* what Arthur Darby Nock once happily characterized as a private line on the heavenly switchboard.[28] In using traditional Roman gods, Diocletian was in fact being more traditional than his predecessors. Early in the century, Elagabalus had ignored the Roman pantheon in favor of the solar deity of his native Emesa, and fifty years later Aurelian, whose victories were sufficiently extensive for him to lay plausible claim to the title *Restitutor Orbis,* took as his *comes* a more vaguely universal version of this deity, now identified as an "unconquered" or "unconquerable" companion, Sol Invictus, making it a new source of legitimacy with which to balance the volatile loyalties of the armies. A tantalizingly brief fragment that survives from a history of Aurelian's reign depicts him dealing with a mutiny by his troops. Here, Aurelian confronts his troops not with the authority of the Senate but with that of his *comes,* telling them that they have no right to challenge his rule because they played no part in creating it. From the sun god it had come, and only the sun god could take it away.[29]

Care must be taken in reading such evidence. It is easy for our intensely secular age to conclude that such statements were mere cynical manipulation, or that the divine ties were developed strictly for political reasons. It is better, however, to see this change as a reflection of a new mood of religiosity, inherent in which is the idea that the source of legitimacy, the proof of a true emperor, must be divine instead of senatorial. In Ecphantus, it is this divine tie that separates true from false kings:

> The king is therefore a being who is sole and unique, as being the reflection of the Higher King; he is always known to his Creator; but by his subjects he is seen in his office of king, as it were in a blaze of light. For by his office he is judged and tested, being thereby as an eagle—the mightiest creature among all birds—when it faces the sun. The like holds good of the office of kingship; it is divine, and difficult to behold owing to excess of light, except for those who are of the true breed. False claimants to kingship, who are of bastard stock, are convicted and condemned, like men who have ascended

Figs. 1–2. The sun has always been a powerful symbol of monotheistic belief, and Christians readily borrowed the image to explain their faith to nonbelievers. In figure 1, Helios, the sun god, easily identified by the rays radiating from his head, drives his four-horse chariot across the sky in a relief from about 300 B.C. In figure 2 (*opposite*), the sun god is replaced by Jesus in a mosaic from an early-fourth-century tomb excavated beneath the Vatican in Rome. A cross superimposed over the sun radiates from his head, and two of the horses of his chariot are still visible. The image, named Christus-Helios, indicates how such comparisons might have helped converts understand their new faith. (Staatliche Museen zu Berlin)

to a height beyond their real powers, dazzled by the many flashes of light about them and the dizziness that comes upon them; but such as have come properly to kingship, by reason of their fitness for it, find it a safe habitation, because they are able to make good use of their office.[30]

The solar ideology of Ecphantus indicates the theoretical base on which Aurelian, who celebrated his relationship to Sol Invictus, rested his claim to independence from the whim of his troops. Its new prominence was a mixed blessing for Christians. Because the sun appears to be everywhere at once, bringing light and warmth to humans without being diminished in any way or contaminated by its contact with the evils of this world, it has always been a powerful symbol of monotheistic belief. The sun was the focus of Akhenaton's monotheistic reforms in Egypt in the 14th century B.C., and Plato used it as the visible

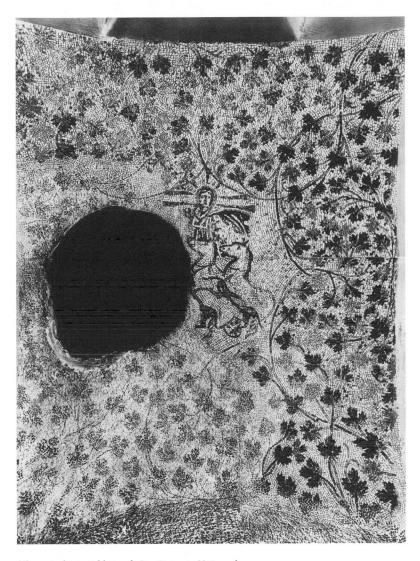

(Photo Archivio Fabbrica di San Pietro in Vaticano)

representation of God on this side of his Divided Line. Christians used solar parallels to deal with pagan doubts that a god like Jesus would suffer earthly contamination, and, as we saw in the preceding chapter, they exploited references in the Hebrew Bible to God as the "Sun of Righteousness" and "Sun of Salvation" to diminish the differences between their belief and solar monotheism. One possible result of this type of religious odyssey survives in a fresco of a Christian tomb demolished by Constantine to build the first Church of Saint Peter on the Vatican. Dubbed "Christus-Helios" by art historians, the mosaic shows Christ in the place of the sun god, driving the solar chariot, from which the rays of the sun radiate in the shape of a cross.[31] This legacy of sacral kingship was shared by Christians and pagans. On the other hand, the greater dependence of late imperial ideology on a divine source of legitimacy increased the political stakes of refusal to acknowledge official religion. Combined with the greater visibility that Christians achieved in the course of the third century, their refusal to participate in ruler cult magnified the threat they posed to imperial stability.

Christianity Spreads

The same age that created so many crises for the Roman Empire was also the age in which Christianity became a substantial force throughout the empire. Although at best the percentage of Christians in the empire had barely entered double digits by the end of the century, what data there are suggest that during these decades the new religion finally broke out of the urban areas in which most of its previous growth had occurred and became established among the much more numerous peasant population in the countryside, particularly in North Africa and Asia Minor.

One factor contributing to the rise in Christian fortunes was the tradition of charity which the new faith inherited from its Jewish forebears, in which almsgiving and care of the poor had always been seen as a religious duty. The letters of Saint Paul show that this tradition had carried over into the earliest Christian communities and by the second century had earned approving notice from pagans who otherwise had no sympathy with Christian goals. The satirist Lucian, whose sharp tongue lashed Christian and pagan with equal zeal, devoted one essay to the Cynic philosopher Peregrinus, who immolated himself in 165 at the Olympic Games, a suicide that drew wide attention. Although scholars now are inclined to see Peregrinus as a deeply troubled but earnest religious seeker, Lucian portrays him as a flamboyant buffoon and con man. At one stage of his career, Lucian tells us, Peregrinus became a Christian and drew many followers for his commentaries on Scripture. Thrown into prison, Peregrinus immediately became the object of even greater attention:

> Well, when he had been imprisoned, the Christians, regarding the incident as a calamity, left nothing undone in the effort to rescue him. Then, as this was impossible, every other form of attention was shown him, not in any casual way but with assiduity; and from the very break of day aged widows and orphan children could be seen waiting near the prison, while their officials even slept inside with him after bribing the guards. Then elaborate meals were brought in, and sacred books of theirs were read aloud, and excellent Peregrinus . . . was called by them "the new Socrates."

To Lucian, of course, such ministrations simply proved the extent of Peregrinus's skills at fakery and the gullibility of the Christians. But they also testify to a well-organized and elaborate relief network that would be impressive by any standards, doubly so by those of the ancient world. Even Lucian felt obliged to comment, "They show incredible speed whenever any such public action is taken; for in no time they lavish their all."[32] His own explanation for this behavior drips with sarcasm:

> The poor wretches have convinced themselves, first and foremost, that they are going to be immortal and live for all time, in consequence of which they despise death and even willingly give themselves into custody, most of them. Furthermore, their first lawgiver persuaded them that they are all brothers of one another after they have transgressed once for all by denying the Greek gods and by worshipping that crucified sophist himself and living under his laws. Therefore they despise all things indiscriminately and consider them common property, receiving such doctrines traditionally without any definite evidence.[33]

For all Lucian's elegant disdain, it is not difficult to imagine how attractive these same qualities—a willingness to lay down all for the sake of others—could be during disasters, of the sort that beset the empire in the third century. This is the picture that emerges in vivid detail from a poignant letter written by the bishop of Alexandria, Dionysius, in the aftermath of a plague that swept the city in 260:

> The most of our brethren were unsparing in their exceeding love and brotherly kindness. They held fast to each other and visited the sick fearlessly, and ministered to them continually, serving them in Christ. And they died with them most joyfully, taking the affliction of others, and drawing the sickness from their neighbors to themselves and willingly receiving their pains. And many who cared for the sick and gave strength to others died themselves, having transferred to themselves their death. . . .
>
> . . . And they took the bodies of the saints in their open hands and in their bosoms, and closed their eyes and their mouths; and they bore them away on their shoulders and laid them out; and they clung to them and embraced them; and they prepared them suitably with washings and garments. And after a little they received like treatment themselves, for the survivors were continually following those who had gone before them.

Dionysius draws a pointed contrast between this treatment and what pagans could expect when they contracted the sickness:

> But with the heathen everything was quite otherwise. They deserted those who began to be sick, and fled from their dearest friends. And they cast them out into the streets when they were half dead, and left the dead like refuse, unburied. They shunned any participation or fellowship with death; which yet, with all their precautions, it was not easy for them to escape.[34]

Even allowing for a certain exaggeration, the general outline conforms to the pattern of organized relief visible in other instances. The care has practical implications for the spread of Christianity. On the basis of studies of modern epidemics, which indicate that such simple nursing even without medications can reduce the mortality rate by two-thirds or more, one scholar has estimated that over the course of a century the Christian percentage of a typical city hit by plague would have nearly doubled, from about 1 in 6 to 1 in 3.5. Such figures posit a static population and a similar birthrate for Christians and pagans. If the Christian birthrate was higher—as seems likely with a higher recovery rate during plague—the proportion would be even more favorable.[35]

Charity played a role as well in cementing the Christian community. Although in theory charitable activity should automatically bind a congregation together, in fact the potential for disruption is very great, not only because of the resentments that disparities in wealth can breed but also, and more important, because wealthy members of the congregation pose at least potentially as large a threat to the authority of the clergy as that posed by freewheeling charismatics. In the event, however, charity served to reinforce the authority of the bishop, for it was established very early that charitable acts were efficacious only if they were offered to God as part of the normal liturgy. This position effectively made the bishop the middleman in such activities, thereby ensuring that the community would look to him, rather than to the donors, as the source of largesse. In effect, it meant that the bishop took on the role of patron of the local Christian community, and moreover that he held the position without fear of potential rivals.[36] The lesson was reinforced at all levels. The apocryphal "Acts of Peter" included several stories whose aim was to guarantee that the thanks for good acts went to Christ and his church, rather than to traditional patrons, by divorcing the gift from its source. One that makes the point as bluntly as possible involves a gift of ten thousand pieces of gold which Peter received from "a very wealthy woman who bore the name of Chryse (the golden), because every utensil of hers was made of gold— for since her birth she had never used a silver or glass vessel, but only golden ones." When his followers protested because she was "notorious all over Rome for fornication," Peter "laughed and said to the brethren, 'I do not know what this woman is as regards her usual way of life; but in taking this money I did not take it without reason; for she was bringing it as a debtor to Christ, and is giving it to Christ's servants; for he himself has provided for them.'"[37] By such lessons, the source of the church's largesse became less important than the purifying agency—Christ and his ministers—which was the ultimate guarantor of its efficacy.

Charity thus became another weapon in the bishop's armory against dissent, the threat of punishment for one's soul in the afterlife reinforced with the more immediate threat of losing food and shelter in this one. In sheer numbers, the potential group affected could be sizable, especially in the larger cities, where it could rival the clientele of the traditional civic elites. One oft-cited set of figures for the city of Rome in the mid-third century shows more than 1,500 persons on the bishop's rolls, and more than 150 clergy of various grades, including 46 priests.[38]

Even without the positive advantages of charity, Christianity was likely to benefit from the negative effect of disasters on traditional bonds of community. With fewer restraints, people attracted to the new faith would find it easier to explore their interest.[39]

Pagan Monotheism

The correlation of Christian success with Roman misfortune in the third century gives ready birth to facile equations and theories of causation: if Christianity was rising, then paganism must have been declining; if at the same time rational scholarship and satire give way to prayer and theological dispute, then Christianity also must be the cause.

Such interpretations depend on a static definition of paganism and of classical scholarship, one that requires both to have achieved a fixed state of development from which they would never otherwise have changed. It is now clear that ancient religion and philosophy were both constantly evolving and adapting to deal with new questions and concerns. In the third century, traditional religion remained quite robust, but it was changing to deal with increasing interest in a personal relationship with a monotheistic deity. Few scholars are any longer sure of the cause for this phenomenon, although it is clear that it goes back at least into the relatively secure second century, if not earlier, which means that the cause lies in something more complex than the greater insecurity generated by the disasters of the third century. The size of the empire and the relative ease with which people might now relocate presumably made it easier to see beyond the deities of one's childhood and loosened the restraints that make individuals in traditional communities reluctant to pursue new interests.[40]

Evidence of such concerns comes at the highest levels in the second century, including the rhetorician Cornelius Fronto, the senator Aelius Aristides, and even the philosopher-emperor Marcus Aurelius himself.[41] From the same century comes Apuleius's flamboyant novel *The*

Golden Ass, the story of a young man, Lucius, whose search for a love potion gets him turned into a beast of burden. After a series of ribald adventures, Lucius receives relief from a personal deity who not only returns him to human form but also, in return for a vow of chastity and obedience, promises him freedom from the tyranny of fate and a happy afterlife. Although fictional, Lucius's experience has long been regarded as an example of religious conversion. But in his case, the deity is not Jesus but Isis, the ancient Egyptian fertility goddess who had become the centerpiece of one of the empire's more prominent mystery religions.[42]

What such evidence shows is not just a growing interest in personal salvation but also that the traditional religions were evolving their own responses to this need, quite independently of Christianity. In Apuleius's novel, Isis reveals another way in which the traditional religions were moving onto the same field. This is the tendency to replace the pantheon of gods with a single chief god, a "Summus Deus," who simply was known by numerous names. Philosophers, of course, had long believed in a single unifying power, to whom the name *God* was not inappropriate. But that deity was distant and impersonal, more a logical construct than an object of worship. Now deities like Isis came to take on the attributes of this single god known by many names. When Isis appears to Lucius, in a dream, she describes herself as "Nature, the universal Mother, mistress of all the elements, primordial child of time, sovereign of all things spiritual, queen of the dead, queen also of the immortals, the single manifestation of all gods and goddesses that are. . . . Though I am worshiped in many aspects, known by countless names, and propitiated with all manner of different rites, yet the whole round earth venerates me."[43]

These glimpses provided by Apuleius or his contemporary Aelius Aristides, a noted orator and world-class hypochondriac who left a detailed record of therapies prescribed by the god Asclepius, show that traditional beliefs were not dying but were evolving and changing to meet new needs. This continued vigor makes the evidence notoriously difficult to reconcile with the static paradigm inherited from the Enlightenment. For instance, in the second century, the satirist Lucian wrote a number of essays debunking false oracles, religious hucksters, and exhibitionists. For a long time, these satires were taken as evidence of the rationalist scorn for superstitious practices of which Gibbon approved. But, since Christians play only a marginal role in Lucian's satires, it is just as valid to take his writings as evidence for the existence of trends in pagan practice which developed independently of Christian influence. And, by making allowance for Lucian's bias, it is also possible to reconstruct amid his peals of laughter evidence of a sincere spiritual turmoil that affected at least some of those who lived in Gibbon's enlightened century.[44]

As in the case of Peregrinus, where the mockery of Lucian confirms both the traditional view of the second century as a period of classical reason and the presence of individuals during that same century who were restlessly seeking answers that civic religion could not provide, so too here it is not enough to take his satires of popular credulity as hallmarks of high-empire rationalism versus late-empire superstition without also taking into account the evidence it provides for large numbers of non-Christians in all classes who, despite Lucian's sneers, evidently needed something that traditional beliefs and institutions could not provide. The high empire, in other words, was an age, not surprisingly, of several currents. The difference between this period and the third century is not that religious concerns suddenly emerged in the later period but that no Lucian survives to counterbalance them. Indeed, it will be many ages before one recurs. In the next century, the likes of Julian and Eunapius are sometimes seized upon as rationalists simply because they attacked Christianity. But in their own way, as we now are aware, these "last pagans" were every bit as inclined as their Christian enemies to accept mystical revelation over empirical reasoning; their attacks on Christianity do not represent a confrontation between classical rationalism and religious superstition.[45]

For just this reason, it is insufficient to point to the continued vitality of traditional oracles and shrines well beyond the period when, according to an older school, paganism was on the wane without also noting that the questions being put to the oracles have also changed— from "Will I find happiness?" to "Will I find God?"[46] Taken as a whole, all this evidence points in the direction of a rise, for whatever reason, in sentiment for a personal religion, a search for the afterlife. Christianity may have been a beneficiary, but it certainly was not the cause of this interest. In fact, it might well be that what made Christianity appear to be a greater threat to Diocletian than it had seemed to Trajan was that now pagans operated on the same premises and assumptions as Christians.

The Pagan Right

There are, at least in retrospect, a number of obvious reasons for such a development. With the emperor's legitimacy increasingly dependent on the support of a protective deity, the tie that had always been maintained between the empire's security and the favor of the gods took on a new urgency. As the situation worsened both militarily and politically, a desire to find and correct the cause of the gods' displeasure was predictable. It is perhaps significant that Decius's persecution had not been overtly directed against Christians. He had merely ordered all citizens to perform sacrifice to the gods. It is possible to say that Christians simply were mousetrapped by this order, for in 212 the emperor Caracalla had made virtually all residents in the empire Roman citizens. An act of immense symbolic importance for Rome's role in Western civilization, Caracalla's edict had the immediate effect of making provincial Christians, the majority of whom would not have held Roman citizenship previously, vulnerable to edicts such as Decius's in 250.

But if Decius had not had at least the collateral intention of targeting Christians with his edict, he could easily have worked out an accommodation for them, as he had for the Jews, who were exempted from the order. And there can be no doubt at all about Valerian's intentions: by singling out bishops and clergy for punishment and ordering the surrender of liturgical materials and Scriptures, he took aim specifically at the church organization. More than the peace of the gods, therefore, appears to have been at stake. Although it is impossible to prove, it seems likely that the wars with Persia had some rub-off effect on Rome. For centuries while this region was ruled by the relaxed and decentralized Parthians, Rome had never had to worry about invasion. But the Sassanids brought with them a fervent commitment to ancestral Zoroastrianism which amounted to a religious revival of sorts and which manifested itself in severe measures against dissident beliefs. It would not have been hard for some Romans at least to conclude that the stunning successes Persia now enjoyed on the battlefield were a result of this religious cleansing.

In other words, one result of the upswing in Christian fortunes in the third century might have been a pagan backlash. Ironically, what could be said about the imperial Senate—that it was a victim of its own success—thus applies to Christianity as well: now that pagans and Christians were responding to the same set of religious values, it was possible to portray Christians as a threat rather than a nuisance—terrorists rather than hippies. Hints of such a position can be found as early as the judicious Pliny, whose letter to Trajan considered in the previous chapter ends with a description of the steps Pliny took to deal with what he calls "this contagion":

> I therefore adjourned the inquiry and hastened to consult you. For it seemed to me a matter worth consulting you about, especially because of the number of those endangered. For many people of all ages and classes, and of both sexes, are being involved in danger and will be so involved. It is not only the towns but the villages too and the countryside which have been affected by the spread of this contagion, which it seems can be halted and put right. Certainly it is sure enough that the temples which have been all but deserted have begun to be thronged again, and sacrificial victims are everywhere on sale for which till now there had been few buyers. From this it is easy to judge what a host of people can be made to mend their ways if only clemency is allowed for repentance.[47]

Pliny's writings enjoyed a certain vogue in late antiquity—his panegyric to Trajan was used as a model by the rhetorical schools in Gaul, and Constantine's use of a phrase from Trajan's response to Pliny's letter on the Christians discussed in Chapter 2 indicates that Pliny's correspondence was being read as well, in which case the firm way in which Pliny dealt with Christian "obstinacy" would have provided a model for what might be called a pagan "hard right."[48] More immediate evidence comes from the dialogue Dio Cassius composed for Augustus's regime. As we saw (Chapter 2), although the dramatic date is 27 B.C., Dio used Maecenas to rationalize the government as it operated in his own world of the third century. Maecenas's advice with regard to the emperor's religious position was that Octavian make worship of "the Divine Power" (τὸ μὲν θεῖον) compulsory. The phrase is vague enough to extend to new beliefs like Christianity, but as the passage continues, Dio seems deliberately to foreclose such an option:

> Those who attempt to distort our religion with strange rites you should abhor and punish, not merely for the sake of the gods (since if a man despises these he will not pay honour to any other being), but because such men, by bringing in new divinities in place of the old, persuade many to adopt foreign practices, from which spring up conspiracies, factions, and cabals, which are far from profitable to a monarchy. Do not, therefore, permit anybody to be an atheist or a sorcerer.[49]

The connection Dio drew between variant belief and insurrection was ominous.

There are strong signs that similar thinking underlay Diocletian's persecution. Many reasons for these extreme steps have been given. Hatred of Christianity or Christian principles—the reason favored in hagiography—cannot have played more than a minimal part, for Diocletian was eighteen years into his reign before he issued the first of the four edicts against Christianity, indicating at the very least that the Christian problem was not high on his agenda when he came to power. Until that time, according to Eusebius, Christians had been allowed to rise to the highest positions in his government.[50]

Lactantius provides the longest narrative account of imperial deliberations during this period in his pamphlet On the Deaths of the Persecutors. Lactantius was for a time professor of rhetoric in Nicomedia on the Asia Minor coast, a city that Diocletian made his headquarters, and therefore may have had access to firsthand information. His account must be used with some caution, however, not only for the obvious reason that he was a Christian writing about the author of a terrible calamity but also because his construction of the event is so evidently thesis-driven. A work designed to demonstrate God's vengeance on those who persecuted his people required a spectacular demise for the author of the Great Persecution. But Diocletian's death had been relatively benign: with all the malice in the world, the most the man known to the Renaissance as "the Christian Cicero" could devise for him was a fatally broken heart.[51] Another of the Tetrarchs, however, died miserably, after a prolonged wasting illness that Lactantius describes in loving detail. This was Diocletian's lieutenant and successor, Galerius, who also, before dying, obligingly issued a proclamation admitting failure and putting a halt to the persecution.[52]

Not surprisingly, Galerius emerges in Lactantius's pages as the moving force behind the persecution: the thesis required no less. But the requirements of Lactantius's script aside, two considerations make such a scenario unlikely. The first is that Lactantius's chief piece of evidence for Galerius's predominance emerges from a private meeting, at which only Diocletian and his Caesar were present and in which Galerius is supposed to have imposed his will on the old man.[53] Scholars have gone to great lengths to explain how Lactantius learned what transpired behind those sealed and sacred doors; but the conventions of ancient historiography, which permitted authors to use such situations to convey their own analyses through fictional speeches— the debate between Agrippa and Maecenas over the type of government Octavian should introduce is a classic of the kind—must also weigh heavily in the balance. Second, Lactantius's scenario requires Diocletian to be a weak and broken man, completely at the mercy of his vicious lieutenant. But every other aspect of Diocletian's tenure suggests a strong and confident ruler with an extraordinarily forceful presence. We know, moreover, from Lactantius himself that the supposedly dominant Galerius was reduced to summoning his browbeaten predecessor from retirement in 308 in a last-ditch effort to patch the rapidly crumbling Tetrarchy back together.[54]

At the very least, Lactantius's account shows that even contemporaries found a need to explain why Diocletian resorted to the drastic policy of persecution so late in his reign. But, while the thought of Diocletian being browbeaten into doing Galerius's bidding is questionable, there are indications that he may have been manipulated into launching a persecution. Although once thought to be radically innovative, Diocletian actually was imbued with a deep sense of conservatism. Possibly in the same year that he launched the persecution of Christians, Diocletian took similar steps against the Manichees, followers of a puritanical and robustly dualistic faith that had grown up on the borders of Rome and Persia. His rescript ordering leaders of the sect burned at the stake and the most persistent followers put to death takes note of the aggressive proselytizing of the Manichees: "They commit many crimes . . . , disturb quiet populations, and even work the greatest harm to whole cities." But it opens with a much more fundamental statement, echoing Dio in its view that "established religion ought not to be criticized by a new one." The rescript continues: "It is indeed highly criminal to discuss doctrines once and for all settled and defined by our forefathers, and which have their recognized place and course in our system. Wherefore we are resolutely determined to punish the stubborn depravity of these worthless people."[55]

Combined with his tendency revealed in the Edict on Prices to see all opposition as treason, the language of the Rescript on the Manichees suggests that Diocletian's views were shaped by a volatile mix of rigid conservatism and moral outrage, of the sort that unfortunately lends itself all too easily to manipulation. In describing the origins of Diocletian's anger against the Christians, Lactantius paints just such a scenario:

> Diocletian's anxious disposition made him an investigator of future events; and while he was busy in the regions of the East, he was once sacrificing cattle and looking in their entrails for what was going to happen, when certain of his attendants who knew the Lord and were present at the sacrifice, placed the immortal sign on their foreheads; at this the demons were put to flight and the rites thrown into confusion. The haruspices began to get agitated at not seeing the usual marks on the entrails, and as if they had not made the offering, they repeated the sacrifice several times. But the slaughter of victim after victim still revealed nothing; and finally their Tagis, the chief of the haruspices, whether through suspicion or on the evidence of his own eyes, said that the reason why the sacrifices were not yielding an answer was that profane persons were present at the sacred ceremonies. Diocletian then flew into a rage; he ordered that not only those who were attending the rites but all who were in the palace should do sacrifice, and that any who declined should be punished by whipping; he also sent letters to commanders ordering that soldiers too should be compelled to perform the abominable sacrifices, and that any who disobeyed should be discharged from military service.[56]

Lactantius places this event at a time when Diocletian was in the East, and other information suggests that the incident occurred in Antioch, possibly as late as 302.[57] Lactantius limits the emperor's reprisals in the aftermath of this event to the imperial administration and the army, and it is usually thought that several years intervened before the first of the general persecuting edicts was posted, although it might only have been a matter of months. In either case, the reaction of the pious and conservative Diocletian rings true.

The real question is, was the test rigged, and if so, by whom? This account is not the only one to connect the new policy with divination and oracles. In a general edict issued in the mid-320s after a successful war had made him sole emperor, Constantine blames the outbreak of persecution on an oracle from the god Apollo: "About that time it is said that Apollo spoke from a deep and gloomy cavern, and through the medium of no human voice, and declared that the righteous men on earth were a bar to his speaking the truth, and accordingly that the oracles from the tripod were fallacious."[58] The oracle, presumably, is the same oracle of Apollo at Miletus which Lactantius says Diocletian consulted following his secret meetings with Galerius.[59] Lactantius says only that the oracle answered "as might be expected from an enemy of the divine religion," and it is hard to believe that Apollo would call Christians "the righteous men" anywhere except in the Christians' own renditions. But it is the coincidence with the reasons given this same emperor by his palace priests which is the real issue. Divine signs and oracles customarily do not show themselves in sharp contours of black and white: there are large gray areas, open to explication by priests and interpreters, of which examples abound throughout antiquity, to the delight of skeptics then and now. So when this venerable communication network appears to suffer a sudden and simultaneous breakdown, with fingers pointed uniformly in the direction of individuals accused of sabotaging the common good for their personal benefit, at the very time when the ruling emperor is known to see red over just such cases, scholars may be excused for suspecting that some parties were giving the hand of Divine Providence a little nudge.

Who would these conspirators have been? A number of clues all point in the same direction. In the immediate aftermath of the Great Persecution, Eusebius of Caesarea, the Christian bishop who later would write of Constantine's conversion, wrote an apologetic work entitled *Preparation for the Gospel* in which he specifically connected the persecuting oracles with philosophers and city elites:

But, you ask, what sort of persons were these (who tortured for false oracles)? Think not that they were any of the outcast and obscure. Some came to them from this wonderful and noble philosophy, from the tribe who wear the long cloak and otherwise look so supercilious; and some were taken from the magistrates of the city of Antioch, who indeed in the time of our persecution prided themselves especially on their outrages against us. We know also the philosopher and prophet who suffered at Miletus the like punishments to those which we have mentioned.[60]

It may just be more coincidence, but oracles are known to have been a particular concern to some followers of a form of Platonism revived in the third century by the great philosopher Plotinus, called Neoplatonism by modern scholars. Neoplatonists, including Plotinus himself, enjoyed both access and influence in the imperial court. They shared a remarkable number of traits with Christian contemporaries—from an abhorrence of animal sacrifice to a scorn for matters of the flesh and a yearning for mystical union with a transcendent, monotheistic divine being. Despite this similarity, or maybe because of it, some Neoplatonists are known to have been vehemently hostile to their Christian counterparts. Porphyry, Plotinus's greatest student, wrote a tract against Christianity which was so effective that it was later ordered burned by Constantine. He also wrote a tract on oracles.

Lactantius is more forthcoming. In The Divine Institutes, a work written about the same time as Eusebius's Preparation, Lactantius writes of his own experience as teacher of rhetoric in Diocletian's capital city of Nicomedia, a post he says he took up just as the persecution began. At that time, he says, two men in the same city prominently identified themselves with the new policy. One of these he identifies as a self-styled "high priest of philosophy" with ready access to government officials who was "so full of vice that, as a master of continence, he burned no less with avarice than with wanton desires; he was so sumptuous in food that . . . [he] dined worse in the palace than at home." The other, whom he labels "one of the first instigators of persecution," Lactantius describes as a high government official and author of an attack on Christianity in which Christ was compared unfavorably to Apollonius of Tyana, a famous first-century pagan holy man.[61] The description fits Sossianus Hierocles, whose book prompted Eusebius to write a rebuttal, Against Hierocles, and who enforced the persecution with particular vigor in a variety of sensitive posts.[62]

The philosopher, who now appears to be none other than Porphyry himself,[63] is the more intriguing figure here, for even after making allowance for Lactantius's rhetoric he obviously was someone who moved freely in what today would be called "government circles." Like Hierocles, this philosopher also wrote a book in which, Lactantius says, "he broke out profusely into praises of the princes, whose piety and foresight, as he himself indeed said, had been distinguished both in other matters, and especially in defending the religious rites of the gods." According to Lactantius, the author's stated goal in writing was "that all men, laying aside and restraining impious and old-womanish superstition, should be free for legitimate practices and should experience the propitiousness of the gods toward them."[64] The words, which appear to be a direct quotation from the work in question, correspond closely to a famous justification Galerius will give in 311 when, on his deathbed, he orders the persecution stopped:

> Among all the other arrangements which we are always making for the advantage and benefit of the state, we had earlier sought to set everything right in accordance with the ancient laws and public discipline of the Romans and to ensure that the Christians too, who had abandoned the way of life of their ancestors, should return to a sound frame of mind; for in some way such self-will had come upon these same Christians, such folly had taken hold of them, that they no longer followed the usages of the ancients which their own ancestors perhaps had first instituted, but, [were] simply following their own judgement and pleasure.[65]

The similarity does not, by itself, prove influence. Our philosopher might well have been reflecting, rather than influencing, government policy. But it does at the very least indicate the line of reasoning which underlay the persecution, and it is one more indication of communication between policymakers and pagan intellectuals on this issue.[66]

The evidence is fragmentary, but it raises a question that is crucial to understanding critical events in the ensuing decades. Because the surviving historical record by and large reflects the animosity between pagans and Christians, it is easy to depict the Great Persecution as inevitable, a "life and death struggle" between Christianity and paganism. It is likely that those who supported the persecution saw matters in just this way. But how representative were they? This would not be the first time, or the last, that government policy was captured by highly articulate and fiercely committed ideologues.

The Right Discredited

Why did the Great Persecution occur? The answer may be glimpsed by asking another question: Why did it not occur two centuries earlier, when Pliny the Younger wrote to Trajan about his interrogations? Why did Pliny not play Porphyry to Trajan's Diocletian? Lactantius's answer to this conundrum no doubt would be that Trajan was a "good emperor" and Pliny a more erudite individual. In this, he would have been following the trend of ancient historiography generally to equate action with the character of individuals. A modern answer must begin elsewhere. Pliny was no philosopher, but he was certainly capable of systematic thought, and his surviving remarks show he held no brief for Christianity. He might just as easily have reached the same conclusions as pagan intellects of the third century about the potential danger of this new belief. Obviously, one reason he did not was that Christianity was a much smaller and weaker organization in his day, with nothing like the influence in political, military, and even cultural circles which it enjoyed in the later period. But such consideration leads too easily into the images of waxing and waning which have been the bane of scholarship on Christian-pagan relations. Less obvious reasons are more fruitful. The first is that the range of activity that the imperial government considered its primary concern had grown considerably since the early empire. Where Trajan only acted in response to Pliny's query, Diocletian took for granted the need for action on his part.

But why did Diocletian act so aggressively? Megalomania is hardly the answer. One reason is, ironically, not that Christians and pagans were more in opposition than they had been under Trajan but that they had grown so much more alike. With increasingly similar assumptions about the importance of the divine in human affairs, pagan intellectuals of the third century were more vulnerable to Christian arguments than their predecessors had been. From this consideration flows the last and most serious reason: Christians now posed a greater threat to the foundations of the emperor's legitimacy. Like Diocletian, Augustus had at least theoretical roots for his power in Hellenistic ideas of divine kingship. But this was at best a collateral justification for his rule, which was anchored squarely in senatorial tradition. In the third century, that tradition went bankrupt, and as a result late Roman emperors fell back more heavily on the alternative tradition of divine favor. This is what accounts for the greater threat that Christianity posed in the late third century.

By the end of that century, then, the elements of a genuine policy debate may be discerned and defined. It was not, as the litany of pagan complaints about Christian disloyalty often leads scholars to assume, over the equation of religious unity with political and military success. The notion that religious unity was a prerequisite for divine favor was a defining feature of late antiquity, to which Christians, as we will see, could subscribe as fervently as pagans.[67] Use of this slogan by pagan intellectuals should be seen rather as a venerable political maneuver, an attempt to cast their objectives in terms that would have the greatest appeal. The real debate was over the definition of *unity*. The pagan hard right defined *unity* narrowly and exclusively in terms of adherence to the traditional gods of Rome and argued that this adherence could be expressed only by the traditional means of sacrifice. Gallienus put into effect an alternative definition, one that was looser and more flexible and, combined with a loosening of boundaries which seems to have been Gallienus's policy in general, applied as much to political and military as to religious affairs.[68] Eusebius claims that emperors during this period relaxed the requirement for governors to perform sacrifice when Christians held that post, indicating that Christians rode the wave of upward mobility generated by the increase in imperial bureaucracy.[69]

Since all these changes worked to the detriment of established interests, it comes as no surprise that partisans of "the old ways" considered anything associated with Gallienus anathema, even though in spirit his pluralist religious policy was closer to those old ways than was their own program. The strands that make up a given policy often are too intertwined for their individual components to be evaluated separately, and relieving Christian governors of traditional religious obligations was simply too ready a target on which to loose more personal, less defensible passions. In this case, Gallienus's "loose unity" was bad simply because Gallienus was bad. It was guilt by association, nothing more and nothing less, which blinded the hard right to forty years of success.

The change in policy was oversold. To hear Christians tell it, from the very start the persecution was a disaster. The day the first edict went up, a Christian in the crowd tore it down, becoming the first martyr produced by the new policy. If Diocletian had thought it would meet with little resistance, this action should have given him pause. Constantine adds some intriguing eyewitness testimony in the Edict to the Eastern Provincials, which has already been quoted for its reference to the oracle of Apollo:

> I call now on thee, most high God, to witness that, when young, I heard him who at that time was chief among the Roman emperors, unhappy, truly unhappy as he was, and laboring under mental delusion, make earnest enquiry of his attendants as to who these righteous ones on earth were, and that one of the Pagan priests then present replied that they were doubtless the Christians. . . . Immediately, therefore, he issued those sanguinary edicts, traced, if I may so express myself, with a sword's point dipped in blood.[70]

Constantine's characterization of Diocletian as unhappy and deluded is mildly exculpatory. He does not go so far as to say the unnamed priests either created or exploited this frame of mind, but he does clearly indicate that the interpretation of the priests, not the oracle itself, triggered the edicts. The overall effect of the passage is to displace at least some of the blame from Diocletian onto his advisers.

Why did the persecution fail? The record of debate and argument echoed in so many scholarly accounts actually obscures the answer, for it is the nature of such discourse to reflect extremist positions that in turn encourage a sense of a society completely polarized, an either-or situation in which there was no middle ground. The real answer is hidden in the margins of contemporary Christian accounts. The martyrs and their torments rightfully hold center stage in these accounts. But off to the side, the attitude of the crowd that witnessed their ordeal shows through. Lactantius claims in his *Divine Institutes*, "The people standing around hear them [martyrs] saying in the very midst of torments that they do not sacrifice to stone statues made by human hands, but to the living God who is in heaven. Many know that this is true and admit it in their hearts." Elsewhere in the same work he claims that many even converted after witnessing such fortitude. Later, when emperor, Constantine would claim that even "the very executioners who tortured the bodies of their holy victims [were] wearied out, and disgusted at the cruelties." Decades later, Bishop Athanasius of Alexandria claimed that Christians fleeing the authorities were given shelter by pagan neighbors who suffered imprisonment and loss of property as a result.[71]

If they were made earlier, during the persecution itself, it might be possible to dismiss such claims as wishful thinking or propaganda. But since they were made in the aftermath, when nothing was to be gained—indeed, at a time when, according to a standard view, Christians were seeking blood and revenge—this testimony by Christians themselves to a lack of popular backing for the policy of persecution, as well as to efforts by pagans to shield Christians, must be taken seriously.[72] If this were the "life-and-death struggle" that it was for so long normal to suppose, then why was there not a greater rallying around the hard-core pagan position? That there was not is, along with the evidence from Christian writers, an important indication of a large, uncommitted middle that then, as always, did not see options in the stark terms in which theoreticians like to frame them. It does not detract from the heroism and suffering of the martyrs to say that the attitude of this middle group was decisive. Eusebius of Caesarea describes the persecution as an event that divided every town and every household, a civil war. The phrase echoes through numerous other writings. Eusebius regularly uses the term "tyrant" for the persecutors, thereby suggesting that they had no legitimate basis for their rule and had to rely on raw power.[73]

What these varied witnesses are describing is a phenomenon that recurs constantly in the history of conflict: whenever a ruling group appears to violate its own principles, to act with blatant injustice, sentiment in the community can swing in support of groups that previously had been ignored or even scorned. Sensitized to the problem, the community demands a resolution. The reaction is so predictable that it became a standard tactic for modern revolutionaries to attempt to provoke just such overt violations of commonly held norms of justice and decency. One political scientist, indeed, has generalized this pattern into a fundamental principle of politics. Conflict, writes Elmer Schattschneider, is more than a fight between two sides. A larger body is drawn into the arena as spectators, and it is the sentiment of this body, because of its overwhelming size, which determines the outcome of the conflict. For this reason, Schattschneider advised, "If a fight starts watch the crowd, because the crowd plays the decisive role." The principle represented by this aphorism, and developed in Schattschneider's pages, is that the spectators can be more important to the outcome of a political conflict than the original contenders, because they will inevitably take sides, thereby adding their weight to the side they favor. For this reason, Schattschneider concluded, "any attempt to forecast the outcome of a fight by estimating the strength of the original contestants is likely to be fatuous."[74]

Diocletian's strength at the outset of his persecution was overwhelming, compared with that of the Christian community against which he moved. But "the crowd," in this case the large pagan community that did not share the ideological hatred of Diocletian's advisers, gave its sympathies to the Christians, rather than to their own governors. Although Christians rightfully credited their own martyrs with the victory, it is an open question whether the resistance of Christians alone, without the support of this pagan "crowd," would have been sufficient to prevail. Ideologically, there was no reason for ancient states to be as sensitive to what might be called "public opinion" as modern mass democracies. Even so, if, as seems likely, only a small segment of the ruling group was involved in the formulation of this policy, then chances were high that other segments were no more than passive supporters. And with the relatively limited enforcement resources at their disposal, ancient states were even more dependent than their modern counterparts on the support at least of local elites for policy to be effective. Christian writers may not be the most objective commentators on the purpose or course of the persecution, but the real significance of their comments is that they portray the reactions of precisely these groups—civic elites and bystanders. It indicates, if nothing else, contemporary awareness of the importance of such groups to their cause.

Although a shift in the sympathies of what today would be called "the silent majority" cannot be documented in detail, these hints are suggestive of what might well be the most significant result of the persecutions: the hard-liners who had advocated use of coercive measures were thoroughly discredited. Galerius's Edict of Toleration acknowledges that the outcome was counter to intentions.

> When finally our order was published that they should betake themselves to the practices of the ancients, many were subjected to danger, many too were struck down. Very many, however, persisted in their determination and we saw that these same people were neither offering worship and due religious observance to the gods nor practising the worship of the god of the Christians. Bearing in mind therefore our own most gentle clemency and our perpetual habit of showing indulgent pardon to all men, we have taken the view that in the case of these people too we should extend our speediest indulgence, so that once more they may be Christians and put together their meeting places, provided they do nothing to disturb good order. . . . Consequently, in accordance with this indulgence of ours, it will be their duty to pray to their god for our safety and for that of the state and themselves, so that from every side the state may be kept unharmed and they may be able to live free of care in their own homes.[75]

It was as rare in antiquity as it is now for rulers to acknowledge a policy error publicly, and the fact that Galerius did so is an indication of the enormity of the misjudgment.

Because Galerius died soon afterward in horrible agony, Lactantius calls this edict his "swan song"—alluding to the popular belief that swans first crooned a melody only heard at the moment of death. It was more than the song of a dying emperor, however. Galerius's edict indicated the decisive failure of persecution as a means of dealing with the Christians. This was the long-range effect of Diocletian's policy, and it must not be forgotten, lest the heady events of subsequent decades be misunderstood. Traditional scholarship describes the paganism of these decades as demoralized and leaderless. But only paganism of a certain sort merits this description—the hard-line paganism that had prompted the debacle of the Great Persecution. The absence of such voices for the next half century is due in no small part to the fact that this approach to Christian-pagan relations was now thoroughly discredited.

This was the long-range effect. The immediate effect, as always in times of such disruption, was to put new issues into play, making people rethink former positions and focusing attention on the need for change. The irony that greater closeness, not greater distance, between Christian and pagan thinking was one reason for the persecution, for instance, was just waiting to be discovered. For some, in other words, the policy of persecution had created opportunities.

Five

In Search of a Vision

With the first edict of persecution posted in Nicomedia on February 24, 303, Diocletian brought to an abrupt end the policy of "benign neglect" instituted by Gallienus in 260. Almost ten years later, on October 28, 312, Constantine fought the Battle of the Milvian Bridge for control of Rome. Traditionally, it was sometime prior to this battle that he experienced the "Vision of the Cross" described in Chapter 1. A line connects these two events, but it is neither as direct nor as predictable as accounts that focus on the miracle, and the conversion that follows, make it seem. In those accounts, an ardent young prince touched by the hand of God marches from the ends of the earth to defend the righteous people and regain his stolen birthright. This is the version that Constantine himself favored, as a long proclamation issued, probably in 325, to the peoples of his newly won Eastern empire reveals:

> And now, with such a mass of impiety oppressing the human race, and the commonwealth in danger of being utterly destroyed, as if by the agency of some pestilential disease, and therefore needing powerful and effectual aid; what was the relief, and what the remedy which the Divinity devised for these evils? . . . I myself, then, was the instrument whose services He

chose, and esteemed suited for the accomplishment of his will. Accordingly, beginning at the remote Britannic ocean, and the regions where, according to the law of nature, the sun sinks beneath the horizon, through the aid of divine power I banished and utterly removed every form of evil which prevailed, in the hope that the human race, enlightened through my instrumentality, might be recalled to a due observance of the holy laws of God, and at the same time our most blessed faith might prosper under the guidance of his almighty hand.[1]

About the same time, he wrote in a similar vein to the king of Persia, in one of the earliest surviving examples of personal diplomacy:

I profess the most holy religion; and this worship I declare to be that which teaches me deeper acquaintance with the most holy God; aided by whose Divine power, beginning from the very borders of the ocean, I have aroused each nation of the world in succession to a well-grounded hope of security; so that those which, groaning in servitude to the most cruel tyrants, and yielding to the pressure of their daily sufferings, had well nigh been utterly destroyed, have been restored through my agency to a far happier state.[2]

Such statements are important to understanding Constantine and interpreting his goals. But as historical accounts they obviously leave many questions unanswered. When last we looked at the imperial system of the late empire, for instance, four men were ruling in what appeared to be a new manner of coping with Rome's far-flung frontiers and stabilizing the process of succession. Why did Constantine's rise, even if for the reason he purports, lead to the return of a system of sole rule? Was Constantine the only person who saw the need to protect the Christians? And why was he already marching on Rome when God chose to make him his champion? For that matter, by what authority did he assemble his invasion army?

As the answers to these questions will show, there were compelling reasons for Constantine to portray his career in the way he did. Doing so allowed him to give a linear and upward cast to his rise, smoothing out all the little kinks and setbacks. Beginning at a point in the farthest extreme of the Roman world, he extended his control in an unbroken string of successes until by 324 he ruled the whole empire. More important, by describing his purpose as one of unity, Constantine gave himself the purest of motives, and by making himself the instrument of a divine plan, he mitigated the fallout from what might otherwise have been perceived as reckless ambition, while at the same time demonstrating that he enjoyed the divine alliance that had become a sine qua non for imperial legitimacy. Finally, and what is the most immediately significant, this narrative sets the point for the start of Constantine's career at a moment when (with appropriate suspension of disbelief) his adoption of the imperial purple could be justified on dynastic grounds, thereby skirting a political situation that was messier and more ambiguous than an older and more secure Constantine cared to reveal.

At the risk of doing violence to the depth of religious sentiment at this time, it might be useful to think of Constantine's vision in a different sense, as the type of vision that helps political leaders resolve issues that have become so mired in conflict that resolution seems hopeless. Such was the situation brought about by Diocletian's two most disastrous policy decisions: first, to persecute the Christians; second, to ignore the claims of two able and experienced imperial sons to a part in the imperial succession. In both cases, Diocletian's mistake was to underestimate the ability of each group to resist. Separately, each decision might have prevailed; together, they created a synergy that destroyed the system he had nurtured into being.

Breaking the Rules

Constantine had much to explain. It is because of this need to rationalize and legitimize his career that we know so little of the details of Constantine's life prior to his assumption of power. Even his birth date is a mystery. Either because of a self-indulgent effort to liken himself to the youthful conqueror Alexander the Great or because of a more immediate need to distance himself from Diocletian's disastrous policy of persecution, Constantine liked to portray himself as having been a mere youth at the time the persecution began. More sober calculations place his birth date between 270 and 280, meaning he would have been in his late twenties or even early thirties in 303.[3] Around this time he produced a son, Crispus, by one Minervina. Eclipsed by the better match Constantine made in 307, Minervina has faded into the obscurity that covers most of Constantine's early years, though the compulsive tidiness of later writers endowed her with a proper wedding license and appropriately tragic premature death. The formalities of marriage, especially among career army personnel to whom they had been denied for so long, were not the issue they became in more genteel ages. The important point is that, despite his new marriage, Constantine always acknowledged Crispus and groomed him for rule, just as his own father had done with Constantine after his dynastic marriage to Maximian's daughter in 293 required him to take his leave of Constantine's mother, Helena.

What the miracle story and Constantine's own reconstruction both ignore is the more mundane but crucial political situation left in the wake of Diocletian's two ill-starred initiatives, regarding the succession and the Christians. Whatever exactly lay behind his plan for the Tetrarchy, it scarcely outlasted his abdication in 305; and as an attempt to enforce a common religious foundation for the throne, the Great Persecution was nothing short of disastrous.

Beyond these immediate conditions, there was a deeper, longer-lived trend in the nature of paganism, and of Christian-pagan relations, which the traditional story of a sudden reversal brought about by Constantine's miraculous conversion serves to obscure. For reasons that had nothing whatever to do with Constantine, or his conversion, or whatever vision he may or may not have had, the effect of this trend was to eliminate conditions, such as blood sacrifice, which had traditionally interfered with Christian participation in public life.[4] In this light, Diocletian's persecution was not only a failure, but it was also unnecessary: he was responding to yesterday's problem, trying to enforce conformity to a situation that no longer existed, without recognizing the richness of the religious stew that in fact characterized his own times.

The best way to understand the change in policy between Diocletian and Constantine is to see the latter as one of a number of younger players who realized the need for a more flexible and imaginative approach to "the Christian question" than the traditional policy of periodic pogrom allowed. The aim in doing so is not so much to question the miracle, far less to dismiss it, as to see the issues that controversy over what is essentially a religious issue (did alliance with Constantine strengthen the church or corrupt it?) tends to obscure.

For the religious question, Constantine's character and the sincerity of his faith are all-important. But from a political standpoint, the question is different: Given the religious basis for legitimate rule, given a sizable group that could not recognize a legitimate ruler on that basis, given the failure of an effort to compel them to do so, what alternatives were open not merely to Constantine but to anyone who was going to rule Rome in 312? Ultimately, Constantine's success depended on the failures of his predecessor and on his vision of a more successful program than that of any of the other contenders. His victory, therefore, testifies not only to the military skills and religious sensitivities that dominate traditional accounts but also to leadership skills that have been less commonly recognized. Of these the ability to put together a successful coalition was not the least important.

Rather than begin with Constantine's march on Rome, therefore, this chapter begins with Diocletian's two policy failures, for by understanding them it will be possible to understand where Constantine was coming from and where he needed to go. Although interrelated, for clarity the two issues will be dealt with separately.

Succession

Two years after beginning the persecution, Diocletian, that conventional ruler with a flair for the unconventional, took yet another step that was entirely without precedent. In an elaborately staged ceremony outside Nicomedia on May 1, 305, Diocletian told the assembled troops and dignitaries that he had decided to retire. Resigning an office that all previous incumbents had held for life, he put the purple on his lieutenant, the Caesar Galerius, descended to a waiting carriage, and departed without further ceremony for his palace at Spalato on the Dalmatian coast, the modern city of Split. In a parallel ceremony, the Western Augustus, Maximian, simultaneously resigned his office in favor of his Caesar, Constantius I. Such an unprecedented act naturally set tongues wagging. The Christian author Lactantius drew a connection between this decision and the earlier one to initiate a persecution and decided that the avenging hand of God had once again intervened in human affairs. Maybe. Diocletian had been severely ill some months before, and according to this same author the man who renounced his power that spring day was but a shrunken shell of his former self. But the record also shows that plans for this day of resignation had been in the works all winter, with messages passing back and forth between Nicomedia and Milan in order to coordinate the simultaneous resignation of both Augusti on the same day. And, as events would show only too well, Maximian, the Western Augustus, did not embrace retirement with the same zeal as his senior colleague.

From the elaborate arrangements he made for this event, it seems clear that the simultaneous resignation of the two senior Augusti was part of a plan for the Tetrarchy which had slowly evolved in Diocletian's mind. In retrospect, at least, its aim appears to have been "strength in numbers." By multiplying the presence of a single imperial power—four emperors in one, as an imperial panegyrist put it[5]— while fragmenting power at lower levels by the separation of civilian and military offices and breaking down the size of the provinces, the Tetrarchy was intended to restabilize the imperial system. There was a single weakness. In order to achieve the flexibility needed to fight wars on more than one front, each Augustus and Caesar had to have undiluted right to exercise imperial authority in his sphere. Anything less would not address the problem created by the absence of full executive authority in a system that had come to rely increasingly on the absolute authority of the emperor. But this same flexibility also posed the potential threat of fragmenting the empire into four separate and competing spheres. While Diocletian ruled, the threat was only potential. By a combination of superior prestige and determination, he was able to achieve the delicate balance of unanimity and flexibility needed for the system he created to work.

As age and illness took their toll, another question seems to have formed in Diocletian's mind: Would the Tetrarchy last beyond his death? Ever since Augustus first started the game of empire, succession had been its most unpredictable phase, the point at which the rules were most subject to dispute. A superb organizer like Diocletian was unlikely to let even death prevent him from tying up this final loose string. Such considerations would explain another event of that May ceremony. As Lactantius tells it, resignation was not the only surprise

Diocletian had prepared, for the thoughts of those assembled, he indicates, immediately turned to the question of who would succeed to the now vacant Caesarships.

> The gaze of all was upon Constantine, no one had any doubt; the soldiers who were present, the military officers who had been chosen and summoned from the legions, had eyes only for him; they were delighted with him, they wanted him, they were making their prayers for him. . . . Then suddenly he [Diocletian] proclaimed Severus and Maximin [Daza] as Caesars. Everyone was thunderstruck. Constantine was standing up on the platform, and people hesitated, wondering whether his name had been changed. But then in view of everybody Maximian [i.e., Galerius] stretched his hand back and drew Daza out from behind him, pushing Constantine away. . . . No one dared to shout out any objection amid the general consternation at this new and unexpected development.[6]

Several things can be said about this remarkable passage. One, the most obvious, is that, if nobody else, Lactantius clearly was on Constantine's side. The other is that, rhetoric aside, the army obviously acquiesced in what had happened. Why should it have done otherwise? The question reveals how dangerously misleading Lactantius can be. Implicit in his account is the notion that Constantine had some presumptive right to the succession, an assumption that points his readers in a completely wrong direction for understanding the situation. Doubtless, Lactantius based this assumption on a traditional understanding of Roman politics as the game had been played since Augustus. Although never officially a monarchy, the empire in fact depended on the presence of the grown son of an incumbent, by birth or adoption, to avoid civil war when he died. But the Tetrarchy had changed those rules, and this is precisely what Lactantius's narrative obscures: following his lead, it is easy to assume that Constantine had a right to succeed which had been stolen from him by Diocletian, whereas the opposite—that Constantine, having been intentionally passed over, had no right to become emperor—would be closer to the case.

What comes through most clearly from Lactantius's bluster is the sense that at least some parties were caught flat-footed by Diocletian's decision and that one of those parties might have been Constantine. Constantine had reason to believe he was being groomed for greater things. Unlike Maxentius, who stayed in Rome with his father, Constantine had gone to Diocletian's court in Nicomedia, where he had served in Galerius's victorious campaign against Persia and received favored treatment from Diocletian himself.[7] By deciding to retire instead of letting Fate determine the date of succession, Diocletian had unsettled the traditional game, but not in a way that would have kept players from knowing what to expect. His action might, indeed, have been predictable, since retirement allowed him to stay in control of the process, while at the same time permitting simultaneous succession in East and West—something certain to appeal to his neat and orderly mind. The existence of four emperors in the Tetrarchy complicated things, but only superficially. In ancient thinking, the only sure loyalty was family loyalty. Diocletian and Maximian had both tied their Caesars to themselves by marriage alliances, and it was all but a foregone conclusion that Galerius would succeed the former and Constantius I the latter. The only question was, who would take their place as Caesars?

Diocletian had no son, but Maximian did, and so did Constantius. Constantine, as oldest son of Constantius I, who in 293 had been first to become Caesar and now, by virtue of these twin resignations, became the new senior Augustus, was an obvious candidate. Lactantius says nothing about the other, Maxentius, who was son of the Western Augustus Maximian. Maxentius soon would prove to be more cerebral, if less daring, than his imperial nephew Constantine.[8] Given the dynamics of imperial politics, similar expectations must have grown up around him as well. Both of these young men were experienced and able, and Lactantius's words indicate that at least some forces had begun to array themselves, in time-honored Roman fashion, around the proverbial "rising suns." By deliberately avoiding two highly qualified heirs, Diocletian signaled that the Jovian and Herculian dynasties were not only a means to display the divine ties that a legitimate ruler now was expected to maintain but also a way to create an alternative to dynasties built along bloodlines. Theoretically, the solution was brilliant. But its practical limitations became apparent almost as soon as Diocletian retired, for the plan meant two well-trained sons in the prime of life had to be passed over.

So the new regime started off with two disgruntled parties. But it would be a mistake to think this was a fatal error. Though it was far from his intention, what Lactantius's account reveals most clearly is just how limited the options of Constantine or anyone else who might have aspired to greater power were, so long as the army and Maximian were willing to accept Diocletian's decision. As the limited uproar in Lactantius's very partisan account makes clear, Diocletian's efforts at restabilizing the empire had won great prestige for the Tetrarchy. In normal times, even flying in the face of convention as it did, his reordered system for elevation to the purple might have worked. It was, after all, the only game in town. Had there been no discontent in other quarters, these new players might never have had an opportunity to challenge the existing order. Given the nature and cause of that discontent, there is little reason to wonder that in later years Constantine discerned the hand of Divine Providence in his rise.

Persecution

Christian legend came to tell the story of Diocletian's resignation and the rise of his Christian successor somewhat differently.

> In that very moment there went forth from heaven Michael the Commander-in-chief of the host of heaven, together with the army of angels. He laid hold of his rod which was in his hand, threw it under the throne of Diocletian, and turned him over upon his face at the third hour of the day. His guards grasped him and lifted him up. And he rose with great anger, and said,
>
> "By my great god Apollo, I will annihilate the entire race of the Christians. For in their wickedness they have sought for these things with their magic arts, and this happened to me. For they think that with their magic I will fear their God and I will cease persecuting them. But they do not know that there is no god as powerful as Apollo, or Zeus, or the rest of our gods, each one. For every man who has many gods, if one goes off to a country to war, his fellows remain, and they watch over his domain until he obtains the victory and returns to his house in good health. But as for this one whom the Christians glorify, and for whose name they are in trouble and are (even) dying, he was not able to save himself from the hands of the Jews. How, then, will he be able to rescue all of [these] from my hands?"
>
> But even while he was saying these things with great arrogance he (Michael) [put] his hand a second time on his face, and the [throne] turned

over upon him. The lawless one [wept] bitterly, and cried out saying, "Woe is [me] today, [for my] kingdom has been quickly taken from me."

And they grasped him, and raised him up a second time, and found him blind in both eyes. The nobles and his friends wept saying, "What happened to you, our lord king?" But he [was] trembling all over his body. And he cried out with a loud voice,

"Summon Constantine to me quickly, for the God of the Christians has already given him the kingdom. For when my throne was toppled under me for a second time, I heard a great voice of multitudes from heaven saying, 'Augustus Constantine, the righteous King, is the one whom the Lord our God has raised up as king over us in the place of the lawless one, the shameless Diocletian, king of [unrighteousness].' "

So goes one version of a popular account that blossomed in the fifth and sixth centuries. As it continues, Diocletian's generals find Constantine "sitting at the third gate of the palace with his bearers," whence they bring him before their broken ruler, who repents of not heeding Constantine's advice.

"[My] brother Constantine, King of righteousness, forgive me. For you spoke with me many times secretly, saying 'Remove yourself from idols; otherwise the God of the Christians will not tolerate you like this forever.' But I did not listen to you. Behold, therefore, my kingdom has been taken away from me today, and has been given to you."

And immediately the generals took him from the palace, and his servants brought him down to the gate of Antioch, and left him in that place begging alms from those who passed by and from those who were coming in and going out, until the day of his death. At the end of his life, he lifted his eyes to heaven [saying], "One is the [God of] the Christians."[9]

With their notorious ability to play fast and loose with fact, legends often can cut to simple truths that the fastidious accuracy of the historical record obscures. The Diocletian legend, nicely embroidered to remove the ambiguities with which Lactantius had to contend, thereby to make the lesson of God's vengeance all the more satisfying, encourages us to make a simple connection between the failure of the Tetrarchy and Diocletian's decision, two years before resigning, to persecute the Christians. Yet a very different lesson is the one to draw here: if the Tetrarchy were the only innovation Diocletian had attempted, it might have succeeded. But the persecution was a further destabilizing factor that also created a significant pocket of discontent.

As shocking and unexpected as Diocletian's decision to return to a policy of forced repression was, it was implemented only in stages. Diocletian's initial reaction to the claim, reported by Lactantius, that Christians were hampering divinatory sacrifices (see Chapter 4) was limited to official circles—the palace and the army—and the first of his four general edicts in 303 took aim at the instruments, rather than the members, of Christianity. It ordered the demolition of churches and confiscation and destruction of Scripture. For Christians themselves nothing more was done than to ban them from meeting for worship. Between the first and second edicts, fire broke out in Diocletian's palace in Nicomedia. Lactantius portrays it as a fourth-century Reichstag fire, deliberately set by Galerius to implicate Christians and provoke Diocletian to sterner measures, but the work of Christian zealots should not be ruled out. In any case, the second edict escalated the persecution, ordering the arrest of all bishops and priests. The effect was to swamp imperial prisons, leading to a third edict ordering that prisoners who sacrificed be released, a mischievous provision that created no end of confusion, especially as desperate officials used every ruse to achieve at least superficial compliance, thereby tainting many innocent (and not-so-innocent) clergy who gained release at this time. In 304, a fourth edict finally revived Decius's call for universal sacrifice.[10]

The relative mildness of the first edict suggests that those who favored persecution believed little effort would be needed to secure Christian obedience. Such confidence may have been more justified than it now seems, for subsequent accounts have been swayed by the outcome, and the inevitable Christian chortling that followed. Our main source, Eusebius of Caesarea, says he does not intend to speak about backsliders, which means a skewed picture, and divisions in the aftermath over how to deal with Christians who compromised themselves during the persecution are enough to suggest that the number who did so was not insignificant. Even so, the increasing severity of the edicts indicates sufficient noncompliance to require additional steps; it is a classic sign of a policy in trouble. In the West, the edicts were not enforced uniformly. Maximian was avid, either out of loyalty to Diocletian or because of a personal temperament that all sources, pagan and Christian alike, agree was vicious. But his Caesar Constantius seems to have dropped the whole thing in his northern territories after a few initial steps that were halfhearted at best. In the East, however, the resisters were sufficient in number to overwhelm an enforcement system that was neither designed for nor capable of dealing with extensive disobedience.

Still, the failure of Diocletian's policy did not mean Constantine was the only, or even the best, alternative. Galerius's "swan song" Edict of Toleration in 311 was a viable and attractive option. With hindsight, it is all too easy to say that it was not enough, that Christians were in no mood to be reconciled. In fact, if no other option had been available, Christians would have found Galerius's offer quite acceptable, and certainly preferable to continued persecution. But by 311 other rulers were on the scene offering more attractive and creative solutions. In such a situation, Galerius's attempt to turn back the clock could be no more successful than Sulla's had been in the last generation of the Roman republic, and for the same reason: there were too many people who stood to gain from the addition of new players. Here is where Constantine becomes significant, because he was one of the people offering a better option. The simple reason that the edict of 311 did not succeed is that the combined disruptions of persecution and succession were simply too much for the system to absorb. The ensuing instability created opportunities for new alliances and strengthened the hands of marginal players. To put it succinctly, by 311 Christians knew they could get a better deal.

Constantine and Maxentius

Diocletian's retirement in 305 thus set into effect a train of events that lead directly to the moment of Constantine's vision. Fractures in the succession he arranged appeared within months, as both Constantine and Maxentius moved to reassert their claims. In retrospect, it was a mistake to freeze out these two heirs-presumptive. But it is hard to see what other step might have been taken. Given the ancient mode of thinking, the new system was fragile enough. It would have taken several uneventful transfers of power for the idea of succession based on any criterion other than birth to have had even the faintest chance of taking hold. To select a direct male heir, no matter how able, the very first time would have meant its doom.

Lactantius would have us believe that the men chosen to be Caesars in the new college, Severus for the West and Maximin Daza in the East, were utterly incompetent, and boors to boot. Eastern Christians might well have wished this were true, for Daza proved to be an able and resourceful persecutor. Of Severus, little can be said. The most woebegone of the new college, he was caught in the subsequent cross fire between Maxentius and Galerius and eventually put to death more or less as an afterthought, without so much as ever entering Rome or enjoying a decent bath. If there is anything at all to Lactantius's waspish report, it lies in his stress on Galerius's role in the selection of the new Caesars, for if true, it means that Diocletian knew that personal as well as institutional ties were needed to make the system he devised work in practice. In any case, with a colleague far off in Gaul and two Caesars in his personal orbit, Diocletian had provided Galerius with firm grounds for a successful transition. Even this much cannot be taken for granted, however, for Christian writers had ample reason in later years to minimize any more active role that Galerius's colleague, Constantius I, might have played in the new college.

Constantius was senior Augustus in the new Tetrarchy. Yet we know of only one occasion on which he asserted the authority that came with that position: after the transfer of power in May 305, he bade Galerius return his son, Constantine, to his side. (In typical fashion, Lactantius diverts the reader's attention with an account of a thrill-packed escape from Nicomedia and has Constantine arrive just as his ailing father was about to expire. From other sources, it is clear that Constantine met up with his father much earlier, while the army was still in Gaul.) Here is where Constantine picks up the story in his own account, for it was while on campaign in Britain, "the remote Britannic ocean" of Constantine's proclamation, that Constantius died, leaving his son, after a ritual show of reluctance, to be elevated to the purple by the troops. It is easy to see, now, the advantage to Constantine of beginning his account at this point, July 306, rather than fourteen months earlier, for by the rules of the Tetrarchy, Constantine began his career as a usurper.

Frozen out of the game, Constantine, like Octavian centuries earlier, used his father's army to change the rules.

Maxentius, the other heir, proved no more compliant. Exploiting the unpopularity of a tax program that removed Italy's ancient privileges, Maxentius won the support of the people, and by drawing his father out of retirement, he won over the Praetorian Guard. Galerius had recognized Constantine's claim, though at the lower rank of Caesar (his army had hailed him as Augustus). Doing so made a certain sense, since Constantius's death had opened a place that could be filled without causing damage to the Tetrarchic façade. But to do the same for Maxentius would have signaled the end of Diocletian's system, and this Galerius was not willing to do. He prepared to invade the peninsula.

The literary tradition makes Constantine and Maxentius out to be polar opposites, natural enemies, and for good reason: it was Maxentius against whom Constantine was marching in 312 when he experienced the famous miracle. But the tradition was created in the aftermath of that event, which at this point was still some five years off. In 307, there were more similarities between Constantine and Maxentius than there were differences. Both had achieved power by trading on a hereditary claim that was pointedly ignored under current rules. Vulnerable, both had to distance themselves from the Tetrarchy and establish new power bases. If they were to stabilize their regimes, they needed to reach out to new constituencies. Evidently, both saw enough common interest at this time to put aside whatever differences they may have had and establish a common front with each other, in the traditional Roman way. In 307, Constantine married Maxentius's sister, Fausta, in a ceremony at Trier, with the bride's father, Maximian, in attendance to grace the proceedings with Herculian dignity.

An oration delivered at the time survives in a unique collection of panegyrics probably put together in Gaul in the late fourth or early fifth century. Because five of the twelve in this collection deal in whole or in part with Constantine—four of the five delivered in the crucial years between 307 and 313, all of these by pagan orators—their potential for opening a non-Christian window into Constantine's thinking is great. For just that reason, care must be taken not to place more weight on them than they can bear. Because they were delivered on state occasions, it is tempting to equate these panegyrics with official propaganda and to pore over every word as if it were part of an official communiqué.[11] But doing so obscures their most important characteristic, which is that they do not survive for any official reason at all. The earliest, delivered in 289, is numbered tenth in the collection; the latest, which was delivered to the emperor Theodosius I in 389, appears second. The nature of the collection allows for two immediate conclusions: since the speeches were put together without regard to chronological order, they cannot have been selected for their historical value; and, since the addressees include the archpersecutor Diocletian and the apostate Julian (panegyric three, delivered in 362) as well as such suitably Christian subjects as Constantine and Theodosius I, the criterion cannot have been a religious one, either.

Because eleven of the twelve were delivered either in Gaul or by Gallic orators, it seems likely that the collector was not a court official but one of the faculty at the schools of Bordeaux or Autun, which were at the peak of their fame during this century. This being so, the compiler's purpose probably was to provide literary models for his students. What seems to confirm this conclusion is the single non-Gallic panegyric, which is also the only one not from the period of the late third to late fourth centuries. It is the oration delivered to Trajan by Pliny the Younger on the occasion of his consulship in 100. The only contemporary relevance of such an ancient work to readers of this collection was as an example of style and language. Its presence strongly suggests that the others were not likely to have been selected for any reason other than the fact that they were successful examples of the genre. Ironically, this conclusion enhances, rather than detracts from, the value of these orations, for when a collection is made officially, whether for historical or political purposes, historians must be on guard against self-serving distortions or omissions. A collection such as this one, made for entirely different purposes, will contain fewer valuable nuggets, but those it does contain can be all the more valuable for being included unintentionally.

But are these orations "historically relevant"? So much of their content consists of typically overblown language and extravagant praise that some scholars would dismiss them as little more than rhetorical fluff. This reaction against some of the more extravagant conclusions drawn by those scholars who depicted the panegyrics as official propaganda is healthy, but it, too, can be misleading. Taking a cue from the anthropologists, historians have now become more sensitive to the significance of such fluff, along with the other rituals of kingship, as affirmations of the existing political and social order. Where an earlier generation pored exclusively over the words spoken on these occasions, newer scholars cast their eyes over the entire setting—the buildings, the motifs on coins and statuary, the arrangement of local and imperial officials—all designed to make the occasion one in which the very act of participation constituted a communal celebration of the benefits of empire.[12] The nature of the occasion and the collection must be considered together to grasp the importance of these speeches and their use to the historian.

Ceremony aside, an important aim of the orator on such occasions was to receive some benefit, either for himself or his city. Obviously, this aim would not be achieved as readily if the contents of his speech were in any way displeasing to the imperial audience. Since it seems reasonable to assume that the speeches that were put into this collection must have been successful if they were to serve as models, they are even better indicators of imperial attitudes than propaganda. Even though a great deal of their content will seem to the historian or political scientist maddeningly vague, pompous, and extraneous, they are not entirely devoid of references to contemporary events, and in those precious instances in which they do touch on matters of policy or controversial issues, the orator's desire to please ensures that he will have treated these issues in a way that the emperor found acceptable. To this extent, such statements can be taken as reflections of imperial thought, or of what the emperor liked to hear, and therefore useful indications of official thought no matter how one-sided, idealized, or rhetorical they might otherwise be.

The wedding oration of 307 is a case in point. Maximian, Fausta's father and Diocletian's former colleague, attended the ceremony, and the surviving oration negotiates the tricky business of massaging two imperial egos simultaneously. On first reading, it is Maximian who appears clearly as the dominant figure, his deeds and the prestige of his Herculian dynasty receiving the bulk of the orator's attention. Constantine plays a distinctly junior role, essentially as the son of his late father, Constantius (also a son-in-law of Maximian, as Constantine was now becoming), who is depicted as smiling down on the ceremony from the chariot of the sun.[13] But Constantine also benefited from an oration that publicly extolled the great achievements of the dynasty of which, by virtue of this wedding, he was now a full-fledged member. In this case, merely in celebrating the relationship, the oration could not do other than strengthen Constantine's right to rule. Unlike Maxentius in Rome, Constantine had the benefit of Galerius's recognition as a Caesar in the Tetrarchy, and now with this wedding he had the prestige of Herculian descent as well. His flank was secure; no matter who triumphed in the coming years, Constantine would be on the winning side.

Maxentius had no such luxury. Probably for this reason, the record shows him as the more innovative of the two in reaching out to new constituencies. As usurpers, both Constantine and Maxentius found it easier to break with unpopular and failed policies of the Tetrarchy. Coins preserve their efforts to do so. The ideology of the Tetrarchy encouraged a bland uniformity in imperial imagery, with Augusti and Caesars alike portrayed in the same facing profile, hair and beard close-cropped in military fashion, often with military cloaks and armor. The reverses displayed the approved gods of the empire—Jupiter and Hercules, of course, and also warrior deities, the traditional Mars and ubiquitous Sol Invictus. Slogans celebrate Tetrarchic themes: the unity of the Roman people and the new Jovian and Herculian dynasties.[14] Constantine's earliest coins conform to this mold, but he soon shed the beard in favor of styles and images that seem intentionally designed to recall the reigns of Augustus and Trajan.[15] For reasons that will soon become apparent, he also cast around for alternative slogans, empha-sizing the dynastic tie to his father and parading the popular battle god Sol Invictus as his special companion. But it was Maxentius who took the boldest steps. Abandoning Tetrarchic conventions in favor of the ancient titles and symbols of the capital he controlled, he pictured himself in Augustan fashion as consul and *princeps* and blatantly re-vived symbols unique to the city of Rome, such as the twins Romulus and Remus and a domed shrine with the slogan "Eternal Memory" (*Aeternae memoriae*). He also named his son Romulus.[16]

Had it not been for the turmoil of the Great Persecution, neither Constantine nor Maxentius might have gotten away so easily with their challenge to the succession arrangement of 305. But now the allegiance of a disaffected minority was available to anyone who was willing to repudiate persecution as a policy. The two groups were practically driven into each other's arms. Success has allowed Constantine and his historians to shape the record of this period in such a way that he, and only he, emerges as the sincere champion of a downtrodden faith. But it took no divine intervention to see that the policy of persecution had failed, and while it is likely that Constantine took the further step of officially ending the persecution in his territories after taking over from his father (this, at any rate, is the most likely meaning of Lactantius's claim that Constantine showed favor to the Christians from the start of his rule), there is no reason to suppose he was the only one who got the message. Unsurprisingly, therefore, the record shows both Maxentius and Constantine reaching out to this new constituency.[17]

Like Constantine, Maxentius abandoned the policy of persecution as soon as he came to power; for the next several years, indeed, he rather than Constantine seems to have been the one to set the pace, perhaps only because there were more opportunities to do so in Rome than in Gaul, where Christians were relatively scarce. Maximin Daza stands in contrast. With his legitimacy as a member of the Tetrarchy intact, Daza persisted in persecution with a resourcefulness and initiative rarely witnessed at the imperial level, devising new ways to demoralize Christians psychologically as well as physically. He made the spurious Acts of Pilate, "full of every kind of blasphemy against Christ," required reading in schools, with the aim of making Jesus an object of contempt and ridicule.[18] At the same time, Daza took positive steps to reform paganism, attempting to imbue it with a structure and moral code to rival Christianity. The changes anticipate by half a century the efforts of another opponent to Christianity, Constantine's nephew Julian.[19] Even after Galerius officially abandoned the policy in 311, Daza used the ancient equivalent of paper committees to circumvent his superior's Edict of Toleration and continue the persecution. In all likelihood, Daza should be seen as the candidate of the intellectual hard-liners who initially sponsored persecution and were too heavily committed to concede its uselessness. But if imitation is indeed the sincerest form of flattery, then what he, as Julian later, really testifies to is the underlying strength of the Christian movement.

Maxentius, on the other hand, not only restored toleration shortly after seizing power but even seems to have restored churches to the Christians of Rome and intervened in internal squabbles to preserve the peace, thereby anticipating a role that later Christian emperors would play.[20] Although it views Maxentius with suitable hostility, the *Book of Pontiffs,* a chronicle of the bishops of Rome first put together early in the sixth century A.D., provides evidence for substantial growth in both parishioners and clergy under Maxentius, neither of which is likely to have happened had he enforced the edicts of persecution. The record of church strife in North Africa also makes clear that the bishopric of that province had been restored while Maxentius was still in control.[21] Constantine's war against Maxentius in 312—the campaign that produced his Vision of the Cross—thus may have ended as a religious crusade, but it clearly started out as something else. How and why did this transformation come about?

A telling piece of evidence comes from Eusebius of Caesarea's Church History. Despite a detailed indictment of the crimes committed by Maxentius, Eusebius concedes that the usurper "feigned Christianity," at least initially, in order to win the support of the Roman populace.[22] Presumably, given the animus with which he treats him, Eusebius would not have identified Maxentius as a Christian, feigned or otherwise, if the evidence of favorable action on the usurper's part had not been so overwhelming that it had to be explained. Some scholars have deduced from his account that Maxentius must actually have converted to Christianity, anticipating Constantine by several years. Doing so, however, merely projects onto his rival the tangle of policy with belief which has so ensnared analysis of Constantine's own history. What this statement actually reveals is a tendency on Eusebius's part to identify policy with belief, a confusion that has been perpetuated down through the ages (see Chapter 10). When it is used instead to recover a political context that contemporaries like Eusebius did not think worth preserving, what the passage shows is a usurper, one of several, trying to shore up his shaky legitimacy by dealing with problems that the legitimate establishment had failed to solve.

But if Maxentius was beneficent to Christians, why their subsequent hostility? The answer to this little conundrum may lie buried in a rambling oration given by Constantine himself, probably some time in the mid-320s, a decade or more after his victory. Reminding his audience of the terrors of the persecution, Constantine remembers how the people of "the dearest city" had once preferred a "champion unworthy of themselves," at least initially, before choosing the right side.[23] The whole passage is vague and puzzling, and there is no one solution on which all scholars agree, other than the obvious one that the "unworthy champion" was an opponent of Constantine's. A good candidate for "the dearest city" would be Rome, and if so, the unworthy champion should be Maxentius. But if a date in the 320s for this oration is correct, is it not odd for Constantine to dwell on a conflict by then more than a decade old? Not necessarily, even though scholars—on the lookout, as ever, for reference to the most recent events—would rather he spoke of something more current. To Constantine, the battle for Rome was the great foundation event of his reign, analogous to Augustus's Battle of Actium, and so far as we can tell he never tired of talking, or hearing, about it. More pertinent is the way Constantine chides "the people of the dearest city" for their bad judgment. If reason is any guide, these "people" should be the Christians of Rome.

Mere embarrassment at having been on the losing side, therefore, may account for the eagerness with which Christians later heaped infamy on Maxentius. But the Church History indicates a better reason for the change in Christian attitudes toward Maxentius. Going through his rival's papers in the aftermath of his victory, Constantine discovered the public relations equivalent of the mother lode: a secret treaty of alliance between Maxentius and the remaining persecutor, Maximin Daza.[24] Such alliances are always matters of convenience—witness Constantine's own alliance between 307 and 310 with the old persecutor Maximian. Constantine had, sometime prior to his march on Rome, allied with Galerius's handpicked successor, Licinius, and it is therefore not surprising that Maxentius should have come to terms with the wily and able Daza. The latter may well have seemed at the time the more brilliant of the two matches, since Daza was the only one of the four with untainted credentials—Constantine's appointment having been regularized only after the fact and Licinius having been appointed Augustus without first serving as a Caesar—and he controlled the rich resources of Egypt and the East as well. But Daza was also a relentless persecutor of Christians. When news of the alliance became known in the aftermath of Maxentius's defeat, it changed the nature of the conflict, in the eyes of at least one constituency, from a power struggle between northern and southern warlords into a crusade. In politics, it is the mood of the moment which counts; to Christians in the East like Eusebius, still suffering when all other parts of the empire had found relief, such an alliance could only mean that Maxentius did not have the interests of Christians at heart. Therefore, his previous good deeds could only be pretense. In a stroke, Constantine became the true champion, Maxentius an unworthy pretender.

Constantine's seeming reference in later years to the misguided loyalties of Rome's Christians is one hint among many that his rise was not as serene as the account he later favored would suggest. Indeed, it would appear that, after his marriage to Fausta in 307, Constantine was left sitting on the sidelines while Maxentius reaped the prestige from the collapse of Galerius's much publicized invasion of Italy. Finding the peninsula well defended and Maximian's armies securely loyal to him and his son, Galerius had no option but to retreat before he, too, suffered the fate of the hapless Severus. The sight of the victor of the Persian campaign reduced to such ignominy endowed Maxentius with Rome's aura of invincibility. Meanwhile, Constantine, tied down by campaigns against barbarians on his northern frontier, could only watch as Maxentius used his control of the symbolic capital of the empire to conduct a high-profile policy of diplomacy and public works.

In 310, Constantine's world fell apart. Maximian had quarreled with his son in Rome and come to live with Constantine in Gaul, where he also became once again a private citizen, having been convinced by Diocletian to put aside the purple he had resumed in Rome. Now, soon after Constantine had taken to the field against the Franks, Maximian once again donned the purple, seizing Constantine's treasury and using it to offer a large donative to secure the loyalty of the remaining troops. Returning by forced marches, Constantine surprised the aging despot, who threw himself into Marseilles but was soon betrayed.

Accounts differ as to what happened next. In the mildest version, Maximian hung himself for shame.

The extent of the crisis generated by Maximian's stunt may still be measured in another surviving panegyric, this one delivered in 310, only weeks after the old Tetrarch's demise. The occasion was Constantine's Quinquennalia, the fifth anniversary of his rule,[25] and the orator—evidently a professor from one of the great schools of Autun—turned immediately to the subject of Constantine's ancestry. This was a normal enough topic, recommended by rhetorical handbooks. But the orator did so by means of an unusual device. Although his speech honors all the emperors in the Tetrarchy, he explained, for the sake of brevity he will speak only of Constantine. This was a stark departure from Tetrarchic protocol, and the orator assumed a mildly self-deprecating manner (his talents simply were not up to the task of doing more) to remove the sting from any presumed snub. But in this genre even an apology can be an insult. Other orations in this very collection simply ignore Tetrarchic etiquette, which required equal treatment for all the rulers; by pointing out the omission, the orator in fact called attention to it, thus setting the tone for a cat-and-mouse game that, the ensuing lines suggest, was intentional. Immediately the orator decided to reveal something that, he claimed, probably was not known to many people, although those (presumably such as himself) who loved Constantine knew it well: Constantine was not merely the son of a senior Tetrarch, but he was also descended from the third-century emperor Claudius II, surnamed "Gothicus" for his successes against the barbarian invaders in 269. No nameless pretender, Constantine thus was a third-generation emperor, with a pedigree that no other public figure of his day could match.

There are many signs that this speech, if not official court propaganda, was something very like. For one thing, there is the standing of the speaker. He was not at this time a member of the court himself, but he made a point of saying that a son ranked high among Constantine's officials, and he even boasted of the number of his former students in the emperor's service.[26] These claims went well beyond the pretensions to intimacy which orators conventionally made. At the very least, they suggest that this speaker was in a good position to know what topics would, and would not, be appreciated. Then there is the skillful balancing act by which the orator asserted the superiority of Constantine's claim to the purple without completely breaking with the standards of the Tetrarchy. "Surely it is a great and admirable fortune that rises to that pinnacle of majesty . . . through service in the ranks," he conceded. "But it is another thing altogether to hold that peak supported by the eminence of one's birth."[27] To think it mere coincidence for a panegyrist to assert this alternative claim to legitimacy within weeks of Maximian's death strains credulity, for a more blatant challenge to the principles of the Tetrarchy cannot be imagined. Echoed many years later by Eusebius, the importance of this claim to a new and greater legitimacy cannot be overestimated. It represents the final victory of the dynastic principle in imperial politics.

But the measure of this orator's skill is the way he handled the delicate matter of Maximian's attempted coup and subsequent death. He acknowledged as much, putting the issue off until late in his oration and then professing an unwillingness to proceed without a nod from the emperor himself.[28] Constantine was potentially vulnerable on two counts: impiety and ambition. In 306, he had turned to his troops as an alternate source of legitimacy, only to learn (as Octavian had centuries earlier) that such loyalty was unstable. It was Maximian, with his status as Augustus and his Herculian dynasty, who had rescued Constantine from this fate, and now Maximian was dead, one way or another at Constantine's hand. The alternative genealogy and dynastic pretensions with which the orator began clearly were designed to head off this argument before the problem that generated it even arose (rhetorically, a maneuver known as preexplication). With this groundwork laid, he was free to go on the offensive. It was Maximian, we learn, who was guilty of overweening ambition and broken oaths, Maximian who failed to show proper gratitude to the kinsman who had taken him in and rescued him from dishonor. Constantine, we know, would have given the ingrate even more and forgiven him even this. But there are some crimes that his subjects, nay the gods themselves, cannot forgive![29]

This much was stock stuff and pretty much predictable. It is in dealing with the most delicate problem of all, Maximian's enduring popularity with the troops, that the orator shows an ingenuity that at some points is breathtaking in its audacity. Maximian, it turns out, was the one who had forgotten the lessons of the third century. "At one time, perhaps, many bad leaders, inferior in arms, competed with bribes, but their popularity was brief and unstable, and whoever imitated them easily overcame them." Forgetting this lesson, Maximian thought he could "employ without a qualm an army which he had taught to take bribes."[30] How different from Diocletian, who never went back on his decision to retire and thus was "a man truly fortunate and blest whom, although he is a private citizen, such princes as you cherish and obey."[31] Rhetorically, the contrast with Diocletian serves to undercut Maximian's prestige while at the same time intimating that Constantine remained in close relationship with the Tetrarchy's senior Augustus. Historically, the phrase stands in significant and embarrassing contrast to what soon was to become the party line on Constantine's ties to the archpersecutor. Maximian's mistake, the orator tells us, lay in not realizing that times had changed. Bribes worked with other troops, but Constantine's "preferred you to all the gifts which he had promised and to all the offers of preferments."[32] So eager were they to defend their leader that Constantine himself could barely keep up with them on the march or restrain their efforts to take the walls of Marseilles by storm. This was an army that practiced what with rare exception philosophers only preached, self-control (*continentia*).

An army of philosopher-kings in any age would truly be a sight to behold. A more likely way to read such fulsome protestations of loyalty is as indicators that Maximian's death did not sit as well with the troops as Constantine might have hoped. Although Maximian was gone, his son Maxentius survived. In the received tradition, Maxentius had become fed up with his father even before the more generous Constantine, but now he denounced his brother-in-law's treachery and ordered his statues overturned. With political stakes so high, honesty counts little in the race for advantage, and Maxentius's rage may have been as calculated as the Constantinian account of events claimed. At the very least, however, it indicates a belief that there was political gain to be made among Maximian loyalists still serving with Constantine.

Then, in the spring of 311, came Galerius's death. As always, the death of an incumbent triggered a new scramble for power. But even for Rome, this time the situation was exceptionally fluid, with four contenders—Constantine and Maxentius in the West, Licinius (named Augustus in 308) and Daza in the East. There was much behind-the-scenes jockeying for position, but Constantine was the first to move. In the fall of 312, some eighteen months after Galerius's death, he launched an invasion of Italy. On October 28, 312, Maxentius fell in the battle for Rome; by the subsequent summer Daza was dead, having been defeated twice in battle by Licinius. The two victors had already allied, sealing the pact early in 313 with a traditional wedding alliance in which Constantine's half sister Constantia became bride to Licinius. Despite the alliance, the next decade turned rapidly into a series of hot and cold wars finally ending with a decisive victory by Constantine in 324. But it was the campaign of 312 that, as Constantine told Eusebius of Caesarea many years later, changed more than his political standing.

Politics and Religion

The political situation that underlay Eusebius's description of Constantine's conversion in Chapter 1 is now much clearer. Constantine was marching to Rome because the death of Maximian triggered a confrontation that, by now, both he and Maxentius probably had come to see as inevitable. Eusebius characterizes the invasion as a moment of great anxiety for Constantine. He had good reason to be concerned, considering that two previous invasion attempts had resulted in death for one leader and shame for the other. It is easy to see why Constantine cast around for an approach that would allow him to avoid a similar outcome. With a better sense of the environment and circumstances, we may now return to that story, one of the most scrutinized in Christian history. In the course of these musings, Eusebius wrote, "The thought occurred to him, that, of the many emperors who had preceded him, those who had rested their hopes in a multitude of gods, and served them with sacrifices and offerings, had in the first place been deceived by flattering predictions, and oracles which promised them all prosperity, and at last had met with an unhappy end, while not one of their gods had stood by to warn them of the impending wrath of heaven."[33] Contrasting their fate with that of his father, "who had pursued an entirely opposite course, who had condemned their error, and honored the one Supreme God during his whole life," Constantine decided his father's god would be the only one for him. "Accordingly, he called on him with earnest prayer and supplications that he would reveal to him who he was, and stretch forth his right hand to help him in his present difficulties." In other words, he sought a personal revelation. The product of this process was the Vision of the Cross.

Eusebius's account has led scholars down many blind alleys, mostly because of the preconceptions and agendas of later periods. Does the reference to his father, for instance, mean that Constantius I was a Christian? Although some scholars have drawn this conclusion, it seems unlikely that Constantine would then have needed to know the identity of his father's deity. Indeed, even after the vision, Eusebius tells us, Constantine remained puzzled. "And while he continued to ponder and reason on its meaning," he reports, "night suddenly came on; then in his sleep the Christ of God appeared to him with the same sign which he had seen in the heavens, and commanded him to make a likeness of that sign which he had seen in the heavens, and to use it as a safeguard in all engagements with his enemies." Even with this personal intervention, Eusebius makes clear, Constantine remained perplexed. Sending for "those who were acquainted with the mysteries of His doctrines," he first learned of the significance of the cross to Christian belief and began a course of religious instruction.[34]

Eusebius's account is not the earliest. He was writing a quarter century after the event, and although he does not make clear exactly when he heard the story, the occasion could not have been before Constantine's defeat of another one-time ally, Licinius, brought him to the East in 324. Lactantius's version is contained in his pamphlet On the Deaths of the Persecutors, which was probably written around the year 315, within three years of the battle. Not surprisingly, Constantine's battle for Rome is a centerpiece of this highly colored account, the aim of which was to demonstrate the awesome power with which God protects his chosen people. Although significantly abbreviated, Lactantius's version also includes a supernatural revelation. This is how Lactantius tells it:

> Fighting took place in which Maxentius' troops held the advantage until Constantine at a later stage, his courage renewed and "ready for either

success or death," moved all his forces nearer to the city of Rome and based himself in the region of the Milvian bridge. . . . . Constantine was advised in a dream to mark the heavenly sign of God on the shields of his soldiers and then engage in battle. He did as he was commanded and by means of a slanted letter X with the top of its head bent round, he marked Christ on their shields.[35]

Lactantius does not dwell on Constantine's state of mind as Eusebius did, but he does say that Maxentius's troops had had the better of the encounters leading up to this moment, so it is reasonable to assume that even with a "mind prepared for every event" Constantine was experiencing some of the same anxiety that Eusebius spelled out in greater detail. Lactantius does not identify the agent in Constantine's dream, but he is more specific about its time and place. He and Eusebius agree, moreover, on the role played by a divine sign in Constantine's victory. It is undeniable that they are both writing about the same event. Missing from Lactantius, however, is any account of the cross, or of the vision in the sky. All the revelation in his version occurs in the dream, and thanks to the discipline of psychology our world has now learned what the ancient world always knew: the importance of dreams, especially those experienced in moments of duress. Here, the ancients thought, is where gods made contact with mortals. Here, we have been taught, is where the unconscious sorts through data that our stressed and bewildered conscious minds overlook. It thus makes as much sense to our world as it did to his to hear that, at a moment when he was under great duress, as yet uncertain how the risk he had taken would turn out, everything came together for a dreaming Constantine in such a way that the god of the Christians seemed the answer to his problems.[36]

Corroborating evidence that something extraordinary happened during this campaign can be found even closer in time to the battle than Lactantius's account. In the spring of 313, less than four months after the battle, Constantine met with his new ally Licinius in Milan and then returned to his Gallic capital of Trier. There an orator celebrated his victory with a speech that survives as another of the collection of *Latin Panegyrics*. Like Eusebius and Lactantius, this orator also saw divine intervention in Constantine's victory, speaking of a "divine mind" that revealed itself solely to Constantine, a "divine power," a "divine prompting," that made him indifferent to Maxentius's superior numbers. In language that scarcely conforms to traditional polytheistic cosmology, he invoked a god who was "the Creator and Lord of the world" and "Highest Creator of the world."[37] The inscription on the arch built by the Senate in Rome to commemorate his victory uses similar language as well, referring to a "divine prompting" (*instinctu divinitatis*) that moved Constantine to free Rome from the tyrant.[38] Such language suggests that pagans as well as Christians knew that Constantine attributed his victory to divine intervention.

With evidence coming from all directions that something must have happened during the course of this campaign to change Constantine in some way, it seems an easy matter to understand Constantine's conversion by assuming that the dream story, which is in both accounts, was the real event and by sending the more spectacular vision back to the human dream factory from which it came. But there is a further complication, for Eusebius's is not the only description of a vision experience involving Constantine; a comparable story is told by the orator of 310.

This is the speech delivered in the aftermath of another crisis, old Maximian's abortive attempt to suborn Constantine's army and deprive him of his rule, the speech in which the "secret" of Constantine's descent from Claudius Gothicus was revealed. Constantine's new ancestry, however, was the least of the bombshells that dropped in the course of this speech. Here we are also told, more than two years before the battle for Rome, of a reassuring encounter between Constantine and divinity. It happened as Constantine marched back to the frontier after aborting Maximian's putsch. Learning that the invading barbarians already had been dispatched, he turned aside to visit a site that the orator identifies only as "the most beautiful temple in the whole world." There he experienced a vision of a god who guaranteed him not only this victory but thirty years of victory, in fact three times thirty years. Unfortunately, the god in question on this occasion was not Christ but Apollo:

> For you saw, I believe, O Constantine, your Apollo, accompanied by Victory, offering you laurel wreaths, each one of which carries a portent of thirty

Fig. 3. Constantine is portrayed in a striking double image with the god Apollo on this coin minted early in 313, within months of the Battle of the Milvian Bridge. Apollo's solar crown emphasizes his identity with the popular sun god, Sol Invictus, and is consistent with solar connections in Constantine's propaganda during these years. The model used for many years to explain Constantine's conversion made his continued use of such images problematic, but the use is consistent with sociological studies that emphasize the gradual nature of such a change.

(Photo Bibliothèque Nationale de France)

years. . . . And—now why do I say "I believe"?—you *saw*, and recognized yourself in the likeness of him to whom the divine songs of the bards had prophesied that rule over the whole world was due. And this I think has now happened, since you are, O Emperor, like he, youthful, joyful, a bringer of health and very handsome.[39]

The account has generated predictable consternation. What can such a claim mean? Apollo was a solar deity, easily identified with the warrior god Sol Invictus, who starts showing up on coins from about 308 as Constantine's special divine companion. Reverses dedicated "To the Companion Unconquered Sun" (*Soli Invicti Comiti*) show the god with his distinctive solar flares placing a laurel crown on Constantine's brow. A gold coin minted for Constantine's meeting with Licinius in Milan early in 313 displays the emperor in twin profile with Apollo. Because gold coins were distributed only to the highest-ranking officials, and because this issue was distributed only a few months after the victory over Maxentius, it suggests a continuing allegiance to the sun god after 312. Indeed, although other pagan symbols gradually disappeared from Constantine's coins after 313, the sun god remained for a decade or more. Similarly, on the arch that was built adjacent to the Colosseum in Rome to commemorate this victory and dedicated about the same time that Lactantius wrote his pamphlet, there are solar and lunar images, but Christian signs are noticeable only by their absence, particularly in the panel that shows Constantine's soldiers in battle, where some indication of the signs he ordered soldiers to wear might be expected. On the basis of such evidence, the argument has been advanced that the vision of Apollo in 310 was the same experience to which Eusebius referred years later in a suitably Christianized version.[40]

But how much is such evidence worth? Classical literature traditionally followed Homer's lead to involve the gods in battle narratives, and on these grounds some scholars dismiss the 310 orator's whole story as merely more rhetoric, saying that at most it literally describes an occasion on which Constantine saw a statue of Apollo; the orator, learning of this episode, simply adorned it with suitable embroidery. Because the encounter occurred after the crisis was over, according to this view, it does not have the same psychological punch as the later, Christian vision that Constantine experienced while the outcome was still in doubt. According to this view, pagan symbols such as Sol Invictus survive after 312 as nothing more than commonplace motifs that had lost their meaning, whereas the use of neutral language such as "divine mind" and "divine instinct" represents an effort by these pagan sources to come to grips with Constantine's new affiliation with the Christian god.[41]

There is a whiff of partisanship in all these explanations. Rhetoric, obviously, is too subjective a criterion for judging the relative veracity of Christian and pagan versions, particularly when dealing with a period whose entire literary output rings rhetorical in the prosaic modern ear. Attempts to bring scientific objectivity to bear by invoking the "halo phenomenon" (an atmospheric condition in which sunlight on ice crystals can produce a cruciform image with the sun in its center), are similarly misguided, for the real issue is not what he actually saw but what Constantine and others made of it.[42]

Although the scholarly debate has been long and sophisticated, the most basic question of all has gone neglected: Given the disruptive effects of a near decade of persecution and the failure of that persecution to achieve its stated objective, what policy options were open to anyone who became emperor in 312, no matter what his religious persuasion? The reason so obvious a question has gone unasked for so long is that the primary interest of the scholars who have dealt with this evidence has been to establish or debunk the sincerity of Constantine's conversion and the strength of his commitment to Christianity. For this reason, they assume not only that everything Constantine did was intended but also that a non-Christian would not have have had to deal with the Christian issue. These assumptions clearly are not warranted. Thanks to the persecution, any emperor, Christian or not, was going to have to devise a way to deal with the Christian population. As we have seen, Daza was the only one who apparently believed to the end that persecution remained a viable option; even Galerius had conceded the failure of that approach before he died. Maxentius and Licinius show signs that they thought it was necessary to come to terms. It is no test of Constantine's sincerity, therefore, to find that he also did so. Eusebius's account of the vision, with its blend of political and religious events, unquestionably has encouraged this confusion. A better starting place for understanding this evidence is those ideas about governance, about the relationship between the ruler and the divine, which were part of the inherited frame of belief of Christians as well as pagans at this period of the fourth century. With these in mind, it becomes easier to see common themes in much of the evidence that, because of its religious content, has been artificially separated into "pagan" and "Christian" categories.

There was political as well as literary incentive for both Christians and pagans to show that Rome's ruler had the support of a divine *comes,* or companion, and for this reason certain topics recur throughout Constantine's career, whether the speaker is pagan or Christian. Both, for instance, celebrated Constantine's close ties with divinity and his sense of mission, and both expressed certainty that his rule would be of unparalleled length. Obviously, the orator of 313 proclaimed, "You must share some secret with that divine mind, Constantine, which has delegated care of us to lesser gods and deigns to reveal itself to you alone." When this orator invoked the "Highest Creator of the World," he did so to ask him to "preserve this prince for all ages." Asserting that "it is a small thing to wish that such great valor and such great piety should have the longest possible course that life offers," he called on that god to "make the best thing which you have given to the human race last eternally, and let Constantine spend all the ages on earth."[43] More than two decades later, Bishop Eusebius of Caesarea repeated all these themes in an oration he delivered on the occasion of Constantine's thirtieth jubilee, in which he pointedly described Constantine not only as God's "friend" (*philos*, a Greek equivalent of the Latin *comes*) but also as his counterpart on earth and even asserted that death would not stop Constantine from ruling.[44]

What makes these expressions so potent is that parallels to all of them can be found in Constantine's own public expressions, suggesting that in this case at least the orators were echoing the emperor's own beliefs. A sense of personal calling and a mission to combat evil pervades the version of his rise to power with which this chapter began. Elsewhere, he describes himself as possessed of divine wisdom from infancy, having "received no aid from human instruction; nay, whatever graces of character are esteemed of good report by those who have understanding, are entirely the gift of God."[45] He uses virtually every occasion to identify himself as an instrument personally chosen by God—as in a letter he addressed to the inhabitants of Palestine: "and surely it cannot be deemed arrogance in one who has received benefits from God, to acknowledge them in the loftiest terms of praise. I myself, then, was the instrument whose services He chose, and esteemed suited for the accomplishment of his will."[46]

This is an aspect of Constantine's religiosity which it would be foolish to ignore. That his concept of a personal relationship with deity should carry strong political overtones was inevitable in a world where Christians and pagans alike conceived of the emperor as a religiously charged individual. It should come as no surprise, therefore, and certainly should not be taken as a reflection on the nature of Constantine's faith, to find public prayers during his reign consistently associating the Supreme Deity with the safety of Constantine and his heirs, such as this prayer, which Eusebius says Constantine ordered his non-Christian soldiers to repeat on the new Sunday holiday he declared in 321: "We acknowledge thee the only God: we own thee as our King, and implore thy succor. By thy favor have we gotten the victory: through thee are we mightier than our enemies. We render thanks for thy past benefits, and trust thee for future blessings. Together we pray to thee, and beseech thee long to preserve to us, safe and triumphant, our emperor Constantine and his pious sons."[47]

In 312, another, perhaps greater problem lay just beneath the surface: the ambiguous state of Constantine's claim to rule. Initially a usurper, Constantine had quickly conformed to Tetrarchic standards of appointment. These he had maintained and even strengthened by his marriage to Fausta in 307. With the death of Maximian, particularly given the circumstances under which it had occurred, that tie was broken, and Constantine was left with his army as the principal support of his claim. The relative ease with which Maximian had been able to turn those troops to his ends is a good example of just how thin a reed that was to lean on. The dynastic alternative asserted by the orator of 310 had somewhat greater currency, but its real effect lay in the future. At the time, its appeal was primarily to the same constituency from which Constantine was trying to distance himself, the military; it was not likely to sway either traditional senatorial sympathies or adherents to the newer criteria of the Tetrarchy.

These circumstances certainly explain another theme common to Christian and pagan orators: Constantine's selection as emperor did not depend on human criteria. "No chance agreement of men, nor some unexpected consequence of favor, made you Emperor," the orator of 310 proclaimed.[48] This is the same orator who revealed Constantine's royal ancestry and who reported his vision of Apollo. But he did not rest his case on either mortal genealogy or Constantine's eyesight. Elsewhere in the same speech he described a banquet of the gods which Constantius I attended while still alive, at which Jupiter himself ratified his choice of his son to succeed him. Thus, he told Constantine, it was not just by his father but "by the votes of the immortals" that he had been called "to the rescue of the State."[49] Similarly, Eusebius in his *vita Constantini* firmly asserted, "While others have been raised to this distinction by the election of their fellow-men, he is the only one to whose elevation no mortal may brag of having contributed."[50]

Conversion

With such extravagant assertions, it is small wonder that some scholars have seen Constantine's conversion more as a power play than a spiritual awakening. But there is no need to deny the political context in order to admit the sincerity of Constantine's belief. Three and a half centuries earlier, under similar pressure to find a more stable counterweight for the heavy reliance he had heretofore placed on the army to support his claim to rule, the first Augustus had turned instinctively to the Senate. In the new climate of the late empire, Constantine turned equally instinctively to the heavens. The problem is that to our age the one explanation seems "rational," while the other does not. Does this mean there was no miraculous vision? Then as now, people see what they expect to see. The safest thing to say is that in Constantine's age miracle was the most rational explanation for an unexpected turn of events.

A better question is, why does there have to be only one vision, either pagan or Christian? The reason may be that scholars have been following a false scent, trying to make Constantine's conversion fit into a highly literary, if not idealized, model of psychological conversion associated with the names of William James and Arthur Darby Nock. Although both Nock and James recognized that conversion was a gradual process, their ideal model requires the subject to experience a sudden, 180-degree turn in religious outlook. As Nock put it in a typically happy analogy, conversion "is like a chemical process in which the addition of a catalytic agent produces a reaction for which all the elements were already present." It creates "a sense of perceiving truths not known before, a sense of clean and beautiful newness within and without and an ecstasy of happiness," emotions that, he added, "are sometimes, and in fact often, accompanied by hallucinatory or quasi-hallucinatory phenomena."[51] With this model as guide, it becomes imperative that Constantine only experience one genuine vision and equally imperative that his subsequent actions demonstrate a consistency and commitment commensurate with such a soul-wrenching experience—hence the problem of dealing with continued representations of the sun god on Constantine's coins or the lack of Christian symbols on the arch dedicated to him in Rome in the aftermath of his victory.

This may not be the best model for understanding Constantine's experience. Although the Vision of the Cross has garnered the lion's share of scholarly attention, Eusebius's *vita Constantini* actually contains several other instances of visions that this emperor enjoyed at various times in his long career. In fact, at one point Eusebius says that the emperor never started a battle without retiring to his tent to await a sign from God. And, Eusebius adds, he was never disappointed.[52] What the totality of Eusebius's account suggests is that Constantine was a very vision-prone emperor, in an age that expected its rulers to manifest these kinds of ties with a divine being.

Other models do a better job of explaining this kind of ongoing revelation. Sociological studies, for instance, suggest that it is much more typical for converts to go through a number of progressive awakenings, rather than a single, blinding change, and thus a more gradual process than the classic model assumes. More important, these studies indicate that there is usually a greater amount of consistency in the belief of the typical convert before and after the moment of conversion than that model would allow, or even than the converts themselves report. Typically, a long period of searching and study both precedes and follows the actual moment of decision. What really determines whether a conversion experience takes hold or not is the process of socialization into a new community, as part of which the convert becomes familiarized with new standards, histories, and reference points. This is a much more gradual process. After years of development, or what one author calls "biographical reconstruction," the convert not infrequently comes to reinterpret his or her earlier career in the light of these new beliefs and to see the moment of conversion as constituting a much greater leap than it was at the time. In other words, the convert constructs more discontinuity than actually existed and in retrospect perceives the conversion experience as a moment of stark change, a dramatic break.[53]

Using this model, what had previously seemed a weakness in Eusebius's evidence—the long lapse of time between the event and Constantine's narrative—now becomes perhaps the most significant evidence for the veracity of his account, bearing in mind that he is only reporting what Constantine remembered. Constantine's memory would conform to this model of the conversion experience, as would Eusebius's description, at several points in the *vita Constantini*, of the emperor's constant study, his continual progress in the faith. These comments serve to confirm the impression that the emperor was recalling his own conversion through the filter of experience in the Christian community. If there was an earlier vision that was transposed, it was Constantine, not Eusebius, who did it.

One effect of changing conversion models is that the search for evidence of a dramatic change in Constantine's religious behavior after 312 can be tempered by awareness that there was more continuity in his development than, in retrospect, an aging Constantine perceived. It also gives perspective on the continuity that does exist. Too much should not be read into evidence for the existence of certain behavioral patterns before 312. Constantine's claim, cited at the beginning of this chapter, that his mission to unify the empire began in Britain, or Lactantius's remark that his first act was to call off the persecution, sometimes is cited as proof that Constantine was Christian as early as 305, when all they actually indicate is that Constantine believed in his destiny and was concerned about the persecution's disruptive effect from the time that he set out on an alternative track to the purple. The evidence for Constantine's beliefs prior to 312 is admittedly scanty, but it is also remarkably consistent. Like many other non-Christians in late antiquity, he seems to have been a monotheist, believing in a Supreme Creator God known by different names to different peoples and worshiped in different manifestations and guises, here as a sky god, there as a sun god. Solar monotheism—the variant of this belief most widely shared by enlightened pagans at this time—is particularly marked on Constantine's coins from about 308 and may have been his father's belief, if the orator who spoke at Constantine's wedding in 307 was accurately reflecting that belief when he pictured Constantius beaming down on the ceremony from his seat in the chariot of the Sun.[54] Debating which of Constantine's visions was the more genuine is a good example of how misleading it can be to make everything hinge on the single event of 312, because the debate ignores the most important feature of these two visions, which is the remarkable consistency between them: in the one, Constantine sees Apollo, a solar deity; in the other, he sees a cross superimposed over the sun. In both, the guarantee of success is an important element, as is the sense of a close, personal relationship.

In a speech delivered years later Constantine provides the following justification for the superiority of monotheistic belief:

> Else how could the author of universal nature ever be known? To whom first, or last, could prayers and supplications be addressed? Whom could I choose as the object of my worship, without being guilty of impiety towards the rest? Again, if haply I desired to obtain some temporal blessing, should I not, while expressing my gratitude to the Power who favored my request, convey a reproach to him who opposed it? Or to whom should I pray, when desiring to know the cause of my calamity, and to obtain deliverance? Or let us suppose that the answer is given by oracles and prophecies, but that the case is not within the scope of their authority, being the province of some other deity.[55]

The pragmatism and concern for clear lines of authority displayed here seem a good reflection of the way Constantine approached problems. The remark, thus, may well reflect the reasoning process that led Constantine himself first to monotheism and ultimately to Christianity.

Far from being the embarrassment it once seemed, Constantine's so-called contradictory behavior after 312 now seems plausible evidence for conversion, since the notion that continued use of non-Christian symbols and images contradicts the sincerity of his conversion also depends on a psychological model that may be overly demanding and not a good predictor of normal behavior. It is also possible now to see a new meaning in the increased use of phrases like Supreme God and Highest Creator by Constantine's panegyrists after 312 and the gradual disappearance of all signs of pagan deities except the sun god from his coins. To use these as signs of Constantine's Christianity, or to dismiss them as hollow echoes of dead beliefs, fails to take into account an important fact: nothing overtly Christian replaced them. Reconsideration of these signs brings out a different facet, that they could represent an effort to reconcile pagan and Christian monotheists.

What happened in 312 will always be a subject of fascination and speculation. A plausible reconstruction of Constantine's religious development is necessary to round out the picture of his religious policy and to demonstrate how belief and policy might have coexisted in his thinking. But in these pages policy is the critical factor, and for this purpose it is better to situate Constantine's religious development in the context of contemporary power politics and political thought. There is no reason to conclude from this process that Constantine's conversion to Christianity was not sincere; but without questioning his sincerity it is still worthwhile to ask how unique his thinking was at this stage of his career. Instead of the lone hero that he became in subsequent tradition, Constantine emerges as one of several talented and ambitious players seeking a formula to reconcile the imperial need for religious justification with the refusal of Christians to pay divine honors to any other deity. He was casting around, in other words, not only for a god in whom to believe but a policy that he could adopt.

What is significant about the year 312 is not a change in his personal belief, which seem to have evolved more gradually over a longer period, but the fact that in that year a policy began to take shape. The miracle would be important later At the time what was far more important was that he had found a unifying theme, a key to the solution of his own and the empire's problems. Would it work? With his conversion, Constantine acquired more than a religion. He also acquired a constituency. How would he deal with it? These questions lay in the future. As he entered Rome after the Battle of the Milvian Bridge, Constantine had every reason to believe that the problems of the Tetrarchy were behind him. He had discovered a common denominator for the problems of imperial unity, religious diversity, and imperial succession, and he had learned how to fuse these ingredients into a powerful expression of personal mission. He was about to learn something else: becoming a Christian was the easy part.

Six

Building a Coalition

onstantine entered Rome the day following his victory over Maxentius with the head of his defeated enemy firmly fixed on the top of a spear and the contours of a Christian policy firmly fixed in his mind. The plan was based on a stunningly simple premise: that there were sufficient grounds for agreement between Christians and pagans for the ties between emperor and divinity which were now a necessary condition for legitimate rule to be defined in terms suitable for Christians, pagan monotheists, and even those polytheists who did not insist on performance of blood sacrifices. Admittedly, this is not a premise that would occur so readily to a modern mind, conditioned by a millennium and more of scholarship to think in sharply divided categories of "Christian" and "pagan." It takes some repositioning—a determined refusal to read backward from the coercive turn that Christianity took later in the fourth century—to see, for instance, that to contemporaries the Great Persecution looked more like a civil war than the "life-and-death struggle" between two utterly unreconcilable belief systems which it became in subsequent scholarship; that, in fact, it was the closeness, not the distance, between Christian and late pagan thinking which triggered the anxieties of anti-Christian intellectuals; that long before the so-called triumph of Christianity, the normal evolution of pagan rite had eliminated some of the practices that most alienated Christians from participating in public life, particularly with respect to the nature of public obligation and ceremony; and, finally, that the spectacular and costly failure of Diocletian's policy of coercion would have made the search for common ground a viable and attractive alternative to a broad spectrum of Christians and non-Christians alike.

Put in modern terms, the policy question raised by the persecution was this: What defines a Roman citizen? What was the minimum act of obedience necessary to demonstrate commitment? Starting in the third century, an attempt was made to define citizenship by means of ritual sacrifice to the official gods of the Roman state. The effort provoked two persecutions, by Decius and Valerian, until Gallienus called it off. For whatever reason, Diocletian revived this policy in 303. Underlying all these events was the problem of how to incorporate Christians into a state that equated security with divine support. A policy of forced support for the traditional deities accompanied by destruction of the Christian network and hierarchy had failed utterly, its sponsors isolated and discredited. Even Galerius had recognized as much. When he abandoned persecution in his edict of 311, his proviso that it would be sufficient for Christians to pray to their God on behalf of the emperors was more than a return to the status quo ante, it was also an attempt to redefine the nature of citizenship, allowing prayer to substitute for sacrifice. The concession opened a wider door than is usually perceived. But the problem remained.

The Edict of Milan

Within months of his victory over Maxentius, Constantine met with Licinius in Milan, the meeting for which that coin of Constantine and Apollo in facing profile was struck. The occasion that brought them together was the marriage of Licinius and Constantia, the traditional manner for Romans to seal an alliance. The two allies also used the occasion to work out the details of their relationship, which included agreement on a postpersecution policy. The conference was cut short by news that Maxentius's newly unmasked ally, Daza, no doubt reckoning that the best defense was a good offense, had exploited Licinius's absence to invade. Licinius hurried east and destroyed the last persecutor in a series of running battles over the next several months. When he returned to Nicomedia that June, Licinius publicly posted a letter to the provincial governor announcing the allies' policy toward religion, whence it found its way into Lactantius's On the Deaths of the Persecutors. Although it survives only in this form (and in a slightly varying Greek translation published by Eusebius), the policy traditionally is known as the "Edict of Milan."[1]

Toleration, a return to the status quo ante, was the minimal alternative solution. The Edict of Milan embodied a far more creative and daring solution, defining state security in terms of a general monotheism, thereby opening an umbrella that would cover virtually any form of worship—a policy with no losers, only winners. The edict constitutes a landmark in the evolution of Western thought—not because it gives legal standing to Christianity, which it does, but because it is the first official government document in the Western world to recognize the principle of freedom of belief. First among all their concerns, Licinius reports, was the need to make arrangements "which ensured reverence for the Divinity." For this reason, the two emperors decided that they "might grant both to Christians and to all men freedom to follow whatever religion each one wished, in order that whatever divinity there is in the seat of heaven may be appeased and made propitious" both to the rulers themselves and to their subjects.[2] It is true, as is often said, that Christianity was the only religion mentioned by name in this edict, and only Christians benefited from its operative clauses, which provided for the recall of exiles and the restitution of seized property. Certainly, in this respect, the Edict of Milan goes substantially beyond the edict of Galerius two years earlier, which showed no willingness to concede that the Christians had been harmed in any way and thus made no provision for restitution. But this result is incidental, in the strict sense of that word: it follows from the fact that Christians were the only group that lacked legal standing and which had suffered exile and loss of property as a result of the persecution. Similarly, the recognition of the importance of Divine Providence to Rome's well-being was nothing new; this is, rather, the most traditional clause in the entire document, the one least likely—especially in the period of the late empire—to provoke disagreement from any quarter. Its effect was to add the Christian god to the tutelary deities who traditionally had been considered responsible for the well-being of the Roman state. Indeed, no more succinct statement of late imperial political theory can be found than in the edict's penultimate sentence, "In this way it will come about, as we have explained above, that the divine favour towards us, which we have experienced in such important matters, will continue for all time to prosper our achievements along with the public well being."[3]

The real departure of this edict lies in the emperors' unwillingness to speak of the divine guarantor of Rome's well-being in any terms more specific than as "the supreme divinity" (*summa divinitas*). Where Diocletian firmly identified the security of the empire with Jupiter, these emperors were content to satisfy "whatever divinity there is in the seat of heaven" (*quicquid [est] divinitatis in sede caelesti*). It is this uncertainty, this willingness to entertain the prospect of more than one avenue to supreme truth, which sets the Edict of Milan apart. As part of this new openness comes the edict's other major departure: official recognition that religion cannot be coerced. The emperors "grant both to Christians and to all men freedom to follow whatever religion each one wished," they write, because no one should be denied the opportunity "to give his mind to the observances of the Christians or to that religion which he felt was most fitting to himself." The religion of the supreme divinity is one to be obeyed "with free minds" (*liberis mentibus*).[4] A few passages later, the emperors explain again that their permission for Christians to worship openly and freely was given "so that each man may have a free opportunity to engage in whatever worship he has chosen." They continue, "This we have done to ensure that no cult or religion may seem to have been impaired by us." Some fifty years earlier, Gallienus's edict restoring property and freedom of worship, which led to unprecedented Christian prosperity, tacitly recognized both the legal existence of the church and the principle of noncoercion, but only with the Edict of Milan do both of these points become an official and explicit part of government policy.

In its recognition of religious pluralism, the edict cleared one major roadblock to incorporation of Christians in the traditional polity. On another level, the provision for restitution of property to Christians, both individually and collectively (a provision that thereby reaffirmed the corporate legality of the church), while not as radical a departure in theoretical terms, was as a practical matter an even more important signal that Christians were now eligible to partake of traditional imperial largesse. But it has to be read with a parallel provision, providing for reimbursement from the treasury to private individuals in possession of such property. Together, these decisions confirm an overall intent of the emperors to put the divisions created by the Tetrarchic policy behind them and to head off potential conflict of interest between Christians and their neighbors by guaranteeing that there will be no financial losers. It is easy to conceive of another policy that would have condemned those who chose to profit from the misfortune of others; instead, with this decision as much as by their general commitment to freedom of choice, the allies signaled a desire to establish their reigns on the most broadly based coalition possible.

The Milan proclamation shows how much the game had changed in the two years since Galerius's Edict of Toleration. But whose policy was it? It is traditional to see Constantine as the accelerator and Licinius as the brakes, the one responsible for the parts favorable to Christianity, the other for the reluctance to identify the deity who now is supreme in Rome and for including the reminders that all other beliefs were equally favored. There is much hindsight in this conclusion: Constantine and Licinius soon had a falling out, and as a result Licinius, like Maxentius, became tainted by the charge of persecution. Lactantius's tract *On the Deaths of the Persecutors* is a caution against such retrospective judgment. Written no more than two years after the Milan meeting, and thus before the split between Constantine and Licinius, it treats Constantine's colleague respectfully, though not, of course, as favorably as Constantine himself. Prior to his decisive battle with Maximin Daza, Lactantius tells us, Licinius had his own dream visitation and received his own inspiration for victory, a prayer to the Supreme God for his troops to recite before the start of the engagement.[5] Scholars have labored to find intimations of a less favorable judgment in Lactantius's account of the way Licinius hunted down and destroyed the families of his opponents following his victory, forgetting the author's own judgment on these events, "Thus all the wicked suffered by the true and just judgment of God the very things which they had done to others."[6] Eusebius of Caesarea, who would later depict Licinius as an archpersecutor, and describe the war between him and Constantine as a showdown between the old gods and the new, referred to the allies in a new edition of his Church History published in the aftermath of Daza's defeat as "two God-beloved emperors, honored alike for their intelligence and their piety."[7]

Another reason for caution in assessing the relative contribution of each emperor to the Edict of Milan is the language of the orator who celebrated Constantine's victory over Maxentius when he returned to Gaul after the meeting with Licinius. As observed in the preceding chapter, the oration is noteworthy for the absence of the traditional gods and the monotheistic flavor of its references to divinity. What must be observed now is the vagueness of those monotheistic references—"divine mind" (*diuina mens*), "divine power" (*diuina numen*), "Highest Creator of the world" (*summe rerum sator*), a god "whose names are as many as you willed the tongues of men to be" (*cuius tot nomina sunt quot gentium linguas esse uoluisti*)—exactly analogous to the language of the Edict of Milan. Just as the nature of the occasion made it likely that the orator one way or another took Constantine's wishes into account in eliminating the names of the traditional deities, so too should his decision to replace them with these generalized terms reflect similar considerations. There is an alternative explanation, that the orator conformed to the new policy only grudgingly and drew the line when it came to uttering the name of Constantine's new god.[8] Implausible on its face, this argument becomes even weaker in light of what we shall see is a similar vagueness in Christian orators. Perhaps the safest thing to say for now is that, at a minimum, the orator of 313 must have been confident that Constantine would not resent his omission of specifically Christian terminology.

Far from being a stumbling block, the vague language of the Edict of Milan and the oration of 313 is one of the surest markers of Constantine's policy, for in conflict resolution, as in diplomacy, intentional vagueness is often the key to success. The language of both documents, therefore, may indicate a consensus over the shape of a new religious policy that, in turn, opens a new perspective on Constantine's vision.

'Instinctu Divinitatis'

Scholars have argued about Constantine's vision for generations. If the aim is to assess the purity of Constantine's faith, and in so doing either to acquit or to condemn the church for the benefits it received at his hands, then the reason for his conversion to Christianity—which is really what debate over the miracle aims to resolve—may be of some value. But often as not these works have argued over the miracle as if it were vital to understanding Constantine's policy and its implications, and for this aim the miracle is nothing less than a diversion, misstating the question and leading investigators off in the wrong direction. Such arguments seem to suggest that another person becoming emperor would not have faced the same problems or had the same need to reach accommodation with Christianity or that Constantine might not have devised a similar solution had he not been converted. This is certainly not the case. The Tetrarchs' systematic effort to resolve the issue had put Christianity on the agenda, and their failure to achieve a goal so visibly set did not mean the Christian problem no longer existed; if anything, there was more need than ever to resolve it. Christians had developed their own institutions, presided over by their own officials. These institutions were organized, however loosely, empirewide, and the bishops were experienced in both organizing opinion and administering resources. The persecutions—and even more the failure of those persecutions—showed conclusively that Christians could not be compelled to offer allegiance to any god but their own. The question now was, under what terms could Christian cooperation be secured?

Far more important than the miracle, under these circumstances, is the indication that in the course of his campaign against Maxentius Constantine had found a means to break the policy gridlock in which everything from his own need to confirm the legitimacy of his rule to the broader public issue of virtual civil war had become ensnared. Constantine remembered this campaign as an important turning point in his career, either because a brand new policy occurred to him (which is doubtful, given the continuities in his behavior) or because during this period he had a sudden insight into a way to achieve all his goals at once.[9] References closest in time to this campaign—the panegyric of 313 and the inscription on the Arch of Constantine—speak not of a miracle but of an *instinctu divinitatis*, the prompting of a god. Perhaps that is the best way for our age to understand this event. Describing politics in a much different venue, a veteran correspondent once wrote that "the vision of a simple idea . . . [is] enough to overcome the opposition of special interests."[10] A vision of flaming crosses and singing angels surely is not what this commentator had in mind. But if we take Constantine's "vision" in this sense for a moment, seeing it as a sudden inspiration for solving a vexing problem, then it would correspond to what in conflict resolution is called the "moment of insight," the point at which the "frustration, tension, and discomfort" created by failure of traditional mechanisms to resolve a problem are dissipated by looking at the problem in a different way and thereby seeing new paths to its resolution.[11]

What was this "simple idea"? It was the concept that a viable coalition could be forged by emphasizing the points of agreement between monotheists of whatever persuasion, a vision of a new kind of commonwealth in which stability, peace, and unity could be achieved by officially ignoring sectarian or theological differences—"small, trivial matters," as Constantine later would call them—and emphasizing the beneficent Providence of a single, Supreme Being, represented on earth by his chosen representative, the Roman emperor.[12] It was a vision that blended common features of Christian and pagan thought to create a polity in which Christians and pagans could participate on equal terms. This is modern terminology, used to help us understand the issue. But there is some indication that Constantine did not see the situation much differently. In later years, he consistently referred to these events as comparable to a "civil war," a cause of unnecessary suffering that brought evil both to the state and to those rulers who devised them. In an edict more or less introducing himself to the inhabitants of his newly acquired Eastern provinces after the defeat of Licinius in 324, Constantine said of the persecutors, "So violent did their malicious fury become, that in the midst of a profound peace, as regards both the religious and ordinary interests of man, they kindled, as it were, the flames of a civil war." It was "a lasting stain" on Rome, he wrote, a cause of "general sorrow," that Roman citizens had to take shelter from their own government with the barbarians.[13] In another edict written about the same time, he cited the persecution as the cause of "grievous wars and destructive devastations," leading in turn to "a scarcity of the common necessaries of life, and a crowd of consequent miseries."[14]

Public pronouncements by political figures are not necessarily the best gauge to their private thoughts, but they do at least indicate which sentiments they think will strike a positive chord in those who hear them. It is noteworthy, therefore, that Constantine stresses how unnecessary the persecution was, coming "in the midst of a profound peace," how it disrupted the course of ordinary life and stripped Rome of the moral superiority it felt over neighboring peoples. His comments also indicate the factors that were on his mind: first, that there was abundant evidence that the persecution was a failure; and second, that there was significant evidence that Christians and non-Christians could and would find common ground for accommodation. The outlines of this common ground also were clear: monotheism and unity. The persecution had served to remove the large amount of common ground that Christianity shared with traditional religion in late antiquity. Its failure had discredited pagans who saw Christians as enemies, and caused the coercive behavior they advocated to be identified with extremism. All that was needed was a leader who could bring the two sides together. A third factor also was present: Constantine was absolutely certain he was the right man for the job. This much political leaders in all ages seem to have in common.

To say this is not to say that Constantine himself was never converted or that he did not sincerely believe that Christianity was a superior path to personal salvation. But it is to say that Constantine's personal belief and imperial policy were not identical and that neither his belief nor his policy should be held to the arbitrary, one-dimensional standard of an inflexible, exclusive, and intolerant Christianity developed in an age of religious polemic to conduct sectarian warfare in the guise of scholarly dialogue. Constantine had both a religious goal and a political one and no reason to believe the one was incompatible with the other.

For all its religious significance, in other words, Constantine's conversion is a problem that lends itself to political analysis. From that standpoint, the question that needs to be asked now is not "Did Constantine become a Christian?" but "What kind of Christian did he become?" An even more pressing need is to account for the active role Constantine began to assume in Christian affairs and the powers he began to assign to Christian bishops. Traditionally, all these questions have been intermingled by the dramatic circumstances of his conversion, so that the answer to that question preempted the need even to ask the others. That is the cardinal error of Constantine scholarship, for a Christian emperor might just as naturally have decided that God's work was best left to God, and the bishops that imperial power, like all earthly temptation, was to be eschewed. That both thought otherwise is a matter of politics, not religion; its explanation lies in a series of assumptions all parties shared about the role of the emperor and in the routines both emperors and bishops had developed for resolving problems.

The Labarum

There may be a way to reconcile the political and religious readings of Constantine's vision. In all the controversy over this event, a small but important discrepancy is often ignored: although his vision was of the cross, it was not a cross that he adopted as the symbol of his divine tie but a monogram composed of the letters *chi* and *rho*, the first two letters of the Greek word Χριστός, or "Christ." Soon, this emblem was carried in front of Constantine's armies as part of a standard called the labarum (a name of uncertain origin). There is no doubt that this symbol was important to Constantine: it appears on his helmet on a coin issued in 315, and it was used increasingly throughout his reign; eventually, it became a major symbol both for the church and the Christian empire.[15] More careful attention to the nature of this emblem can help us understand the role the miracle played in the development of Constantine's policy. Eusebius describes it as "a long spear overlaid with gold" which formed a cross by means of "a transverse bar laid over it." At the top was the Chi-Rho: "a wreath of gold and precious stones; and within this, the symbol of the Saviour's name, two letters indicating the name of Christ by means of its initial characters, the letter P being intersected by X in its centre: and these letters the emperor was in the habit of wearing on his helmet at a later period."[16] Although he included this description of the labarum with his account of the miracle in 312, Eusebius obviously was describing a version as it existed many years later, because his account includes portraits of Constantine's sons as Caesars hanging from the crossbar, and these sons were not even born in 312, much less elevated to the rank of Caesar. It is clear, moreover, that most of what Eusebius described was a familiar item, the vexillum, the standard that legions had carried into battle for centuries. The Chi-Rho was the novelty; its addition to the top of the standard was what turned the vexillum into the labarum.

Lactantius's account of Constantine's conversion, as we saw in the preceding chapter, is both earlier and briefer than Eusebius's. Here it is in J. L. Creed's English translation: "Constantine was advised in a dream to mark the heavenly sign of God on the shields of his soldiers and then engage in battle. He did as he was commanded and by means of a slanted letter X with the top of its head bent round, he marked Christ on their shields."[17] It is noteworthy that Lactantius does not describe a cross but something else. What that something else was has been a matter of some controversy, primarily because of the awkwardness of Lactantius's prose at this point: *transversa X littera, summo capite circumflexo.* The problem is with *transversa,* an adjective whose common meaning is "intersected." To take it in that sense here would require an emendation of some sort, since "the letter X intersected" makes no sense. Creed reads *transversa* as "slanted"; if, in that sense, Lactantius meant something like "tipped over," or "tipped on its side," then he would be describing the Staurogram, ⳨, a cross with a hooked top which was sometimes used as a monogram for the cross by early Christians. This is the best sense that can be made of the existing text and is thus the most conservative reading. But it is not without problems. For one thing, Lactantius calls the symbol he describes a sign of Christ, which would suggest a monogram for Christ's name, a Chi-Rho, rather than a monogram for the cross, as the Staurogram would be. The simplest explanation may be that Lactantius was not as concerned about carefully describing the object as he was to be as clear and explicit as possible about its meaning.

The problem is not simply philological, for the Staurogram is not the sign that came to be associated with Constantine's vision or which is depicted on his helmet in the earliest-known coin representation; this is the Chi-Rho, ⚚, the monogram of Christ's name. No suitable explanation for this change has ever been given, and if the circumstances of stress and doubt under which Constantine received his sign are anything like what they have traditionally been taken to be, then it is difficult to imagine what conditions might have induced him to tamper with a talisman that had proved its potency in such singular fashion. It may be that Lactantius's awkward language simply means that he was not too sure of what he was describing, that he had not yet himself seen the talisman; but he was sure of its significance to Christians. The difference is more than academic, for unlike the Staurogram, which had been used by Christians, the Chi-Rho sign was a novelty, with no long association to Christian belief. Perhaps this was the reason Lactantius felt obliged to make its Christian meaning clear to his readers. With slight alteration, the words he uses also describe the solar disk, an emblem of sun worship from Constantine's Danubian homeland, usually depicted as it rose over mountains schematically represented by something like an *X*: ⚚. In any case, it would appear that throughout Constantine's reign the Chi-Rho was understood more as a dynastic symbol, a sign for himself and his house, than as a religious proclamation.[18]

There is another point in Eusebius's account of the vision which is easily overlooked: even after the experience, Constantine "doubted within himself what the import of this apparition could be," and only subsequently, when Christ appeared to him in a dream, did he understand that "a likeness of that sign which he had seen in the heavens" would protect him from all his enemies. Sending "for those who were acquainted with the mysteries of His doctrines," Eusebius continues, Constantine asked who the god was which he had seen and what the sign signified. Only then did he learn about the Advent and Incarnation of the Only Son of the Only God, and that the sign was both "the symbol of immortality" and "the trophy of that victory over death which He had gained." Upon hearing this explanation, Constantine compared "the heavenly vision with the interpretation given" and "found his judgment confirmed." He was persuaded that "the knowledge of these things had been imparted to him by Divine teaching" and decided to commit himself to the study of this faith.[19]

Eusebius's full report produces a more nuanced understanding of Constantine's vision experience than occurs when only reading the part of his account pertaining to the vision itself. The full passage supports a gradualist view of Constantine's conversion, with instruction and reflection deepening his experience, over the idea of a sudden, blinding change. More pertinent, what these words suggest is that, at least initially, Constantine himself was not sure what the new sign signified. By the time he told the story to Eusebius, Constantine had had many years to ponder this experience and to refract it through the lens of the Christian community. If initial doubt can still be detected in a story that had gone through such a filtering process, then it is not unreasonable to conclude that at the time its novelty and ambiguous meaning were no less pronounced, and to suggest that the very ambiguity of the sign is what makes it the key.

The significance of the labarum, then, lies in its ambiguity. Like so much else that Constantine did in these years, it could mean many things to many people. Was this the "divine inspiration"—a symbol that could resolve divisions between right-thinking people which had unnecessarily traumatized the empire and jeopardized its unity?

Shared Vocabulary

In the labarum, Constantine's belief and his policy come together. The safest conclusion to draw from the different interpretations of his sign is that it was a sign capable of more than one meaning. It is a small step from this conclusion to another: that the ambiguity was intentional. The polemical roots of Constantine scholarship explain why so simple a step has been so hard to take. To speak of ambiguity when the definition of good Christian behavior required Constantine's stance to be unflinchingly definite, his conversion to be immediate and complete, was to taint the first Christian emperor with goals that were incompatible with sincere belief. But, as we have seen, the Christian movement itself had internal ambiguities, and these ambiguities were a critical component of its success as a movement. As political behavior,

Constantine's resort to ambiguity is absolutely unimpeachable. It need not have been as conscious as described here, of course, but the choice of a symbol that was capable of bringing together a number of disparate groups to achieve the larger goal of imperial unity and stability was a shrewd and statesmanlike move. It has nothing to do with the sincerity of Constantine's Christianity, but it is a sure sign of the accuracy of his political instincts.

Galerius had tried one way of defining Rome to include the Christian god by offering a system that was more or less "separate but equal," with Christians praying to their god in their way but on Rome's behalf. Constantine now tried another way, a definition of Christianity which would include a broader array of Roman beliefs. Was it realistic to think that Christians and pagans could unite behind a common goal of a divinely favored, monotheistic empire? Constantine's policy makes more sense once we consider the full terrain of Christian-pagan relations. At either extreme were Christians and pagans who defined themselves just as we define them today (using, by no coincidence, their own writings to do so). Between these two extremes were varying degrees of Christians and pagans largely lost to the historical record who mingled comfortably on a middle ground of familiar images and terms. Constantine's "inspiration" was to see this ground as the basis for a new consensus around which the Roman state could coalesce. It meant removing those practices that traditionally had kept Christians from participating in public life, the most important of which was the offering of sacrifice. Newer research indicates that this process already was well under way as a result of economic and social changes unrelated to his conversion, making the task easier than it otherwise might appear.[20] All Constantine's program required was a willingness to limit public discourse to broad points of agreement—that there was a Supreme Being, a Creator God, a Savior who cared for the Roman empire and who worked both to choose and to protect its emperor—while leaving more specific definitions of this deity and the means of his worship to the private sphere. If he had found his own way to Christ through this territory, then there was all the more reason for him to believe that others would, too.

Such hopes were not unrealistic. The interaction between pagans and Christians, most easily recovered by examining the writings of

Christian apologists, resulted in mutual influences, a shared vocabulary, and a shared iconography. But it is important to realize that this shared environment was not due exclusively, or even primarily, to the apologists. Much, if not most, was simply the result of living in a common setting, being exposed to the same orientation and way of life. In an insightful study of early Christianity, Ramsay MacMullen captured this aspect of the conversion process in a memorable phrase, referring to the general instinct "when obliged to admit some urgent novelty," such as a new faith, "to make the least possible tear in the fabric of already held beliefs." These are not the converts of the textbook and the academy, intellectuals who need to understand, in Saint Paul's words, "what is the breadth and length and height and depth" of their actions. They are the people who Alan Wardman identified in an equally insightful book as "the church of the multitude," Christians "with the habit of compromise." We can glimpse them still in such survivals as the Christus-Helios mosaic already encountered in Chapter 4 (see figs. 1 and 2).[21] Here, a person identifiable as Christ stands at the reins of a four-horse chariot—the traditional vehicle driven by the sun god—superimposed over rays of light in the form of a cross. Elsewhere, Christ appears in the floor mosaic of a private house in the guise of Orpheus, charming the beasts with his lyre, and Mary in a pose reminiscent of Isis suckling the infant Horus.[22] Such similarities bring out something that is easily forgotten in an age in which the Chi-Rho automatically appears as a Christian symbol, which is that this sign, and many other symbols that now have an exclusively Christian connotation, such as the Nikes or "Winged Victories" on the Arch of Constantine which viewers now take to be angels, were then part of a much larger vocabulary and iconography that both Christians and pagans shared.

This shared vocabulary, rather than mere awkwardness in adapting to Constantine's new Christian belief, is what seems to lie behind the phrases of the orator who addressed the emperor in 313. In all the debate over the extent to which the pagan orators in the Latin panegyrics reflected Constantine's own beliefs or compromised their own in order to satisfy his Christian sympathies, a simple and obvious point has been forgotten: evidently, these panegyrists had little difficulty conforming to such a plan. The changes show how ready pagans were to collaborate in his program.

But, at least according to one prominent view, pagans were not the problem. It was Christians who, in the aftermath of the sudden reversal brought about by Constantine's conversion, were governed by "a mood of resentment and vengeance."[23] To such scholars, it may seem that the opposite view presented in these pages has been too theoretical, too general, to counter such a well-entrenched judgment. Is there any hard evidence that at least some Christians were equally willing to compromise for the sake of Constantine's greater good? One extensive piece of evidence survives in the lectures on Christian government which Constantine had been hearing from none other than Lactantius, the Christian author of On the Deaths of the Persecutors. These lectures Lactantius subsequently published as *The Divine Institutes*. Unlike his pamphlet on the persecutors, a quick and tendentious rereading of three centuries of Roman-Christian history, *The Divine Institutes* is Lactantius's masterwork, an ambitious attempt in seven books to provide a Christian analogue to the "institutes" that Romans wrote for the study of law and government. This is the work that gained for Lactantius the title of the "Christian Cicero," and his debt to Cicero and Vergil, as well as other luminaries of Rome's Golden Age, is evident on practically every page.[24]

A rhetorician of some note, Lactantius had been recruited by Diocletian for the chair of Latin rhetoric in Nicomedia prior to the outbreak of the Great Persecution. His situation there soon became untenable, and his whereabouts for the next several years are a mystery. Eventually, he came into Constantine's orbit and became tutor to the emperor's son Crispus.[25] He dedicated a new edition of *The Divine Institutes* to Constantine, "the first of the Roman princes to have repudiated errors and to have come to know and honor the majesty of the one true God."[26] Standard studies place this dedication, and Lactantius's relationship with Constantine, quite late, well after publication of On the Deaths of the Persecutors in 315, but there is now good reason to believe that he was at Constantine's court and delivering the substance of *The Divine Institutes* in the traditional form of oral presentation, even before the decisive Battle of the Milvian Bridge.[27]

More important here than the precise date is the tenor of *The Divine Institutes,* which differs sharply from that of On the Deaths of the Persecutors. Where that work focused on conflict between Christians and pagans and exulted in signs of God's vengeance on those who would oppress his people, *The Divine Institutes* reaches out to non-Christians in a typically apologetic search for common ground. The first three books give an argument for monotheism and the search for true wisdom, and only in the fourth book does the discussion turn specifically to Christ and his mission, which Lactantius describes as finally making possible the dream of a state built on true justice, the topic of book V. Only after this lengthy foundation does Lactantius discuss, in the final two books, the way to a Christian life and his picture of the Last Days.

Unlike earlier apologists, Lactantius specifically targeted the traditional Roman intelligentsia, to the point of criticizing his predecessors for failing to take into account the criteria of this class, especially the value they placed on style and reasoned argument. "This reason is one of the first why the wise and learned people and the princes of this world do not place any sacred trust in the Scriptures; the fact that the prophets spoke the common and simple speech, as though they were speaking to the people," he observed. "So they are despised by those who wish to hear nothing or read nothing except what is polished and eloquent."[28] Not only does Lactantius lard his pages with references to familiar authors of the classical curriculum and draw on the pagans' own philosophers and seers in support of Christian doctrine, but, even more important, he stretches his definition of Christian belief to the point where it would at least be congenial to those who had taken the first step toward true belief, which he defined as recognition that there is only one Highest God (*Summus Deus*). In Lactantius's view, as Elizabeth Digeser has concluded, conversion "is not a sudden change or transformation, but a series of steps toward enlightenment, a view that allows Lactantius to see the whole population as falling somewhere along the path to truth, i.e., toward becoming a Christian."[29]

Because of the importance of this particular class of pagans to his design, the way Lactantius uses the persecution to illustrate his point that the polytheistic state was unjust is highly significant. Comparing the martyrs to Romans who, in the glory days of the republic, had sacrificed their lives for the good of the state, he hammers away at the point that now it was Christians who were upholding the commitment to justice and duty which had made Rome great. "Robbers and men of robust strength cannot endure lacerations of this sort," he writes, continuing,

> But among us—and I will not speak of the men—children even and frail women silently vanquish their torturers, nor was fire able to extract a groan from them. Let the Romans go and glory in a Mucius or a Regulus. The one handed himself over to the enemy to be killed because he was ashamed to live as a captive. The other, seized by the enemy, when he saw that he could not avoid death put his hand into the fire to satisfy for his crime to the enemy whom he wished to kill, and he gained thereby the pardon which he had not merited. Lo, the weak sex and fragile age suffer laceration of the whole body and burning, not of necessity, because they could avoid it if they wished, but of will, because they trust in God.[30]

It is no coincidence that these are the pages in which Lactantius provides the evidence for pagan revulsion at the excesses of the persecution, discussed in the previous chapter. In the context of his overall purpose to attract a sympathetic hearing for Christianity from educated pagans, and his specific purpose in book V to argue the superiority of Christian justice, it is obvious that the reason Lactantius dwelled so much on the brutalities of the persecution at this point cannot merely have been to give vent to a smoldering hatred for the pagan "enemy." Rather, it was to solidify the bond he wanted to forge between his faith and those pagans who were both shocked and humiliated by the patent injustice with which the champions of their own traditions had behaved. Lactantius did not need Elmer Schattschneider's advice; his eyes were firmly fixed on the crowd.[31]

Lactantius was relentless in his efforts to show educated pagans that the persecution was a violation of their own highly cherished rules, according to which victory on the field of ideas could only be won by eloquence and reasoned argument. A century and a half earlier, the pagan Celsus had berated Christians precisely with this point, mocking their unwillingness to engage in debate with their betters:

> Their injunctions are like this. "Let no one educated, no one wise, no one sensible draw near. For these abilities are thought by us to be evils. But as

for anyone ignorant, anyone stupid, anyone uneducated, anyone who is a child, let him come boldly." By the fact that they themselves admit that these people are worthy of their God, they show that they want and are able to convince only the foolish, dishonourable and stupid, and only slaves, women, and little children.[32]

Now it was Lactantius's turn to attack. Why is it, he asks, that "the right of defending themselves is given to sacrilegious persons, and to traitors and sorcerers," but not to Christians? The answer is obvious: "they fear lest they should be overcome by us, and be compelled at length to yield, truth itself crying out." Their use of coercion, he continues, means that "they themselves plainly show their distrust in their own abandoned system, since they neither venture to investigate, nor to engage with us, because they know that they are easily overpowered. And therefore, discussion being taken away, 'Wisdom is driven from among them, they have recourse to violence,' as Ennius says." These are the men, Lactantius writes, with whom he now seeks to debate, men "who would more readily drink blood than imbibe the words of the righteous."

Lactantius's strategy was risky. His aim clearly was to make non-Christian listeners so uncomfortable that they would feel no wish to be associated with so patently cruel and unjust a policy, much less defend it. But having painted such a bloody picture of the opposition, he risked alienating the moderate pagans he wanted to reach by making them feel unjustly accused. Thus he quickly followed these stinging words with an appealing concession: "But we must not lose hope. Perhaps 'we do not sing to deaf ears.' For things are not in such a bad condition that sane minds are lacking which delight in the truth and which see and follow the way pointed out to them as the right one."[33] With his audience thus prepared, Lactantius laid down a direct challenge. "Let them invite us to the assembly," he declares. "Let them urge the acceptance of the cults of their gods; let them persuade that there are many by whose power and providence all things are ruled." It was a loaded challenge, for Lactantius added an important qualifier: "Let them confirm all these points, not by their own personal assertion, for the authority of mortal man avails nothing, but by some divine testimony, just as we do." In other words, the debate that he proposed would be based on Scripture, not reason. Celsus would have scoffed at such a proviso. But the late empire was a different place, one that put great weight on written texts, the older the better; one that sent pagan intellectuals scrambling for their own holy texts to hold up alongside those of the Christians.[34] Although Lactantius's condition put the debate he proposed on comfortable ground for a Christian, it would no longer have seemed an unreasonable one for him to make.

More significant than the condition he demanded is the reason Lactantius gave for the debate to be held in the first place. The reason, Lactantius explained in disarmingly simple prose, was that true belief cannot be coerced. "There is no occasion for violence and injury," he claimed, "for religion cannot be imposed by force; the matter must be carried on by words rather than by blows, that the will may be affected."[35] His was a clear-cut statement of the principle of religious toleration. Digging deep into the wellsprings of Christian thought, Lactantius here developed a case for toleration of other beliefs which puts the lie to modern assumptions about the roots of Christian intolerance.[36] He did so, moreover, in a way designed to drive a wedge between educated pagans and the leaders of the persecution, claiming for Christianity the commitment to rational exposition which had been the hallmark of classical thought. "Let them imitate us, that they may expose the plan of the whole matter," Lactantius demanded, "for we do not entice that they may object to it, but we teach, we prove, we explain." For this reason, he added in a final dig at the coercive practices of the Tetrarchs, "no one is retained by us against his will—for he is useless to God who is without devotion and faith."[37] The turnabout is a sign of just how much moral high ground paganism had lost as a result of Diocletian's persecution.

As the Edict of Milan shows, these were words that Constantine was ready to hear. It is a premise of that document that the right way to ensure proper reverence was not to compel allegiance, as the persecution had done, but to "grant both to Christians and to all men freedom to follow whatever religion each one wished," and that the religion of the supreme divinity was one to be followed "with free minds."[38] The principle that true belief must be freely held became a key part of the

211

Constantinian program. But even before the meeting at Milan took place, events had been set in motion which would test Constantine's commitment to this principle.

The Donatist Schism

When Constantine entered Rome, he may have had a policy, but it is unlikely that he had specific plans for how to implement it. His immediate needs would have been to mend fences with Maxentius's partisans—the senatorial leadership and, possibly, the Christians of Rome, for if, as the reading above suggests, Maxentius only became thought of as a persecutor in later years as a by-product of his alliance with Maximin Daza, then this group had no immediate reason to greet Constantine as a liberator. Still, they would not have been ignorant of his father's relatively mild policy toward their brethren in Gaul, which stood in sharp contrast to that of Maxentius's father; presumably, they also would have known that Constantine had continued, and even expanded, those policies during his years in Gaul. So Christian support, while not the given it became in later tradition, was certainly Constantine's for the asking, so long as he did nothing to alienate the community in Rome and Italy. While it was clear to Constantine that Christians were not to be excluded from any new coalition, the terms on which they were to be included had yet to be worked out. For the Christians, there were as many uncertainties. An emperor of their own faith was an entirely new phenomenon. Whatever rules might have applied to ordinary converts, we can safely assume, did not apply to him. Accommodation was necessary while Constantine adjusted to his new role, and his various Christian constituencies got used to the idea of having a new, and very powerful, player on their board. The years 312–25, thus, were pivotal for working out the means by which the emperor would be involved in Christian decision making.

While in this unsettled stage, Constantine was called upon to resolve a dispute between the Christians of North Africa. Since this schism demanded Constantine's attention at just the time when he seized control of Rome, and because it is the first interaction for which any significant documentation survives, it has received abundant scholarly attention.[39] The problems raised by this dispute led to a number of decisive modifications in imperial procedures; at the same time, they plunged Constantine into the middle of ecclesiastical politics earlier than might otherwise have been the case and forced him to make choices that have much to say about the type of Christianity he was prepared to support. In this sense, it inaugurated the whole trail of events which brought Constantine and the bishops together in Constantinople a quarter century later, in the confrontation with which this book began. As we will see in Chapter 11, it was also an issue that triggered Christian rethinking about the use of coercion to compel belief, and thus it pertains directly to the understanding of Christian intolerance. For all these reasons, then, this dispute can serve as a case study of Constantine's Christian policy.

The controversy came to be named after Donatus, who assumed leadership of the breakaway church in Carthage right around this time, and it would consume the African church in debate and disorder for a century and more. Donatus was the type of rebel who is every ruler's worst nightmare: charismatic, eloquent, tireless, and utterly convinced of the justice of his cause. Decades later, when Constantine's son and successor made a clumsy attempt to buy a solution to the controversy, Donatus replied with a bitter question that soon became a battle cry, "What has the Church to do with the emperor?"[40] Ostensibly, the dispute was over clergy who had surrendered copies of Scripture and sacred vessels to Roman officials during the persecution, thereby becoming *traditores* (handers-over), root of the English word *traitor*. But more obviously was involved, since both sides agreed that clergy who had so acted were thereby disqualified from office, and even subsequent proof that some of the movement's most vocal leaders had themselves been *traditores* failed to dampen enthusiasm for the cause, or even to prevent the faithful from revering as martyrs some of the men so disgraced.

The controversy extended to the actions of the tainted clergy— were these valid? Were clergy consecrated and sacraments performed by such individuals legitimate? Who besides the offending parties had to be expelled in order to maintain the purity of the body? Tainted bishops had consecrated others, for instance, and clergy had administered sacraments that, in Donatist eyes, were invalid. Following precedent in the African church, the Donatists argued that rebaptism was the only solution; their opponents held that churches elsewhere only recognized one baptism and that in any case the option of rebaptism was not open for deceased Christians who had received last rites from compromised clergy. Why should blameless lambs suffer eternal damnation for alleged sins of their pastors? Beneath the charges and countercharges with which the record is larded there seems to lie the conflict between rigor and forgiveness which always lurks just beneath the surface in Christian communities. On this level, Donatism was but another manifestation of the perennial Christian need to reconcile the sanctity of the clerical office with the personal quality of individual clergy. At its deepest level, the Donatist controversy was a fight over the soul and substance of the church, a renewal of the ongoing battle between the beacon and the ark, the church of the elect and the church of the masses.

At least initially, personality conflict fed the flames. Caecilian had been a deacon at Carthage during the persecution, and in that capacity he had taken steps that his opponents interpreted as interfering with attempts by members of his congregation to bring food to other Christians imprisoned by the authorities. He had also offended a wealthy parishioner by forbidding her from fondling relics of her favorite martyr in church. Many reasonable explanations can be given for Caecilian's actions, but all would miss the point. In the North African church, martyrs had always been revered even more than elsewhere, and even one of these charges by itself was enough to ruin a cleric's career. When Caecilian became bishop of Carthage, around 311, with a hasty consecration that prevented bishops from neighboring Numidia (modern Algeria), where Donatist sentiment was strongest, from exercising their traditional rights to participate, his enemies exploded. Instead of taking steps to defuse the situation, Caecilian coolly informed the furious Numidians that they could exercise their rights by confirming his appointment after the fact.

All this happened before Constantine seized control of Rome. His earliest-known response to the issues raised by this controversy is contained in a letter he sent after that victory to Anulinus, the proconsular governor of the province of Africa (roughly, modern Tunisia). In it, Constantine instructed Anulinus to restore property to "the Catholic Church of the Christians" which was now in the possession of others. A date on the letter would answer many crucial questions. It would, for instance, give us a sense of how to read his reference to "the Catholic Church of the Christians." Was this, as it sounds, an awkwardly innocent reference by someone newly introduced to the way Christians generally defined themselves? If so, then his instruction would have been a simple order to restore property seized in the persecution. But if it was something more, a specific phrase, it would suggest that Constantine already knew about, and had taken sides in, the controversy, ordering Donatist churches to be turned over to their Catholic rivals.[41]

There is a significant sentiment in favor of the conclusion that Constantine wrote this letter even before the meeting in Milan. But whether or not he had yet identified Christianity as a vital personal interest at the time he wrote it, this letter shows Constantine engaged in a set of difficult issues that would force him to choose among the different factions of Christians which now competed for his attention. What criteria would he use to support one Christian group and oppose another? And what means would he employ to make and enforce such decisions? From the standpoint of policy, these are the relevant questions. They are critical to determining what kind of Christian he had become. Since nothing promotes record keeping like sheer visceral hatred—especially when, as in this case, property is involved—we are unusually well informed about the progress of this case and can extract, as a result, some of the factors that influenced the course of events and criteria that Constantine used in choosing the side to support.

If it is questionable whether Constantine had taken sides when he first wrote Anulinus, two other letters included by Eusebius in the Church History leave no doubt at all that he subsequently did so. One of these letters went to Caecilian to inform him that three thousand *folles* had been allocated to him for support of Catholic clergy in Africa, Numidia, and Mauretania and that more was available if he needed it.[42] The other went to Anulinus, instructing him to exempt clergy "in the Catholic church over which Caecilian preside[d]" from all public obligations.[43] These were enormous concessions: one *follis* could feed a person for an entire year.[44] The exemptions were, if anything, even more generous, since they freed clergy not only from all taxes but also from the burdens of liturgies and service on town councils.

Together, these decisions represent Constantine's first attempt to resolve the Donatist problem. They have been carefully vetted for evidence of his new faith, but what may be more significant is the utterly traditional reasoning they reveal. In his second letter to Anulinus, for instance, Constantine justifies exempting Caecilian's clergy from public duties on the grounds that "when they show greatest reverence to the Deity, the greatest benefits accrue to the state." Indeed, he begins the letter by observing that "when that religion is despised, in which is preserved the chief reverence for the most holy celestial Power, great dangers are brought upon public affairs; but that when legally adopted and observed it affords the most signal prosperity to the Roman name and remarkable felicity to all the affairs of men, through the divine beneficence."[45] Although the religion now is Christianity, the premise that proper regard for religion was vital to the security of the state is exactly the same as the one Galerius gave two years earlier to justify Diocletian's persecution. There is another way in which Constantine's thinking was completely traditional: his gift to Caecilian of three thousand *folles* followed a principle as old as Xenophon's Cyrus, showing which side had won his favor by conferring on it marks of signal favor. Thus, the novelty in these letters is not what Constantine did but for whom he did it. The distinction will be worth remembering.

Donatus's famous complaint can be misleading. As their Catholic adversaries never tired of reminding them, it was the Donatists who first appealed to the emperor, and no issues of conscience at this junction seem to have prevented them from doing so again. In April 313, Anulinus forwarded to Constantine two petitions that had been brought by "a crowd of people" who begged him to transmit them to the emperor. One of the petitions, sealed in leather, contained charges against Caecilian; the other asked the emperor to provide judges from Gaul, where, thanks to his father's refusal to implement the persecution, clergy were "immune from this outrage."[46] The Donatist appeal is not difficult to understand, for at that point they had little choice and nothing to lose. Although it was effective in the blame game to taint the Donatists' appeal as an attempt to involve the emperor in the affairs of the church, the charge is not a little misleading, since the emperor already had gotten involved before they chose to appeal. They appealed because they had already lost the battle in Carthage and therefore needed to widen the conflict to even the balance.[47] Moreover, as the terms of their petition make clear, they were not thinking of Constantine as a Christian when they appealed to him but as an emperor. It was easy to blur this distinction in later years, when the complications created for the independence of church governance by having an emperor who was a Christian were more evident than they were in 313. At this time, Christians, like everybody else, thought of the emperor as the ultimate source of justice. Moreover, there was precedent for Christians to appeal for the emperor's help in resolving church disputes. Almost half a century earlier, the bishops of the Middle East had appealed to the emperor Aurelian for help in driving Paul of Samosata from the church buildings of Antioch after they had deposed him from office.[48]

With their appeal, the Donatists hit the jackpot. The duty to provide justice to his subjects was one that, as we shall see in Chapter 9, Constantine took with the utmost seriousness and one that he wrestled with for his entire career. In a letter written to the vicar of Africa at a later stage in this dispute, Constantine revealed just how great a role this obligation played in his thinking. "What else could I do," he asked, "given my principles and the duty of emperor itself?"[49] The isolation in which late Roman emperors were enveloped also helped the Donatist cause. Emperors knew that the layers of ceremony which protected them from assassins also made them dependent for information on others whose loyalties or interests might lead them to shade or conceal the truth. This was a particular concern of Constantine's. A panegyrist who celebrated the imperial anniversary in 321 contrasted Constantine's efforts to be open and accessible with the secrecy and aloofness of his predecessors, and several surviving laws testify to his frustration with the reports of his subordinates.[50] In choosing to give support to Caecilian's party, Constantine appears to have relied on advice from Bishop Ossius of Corduba, for his offer of state resources to Caecilian refers to a list carried by Ossius which Caecilian was to use for distributing the new funding. Now, in accusing Caecilian of wrongdoing, the Donatists were also raising doubts in Constantine's mind about the reliability of Ossius's findings.[51]

The appeal was a political hot potato. Constantine could not ignore it, if for no other reason than the potential threat the conflict posed to the peace of the North African province. Neither, however, could he afford to ignore the sentiment of Christians in Rome. Even if there were not bruised feelings over Maxentius, the bishop of the capital city enjoyed formidable assets—prestige, proximity, access, and familiarity—and Bishop Miltiades was an ally of Ossius. He had to tread carefully.

No more than a month or two after receiving their petitions, Constantine gave the Donatists everything they requested. He wrote Miltiades, informing him that he had summoned Caecilian along with ten supporters of his choice and an equal number of accusers to Rome, to be judged by Miltiades and a panel of three bishops Constantine was sending from Gaul.[52] In writing Miltiades, Constantine appears, like the Donatists, to have followed precedent, for in the earlier case Aurelian had likewise delegated the decision to "the bishops of Rome and Italy."[53] But Constantine went significantly beyond precedent in selecting the bishops from Gaul who would sit with Miltiades. The significance of this initiative should not be overlooked. The three bishops named by Constantine were from Arles, Cologne, and Autun—cities to which Constantine was a frequent visitor during the previous decade. Whatever his personal religious sentiments during those years, it is inconceivable that he would not have established relations with the leaders of such important communities. Constantine had seen to it that a majority of the group that would hear the Donatist case would be composed of bishops he knew and whose judgment he presumably trusted.

There is no telling how the Donatist controversy might have played out had Miltiades simply followed Constantine's script. But bishops of Rome always took great care to protect their claim to a unique status in the church as the heirs to both Peter and Paul, the former of whom had been vested with special authority by Jesus himself, and Miltiades was no exception. Unable, or unwilling, directly to jeopardize his relationship with the new ruler of Rome, Miltiades was equally unwilling to preside over a council of whose outcome he could not be certain. When the council opened in October, an additional fifteen bishops were present, all from Italy, all of his own choosing. Miltiades took further steps to control the outcome, opting to follow the strict rules of evidence and argument as laid down for Roman civil proceedings. This decision evidently caught the Donatists flat-footed. Expecting the looser rules of an arbitration process, they found themselves instead expected to mount a full-fledged court case. Prevented from offering any but the narrowest outlines of their charges, the Donatists quit the meeting in disgust, and Miltiades declared Caecilian innocent by default.[54]

Strictly, Miltiades was within his rights. Consultation presumably took place before Constantine dispatched his letter to Miltiades, for the bishop had won some important concessions. The hearing, Constantine wrote, was to take place "as you may understand to be in accordance with the most holy law," adding that Miltiades could "consider in what way the above-mentioned case may be most accurately investigated and justly decided."[55] Presumably, had he been challenged, Miltiades could have pointed to the same precedent of Aurelian which governed the Donatist appeal and Constantine's decision to refer the matter to him, for Aurelian's ruling had specified the bishops of Italy as well as Rome. It is impossible with such a remove of time and with evidence so tainted by partisanship to know how much leeway Constantine thought he was granting with these instructions, but it would be a mistake to assume that he concurred in, or even knew about, the changes that Miltiades adopted. In the fall of 313, Constantine was far to the north in Trier and may even have been visiting Britain when the council was held.[56] What can be said for certain is that when the Donatists again turned to the emperor in the aftermath of this fiasco, they found him receptive. Constantine responded by summoning a new council that would be made up of bishops from all the provinces under his rule, to meet not in Rome but in Gaul. Either by chance or design, the bishop of Rome was not present at this council. Neither was Ossius of Corduba.[57]

The council that opened in Arles on August 1, 314, was a major departure. Not only did Constantine take the initiative in summoning the council himself, but he also gave the bishops access to the public post—a highly prized perquisite because of the relative comfort and efficiency of this service compared with the normal means of travel; it signaled the elevated status of Christian leaders in the new regime, as well as the benefits that could flow from imperial favor. The meeting was a milestone in the development of church organization as well, for it was the first to include representatives from all the provinces of the Western empire. With changes so many and so profound, it is understandable if one other offshoot of this council often fails to get the attention it deserves. By listening to the Donatist appeal and summoning this council, Constantine effectively nullified, or at least ignored, the decision of the Council of Rome.

Despite its somber implications, Constantine's unilateral decision does not receive much attention because the Council of Arles unanimously confirmed the decision of the Rome council, and Constantine showed no anger when it did so. To the contrary, when the Donatists appealed yet again, it was they whom Constantine blamed, in a letter to the Catholic bishops subsequent to the Council of Arles which is justly famous for what it reveals about his intentions. "They demand my judgment," Constantine wrote, "when I myself await the judgment of Christ. For I tell you, as is the truth, that the judgment of the priests should be regarded as if God himself were in the judge's seat. For these have no power either to think or to judge except as they are instructed by Christ's teaching."[58] The letter says much about Constantine's intentions but little about his actions, for despite the eloquence of these heartfelt protests, Constantine once again gave in to the Donatist demands and agreed to hear their case personally. Dismissing the bishops from Arles, he ordered both Caecilian and his accusers to his court, where they attended his pleasure for the better part of a year. In the spring of 315, Constantine returned to Rome, and the pace of events quickened. First, the Donatist bishops were given permission to return home, only to have that permission revoked within a matter of days. The cause for the sudden about-face evidently was that, in the interim, Constantine had received the findings of an inquiry he had ordered in North Africa which not only exonerated Caecilian of a major charge but also produced a confession from one of his accusers that he had forged the incriminating document. Triumphantly, Constantine ordered the guilty party to Rome and confidently told the Donatists that he would find in their favor if they could prove even one of their charges against Caecilian. Caecilian knew either too little or too much about these events; before the hearing could be held, he slipped away from Rome and returned to Carthage. The Donatists soon followed.

Amid reports of widespread rioting in the province, Constantine wrote the vicar Celsus that he intended to come to Africa himself and show all sides just how swift imperial justice could be. He never came.[59] The Donatist issue dragged on. His patience at an end, Constantine for a time unleashed the coercive machinery of the state against a group that he now characterized as false Christians, agents of the devil, stubborn militants. In his anger, he even sought to close off Donatists from the reward of martyrdom, as if he, as emperor, had the right to decide what was true and what was false martyrdom.[60] This was a claim that the bishops had advanced, with some success, a century earlier, but Constantine's gambit was premature. After exhausting every traditional means of bringing an unruly constituency into line, Constantine wrote to the bishops of Africa that the only thing left to do was to "cultivate patience" and wait "until the heavenly medicine manifests itself," ending his letter with a categorical denial of coercion, "Let nothing be done to reciprocate an injury; for it is a fool who would usurp the vengeance which we ought to reserve to God."[61] It is all too easy to say that Constantine wrote out of desperation, rather than conviction, at a time when he was about to launch a decisive offensive against Licinius for control of the East. But almost ten years later, at a time when he had been in sole control of the empire for several years, and when according to conventional wisdom he had entered the most unrestrainedly Christian phase of his rule, he wrote in the same vein to the bishops in Numidia, while promising to build a new basilica for one that had been seized by the Donatists: "Indeed it is by this that the judgment of God appears manifestly more great and righteous, that he bears them [Donatists] with equanimity and condemns by his patience, enduring all the things that come from them. God indeed promises to be the avenger of all; and thus when vengeance is left to God a harsher penalty is exacted from one's enemies."[62] It may well be that Constantine was motivated by expediency, that he was merely putting the best face on an embarrassing demonstration of the actual limits of imperial power. But even so, it remains significant that the face he chose was that of Christian love and endurance, that the principle he chose was one compatible with the Edict of Milan. It is just conceivable that in the course of the Donatist conflict he had grown to appreciate the importance of that principle.

The Christian Establishment

Evidence for Constantine's continued commitment to the principle of noncoercion comes from the last months of the reign. On July 25, 335, Constantine opened a year-long celebration of his thirtieth jubilee. As part of the closing ceremonies a year later, Bishop Eusebius of Caesarea delivered an oration that he saw fit to append to the *vita Constantini* that he published after Constantine's death in 337. The speech has been called an aggressive appropriation of traditional themes by a newly confident Christianity,[63] and in a way it was: Eusebius was a much more complex figure than Lactantius, as we will see in Chapter 10. But what is striking about the speech at this moment is the number of Constantinian themes crammed into its pages. Eusebius restricted all his references to deity to terms familiar from centuries of such speeches on Hellenistic kingship, terms such as *Savior* and *Logos*. In keeping with the monotheistic emphasis of the day, he celebrated the "Supreme Sovereign," the "Universal Creator," the "Highest of All."[64] Like the pagan orators, he never once used the specific name of Christ, and his only direct reference to the Incarnation was a clumsy circumlocution, in which he spoke of "a certain new epiphany."[65]

Eusebius shares other points with Constantine's pagan orators: a predilection for solar imagery, emphasis on the longevity of his rule, the role of divine selection, the criteria for a good king.[66] It can, of course, be said that all these points were commonplaces, that they do not necessarily say anything significant about either Constantine or Eusebius. Still, when every excuse has been made, the fact remains that these sentiments and phrases recur in the writings of Lactantius and Eusebius, the two Christian authors whose names come down in close association with that of Constantine. That is a coincidence worthy of notice. Lactantius and Eusebius have both been identified at various times as major influences on Constantine, chief advisers and architects of his policy.[67] More hostile observers might prefer to dismiss them as "court Christians" trying to ingratiate themselves with a willful monarch. Fortunately, the case does not need to rest on their evidence alone, for there are other indications that these writers represented a significant trend in mainstream Christianity.

There are abundant signs that by the third century more and more

Christians were coming from "mainstream" culture, bringing with them the education and affluence that were markers of that culture. Eusebius writes in the Church History of Christians who had reached the highest offices prior to the persecution, and Lactantius remarks that the persecution was especially hard on intellectuals. His description of Diocletian's destruction of the church in Nicomedia at the outset of the persecution is significant for what it takes for granted: that the church was a prominent structure, in close enough proximity to Diocletian's palace for him to watch it being razed from the roof of that building.[68] It is predictable under such circumstances that at least some Christians would have sought ways to lower the barriers that in the past had kept the more affluent members of the faith from enjoying the traditional rewards of their status.[69]

One piece of evidence for just such an attempt exists in a set of eighty-one canons issued by a council of bishops who met in the city of Illiberis (Elvira) in southern Spain sometime early in the fourth century. Scholars have been unable to agree on precisely when this council met, and its eighty-one canons pose thorny problems. There is good reason to believe they are a compilation of the decisions of a number of councils.[70] Fortunately, for present purposes the issue is unimportant, because what is of interest is the information this document provides about the relative wealth and social standing of members of the Christian community in that part of Spain, and many of the canons that yield this information still appear to date to this period; thus, even if others do prove ultimately not to have been adopted until later in the century, a sufficient number would remain to form a picture of this community.

The information in these canons is indirect, of course, for the object of the synod was church discipline, not sociological record keeping, and the bulk of the canons deal with matters that crop up over and over in the premodern world—regulating licentious behavior, for instance, and the conduct of clerics, and prescribing appropriate punishments for perceived misconduct. It is in the course of making these prescriptions that the document reveals its treasure, for it may be taken as given that the punishments would not have been prescribed if the acts they name were not actually being committed.

While the immediate purpose of the canons of church councils was to deal with questions of doctrine or discipline, their incidental effect is to reflect the concerns of the Christian community and to define the boundaries of acceptable behavior at any given moment. In this way, the canons of a council can serve as a snapshot of the community they address. What this particular snapshot shows is a community living cheek by jowl with non-Christian neighbors, on friendly enough terms for pagans to borrow Christian finery for festivals (can. 57) and for Christians to witness the sacrifices on the capitol (can. 59). Christians in this community were wealthy enough to rent land to pagans (can. 40) and to have pagan slaves (can. 41). If the theory that a privileged class will seek to reduce barriers has any merit, there should be signs in these canons of attempts by Christians to engage in the pursuits that traditionally brought prestige and status in their world.[71]

There are, in fact, a surprisingly large number that do just that. Canon 56 deals with Christians who hold the office of duumvir, a local magistracy analogous to the consulate at Rome and, like the consulate, held by the most distinguished members of the local elite. Because the ancient state did not distinguish between civil and religious functions, many of the duumvir's duties would naturally have brought him into contact with the pagan gods. Even if he did not perform the sacrifices or inspect the auguries himself, he would have had to supervise the priests who did so, or at the very least sanction their practices. At an earlier point in their history, as we saw in Chapter 3, it was impossible for a Christian even to mingle with the crowds at a pagan festival: to hold offices that obliged them to assume responsibility for the performance of those very rites, even if they had the means to do so, would have been unthinkable. Yet the only punishment provided by this canon for holding the office of duumvir is that Christians who did so had to refrain from attending church during their year of office. Other canons (2–4, 55) deal with Christians who hold public priesthoods; although it remained a mortal sin to sacrifice to idols or preside over public games, readmission after two years was possible for those who held this office without committing those sins.

The canons of Elvira contain another decision that undermines the case for attributing Christian coercion to inherent intolerance. In canon 60, the bishops ruled that Christians killed for attacking idol temples were not to be considered martyrs. Whether this decision was taken before, after, or even during Diocletian's persecution is immaterial to its import; indeed, the later in the century this canon is dated, the more significant it becomes, for it does not reflect a community that saw itself in a life-and-death struggle with its pagan neighbors. It was, rather, the decision of a community that wished to eliminate sources of unnecessary friction. In the Council of Elvira, we hear the voice of a community that had arrived. The signal these penalties send is that the Christians of southern Spain were finding ways to live up to their means, to achieve status and distinction in a pagan world; they were a group that was ready, and willing, to play. Even more important is the justification the bishops gave for their decision not to recognize Christians killed in assaults on temples as martyrs: the perpetrators did not deserve such esteem, "since this is nowhere written in the Gospels and is never found being done by the apostles."[72] Whatever the motivation for their ruling, the critical point is that they were able to find justification for it in the core texts of Christian belief.

The Donatists and the Christian elite of Elvira represent points on a spectrum of Christian opinion. In deciding where to place Constantine on the same spectrum, it may not be inconsequential to note that one of the bishops whose name appears on the list of those who attended the Council of Elvira was one Constantine soon found to be an appropriate emissary, Ossius of Corduba.

Games

Like Augustus's "Principate" and Diocletian's "Dominate," the system that can be seen in place at the end of Constantine's reign, when the events with which this book opened transpired, was not so much the result of systematic planning as of ad hoc responses to unexpected situations. This is the significance of the Donatist schism. Politically, the Donatist affair was fraught with pitfalls for Constantine. While Constantine is not likely to have been as ignorant of church affairs as later tradition made him, neither would he have known right away how to resolve a question that cut to the heart of Christian identity and values. He needed cover. In the modern world, leaders in similar situations make use of special committees, or "blue ribbon panels," to put distance between themselves and controversial issues. The tactic might not be as old as time, but it certainly was well known in the fourth century. Describing the steps Diocletian took to implement the persecution, Lactantius writes: "For Diocletian had the kind of malice which consisted in acting without consultation when he had decided to do something good, so that he could get the credit himself, but in calling on a number of people for advice when he was planning something evil which he knew would merit censure, so that his own misdeeds could be blamed on others."[73]

For Constantine, turning the problem over to Miltiades must have seemed an easy way out, covered by both Christian and imperial precedent. When it failed, for the reasons the Donatists alleged, his own sense of fairness came into play, requiring him to take a more direct hand. But how? The world of politics is a world of appearances, prestige being the most important appearance of all. As the emperor Tiberius knew centuries earlier when he constantly delayed dealing personally with mutiny in Gaul, nothing can be more damaging to a ruler than to weigh in with all his resources only to prove ineffective.[74] If he needed one, Constantine had the more immediate example of Galerius's disastrous campaign into Italy to remind him not to commit his prestige without being certain of success.

In the high empire, the Senate provided the emperor not only with legitimacy but also with the cover that he needed from time to time to take risky or unpleasant actions. At his option, the emperor could preside over the Senate and seek its counsel, or he could stay in the background and let the Senate bring a decision to him. The emperor was a member of the senatorial class, and thus of the Senate, but Constantine was not a bishop. When he took the initiative to summon the Council of Arles, he must have had something analogous to the magistrate's right to summon a meeting of the Senate in mind. In the *vita Constantini,* written some two decades later, Bishop Eusebius mentions how Constantine, "like some general bishop constituted by God, convened synods of his ministers."[75]

The passage occurs in a part of the essay where Eusebius was writing specifically of the Donatist problem, and it is reasonable to suppose that he had the Council of Arles in mind when he described the emperor's conduct at these meetings: "Nor did he disdain to be present and sit with them in their assembly, but bore a share in their deliberations, ministering to all that pertained to the peace of God. He took his seat, too, in the midst of them, as an individual amongst many, dismissing his guards and soldiers, and all whose duty it was to defend his person; but protected by the fear of God, and surrounded by the guardianship of his faithful friends." In these details, Eusebius may have been influenced by later developments, just as he was in his description of the labarum, so it cannot be said for certain that Constantine even attended this particular council. But just as there was no reason to doubt that the labarum existed in some form at the earlier time despite Eusebius's elaborations, so this passage can be taken at the very least in a general sense as an indicator of the relationship Constantine began working out with the bishops in the years following his capture of Rome. What it shows is an emperor pulling out all the prestige stops, working the bishops the same way Augustus worked the Senate, shunning the trappings of his office with the same ostentatious denial that his predecessors had used to show senators that they were, in Pliny's phrase, "one of us."

Thus did a formidable and unusually durable relationship begin to take shape. Later in the *vita Constantini*, Eusebius quotes Constantine as telling a group of bishops with which he was meeting, on some occasion that Eusebius does not identify, "that he himself too was a bishop." Eusebius, who was among those present, quotes the emperor as saying, "You are bishops whose jurisdiction is within the Church: I also am a bishop, ordained by God to overlook whatever is external to the Church."[76] As observed in Chapter 2, the phrase is pregnant with meaning for the future of church-state relations in the West. With that history in mind scholars have chewed over it for centuries, looking for theological nuances and programmatic vision that Constantine could not possibly have intended. But whatever else may be encoded in Constantine's self-allocated role as "bishop of those outside," the phrase certainly shows an emperor who was reaching for a way to establish the same commonality with this class of Christian leaders which previous emperors had established with the senatorial class.[77]

There is more to be gleaned from Eusebius's description of Constantine's behavior at councils, for the bishop concludes this passage with a statement that reveals much about the emperor's goals and method of decision making. "Those whom he saw inclined to a sound judgment, and exhibiting a calm and conciliatory temper," Eusebius

227

writes, "received his high approbation, for he evidently delighted in a general harmony of sentiment; while he regarded the unyielding with aversion."[78] For this sentiment there is abundant confirmation in the Donatist record. Constantine consistently characterized the Donatists as quarrelsome and unreasonable men who were exhausting his patience. "I found it evident that they declined to have before their eyes either respect for their own safety or, what is more, the worship of Almighty God," he sniffed to Aelafius, the vicar of Africa, and he exclaimed to the bishops at Arles, "How great their madness! . . . What powerful wickedness abides in their hearts!"[79]

These instances, which could easily be multiplied, show that the Donatists progressively alienated Constantine with their antics. Why? At first glance, the behavior of the Donatists throughout this affair appears bizarre. They appeal repeatedly to Constantine, spurning all attempts at compromise and making no effort whatsoever to appear conciliatory, or even rational, themselves, only to wind up denying the legitimacy of the very process that they themselves had initiated. The Donatists were not playing by the rules of the game. It even seems at times as if they wanted to lose. Some of the answer for the Donatists' actions assuredly lies in the lopsidedly orthodox nature of the evidence that has come down to us; with a little distance, their tactics become much more understandable. In using the appeal process, for instance, they sought to widen their conflict with Caecilian by involving third parties. By calling for Constantine's personal involvement, they were behaving no differently than the Christians of Antioch when they appealed to Aurelian against Paul of Samosata some forty years earlier. And they certainly had reason to protest Miltiades' heavy-handed attempt to deny them a full airing of their grievances at the Council of Rome. Even their stridency had a method behind it, for its effect was to motivate the emperor to seek resolution. The tactic could be traced back to Jesus himself: "He that is not with me is against me"—the *locus classicus* for an activist agenda that seeks to advance by polarization.[80]

In painting the issue in black and white and refusing all attempts at compromise and reconciliation, the Donatists certainly were following this plan. But what about their use of the appeal process? Here, too, they followed a recognizable tactic. "No organization, including organized religion, can live up to the letter of its own book," Alinsky wrote.

"You can club them to death with their 'book' of rules and regulations."[81] The rules in this case were that everyone, but particularly the underdog, had the right to appeal to the emperor. In appealing to Constantine's personal sense of duty as a ruler to ensure that his subjects received justice, the Donatists were merely adopting a strategy as old, and as effective, as the one he had adopted in using imperial resources to boost the prestige of Caecilian's party.

Only in resisting all efforts to find an equitable resolution do the Donatists appear irrational, but the difference may simply be that compromise and settlement were not on their agenda. Their aim was to delineate the differences between themselves and what they regarded as the impure and worldly faction of Caecilian, and they spurned earthly goals for the treasure that they firmly believed their fidelity was storing up for them in heaven. What the Donatists represent are the fault lines developing out of Christianity's very success. Sociologists who study the development of new religions and cults have observed that a split regularly develops between those members who have achieved some standing in the world outside the church and those who continue to relate to that world as outsiders. The one group will be eager to reduce the tensions that originally separated their organization from the surrounding culture, while the other will continue to define that culture as foreign, hostile, and corrupt. To these, those members who start bending rules in order to make the process of assimilation easier inevitably will seem suspect and "worldly."[82]

To see signs of a social split between Donatists and the body that came to be known as the universal, or Catholic, church is not to say, as once was fashionable, that the Donatists were motivated more by social or nationalist than by religious concerns.[83] But it is to say that attention to social divisions can illuminate Donatist behavior, as it can Christian behavior in general. The social distinction between Donatist and Catholic emerges more clearly later in the century in the guerrilla activities of a radical offshoot, the Circumcellions, who specialized in terrorist acts against wealthy Catholic landowners. But it is already evident here in the intransigence of the Donatists; their readiness to believe the absolute worst of rival Christians; their refusal to doubt the integrity of their own leaders even in the face of seemingly plausible evidence; their indifference to political realities; and their overall sense of alienation, for these are classic symptoms of the politically dispossessed.[84]

The Donatists, then, would represent those Christians in the North African church who remained committed to a world of sharp divisions, who continued to think of themselves as outsiders. Whereas the one group, represented here by the citizens of Elvira, was ready to make its peace with the dominant culture, the other, represented by the Donatists, was not. Looked at in this way, Constantine's decision to support the church of Caecilian becomes highly revealing.

Choosing Partners

It never comes out stated this way, but in fact the Donatists are the type of Christians scholars think of when they characterize the church in the age of Constantine as bent on revenge, thirsting for blood, intransigent, and intolerant. This being so, it is important to note that, in his first opportunity to use imperial prestige and largesse to influence the direction Christianity would take, Constantine did not choose the Donatist side in this controversy. Constantine had a rigorist strain in him, and his support for Caecilian, at least initially, does not appear to have been unqualified. But if there was one thing the Donatists' blunt and insistent opposition did not do, it was signal a willingness to belong to a harmonious and smoothly running coalition. Indeed, Donatus's scornful question "What has the Church to do with the emperor?" reflects the same readiness to challenge imperial authority which Christians had shown in earlier ages.

No greater contrast could be made than with the actions of the party Constantine chose: the group now calling themselves "Catholics," while itself reflecting a variety of attitudes toward the state and non-Christian society, was nevertheless far more prepared to work with the existing power structure than were the Donatists. As the contretemps with Miltiades already suggested, the union was not a seamless blend. The Council of Arles sent similar signals. The bishops, before coming to the Donatist dispute, found time to make provisions for Christians who held public office (can. 7) and, apparently, for Christians in the military (can. 3). The latter decision is open to more than one interpretation, but the one most widely accepted is that it created a loophole for taking up arms in time of war.[85] The topic of holding public office had already been broached at the Council of Elvira, where the bishops decided that it would be sufficient for the official to absent himself from church during his year of office. The bishops at Arles took a different tack, ruling that Christians who held public office only needed to carry letters from their bishops to present to the bishop of the place they would govern, and would not need to be excommunicated unless they acted in a way contrary to Christian principles.

At first glance, this canon appears to make an even greater concession than that made by the Elvira council, since it envisages circumstances in which service might last longer than a year or even be continual. The bishops evidently were thinking beyond the horizons of municipal office and envisioning Christians in imperial service. But their concession came with a sting, since it gave the bishop a virtually unrestricted hold over Christian officials in his district. Although it may have been meant merely as a check on the appointment of heretics, this canon contained within it the seed of a potentially revolutionary principle, the right of bishops to judge the actions of public officials. Latent, it will reemerge with explosive force at the end of our study. But at this point, with the first decade of Constantine's sole rule in the West coming to a close, such considerations were less important than the contours of a religious policy that now was clearly in place: a policy with a goal of inclusive monotheism which would be based on the use of councils, rather than coercion.

PART III

CONSEQUENCES

Rule number one of the coalition game:
Secure your political base first.
H. Smith (1988)

Seven

Consensus Politics

t is unfortunate that after Milan a blind falls over Licinius's relations with the church. When it rises again, some ten years later, he has somehow become an incarnation of the demons he had helped to destroy, persecuting Christians and thereby bringing down upon himself the avenging wrath of Constantine. No doubt to avoid the messy implications raised by this denouement, scholars have pictured Licinius as at best a grudging partner in Constantine's Christian policy, never truly committed to the equal treatment guaranteed by the Edict of Milan. There is, however, no reason to think Licinius was forced by Constantine to concede more than he wished. Indeed, Licinius's provinces held the vast majority of the Christian population of the empire, and he was, if anything, the more zealous of the two in punishing persecutors, at least at the start.[1]

Nevertheless, in late spring of 324, after years of hot and cold war between the two, Constantine invaded the territories of his former ally. Defeated on land, Licinius took refuge in the ancient city of Byzantium, which Constantine promptly put under siege. Two months later, Licinius risked all on a naval battle, in which he was decisively defeated by a fleet commanded by Constantine's son Crispus. On September 19, Licinius surrendered and was sent into exile at Thessalonica. Six months later, in terms uncannily reminiscent of the fate of Maximian some fifteen years earlier, Constantine had Licinius put to death, on the grounds that he was attempting a coup. Nor was Licinius's demise the only echo of earlier battles. Constantine justified his invasion on the grounds that it was necessary to protect Christians in the East from another persecutor.

What accounts for the turnabout in Licinius? It is clear that rivalry with Constantine, ending in 324 but manifesting itself as early as 314, was a factor. Looking at the details of Licinius's "persecution" reveals that it was much more limited in scope than the earlier ones. It may be that Licinius's real crime was to adhere scrupulously to the Milan accords in his territories when Christians in the West were becoming accustomed to a much richer diet. What once could seem like liberty simply came to appear as restraints. It is noteworthy that Eusebius of Caesarea, who casts Licinius among the persecutors in his *vita Constantini,* explains Licinius's actions as due to his perception "that all we did, and all our endeavors to obtain the favor of God, were on Constantine's behalf."[2]

One further tantalizing piece of evidence opens the possibility that Licinius's "persecution" may have been, at least in part, a reaction to Christian squabbles. After he gained control of the East, Constantine wrote an angry letter to the Christian community of Nicomedia, denouncing their bishop, Eusebius, as "a client of the tyrant," evidently Licinius, who abetted his persecution.[3] The charge cannot literally be true, for Eusebius of Nicomedia sat at the middle of one of the most brutal controversies in Christian history for more than twenty years, and if there were even a hint of such compromising behavior on his part, his enemies certainly would have used it against him. What Constantine's next statement does indicate is that Eusebius had allied himself in some fashion with Licinius: "I shall say nothing about the outrageous actions against myself. At the moment when the clash of the opposing armies [i.e., his and Licinius's] was at hand, he [Eusebius] sent surreptitiously 'eyes' to spy on me, and all but afforded armed assistance to the tyrant. Do not imagine that I am not prepared to prove this. There is an accurate proof, because it is well known that the presbyters and deacons who came with Eusebius were publicly arrested by me."

The context for this outburst was Constantine's efforts to resolve a theological dispute over the views of an Alexandrian presbyter, Arius, who was being supported by Eusebius of Nicomedia. The controversy had been growing since at least 318, and it is hard to see how Licinius would not have been touched by it. It quickly engulfed Constantine. One of the proofs subsequently used to show that Licinius was a persecutor was a ban he instituted on synods and assemblies. If, instead, his motive was to enforce a cooling-off period in the rapidly spiraling controversy over Arius, it would not be unreasonable to assume that he acted on the advice of Eusebius of Nicomedia and that this was the basis for Constantine's angry charge.[4]

While these events were unfolding, Constantine suffered—and inflicted—severe personal tragedy. For reasons that remain obscure, he ordered the execution of his eldest son, Crispus, while en route to celebrate his vicennalia in Rome. In Rome, Constantine's wife, Fausta, fell victim to the emperor's wrath in a particularly grisly way, locked into a steam room and poached to death. Under such circumstances, it comes as no surprise to learn that Constantine's vicennalia was a disaster. His mother, Helena, subsequently undertook a pilgrimage to Jerusalem, where she spent lavish amounts endowing holy sites and, incidentally, touched off a wave of fashionable tours to the Holy Land.[5] Almost from the start, scholars have tried to connect changes in Constantine's policy to these events. Pagans, beginning apparently with Constantine's own nephew, the emperor Julian, dated his conversion to this period, claiming that he turned to Christ only after horrified pagan priests refused to promise him expiation for his sins. Modern scholars have not followed this lead, but they have connected these events with an increasing "orientalization" of his government and greater rigor and instability in his pronouncements. More recent scholars, influenced no doubt by the cynicism of late-twentieth-century politics, have described Helena's pilgrimage as a propaganda stunt to divert public attention from these unseemly events.[6]

It is true that Constantine threw himself into Christian politics subsequent to these tragedies, but he had little choice; indeed, he can be said to have acted in spite of, not because of, these misfortunes. What the death of an incumbent emperor was to Roman politics, the charge of heresy was to Christian belief—a flashpoint that threatened to destabilize the entire system. As soon as he took control of the

Eastern empire after his defeat of Licinius in 324, Constantine encountered just such a controversy embroiling virtually the entire Eastern church. The Arian heresy is what led to the Council of Nicaea, which subsequently became a watershed in the development of Christian theology. More than theology was at stake, however. In very fundamental ways, the controversy determined the type of movement Christianity was going to be, the way it was going to relate to the state and how it would deal with dissent in the future. Politically, it was a debate over whether and how to join the mainstream.

The Heresy of Arius

The central point of Christian teaching hinges on the belief that Jesus Christ is both fully god and fully human; in no other way could he have performed the redemptive act that brought the "good news" of eternal life and freedom from death. On a more practical level, it was also the most effective way to distinguish Jesus from the galaxy of dying and resurrected gods who populated ancient mythology, as well as from the sons of philandering gods in the heroic pantheon. But by human reckoning, 100 percent man and 100 percent god adds up to 200 percent. That, and very real fears that the majesty of god would be compromised by too much human feeling, on the one hand, versus concern that Jesus' sacrifice would be belittled if his suffering was denied, on the other, meant that any attempt to adjust the equation one way or the other inevitably stirred deep and bitter passions. More than matters of taste and judgment were involved, for the controversy went to the very heart of Christian belief, and in Christian thought the connection between correct belief (*ortho-doxa,* hence orthodoxy) and salvation was deep seated and implacable.

Arius, a priest in Alexandria, was by no means the first Christian to be tripped up by efforts to express more clearly and carefully the relationship of Father and Son in the Christian Trinity. What exactly he taught is hard now to discern from all the polemic and parody under which it has been buried for so many centuries. Recent efforts to do so have led to surprising conclusions, including one that his was the conservative side in the debate, another that his views were in fact orthodox.[7] Fortunately, to analyze the political implications of the process, it is sufficient to know what his opponents claimed Arius was doing and how they went about establishing their own position as the one that represented right belief, or "orthodoxy." In the simplest terms, Arius is said to have argued a set of logical propositions: first, if there is a "Father" and a "Son," then in some way the one must have preceded the other; and, second, that there must have been a point at which the Son did not exist. A third proposition would have been equally self-evident in the traditional environment of antiquity, though less so in the more permissive modern world: that the Father automatically took precedence over, and was by definition greater than, the Son.

Harmless as these propositions might seem, especially when accompanied by the requisite avowals that all of this happened before there were such things as time or normal creation and that both Father and Son were infinitely greater than anything mortals could imagine, they were nonetheless alarming to Arius's bishop, Alexander, whose own clumsy theology is supposed to have provoked Arius's lectures. Basically, what Alexander saw, and what allowed his to become the orthodox position, was the deeper truth that, despite all the qualifiers, the effect of Arius's teaching was to make Jesus a secondary god and thereby minimize the difference between his role and that of the heroes and demigods of pagan belief. Alexander ordered the dissident priest to desist and, when he persisted, summoned a council that excommunicated Arius and banished him from Alexandria. Arius did not accept the punishment. Instead, he traveled to the bishops of other Eastern cities, many of whom evidently had been classmates of his in the school of the great Lucian of Antioch, and gained their support for his theological position. Angry letters traveled throughout the East as both sides now sought to line up additional support.

One member of Arius's old school network was Eusebius, the bishop of Nicomedia and subject of Constantine's bitter reproaches. Evidently, Eusebius had used his position as bishop of the Eastern capital well, for an early letter of Bishop Alexander identified him as a prime mover of Arius's cause, while at the same time questioning the sincerity of his motives. "He affects to write in [Arius's] behalf," Alexander warned other Eastern bishops, "while the fact itself plainly shows that he does this for the promotion of his own purposes." The fifth-century church historian Socrates Scholasticus, who included this letter in his account, claimed that this "personal and censorious" attack was what made Eusebius a bitter enemy.[8]

If he had not been before, Constantine was certainly aware after his experience with the Donatists that not all Christians were alike. But at this time he had every reason to believe he had negotiated the Donatist issue successfully, and compared with the machete tactics of those combatants, the stilettos wielded in this debate must have seemed far less lethal to him. Or so it would appear from a letter Constantine wrote to the two adversaries in his first attempt to defuse the conflict:

> I understand, then, that the origin of the present controversy is this. When you, Alexander, demanded of the presbyters what opinion they severally maintained respecting a certain passage in the Divine law, or rather, I should say, that you asked them something connected with an unprofitable question, then you, Arius, inconsiderately insisted on what ought never to have been conceived at all, or if conceived, should have been buried in profound silence. Hence it was that a dissension arose between you, fellowship was withdrawn, and the holy people, rent into diverse parties, no longer preserved the unity of the one body.[9]

These "points of discussion," as he called them, "are enjoined by the authority of no law." They are the product of "misused leisure," "merely an intellectual exercise." In a judgment certain to astound the recipients, he wrote,

> The cause of your difference has not been any of the leading doctrines or precepts of the Divine law, nor has any new heresy respecting the worship of God arisen among you. You are in truth of one and the same judgment: you may therefore well join in communion and fellowship. . . . For since you have, as I said, but one faith, and one sentiment respecting our religion, and since the Divine commandment in all its parts enjoins on us all the duty of maintaining a spirit of concord, let not the circumstance which has led to a slight difference between you, since it does not affect the validity of the whole, cause any division or schism among you.

Constantine even went so far as to urge the feuding priests to learn from the example of pagan philosophers who, though they were "frequently at issue on certain points, and differ[ed], perhaps, in their degree of knowledge," nevertheless were "recalled to harmony of sentiment by the uniting power of their common doctrines."[10] In the same way, he argued, "The dignity of your synod may be preserved, and the communion of your whole body maintained unbroken, however wide a difference may exist among you as to unimportant matters." Constantine concluded with an explicit statement of his own priorities: "As far, then, as regards the Divine Providence, let there be one faith, and one understanding among you, one united judgment in reference to God. But as to your subtle disputations on questions of little or no significance, though you may be unable to harmonize in sentiment, such differences should be consigned to the secret custody of your own minds and thoughts."[11] The letter has been scorned for its naiveté; but what it actually reveals is a Constantine more concerned for unity than theology, with a personal agenda that required no more specific definition of worship than acknowledgment of a single "Divine Providence." Everything else, including the nature of the Son and his relationship to the Father, was "trivial," "of no consequence," "truly insignificant"— words that, with their like, he repeats over and over.

How much "unity" did he have in mind? His concern to unify all Christian parties is so well documented that it may be taken as a given. But, as indicated in the last chapter, many of Constantine's actions suggest he had conceived a broader unity, a consensus of pagans and Christians who would put aside specific differences in order to achieve a stable and harmonious empire based on two general principles: the legitimacy of Constantine and his dynasty, and the existence of a Supreme God who underwrote both the empire and the dynasty. Constantine's advice to Arius and Alexander in this letter to settle in public for "one united judgment in reference to God" and leave more specific characteristics to the private arena becomes more coherent if taken as a specimen of this policy.

Even though the letter is written in the context of a specific dispute among Christians, it contains references to the broader policy in its opening sentences. Here, Constantine identified two reasons for undertaking his recent conquest of Licinius's territories: "to restore and rejoin the body of our common empire which had been stricken as if with a terrible wound," and, as his primary goal, "to unite the inclination of all peoples regarding divine matters into a single sustaining habit." Did he mean by this phrase that he wanted everyone to become a Christian? Yes, presumably, for he must have known that Christians certainly were not prepared to abandon the tenets of their faith. But as the remainder of the letter, with its exhortation to settle for agreement on the outlines of monotheism, makes clear, Constantine thought of Christianity in broadly inclusive terms, as a faith for which the threshold for admission could be quite low. This introductory paragraph also included a significant distinction with regard to means. Whereas the physical union of the empire required "the power of military arms," Constantine described spiritual unity as something that must be accomplished "through the hidden eye of the mind"—an ambiguous phrase, but certainly one that he meant to contrast with the force of arms needed to achieve the other goal.

Constantine practiced what he preached. Upon taking control of the Eastern empire, he circulated a general edict to all the provinces— one of two that he wrote at the same time, according to Eusebius, who included a copy in the *vita Constantini*. The other (which Eusebius does not include) was addressed specifically to the churches. The copy Eusebius included was addressed to his own province of Palestine, and for that reason it is usually referred to as the Edict to the Palestinians, less frequently as the edict On Piety, which is the subject assigned to it in the chapter heading of the *vita Constantini*. Since that heading was not written by Constantine, it is best to use the more neutral designation.[12]

The circumstances of this edict, which takes up nineteen of the seventy-three chapters in the *vita Constantini*'s second book (chs. 24– 42, inclusive), are important to understanding its contents. If, as seems likely, Eusebius inserted it in the appropriate place chronologically, this was Constantine's first occasion to address his subjects since completing the war against Licinius. This is the edict quoted in Chapter 5, wherein Constantine heralded his rise "from the remote Britannic ocean" in response to God's call, and its operative clauses make provisions for the return of exiles and restoration of property.

With this purpose in mind, two points in the edict stand out. The first is how quickly Constantine moved to associate Licinius with the policy of persecution followed under the Tetrarchy, thereby blurring any distinction that might have been made between the general policy instituted by Diocletian and whatever specific acts of which Licinius might himself have been guilty—an imprecision that makes it difficult

Fig. 4. This gold medallion, minted for the dedication of Constantinople in 330, provides a visual summary of Constantine's agenda. In the center, the emperor receives a crown from a hand reaching down from the heavens. He is flanked by two of his sons, who receive crowns from a soldier and Nike, respectively. The scene brings together Constantine's central themes of divine selection, military victory, and dynastic succession. The unidentified heavenly hand symbolizes the vague monotheism around which he built a consensus of pagan and Christian support. The legend reads Gaudium Romanorum, "Joy of the Romans."

(Kunsthistorisches Museum, Vienna)

to identify when the acts of injustice which Constantine offers in the letter as justification for his own actions actually occurred, although for the most part scholars have assumed, perhaps too hastily, that they were all Licinius's doing. The second point is that, despite Eusebius's assurance (2.23) that Constantine used this letter to proclaim "openly to all the name of Him to whose bounty he owed all his blessings," Constantine himself refers only to a "Supreme God" (five times), a "Supreme Being," "Almighty God," "the Divine Will," "the Divine spirit," "that God who is the source of all blessing," "God the Liberator of

243

all," "Divinity, alone and truly God, possessor of almighty and eternal power," and the like. This is precisely the protocol he was soon to urge on Arius and Alexander. His imprecision need not be taken to mean that he had anything but the Christian god in mind—the whole thrust of the edict, after all, was to spell out the means of restitution to a people that, Constantine believed, had been terribly wronged. He devoted several passages to a feeling description of the sacrifices borne by the martyrs and confessors. But his use of phrases common to Christians and pagans alike is consistent with the search for a common denominator that was the hallmark of his religious policy.

Similar themes emerge from another general edict circulated during this same period, the Edict to the Eastern Provincials, also reproduced by Eusebius in the *vita Constantini*.[13] Here Constantine set out "to lay before you all as explicitly as possible the nature of my own hopes for future happiness." Presumably for that reason, when Eusebius put this edict in the *vita Constantini,* he described it as dealing with the error of polytheism, for which reason it is now sometimes referred to as the Edict on the Error of Polytheism. The title is not wrong, but it can be misleading, especially if taken in conjunction with Eusebius's immediately preceding claim that the edict constituted a call on all Constantine's subjects "openly to profess their allegiance to his Christ as their Savior," for Constantine did not proceed, as Eusebius's introduction and Constantine's own preliminary statement might lead one to expect, to speak of the happiness of the life to come. Instead, he speaks of the misery generated by the persecution, the shame of seeing Roman citizens forced to seek protection from the barbarians, and the miserable fate suffered by those who followed this policy.[14] The "error," then, at least as far as Constantine was concerned, pertained to this world, not the world to come.

In the remainder of this edict, Constantine reiterated his commitment to a policy of peace and unity. It was for this reason that he led the armies "preceded by thy sacred sign" to victory, and he invokes "the most mighty God" with a prayer: "For the common benefit of the world and all mankind, I long for your people to be at peace and to remain free from strife," adding, "Let those who delight in error alike with those who believe partake in the advantages of peace and quiet. For this sweetness of common benefit will have strength to correct even these and lead them to the straight road. Let no one disturb another, let each man hold fast to that which his soul wishes, let him make full use of this."[15] This we may take as a succinct statement of Constantine's program: debate and exhortation will show the way to God; coercion will not. A little further, he says again:

> As for those who will not allow themselves to be cured of their error, let them not attribute this to any but themselves. For that remedy which is of sovereign and healing virtue is openly placed within the reach of all. Only let not any one inflict an injury on that religion which experience itself testifies to be pure and undefiled. Henceforward, therefore, let us all enjoy in common the privilege placed within our reach, I mean the blessing of peace, endeavoring to keep our conscience pure from all that is contrary.[16]

Thus in two general edicts issued in the immediate aftermath of his victory over Licinius, Constantine described himself as an emissary of peace and renounced the use of coercion to compel belief. The reason can hardly be coincidence. The intent was to reassure his new subjects, pagan and Christian alike, by explaining his motives and distinguishing them from those of his predecessors. This is the context in which to read his more elliptical comments in the letter to Arius and Alexander, written in this same period, in which he carefully distinguished between military and spiritual goals and the means whereby to accomplish them. In that letter, Constantine gave one overarching goal for both the reasons that he undertook the conquest of the Eastern provinces: "If I were to establish through my prayers a common agreement among all the servants of god, the conduct of public affairs would enjoy a change concurrent with the pious sentiments of all."[17] All pious sentiments, not just those of a particular belief.

A unified Christianity obviously was important to Constantine, but as a prerequisite, not as an end in itself. He thought of it as part of a program to achieve unity in the empire as a whole.

Pagan Consensus

How did pagans react? It was once a given that pagans were shocked and demoralized by the dramatic reversal that occurred under Constantine and were in full retreat until the accession of Constantine's nephew, the apostate emperor Julian, in 361. Julian's efforts to restore paganism were cut short by his untimely death in a war against Persia in 363, but, according to this reading, they were sufficient to spark a "pagan revival" that lasted until the Battle of the Frigidus River in 394, in which the Catholic emperor Theodosius I defeated Eugenius, a usurper who had vowed to restore the old gods if he was successful.[18] But it is now clear that those later conflicts do not belong in the Age of Constantine. Far from being inevitable, Diocletian's Great Persecution appears more and more an aberration, interrupting almost half a century of peaceful coexistence between pagans and Christians. Its most important effect was not to polarize pagans and Christians but to discredit coercion as a viable means for settling religious differences. It is premature, and misleading, to think of a "life-and-death struggle" between two monolithic religious systems as the guiding motif of this period. Certainly there were pagans and Christians who saw the issue in such terms, but the evidence of pagans who sheltered Christians during the persecution and who were revolted by its excesses, as well as the number of Christians in the Roman Empire who argued that true belief could not be forced, should have raised doubts long ago that everybody in the Age of Constantine saw the issue in as coldly logical terms as the trained disputants whose writings have helped frame the record for future ages.

Much scholarship has seriously undermined the "conflict" model of Christian-pagan relations. Even one of the more eloquent spokespersons for this view admitted that the contemporary record contained little evidence of such a struggle, though he considered this absence more ironic than questionable.[19] Since then, a great deal of healthy stocktaking has gone on, resulting in a much more nuanced understanding of the relations between Christian and pagan during this critical century. The year 1961 was a watershed. In that year Peter Brown published an article in which he pointed to an anomaly created by relying exclusively on this model of pagan-Christian relations: the speed with which members of a Roman aristocracy that was supposedly fiercely pagan at one moment had become almost uniformly Christian a moment later. The only way to understand this sudden change, Brown argued, was to take into account a "drift into a respectable Christianity" which he felt "led to a blurring of the sharp division between a pagan past and a Christian present."[20] In the same year, Friedhelm Winkelmann published an exhaustive review of the sources, during which he came to the then startling conclusion that to most pagans of the Age of Constantine the emperor's actions in support of Christianity were, at worst, a "bearable evil."[21] Since then, increasing numbers of scholars have come to the conclusion that the best way to make sense of the highly contradictory evidence from this century—from the presence of pagan officials and orators at Christian courts to the friendships between Christian bishops and pagan grandees and the mixture of pagan and Christian motifs in such varied venues as calendars and funerary art—is to posit that, at least on a number of levels, Romans for most of the fourth century did not see religion as the critical issue it subsequently became. As Brown has put it more recently, members of the fourth century's high culture would have been horrified to learn what modern scholars have assumed about their commitment to such a conflict.[22] In such an atmosphere, a search for consensus is not the quixotic policy it once might have seemed; indeed, all the signs of peaceful intermingling of pagan and Christian thought may instead be thought of as proof of the success of such a policy.

Because of the nature of the sources, evidence of pagan participation in the Constantinian consensus is harder to come by. Eusebius of Caesarea drops a hint in his otherwise carefully Christianized essay on Constantine's life when his enthusiasm for the emperor's eloquence leads him to mention that "even pagan philosophers who were present" at the emperor's regular salon testified to the truth of his sentiments.[23] We know the name of one of these philosophers, Sopater of Apamea, regarded as the most prominent Neoplatonist of his day. According to his biographer, Eunapius of Sardis, Sopater abandoned the academy in the 320s and sought fame and fortune at Constantine's court—a career move of which Eunapius strongly disapproved. Sopater eventually fell victim to a court conspiracy that Eunapius, a bitter anti-Christian, blamed on religious rivalry; but at one point his stock with Constantine was so high that even in Christian accounts he is credited with performing rites at the foundation of the emperor's new capital, Constantinople.[24]

One significant piece of contemporary testimony to Constantine's policy comes from a surprising source. Julius Firmicus Maternus was a barrister under Constantine and, according to his own account, a firm believer in the emperor's policy of social justice until disgust at the greedy and corrupt practices of the day drove him into early retirement.[25] Firmicus will reemerge in a later chapter as one key to the puzzle of Christian intolerance. While Constantine was still alive, he wrote, at the request of a highly placed official, the *Mathesis,* the most thorough study of astrology in Latin to survive from the ancient world.[26] A striking number of Constantinian themes can be found in its pages, particularly those that stress the emperor's closeness with a special deity. *Mathesis* is replete with such neutral religious terms as *numen fabricator deus, deus summus* and *divina mens,*[27] and two passages in particular contain multiple echoes of phrases that cropped up in the pagan orations considered in Chapter 5. In book I, he begs the Sun, "best and greatest, . . . Mind and Moderator of the universe," to preserve Constantine, "the Most Great Princeps and his unconquered children, our lords and Caesars," so that "the human race may enjoy everlasting peace and prosperity."[28] And in the preface to the fifth book, Firmicus prays to an unknown god:

> Whoever Thou art, God, . . . who strengthens the body's weakness with infusion of the Divine Mind, . . . Sole Governor and Chief of all, Sole Emperor and Lord, to whom the entire force of the heavenly powers is subservient, whose Will is the essence of finished creation; by whose unbreakable laws the organized nature of the world had imbued all things with eternity, Thou, Father of all and at the same time, Mother, Thou Father and Thine own Son, bound together by the chain of fate, to Thee we stretch out hands in prayer, Thee we worship with trembling supplication.[29]

Firmicus may, as he says, have written the *Mathesis* merely to satisfy the interest of his friend Lollianus Mavortius. But he fully expected Mavortius to become consul at the time he wrote, and there is a long tradition in Roman politics of seeking plum appointments by just such literary devotions.[30] Whether or not such considerations influenced Firmicus's selection of themes to emphasize, either he had the dullest antennae and tinniest ear of any member of the elite in Rome's thousand-year history, or his book is evidence that at the very end of Constantine's reign, in what is universally regarded as the most fully realized point of the emperor's Christian policy, an experienced and well-connected member of the governing class still believed he could advocate his faith in astrology with impunity and even dedicate the product of his devotion to a key figure in Constantine's government. But the best evidence for Constantine's consensus may be negative—the lack of any strong pagan outcry against his pro-Christian policies in the surviving record, and the refusal of his successors for almost fifty years to take any but token steps against pagan practices. Additional evidence comes from the arguments pagans used once that policy started to change in the last quarter of the century. Speaking against unchecked attacks on the temples by bands of monks, the great Antiochene orator Libanius deliberately evoked the Christian tradition of the martyrs, claiming that, "as everyone knows," suffering simply confirms people "more strongly than ever in their faith."[31]

Other pagan orators in these later years delivered ringing defenses of the principle of toleration. Themistius, who was more or less "orator laureate" for the middle decades of the century, resorted to the ancient rules of "good king" panegyric to praise Julian's successor, the Christian emperor Jovian, as a ruler who was "aware that a king is not able to apply compulsion to his subjects in all things . . . and especially the virtue of reverence for the Divine." God himself created diversity of belief, Themistius argued, and in subscribing to this principle Jovian makes himself "the most godlike of kings."

> The law of God and your law remains unchanged for ever—that the mind of each and every man should be free to follow the way of worship which it thinks [to be best]. This is a law against which no confiscation, no crucifixion, no death at the stake has ever yet availed; you may hale and kill the body, if so be that this comes to pass; but the mind will escape you, taking with it freedom of thought and the right of the law as it goes, even if it is subjected to force in the language used by the tongue.[32]

In the Latin West, Symmachus, urban prefect and senatorial spokesman, uttered the phrase that has since become a watchword for religious toleration, "Not by one avenue only can we arrive at so tremendous a secret [as the nature of God]."[33]

One of the nicer ironies of this whole question is the way that these speeches have become proof of paganism's tolerant spirit. No such argument can be found during the heyday of classical paganism, and the reason it occurs now is because these authors were deliberately drawing on themes that they knew would resonate with a Christian audience.[34] Libanius, for one, knew exactly what he was doing. In his speech For the Temples, he asked Theodosius why constraint was being used and then observed, "It is said that in their [the Christians'] very own rules it does not appear, but that persuasion meets with approval and compulsion is deplored. Then why these frantic attacks on the temples, if you cannot persuade and must needs resort to force? In this way you would obviously be breaking your own rules."[35] Libanius was not asserting a pagan tradition of toleration against a new Christian policy of coercion but using a Christian emperor's own tradition to convince him that coercion was wrong. It is a tactic that disempowered peoples all through history have used to win concessions.[36]

Although it was once commonplace to postulate howls of pain from pagans in reaction to Constantine's policy, what the record suggests is that pagans found Constantine's policy, in Winkelmann's words, a "bearable evil."[37] The bigger task for Constantine was to strengthen the hand of Christians who favored an inclusive policy.

The Council of Nicaea

Theologically, the Donatist schism and Arian heresy were entirely different in nature and import: one concerned discipline and, perhaps, social divisions; the other went to the heart of Christian faith and belief. Politically, however, the two had one thing in common: they both presented Constantine with choices that, as much as his writings, can be used to reveal his own preferences and priorities. In both cases, he showed a consistent tendency to come down on the side of Christians who would be inclusive, who were "team players," who worked for consensus.

Constantine entrusted his letter to Arius and Alexander to Bishop Ossius of Corduba, who had either accompanied him on his campaign or joined him in the East after the victory. From Alexandria, Ossius went to Antioch, where he participated in a council that provisionally excommunicated three bishops, including Eusebius of Caesarea, for refusing to support the position of Bishop Alexander. A letter sent from the council refers to an upcoming "great council," to be held at Ancyra, where all these problems would be resolved. Scholars have long postulated that Constantine must have been the one who called this council, a view disputed by T. D. Barnes.[38] It would not be surprising, given his experience with the Donatists, if Constantine had already thought of a council as the right mechanism for settling this issue should his plea to the disputants go unheeded, but Barnes might be right to think he had not settled on a venue, since the atmosphere in which the debate was conducted could have a crucial effect on the outcome. Ancyra, whose bishop, Marcellus, was a vehement opponent of Arius, might have been chosen by Ossius after consultation with Bishop Alexander, as a means of gaining his commitment to attend.

But Ossius's mission should be seen as part of a two-pronged effort to lay the groundwork for reconciliation. While Ossius soothed the bishops allied with Alexander, Constantine worked just as diligently on Eusebius of Nicomedia. The evidence for this effort is buried in Constantine's letter to the congregation of Nicomedia, written to justify his decision to exile their bishop in the aftermath of the Council of Nicaea. Here, Constantine claimed that prior to the council Eusebius "secretly sent different messengers" to solicit Constantine's support, "because he was afraid that his being detected in so great a sin would result in his expulsion from his honourable office."[39] The part about Eusebius's motives was obviously after the fact; at the time, Eusebius's messages seem to have convinced Constantine that Ancyra would not be a level playing field.

Constantine's subsequent actions show how well he had learned from his first experience with church councils ten years earlier.[40] Instead of letting Ossius and Alexander proceed with a stacked meeting, as he had done with Miltiades in Rome in 314, Constantine abruptly intervened, changing the site for the proposed council just months before it was to begin from Ancyra to Nicaea, in the province of Bithynia. Ostensibly, the reason was because the coastal city was more accessible and the weather better. Coincidentally, however, Bithynia was also the province that Eusebius presided over as metropolitan bishop, giving him precedence in any proceedings within its borders, and Nicaea's bishop, Theognis, was a close ally. Constantine had learned from his experience with Miltiades' abortive Council of Rome that broad representation was the best way to isolate the losing side and limit their appeals.

When the Council of Nicaea opened on June 1, 325, Constantine had every reason to believe he had events well in hand. No detailed record of the proceedings survives, but Eusebius of Caesarea has left a description of the opening ceremony, how the bishops were seated to the right and left according to rank in the palace's great central hall, how a hush of anticipation fell over the assembly as the time arrived for the emperor to appear. His own words capture better than any summary the impact of the moment:

> And first of all, three of his immediate family entered in succession, then others also preceded his approach, not of the soldiers and guards who usually accompanied him, but only friends in the faith. And now, all rising at the signal which indicated the emperor's entrance, at last he himself proceeded through the midst of the assembly, like some heavenly messenger of God, clothed in raiment which glittered as it were with rays of light, reflecting the glowing radiance of a purple robe, and adorned with the brilliant splendor of gold and precious stones.[41]

While Constantine waited, Eusebius continues, "a low chair of wrought gold" was brought for him to sit on. Even then, Constantine did not sit, until "the bishops had beckoned to him," after which the bishops in their turn sat.

Constantine's entrance was enviably well orchestrated, with just the right combination of majesty and modesty to overawe the assembly. The detail with which Eusebius recorded it is testimony enough to the impression it made. A bishop identified by Eusebius only as the one "who occupied the chief place in the right division of the assembly," but who should have been either Eusebius of Nicomedia as metropolitan or Theognis, the bishop of Nicaea, gave a brief address of welcome, after which Constantine himself spoke. This speech, reported by Eusebius of Caesarea in his *vita Constantini*, is seldom reprinted, much less analyzed, for it is devoid of theological content and reads like but another piece of ceremonial fluff. As a political document, however, it is extremely revealing of Constantine's motives and methods.

When the welcoming bishop had finished speaking, Eusebius writes, all eyes turned to the emperor. Constantine milked the moment. According to Eusebius, he first "looked serenely round on the assembly with a cheerful aspect" and took a long moment to collect his thoughts before beginning to speak. He spoke in Latin, with an interpreter who, presumably, translated whenever the emperor paused. This, in itself, is significant. It was customary for emperors to deliver formal addresses in Latin, even if they were fluent in Greek: Augustus had set the standard here, as in so much else, long ago.[42] In this case, the tradition allowed Constantine to add the distant majesty of the language associated with justice and government to the aura of impartiality which was important to the role he would play in events. It also allowed him to pause frequently, and at the right points, for applause.

His opening sentences are particularly admirable: "It was once my chief desire, dearest friends, to enjoy the spectacle of your united presence; and now that this desire is fulfilled, I feel myself bound to render thanks to God the universal King, because, in addition to all his other benefits, he has granted me a blessing higher than all the rest, in permitting me to see you not only all assembled together, but all united in a common harmony of sentiment."[43] With remarkable economy, Constantine managed both to identify with his audience and to slip his own agenda onto the table. His words were designed to create harmony but also to play on the sentiments of the majority of the bishops present, who were not vested in either side of the theological controversy and wanted nothing so much as to restore harmony to their communion. These centrist bishops were vital to Constantine's plan, and his speech was designed to win them to his side. He followed his opening statement with a discernible pattern of applause lines: dissension is the work of the devil; strife within the church is far more evil and dangerous than any kind of war; his victory over the enemies of the church will mean nothing if he does not see the bishops "all united in one judgment" with the "common spirit of peace and concord." Moving swiftly to his conclusion, Constantine assured the bishops that, by settling this controversy, they would "at the same time be acting in a manner most pleasing to the supreme God, and [they would] confer an exceeding favor" on Constantine, who was, in his words, their "fellow-servant."[44] The reaction that surely punctuated each of these lines must have given pause, as it was meant to do, to all those bishops who had come to the council thirsting for blood.

Constantine's speech was designed to evoke a spirit of moderation, and Eusebius's subsequent account, although it offers little other detail of the proceedings, demonstrates how the emperor worked to restrain extremists on both sides. The debate threatened at the outset to break down in mutual recriminations, Eusebius writes, but Constantine, "by the affability of his address to all, and his use of the Greek language, with which he was not altogether unacquainted, appeared in a truly attractive and amiable light, persuading some, convincing others by his reasonings, praising those who spoke well, and urging all to unity of sentiment, until at last he succeeded in bringing them to one mind and judgment respecting every disputed question."[45] Eusebius clearly approved of this influence. Another participant who did not was Eustathius of Antioch, who wrote darkly of how "the Eusebian gang" was saved from utter ruin by those who "under the pretence of preserving peace, imposed silence on all the ablest speakers."[46] But then Eustathius had more reason than most to be bitter, for in the aftermath he was the first to fall victim to those enemies who in his view should have been crushed at Nicaea.

Eusebius of Caesarea's narrative moves swiftly past such unseemly matters to the closing ceremony—a magnificent feast to celebrate the emperor's vicennalia. Although he omitted details of the debate from the *vita Constantini*, Eusebius was more forthcoming in a letter he wrote to his congregation in the aftermath to justify his own actions. The letter begins by expressing concern that the congregation might have been misled by rumors and false reports about the council; it then reproduces the traditional creed of his congregation at Caesarea which Eusebius reports he presented to the council, neglecting to mention that he did so to purge himself of the charges of heresy with which he had been indicted by the Council of Antioch. He continues: "On this faith being publicly put forth by us, no room for contradiction appeared; but our most pious Emperor, before any one else, testified that it comprised most orthodox statements. He confessed moreover that such were his own sentiments, and he advised all present to agree to it, and to subscribe its articles and to assent to them, with the insertion of the single word Consubstantial (*homoousios*)."[47] The letter in its entirety is so disingenuous that it is best not to put too much weight on any of its parts. Eusebius clearly was embarrassed, and it is significant that the letter survives only in the work of an enemy, Athanasius, who used it years later to discredit Eusebius's successor as bishop of Caesarea, Acacius. There is no particular reason to doubt that Constantine found Eusebius's creed acceptable, but if he did, indeed, approve it with as strong a testimony as Eusebius represents, then it is one further proof of both a prior plan to control the debate and Constantine's immense political skills. Any bishop who intended to attack Eusebius's orthodoxy certainly must have had second thoughts after so ringing an endorsement,[48] and Eusebius was, in fact, allowed to take his place in the assembly. No doubt the bishop of Caesarea felt both relief and gratitude for Constantine's intervention; this was psychologically, therefore, just the right moment for Constantine to drop the bombshell that Eusebius tries to pass off to his congregation as the mere insertion of a single word.

Homoousios—"Consubstantial" in the Latin, "of the same substance"—emerged as the term over which battle lines became drawn. Athanasius reveals in his work *On the Council*—the work to which he attached Eusebius's letter—that it was inserted specifically into the debate to confound the Arians, who had been able to find an acceptable meaning in every earlier attempt to devise a statement of faith. With each attempt, he writes, "Eusebius [of Nicomedia] and his fellows . . . were caught whispering to each other and winking with their eyes, that 'like,' and 'always,' and 'power,' and 'in Him,' were, as before, common to us and the Son, and that it was no difficulty to agree to these."[49] There were several reasons why they could not do the same with *homoousios*. Theological objections aside, the term was not scriptural, and by common consent phrases that could be found in the New Testament canon were the most reliable indicators of Christian faith. Even two decades later, Athanasius was forced to defend its use, which he did by arguing that "Eusebius and his crowd" (his favorite phrase for the opposition) subscribed to it at the time—as Eusebius of Caesarea's letter proved. But there was an even more serious defect: in the careful fine-tuning that was always necessary to distinguish the Person of Christ without separating him from the Oneness of the Father, *homo-*

ousios had already been judged and found wanting. It was linked with Sabellianism, the most prominent heresy of the previous century, whose error lay precisely in the failure to distinguish sufficiently between Father and Son. A council in Antioch had condemned the term as heretical in 268; how, the Arians demanded, could it now become an article of faith? They could accept *homoiousios*, "of a similar substance," but they would not discard the iota of difference which separated the two terms. It was a matter of principle as well as theology. As Athanasius's explanation makes clear, his party sensed a tactical advantage in the discomfiture of their opponents and accordingly chose this ground on which to make their stand.

Eusebius of Caesarea's letter to his congregation must be understood to have compressed all this maneuvering and debate into a single moment if it is to be reconciled with the account given by Athanasius. But even though Constantine may not have suggested the word at the precise moment that Eusebius describes, and may not even have been the first to suggest it at all, he must have given his support to it at some point or Eusebius would not have dared to hide behind his authority. Why? Why would Constantine support insertion of such a troubling and controversial term? From the letter he wrote to the principals only months earlier, it is safe to say that the theological implications, one way or the other, would not have bothered him. But the whole purpose of the council, to his mind, was unity, and *homoousios* was chosen specifically to drive a wedge into the assembly.

Two considerations bring the dynamics of the debate into focus. First, it is necessary to discard the assumption of a clear divide between orthodox and Arian positions, such as came to be perceived in retrospect, when positions had hardened and a more sophisticated theological vocabulary developed. At the time, not only were there compelling arguments on both sides, but also the technical language did not exist to bring into sharp relief the cause of the division. Both sides, for instance, were accused of "Judaizing"—in fourth-century Christian vocabulary the equivalent of seeking *regnum* in the Roman republic or being a Communist or Fascist in twentieth-century American politics. The Arians were like the Jews because they minimized the divinity of Christ, the Nicenes because they emphasized the Oneness of the Divine Being. The reaction of any Jewish listener to this aspect of the debate can only be imagined, but a century later, Christians looking back on the charges and countercharges leveled during this period likened the two sides to armies groping their way in the dark, neither side exactly clear what it was fighting about.[50] The majority of bishops at the council, it is generally conceded, were as confused by the theological intricacies of the question as a modern layperson is likely to be, and they were ready to support anything that was not patently heretical. It is usually thought that Eusebius of Caesarea omitted theological details because of his personal embarrassment. But his account might well reflect the aspects of the council which most impressed the majority of participants. It is certainly this center he was thinking of when he described the reaction of the bishops to the emperor's summons: "As soon then as the imperial injunction was generally made known, all with the utmost willingness hastened thither, as though they would outstrip one another in a race; for they were impelled by the anticipation of a happy result to the conference, by the hope of enjoying present peace, and the desire of beholding something new and strange in the person of so admirable an emperor."[51]

This consideration explains the mood of the assembly. Constantine's motive is a bit harder to tease forth, only because it must be deduced from the scanty evidence that survives. His preparations for the council, and the outcome he desired, involved concessions to both sides. The outline of his concessions to "the party of Eusebius" is fairly clear: he gave them the choice of venue and undertook to restrain the more virulent voices of the opposition. What had he given to bring "the party of Alexander" to the table? Only one conclusion accords with the outcome. At the end of the day, they would have a creed that clearly branded Arius a heretic. Like all catchwords, *homoousios* was defensible only in the entire context of debate and study that led to its choice. But it had the one advantage of being a word that exposed and isolated Arius. When all the arguing and cajoling was done, only two bishops, both of them among Arius's original supporters, refused to sign. By imperial decree, they were sent into exile, along with Arius (who, as a presbyter, did not participate in his own condemnation) and a miscellaneous group of priests and students loyal to his cause.

To Tyre and Beyond

By all accounts, Constantine at Nicaea was at the top of his form. Yet the unity he achieved at that moment soon came unraveled, setting in motion a train of events which leads to the Council of Tyre, and from there to the meeting in Constantinople with which this book began. A very different Constantine appears in standard accounts of the next ten years—choosing one side, then another; exonerating Athanasius with the highest praise at one moment, only to condemn him and embrace Arius at the next; calling one council after another, never able to make up his mind, whining and blustery in turns, a pitiful spectacle, wavering and indecisive—"un pauvre homme qui tâtonnait," in the memorable phrase of André Piganiol.[52] The contrast with his commanding presence at Nicaea is immediate and predictably read as deterioration.

The trend is already visible in the work of Eutropius, one of the new aristocracy of the fourth century who became *magister epistularum* under Constantine's son, Constantius II, and eventually praetorian prefect and consul. A pagan who is regarded as one of the more balanced observers of his age, Eutropius wrote of Constantine in his *Breviarium,* a précis of Roman history dedicated to the emperor Valens (364–378), that "he was a man who at the beginning of his reign was comparable to the best of rulers, in the last period to those of the middle rank."[53] Church historians depict Constantine as unable to put a halt to the sniping of the different episcopal factions and increasingly misled by a pro-Arian faction, while others see him as frittering away the resources of both church and state, miring his successors in religious squabbles when their attention was desperately needed elsewhere.

The shifts and turns during this final period of Constantine's reign make him appear either Machiavellian or inept, depending on the observer, inconstant or feckless, subject to whichever dominant personality saw him last. But appearances can be misleading. One trait that immediately leaps out at any student of the age, for instance, is Constantine's readiness to submit and resubmit issues of Christian doctrine to different church councils, which has been interpreted as everything from vacillation to a cynical plan to "divide and conquer." But these judgments rarely take into account either the novelty of the conciliar arrangement being worked out between Constantine and the bishops or Constantine's own agenda. In this case, much of the inconsistency depends on unspoken assumptions about what Constantine must have intended. Looked at without these preconceptions, the record yields a very different picture.

The exact sequence of events in the decade that separates the meetings in Nicaea and Constantinople is murky. Athanasius himself wrote several detailed accounts, at least one of which was never meant to be seen by any but his most loyal supporters. Rich in documentary evidence, his story is nevertheless incomplete and fuzzy about the meaning, and even the timing, of key details—not surprising, given the partisan motives of the author. His witness nevertheless long went unquestioned, and only patient sifting by the keenest and most determined scholarly minds has brought some order to a jumbled record of fragments, hints, innuendo, and precious details inadvertently recorded.[54]

It is clear that the unity of Nicaea soon dissipated. Within a few months, two more bishops joined the list of exiles, none other than Eusebius of Nicomedia and Theognis of Nicaea. Their crime appears to have been a continued willingness to communicate with Arius and his followers, for when he sought permission to return from exile two years later, Eusebius pointed out that, whereas he had demonstrated his orthodoxy by signing the creed, he had refused to sign the accompanying anathema on Arius, because he did not consider Arius guilty of the theological errors of which he was accused.[55] Such reasoning would explain why he saw no contradiction between signing the creed and continuing to communicate with Arius. Eusebius may indeed have acted in good faith, but Constantine clearly felt betrayed. This was the occasion that prompted his scathing letter to Eusebius's congregation in Nicomedia in which he all but accused the bishop of high treason. Yet his anger soon was to shift in other directions.

The turning point came near the end of 327 when Arius himself signaled to Constantine that he could live with the creed. His confession of faith is a small milestone in the art of diplomacy:

> This faith we have received from the holy gospels, the Lord therein saying to his disciples [Matt. 28:9]: "Go and teach all nations, baptizing them in the name of the Father, and of the Son, and of the Holy Spirit." If we do not so

believe and truly receive the Father, the Son, and the Holy Spirit, as the whole Catholic Church and the Holy Scriptures teach (in which we believe in every respect), God is our judge both now, and in the coming judgment. Wherefore we beseech your piety, most devout emperor, that we who are persons consecrated to the ministry, and holding the faith and sentiments of the church and of the holy Scriptures, may by your pacific and devoted piety be reunited to our mother, the Church, all superfluous questions and disputings being avoided: that so both we and the whole church being at peace, may in common offer our accustomed prayers for your tranquil reign, and on behalf of your whole family.[56]

Arius obviously had done his homework. In reminding Constantine of God's ability to punish wrongs done himself, his confession picked up the refrain from a long tradition of pagan and Christian toleration which Constantine himself had learned to use, and in asking for nothing more than peace and unity while stressing the importance of prayer for the imperial family and dismissing all else as "superfluous," it addressed itself directly to the emperor's personal agenda.

Constantine was beside himself with joy. "Arius, I say, that Arius, has come to me, the Augustus, in accordance with the exhortation of very many persons, announcing that he thinks about our Catholic faith those things which in the synod at Nicaea have been defined and confirmed," he wrote Bishop Alexander of Alexandria. Thinking the unanimous support he had long sought was now achieved, Constantine stressed how he had personally examined "the suppliant man" in front of witnesses and, being fully satisfied, begged Alexander to receive him back: "For if you should make provision for these things, you would conquer hatreds by concord. I beg, therefore, aid concord; cooperate in the beauties of friendship toward the persons who do not doubt the matters of faith; make me to hear those things which I wish and desire: the peace and the concord of you all."[57]

There was consternation in Alexandria. Despite the fervor of its words, Arius's confession effectively sidestepped the real issue of the council, and anyone who knew his unyielding temperament must have remained skeptical of the sincerity of his newfound commitment. Eusebius of Nicomedia, on the other hand, was elated by Constantine's change of heart. He immediately petitioned for permission to return from exile, on the plausible grounds that his offense had not been theological—he had, indeed, subscribed to the statement of faith at the Council of Nicaea—but personal, continuing to communicate with Arius after he had been denounced as a heretic. How, Eusebius now argued, could he be left in exile for standing by a man whom the emperor himself now deemed orthodox? The appeal worked. Once reinstated, Eusebius skillfully exploited the access that being bishop of Nicomedia provided him, as Socrates Scholasticus recognized: "Now at this juncture," he wrote, "Eusebius possessed great influence, because the emperor resided at Nicomedia. . . . On this account therefore many of the bishops paid their court to Eusebius."[58] Eusebius lost no time organizing his allies. In swift order, two of the most outspoken and vulnerable champions of the Nicene position, Eustathius of Antioch and Asclepas of Gaza, were deposed, along with a number of their supporters.[59] But the backlash swiftly came to focus on one person in particular, Athanasius of Alexandria, who succeeded Bishop Alexander upon his death in 328, bringing with him a mind as resourceful, and a spirit as inflexible, as Arius's own.

Athanasius's ordination was a portent of things to come. He had been in Constantinople when Alexander died, but he hastened back to Egypt as soon as he heard the news. A council of bishops had been summoned to choose a successor, yet even though Alexander was reported to have named Athanasius on his deathbed, it proceeded with more deliberation than the young cleric thought necessary. According to his detractors, Athanasius preempted the council by taking himself to the church of Dionysius with a handful of like-minded bishops and, in circumstances eerily reminiscent of Caecilian's earlier action in Carthage, undergoing the ceremony of installation—having first taken the sensible precaution of barricading the church's doors to deter interlopers. While rivals fulminated against this extraordinary procedure, and complained further that the preemptive bishop had not even achieved the minimum age of thirty prescribed by canon at the time of his elevation, Athanasius set about putting his new house in order.[60]

One target of his housecleaning was the Meletians, a breakaway sect of rigorists who, like their Donatist counterparts to the west, had broken with the established church over treatment of lapsed Christians and set up their own churches and chain of command. But the Meletians had received more generous treatment from the Council of

Nicaea than the Donatists had from the Council of Arles. The canons of
the council provided that the Meletians should be reunited with the
Catholic Church, that their bishops should be confirmed in their
station in cities that had no Catholic bishop, and, in cities that did, they
should maintain the dignities of their former office and be eligible to
succeed should the Catholic bishop predecease.[61] Athanasius would
have none of it. When a delegation of Meletian bishops came to the
capital to complain, Eusebius of Nicomedia was ready for them. In
return for sharing communion with Arius, Eusebius would put the
considerable powers of his office, and the entrée that his position gave
him to the imperial court, at their disposal. Opponents naturally called
it an unholy alliance. But by this time Arius had been restored to the
fold by the declaration of both the emperor and an episcopal council,
and Athanasius's refusal to honor the accord reached with the Meletians flaunted the authority of the Council of Nicaea at least as patently
as had Eusebius's earlier communion with Arius.

Suddenly Athanasius was on the defensive. Now the charge that
would haunt him for so many years surfaced—that his agents had
invaded a Meletian church, overturned its altar, and broken a sacred
chalice. In the context of the vigorous campaign Athanasius was wag-
ing against the Meletians, such charges were instantly plausible, and
Athanasius never did, in fact, completely and unequivocally deny the
affair of the chalice (even if items were broken, he once conceded, they
could not be considered sacred because the building in question was
not a properly consecrated church).[62] But it is Constantine whose
actions have attracted the most comment. In 331, the Eusebian-
Meletian alliance prevailed upon him to hear these charges against
Athanasius, as well as others alleging corruption and abuse of power.
The result of this hearing was a victory for Athanasius—a letter from
Constantine to the Christians of Alexandria which reviled those who
had brought charges against their bishop, whom he praised as a man of
rare piety.[63] To make the victory all the more sweet, Constantine soon
turned against Arius, denouncing him as a "Porphyrian," by which he
evidently meant that Arius, like the Neoplatonist enemy of the church,
minimized the divinity of Christ, and perhaps also that like Porphyry
Arius was standing in the way of a peaceful resolution. Insisting that
the priest he had received so joyfully only a few years earlier was as

implacable an enemy of Christianity as the author of Against the Christians, Constantine ordered all of Arius's writings burned.[64]

Athanasius's triumph was short lived. Two years later, he was back in Constantinople to answer renewed charges, this time including the murder of the priest Arsenius. Once again, Constantine dismissed the charges, and sober scholars believe that it was on this occasion—not the Council of Tyre two years later—that Arsenius turned up alive and with both arms intact.[65] Yet despite such convincing proof, in 334 Constantine again turned against the bishop of Alexandria, ordering him to trial before a council of bishops summoned to sit in Caesarea in 334. The decision sent Athanasius virtually into open revolt. He ducked the imperial summons by hiding out with the monks in Upper Egypt—a tactic he would use time and again over the next forty years. When the bishop proved contumacious, Constantine ordered another council for Tyre in the following year, this time warning darkly, "Should any one, though I deem it most improbable, venture on this occasion to violate my command, and refuse his attendance, a messenger shall be despatched forthwith to banish that person by virtue of an imperial edict, and to teach him that it does not become him to resist an emperor's decrees when issued in defense of truth."[66] Thus was set in train the string of events that led in rapid succession to Athanasius's exile to Gaul in November 335.

These are the inconsistencies and about-faces that have so sullied Constantine's record in this period, and indeed it is easy to conclude even from this brief outline that the emperor was out of his depth, mere putty in the hands of a sophisticated thinker like Arius or a charismatic personality like Athanasius. Yet this outline is also sufficient to show that these judgments have measured the emperor according to a theological yardstick, assuming that his agenda was identical to that of the church.

It is better to see Constantine as following his own agenda and using the resources at his command to persuade Athanasius and Eusebius of Nicomedia alike to conform to it. What was Constantine's agenda? Eusebius's letter to his congregation in Caesarea can be our guide. Evidently anticipating objection to his decision to sign the creed, Eusebius points out that the meaning of *homoousios* was the subject of prolonged discussion: "And they professed that the phrase 'of the substance' was indicative of the Son's being indeed from the Father, yet without being as if a part of him. And with this understanding, we thought good to assent to the meaning of the pious teaching suggesting that the Son was from the Father, not, however, a part of His substance." In any language, these words are nonsense, claiming that the term "of the substance" means anything but "of the substance." If Eusebius was not aiming at deliberate obfuscation, his words must mean that, despite Athanasius's gloating, significant qualifications had to be put on the term *homoousios* before it would prove acceptable to a large enough number of centrist bishops to isolate Arian hard-liners. Eusebius might have fooled himself into believing he had been given as much wiggle room as he reported—he ends this section of his letter with the candid admission that "peace [was] the aim which we set before us, and steadfastness in the orthodox view"[67]—but it seems likely that in some way Constantine had communicated to the assembly the same principles he had articulated in his letter to Arius and Alexander: that there was no need to require "entire unity on this subject" and that it would be sufficient to have "one faith, and one understanding among you, one united judgment in reference to God," with room for differing interpretations of detail.

Before closing his letter, Eusebius invoked the emperor's authority once again, writing with regard to another contested point, "Our most religious Emperor did at the time prove, in a speech, that He was in being even according to His divine generation which is before all ages, since even before He was generated in energy, He was potentially with the Father ingenerately, the Father being always Father, as King always, and Saviour always, being all things potentially, and being always in the same respects and in the same way."[68] Either Eusebius omitted a significant, and substantive, portion from his account of Constantine's welcoming address in the *vita Constantini*, or the emperor spoke to the council on more than one occasion. Either way, this additional information confirms Eusebius's claim in the *vita Constantini* that Constantine took an active role in the proceedings, listening patiently to all the speeches, flattering each speaker with his full and undivided attention, so that "by occasionally assisting the argument of each party in turn, he gradually disposed even the most vehement disputants to a reconciliation . . . , praising those who spoke well, and urging all to unity of sentiment, until at last he succeeded in bringing them to one mind and judgment respecting every disputed question."[69]

Constantine was playing the game of consensus politics. In this game, winners are players, like Eusebius of Caesarea, who place peace at a higher value than quibbling over abstract terms; losers are players, like Arius, who cannot find it in themselves to compromise. For the game to work, everybody must give up something. This is the reason for the sense of betrayal which permeates Constantine's letter to the congregation in Nicomedia to explain why he exiled their bishop. "My sole desire [in calling the Council of Nicaea] was to effect universal concord," he wrote. Eusebius had asked Constantine's protection and thereby "perverted my judgment and got round me in an underhand way, as you also shall get to know. For everything was done at that time as he wanted—and he concealed all his evil intention in his own mind."[70] Making allowance for the flourishes of Byzantine rhetoric, Constantine's account is perfectly clear, and highly revealing. With bishops Alexander and Ossius evidently in complete agreement and the council scheduled to be held in Ancyra, the see of a fervently anti-Arian bishop, Eusebius complained that his side would not receive a fair hearing. Constantine did "everything . . . as he wanted," moving the site to Nicaea and probably promising that he would rein in the extremists. In return, he expected Eusebius to facilitate a compromise. Instead, the bishop behaved treacherously, at least in Constantine's eyes—raising objections, holding out until the last minute, and then using a technicality to share Holy Communion with individuals who had been stigmatized as public outlaws. Eusebius may have run afoul of his own logic in thinking that he could condemn the heresy but continue to communicate with the heresiarch. To Constantine, this was mere hairsplitting, a self-indulgent cleverness that put the carefully crafted arrangement of Nicaea in jeopardy. No wonder he was furious: he had conceded everything to the bishop of Nicomedia and received only high-handed treatment for his pains.

How could so skilled a player as Eusebius undoubtedly was have stumbled so badly? The simplest answer is that he had misread the rules at Nicaea and allowed himself to be marked as a troublemaker. Athanasius's account of the council may well exaggerate his own role, since he was only a presbyter at the time and it would have been unseemly for him to play as visible a role as he gives the impression of having done. But the tactic his account describes is clear: its aim was to maneuver the Eusebians into a position where they would have to decline on principle, and in the consensus game, principle, while useful for gaining concessions, is not in the end a winning ticket. The rule of consensus requires all players to recognize the supreme value of the common goal. Consensus politics, in other words, places a premium on team players, and Eusebius of Nicomedia, unlike his namesake of Caesarea, had placed himself before the team.

This was a mistake Eusebius would not make twice. Once he realized that the reason for Constantine's support of the Nicene formula was not so much theology as a commitment to unity and consensus, Eusebius skillfully turned the tables on Athanasius, using a series of councils to maneuver him into a position where he would become the obstructionist in Constantine's eyes. Athanasius's own account shows how vulnerable he was to this strategy, for it makes clear that he was no more inclined to compromise than his opponents. Moreover, it shows him unwilling even to concede them honorable motives or to seek common ground. It shows, in fact, exactly the opposite: so certain was he that the Eusebians were not sincere that every time he saw a formula was acceptable to them, it immediately became suspect in his own eyes. On that occasion, the dynamics of the room had worked in his favor. But what option would he have if they now accepted the Nicene formula? The rule of consensus does not allow for a litmus test—there is to be no prying, in Constantine's words, into "the secret custody of your own minds and thoughts." Lip service is sufficient. Players who acknowledge the common goal must be accepted without further challenge to their sincerity or commitment. Surface consent—what a principled person would call superficiality—is a necessary, but also a sufficient, condition. What Athanasius's account shows most of all is how much difficulty he would have playing that game. Soon Constantine was writing Athanasius to "grant free admission to all who wish[ed] to enter the Church." The emperor continued, "If I learn that you have hindered any who lay claim to membership, or debarred them from entrance, I will immediately send someone to depose you at my command and remove you from your place."[1]

Athanasius cites this letter in a context that would limit Constantine's order specifically to Arius, and Arius may indeed have been its primary beneficiary. But it should be noted that Constantine's language is more general, suggesting a policy that envisioned few restrictions on Christian membership. Here, Athanasius was a godsend to Eusebius of Nicomedia. As events would show, Constantine's threshold for the definition of Christian belief was to prove far too low for any of the disputants to accept.[72] But by taking the stand he did on Arius, Athanasius relieved the Eusebians of any need to compromise the essentials of their belief in order to maintain their ties with Constantine. All they needed to do was to depict Athanasius as the bar to unity within the Christian fold, and this they could do handily by professions such as Arius had used to win Constantine's heart. So long as Athanasius was unwilling to compromise for the sake of unity even within the Christian community, it was an easy matter for the Eusebians to position themselves as the party most suitable to Constantine's plans.

This explication of the dynamics of Nicaea and its fallout also clarifies the subsequent behavior that Constantine scholars have frequently characterized as either inconsistent or contemptible. The reason it has seemed so bizarre is that scholars have been following the wrong map, reading Constantine from theological signposts, so to speak. With Constantine's own agenda in the foreground, his behavior is both coherent and consistent. However crucial they might have been to the cause of orthodoxy, the charges against Athanasius in fact meant nothing to Constantine; they were merely a convenient lever to bring a recalcitrant bishop to the negotiating table. On each of the occasions that resulted in exoneration and praise, Athanasius must have delivered, in addition to ringing defenses of orthodoxy, sufficient evidence of flexibility, a willingness to reconsider or be persuaded, to convince Constantine that he was being reasonable. In return, on each occasion the emperor dismissed the charges, only to reinstate them when Athanasius subsequently reneged.

Athanasius maneuvered as much as he could, elevating the decisions of Nicaea above those of any other council in order to claim that someone excommunicated, as Arius had been, by the Nicene council could not subsequently be reinstated by any lesser council.[73] For this reason, the Meletians were a greater threat to him than Arius: the same Nicene council had ordered that they be reintegrated into the Egyptian church, and this Athanasius was equally determined to prevent. Had he compromised on one or the other, Athanasius might well have kept in Constantine's good graces. But his steadfast rejection of both Arius and the Meletians exposed a contradiction in his argument which the bishop of Nicomedia had no trouble exploiting to hang the label of dissenter and troublemaker on Athanasius.

Arius proved time and again to be as rigid and unyielding as Athanasius, and Eusebius's influence may be discerned in his eventual willingness to play down the extent of his nonconformity in order to regain Constantine's favor. At one point, however, he overplayed his hand. Probably in 332—after suffering Athanasius's efforts to avoid reinstating him for some five years—he wrote Constantine an ill-tempered ultimatum, reminding the emperor of his own hold over the masses and threatening to form a breakaway church if Athanasius was not brought into compliance.[74] This letter was what provoked Constantine's own angry conclusion that Arius was no better than Porphyry.[75] It presumably required all of Eusebius of Nicomedia's considerable diplomatic skills to refocus the emperor on Athanasius as the true obstacle. But once that was done, the road to Tyre was opened—a much straighter and better signposted road than shows on the theological map.

Political Consequences

The Christian organization posed distinct and novel challenges for an emperor who would aspire to a leading role in that community. Effective leadership of such an organization required skill at finding common ground—building consensus and smoothing over differences. At Nicaea, Constantine had exhibited a rare gift for accomplishing such goals, and in the decade following he continued to use the levers of his office in order to achieve a consensus that was, to him, as important as the ideological purity sought by both Athanasius and Arius. It was in this atmosphere that the roles of emperor and bishop were further defined. Attempting a formal and rigid constitutional definition of Constantine's relations with the bishops is as futile as bygone efforts to do so for Augustus and the Senate. The relationship was fluid, and Constantine held the upper hand. He did not hesitate to involve himself where appropriate, nominating candidates for the bishopric and even intervening in episcopal decisions. But, like Augustus, he always did so with great deference and even protest. The only difference is that Constantine had no need to cover his tracks with ex post facto precedents, for the whole relationship was at once both familiar (a part of the emperor's duties as pontifex maximus) and unprecedented.

Many anecdotal stories circulated in the aftermath of Nicaea, most of them patently apocryphal. One in particular, however, has the ring of authenticity, and it is a story that illustrates Constantine's agenda. The story is of an interview Constantine had with the Novatian bishop Acesius. The Novatians were another rigorist sect that had broken with the main church in Rome in the previous century. Constantine evidently did not know much about them, for he was surprised to learn that Acesius had no objection to signing the creed. "For what reason then do you separate yourself from communion with the rest of the Church?" he asked. Acesius replied that his sect did not agree with the policy of forgiveness after penance which governed the treatment of Christians who lapsed during persecution, because "it is not right that persons who after baptism have committed a sin, which the sacred Scriptures denominate 'a sin unto death' be considered worthy of participation in the sacraments." Hearing this, Constantine dismissed Acesius with the comment, "Place a ladder, Acesius, and climb alone into heaven."[76]

The story is told by Socrates Scholasticus in the church history that he wrote little more than a century after the Council of Nicaea. He says that he heard the story from an aged Novatian priest, Auxanon, who had accompanied Acesius to the council as a youth. What makes the story more plausible than most is not so much the genealogy Socrates gives it as the fact that he says the old man, who was "by no means prone to falsehood," had simply repeated it "in the course of a narrative about the Council." In other words, Socrates was aware, and wanted his readers to be aware, that Auxanon was not telling the story to make a particular point. No record was kept of the proceedings of the Council of Nicaea, and Socrates' comment suggests he had learned to suspect those stories in circulation which did have a point—such as one about the illiterate priest who shamed a mocking philosopher into confessing the truth of Christianity.[77] Socrates' own purpose for repeating the story is useful as well. He says that he wanted "to show how much he [Constantine] desired peace," which means that he was not particularly interested in the part of the story which clinches the case for its authenticity, which is the fact that Constantine behaves in a way that does not conform to expectations, ancient or modern. The ancients made Constantine a model Christian emperor, generous to the church and reverent to its leaders. Much of this ancient view was carefully nurtured by Constantine himself and dutifully recorded by his biographers. In modern interpretations he has been everything from calculating and power-hungry to superstitious and befuddled. Nowhere else, however, does he appear quite as he does in this anecdote: relaxed and self-confident, with an unexpected capacity for both humor and decisiveness. No wonder that Socrates found the story so intriguing.

Juxtaposed against the rendering of Constantine's diplomatic skills in Eusebius's account of his activities at the council, Socrates' story opens a new window on Constantine's political abilities. Others will be quick to point out that elsewhere Constantine showered Acesius with signs of respect and specifically exempted the Novatians from punitive measures taken against other breakaway sects.[78] This was the diplomat Constantine, always courting the opposition and doing his best to neutralize what he could not win over. The moment captured by Socrates shows just as clearly, however, that Acesius did not represent the type of Christianity to which Constantine had converted, and it leaves us little surprised that the Novatians played no part in the formulation of his policies. It straightens, at least a bit, the road between Nicaea and Tyre, revealing amid the twists and turns of Constantine's support a surprising consistency in what it was he supported. Each time he acted for or against Eusebius, Athanasius, or Arius, he was acting for a church that would be inclusive and flexible, an umbrella organization that would not ask too many questions of any person or group willing to commit to play by the rules.[79] He preferred, in other words, pragmatists over ideologues. It is possible to be even more specific about the type of harmony he sought, for Constantine's reaction to the pious mouthings of Acesius is consistent with the position he took during a string of clashes with Donatist rigorists, unyielding Arian theologians, and purist Nicene fathers. In all these situations, Constantine favored not only peace and harmony but also inclusiveness and flexibility.

For all the reasons discussed at the outset of this study, politics has been the forbidden topic of Constantine scholarship, discredited in the aftermath of Burckhardt's tendentious analysis as anachronistic and unjust, foreign to the thinking of Constantine's age and a slur on his religious sincerity. That judgment, however, should be limited to religious polemic masquerading as political inquiry. Politics properly studied points the way out of the contradictions of Constantine's policy and proves the sincerity of his motives. The political concept of leverage, for instance, explains how a numerically small but organized and concentrated group like the Christians could yet play a significant role in imperial politics, especially during the breakdown of the Tetrarchy, when rival pretenders sought Christian support for their imperial candidates. After the defeat of Licinius, however, this option was foreclosed. If Constantine were, as Burckhardt reasoned, only interested in using Christianity to consolidate his personal power; if, as subsequent scholars have argued in the Burckhardt manner, he wanted to construct an imperial church, a *Reichskirche*, then the easiest game for him to play once he was in sole control would have been "divide and conquer." Constantine should have let dissidents go their own way, as he had with the Donatists, and simply concentrated his energies and resources on strengthening those factions that would give him what he wanted. Certain aspects of subsequent European history arguably would have been far less somber had he done so. Only a sincere commitment to the elusive goal of religious unity can explain his persistence in the face of singular and mounting political costs.

In his treatment of both Arius and Athanasius, Constantine was consistent: neither theology in Arius's case nor the various criminal charges in Athanasius's were as important to him as the willingness of the defendant to compromise for the sake of unity and consensus. The type of players Constantine was looking for were those who would advance his agenda for a moderate and inclusive Christianity, who would in turn be part of a coalition of Christians and pagans united behind a policy that provided a religiously neutral public space. Athanasius had been as successful in convincing Constantine of his good intentions when they met in 331 as Arius had been earlier, and in both cases Constantine produced a "forgive and forget" letter. When Athanasius subsequently balked at the terms for implementing this agreement, Constantine did not hesitate to reinstate charges that he had earlier dismissed as groundless. The policy shifts of these years are apparent, not real; they do not show a hapless emperor being swayed first by one group, then by another, but an emperor who knew his own mind and was fully intent on carrying out his program. What these events do show, however, is that during these years Constantine lost control of the agenda, and, ultimately, he lost control of the message.

It would prove, in the end, his undoing.

Eight

Controlling the Message

B y September 335, the bishops at Tyre had adjourned their inquiries into allegations of misconduct against Athanasius and taken themselves to Jerusalem in response to a summons from the emperor. There they joined in an elaborate, eight-day celebration to dedicate Constantine's new Church of the Holy Sepulchre, built over what they fervently believed to be the site of Christ's tomb. The Encaenia festival lasted from September 13 to the 20th, deliberately timed to coincide with, and supplant, the similar rite by which Solomon had dedicated his temple some thirteen hundred years earlier. Solomon's temple, of course, was long gone, but the ruins of the Second Temple of Jerusalem, built in the sixth century B.C. and magnificently enlarged by Herod the Great, only to be razed in the aftermath of the disastrous Jewish revolt of A.D. 66–70, were fully visible from the gates of this new symbol of Christian triumph, standing in mute testimony to the reversed fortunes of the two faiths. In future centuries, especially in the Latin West, the church built over the traditional site of Saint Peter's tomb on the Vatican Hill would become the symbol of the Christian state, and the bishop of Rome one of the most powerful leaders in Christian Europe. But at this time, the Holy Sepulchre was the most spectacular of Constantine's accomplishments: representations of its buildings show up all over the empire as models of the afterworld, increasingly known from this time as "the heavenly Jerusalem."[1]

In typical fashion, Constantine's biographer, Eusebius of Caesarea, attributes the construction to the emperor's foresight and zeal for the faith. Following the Council of Nicaea, he writes, Constantine, "being moved in spirit by the Saviour himself," decided to make "the blessed locality of our Saviour's resurrection an object of attraction and veneration to all." Removing the Temple of Venus that had been built over the filled-in site long ago by "impious and wicked men," the workmen discovered, "contrary to all expectation," a rock-cut cave closed by a round stone such as was known to be used for burial tombs in the time of Jesus. On news of the discovery, Constantine immediately ordered no expense spared in construction of the church whose dedication was celebrated in 335, a magnificent complex of buildings and gardens through which the visitor passed to reach the cave itself, "the chief part of the whole," which Constantine "beautified with rare columns, and profusely enriched with the most splendid decorations of every kind."[2]

Eusebius's account masks a more activist role played by the bishop of Jerusalem, Macarius, who saw an opportunity in Constantine's victory over Licinius to regain property seized almost two centuries earlier when Hadrian refounded Jerusalem as Aelia Capitolina in the aftermath of the Bar Cochba revolt of 132–35. This would be the action of "impious and wicked men" to which Eusebius referred, since, if Christian calculations were correct, Hadrian's grading operations for his new forum would have covered both the garden in which Jesus had been buried and the adjacent hill of Golgotha. Despite Eusebius's contention, there is no reason to believe Hadrian acted deliberately to obliterate Christian sites, and however repugnant the Venus temple that he raised on the newly leveled ground was to Christian sensitivities, it served the useful purpose of securing the location of the tomb in the minds of future generations. Thus, when Constantine ordered the return of Christian tombs and cemeteries subsequent to his own victory, Macarius seized the opportunity to ask for the return of this most important of all tombs, even though Constantine undoubtedly had more recent confiscations in mind when he issued his edict. Assuming Eusebius was following chronological order in his narrative, Macarius probably used the occasion of the Council of Nicaea to advance his claim in person.[3]

Eusebius's mind was not on such mundane activities when he wrote the *vita Constantini,* and it seems not to have been on another discovery connected with this event, either. Within a decade of Constantine's death, wood purported to be part of the true cross began circulating in the Mediterranean, and by the end of the century the cross itself was the centerpiece of an elaborate Easter liturgy witnessed by a pilgrim who kept a record of the event for her colleagues in the West. At that time, the wood was taken out of the gold and silver box in which it was kept and placed on a table in front of the bishop, who held it by both ends while the faithful filed pass to kiss it, under the eyes of the deacons. "They guard it like this because . . . on one occasion (I don't know when) one of them bit off a piece of the holy Wood and stole it away, and for this reason the deacons stand round and keep watch in case anyone dares to do the same again."[4] The author of this account, Egeria, was one of the many inhabitants in the later Roman Empire spurred by Constantine's attentions and the example of his mother, Helena, to visit the region rapidly becoming known as "the Holy Land."[5] It was during this visit that, later legend records, Helena discovered the remains of the cross. Eusebius records Helena's pilgrimage, but he says nothing about discovery of the wood—a vexing silence, which Gibbon with typical skill used to cast doubt on the entire episode: "The silence of Eusebius," he wrote, "which satisfies those who think, perplexes those who believe." The problem is more complex, for Eusebius is equally silent about uncovering the hill of Golgotha and, later, the cruciform shape of Constantine's resting place, the Church of the Apostles in Constantinople, both of which are attested by other observers.[6] He obviously knew more than he disclosed in the *vita Constantini,* for in a speech he delivered in Constantine's presence he alluded to both the hill and the wood.[7]

Various solutions for Eusebius's lapse have been proposed, the simplest of which is that his thinking, formed in an earlier age, did not give as much weight to the cross, much less to the cult of relics, as later ages were to do. But, as the obvious pride with which he details benefactions such as the Church of the Holy Sepulchre shows, Eusebius fully understood what these signs of imperial favor meant to his contemporaries. By such largesse, rulers as early as Xenophon's Cyrus had signaled their favor and approbation, and in this sense Constantine's churches served as a sort of visual propaganda for his new commitment. Constantine's churches changed the landscape of the Roman Empire, as surely as his predecessor Augustus's buildings changed that of the Roman republic.[8] Just as surely, they signaled a change in the priorities of government. In place of senatorial *amici* Constantine had substituted, or better adlected, episcopal ones.

As Solomon might have been able to warn him, however, the Christian movement was unlike any that emperors before Constantine had ever attempted to cultivate. Its priests had lines of authority—to God, and to their congregations—none of which depended on the emperor's favor.[9] Favor would not be enough to control this movement, which differed radically in certain key ways from anything with which a Roman emperor would have been prepared to deal. Christianity differed from classical standards not only in the nature of its organization but also in the criteria by which it judged individuals and leaders, and by which it measured success in this world. Next to the humblest of these, Solomon in all his glory would have to yield. Constantine rose to this new challenge with an energy and skill that have rarely received their due.

The Bully Pulpit

Eusebius's *vita Constantini* presents an emperor who diligently studied Scripture and surrounded himself with men of God in order constantly to deepen his understanding of the faith.[10] It is all part of an idealized version of Christian kingship which Eusebius aims to convey. It smacks of an Old Testament flavor, with the king serving primarily as a student of Scripture whose ideal purpose is to aid the priestly class.[11] In one way, however, Constantine goes beyond this model to take an activist role. The emperor, Eusebius writes, "conceived it to be incumbent on him to govern his subjects by appealing to their reason, and to secure in all respects a rational obedience to his authority. Hence he would sometimes himself evoke an assembly, on which occasions vast multitudes attended, in the hope of hearing an emperor sustain the part of a philosopher."[12] The passage caught Jacob Burckhardt's eye. Why, he mused, "would Constantine, who preserved the Diocletianic fashion of imperial appearance so zealously, and who set such great store by his personal majesty, condescend to show himself before the crowds in the capital? . . . Why speeches, when the Emperor possessed the fullest power to act?"[13]

Why, indeed? The emperor had cultural duties that were important to maintaining his bond with the civic elites of the empire. For this reason, even the most unpolished emperors listened appreciatively to interminable speeches in praise of this value or another, even if they were delivered in a language they understood barely, if at all. Oftentimes, the ceremony was more important than the speech itself, but just as often the emperor's decision simply to hear a speech was an important signal of his willingness to grant a favor or yield to a request. When he responded appreciatively to a well-turned phrase or nicely made point, he reassured the elites who ran the cities and kept order in the provinces that the standards and values by which they had been raised were still strong enough to restrain the arbitrary and despotic alternatives that lay at his disposal. This capacity to assert his will by force had been present in the empire from the start, as the occasional Nero or Commodus showed, and by the late empire the elites no longer asserted even a theoretical right to control it: it was in the emperor's power to do as he willed. Paradoxically, such license made it more necessary than ever before for emperors to demonstrate that they would not rule by anger or caprice, that their anger would yield to the silken bonds of classical culture.[14]

Emperors were also known to take a more active role, one that included speech making as well as composing plays and poems. Augustus set the pace, and Constantine maintained it, presiding over something that Eusebius refers to as "his usual auditory," a sort of salon devoted to philosophical and theological topics at which the emperor himself occasionally delivered papers.[15] But the venue for these imperial performances differed significantly from the one Eusebius describes for Constantine's public exercises. Emperors spoke to the Senate, not the masses, and their literary and philosophical activities— always excepting, of course, a Nero or a Commodus—were similarly restricted, as evidently was Constantine's own salon. It is tempting to think, therefore, that Eusebius merely engaged in poetic license when he referred to an audience of "multitudes," but confirmation of the nature of these occasions comes from an unexpected direction. At the end of the fourth century, a pagan historian, Eunapius of Sardis, wrote a series of lives of philosophers with the polemical intent of holding up exemplars of true wisdom against the upstart Christians. Discussing the fate of the Neoplatonist philosopher Sopater, who fell victim to a conspiracy in Constantine's court, Eunapius digresses into the history of Constantinople, a city he says was filled with "the intoxicated multitude which Constantine transported to Byzantium by emptying other cities, and established near him because he loved to be applauded in the theatres by men so drunk that they could not hold their liquor. For he desired to be praised by the unstable populace and that his name should be in their mouths, though so stupid were they that they could hardly pronounce the word."[16]

Making allowance for the invective, to which accusations of drunkenness were commonplace,[17] Eunapius's account corresponds to Eusebius's in its indication of a large, public audience made up primarily of common people—not the sort before whom emperors ordinarily chose to display their cultural attainments. Eusebius, in his turn, confirms something of what Eunapius claims. Speaking on the occasion of Constantine's thirtieth jubilee, the bishop proudly noted that Constantine reckoned "the acclamations of the people, and the voice of flattery . . . rather troublesome than pleasing, because of the steady constancy of his character, and genuine discipline of his mind." Such, of course, was how an emperor should behave, in a panegyric at least. But it was not incumbent upon the panegyrist to call attention to this particular virtue, and most panegyrists managed not to do so. By the convoluted rules that governed such addresses, Eusebius's decision to include praise for this virtue—along with notice of Constantine's scorn for fine apparel, in fact one of the emperor's more notorious weaknesses—suggests it was one Constantine honored more by the breach than the observance.[18]

What accounts for Constantine's speeches? In the theories of kingship which permeated the ancient world, good rulers were expected to lead their subjects to knowledge of better things, to serve as a beacon or even living image of the Higher Good. In the heyday of the Principate, Dio Chrysostom spoke approvingly of the man "who, having managed his own life admirably, endeavours by the persuasion of speech combined with good-will and a sense of justice to train and direct a great multitude of men and to lead them to better things."[19] This seems to be the image at which Eusebius aimed when he spoke of the crowds "hearing an emperor sustain the part of a philosopher." But still there is an important difference, for Dio, a true son of the Principate, also speaks with scorn of the ruler who covets "the praise of the vulgar and the loungers about the market-place," rather than "that of the free-born and noble, men who would prefer to die rather than be guilty of falsehood."[20] In the same discourse in which he praised leading the multitude to better things, Dio expressed nothing but pity for the man who is "ever turning and revolving, a flatterer of peoples and crowds, whether in public assemblies or lecture halls."[21] Clearly, Dio would have had nothing better than Eunapius to say about the types of assemblies Constantine convoked.

But ancient kingship theory also had a more radical edge that may at least partially explain Constantine's behavior. This consisted in the belief that a good king would be loved by his subjects. In a version attributed to a Pythagorean philosopher named Ecphantus, the theory emerges as the answer to a very real problem: How, when there are many pretenders and challengers to power, does one tell a genuine king from an imposter? True kingship is an inner quality, Ecphantus explains; it allows the genuine ruler to gaze upon the divine archetype by which his rule must be guided without being blinded. In this way and more does Ecphantus reflect the exaltation of the ruler's qualities which was elaborated during the Hellenistic period. But then he adds,

> Beauty at once shines out of his government; and the king who has copied beauty by virtue of his excellence is beloved both by Him whom he has copied and, even more, by his own subjects. For no one beloved by God would be hated by men—any more than the stars and the whole universe hate God; for if they had hated their Leader, they would not have followed Him in obedience—as now they do because the goodness of His government is the cause of their being well governed.[22]

At first just more pious nonsense, the passage on reflection conveys a stunning point: to be a true king, the ruler must be beloved by his subjects, for it is as impossible for the people to hate a true king as it is for such a king to hate his divine counterpart.

What makes this piece of Hellenistic reasoning stand out is that, in all its theoretical musings about the qualities that the king must possess, this is the only empirical test that it provides. To know whether or not a ruler is genuine, therefore, one need only observe how his subjects think of him.

Startling as it is, Ecphantus's theory remained just that, for it provided no mechanism for the people to express their sentiments. It was elegant but toothless, and easily deflected by Establishment orators like Dio, who turned it into nothing more than another aphorism for harmony with the upper classes. Dio speaks, for instance, of the way "they who come into his [the good king's] presence and behold him feel neither terror nor fear; but into their hearts creeps a feeling of profound respect, something much stronger and more powerful than fear. For those who fear must inevitably hate and want to escape; those who feel respect must linger and admire."[23] Elsewhere, Dio points to the practical advantages that derive for a king who maintains the "loyalty of his friends," since such reliable support allows him to extend his reign to more regions than he could control personally.[24] The reference to "friends"—*amici, comites*—is a signal that the discourse has changed from the common people of Ecphantus's vision to the more familiar circles on which emperors relied for administration and advice. In such ways, Dio smoothed out the rough edges of Ecphantus's radical proposal, making it but one more tool in the arsenal of elite values.

Though heavily sedated, Ecphantus's theory survived into the later empire, and it would not be surprising if, amid the general leveling of privilege which took place in the third century, emperors began to define their obligations more broadly. Certainly, Constantine on more than one occasion showed an interest in making officials more accountable to the provincials. In one surviving law, he ordered his governors to submit public acclamations to him, so he would know which to promote and which to condemn.[25] In another, he encouraged citizens "of any position, rank, or dignity whatever" who had been wronged by an imperial official not to be intimidated by high office: "I Myself will avenge Myself on that person who has deceived

Me up to this time with feigned integrity."[26] Historians have not exactly covered themselves with glory in their analysis of such laws. Gibbon thought them due to emotional imbalance; others have postulated fear of a conspiracy. Few seem to have thought sincere outrage at misconduct or a genuine desire to encourage common people to voice their dissatisfaction a possibility worth entertaining.[27] Yet in the context of Hellenistic kingship theory, what Constantine's speeches and laws alike provided was precisely what was missing from Ecphantus: a mechanism for the expression of popular views.

Constantine was, to be sure, naive in his belief that such procedures could not be manipulated, content with the warning that "We shall carefully investigate whether such utterances are truthful, and are not poured forth effusively and wantonly by clients."[28] But the same holds true for his thinking about almost anything that today would be considered the province of the social sciences. In a speech that will receive more attention below, he explained the scarcity of precious metals like gold and the abundance of others like iron or copper as the result of God's Providence.

> For the searchers for metals, were those which are employed for ornament procured in equal abundance with the rest, would be impelled by avarice to despise and neglect to gather those which, like iron or copper, are serviceable for husbandry, or house-building, or the equipment of ships; and would care for those only which conduce to luxury and a superfluous excess of wealth. Hence it is, as they say, that the search for gold and silver is far more difficult and laborious than that for any other metals.[29]

Another such amiable mixture of canny insight into human nature and utter indifference to the laws of supply and demand would be hard to find. The point should not be lost, however. Previous emperors had expressed concern for the plebs, with varying degrees of sincerity. Constantine's utterances on the popular will go beyond such traditional expressions; they indicate an intention to encourage popular involvement in the decision-making process, at least to the extent of expressing approval or disapproval of magistrates.

In the absence of a similar record of the edicts of earlier emperors, it is not possible to say such an intention was unprecedented. But if any of Constantine's predecessors had made similar attempts, the jurists whose writings later were considered canonical did not rush to incorporate such thinking into their own theories. Coming closest is Ulpian's statement that the decisions of the emperor have the force of law, because by virtue of something he called—to the chagrin of generations of analysts who have tried to establish its existence—the *lex regia,* the people have vested the emperor with their sovereignty. Ulpian's argument that the power of the ruler derived from the people had incalculable impact on the development of modern theories of democracy when it was discovered after centuries of absolutism based on the theory of the ruler's "divine right." But this ultimately beneficial influence should not blind us to its actual thrust, which was to rationalize the anomaly posed by the legislative activity of emperors. Unlike Constantine's efforts to involve the public in government, Ulpian's theory effectively removed the last theoretical impediment to dispensing with popular participation.[30]

The Great Persecution seems to have been responsible, at least in part, for this increased attention to public opinion, for the pagan militants who backed that policy took extraordinary pains to mobilize popular support. No less a figure than the Neoplatonist philosopher Porphyry seems to have been the author of a paper that Diocletian used as a rationale for the persecution, and his henchman Hierocles attempted to promote the pagan sage Apollonius of Tyana as a superior alternative to Jesus. Maximin Daza went further, not only modeling a new state church on Christianity's hierarchical organization but also introducing propaganda into the school curriculum in the form of the forged Acts of Pilate, which he made mandatory reading.[31] In such a charged environment, Constantine easily became sensitized to the importance of popular support, as the unprecedented variety of his coin images and slogans testifies.[32]

The Great Persecution charged the atmosphere, but even if it had never taken place, the internal makeup of the Christian community would still have required Constantine to seek more of a public forum for his speeches than earlier emperors had used. Burckhardt's own answer to the question he posed is instructive. "In this period of religious crises," he decided, "the spoken word, previously confined to rhetorical exercises and eulogies, now delivered from the preacher's pulpit, must have won so enormous an influence that Constantine could not entirely forgo it as an adjunct of power."[33] Burckhardt's insight into the importance of the preaching function was characteristically prescient, but his analysis was cast exclusively in terms of a power struggle between Constantine and the bishops, based on his assumption that Constantine grasped the potential of the Christian movement as a means to strengthen his political power. This view, as we saw in Chapter 1, was based on an even older premise that the church became "worldly" as a result of Constantine's conversion and lost its spiritual purity. Burckhardt modernized this religious argument with a political veneer, according to which the church became not only worldly but also subservient, a tool of the secular power, an "imperial Church."

The unspoken premise of such reasoning is that nonintervention was an option. Conceivably, Constantine could have adopted a hands-off approach, but to do so not only would he have had to deny three centuries of imperial tradition concerning the religious role of the emperor, but he also—given the common belief of his age in the direct role played by deity in the success or failure of imperial plans and the need to consult deity before the simplest duties could be discharged— would have had to surrender his control over important sectors of government policy. Roman rulers extending back to the earliest days of the republic and beyond had always been responsible for maintaining the *pax deorum,* the "peace of the gods," and it was natural both for Constantine to assume a position of leadership in the Christian organization once it became one of Rome's legally recognized religions and for Christian leaders to accept him in that role. It is anachronistic to see the authority Constantine asserted either as a power grab on his part or as spiritual capitulation by the bishops on theirs. Religious matters in the ancient world were no more clearly defined than secular ones, and in such an environment, participation by the emperor was not only normal and expected but even demanded.

In calling attention to "the preacher's pulpit," however, Burckhardt was closer to the mark. The bishop's obligation to guide and instruct his flock provided him with a unique source of strength. Bishops undertook the instruction of catechumens and provided regular guidance in the form of homilies and sermons. In strictly organizational terms, nothing in the Greco-Roman world could compete in frequency or authority with the opportunity afforded the bishop by Christian liturgy to shape the thinking of his community, the power of the pulpit. Saint Jerome remembered fondly an incident from his earlier days, when he posed a theological question to one of the greatest of these fourth-century orator-bishops, Gregory of Nazianzen, only to receive the following taunting response: "I will tell you about that in church, and there, when all the people applaud me, you will be compelled against your will to know what you don't know, or else, if you alone remain silent, you will undoubtedly be put down by every one as a fool." Although Jerome received the taunt in friendship, it is not difficult to imagine just how important the ambiance of the liturgy could be in less amiable situations.[34]

To assume a leadership role in this community, Constantine could not merely listen to others deliver speeches; he had to become an advocate himself: he had to create his own pulpit. But rivalry with the bishops does not sufficiently explain his need to do so. The bishop's power of the pulpit was real, but none of Constantine's successors worked quite as assiduously as he did to emulate it. Something more is needed to explain Constantine's penchant for public speaking. The glimmer of an answer lies in an argument Norman Baynes developed in opposition to Burckhardt, that benefactions like the Church of the Holy Sepulchre represent Constantine's sincere desire to achieve the "triumph of the Church."[35] As stated, Baynes' conclusion shares with Burckhardt the premise that Constantine had only one Christianity with which to deal. By modifying the argument to take into account the spectrum of Christian sentiment which Constantine faced—saying not that he desired the triumph of *the* church but the triumph of a particular kind of church—a plausible reason emerges for his oratory: he was working to ensure the success of the type of Christianity which he favored. In modern parlance, he wanted to control the message.

Conflicting Messages

Like all other mass-based organizations, Christianity consists of not one but several messages. There is the central message of salvation which unites all members of the Christian community, making them "one body in Christ." Beneath this central and overarching belief, however, lie a myriad of what it would be tempting to call fine points or implementing details, were it not for the fierce and sometimes bloody conflicts they have generated. Those of these details which pertain to theology have always claimed attention; but others whose application is more practical or social are of concern here. For ease of analysis, these may be sorted into two opposing categories, headed by the great commandment to "love thy enemy" on the one hand and the equally strong injunction to "resist Satan" on the other. As indicated in Chapter 3, the one can be said to have motivated the apologists, the other the martyrs. In the same simple and generalized sense, it is possible to speak of one group of Christians who were inspired by the message of love to seek common ground with non-Christians, to minimize differences and emphasize similarities, and others who regarded non-Christians with suspicion and hostility, as enemies, agents of the great Satan.

These latter Christians are the ones that scholars usually have in mind when they identify Christianity as intolerant. They are the ones whose view came to prevail at the close of the fourth century, and it therefore has been easy to assume that theirs was the normative Christian view, that intolerance is inherent to Christian belief, and that therefore Christian coercion of other forms of belief was the natural and predictable outcome of the conversion of Constantine. To support this thesis, it has been necessary to minimize or even ignore the oft-stated position of early Christians that true belief cannot be coerced.

The argument of this book has not been to deny that such Christians existed, or even that they were able to base their views on core Christian texts. To the contrary, their existence is necessary to understand both what Constantine did and why he did it, for, as should by now be clear, the type of Christianity to which Constantine converted, and the type whose triumph he sought to secure, was one that was both noncoercive and inclusive. Constantine set out this agenda in the letters and edicts discussed in the previous chapter which he issued in the aftermath of his victory over Licinius. It consisted of three parts. The first was that he was chosen by God to carry out a mission. By this time, such a claim was nothing more than the expected language of imperial legitimacy, although to say this is not to say that Constantine did not firmly believe it to be true. Second, that he intended to unify the empire. This had a double edge—to bring both halves of the empire back under the same ruler, but also to bring together Christian and pagan. Third, to bring peace. This could only have one meaning. He sought "a common agreement" that would be "concurrent with the pious sentiments of all."[36]

This program was a risky one that could have cost a less skilled emperor his credibility with both groups, Christians and pagans alike. Instead of the large middle ground that he succeeded in creating, Constantine might well have found himself with no base at all. In the event, his success was so complete that the risks he ran rarely receive the attention they deserve. Yet it is precisely Constantine's vulnerability that explains seemingly contradictory statements in his public utterances.

Constantine's Edict to the Eastern Provincials, the general policy statement discussed in the previous chapter in which he repudiated Diocletian's persecution policy in the aftermath of his victory over Licinius, is a case in point. This edict has been the subject of widely varying interpretations. Hermann Dörries called it an edict of toleration to which Constantine adhered throughout his reign, a view roundly censured by T. D. Barnes, to whom it is no more than a grudging concession of minimal significance.[37] In support of his view, Dörries pointed to those sentences in which Constantine repudiated the use of force to compel belief, telling both Christians and pagans to refrain from the use of force and urging them to "partake of this proffered benefit, that is, the beauty of peace, consciously avoiding all confrontation." Constantine followed this exhortation with an eloquent statement of the traditional Christian belief that true faith must be voluntary: "What each man has adopted as his persuasion, let him do no harm with this to another. That which the one knows and understands, let him use to assist his neighbor, if that is possible; if it is not, let it be put aside. For it is one thing to undertake the contest for immortality voluntarily, another to compel it with punishment."[38] Barnes, by contrast, was particularly struck by the angry language with which Constantine condemned pagan rites and the absence of any specific reference to the abhorrent practice of blood sacrifice. These, he thought, made the edict's hortatory clauses nothing more than grudging concessions.

The final paragraph of the edict supports both interpretations. "I have said these things and gone through them at greater length than my customary concern requires," Constantine wrote, "since I did not wish my belief in the truth to be hidden, and especially because I hear some people are saying the customs of the temples and the power of darkness have been taken away. I should, indeed, have advised this very thing to all men, if the violent opposition of wicked error were not immoderately embedded in some souls, to the detriment of our common salvation."[39] Although Constantine here specifically repudiated a policy of force, he also indicated that he would have liked to use it, had not the opposition been so entrenched. The statement suggests that he was being tolerant because he had to, rather than because he wanted to—indicating that his was the type of de facto toleration which sometimes results when opposing sides are so evenly balanced that those who would coerce must concede that they cannot.[40]

In the same document, therefore, evidence can be found for conflicting, even diametrically opposite, positions. From this it follows that Baynes' important axiom that "the true starting-point for any comprehension of the reign must be Constantine's own letters and edicts"[41] requires a corollary: it is not sufficient to pay attention just to what the emperor says; attention must also be paid to whether he did what he said. Analysis of this emperor's own letters and edicts must always take into account his considerable political skills. Just as his letter to the bishops at Arles shows that in cultivating the bishops Constantine developed a rhetoric of deference which does not always correspond to his actions,[42] so too the Edict to the Eastern Provincials reveals that the emperor mastered a vocabulary of condemnation which also must be measured against his actions before drawing any conclusions about the relevance of that language to his policy. More careful attention to his actions will show that in both cases Constantine was catering to a constituency.

Constantine ascended the pulpit not to compete with the bishops but to compete for control of the message. The ambiguities and contradictions that hold any mass-based organization together also create a situation in which particular acts can be understood in more than one way. In a sharply ideological movement, with a heterogeneous base and a core message shrouded in ambiguities, interpretation of the message—hermeneutics, or "spin control"—is all-important. Only when opinion crystallizes can a given position or action be called with certainty orthodox or heterodox, astute or foolhardy, virtuous or vicious; until that moment, discourse will be characterized by verbal warfare to control the message.

Here is a familiar example from modern politics. One side is concerned about the rising national debt and the tendency of bureaucrats to make work for themselves, protecting their jobs by imposing meaningless regulations that merely add unnecessary costs and thereby reduce the ability of businesses to compete. The other believes that a relatively small investment now in the health and housing and education of children will head off much higher costs in the future while also making the nation more able to compete and more democratic. Both positions reflect legitimate concerns; in a rational environment, both would have to be addressed and priorities established for implementing them. In the political world, however, there are only "winners" and "losers." Which is which depends on who is more successful at framing the issue in a way that wins the backing of others. So one side calls the other a tool of the rich and selfish, the people who have taken the most and want to return the least. The other replies by calling opponents Communists (in the good old days) or says they are attempting to inject foreign ideas about class warfare into domestic politics. One side talks about the wastefulness of taking money from productive people and giving it to those who have no sense of responsibility, or rails against big government, waste, and corruption, while the other talks about windfall profits and the influence of big money.

In short, both sides attempt to find a way to align their own position with generally approved sentiments and to characterize the opposition as either self-interested or in some other way a threat to the common good—a tactic known as "taking the moral high ground." They do so by exploiting the ambiguities and contradictions in their core messages which give large, heterogeneous groups the flexibility they need to hold together and adapt to varying conditions. It is well to notice here another characteristic of these examples which will prove significant to understanding the process of coercion: they support their own position by attacking the other.[43]

Actually, given the tenor of late-twentieth-century politics, observers would probably refer to this example as a fairly principled debate that "stuck to the issues." But is an example from a mass-based political system relevant for an empire in which common people had long ceased to play an active role? The importance of public opinion in the empire as a whole might be debated, but in the Christian community in these early centuries popular participation was rampant. Ordinary Christians could be expected to have opinions about the most obtuse points of theology, as is made clear by an oft-quoted account by Gregory of Nyssa of his experience in Constantinople: "If you ask about your change, the shopkeeper philosophises to you about the Begotten and the Unbegotten; if you enquire the price of a loaf, the reply is: 'The Father is greater and the Son inferior'; and if you say, 'Is the bath ready?' the attendant affirms that the Son is of nothing."[44] Gregory's words do not need to be read as literally as they often are to recognize that Christianity restored to common people an outlet for popular participation which they were denied in imperial politics. Eusebius's awkward letter to his congregation from Nicaea, Constantine's frequent letters to the Christians of Nicomedia, Alexandria, or Antioch—no matter how varied their format or contents, what the very existence of these letters testifies to first of all is the need of Christian leaders to justify their actions in a way that had long disappeared from other arenas of public life. Bishops had constituencies to which they were in some degree accountable; but an emperor who wished to exert influence over this body did not begin with, nor could he limit himself to, his own congregation. He had to develop a means to influence any Christian community in his empire, a superepiscopate; to do this, he, too, needed to justify his actions and persuade his constituency of his qualifications to rule.

This was no small feat for a Roman emperor to accomplish. Like everyone else, Christians in the late empire recognized the emperor as a sacrosanct individual, with the right and duty to regulate religious affairs. But they also had several centuries of reasons to be distrustful of the emperor, Saint Paul's injunction that all kingship is from God notwithstanding.[45] Only the enormous success of the miracle story in later centuries can explain why so little attention has been paid to how vulnerable Constantine was in his chosen role. Not only was he associated with rulers who had sponsored the most recent of the persecutions, but his own conversion had only come recently, when he was already middle aged. By far the safer position for him to take would have been one that covered his flank against charges of being "soft on paganism." It was an act of no small courage to embark instead on a program of coalition and consensus: to do so meant to put his prestige on the line, something a Roman emperor did at great risk. What if the militants succeeded in portraying him as a less-than-sincere Christian, an agent of Satan?[46]

Constantine's public speaking is a sign that he was determined to avoid such an outcome. He set about winning the support of the Christian leadership with all the practical and traditional means of patronage and resource distribution by which Roman emperors, like their counterparts before and since, have always signaled their favor, and in return he found a suitable instrument for achieving consensus in the councils of bishops. But Christianity was a volatile religion, with an organization that, as the Donatists showed, was subject to fissure at any point. It was a movement in which individual commitment counted for much. Because of this populist aspect, Constantine had to establish a broader base for his leadership to ensure the success of his program. Yet in the Christian community, a different set of values and expectations of leadership prevailed. All the criteria that entitled one to power in the classical world—family, education, wealth—paled before the one necessary requisite of personal piety, which was itself compounded by the value placed on humility and meekness.

Constantine mastered this new vocabulary and used it to particular effect. Whenever the crowds at his public lectures "greeted him with shouts of acclamation," Eusebius writes, "he would direct them by his gestures to raise their eyes to heaven, and reserve their admiration for the Supreme King alone, and honor him with adoration and praise." Eusebius also records an instance when "one of God's ministers presumed so far as in his own presence to pronounce him blessed, as having been counted worthy to hold absolute and universal empire in this life, and as being destined to share the empire of the Son of God in the world to come." Constantine reacted to such comments "with indignation, and forbade the speaker to hold such language, exhorting him rather to pray earnestly on his behalf, that whether in this life or in that which is to come, he might be found worthy to be a servant of

God."[47] Evidently, from reading Eusebius's own speech, which makes exactly these points and more, as we will see in Chapter 10, it was not what was said that earned the rebuke but how it was said.

Constantine also mastered the difficult political trick of identity transfer which great leaders often seem to achieve between themselves and a larger entity. Just as observers noticed that whenever French president Charles de Gaulle said "France wants" he usually meant "I want," so in the same way, when Constantine said "God wants," his words often must be taken in the sense of someone who identified God as his own "helpmate" and himself as God's chosen champion.[48] At the same time, and in the same way, he always spoke of the wrongs suffered by the Christians as an evil inflicted on the empire as a whole, thereby avoiding precisely the divisiveness so favored by modern scholarship.[49] Eusebius's account of Constantine's speech making includes one of those occasional slips whereby the bishop inadvertently reveals more than he intended. "And if in the course of his speech," he wrote, "any occasion offered of touching on sacred topics, he immediately stood erect."[50] In this sentence, Eusebius obviously intended to underline the emperor's piety. But in emphasizing how Constantine behaved when he came to matters of religion, he indirectly tells us that the emperor's speeches did not deal exclusively with sacred topics. Much of Constantine's speech making evidently was devoted to the important and traditional practice of legitimizing his rule, for Eusebius remarks that his assemblies were designed to instill "a rational obedience to his authority," which is just another way of stating the principle first articulated by Xenophon of "ruling over willing subjects."[51]

To achieve his goals, Constantine tapped into the Christian tradition that true belief could not be compelled. By means of this tradition of noncoercion, he hammered home the lesson of the Great Persecution that to coerce belief is to invite disaster. The rhetorical tidbits Constantine threw to Christian militants must be read in the context of this larger message, as two prongs of a sophisticated strategy whereby he neutralized militants by asserting the irenic elements of the Christian message while at the same time protecting himself from a charge of being "soft on paganism" by feeding their hatred of Satan with protestations of solidarity.[52] Thanks to Eusebius, there is an opportunity to study his method in some detail.

Speaking with Saints

At the point where he describes Constantine's public speaking, Eusebius also gives a summary of the typical sort of oration the emperor would give. Constantine, he says, "usually divided the subjects of his address, first thoroughly exposing the error of polytheism, and proving the superstition of the Gentiles to be mere fraud, and a cloak for impiety. He then would assert the sole sovereignty of God. . . . Proceeding next to the dispensation of salvation . . . [and] entering next in order on the doctrine of the Divine judgment."[53] Such, Eusebius concludes, was Constantine's "constant testimony." Shortly afterward, Eusebius promises to append a specific oration "by way of specimen," in order that "no one may have ground for deeming [his] testimony on this head mere empty praise." This was an oration that, Eusebius says, the emperor entitled To the Assembly of the Saints.[54]

A number of the manuscripts of Eusebius's vita Constantini do include an oration bearing that title. Its history is a microcosm of classical scholarship in the modern age. Its authenticity questioned during an earlier period of hypercriticism (during which scholars freely dismissed whole passages for not conforming to what their science told them the emperor should have said), it then became cautiously admitted as a representative piece of fourth-century propaganda, though still held unlikely to be Constantine's own. Recent scholars have been more willing to concede authenticity, although the enthusiastic identification of parallels in other writers such as Lactantius was beginning to sound like yet another search for alternative authors until T. D. Barnes came to the sensible conclusion that words delivered by the emperor, no matter who wrote them, could safely be considered to be the emperor's own.[55]

The most serious obstacle to authenticity was posed by a long section in which the emperor gives a Christian interpretation to Virgil's famous Fourth Eclogue, with its prediction of a birth that would bring peace to the world. According to Eusebius, Constantine wrote his orations in Latin, whence they were translated into Greek by "interpreters appointed for this purpose." This process alone explains much of the oration's misuse of Virgil. (Robin Lane Fox has offered the engaging comparison of using a Russian translation of "A Midsummer

Night's Dream" to prove the theory of class struggle.)[56] But more than misuse, the commentary on Virgil appears in places to depend on the Greek text, reading into it ideas that, however strained, might never have been derived from the Latin. Such an anomaly would suggest that the speech we have never existed in a Latin original, as Eusebius says Constantine's oration did, and that it must therefore be a forgery. This seemingly fatal objection now appears to have been solved by careful attention to the details of translation.[57]

With authenticity more secure, a great deal of effort has been devoted to identifying the place and date of the oration, as well as the audience that would have composed an "assembly of saints." Such a title suggests a Christian audience, and this seems confirmed by internal evidence: Constantine begins, for instance, by saluting a presider whom he describes as a model of chastity, and in the same passage he characterizes his listeners as sincere worshipers of God who are also "best instructed in the mysteries of God," begging them to attend to the sincerity, rather than the perfection, of his own humble efforts.[58] For all these reasons, the Council of Nicaea long seemed the most appropriate setting. But one of the precious few internal indications of a date belies this conclusion. Constantine begins by acknowledging the arrival of Good Friday, which occurred on April 18 in the year 325, whereas the Council of Nicaea did not open until June 1.[59] Moreover, Constantine indicates in his opening remarks that the audience was a large one that also included laypeople, "blessed multitudes, who worship him who is the author of all worship, and praise him continually with heart and voice."[60] Although a Christian audience is still the most likely, one that included at least some monotheistic pagans cannot be ruled out.

Similar precaution needs to be exercised with regard to the date. Most scholars have settled on a date in the mid-320s, if for no other reason than that there are a number of correspondences between sentiments expressed here and in edicts Constantine issued subsequent to his takeover of Licinius's domains. The fact that the oration was translated into Greek is itself some indication that Constantine was in the East when he delivered it, and this too indicates a time after Licinius was put aside. But diminishing returns set in with attempts to determine a more precise date. It has been argued, for instance, that the oration must have been delivered prior to the Council of Nicaea, since its theology would have been suspect afterward; but this line of reasoning presumes that Constantine's thinking was deeply affected by that council, a position that is otherwise difficult to prove. Other threads—lack of a title here, or reference to Licinius there; cryptic references to a "great city" and an "unworthy opponent"—all have been used to weave elaborate garments.[61]

It would be nice to have a precise place, date, and audience, but in this case they may not be crucial. Such factors usually help historians understand the author's purpose and how his or her thinking developed over time. But the most important characteristic of this speech may in fact be its timelessness. This is certainly the way Eusebius of Caesarea understood it. The passage in which he describes this speech and gives his reasons for including it reads as follows: "The emperor was in the habit of composing his orations in the Latin tongue, from which they were translated into Greek by interpreters appointed for this special service. One of the discourses thus translated I intend to annex, by way of specimen, to this present work, that one, I mean, which he inscribed 'To the assembly of the saints,' and dedicated to the Church of God, that no one may have ground for deeming my testimony on this head mere empty praise."[62] His language suggests that Eusebius knew no more about the precise circumstances of this speech than we do—something that would by itself rule out delivery at any gathering at which he himself might have been present. Indeed, by elaborating on the title, Eusebius indicates that he did not expect his audience to know immediately what an "assembly of the saints" was. It seems likely that Eusebius found the speech while going through a dossier of Constantine's speeches in the imperial archives, possibly in preparation for writing the *vita Constantini*.[63] These words become even more significant when they are tied in with his comments just a few paragraphs earlier about the emperor's speech-making activities.[64] Together, they indicate that Eusebius's purpose in attaching the oration was not historical, in the sense of documenting a particular moment in the emperor's reign; rather, it was typological, to substantiate his description of the type of speech that, he says in that earlier passage, the emperor was always giving.

More might be learned, therefore, by reading the Oration to the

Saints not as reflecting a particular moment but as Constantine's version of the stump speech modern politicians use during campaigns—the basic speech that gets modified as needed to suit a particular audience or occasion but otherwise stays much the same year in and year out—codex pages serving in this case as a fourth-century equivalent of a politician's note cards. The state of the document offers some small confirmation that this was so. It appears in the manuscripts with its thirty-nine printed pages divided into twenty-six chapters. These vary in length, half of them being no more than a page in length, the average being one and a half pages long. However, one chapter, the eleventh, is significantly longer, covering more than five pages, or 13.5 percent of the whole. Length is not the only thing that makes chapter 11 stand out from the rest. A discussion of the nature of Christ, it serves as introduction to a longish section dealing with the Second Person of the Trinity as the oration now stands. But it repeats arguments found elsewhere in the oration and concludes in a way that also would allow it to stand by itself as a separate, shorter treatise. This is precisely what makes its anomalous length so suggestive. There is no inherent reason for chapter 11 to have been kept intact; indeed, with far less reason the discussion of Virgil is distributed across three chapters (19–21). Most likely, the chapter divisions were made by Eusebius himself.[65] It is tempting to wonder, therefore, if there was something in the state of the manuscript that Eusebius saw—a difference in the size or age of the sheets, or in handwriting—which made him decide that this section needed to be set off by itself. Such a suggestion—and it can be nothing more than that given the present state of the evidence—would be some material confirmation that this was a speech that Constantine kept reworking over an extended period of time and delivered over and over in different versions to suit various occasions.

Reading the Oration to the Saints as a much-reworked version of one basic speech both explains some of its peculiarities and heightens our appreciation of the emperor's speech-making activity. It explains, for instance, why the speech does not conform exactly to the outline Eusebius gives in the *vita Constantini* (at 4.29). There, the bishop would be describing the generic or basic speech, of which he recognized the Oration to the Saints to be only one particular variant. A more important result of this approach is a new attention to the oration's purpose. For many years now, it has been known informally as Constantine's "Good Friday Sermon," because of its opening salutation to "the day of the Passion."[66] What such a title obscures is the fact that it is not a sermon at all, much less a speech about Easter, a topic to which Constantine never returns in all his thirty-nine pages of text. Along with his acknowledgment of the audience and chairmen, this salutation should be ignored as nothing more than a perfunctory variant to adapt to the occasion.

The real subject of the speech is not Easter but Providence: it aims to demonstrate the care that God exercises on behalf of those who worship him with true piety. Constantine is careful to remind his hearers of his own intimate association with this deity, saying at one point, "Be it my special province to glorify Christ, as well by the actions of my life, as by that thanksgiving which is due to him for the manifold and signal blessings which he has bestowed,"[67] and at another, "We, however, have received no aid from human instruction; nay, whatever graces of character are esteemed of good report by those who have understanding, are entirely the gift of God."[68] In language that echoes his earlier description of response to the coming of the Savior, Constantine says of his own success: "The cosmos itself celebrates, the procession of the stars appears brighter and more visible—rejoicing, I believe, at the fitting retribution of the unholy deeds—and the very seasons which have succeeded the wild and inhuman life are themselves accustomed to rejoice at their own good fortune and make plain the beneficence of God for mankind."[69]

Such assertions would be shameless self-promotion if made by modern politicians. But close association with divinity was an important part of a late Roman ruler's claim to legitimacy, and making that relationship known to his subjects as normal as an American congressperson reminding her constituents of what she has done for them lately. If it seems startling for such assertions to be made to a Christian audience, that is only because the modern Western world only knows of a Christianity that has existed some fifteen hundred years without a Roman emperor. Roman Christians shared with their pagan counterparts the ideology of the emperor's sacral role. While the emperor only associated with pagan gods, Christians perforce had to distance themselves from that role. But not the smallest effect of Constantine's conversion was that it removed this obstacle for Christians. The modern Western world has made up a label for imperial intervention in church affairs, *caesaropapism,* applying it pejoratively and anachronistically. At the time, a Christian emperor seemed simply to have put things back in their right order again. When Eusebius of Caesarea delivered his jubilee oration near the end of Constantine's reign, he had no difficulty describing the emperor in terms that virtually made him a fourth member of the Trinity. Often described as the foundation of one thousand years of Byzantine political theology, Eusebius's speech relies heavily on principles developed over practically as long a spread of Hellenistic thinking about kingship.[70]

Naturally, in Constantine's own speech, glimpses into the first Christian emperor's personal religious makeup are the ones that have been most eagerly sought, especially any that might confirm or deny his conversion experience. One passage in which Constantine describes his lifelong search for a revelation, coming as it does in the midst of a description of the benefits of conversion, has generated much attention.[71] But far more revealing, and original, is another section in which he gives his reasons for rejecting polytheism: "For if the dominion of these things [in heaven and earth], numberless as they are, were in the hands, not of one but of many, there must be a partition and distribution of the elements, and the old fables would be true; jealousy, too, and ambition, striving for superior power, would destroy the harmonious concord of the whole, while each of the many masters would regulate in a manner different from the rest the portion subject to his control." This obviously unsettling paradigm for political strife in lower spheres occurs in the same part of the speech already looked at in Chapter 5 where Constantine describes the personal dilemma he perceived in polytheism: "To whom first, or last, could prayers and supplications be addressed? Whom could I choose as the object of my worship, without being guilty of impiety towards the rest? Again, if haply I desired to obtain some temporal blessing, should I not, while expressing my gratitude to the Power who favored my request, convey a reproach to him who opposed it? Or to whom should I pray, when desiring to know the cause of my calamity, and to obtain deliverance?" Such a messy system, Constantine decided, hardly needed to be refuted.[72]

The High Ground

Such a justification for monarchy undoubtedly will strike modern ears as overly political. But in a world that had not yet come to distinguish between "church" and "state," Constantine's reasoning would not have seemed as out of place as it does now. More important to the present discussion is that Constantine's "political theology," as modern scholars call this kind of thinking, includes a passionate argument for a sophisticated religious policy of pluralism and toleration. It comes in the same chapter 11 whose length is so curiously disproportionate. Here, Constantine undertook a defense against those who mock the idea of God having been condemned to death as meaning that "he who is the cause of life for all living things was himself deprived of his own life." Such talk, he says, merely shows how witless and depraved such individuals are.[73] This much is standard apologetic material. But then the emperor continues, "But that they appear to have persuaded themselves that God, who is incorruptible, was overpowered by man, or that fierceness became master of benevolence, this transcends all foolishness. They do not realize that the great-spirited and forbearing one is never deterred by insolence, nor is one with the greatest innate strength moved by shameful treatment." The remainder of this passage has suffered something in transmission. But its sense is that such a being always is able to overcome "the wildness of those who go against it, breaking [it] down with the confidence of reason and magnanimity."[74]

A defense of Christ's suffering certainly is nothing unusual by itself, though there is something unusual about its being put forward in this place, that is, as an explanation for the Incarnation. The standard apologetic answer runs somewhat differently: the need to recover human beings from the error of idol worship, for instance, or the need to expunge sin and triumph over death in order to win immortal life for all. But here the issue is not so much suffering as forbearance, and even more important than either suffering or forbearance is the indication that, in Constantine's mind, the behavior of such "witless and depraved" individuals was to be met with "reason and magnanimity." In other words, the important lessons to Constantine did not apply to salvation so much as to governance. The Incarnation, he says, occurred because "the philanthropy of God had intended to wipe out injustice and to exalt decency and justice," so that "good and blessed men should seek to emulate his own providential guidance of the world," and he proceeds to define "the holy victory, the true conquest and the greatest act" not as the redemption of humankind or the triumph over death but instead as "the moderate governing of the entire populace."[75]

It is never wise to separate political from religious thinking in the ancient world, particularly in the case of a figure like Constantine. But to the extent that any such distinction may be made at all, it seems fair to say that the lesson the emperor here attempted to derive, the moral for which he saw the Incarnation as the paradigm, was one that had a distinctly temporal application. This being so, then the question arises, was this argument merely theoretical, or might Constantine's remarks legitimately belong in a more immediate context, one that required him to make the case for a policy that emphasized not only inclusion over exclusion but also persuasion over coercion?

The Edict to the Eastern Provincials (VC 2.48–60) is one reason to think that a policy debate was involved. Here, as we saw above, Constantine also praised "the advantages of peace and quiet" and "the beauty of peace." In what appeared to be a call for mutual toleration, he wrote, "Let no one disturb another, let each man hold fast to that which his soul wishes, and make full use of this."[76] Constantine clearly meant these words to apply to pagans as well as Christians, for he specifically described "the advantages of peace and quiet" as belonging to "those who delight in error alike with those who believe" (VC 2.56.1). Such sentiments closely parallel the lessons Constantine draws in the Oration to the Saints. But there are other parallels as well, and these are more problematic, for the edict also includes an angry and scornful dismissal of traditional religion's "temples of lies" (ψευδολογίας τεμένη) which to at least one scholar has seemed a truer indication of Constantine's mood.[77] Like the edict, the oration also has its angry moments. In the very same passage in which he praises generosity and benevolence so lavishly, Constantine also scorns these "impious ones" for "the butchery of your sacrifices, your feasts and great festivals," where, he sneers, worship is merely a pretense for "pursuing pleasure and licentiousness, and pretending to conduct holy rites but serving your own pleasures." Labeling their rites the work of "base and shameless Blasphemy," Constantine dismisses them as fit only for "adolescents and those who have the nature of adolescents," deceits that have led these innocents "away from worship of the real God."[78]

In both documents, then, Constantine sends contradictory signals, urging mutual toleration while at the same time using inflammatory language that seems to undermine his praise for moderation and restraint. The dichotomy is not as complete as it may appear, for toleration is not tantamount to approval, or even neutrality; indeed, strictly speaking, true toleration would entail precisely the kind of disapproval which Constantine expresses in these documents.[79] But fiery and intemperate language was not required, and Constantine surely knew that it was not the best way to assure adherents to the old ways of the sincerity of his promise. Why did he indulge in it? The oration may provide an answer, not only to this question but also to the larger question of whether these statements belong to a larger policy debate, for, between his attack on Blasphemy and warning to the "impious ones," Constantine inserts a rhetorical question. Is not our God, he asks, the one who is "properly worshipped by the wisest and most sensible peoples and states, who possesses manifold power and who surpasses every superlative, whose praise is greater and miracle more astounding, in that he does not abuse his power to punish insolence, but forgives men their foolish notions, deeming folly and error inbred human traits, while he himself abides by his personal resolve and never at any time lessens his innate benevolence?"

Constantine's use of the intensive "never at any time" (οὐδοτιοῦν in the Greek) stands out for the firmness and resolve that it conveys. But what makes the whole passage so significant is the priority Constantine gives to God's forgiveness, all the more praiseworthy because of his power to punish. Considering the close and personal terms in which Constantine always conceived his own relationship to deity, it probably also is significant that he should depict this forgiveness as a "personal resolve," an innate trait that he could not attribute to his god without also asserting it for himself. Suddenly, his ensuing threat to the "impious ones" is less significant for its negative portrayal of their rites as for a parenthetical comment, "for it is permitted to you that your sins go unpunished."[80]

This theme of toleration, once identified, emerges as a prominent subtext of the oration, showing up as early as the opening chapter, in which Constantine reminds his hearers of the "violence and cruelty" that accompanied error and superstition, "in that the will of princes encouraged the blind impetuosity of the multitude, or rather itself led the way in the career of reckless folly."[81] With this transparent reference to the persecutions, Constantine deftly placed all such behavior beyond the pale of correct belief. In chapter 13, Constantine continued his rebuttal of "blasphemers" who did not understand true piety; but at this point his argument takes an important twist. He had just ended what is now chapter 12 with a ringing endorsement of martyrdom as the ultimate proof of "pure faith and genuine holiness before God"—a guaranteed applause line. Now he turns to others who, he says, "show their immaturity by criticizing God in this way: why in the world did He resolve and devise not one and the same nature for all, but instead bid the creation of beings different and completely opposite in nature, which accounts for the different customs and principles of mankind?"

Such persons, he retorts, might as well complain that there is night as well as day, sea as well as land, mountains as well as valleys. "Wanting all men to be the same character," the emperor sneers, is "entirely laughable." It is a wish that shows ignorance of both physics and ethics. Instead of making everybody the same, God gave humans the ability to reason, to distinguish good and evil; having done so, he also gave free will and to each "the right to determine the outline of his own life." Such things were given equally to all.

> Whence, then, the difference in customs? Whenever, I think, we pay no heed to the foreknowledge of good that has been given us and yield to appetite or desire, we choose the worse over the better. For appetite is no small spur to passion, and desire is also overpowering, and they lead thoughtless ones to disaster, whenever they prevail over reason. One should train, therefore, like a good charioteer who draws the reins of an undisciplined and runaway team. From this result faith and piety toward God, justice and moderation and a wealth of all sorts of virtue.[82]

Against whom were these remarks directed? The natural inclination of modern readers is to assume that all criticism must be directed against pagans. Certainly, it was they who were responsible for the only persecutions to date. Such an interpretation, however, ignores the broad spectrum of thinking within the Christian community. In the aftermath of persecution, and with a government now favorable to their interests, it would be odd if there were not at least some of those Christians pressing for revenge and retribution such as modern scholarship has long posited, as well as others whose passion for truth made variant belief intolerable. Constantine, thus, may well have had these rigorists as much in mind as the now discredited pagan right. His ridicule of those who seek uniformity in nature in these passages is of a piece with the frame of mind he revealed in his retort to the Novatian bishop Acesius at the Council of Nicaea.[83] In both cases, Constantine spoke against a habit of thought, not a form of belief.

The object of Constantine's scorn may be conjectural, but the thrust of his argument is not. As elsewhere in the speech, his brief is monotheism; but in this section the choice between monotheism and polytheism is not at issue; rather, the choice is between uniformity or diversity. In arguing for diversity, Constantine also argues for toleration. Thus, his opening rejection of persecution is phrased as a statement of principle rather than a specific reference to recent events. "Yes," he concedes at the outset, "it would perhaps be better, for both carrying out His commandments and the correct understanding of Him, as well as for maintaining the faith of each individual, if all men were of the same character." But, he adds immediately, "mighty is the work of God." His successive images of the varieties in nature all speak to the same point—diversity is part of God's plan. Free will is part of that plan, and it is better to understand and control the passions that lead men to act against their best interests—here, an image from the chariot races to which fourth-century Romans were so passionately attached nicely underscores the point—than it is to hold everybody to one and the same standard. Thus, Constantine here rejected, as firmly as he did in the letter to Arius and Alexander, Christians who insisted on a narrow, rigorous, and exclusivist interpretation of the faith.

The Edict to the Eastern Provincials points in a similar direction. Despite its pejorative remarks about the value of traditional rites, nothing in it indicates that non-Christians were being hampered in the practice of their beliefs. On the contrary, when Constantine asserts, "What each man has adopted as his persuasion, let him do no harm with this to another," he justifies his position on the basis of principle, not expediency: "For it is one thing to undertake the contest for immortality voluntarily, another to compel it with punishment." Here, the finger seems to point clearly in the direction of the Christians, immortality being a goal more readily associated with their practices than with those of traditional religion. The same source of trouble is suggested by the edict's closing words: "I have said these things and gone through them at greater length than my customary concern requires, since I did not wish my belief in the truth to be hidden, and especially because I hear some people are saying the customs of the temples and the power of darkness have been taken away. I should, indeed, have advised this very thing to all men, if the violent opposition of wicked error were not immoderately embedded in some souls, to the detriment of our common salvation."

As always, the language is opaque. But the force seems clear enough. Rumor or misunderstanding had prompted some persons to believe that Constantine had or would act against pagan rites. To set the record straight, and either to prevent or stop acts of violence against the temples from occurring, Constantine issued a clear statement of policy, "since I did not wish my belief in the truth to be hidden"—a phrase that now has more than one meaning.

Both psychology and context, therefore, indicate that a secondary purpose of the Oration to the Saints was to argue in favor of diversity of belief, an argument that would have been pointed against certain Christians at least as much as, if not more than, pagans. It makes the case for a party of the center, rejecting coercion whether by Christians or pagans in favor of a broadly inclusive and tolerant monotheism. The oration can be read with a new appreciation of the difficulties Constantine faced once this secondary purpose is realized, because in certain ways such a purpose conflicts with the primary one of demonstrating Constantine's legitimacy to his Christian constituency. How was he to do this and at the same time restrain those militants who might easily interpret his reluctance to press their interests as proof of insincerity?

Angry and abusive language is certainly one way in which he did so. Even in a later and more triumphantly intolerant period, Christians were content with what Peter Brown has called "rhetorical humiliation" of their opponents,[84] and a key component of successful leadership in all ages has been an ability to mollify the faithful with appropriate noises without losing the flexibility to deal with the opposition. Not only strong language but also wistful expressions that things might be different—such as Constantine's assertion at the end of the Edict to the Eastern Provincials that he "should, indeed, have advised this very thing to all men" if it were not for the powerful interests ranged against them—served both to reassure militants that Constantine was theirs in spirit and to remind them that the world they lived in was not yet perfect.

But Constantine also tackled the problem in another and far more creative way. His solution was to use what might be called a reverse *speculum principis*; taking a page from the court orators who used the image of the "good king" to influence imperial behavior, he held up to Christian militants a mirror of ideal Christian behavior to show them the flaws in their own agenda.[85] Doing so allowed Constantine to seize the high ground in this debate, depicting his policy not as his own but God's, and putting those who opposed it in a position in which they would have to justify transgressing their own commandments. The usurpation is so thorough that, before the speech ends, Constantine even ranges on his side the most exemplary type of Christian and natural role model for uncompromising resistance, the martyr. Reminding his hearers of the way Christ rebuked Peter for drawing his sword to defend him, "reproving him for his distrust of refuge and safety in himself, and declaring solemnly that all who should essay to retaliate an injury by like aggression, or use of the sword, should perish by a violent death" (Matt. 26:52), he continues, "This is indeed heavenly wisdom, to choose rather to endure than to inflict injury, and to be ready, should necessity so require, to suffer, but not to do, wrong. For since injurious conduct is in itself a most serious evil, it is not the injured party, but the injuring, on whom the heaviest punishment must fall."[86]

In a stroke, the martyrs have been changed from prototypes of resistance to models of Christian suffering and endurance.

Constantine's Oration to the Saints illustrates how he used core Christian texts both to provide moral cover for his policy of toleration and to discredit the case for coercion, while at the same time making the case for an umbrella Christianity that would cover much classical belief as well. His account of Jesus' "heavenly wisdom" restates the phrase "all they that take the sword shall perish by the sword" as a decision "to choose rather to endure than to inflict injury, and to be ready, should necessity so require, to suffer, but not to do, wrong"—words reminiscent more of Plato's Apology of Socrates than of the gospel.[87] In another passage he singles out as God's greatest attributes both his capacity to forgive the "foolish notions" of mankind and the firmness with which he refuses at any time to lessen "his innate benevolence." To do otherwise, Constantine says, is "witless and impious."[88] By describing such a policy as Christ's, rather than as his own, Constantine was able not only to advocate a position certain to disappoint at least a segment of his hearers, but also to vindicate it. With such language, Constantine turned the image of the martyrs to his own purposes.

Constantine's treatment of the martyrs suggests, then, that despite its theological veneer the oration may be read for signs of a more immediate, more political, conflict—for control of the message. The oration shows two things of direct relevance: first, where Constantine placed himself among the variety of positions Christians took in defining themselves in relation to outsiders; second, an underrated skill for putting his position in a way that was likely to gain the broadest approbation. When he defined God as the Being "properly worshipped by the wisest and most sensible peoples and states," Constantine opened the door to a broader spectrum of beliefs than Christian rigorists likely would have accepted, while at the same time putting those who would refute it in the uncomfortable position of seeming to deny that the Christian position was the "wisest and most sensible." Similarly, when he ridiculed those individuals who were complaining that God did not make all men of one character and one faith,[89] he managed to isolate hard-line Christians as well as pagan unbelievers, lumping them both together in the category of "critics of God."

Finding the Center

Careful reading of the Oration to the Saints gives a new meaning to Eusebius's description of an emperor who played the role of a philosopher. It might be that Constantine's persistent oratory did not fully persuade Christian militants. Still, it neutralized them, which is one reason why they do not loom large in the record of this age, being drowned out in a chorus of praise for the first Christian emperor. Even more important, Constantine's aggressive advocacy of an alternative, and morally unassailable, interpretation of Christian virtue provided leadership and a rallying point for centrists. Of these, there were many. They provide the answer to the contradictory juxtapositions of fierce and mild language which characterize so many of Constantine's utterances, for words do not have a life of their own; if they are to mean anything, at some point they must correlate with action. Constantine was wholly consistent in his actions, with one exception that will be discussed in the next chapter: he favored an umbrella faith of compromise and inclusion. The contradiction, then, consists in the disparity between fierce language and mild action, a condition suggesting that scholars err when they take his language too literally. This behavior pattern is not limited to actions involving pagans; it extends to Jews and even to other Christians.[90] This is puzzling behavior to those historians who believe in tidy, rational action. But it is instantly recognizable to practical politicians as a favored way to placate a difficult constituency. As in the case of the martyrs, Constantine neutralized extremists by stealing their rhetoric.

Situating Constantine as the leader of a large and potentially volatile movement resolves the problem posed by his seemingly contradictory behavior. The answer lies not in theology but in the nature of Christianity as a mass movement with a militant wing. Constantine kept the loyalty of this wing by throwing them rhetorical tidbits, while at the same time exploiting the irenic side of the gospel message to lead the movement onto broader ground. In this way, he created a coalition around the idea of a faith that would be tolerant, broadly based, and inclusive. In modern parlance, he seized control of the discourse, using the structural ambiguities in the Christian message to isolate Christians who advocated coercive measures, making them appear to be at variance from the faith's core teachings and thereby vulnerable to a charge of extremism. Doing so, he neutralized the potential liability that his policies entailed. Even the most hard-line rigorist would have difficulty opposing a policy that seemed to flow directly from the Master's teaching.

In the years since he first seized power, Constantine had evolved a policy of unity and peace which was now quite clear and consistent. First articulated, for us, by pagan panegyrists, the policy was developed and informed by the emperor's decision to enroll the Christian god among the legitimate protectors of the state and by his own personal commitment to that god. Constantine was converted, but to what? Every indication is that he conceived of Christianity as a faith that wanted, and practiced, toleration. Subsequent history would show that the creation of a "vital center" might well be regarded as his most important achievement.

Constantine died on Whitsuntide, May 22, 337, with his place in history already secure. Eusebius of Caesarea, who records the emperor's last days in his *vita Constantini,* is circumspect about the nature of the illness and its symptoms, reporting only that it began as a "slight bodily indisposition" and then, sometime around Easter, took a turn for the worse. Despairing of a cure in Constantinople, Constantine crossed the Hellespont and went first to Drepanum, a city that he had renamed Helenopolis in his mother's honor, famous for its hot springs and the site where lay the powerful bones of the martyr Lucian of Antioch. There he exhausted himself in prayer and supplication. With the end fast approaching, Constantine began a progress to the sea but was forced to stop at the outskirts of Nicomedia, where he summoned the bishops and begged for the solemn rite of baptism. Even in his last days, Constantine's wonderful sense of theater did not desert him. "At the conclusion of the ceremony," Eusebius writes, "he arrayed himself in shining imperial vestments, brilliant as the light, and reclining on a couch of the purest white, refused to clothe himself with the purple any more." In this state, he received a steady stream of courtiers and army officers, urging them to put aside their grief, for "he was now in possession of true life."[91]

Typically, Constantine died with a message on his lips. For some time, he had been building a church in Constantinople to be dedicated to the Twelve Apostles, but only in the last months of his life, according to Eusebius, did he reveal his intention to be buried there, leaving Rome as a consolation prize the remains of his mother, Helena, for the magnificent porphyry sarcophagus that awaited him in the old capital. Leaving little to the imagination, Constantine arranged for his body to be placed in the middle of relics and memorials for each of the apostles.[92] The arrangement performed a double task, surrounding his mortal remains with the protection of Christ's most powerful intercessors while also signaling the role Constantine himself had played in the historic growth of the Christian movement. A dutiful church responded with the honorific title of *Isapostolos,* "the equal of the apostles." In other ways, however, Christians proved far less pliable. With gestures such as his choice of the Church of the Apostles for his tomb, Constantine appears to have tried to control the message even in death. But it was not to be. He soon lost control of his message, and with it, control of his agenda.

Nine

Controlling the Agenda

Constantine was still very much alive in September 335, when Athanasius decided to make his getaway. The emperor was, indeed, at the height of his powers, at least in the eyes of the bishops who attended the dedication of his new basilica in Jerusalem, a rival to the glory of Solomon. Athanasius, however, was not among those on hand to admire "the New Jerusalem," for despite the urgency of the emperor's summons he had remained in Tyre. Conceivably, the bishops had deliberately excluded him from the ceremonies as being under charges. But it is more likely that he stayed behind through his own choice, for the bishops, now sitting as the Council of Jerusalem, used their time well. Following Constantine's instructions, they readmitted Athanasius's archenemy Arius to communion and bade all other churches in the East to do likewise. Athanasius doubtless would have preferred isolation to the alternative of sharing communion with the hated Arius. The other bishops seem to have been wary of Athanasius's intentions, for they had posted a guard to watch over the harbor in their absence. He eluded it by slipping out at night, using one of the open boats that served for local transportation.

Athanasius's departure shows that, despite stories such as the dramatic introduction of Arsenius with both hands intact which circulated in the aftermath, things had not gone well for him at Tyre.[1] Constant protests from supporters he had brought from Egypt had availed nothing more than a mild admonition from the imperial representative, Count Dionysius. More seriously, the bishops had brushed aside complaints of meddling and decided to send a commission drawn from their own number to collect depositions in Egypt concerning the affair of the broken chalice and other allegations. Athanasius knew only too well what this group would find. The bishops must have been informed of Athanasius's flight, but they do not appear to have been overly concerned. They returned to Tyre, there to await the commission's findings before taking further action.[2] Presumably they thought he was making his way back to Egypt, where he had both resources and opportunities. But Athanasius had determined on a more dangerous game. Twice before, when cornered, he had managed to win over the emperor through a personal appeal; now he would risk all on the chance it would work again.

And so we return to the encounter with Constantine with which this book began. Mystery enshrouds Athanasius's whereabouts for the almost two months between the time he departed Tyre and surfaced again in the streets of Constantinople. If he had traveled the entire distance by sea, as is usually assumed, he should have reached the capital in no more than twenty days; more likely, then, he went by land at least part of the way, traveling on the great road from Tarsus to Ancyra—where he would have been sure of a warm welcome by Bishop Marcellus—and thence to Constantinople.[3] Conceivably, the trek had been difficult, for Constantine writes in his letter to the bishops at Tyre that he did not immediately recognize Athanasius. But Constantine was not the only player in this period with an outstanding sense of theater, and Athanasius certainly would have wanted a physical appearance that would underline the jeopardy his soul was in. With a better sense of the undertones, it is well now to return to Constantine's letter, picking up at the point where he has summoned the bishops to account for "the tumult and fury of [their] synod":

> The reason I have thought fit to write these things to you and summon you to me by this letter you will know from the following.

As I was going into our eponymous and all-blessed city of Constantinople (as it happened, I was on horseback at the time), suddenly the bishop Athanasius came into the middle of the street with certain others whom he had with him, so unexpectedly as even to give cause for alarm. For as God who sees all is my witness, I neither recognized him nor was I able to tell at first sight who he was, until certain of our companions, when we asked to be informed, as was fitting, reported to us both who he was and the injustice he had suffered.

I neither conversed with him at that time nor agreed to a meeting. But although he kept demanding to be heard, I declined and was about to order him driven away, when with greater outspokenness he claimed he wanted nothing more from me than your summons, so that he could complain in your presence about what he had been forced to suffer. Since this seemed reasonable to me and fitting to the times, I readily ordered these things be written to you, so that all you who made up the synod that met in Tyre would immediately hasten to the court of my Clemency and show clearly by the very facts the pure and unperverted nature of your judgment to me, who you would not deny am a true servant of God. For through my service to God, peace reigns everywhere and the barbarians themselves, who until now were ignorant of the truth, truly bless the name of God.

After a further sentence lamenting the fact that the barbarians "know God and have learned to reverence him, who they have seen by the very facts shields me and everywhere provides for me," whereas the men of God "do nothing but that which encourages discord and hatred and, to speak frankly, which leads to the destruction of the human race," Constantine concludes:

So hasten, as already has been said, and take care that all may come to us swiftly, persuaded that I will try with all my might to set things straight, so that those things may be protected which in God's law are especially inviolate, against which neither blame nor any ill repute will be able to be attached, when the enemies of the law—whoever under the guise of the holy name proffer many and varied blasphemies—are clearly scattered and wholly crushed and completely obliterated.[4]

It is important to remember the source of this letter: Athanasius included it as part of the proof for his case in his Apology against the Arians. Like any document that survives in a source that is using it for a tendentious purpose, therefore, Constantine's letter may well have been modified to make it better suit that purpose. But it is not likely that Athanasius would have tampered with it in a way that weakened his case; that is, he would not have removed passages favorable to himself or added any that strengthened the case of his opponents. We can be reasonably certain, therefore, that anything in this letter which works against Athanasius and in favor of his enemies was in the original.

Athanasius characterizes it as an angry letter, one that struck fear in the hearts of his accusers, and his lead has been followed by most commentators. But is the letter what Athanasius says? Certainly it starts that way, with its references, quoted in Chapter 1, to the "tumult and fury" of the council and the suggestion that "love of strife" was more important to its proceedings than the discovery of truth. It also, incidentally, indicates that Constantine had none of the doubts raised by modern scholars about his right or ability to judge the proceedings of a church council. But after this paragraph the tone becomes decidedly different—conciliatory, even defensive. Far from issuing a peremptory order, Constantine goes to considerable lengths to explain why he was acting in this manner, and in the course of this explanation he says several times that he had no wish to meet with, or even speak to, the Alexandrian bishop. Despite Athanasius's startling and dramatic behavior, he writes, "I neither conversed with him at that time nor agreed to a meeting." The implication is that had he known it was Athanasius he would not even have stopped. Only after Athanasius made clear that he simply wanted to face his accusers in Constantine's presence—in other words, that he was not attempting to circumvent the council—did Constantine relent, "since this seemed reasonable to me and fitting to the times." After reminders of his goodwill and past services, Constantine almost pleads with the bishops to "come to us swiftly" so that he can "try with all my might to set things straight." The final sentence is nothing short of a gem of diplomatic gobbledygook, in all likelihood designed to convince both Athanasius and his opponents that the emperor shared their views.

Is Constantine's anger directed exclusively at the bishops? He seems more to be engaged in preexplication, as if assuring the bishops that he had not broken his word. Probably, he was doing precisely that. The fight between Athanasius and his accusers had been going on for some years. On at least two former occasions, Constantine, who originally supported an inquiry, had abruptly reversed course and vindicated Athanasius after granting the bishop a private audience. After the debacle in the preceding year, Constantine had taken special pains with this year's preparations, even sending the imperial Count Dionysius, a former governor of Syria and therefore knowledgeable of regional matters, to preserve order. Presumably, he did so in order to satisfy Athanasius's objections and doubts, even though Athanasius ever after used the presence of this imperial official to challenge the legitimacy of the proceedings and taint its verdict. It is reasonable to assume that this time the other bishops had demanded some assurances from Constantine as well before they took on yet again the unenviable task of trying to bring this wily street fighter to heel. Constantine therefore needed to assure the bishops at Tyre that he had lived up to his side of the arrangement.

The pains Constantine took in his letter to assure the bishops that he would not so much have stopped had he known the intruder was Athanasius, and that he granted him nothing more than any of his subjects had a right to expect, suggest that they had extracted from him as the price for their own continued cooperation a pledge not to engage in "personal diplomacy" with the bishop of Alexandria. In this part of the letter, then, Constantine's first concern seems to have been to assure the bishops that he had lived up to his side of that bargain. Clearly, he had been unsettled by Athanasius's assault. But, as the event showed, he had kept his presence of mind. What really disturbed him, it would seem, was not the bishops themselves but the way they let the proceedings get so out of hand. But he also let the bishops know in no uncertain terms that he wanted an end to this dispute. If Constantine was angry at anything, it was with the constant squabbling into which relations with the bishops, in his eyes, had degenerated.

Athanasius's own account of this letter's impact is clearly flawed. According to his reconstruction, it struck terror into the bishops, still at Tyre, and only the small handful who confronted him in Constantinople dared to face the emperor's wrath, despite his order for the whole body to appear before him. The chronology is impossible to reconcile with this reconstruction, for it would mean that Constantine's letter was drafted, sent, and received, and the delegation traveled from Tyre to Constantinople, all in the space of no more than the eight days that intervened between the encounter and Athanasius's exile—a feat that would be difficult to accomplish even in the twentieth century, before the conveniences of electronic correspondence and air travel.[5] The most likely scenario for this time frame is that the bishops were already en route to Constantinople to report on the council. At the very least, they would have wanted to inform Constantine of Athanasius's contumacy. But it is also conceivable that, since they were by now familiar with Athanasius's penchant for personal appeals, the possibility that he was making for the capital had not escaped them. Their arrival made Constantine's letter, which had already been dispatched, irrelevant, but Athanasius subsequently found its mention of discord at the council supportive of his position.[6]

This reconstruction does not explain why Athanasius represented the sequence of events so differently. The kindest explanation, which has some supporters, is that, because he was writing decades afterward, his memory of the precise order of events had faded.[7] It was, to say the least, a convenient lapse. The arrival of the bishops might well have thrown a crimp into Athanasius's plans and precipitated a meeting before he had expected. His own account focuses on irrelevant charges—not of sacrilege but treason. Assuming that Constantine's letter accurately reflects his mood, the emperor's longstanding demand that communion be restored with Arius must also have been on the agenda. In previous meetings, Athanasius had been able to sidestep a clear yes or no, but the bishops certainly would not have allowed him to do so this time. The dance was over.

Cornered, Athanasius lashed out. "The Lord will judge between me and you, since you yourself agree with those who calumniate your humble servant."[8] The audacity of these words would have provoked Constantine in any case, but if his study of Scripture had been anywhere near as diligent as his biographer Eusebius claims, he should have been doubly affronted, for Scripture abounds with claims by the righteous of vindication by God's judgment.[9] Under the circumstances, Constantine's reaction was remarkably restrained. Despite the importuning of the bishops, he refused to depose Athanasius. Instead, he sent him to Gaul to rethink his position. It was a canny judgment.

Denied martyrdom, Athanasius could anticipate no fate other than that of becoming more and more irrelevant for so long as Constantine lived. He had to choose, in other words, between the power he would retain by compromising and the pleasure of a good snit. This was surely not the outcome he had intended, but it was one for which he had helped write the script. Just as it had for his Arian opponents at the Council of Nicaea a decade earlier, now his own refusal to compromise had led to exile. The circle was complete.

Defining Agendas

Just as one journey ends, another must now begin. Political analysis has been the thread for guiding us through a maze of Constantinian problems and avoiding such blind alleys as the idea of "the church" as an abstract, monolithic entity. Looking back from the center of this maze, an imperial policy that too often has looked twisted and confused now looks relatively straightforward and consistent. But the way out leads through an even more twisted trail, one on which Christians, who up to now have appeared as eloquent advocates for freedom of worship, turn instead to the systematic use of the coercive powers of the state to suppress alternative forms of belief. The simplest explanation for this coercive turn is Lord Acton's dictum about the tendency of power to corrupt; oddly, however, this is not the explanation on which modern scholarship relies. Instead, as we have seen, it favors an explanation that seems even simpler: the idea that Christian rejection of other gods amounts to an intolerance that in turn led inevitably to coercion.

But the seemingly obvious path to this explanation has an obstacle that no amount of scholarly engineering has been able to remove, for Constantine, who according to this view first diverted the state to the coercive purposes of the church, actually refused to persecute, with one important exception to be dealt with below. There is, moreover, every reason to believe that his refusal was not merely tactical but the product of a conscious policy to achieve Christian objectives by concentrating on the broad areas on which Christians and at least educated, monotheistic pagans could agree—a policy that might be given the shorthand identity of "the Constantinian consensus." It is well to recall that this failure to persecute, combined with his continued support of state cults and pagan philosophers, forms the basis of the Burckhardtean argument that Constantine was not sincerely converted to Christianity but only took advantage of the church's political assets to further his personal drive for power.

This is a good point at which to pause and take some bearings. The fourth century produced a first-rate historian, Ammianus Marcellinus, a seasoned observer and friend of the emperor Julian. The early books of his history, including the ones that covered the reign of Constantine, are unfortunately lost, but comments he makes about Constantine's successors—his son Constantius II and nephew Julian—are capable of taking this inquiry in two very different directions.

Ammianus writes that Julian, who turned away from Christianity, recalled all the bishops sent into exile by his predecessors—ostensibly because he was guided by the principle of religious freedom but also because he knew that the internal dissension created by these recalls would make Christians weak and easy to control: "On this [freedom of all Christians to observe their own beliefs] he took a firm stand, to the end that, as this freedom increased their dissension, he might afterwards have no fear of a united populace, knowing as he did from experience that no wild beasts are such enemies to mankind as are most of the Christians in their deadly hatred of one another."[10] This was true mischief. Showing how an emperor could exploit the differences between Christian factions to his maximum advantage, Julian fits Burckhardt's expectations much better than Constantine ever did, while at the same time revealing the flaw in the great Swiss historian's estimate of the first Christian emperor. Unlike Julian, Constantine devoted considerable personal resources to achieving Christian consensus and in the process weakened considerably his own capacity for independent action—his own, and that of his successors. In this passage, then, Ammianus shows how political analysis can actually confirm, rather than refute, the sincerity of Constantine's beliefs.

However, Ammianus is also the source for a point of view that is much more pervasive in modern scholarship and poses a much thornier problem. Writing about Julian's predecessor, Constantius II, Ammianus complains that the public transportation service was clogged with bishops, preventing the government's business from getting done.[11] Ammianus's comment shows that contemporaries were aware that the interminable wrangling over increasingly obtuse and obscure theological questions was diverting both vital resources and imperial attention from the pressing problems that eventually led to the fall of Rome. It accords so well with post-Enlightenment evaluations of the role of religion in government that the judgment of its author rarely is questioned. This is the reason, indeed, that other critics write so disparagingly of Constantine's last years, deriding him as a mere tool of clerical ambition. It is the reason, as well, that critics down to the present day deplore the waste of imperial energies on internal Christian squabbles.

But in many ways Ammianus, for all his skill as a historian, reflects a provincial and traditional view that caused him to underrate, or miss completely, some of the key developments of his age.[12] Popular involvement in theological issues suggests that they were not as irrelevant as they now seem; on the contrary, that they were a key component of the renewed vitality of popular interest in government. And if, as everyone in the fourth century believed, God's favor was the most important determinant of success, then the bishops traveling from council to council were in fact conducting the government's most important business.

Even here, however, Ammianus can be a guide of sorts. By pointing to the new importance of bishops and councils in the post-Constantinian period, he introduces a concept that will be as important to the understanding of Christian coercion as was that of players to understanding Constantine's policies. It is the concept of agendas.

What Ammianus did not need to tell his contemporaries was how great a boon it was to be able to command seats on the imperial post, how much more convenient and comfortable such travel was, how it marked off its users from the ordinary traveler, and how jealously in consequence the privilege was guarded by those who held it.[13] Constantine's distributions to the bishops clearly marked them out as favored members of the new order, significantly enhancing their prestige. From this time bishops begin to adopt the ceremonies and even raiment of the late imperial court. Even the image of Christ was not immune, as Christ the youthful shepherd of third-century catacomb paintings yields to Christ the Lawgiver and Christ the Judge, sitting on

Figs. 5–6. Christian art reflects the changing fortunes of the church. In figure 5, a third-century fresco from the Catacomb of Priscilla in Rome shows Christ as he was commonly represented prior to Constantine's conversion, in the guise of a youthful shepherd. In figure 6 (*opposite*), a mosaic from the fifth-century Church of San Apollinare Nuovo in Ravenna shows him endowed with the dignities of a Roman emperor, seated majestically amid angelic counselors. (Deutsches Archäologisches Institut, Rome)

a jeweled throne and wearing imperial regalia, flanked by angels or apostles arrayed like so many imperial counselors, in churches built from the late fourth century onward.[14]

Ironically, this rapid transformation in the political and material circumstances of Christianity underlies the two diametrically opposite conclusions modern scholars have reached about Constantine's intentions—that he cared nothing for Christianity and only used the

318

(Deutsches Archäologisches Institut, Rome)

church to achieve personal power, and that he slavishly placed the empire at the feet of the church. Whether they see Constantine as a master manipulator or an utter fool, these conclusions take it as given that the outcome was the result of a deliberate intent. The circumstances surrounding the Council of Tyre allow a more accurate impression to be formed of the turmoil and confusion in which this transfer of power occurred, opening the door to thinking of it as an unintended consequence of Constantine's policies.

There is an even more important premise that the manifold judgments about Constantine and the clergy share: they assume not only that both sides were willing participants but also that both sides shared a common goal, something usually referred to as "the triumph of the church." That is, they assume that the agenda of emperor and bishops was the same—that, in modern political parlance, both were "singing from the same page."

Thus, the most important lesson to be drawn from the sordid events of 335 is also the simplest one: they show that the agendas of Constantine and the bishops were not identical. Whereas Constantine's repeated wish was for an end to bickering and conflict, the bishops placed a far higher value on conformity and obedience. Unity was also a goal of the bishops, but it is obvious that their idea of unity was not identical to Constantine's. Whereas Constantine's idea of unity extended beyond Christianity to embrace pagan notions of a Supreme God, the organizational thinking of the bishops did not extend beyond the confines of their faith, and they insisted on raising the threshold for their definition of monotheism to the point where even variant Christian belief would be excluded. Moreover, while both Constantine and the bishops placed a heavy premium on unity, he defined this goal in traditional terms of the body politic, according to which all members must be preserved intact, while the bishops thought of unity in terms of the body of Christ, to which purity was more important than wholeness: "And if your hand causes you to sin, cut it off," Jesus taught; "it is better for you to enter life maimed than with two hands to go to hell, to the unquenchable fire."[15] Thus, though both bishops and emperor could speak of "unity" as a goal, each side used this term in a critically different sense: Constantine sought unity in order to achieve the traditional imperial goal of peace and legitimacy through divine favor, whereas the bishops sought a unity based on right belief as a means to divine favor. The result is a slight but noticeable misalignment that created grounds for significant friction: Constantine's agenda called for the inclusion of the greatest possible number as a goal in itself, whereas to the bishops inclusion was no more than a means to reach the greater end of the kingdom of the saints.

Another obvious lesson: if Constantine and the bishops could have separate goals over something as basic as the composition of their mutual faith, then there is no reason to believe that their agendas were identical on other matters. To be more precise, although scholarship encourages us to think of the benefactions that Constantine bestowed on the church as motivated primarily by his commitment to Christianity, some of these are likely to have been the product of a different agenda altogether, one in which the church as represented by its bishops was a means rather than an end. Indeed, abundant evidence survives of a social agenda to which Constantine attached as much importance as he did to matters more directly related to Christian belief. Only the impermeable wall between religion and politics thrown up by modern scholarship has prevented the question from being asked of whether there was not a more direct link between these two agendas than perceived by overly narrow concentration on the religious one to the exclusion of all else.

For the remainder of this chapter, one of Constantine's most controversial laws will serve as a case study of the very different results that can be achieved by assuming that Constantine's agenda was not identical to that of the bishops and that his actions were not always motivated by religious concerns. This law, now known as the First Sirmondian Constitution, appears to surrender important judicial rights to bishops, in reckless disregard of both principle and precedent. But, by a sheer accident of historical preservation, it yields instead a lost Constantinian agenda that addresses an entirely different set of concerns.

Compiling the Record

The best evidence for a broader Constantinian agenda lies in two great compilations of late Roman law, the Theodosian Code, completed in 438, and the Code of Justinian, completed about a century later. The jurists who compiled the Theodosian Code proceeded in accordance with a certain set of guidelines and restrictions that frequently are not taken into consideration when using the results of their labors, even though these parameters strongly influenced what went into the code, which is by no means a compilation of all preceding laws, and also influenced the way those laws selected for inclusion appear. In minutes of the meeting of the Roman Senate at which the completed code was introduced, along with the precise record of the Senate's laudatory acclamations noticed in Chapter 2, is Theodosius II's own statement of the principles under which the jurists operated. Theodosius II instructed his codifiers to compile the laws issued "by the renowned Constantine, by the sainted Emperors after him and by Us" according to a hierarchy of titles and headings.

The codifiers were asked to include contradictory and outdated laws, with the exception of those that could no longer be cited in court, but otherwise Theodosius II gave them a great deal of latitude. Some laws they condensed to bring out the essential point; others they broke into several parts in order to fit the code's preconceived categories.[16] In other words, they acted as lawyers, not historians, aiming to create a handy reference for precedents on issues of legal dispute, not an accurate reflection of the interests and intentions of Theodosius II's imperial predecessors. One immediate casualty of this procedure was the background—the circumstances that originally brought the case to the emperor's attention and which led to the decision recorded. Another was any explanatory matter that an emperor might have included to clarify his decision.

Since almost all imperial legislation came in response to requests from officials for clarification or appeals from decisions in specific cases, rather than as the result of an emperor's intention to articulate a program of initiative or reform as is the familiar scenario in the modern world, removing such material can have the effect of significantly skewing the contents, misleading researchers about the emperor's intent or purpose.[17] In the absence of such material, it becomes altogether too easy to forget that the motive and intent of a given piece of legislation may have had nothing to do with where it finally appears in the code. It is, accordingly, rare to be able to recover the original context of a law that survives in this way, but a unique set of circumstances permits us to do so with regard to a set of Constantine's most important, and controversial, decisions, in which he extended judicial powers to the bishops. The extension of these powers traditionally constitutes proof of Constantine's efforts to achieve "the triumph of the church." But this conclusion may have been arrived at too hastily, without taking into account the emperor's own agenda.

A law of 316 confirms that bishops may sanction the manumission of slaves by their owners even if other witnesses are not present, and another that may have been issued as early as 318 permits a litigant to transfer jurisdiction in his case to a bishop's court even if proceedings had already begun in the civil court. This second law reads as follows:

> Pursuant to his own authority, a judge must observe that if an action should be brought before an episcopal court he shall maintain silence, and if any person should desire him to transfer his case to the jurisdiction of the Christian law and to observe that kind of court, he shall be heard, even

though the action has been instituted before the judge, and whatever may be adjudged by them shall be held as sacred; provided, however, that there shall be no such usurpation of authority in that one of the litigants should proceed to the aforementioned tribunal and should report back his own unrestricted choice of a tribunal. For the judge must have the unimpaired right of jurisdiction of the case that is pending before him in order that he may pronounce his decision, after full credit is given to all the facts as presented.[18]

The language of this law is particularly confusing, seeming to some readers even to permit only one party to the suit to make such an appeal, and it may have been in response to questions it raised that Constantine's prefect Ablabius, himself a Christian, wrote the emperor in 333 seeking clarification. Ablabius's inquiry does not survive, but Constantine's ruling does. In it, he confirms that "whoever, therefore, having a suit, whether defendant or plaintiff, either during the start of the suit or after the circuits of time have passed, whether when the matter is drawing to a close or when sentence already is going to be pronounced, should choose the judgment of the high priest of the sacrosanct law, instantly, without any hesitation, even if the other party is opposed, let the parties to the suit be directed to the bishop." This is startling language. Not only does it explicitly permit one party to a suit to take the case to a religious tribunal, but it also allows the appeal to proceed even if the other party to the suit should object. As if this were not enough, Constantine went on in this new ruling to say that any matter decided by a bishop was not subject to appeal and that judges not only could accept testimony from a single bishop without need for further witnesses but must not even hear other witnesses once a bishop had testified. It would be difficult to find a similar instance in which so many principles of Roman jurisprudence were cast aside in so few words.[19]

On a minimalist reading, the manumission law of 316 merely extended to bishops rights held by other priesthoods, and the later appeals law gave them standing as arbiters and no more—assuming, despite use of the singular, that agreement of both parties must have been necessary, or at least that both parties must have been Christian.[20] But no amount of weaseling can escape the revolutionary implications of Constantine's response to Ablabius in 333. Its endorsement of appeal by only one party to a suit is specific and unambiguous, stipulating that the change of venue must be allowed even if it is against the will of the other party. Like its insistence on the sole testimony of the bishop, this was a ruling that ran counter not merely to Roman but also to Jewish and Christian jurisprudence.[21]

What makes this law even more explosive is that Constantine's judgment was not delivered in a constitution, a new law, in which case its radical orders might be attributed to impatience or dismissed as a temporary aberration; instead, these orders were issued in a rescript, a reply to a query by a high-ranking official concerning the interpretation of some previously established law. Since it was customary for a response to take its cue from the referral, it is safe to assume that Ablabius's inquiry raised precisely these points. Constantine's use of the phrase "Our Moderation" (*moderatio nostra*) was probably also lifted from Ablabius's petition, since it is not a usual occurrence in the repertoire of imperial titles. Given the hortatory nature of such epithets, Ablabius's decision to petition not "Your Wisdom" or "Your Sagacity" but "Your Reasonableness" suggests that he was not so much in doubt about the meaning of whatever earlier law had raised his eyebrows as indulging in the time-honored ploy of prudent administrators to ask for clarification in a way that gave their superiors a face-saving opportunity to reverse an ill-advised decision—the same device that Pliny the Younger may have used two centuries earlier to guide Trajan's Christian policy (Chapter 3).

If this was Ablabius's intent, Constantine's response shows that he was in no mood for second thoughts. "We are not a little surprised, Ablabius, dearest and most beloved parent," he begins, "that your gravity, who is full of justice and proper reverence, has wished to inquire of Our Clemency, either what Our Moderation previously advised regarding judgment by bishops or what we now desire to be observed." In the next section, his language is even more impatient: "We ordain, therefore, just as the appearance of our edict revealed, that the judgment of bishops issued any where or way without any distinction of age be preserved inviolate and uncorrupted; that is to say, that whatever judgment shall have been determined by the bishops be held ever sacred and venerable."

Ablabius may have hoped for a more favorable reading, but what he got was a more vigorous and unambiguous restatement of the very points at issue. Constantine now specified that appeal to the bishop's judgment may be made even after trial in the civil court had already begun, and indeed at any point up to the actual pronouncing of sentence, and that such an appeal must be allowed "instantly, without any hesitation, even if the other party is opposed." The judge's decision, moreover, is to be inappellable—"all cases . . . upon being terminated by the judgment of bishops may be confirmed by perpetual and permanent law, nor is it permitted that a matter which the judgment of bishops shall have decided may be reconsidered further"—and when bishops themselves testify in civil court, "every judge may accept without doubt testimony by a single bishop, nor should any other witness be heard when testimony by a bishop may have been pledged by whichever party."

Instructions to accept the testimony of a single bishop without further evidence, coupled with a specific injunction that such testimony should not merely preclude the need for additional witnesses but actually prevent others from testifying, seem to confirm the case for a Constantine engaged in a massive redirection of authority with the aim of securing the triumph of the church.[22] But does it? If this ruling had come in the same fashion as others that appear in the codes, it would be impossible to decide what Constantine's motives were and plausible to argue that his aim was to benefit Christian litigants and their bishops. But the law of 333, "On the Judgment of Bishops" (*De episcopali iudicio*), does not come down in the Theodosian Code. It survives as part of a set of eighteen Roman laws, ranging in date from 331 to 425, discovered early in the seventeenth century in a manuscript of the canons of church councils held in Gaul and North Africa in the fifth and sixth centuries. Named after the scholar who found and published them, Jacques Sirmond, the collection is now known as the Sirmondian Constitutions.[23] "On the Judgment of Bishops" is the first in that collection—the First Sirmondian Constitution (hereafter CS 1); it is the law that makes possible a reappraisal of Constantine's intentions.

Sifting the Record

The laws in the Sirmondian collection survive through an independent tradition, having been copied down in their entirety before the Theodosian Code became the standard source, probably for the use of bishops at one of the councils in whose manuscript record they were found. For this reason, "On the Judgment of Bishops," or CS 1, contains the background and explanatory matter eliminated or moved elsewhere by the codifiers and, especially, the emperor's own rationale for so acting. If Constantine's intent had been either to augment the power of bishops or to give an edge to Christian litigants, his explanation should be expected to say so, directly or indirectly: perhaps "thus may the Supreme Deity be ever propitious to us," as in the Edict of Milan, or "for it ill behooves a Christian to face judgment by an unbeliever," on the lines of a ruling he gave regarding Christians enslaved to Jews.[24] But instead, Constantine wrote that he had come to this decision in order to curtail "the wicked seeds of litigation, so that wretched men, entangled in the long and nearly endless snares of legal procedure, may have a timely release from mischievous pleadings or absurd love of disputation." The position of this sentence is significant. It follows immediately his startling demand that a bishop's testimony be considered both sufficient and exclusive—precisely the provision that made Ablabius's eyebrows jump—and thus indicates that Constantine's mind was on an entirely different set of issues than the church or religious policy when he ruled in this case.

There are further indications in the body of this ruling of the nature of the case that prompted CS 1. Constantine writes, for instance, that Ablabius must honor the bishop's decision "without any distinction of age" (*sine aliqua aetatis discretione*) and enforce it whether the case was "between minors or between adults" (*inter minores sive inter maiores*), phrases that indicate the point at issue was not so much the jurisdiction of the bishop as whether that jurisdiction extended to suits involving minors. Such a question would have been neither idle nor esoteric. If the number of cases that survive not only in the codes but also in literature and papyri are any indication, wards were routinely victimized by unscrupulous or incompetent guardians and also by attorneys who sought fat fees. Ammianus Marcellinus described these latter as "the most violent and rapacious classes of men," who "wear out the doorposts of widows and the thresholds of orphans, and create bitter hatred among friends, relations, or connections, who have any disagreements, if they can only find the least pretext for a quarrel."[25]

Minors had to stand by helplessly until reaching legal age while their estates were squandered away, and it seems likely that one such (or his attorney) had tried to get an early start on the process by exploiting some powers that Constantine had assigned to bishops. Those powers might be the ones spelled out in the law of 318, which is, at least in its surviving form, silent with regard to the age of appellants to the bishop's jurisdiction. Thus, a minor who had no standing in civil courts might have tried to exploit this ambiguity by taking his case to the bishop's court. But there are other indications that a more recent law might have triggered these events, for Constantine refers impatiently in his reply to Ablabius to an edict that he thought already answered his prefect's questions (*sicut edicti nostri forma declarat*, "just as the appearance of our edict revealed," or better, perhaps, "just as it says in black and white"), wording that sounds more appropriate to a recent decision than a law already on the books for fifteen years.

Another clue as to the nature of this more recent edict lies in Constantine's evident concern in CS 1 to provide fair and speedy trials, "a timely release from mischievous pleadings" in his own words. This, he says, is the reason he permitted only one party to the suit to take the case to the bishop, "even if the other party is opposed," for, he writes, "many things which in a court of law the captious bonds of legal objection do not allow to be brought forth, the prestige (*auctoritas*) of the sacrosanct religion finds out and makes known." Freed from the limited perspective imposed by overconcentration on Constantine's religious beliefs, a picture of this legal initiative begins to take shape. Constantine was not concerned with the power of the bishop or of the church but with the administration of justice. For this reason, he forbade appeals from the decisions of bishops and ordered that a single bishop's testimony be sufficient to preclude the testimony of other parties. The bishop was "a sacrosanct man," someone "of unimpaired memory," whose truthfulness was both authoritative and incorruptible: "That is truly confirmed by the authority of truthfulness, that is incorrupted, which the recollection of unimpaired memory shall have brought forth from a sacrosanct man."

From Constantine's vantage point, if bishops were trustworthy and reliable, what need was there for additional witnesses in a trial? If they agreed with the bishop, their testimony was redundant, and if they did not, they must be lying. The reasoning might seem naive, and remarkably credulous, but to a man who never grasped the relationship between the scarcity of precious metals and their value, and who once tried to deal with the problem of appeals by ordering his judges only to accept them from innocent litigants, the logic would be hard to deny.[26] The point in any case is that, simplistic or not, Constantine's reasoning suggests an entirely different framework for CS 1, one in which the bishops were secondary, rather than primary—a means rather than an end. Constantine's primary concern was with legal delays that worked against vulnerable litigants. The term Constantine used for those trapped in the snares of litigation, *miseri homines,* "wretched men," would have relevance for all victims of the judicial process, of course; but it indicates a special concern for the lower classes of the empire, judicially known as *humiliores,* "more humble." If Constantine was thinking of cases involving poor and rich litigants, and not of episcopal privileges, the peculiar provisions of this law fall into place. One-sided appeal, for instance, becomes not only desirable but necessary, since the rich party surely would resist losing the built-in advantages provided him by the regular courts. And, since a bishop had utterly no reason to lie, the problem of tainted or conflicting evidence, the basis of so many appeals, could be avoided simply by allowing only the bishop to testify. CS 1 needs to be read as part of a social agenda, not a religious one.

The appeal process was a particularly effective device for litigants with the resources to use it. Since appeals could be made even before judgment was handed down in the original case, a litigant who did not like the way things were going could bring an immediate halt to proceedings by interjecting one, thereby tying up the case without issue. Faced with the prospect of relocating to a distant and expensive metropolis until such time as the calendar of a busy higher official permitted a hearing, less favored litigants settled if they could, or simply threw in the towel.[27] This loophole plagued Constantine for his entire reign. As early as 314, when he was still wrestling with the Donatists, the emperor complained of their use of this tactic when they appealed the decision of the Council of Arles. "Just as is wont to happen in the cases of the heathen [*gentilium*]," he wrote in exasperation to the bishops there, "they have made an application of appeal! It is true that the heathen, fleeing from a lesser tribunal, where justice can be soon obtained, are wont to betake themselves to an appeal, since authority intervenes more for greater tribunals."[28] In the same year, he ruled that "dilatory and frustrating deferments that are not appeals but mockeries" should be denied.[29] The problem was easier to identify, however, than to resolve. He could, of course, forbid appeals completely, as at one time he did.[30] But then how was he to know he was not abandoning poorer citizens to local corruption? Hence emerged another law, charming in its simplicity, which instructs judges to refuse appeals from guilty persons and only accept them from innocent ones.[31]

Appeal, in fact, often had to be encouraged instead of discouraged, for given the disabilities it imposed on them, poorer citizens were reluctant to exercise this right even when their case was airtight. In one law, Constantine threatened to punish citizens who did not appeal when they suffered injustice. In another, he ordered a governor he evidently did not trust to forward all his case books for review automatically every six months. In 325, he encouraged his subjects to appeal mistreatment by such governors, writing the prefect Constantius, "By edict We remind all provincials that, if they have been treated with contempt when appealing to their own governors, they shall have the right to appeal to Your Gravity, so that, if it should appear that this mistreatment occurred by the fault or negligence of the governors, Your Gravity shall immediately refer them to Our Wisdom, in order that it may be possible for such governors to be fittingly punished."[32] It was a frustrating dilemma, the attempts of various emperors to deal with it forming one of the more depressing subthemes of the codes. The Oration to the Saints reveals Constantine's own preoccupation with legal issues in its striking number of courtroom images, especially ones dealing with sharp practices and unjust defenses, and in a singular passage of his peroration, where he characterizes his success as a victory for freedom and "the adjudication of contracts."[33]

These are important leads that have not been pursued because of the narrow focus on religious issues. When the search for the antecedent to CS 1 is extended to include other matters—minors and orphans, speedy and fair trials, the abuse of the appeal process—strong hints emerge from the Theodosian Code of the law that might have prompted Ablabius's letter to Constantine. A number of laws attributed to Constantine, all bearing the general address "To the Provincials" (*ad provinciales*), all concerned with the rights of minors, fair trials, and appeals, now appear under various titles of the code, and all bear a date in 331 which suggests they might originally have been part of a single piece of legislation. Laws in the codes are not dated uniformly. Some show the date when the decision was handed down, or "given" (*data*), others the date when it was published, or "posted" (*praeposita*). Some include both dates but omit the place "given" or "posted." Mistakes, furthermore, were commonplace. Under such circumstances, certainty is impossible. But so many of these are listed as either given on August 1 and posted on September 1, or posted on dates such as October 1 and November 1 which are within tolerable bounds for the slowness of circulation and idiosyncrasies of local officials, that there is an active possibility that all, or most, were originally part of a single omnibus law that became separated when the codifiers took out the parts that pertained to particular sections of the code. Even if not, the laws certainly indicate that these topics were very much on Constantine's mind during those months.[34]

Whether one law or a series, Constantine's decisions in the year 331, taken together, constitute a sweeping effort at reform. The problems they address continued to be subjects of legislation between 331 and 333. Just eighteen days before the date of the First Sirmondian, Constantine dealt again with the rights of minors, and on the same day, May 5, 333, he reduced the status of subordinate officials (in this case military accountants), the effect of which, as a subsequent law reveals, was to make officers of the court subject to torture for malfeasance.[35] In addition to being consul in 331, Ablabius was also praetorian prefect, which means he would have attended meetings of the consistory where this legislation was formulated—hence Constantine's expressions of surprise and irritation at the disingenuous inquiries of this same Ablabius two years later.

Nothing survives to suggest that other parts of this initiative included the alternative of bishops' courts. But Constantine's response to Ablabius in 333 and the fact that he continued to deal with these problems after 331 provide a strong inference that Ablabius was moved by something recent when he wrote to Constantine in 333. This event may have been nothing more than a lawyer's gambit, but Constantine's reference to "the form of our edict" suggests that it was rather another imperial initiative. A plausible explanation would be that the reform effort in 331 failed and that in the aftermath of that failure Constantine attempted to implement the same reform, this time by means of the bishops. The absence of such an effort from the codes need not be significant because, as we will see, it was soon abrogated, and the compilers of the Theodosian Code were specifically instructed not to include decisions that no longer could be cited in court. Abundant reason for Constantine to have taken this further step is provided by the most famous of these laws of 331, in which he threatens to cut off the hands of greedy judges: "The rapacious hands of the apparitors shall immediately cease, they shall cease, I say, for if after due warning they do not cease, they shall be cut off by the sword." Constantine's frustration, evident in these opening words, continues in a series of lapidary commandments:

> The chamber curtain of the judge shall not be venal; entrance shall not be gained by purchase, the private council chamber shall not be infamous on account of the bids. The appearance of the governor shall not be at a price; the ears of the judge shall be open equally to the poorest as well as to the rich. There shall be no despoiling on the occasion of escorting persons inside by the one who is called chief of the office staff. The assistants of the aforesaid chiefs of office staff shall employ no extortion on litigants; the intolerable onslaught of the centurions and other apparitors who demand small and great sums shall be crushed; and the unsated greed of those who deliver the records of a case to litigants shall be restrained.

Before he finished, Constantine threatened "armed punishment" of those who "suppose that anything ought to be demanded by them from those involved in civil cases," calling them "scoundrels" who will lose their "heads and necks" if they fail to provide access to "all persons who have suffered extortion": "If they [the governor's staff] should dissemble, We hereby open to all persons the right to express complaints about such conduct before the counts of the provinces or before the praetorian prefects, if they are closer at hand, so that We may be informed by their references to Us and may provide punishment for such brigandage."[36]

Constantine even tried religious sanctions. In his frequent lectures on salvation, Eusebius reports, he would denounce the greed and rapacity of his own officials: "As if smiting and scourging them with words, he made certain of the nobles in attendance bow down their heads, being stricken in conscience. Testifying against them in ringing tones, he would bid them render account to God of the things entrusted to them."[37] On one occasion, Eusebius adds, Constantine went so far as to scratch the dimensions of a grave on the ground for one of his officials, thereby to remind him of a fate from which no amount of wealth could save him. Given an emperor reduced to such feeble devices as public humiliation of his officials, Eusebius's rueful judgment on these efforts comes as no surprise: "But they were poor learners and deaf to goodness, in word applauding his sayings with laudatory cries, but in deed scorning them utterly through their greediness."

Eusebius's comments confirm a tendency already visible in Constantine's laws to analyze problems in terms of moral failing. Yet it was not so much avarice that made the courts venal as the need of career officials to please those of higher standing in a society that naturally believed in the perquisites of rank, combined with the very real need to make a living. There is an instructive parallel in the life of Saint John the Almsgiver, seventh-century bishop of Alexandria. Informed, his biographer tells us, "that the stewards of his church, being corrupted by bribes, were becoming respecters of persons in their administration of justice," John immediately convened the group, and, "without bringing any charge against them, he increased the salaries they had received hitherto, and at the same time made it an inflexible rule that they should not take a gift from anyone whatsoever."[38] In Constantine's case, legislation, exhortation, and threats failed, because unlike John he did not accompany them with realistic steps to correct systemic causes of the problem.

Constantine must be forgiven for seeing corruption where instead he should have seen chronic undercompensation combined with the need to maintain a standard of living appropriate to one's class. It was one thing for Saint John to think this way—his was exactly the kind of nontraditional thinking which Christian leadership at its best had to offer—but a Roman emperor would have had to be some kind of prodigy to think this way, and prodigies (as Julian was to show) do not necessarily make good emperors. Everything in ancient education, every one of the interminable speeches that the emperor endured, defined problems in terms of virtue and vice. Within these parameters, vice and its attendant corruptions were the obvious explanations for what was really a deep-seated bias of the ancient system of justice in favor of wealth and influence.

For present purposes, the inadequacy of Constantine's solution is far less important than his evident determination to deal with one of the most intractable problems of late antiquity, a judicial system that worked to the advantage of the rich and powerful, a system that in practice frequently robbed poorer citizens of the justice to which they were entitled.[39] Saint Augustine gives a vivid example of influence peddling to illustrate the probity of his friend Alypius:

> At Rome, he served as assessor to the count who had charge of the Finances for Italy. At that time, there was a certain very powerful senator to whom many men were obligated because of benefactions and many were under his control out of terror. He wished to gain some special privilege for himself, as is customary with a man possessing his influence, and it was something that was illegal before the law. Alypius opposed it. A bribe was offered; he rebuffed it with spirit. Threats were made; he spurned them roughly.[40]

In this instance, an attempt to undermine justice failed. But jurists with the principles of an Alypius were few and far between, which is precisely why Augustine could use such a story to illustrate the uniqueness of his friend's character.

No doubt it was Alypius's indifference to matters of this world which made the senator in this case resort to so blunt an instrument as bribery (and Augustine admits his friend was briefly tempted by an offer to buy books at government rates). Subtler signals of influence and preference, combined with a natural inclination to defer to men of rank and authority, were usually sufficient to win the favor of young officials eager to advance their own careers. In the face of a determined litigant, men of influence could always make use of their superior resources to exhaust their opponents and win through default a case that justice impartially applied would have denied them. As the weakest of the weak, widows and orphans—the precise objects of Constantine's attention in CS 1—were the proverbial losers.

The venal image of late Roman law handed down in the sources needs to be put in perspective. Unscrupulous guardians, scheming lawyers, and biased courts were hardly new to the late empire (in the Gospel of Mark, Jesus warns his disciples, "Beware of the doctors of the law, who love to walk up and down in long robes, receiving respectful greetings in the street; and to have the chief seats in synagogues, and places of honour at feasts. These are the men who eat up the property of widows, while they say long prayers for appearance' sake, and they will receive the severest sentence"), and the appeal process has been subject to abuse in every society—the more hierarchical, the more the abuse. In tsarist Russia, young Vladimir Ilyich Ulyanov won his only case as a lawyer, and showed the mettle of the future Lenin, by pursuing a case against an unscrupulous merchant in his provincial town despite efforts to drag it out through frequent postponements and transfer of jurisdiction to a town almost seventy miles away.[41]

Although the instances of such behavior multiply in sources for the later empire, the reason may be due to a greater sensitivity to the abuses suffered by lesser citizens rather than an increase in the abuses themselves. A story is told about the philosopher-king Marcus Aurelius, during the Golden Age of the second century, sitting in judgment on a case brought against his friend, the rhetor and powerful magnate Herodes Atticus. The case was brought by the citizens of Athens, who had refused to yield to the obstacles a man with Herodes' resources could put in their way, and had pursued their case all the way to the emperor. As Athanasius was to do 150 years later, Herodes bitterly rebuked the emperor and stormed from the tribunal. Marcus proceeded with the hearing and burst into tears on hearing of Herodes' misdeeds. But no banishment resulted from this confrontation. Instead, the breach of protocol was patched up with a cover story (Herodes was distraught at the untimely death of his freedman's twin daughters), some of his other freedmen got slapped on the wrist for their master's improprieties, and for some months Herodes was forced to endure the agony of not knowing whether the emperor would accept his next dinner invitation. Philostratus, who tells this story, gives not the slightest hint of irony or censure; rather, his intent was to illustrate Marcus's philosophical temperament. But it is all too easy for a more cynical age to read beneath the surface of Philostratus's edifying tale the working of an elite brotherhood, whose self-interested exploitation of the judicial system was masked by a shared commitment to rhetoric and the Muses.[42]

In the fourth century, the praetorian prefect Petronius Probus might have come down as a late-empire analogue to Herodes Atticus. In addition to his lengthy public service, he was a poet and litterateur, on intimate terms with the high and mighty. But instead of an admiring Philostratus as his Boswell, Probus had the misfortune to fall under the withering gaze of Ammianus Marcellinus, who left the following portrait of a man who, he conceded, was decent enough in his own behavior but

> was driven to be solicitous for [positions of authority] by the squabbles of his troops of clients, whose boundless cupidity prevented their ever being innocent, and who thrust their patron forward into affairs of state in order to be able to perpetrate all sorts of crimes with impunity. For it must be confessed that though he was a man of such magnanimity that he never desired any dependent or servant of his to do any unlawful thing, yet if he found that any one of them had committed a crime, he laid aside all consideration of justice, would not allow the case to be inquired into, but defended the man without the slightest regard for right or wrong.[43]

Constantine may have been naive about many things, but his surviving laws leave little doubt how he felt about such use of influence. In a ruling dated 328, Constantine wrote, "If any very powerful and arrogant person should arise, and the governors of the provinces are not able to punish him or to examine the case or to pronounce sentence, they must refer his name to Us, or at least to the knowledge of Your Gravity [the prefect Maximus, to whom the ruling is addressed]. Thus provision shall be made for consulting the interests of public discipline and the oppressed lower classes."[44]

This commitment to alleviate the lot of "the oppressed lower classes" is the key to CS 1. Constantine's efforts to make government officials more responsive to the poorer classes had been strenuous. In a notoriously misunderstood constitution of 325, he had offered direct access to himself to any person with evidence of misconduct by any of his officials:

> If there is any person of any position, rank, or dignity whatever who believes that he is able to prove anything truthfully and clearly against any judge, count, or any of My retainers or palatines, in that any of these persons has committed some act which appears to have been done without integrity and justice, let him approach Me and appeal to Me unafraid and secure. I Myself will hear everything; I Myself will conduct an investigation; and, if the charge should be proved, I Myself will avenge Myself. Let him speak with safety, and let him speak with a clear conscience. If he should prove the case, as I have said, I Myself will avenge Myself on that person who has deceived Me up to this time with feigned integrity. The person, moreover, who has revealed and proved the offense I will enrich with honors as well as with material rewards. Thus may the Highest Divinity always be propitious to Me and keep Me unharmed, as I hope, with the State most happy and flourishing.[45]

The language of this edict is so wrathful that scholars have suggested Constantine must have been worried about plots against himself. But it is mild compared with that of the 331 law quoted above, where he threatens to cut off the hands that court officials held out for fees. What this law in fact shows is Constantine attempting to correct the notorious tilt of Roman courts in favor of the rich and powerful, in the belief that by this means he will secure divine favor. While none of the other rulings betray quite this intensity of feeling, they have one common characteristic: all deal with aspects of the same problems addressed in the First Sirmondian Constitution—the rights of minors, fair trials, and appeals. When bound, as here, with Constantine's eagerness to maintain the goodwill of divinity, and the belief that such favor brought peace and prosperity to his subjects, Constantine's commitment to "integrity and justice" emerges as a potent agenda.

Implementing the Agenda

There is no direct evidence to explain why Constantine's court reforms would have failed, but there is a certain amount of indirect evidence by means of which a reason can be inferred. The success of any such reform would have been made unlikely by the mere fact that the career officials who staffed the courts were bound by both personal bias and enlightened self-interest to be partial to the class on which the success of their careers depended. Augustine reveals as much in the story about his friend Alypius, for after narrating this instance in which a senator got his comeuppance, Augustine adds, "All were amazed at such unaccustomed spirit, which did not crave such a man as a friend, or fear him as an enemy, even though he was much noted for his innumerable ways of giving help or doing harm." With considerably less fanfare, Augustine also lets the reader know that, after this incident, Alypius was unable to find employment as a jurist.[46]

There is one way in which the operation of interest differed in the late empire as opposed to earlier periods: the layers of court ceremonial formalized by Diocletian succeeded not only in protecting the emperor from assault but also in isolating him even further from contact with the general public. The more they relied on subordinates as gatekeepers, the more dependent emperors became on subordinates for advice on whom to favor, whom to shun. Had it not been for the intervention of officials in Constantine's party, Athanasius's piece of street theater in Constantinople would have come out quite differently. This isolation created a dilemma that was at the heart of late Roman rule, for even an emperor who sincerely wanted to protect the lower classes had to rely ever more heavily for both information and enforcement on officials who came from the very class that was most likely to resist and seek to thwart such policies. The result of this tension was a fundamental distrust that still reverberates in the codes.[47]

The *Historia Augusta* is a set of imperial biographies which purports to have been written by several hands early in the fourth century but which was in fact written by a single author toward the end of that century in what now appears to have been a massive hoax.[48] In the Life of Aurelian, the author, supposedly "Flavius Vopiscus of Syracuse," mused about the problem of "bad emperors" (*malos principes*): What accounts for them? After listing the obvious reasons—power and wealth—the author focused on the influence of "unscrupulous friends, pernicious attendants, the greediest eunuchs, courtiers who are fools or knaves." His description of the means by which such influence was practiced remains a valuable tutorial in late Roman politics:

> Four or five men gather together and form one plan for deceiving the emperor, and then they tell him to what he must give his approval. Now the emperor, who is shut up in his palace, cannot know the truth. He is forced to know only what these men tell him, he appoints as judges those who should not be appointed, and removes from public office those whom he ought to retain. Why say more? As Diocletian himself was wont to say, the favour of even a good and wise and righteous emperor is often sold. These were Diocletian's own words, and I have inserted them here for the very purpose that your wisdom might understand that nothing is harder than to be a good ruler.[49]

At about the same time that pseudo-Flavius was passing on such advice, the famous pagan orator Libanius played on this very fear when he attempted to convince the emperor Theodosius I that counselors who had advised him to allow the temples to be attacked had played him false. Whenever the emperor's actions provoke an outcry, he warns, "In public they disclaim such responsibility, but in private conclave with you they claim that none of their other actions has served your house so well."[50]

Constantine's threats against his courtiers, his efforts to regulate the judicial system, and his steps discussed in the previous chapter to create an alternative means of evaluating governors through popular acclamation all testify to his determination to break the pattern of elite influence and alleviate the lot of the poor. This is the agenda that underlay CS 1 and which, in turn, makes CS 1 a singular artifact. It reveals, first, a situation in which action favorable to the church—in fact, so favorable that even orthodox scholars have doubted its authenticity—apparently was undertaken for reasons that have little directly to do with religious policy. Constantine's interest, rather, was for justice and honest trials; the bishops were a means, not an end. Second, as a result of this understanding, it is now possible to come to a better understanding of the dynamics of Constantine's relations with the bishops and the effect of that relationship on his agenda.

Defining a Relationship

Why did he turn to the bishops? His reverence for the clergy has often been remarked, and it certainly was real.[51] But it is a mistake to conclude from these examples that CS 1 reveals an emperor so blinded by religious awe that he was willing to deliver the empire into the hands of the church. From another perspective, requiring bishops to testify in court runs counter to a truly reverential spirit. Later in the century, Theodosius I showed a more proper attitude when he avowed that it was dishonorable for a bishop to give testimony, a sentiment echoed a century and a half later by the more magisterial Justinian. The sentiment is, in fact, very old: ancient Hindu law said that priests "of deep learning in scripture," as well as students of theology, and anchorites "secluded from all worldly connections" should not testify in court at all.[52]

The comparison with Constantine's reverence is striking: whereas in these other cases the intent was to protect sacrosanct individuals from contamination by the grimy business of secular affairs, Constantine's was to plunge them into the middle of this pollution, in the hope that their personal qualities would help clean up the mess, as he wrote in a passage already quoted from CS 1: "For many things which in a court of law the captious bonds of legal objection do not allow to be brought forth, the prestige (*auctoritas*) of the sacrosanct religion finds out and makes known." The difference is utility. Frustrated in his efforts to reorient the values of his own officials, Constantine sought to address the problem by creating an alternate judiciary free of the biases and material concerns of the careerist. His aim was neither to harness the bishops to his own lust for power nor to put the empire at their feet but to use them to cut through the Gordian knot of bias and interest which prevented "miserable men" from receiving due process. His aim was not to empower Christians but to empower the poor.

Modern scholarship has been so tightly focused on the rapid growth in wealth and power of the bishops during the course of the fourth century, the infighting of great prelates like Athanasius and Eusebius of Nicomedia, the bloody ambitions of a Damasus of Rome, that it is difficult now to entertain the proposition that Constantine might have been so blind or naive as to believe that such figures could be the cornerstone of a new judicial system. When Edward Gibbon sought to compare the ambitions of such bishops to "the fervour of the first Christians," he found an apt quotation in the early-fifth-century writer Sulpicius Severus, who commented that these early Christians "desired martyrdom with more eagerness than his own contemporaries solicited a bishopric."[53] But despite these images of greed and ambition, it is important to remember that the vast majority of bishops were humble men, whose devotion to Christian values and lack of interest in worldly advancement placed them outside the traditional social code, making them honest and independent judges. Ammianus Marcellinus, who as we have seen could be a devastating critic, and whose biting and widely quoted comments about the powerful bishops in the major cities of his day show that he held no brief for the clergy, wrote quite differently about their country cousins. After describing the perquisites that made the bishopric of Rome such a desirable prize, he continued, "And they [rivals for that office] might be really happy if, despising the vastness of the city, which they excite against themselves by their vices, they were to live in imitation of some of the priests in the provinces, whom the most rigid abstinence in eating and drinking, and plainness of apparel, and eyes always cast on the ground, recommend to the everlasting Deity and his true worshippers as pure and sober-minded men."[54]

If Constantine's purpose was to supplant a corrupt bureaucracy, then the bishops were a logical, indeed a brilliant, choice. In number and distribution, there were enough of them in place for the reform to take effect immediately, at virtually no cost to the state. More important, bishops were far more independent and more likely to identify with the problems of the poor than were secular officials.

Even better testimony than Ammianus's, because it is so grudging, comes from Constantine's nephew and eventual successor Julian, who renounced Christianity after he became emperor in 361, thereby earning the title "the Apostate" from his former co-religionists. Julian hated his former faith with a rare zeal and devoted his brief career to the task of replacing it with a renewed paganism. For this reason, anything Julian said in any way complimentary to Christian clergy has to be taken seriously. Some of these compliments are, indeed, indirect. For instance, he insisted that his new priests conform to the highest standards of personal morality, forbidding them to attend the games or read licentious literature, and he also acknowledged the importance of humble behavior to the success of his new priesthood, writing that "any priest who behaves unjustly to his fellow men and impiously towards the gods or is overbearing to all, must either be admonished with plain speaking or chastised with great severity."[55] In both of these cases he surely would have said he was doing nothing more than enforcing traditional standards, although in the latter case at least Christian influence would be hard to deny, since nothing in either the old code or the new morality required the holders of pagan priesthoods to behave with such humility. But in one other instance, he was disarmingly specific about the source of his inspiration. On this occasion, he complained to Arsacius, his new high priest of Galatia, "Why do we not observe that it is their benevolence to strangers, their care for the graves of the dead and the pretended holiness of their lives that have done most to increase atheism?" "Pretended holiness" was as close as Julian could come to acknowledging the perceived piety of the Christian clergy, but it is for present purposes close enough.

More significant as a way of understanding Constantine's agenda is the importance Julian attached to organization (evidenced by the network of high priests which he tried to create for each province) and even more to acts of charity. In his letter to Arsacius, Julian allowed that

> it is disgraceful that, when no Jew ever has to beg, and the impious Galilaeans [his preferred term for Christians] support not only their own poor but ours as well, all men see that our people lack aid from us. Teach those of the Hellenic faith to contribute to public service of this sort, and the Hellenic villages to offer their first fruits to the gods; and accustom those who love the Hellenic religion to these good works by teaching them that this was our practice of old.[56]

In another letter, Julian admitted the superiority of Christian caretaking: "For when it came about that the poor were neglected and overlooked by the priests, then I think the impious Galilaeans observed this fact and devoted themselves to philanthropy. And they have gained ascendancy in the worst of their deeds through the credit they win for such practices."[57]

Julian did more than encourage acts of charity. In what must be seen as a direct imitation of his uncle's policy, Julian announced to Arsacius that he was allocating him thirty thousand *modii* of wheat and sixty thousand pints of wine, with instructions that "one-fifth of this be used for the poor who serve the priests, and the remainder be distributed by us to strangers and beggars."[58] If Julian's reforms could be motivated at least in part by the belief that the poor had been effectively served by Constantine's diversion of patronage resources to Christian bishops, then it surely is not unreasonable to think that when Constantine himself diverted those resources he might also have had this immediate social concern in mind, as much as some abstract "triumph of the church." A charitable program, then, must also be considered a part of Constantine's agenda to which the bishops were as much means as ends, a relatively honest and efficient network for the distribution of poor relief as well as justice.

The resources devoted to this purpose could be substantial, as the records of the *Liber Pontificalis* indicate just as well as Julian's letter to Arsacius.[59] While they greatly increased the ability of bishops to care for the poor, however, these resources also provided bishops with the ability to expand greatly their patronage networks, helping to make them in large cities like Alexandria a virtual countergovernment. To Julian's shrewd eyes, in any case, this action explained much of the success Christianity enjoyed in his day. If here, too, Constantine's agenda was at least as much social as religious, both the power and the resources that characterized the church in later years would better be seen as unintended consequences of a different agenda. It would also mean that the charge against Athanasius made to Constantine by his rivals, that he diverted charitable distributions to his own use, had more bite than might otherwise seem the case.

This much can be said: Lactantius, whose *Divine Institutes* resonated in so many other ways with Constantine's agenda, pointedly criticized in that work the lack of justice of "those who worship the gods," complaining, "If they sit as judges, either they destroy the guiltless because they have been corrupted by bribes, or they let the guilty go unpunished." Conversely, Lactantius stressed the importance of protecting the weaker members of society, naming in particular minors and widows: "It is no less a great work of justice to protect destitute children and widows and to defend those needing help which the divine law so prescribes to all, since all the best judges think it pertains to their office to favor them with natural humaneness and to strive to be of help to them."[60] It was therefore no idle compliment for Constantine to begin his Oration to the Saints by apostrophizing the church as "the cherisher of tender and inexperienced age, guardian of truth and gentleness."[61]

Such concerns may also have governed an attempt by Constantine to restrict the entry of wealthier Romans into the clergy. His law, which dates from the latter half of the 320s, denied exemption from compulsory public service to individuals who took orders. It is usually (and rightly) read as an effort to close a loophole through which local elites evaded their increasingly burdensome civic responsibilities, a premodern version of a tax shelter. But the same law also sought to limit replacement clergy to candidates who came from lower ranks of society: "For the wealthy must assume secular obligations, and the poor must be supported by the wealth of the churches."[62] Once again, Julian can provide an insight into his uncle's policies. In establishing criteria for the selection of his reformed priesthood, the Apostate demanded that preference be given to "those who show most love for the gods, and next those who show most love for their fellow men, . . . whether they be poor or rich," adding,

> And in this matter let there be no distinction whatever whether they are unknown or well known. . . . Even though he be poor and a man of the people, if he possess within himself these two things, love for God and love for his fellow men, let him be appointed priest. And a proof of his love for God is his inducing his own people to show reverence to the gods; a proof of his love for his fellows is his sharing cheerfully, even from a small store, with those in need, and his giving willingly thereof, and trying to do good to as many men as he is able.[63]

Julian frequently showed an uncanny insight into the springs not only of the Christian priesthood but also of his uncle's policies. His concern to create a humble priesthood as well as a charitable one thus might also echo Constantine's intentions. Even if not, Constantine's own law at the very least once again reveals a difference between his agenda and that of the bishops, who increasingly came to place a premium on the traditional markers of class and education in selection for the priesthood. By the second half of the century, Bishop Gregory of Nazianzen could cast scorn on the lowborn origins of the bishops who had helped depose him from the bishopric of Constantinople.[64]

Redefining the Agenda

The First Sirmondian Constitution has not finished telling its secrets. Nothing in the surviving laws indicates that in subsequent years bishops' courts continued to possess, or in fact ever held, the most controversial privileges confirmed in this law—one-party appeal and exclusive testimony. Those who study these matters assume that these would have been canceled by Julian when he abrogated other privileges and were never reinstated.[65] But there is some indication that they were revoked by Constantine himself. Two laws dated to the year 334 deal with matters that came up in CS 1. Little more than a year after his response to Ablabius, on June 17, 334, Constantine ruled once again on the problem of appeals in a way that shows he was still struggling with the problem of how to guarantee justice in a way that would not work to the detriment of the poorer classes. Here, Constantine ordered that appeals to the emperor of cases involving widows, orphans, and those disabled by illness must be heard in their own provinces, in order to spare these classes the cost and effort of travel to the capital—obviously a direct attempt to short-circuit a favorite legal device of the rich. However, Constantine allowed an exception if the appeal for trial before the emperor was made by widows, orphans, and the ill, plus any others "made wretched by the wrongs of fortune." These, he said, may do so, particularly if "they are in terror of the power of any person."[66] Two months after this law, on August 25, 334, Constantine gave another ruling on witnesses, in response to a question posed by the governor Julianus. Here Constantine strongly confirmed the principle that evidence must be supported by the testimony of more than one witness, no matter how exalted his rank: "In a similar manner, we sanctioned that no judge should easily allow the testimony of only one person to be admitted in any case whatever. We now manifestly sanction that the testimony of only one witness shall not be heard at all, even though such witness should be resplendent with the honor of the glorious Senate."[67]

Nothing in either of these laws directly negates the regulations of the First Sirmondian. Neither mentions bishops directly, and the first law of the two actually confirms a principle enunciated in CS 1 by, in effect, denying appeal to one party or class of litigant while at the same time guaranteeing it to another. But the class of litigant being protected by this law—widows, orphans, and the ill—corresponds so nicely to the "miserable men" (and in the case of minors with guardians, i.e., orphans, exactly the same group) whom CS 1 intended to aid that at the very least this law signals that Constantine did not conceive the provisions of CS 1 as pertaining exclusively to bishops. In the second law, the terms excluding testimony that cannot be corroborated by other witnesses are so categorical that Constantine would merely have been inviting further requests like Ablabius's if he meant to continue to exempt bishops from its provisions. While the relationship of these laws to CS 1 is debatable, taken together they show that Constantine did not consider CS 1 the last word on the subject of appeals or testimony. More than that, the first shows him attempting to deal with the issue of justice for the poorer classes once again within the framework of the civil apparatus, while the second might be the closest thing to an admission of error which someone like Constantine was ever likely to make.

What does all this mean? If these subsequent laws do indicate Constantine was backing away from the conditions of CS 1, one probable reason is that it was pressure from his own bureaucracy which forced him to do so. However, it is also possible that he no longer regarded the bishops as the solution that he once expected them to be. These were the very years when the conflict between Athanasius and his enemies was putting the goal of unity ever further out of reach, provoking the exasperation that can still be read in his letters summoning bishops to the Council of Tyre and bishops from that council to Constantinople. It may be significant, too, that one of the charges leveled against Athanasius during the meeting in Constantinople was that he was diverting charitable supplies to his own resources. This would not have been the first time such a charge had been made, nor was Athanasius the first object: earlier letters boil with indignation at what Constantine took to be corrupt dealings by Eusebius of Nicomedia and Arius.[68] How many such charges would it take to disabuse Constantine of the notion that the bishops were immune to the systemic abuses of the civil bureaucracy? Or might it simply be that Constantine decided the cost of the bishops' support had gone too high—that what the bishops had to offer was not worth what they wanted in return?

The Origins of Coercion

In the scholarship on CS 1, the reaction of the bishops to Constantine's initiative rarely is questioned. Implicitly, the assumption is that they sought, or at least welcomed, these powers. It is all part of a standard model that governs study of the transformation of church and state which began during Constantine's reign, a model of the emperor giving (for reasons of personal power, à la Burckhardt, or personal devotion, à la Baynes) and a grateful church receiving. Yet from later complaints it would seem that even the much less extensive judicial duties of later ages were a constant drain on the bishops' energy and resources. Every mention of these activities which survives is cast in terms of the great and unwelcome burden it posed. Augustine was particularly bitter, and typically eloquent, in giving voice to that sentiment.[69]

What difference does it make whether or not the bishops were agreeable to Constantine's design? If they did, in fact, see these juridical powers as more of a burden than a boon, as more a part of Constantine's agenda than their own, then another factor must be taken into account in assessing the developments of the later part of Constantine's reign: the working of the inflexible political law of quid pro quo. The difference would be that, instead of taking the bishops' support for granted, Constantine had to woo them. The resources with which he endowed churches and charitable endowments certainly were attractive to the bishops, but even more so was the imperial support that he now provided for their internal disputes.

This analysis points the way to resolution of a conundrum raised by Constantine's refusal to coerce non-Christians to adopt his faith. By the end of the fourth century Christians clearly were intent on removing paganism from the political landscape. With the benefit of hindsight, it has been a relatively easy matter for scholars to find Christians at all times who were intent on doing so and to trace the origins of Christian coercion to an intolerance that is deeply embedded in the faith. But if Constantine succeeded in creating a consensus of pagans and Christians in favor of an imperial dynasty built around a vague monotheism that, as he said in his letter to Arius and Alexander, each person could define as much more specifically as he pleased in "the secret custody of your own minds and thoughts,"[70] if he succeeded in neutralizing Christian militants, then inherent qualities are insufficient to explain the success of a militant agenda in subsequent decades.

The remaining chapters of this book are devoted to an attempt to direct the inquiry into Christian coercion away from such inherent qualities and into the study of group behavior and mass movements, thus completing the alteration begun two centuries ago by Edward Gibbon when he denied himself the theologian's method "of describing Religion as she descended from Heaven, arrayed in her native purity," in favor of a search for answers in the human condition, "the inevitable mixture of error and corruption which she [Religion] contracted in a long residence upon earth, among a weak and degenerate race of beings."[71] As part of that redefinition, it will be important to observe that the first step in the direction of coercion was taken during Constantine's reign, and—in what will be seen as a regular pattern—the object of that coercion was not, as might have been expected, pagans but other Christians.

Heresy is the one important exception Constantine made from his commitment to a noncoercive approach. In his *vita Constantini*, Eusebius of Caesarea reproduces an edict in which Constantine attacked the "venomous errors" of Christian heretics, seized their meeting places, and declared unlawful any form of meeting, public or private, in which they might attempt to engage in the future.[72] Although Eusebius records it nonchalantly, and with obvious satisfaction, the decision cannot have been an easy one for Constantine to make, since it meant abandoning the principle that he stated so eloquently to the bishops of North Africa and in the Oration to the Saints that true godliness is shown by acts of forbearance and toleration. More pointedly, it also contradicted his own advice to Arius and Alexander to leave conscientious objectors free to pursue the privacy of their own thoughts.[73] Now, in this edict, an entirely different rhetoric prevails. Constantine characterizes the beliefs of the heretics as "venomous," a term implying that those who held such beliefs were snakes; he likens heresy to a disease, something capable of infecting healthy souls. Such images are important as labels that serve both to identify and to stigmatize a group, making it easier to single out its members and deny them humane treatment.[74] Moreover, Eusebius indicates that the edict convinced many to return to the true faith.[75] The smugness of his assessment is an indication of the edict's worst precedent of all: it was successful. This step, however limited in scope and duration, opened the door for the more massive coercion campaigns that would occur at the end of the century. Why did Constantine take it?

So long as coercion could be defined as a natural by-product of Christian belief, this was a question that did not need to be asked. But the inconsistency of Constantine's edict against the heretics with the rest of his carefully articulated program now demands explanation. The simplest one is that the emperor was inspired by the success of his strong actions against the holdouts at the Council of Nicaea to adopt similar measures with regard to other dissidents. Eusebius attaches no date to the edict, but he places it amid other events that can be dated to the late 320s, and this date would mean that the consensus Constantine forged at Nicaea had not yet come unraveled; he could still have believed that the unity he sought was within his grasp.

Such a scenario would certainly sit well with the standard model employed for this period, making this edict yet another example of the imperial initiative that determined the future of church and state. Indeed, in this edict, Constantine equates "that prosperity which we enjoy through the favor of God" with the need to restore heretics to the right path, suggesting that he was also motivated by the traditional duty of Roman emperors to protect the *pax deorum* by enforcing right worship. But the First Sirmondian Constitution suggests that the bishops should not be left out of the scenario so readily. If Constantine did need to win the support of the bishops for his goal of an alternative judiciary, then there would be another reason for him to have moved against the heretic: it was an act of political horse trading. Vulnerable both as a leader of that polity that had for so long represented, at least to one strand of Christian thought, the forces of evil and as a late and still-unbaptized convert, Constantine needed to make a gesture that would protect his flank against attacks by militant Christians and win the support of the bishops for his social and judicial initiatives. Heretics were an ideal target for both objectives, and moving against them had the additional advantage that it could be explained to pagans in nonalarming ways, as a traditional duty of Roman rulers.

Thus, just as the preceding chapters revealed an underlying consistency to the seemingly wild swings in Constantine's post-Nicene behavior, showing instead an emperor skillfully shifting his weight from one side to the other and using the leverage of criminal charges as well as the velvet murmurings of a respectful and irenic rhetoric to massage the bishops into a condition of inclusive harmony, so now awareness of his need for the bishops to carry out a social and legal agenda reveals that the bishops had some leverage of their own. It certainly should not strain the bounds of credulity to suggest that they applied that leverage to obtain the more aggressive posture that Constantine displayed in the edict against the heretics. With heresy, both imperial and episcopal agendas came together. Punishment of improper worship was the one action that Constantine would have been prepared by centuries of imperial procedure to take, and the one that, in his eyes, a new and important constituency had the most right to demand. It had the additional advantage of demonstrating his toughness to militant Christians at very little cost.

Constantine certainly saw the attention he gave to disputes between the clergy—disparaged then and now—as a duty. But it was also, at least in some small way, a price.

CS 1 thus shows an alternative way of understanding the relationship between church and state which was forged during Constantine's years. The model that scholars have used in the past to explain the growth of the church's power during these years implicitly or explicitly has been one of Constantine giving and the bishops taking. That is, all concern has been devoted to the nature and extent of Constantine's motives, a method that in turn suggests that all initiative and all decision were his, entirely. The context of CS 1, however, is one in which Constantine had need of the bishops for ends that were not primarily religious, a context that shows bishops as more suitable to his mission than theirs. In this context, the new relationship being forged between church and state during this emperor's reign takes on an air of improvisation, one in which, in return for services that they, and they alone, could offer, the bishops were able to demand from Constantine concessions he otherwise might not have been so willing to make. A convergence of interests thus underlay the Constantinian settlement, creating a situation better characterized as one that required give-and-take on both sides, rather than as one in which all initiative lay with one side or the other. This is the proper basis on which to begin to understand the otherwise perplexing actions of Constantine's last decade and the use of coercion to which Christians from this time forward increasingly turned.

Defining an Era

The speed with which Constantine became involved in Christian disputes can be deceptive. Combined with the natural tendency of scholars to concentrate on those actions that best explain the church's subsequent dominance, this involvement leads to the easy conclusion that Constantine's prime interest was to promote the type of Christianity known to later ages, a coercive and intolerant Christianity that, with its "triumph," forged a stranglehold over secular as well as religious life. Yet the foregoing suggests that Constantine had something very different in mind when he turned judicial and patronage powers over to the bishops, not only a different kind of Christianity but also a social program for which he thought the bishops would be instrumental. The First Sirmondian Constitution offers a rare opportunity to look at Constantine's actions not just in terms of results but also in terms of intentions; to separate means from ends, remedy from problem. In this case, Constantine took action favorable to the church—so favorable, in fact, that even orthodox scholars have doubted the law's authenticity—for reasons that have little to do directly with modern ideas of religious policy. Although this law certainly would have incidentally advanced the interests and power of the bishops, its primary purpose was to remedy a longstanding defect in the Roman judicial system. Constantine may have had some notion that doing so would contribute to the success, and maybe the triumph, of Christianity, but his primary purpose was more immediate and more pragmatic. He needed the bishops in order to carry out his social, political, and juridical agenda.

In an oft-cited passage, Eusebius of Caesarea proclaims that Constantine "rated the priests of God at a higher value than any judge whatever."[76] The greatest significance of CS 1 may be that it provides an alternative to the theological context in which Eusebius puts this observation, by indicating that, in addition to whatever religious and imperial ambitions he harbored, Constantine had social and administrative goals that his Christian supporters were in a position to help him attain. Consequently, they were also in a position to press their own agenda on an emperor whose claim to their support rested on an avowed identity of interests. But this is only part of the picture, for in taking on the burden of enforcing orthodoxy Constantine also showed the bishops the advantages that would accrue from cooperation with his goals. Constantine needed the bishops, but the bishops also needed Constantine. This mutual need is what defines the Age of Constantine.

Constantine's agenda was flawed. As his letter to Alexander and Arius shows, his own goals were vague, going little beyond a wish that there be "one faith, and one understanding among you, one united judgment in reference to God."[77] He left it to the bishops to work out the fine print of the arrangement, and he thereby forgot a cardinal rule of politics: the power to define is the power to redefine. Not by any great plan nor by any will to power was the great superstructure of church and state erected in this decade, but in the more familiar political atmosphere of last-minute and ad hoc decision making. During this same period, the same Constantine who had won control of the message so brilliantly lost control of his agenda. By leaving details to the bishops, he allowed them to advance their agenda even when it ran counter to his own; he had successfully contained the militants, but he could not contain the bishops. An observer of late-twentieth-century politics, describing the way subordinates far down on the chain of command can make decisions that affect the outcome of policies, drew the following moral from this process: "Never underestimate the power of writing the fine print."[78] The moral of this story is the same.

This was one way that Constantine lost control of his agenda. There is another important way, also involving "the fine print," but here in a less literal sense. It is a way that would have been hard then to predict and is hard even now to see, for it was accomplished through the simple matter of record keeping. As Christians increasingly took charge of the record, they quite naturally focused their attention on those parts that helped them understand and make sense of their own complicated past. To this delicate process of memory and interpretation we must now turn, for at its center sits, not surprisingly, yet another bishop.

PART IV

UNINTENDED CONSEQUENCES

> When political sects have been too long in office they
> start believing they know what is good for you.
> Russell Baker (1992)

Ten

The Fine Print

The years 335–37 would have tested the strength of a man half the age of Eusebius of Caesarea. Between July 335 and Constantine's death on May 22, 337, Eusebius presided over the unruly Council of Tyre that sat in judgment on Athanasius;[1] played a prominent role in the eight-day Encaenia festival to dedicate Constantine's Church of the Holy Sepulchre in Jerusalem; traveled to Constantinople to report on the council to Constantine and repeat the oration he delivered at the time of the Encaenia; journeyed again to Constantinople to participate in the Council of Constantinople that brought down Bishop Marcellus of Ancyra in the spring of 336; prepared and delivered a state oration for the closing festivities of the emperor's thirtieth jubilee in July 336; and wrote *Contra Marcellum* in two books and *De ecclesiastica theologia* in three. During this same period, Eusebius began work on another project that he may have had in mind for at least a decade, the *vita Constantini*.

All this, when Eusebius was well beyond his seventieth year. From references he makes in the Church History to events "in my own lifetime," it would seem that he was born around 260, though as is often the case in antiquity we know next to nothing of his early life.[2] Eusebius emerges from the shadows as a student in the school of

Caesarea founded originally by the great Origen during his exile from Alexandria and maintained by his devoted follower Pamphilus, a wealthy member of the community who was imprisoned and eventually martyred during the Great Persecution. Eusebius himself managed to escape this fate, even though he attended Pamphilus constantly while in prison, where the two of them collaborated on a biography of Origen, the last book of which Eusebius completed by himself. After the persecution, probably around 314, Eusebius became bishop of Caesarea.

The persecution also started Eusebius on the path to scholarly immortality. Evidently in response to the polemics surrounding that misfired policy,[3] Eusebius produced The Chronicle, a work in which he created a common calendar for the tangled histories of five different nations—the Chaldaeans, Assyrians, Hebrews, Greeks, and Romans—by establishing common points (such as the fall of Troy, the first Olympiad, and the death of Jesus) and then arranging the events of each nation in parallel columns synchronized at these points. Only one other person—Julius Africanus, at the beginning of the third century—had ever attempted such a complex task, and Eusebius's dwarfed that effort in both design and execution. He followed this achievement with an even more original and valuable work, a history of the church from its origins to his own day. This was a subject that had never before been attempted; Eusebius literally had to create it out of the scattered and incomplete records of a people who did not define themselves by traditional categories of political, social, or cultural identity. The closest model for what Eusebius had in mind was the histories of the philosophical schools, which concerned themselves with the preservation of a body of ideas as represented in a succession of legitimate teachers. But no philosophical school came anywhere near Christianity either in the size and scope of its organization or in the diversity of its adherents (whether defined geographically, ideologically, or socially).[4]

Eusebius settled on five unifying themes, which he announced at the beginning of the work: for each generation, he would report the bishops of the most famous sees, the works of those who proclaimed the Word of God, the fate of the Jews, heresies, and persecutions and martyrs.[5] He ignored the events and leaders that made up the stuff of traditional accounts, and in a further departure from classical history he made extensive use of documents, which he quoted verbatim. The choice of themes is revealing. Instead of miracles and relics, Eusebius chose to concentrate on topics that were essentially institutional and clerical, thereby anticipating by more than a century the principle that came to govern the writing of church history: *in sacerdotibus ecclesia constat* ("the Church consists in the clergy").[6] His was a new history for a new type of people, and he rightfully described himself as "attempting to traverse as it were a lonely and untrodden path."[7] The Church History was an instant success, propelled no doubt by the failure of the persecution that Eusebius documents so vividly in the closing books of this work. Successive editions carried the story up to Constantine's victory over Licinius in 324. Like Thucydides, the "father of scientific history," Eusebius succeeded in establishing a new field of study, and like Thucydides, the "father of church history" was paid the ultimate compliment by those who wrote after him: rather than attempt to improve on what he had written about the first three centuries of the church, they all opted to pick up the story from the reign of Constantine. It would be difficult to overestimate the influence of this work on subsequent scholarship, down to the present day. As Brian Warmington has observed, without it "we would know less of the first three centuries of Christianity than we do of Mithraism."[8]

Eusebius of Caesarea is key to another important way in which Constantine lost control of his agenda. Derailed by the aggressive use to which bishops like Athanasius and Eusebius of Nicomedia put Christianity's new political powers, it now virtually disappeared from the historical record through the quieter labors of bishops like Eusebius of Caesarea. The Constantine of the present study—the artful negotiator, patient consensus builder, and ardent judicial reformer— appears on Eusebius's pages in only the briefest of glimpses. Instead, what emerges from his pen is a loyal son of the church, bent entirely on confessing his faith and eradicating "the filth of godless error." The certainty with which Eusebius advocates this position is the crux of a longstanding problem. It is what led Jacob Burckhardt to dismiss him as "the first thoroughly dishonest historian of antiquity," and others to respond, in turn, that Eusebius's painstaking accuracy in the scrutiny and reproduction of documents acquits him of this charge.[9] Though few today would want to go as far as Burckhardt, it is obvious that Eusebius did not write with disinterest. Despite his care in citing documents, he was selective in his use of them, and even one of his firmer admirers has cautioned that "it is unwise to rely on Eusebius's reports as reproducing exactly the precise tenor, or even main purport, of lost evidence."[10]

The preceding chapter ended with a warning from a veteran Washington correspondent about "the fine print." What Hedrick Smith meant was the importance of detail to the determination of policy. "Policy gets defined just as much by implementing details as it does by deciding the broad sweep," he wrote, with the stern conclusion that "any president or top policymaker who does not know that just doesn't understand the game of governing."[11] Smith's remark points the way out of this apparent dilemma with Eusebius, for the concept of "the fine print" extends beyond contracts and legislation. Historians have their fine print as well, which they convey overtly by interpreting events and looking for their underlying causes (as this book is attempting to do), but also covertly when they decide which of the myriad pieces of information that pertain to their topic deserves to be included and which can be left aside. The study of a historical work cannot end with verification of its documents and sources; thought must be given both to the choice of documents and to the way they are interpreted. In his writings, Eusebius took control of "the fine print" of Constantine's policy; that is, he interpreted it according to his own conceptual scheme, according to which some things the emperor did seemed more important to him than others, and these were the things that, he believed, gave meaning to Constantine's career. It is far more useful to understand what that scheme was than it is to criticize Eusebius for doing what all historians do.

Reading Eusebius

Just as there have always been facts, there have always been different ways of interpreting and explaining those facts. The need to explain the new thing they were attempting is one reason why Christians from the earliest times excelled in writing the fine print. The apologists brought the art of explanation to a new level, and the need to explain, to defend, to justify assured that every Christian, no matter what else he or she was, was also a little bit of an apologist. Eusebius prepared his *Chronicle* with admirable sensitivity to the limitations of his materials and rigor in his use of them, but he undertook the project to begin with to support Christians in a longstanding argument with Greeks and Jews about the antiquity of their faith. Hence, as Arnaldo Momigliano put it in a seminal essay, in Eusebius's mind "chronology was something between an exact science and an instrument of propaganda."[12]

Christians had a sense of the meaning of events which was so strong that it vested their work with an obvious bias. For instance, the deaths of the persecutors—the thesis that sought to prove the potency of the Christian God by showing how he struck down those who harmed his people—were as important an arguing point for Eusebius as for Lactantius. Constantine himself used it in his Oration to the Saints. The point has been made successfully for centuries. Yet, strictly speaking, it is clearly wrong. The first of the Tetrarchs to die was not the fearsome Daza or the violent Galerius or even the malevolent Diocletian but, in fact, the pious Constantius I, Constantine's father, whose participation in the persecution had been minimal at best. Another lesson from the persecution was that those who raise their hands against God die without heirs, whereas both Constantius I and Constantine had heirs in abundance. But Constantine put his own eldest son to death, and no sooner had he died himself than all his relations but his three surviving sons and two negligible nephews were put to the sword, and in fewer years than Constantine himself had reigned his line would end in the person of one of those two nephews, Julian, who turned his back on Christian belief. At the end of the century, the rabidly Catholic Eastern prefect Maternus Cynegius died in the middle of a campaign to destroy the temples, and a quarter century after that Christian Rome itself would fall into enemy hands, suffering a fate that pagan Rome had avoided for a millennium. Yet save for this last, Christians were able safely to ignore the contrary implications of these reversals to their theory of history. The last provoked Augustine of Hippo into a dramatic rethinking of that theory, the result of which was a book that remains a cornerstone of Western thought about the relationship between God and man, *The City of God.*[13]

Bias this palpable makes it easier to understand the ferocity with which Jacob Burckhardt attacked Eusebius as a liar. Were he alive today, Burckhardt would undoubtedly have made use of more euphemistic late-twentieth-century terminology and called the bishop of Caesarea a "spin doctor" instead. But the mistake would still be the same. Liars or spin doctors have no interest in the truth, no belief other than to present their case in whatever way will gain their end. Eusebius was looking for an underlying truth in history, and he gives every indication of having believed fervently in the answer he discovered. Christians like Eusebius are better seen as working within what critical theorists now call a "totalizing discourse," a phrase that sounds much nicer than "ideological blinders" but which means much the same thing: an explanatory mode that encompasses, and eclipses, all other forms of explanation. It is, in the simplest sense, a way of looking at the world in which one answer fits all. It is significant to note that a "totalizing discourse" defines the agenda not merely by deciding which topics are important and which are not but by doing so in such a complete way that topics and points of view that are not considered important are not even heard—they are simply excluded from the discourse.[14]

This discourse governs the Church History in the most obvious of ways, for to write the history of a people who were not defined by birth ties or nationality, Eusebius had to ignore all the standard sources of information, the characters and events who filled the pages of Greco-Roman historiography. In his book, the events of the Roman Empire are peripheral, important only to the extent that they affect the people of the church. The point is obvious once it is made, but when it is not, the result is often either a naive misapprehension of the relative importance of Christianity in the Roman world or the misguided fury of a Burckhardt, for Eusebius's viewpoint governed the Church History in less obvious ways as well. His decisions on whether to accept or reject a source of information, for instance, could be influenced as much by the orthodoxy of the author as the soundness of the text, and he was notoriously indifferent to explanations that detracted from the central position of the church.[15] A relatively innocent example is his treatment of a pivotal event in Marcus Aurelius's campaign against the Quadi, when a providential storm blinded the enemy and abetted Marcus's victory. The incident is well known—it is recorded by the historian

Dio Cassius and illustrated on the column Marcus erected after his victory. In both instances, the credit for what was seen as a divine intervention was given squarely to Marcus, who is depicted making an offering to the gods on his column. Eusebius cared nothing for this explanation, if he even knew of it. Instead, in his pages, all the credit is given to a legion of Christian soldiers, who in return were given the title of "the thundering legion" by a grateful emperor.[16]

Christians inherited from Judaism a deep belief that the meaning of human history lies in the working out of God's plan. Consequently, in Momigliano's words, "Christian chronology was also a philosophy of history."[17] The influence of this worldview on Eusebius shows clearly in his explanation of the persecution that Diocletian inflicted on a Christian community that had enjoyed peace for some forty years. Because of "the abundant freedom," he wrote,

> we fell into laxity and sloth, and envied and reviled each other, and were almost as it were, taking up arms against one another, rulers assailing rulers with words like spears, and people forming parties against people, and monstrous hypocrisy and dissimulation rising to the greatest height of wickedness. . . . Then, truly, according to the word of Jeremiah, "The Lord in his wrath darkened the daughter of Zion, and cast down the glory of Israel from heaven to earth, and remembered not his footstool in the day of his anger. The Lord also overwhelmed all the beautiful things of Israel, and threw down all his strongholds."[18]

The contrast with traditional Greco-Roman histories is immediate. The ancients, for the most part, were content to explain events in terms of the virtue or vice of particular individuals. In this, Eusebius varied only little, attributing the vice to an entire group rather than an individual; and the notion of divine judgment falling on a community, rather than on individuals, was anything but new. But Eusebius differed substantially in identifying this vice as an offense against God, a sin. The difference becomes even more profound when the two parts—sin and retribution—are combined, as they are here, into a motive force to explain historical events. When classical historians looked for transcendent causes, they rarely went beyond stock appeals to Fate or Fortune which owe as much to the influence of the dramatists as to a philosophy of history: "Fortune ceased to smile upon" or "Fate had ordained." Christian history needed a greater sense of purpose and meaning than either of these old standbys could provide. Drawing on the great Judaic interpretations of Israel's travails, Eusebius concluded that Christians themselves were responsible for the persecution, by provoking God's wrath with their sins, and thereby turned the event of Diocletian's persecution from what might have been read as proof of the weakness of the Christian God and his failure to protect his chosen people into a chastisement that proved the opposite—the omnipotence of that God and the sureness of his plan.[19]

The nature of the sins Eusebius identified is significant—not adultery or greed but strife and contention. Even the bishops, Eusebius writes, "those esteemed our shepherds, casting aside the bond of piety, were excited to conflicts with one another, and did nothing else than heap up strifes and threats and jealousy and enmity and hatred toward each other, like tyrants eagerly endeavoring to assert their power."[20] The internal unity of the church was, for Eusebius, a matter of prime importance. Thus, the passage demonstrates more than God's plan; it also demonstrates Eusebius's own priorities and agenda, as does another statement in the same place. After pointing out that Christians failed to see the signs of God's anger, Eusebius writes that "some, like atheists, thought that our affairs were unheeded and ungoverned; and thus we added one wickedness to another."[21] To Eusebius, signs of God's plan were everywhere, waiting only for the right exegete, the learned mystagogue, to explain them. To think there was no divine plan was wicked and sinful.

Eusebius interpreted the first three centuries of Christian organization with a singleness of purpose which would be hard to overestimate. His criteria of apostolic succession and canonical truth, for instance, allowed him to isolate a mainstream Christianity from the many variants by which it was threatened, but they also made it harder for scholars in subsequent generations to appreciate the variety of local traditions that made up the early church, and thus explain why it has been so easy for scholars to think of the Christianity Constantine encountered as a single, monolithic "church."[22] With twenty-twenty hindsight, Eusebius created the notion of a central, unified, monolithic orthodoxy, albeit one occasionally pestered by heresies that by definition were at once marginal, easily identified, and quickly isolated from the mainstream. The difference is a matter of degree, rather than kind. There were, of course, local traditions that were more "mainstream" than others, and there were variants of that belief which were definitely heretical. But where Origen in the third century could not only admit but even defend the proposition that there had always been division even within mainstream Christianity, Eusebius removed this dynamic shadow ground of faith and replaced it with a starkly demarcated border that always separated the one central, clearly defined orthodoxy from error.[23]

Equally strong in Eusebius's thinking was the idea that God's plan portended a dual mission for Rome and Christianity. As early as the second century, the Christian apologist Melito of Sardis made this claim, offering as evidence the close proximity in time between the reign of the first emperor, Augustus, and the birth of Jesus. "And the most convincing proof," Melito argued in an apology addressed to the emperor, "that our doctrine flourished for the good of an empire happily begun, is this—that no evil happened since Augustus' reign, but that, on the contrary, all things have been splendid and glorious, in accordance with the prayers of all."[24] It is by no mere coincidence that Melito's argument comes down via Eusebius's Church History, for it can also be found in the works of Origen,[25] Eusebius's intellectual progenitor, and it runs through Eusebius's works, literally from first to last. The Chronicle reflects this outlook in the organization of its time lines, which Eusebius reduced from five to two—Christianity and Rome—once he came to Augustus. In the speech Eusebius gave at the dedication of the Holy Sepulchre in 335 and then repeated in Constantine's presence, he took this correlation much further than either Melito or Origen had done. Not only does he have Rome and Christianity "proceeding as if from a single starting point," but now the two are joined in the same mission: "For while the power of Our Savior destroyed the polyarchy and polytheism of the demons and heralded the one kingdom of God to Greeks and barbarians and all men to the farthest extent of the earth, the Roman Empire, now that the causes of the manifold governments had been abolished, subdued the visible governments, in order to merge the entire race into one unity and concord."[26]

By yoking the mission of Rome to subdue the barbarians on earth with Christ's divine mission to fight demons in the spiritual world, Eusebius fused what had been a simple chronological correlation into a powerful, cosmic model of causation, a "political theology" that equated polytheism with polyarchy and division, monotheism with monarchy and unity. In other passages, Eusebius regularly links polytheistic belief with moral degeneracy and sexual license, thereby forging a stereotype that has remained unshakable through the ages, despite abundant evidence that an ascetic, almost puritanical morality was as much a part of pagan as Christian teaching in the fourth century.[27] He made one more equation, so subtle and transparent that it is rarely noticed: by speaking only of "monotheism" and "polytheism," he wiped out the large middle ground that Christians shared with other monotheists. It is one of the most influential equations in the history of political theory: polytheism equals pluralism, which equals strife and, of course, moral degeneracy—all springing from the same root, subsumed under the single heading that we now label "paganism." Conversely, monotheism is synonymous not only with empire and unity and moral behavior but also with Christianity. At a stroke, the consensus Constantine built between Christians and other monotheists disappears from the record.[28]

It is now obvious, given the faith he placed in the joint mission of Rome and Christianity, why Diocletian's persecution was such a shattering experience for Eusebius. Amazingly, he came through that nightmare with his confidence intact. In the decade following the death of the last of the persecutors, Eusebius dedicated himself to the task of rebutting the charges that had helped bring on the persecution, again writing in a typically innovative way. Within a few years of Maximin Daza's death, Eusebius completed the *Praeparatio Evangelica* (*Preparation for the Gospel*), a monumental work in fifteen books designed to show the superiority of Christian to Greek teaching. This was soon followed by an even lengthier undertaking, the *Demonstratio Evangelica* (*Proof of the Gospel*) in twenty books, which aimed to do the same with the Jews. In the introduction to the *Preparation,* Eusebius still argued that the Roman peace was part of God's plan for the spread of Christianity.[29]

Such works won for Eusebius a reputation as the most learned Christian of his day. But the bishop of Caesarea came out of the persecution with something more, a sense of personal mission. Others have dated a growing intolerance of pagan practices in his writings from this time.[30] He himself attributed his survival to the need for someone to preserve the memory of the martyrs, a task that by itself might account for the determination of his later works. In a speech he delivered on the occasion of Constantine's thirtieth jubilee, Eusebius described the heavenly rewards God gave those who died in the persecution, then added, "Those yet on the earth He preserved to be a spark, a seed of piety for posterity, to become alike spectators of His judgment against the godless and interpreters of what had taken place."[31]

Eusebius also came to see Constantine as the instrument of God's plan—a concept of which, as we have seen, Constantine himself was not unmindful. It is therefore not surprising either that Eusebius should see himself as the interpreter of this emperor's reign, or that Constantine should have found Eusebius a congenial companion. Yet, to borrow a famous witticism, there may be less here than meets the eye.[32]

Beginning with the later editions of the Church History, Eusebius set out to fix Constantine's place in the history of Christianity, and he died while finishing an encomiastic essay on that emperor. His *vita Constantini* has been called, with justice, "perhaps our most valuable source for the activities of any emperor."[33] Other ancient authors treat Constantine's reign, but none can match either Eusebius's credentials as a contemporary and experienced observer or the length of his account. Non-narrative sources, such as coins, laws, panegyrics, or inscriptions (particularly those that give the names or religious orientation of Constantinian officials), give a far less definitive picture of imperial policy. Scholars still must use Eusebius as a touchstone and decide in those cases in which the alternative sources differ whether these sources need to be forced into the Eusebian mold or whether Eusebius himself must be doubted or revised.

Since the fifth century, when the church historian Socrates Scholasticus wrote of Eusebius's "reputation of disingenuousness," those who have used the *vita Constantini* (hereafter cited in this chapter as *VC*) have known that it is not a full or impartial study. Eusebius himself says as much, writing that he intends to "select from the facts which have come to [his] knowledge such as are most suitable, and worthy of lasting record." The intent earned a snide comment from Gibbon and the withering scorn of Burckhardt. It was in part because of Eusebius's silences and the internal contradictions in which he can occasionally be caught that Burckhardt came to the devastating conclusion about the bishop's honesty which was discussed in Chapter 1. Others, unable to accept such a judgment on the "father of church history," preferred to conclude instead that the *VC* could not have been written by Eusebius but was instead a later forgery.[34] But it is of limited use either to censure a fourth-century bishop for not being interested in topics that capture the fancy of later ages or to pretend that his work is other than it is. For all the criticism to which he has been subjected over the ages, and for all the flaws in his work, the conceptual framework of the Age of Constantine we use is still the one Eusebius created for us: we see Constantine through the eyes of Eusebius of Caesarea.

As with the Church History, it would be a useful exercise to imagine what our idea of Constantine would be without the information Eusebius supplies in the *VC* and its various documents and appendices. In this case, it would be even more useful to perform a slightly different exercise as well, and imagine what our picture of the first three centuries of the Roman Empire would be like if the Church History, with its deliberate emphasis on Christian issues and indifference to the topics of traditional historiography, were the only narrative source to survive for that period. Together, the two exercises reveal not just how important a source Eusebius is but also how dangerously misleading it is to think that the outline he provides simply needs to be filled in more precisely. It is all the more important, therefore, to pay attention to the limitations of the *VC* and to understand what Eusebius intended to do in it, and why.

In his introduction, Eusebius compared Constantine to Cyrus, a name that (thanks to Xenophon) would immediately have conjured in the minds of his readers the notion of an ideal ruler. At once, these readers also would have known that Cyrus was going to come off the loser in this comparison, for they had learned from the same handbooks as Eusebius, and they knew that comparison with great rulers of bygone days was the standard way to elucidate the greatness of one's own subject. So when they read that, whereas Constantine "with the greatest facility obtained the authority over more nations than any who had preceded him, and yet retained his power, undisturbed, to the very close of his life," Cyrus "met with an inglorious and dishonorable death at the hands of a woman," they knew precisely what they were in for: an encomiastic treatise on the subject of the model ruler.[35]

Reading Constantine

The VC follows a simple plan. "It is my intention," Eusebius writes at the outset, "to pass over the greater part of the royal deeds of this thrice-blessed prince . . . [and] speak and write of those circumstances only which have reference to his religious character."[36] This sentence once fueled a vigorous debate over the authenticity of the VC, for despite Eusebius's disavowal its pages include several accounts of Constantine's victories over barbarian tribes and other details that seem, to modern readers, inappropriate to "religious character." But such intense literalism is misguided. Far more important is the need to understand what a phrase like "religious character" (τὸν θεοφιλῆ . . . βίον) would have meant to Eusebius, for it held a meaning at once broader and narrower than will occur to a modern reader—broader in that the ancient state did not separate "religious" and "secular" activities as nicely as the modern one; narrower in that to Eusebius's way of thinking the only true religion was Christianity. Hence, steps Constantine took in favor of traditional religion would not, to his biographer, shed any meaningful light on his "religious character."

More important, Eusebius meant by this phrase that he would pay no attention to the multiple meanings that, given the fluid religious terminology of the day, many of Constantine's actions were bound to have. Here, just as in the Church History, Eusebius will only be interested in the way Christians understood Constantine; how pagans reacted was not his concern. Readers who do not keep this purpose in mind therefore run the risk of assuming that the examples of Constantine's piety Eusebius provides have an exclusively Christian meaning when in fact pagans would have found many of them just as praiseworthy. Some famous examples include Constantine's Sunday law, the religious pose on his coins, and a consecration coin issued after his death which depicts a hand from heaven reaching down to meet the emperor's heaven-bound chariot. In each of these cases, Eusebius postulated a single and explicit Christian meaning for images that had, in fact, much broader connotation.[37]

These "sins of omission," if they may be so called, are the hardest to see, simply because by design the counterevidence is not there. The result is not so much a lie as a half-truth, something that has been developed into a high art form in modern politics but which has its roots as far back as the sophistic movement in fifth century B.C. Greece. It is the tactic that led Louis Duchesne to describe the *VC* as a "triumph of reticence and circumlocution."[38]

To appreciate the effect of Eusebius's plan on the portrayal of Constantine in the *VC*, we must return for one last time to the account of his conversion. The sequence of events in that account was that Constantine first decided he needed divine support if he was to win the struggle with Maxentius, then gave thought to which deity would best meet these needs. After deciding that his father's successful reign was due to the honor he paid to "the Supreme God" and that the failure of the other Tetrarchs was due to their trust in "a multitude of gods," Constantine "felt it incumbent on him to honor his father's God alone" and began a regimen of prayer and supplication to that deity to "reveal to him who he was, and stretch forth his right hand to help him in his present difficulties." At this point, he experienced the vision of "the trophy of a cross of light in the heavens, above the sun, and bearing the inscription, CONQUER BY THIS," followed by a visit from Christ as he slept, instructing him to make a likeness of the sign he had seen and "to use it as a safeguard in all engagements with his enemies."[39]

With a better sense of Eusebius's style and habits of thought, problems raised earlier by this passage dissipate.[40] Given Eusebius's political theology, for instance, and his strong sense of the joint mission of empire and faith, it is no longer unusual to see a Christian bishop take it for granted that Constantine would seek divine aid for his imperial aspirations or that the Christian god would help him in that design.

Eusebius's treatment of the miracle also helps explain some of the controversy raised by the *VC*, for Eusebius claimed to tell the story as he heard it from the emperor himself, at a time "when he was honored with his acquaintance and society."[41] This is one of several places in the *VC* where Eusebius suggested a certain closeness between himself and the emperor. At the outset, he used a similar phrase to explain that he undertook the work because "God has permitted me to come into his presence, and enjoy his acquaintance and society." Here he added a further claim, "Wherefore, if it is the duty of anyone, it certainly is mine, to make an ample proclamation of his virtues to all in whom the example of noble actions is capable of inspiring the love of God."[42] The effect of this claim is to suggest that there was no one more qualified than Eusebius to perform this task. As if to support such a contention, almost half the documents that Eusebius reproduces verbatim in the VC were either addressed to or written about himself—seven out of fifteen. Since he indicates that he selected these documents for their importance and representative nature out of a larger number that were available to him, it is easy to infer that Eusebius was in close and prolonged contact with the emperor.[43] The intimate knowledge Eusebius appears to convey not only of Constantine's acts but even more of his plans and intentions long led scholars to postulate just such a relationship between the two, one in which Eusebius became promoted successively into a "courtly bishop," a "worldly adviser," and even "chief architect of Constantine's Christian policy."[44]

No doubt this is the reason that, for centuries, scholars took it as given that the author of the VC was not only an intimate of Constantine's but also a major influence on his policy. In the fifteenth century, Reginald Pecock described Eusebius as being "as priuey with Constantyn in the counceilis of his herte and of his conscience, as a confessour," and in the eighteenth Edward Gibbon, whose favorite phrase for Eusebius was "the courtly bishop," imagined him as someone "more practised in the arts of courts, than that of almost any of his contemporaries."[45] The relationship seemed to be more than confirmed by documents in the VC. In one of these, a letter to the congregation at Antioch when they attempted to translate Eusebius from Caesarea to their own bishopric in 328, Constantine writes of Eusebius as one "whom I have myself long well known and esteemed for his learning and moderation."[46] In two other letters, both probably written around 335, Constantine calls on Eusebius to prepare accurate copies of the Bible for his new capital of Constantinople and praises the bishop for a treatise on Easter which he undertakes to copy and distribute. Add to these testimonies such prima facie evidence as Constantine's selection of Eusebius to speak at his thirtieth jubilee and the *VC* itself, with its abundance of personal anecdotes and apparently complete knowledge of the emperor's thinking, and Eusebius easily emerges as the quintessential insider.[47]

There is another way to read this evidence. If the literary model of the *VC* was not biography but panegyric, then intimation of a close familiarity with the subject becomes not a statement of fact but a reflection of a well-known characteristic of the genre; that is, panegyrists were permitted to imply such intimate knowledge, even when both the audience and the subject knew it to be untrue.[48] A closer look at the documents included by Eusebius in the *VC* also reveals a more limited acquaintance than at first appeared to be the case. The number relating to Eusebius clearly is a disproportionately large amount of the whole, especially given the scope of the work. Recognizing this disproportion leads to the further observation that, with only one exception, all the documents are either the sort that would have come to Eusebius routinely as part of a larger and more general circulation, rather than as personal communications, or the type that deal with matters in which he had a personal involvement but do not necessarily have a more general significance.[49] It is not safe, in other words, to assume that the documents were selected from a broad sample as representative of Constantine's writings, in the manner of an impartial biographer using modern principles of historical study; on the contrary, it might be safer to assume that they were included because they were documents that Eusebius had at hand in Caesarea.

On this basis, T. D. Barnes has noted that personal contact between Eusebius and Constantine can be documented on no more than four occasions. Far from being the recollections of an insider at the heart of imperial politics, Barnes concluded, the *VC* represents nothing more than the view of a distant and not always well-informed provincial.[50] The effect of this line of argument would be to salvage Eusebius's reputation for integrity by limiting the sources of his information. It is clear in retrospect that Jacob Burckhardt's accusation of dishonesty was based on the assumption that Eusebius knew better; similarly, those scholars who once cast doubt on the authenticity of the *VC* did so on the basis of errors that they presumed a historian with Eusebius's credentials would not have made. If, however, Eusebius's knowledge of the events was in any way incomplete or secondhand, his account, while more limited, still may be taken as authoritative.

The effort to achieve a more realistic estimate of his biographer's ties to Constantine is a useful correction to the excesses of Eusebius's critics. But such an approach still presumes that Eusebius operated as an impartial observer who proceeded on assumptions of scientific objectivity more appropriate to the nineteenth than the fourth century. It ignores, or papers over, inconsistencies, inaccuracies, and omissions that may be due not merely to such circumstantial factors as time and material at his disposal but also to the same single-minded focus on Constantine's Christianity which the Church History maintained on the larger question of Christian development. It precludes, in other words, the possibility that Eusebius omitted types of information for reasons other than lack of knowledge.

It may be that the reversal of Eusebius's connection to Constantine has gone too far. Four or five known contacts is, in fact, rather a lot, given the limited amount of information on such topics which has come down from antiquity. It is, as Brian Warmington has noted, a larger number of contacts than is attested for an even more famous "adviser," Ossius of Corduba.[51] Thus it may be better to regard these known contacts as a safe minimum, rather than as an absolute maximum.

In addition to the documents, there are five instances of direct or indirect quotation in the *VC*, including the account of the vision, which also may be taken as indications of personal contact. These, along with the one document whose presence cannot readily be explained as part of Eusebius's personal collection, point in the direction of a period of more extended contact. The document is a letter Constantine wrote to the Persian king Shapur II, probably in the mid to late 320s. Given its likely date, its place in the *VC* is anomalous: Eusebius placed it in the fourth book, although he dealt with other events of the late 320s in book III. Two of the other documents stand out for the way Eusebius refers to them as either being in the emperor's own handwriting or containing his autograph.[52] Eusebius no doubt intended such information to reinforce the authority of both the documents and his account, and if nothing else it does serve to remind how little we know about the mechanics of imperial proclamations. Did the emperor personally sign all copies and even write some of them out in his own hand?[53] Perhaps. But another plausible explanation is that these copies came from the imperial archives. A second-century inscription records the permission of the emperor Antoninus Pius to make a copy of a judgment of his predecessor Hadrian. From the language, it would appear that Antoninus signed the original, a procedure that might explain why Eusebius refers to his two documents in the way he does.[54] But if Eusebius was doing archival research while Constantine was still alive, then the *VC* must have been something more than a last-minute project, hastily pulled together out of materials Eusebius had at hand in Caesarea in the interval between the emperor's death and his own no more than two years later.

Barnes has suggested that the bishop was already thinking of a biography of the emperor as early as 325.[55] Of course, Eusebius could have written the *VC* without Constantine's permission. But in addition to the opportunity for personal interviews, permission also might have been necessary for access to the imperial archives. The emperor's permission also would have provided the "authentic seal" that Eusebius was eager to place on the emperor's religious history.[56] There are further indications of this plan.

The documents and personal references are not the only reason that Eusebius has been linked so closely to Constantine. Eusebius never intended the *VC* to be read by itself. At several points, he expresses the intention of publishing it together with one of Constantine's own speeches, the Oration to the Saints, and two speeches of his own—one that he delivered at Constantine's thirtieth jubilee, the oration *Laus Constantini*, or *In Praise of Constantine* (hereafter simply *LC*), and another that he delivered at the dedication of the Church of the Holy Sepulchre in Jerusalem and subsequently repeated for Constantine's enjoyment in Constantinople. This speech, which may now be entitled *De sepulchro Christi* (*SC*), was long considered lost, but it seems instead to have been commingled in the manuscripts with the *LC*, where it appears as the last eight chapters of that work (11–18).[57] Barnes has concluded that Eusebius intended the package to "establish two crucial theses: Eusebius is the authoritative interpreter of the Constantinian empire, and emperor and bishop agree on fundamental theological issues."[58] Ironically, given this intent, Eusebius's two speeches actually provide the means both to understand the conditions under which Eusebius wrote the *VC* and to separate Constantine's views from those of his biographer.

Although it appears in the manuscripts after the *LC*, the *SC* is actually the earlier of the two speeches, having been delivered almost a full year before the *LC*. Eusebius writes of the occasion in book IV of the *VC*, as one on which,

> emboldened by the confident assurance I entertained of his piety, I had begged permission to pronounce a discourse on the subject of our Saviour's sepulchre in his hearing. With this request he most readily complied, and in the midst of a large number of auditors, in the interior of the palace itself, he stood and listened with the rest. I entreated him, but in vain, to seat himself on the imperial throne which stood near: he continued with fixed attention to weigh the topics of my discourse, and gave his own testimony to the truth of the theological doctrines it contained.[59]

The most likely time for this to have occurred is when Eusebius came to Constantinople in November 335 as part of the delegation from the Council of Tyre.[60] The timing is significant, because at two points in this speech Eusebius expresses an interest in telling Constantine's story. In the first chapter of the *SC*, which is chapter 11 of the combined work, he says, "I pray that I may be a kind of interpreter of your intentions and become the reporter of your devout soul," and in the concluding chapter, he outlines a list of topics on which Constantine himself, "should leisure permit," might provide information: "the countless manifestations of your Savior and his countless personal visits during sleep," the support he has received from his "Champion and Guardian God" in peace and war, his projects and intentions.[61] It was customary for those who delivered speeches before emperors to petition for a favor, and these comments by Eusebius come at precisely the points—introduction and conclusion—where such favors typically were solicited.

Eusebius writes that after delivering his speech on the Holy Sepulchre he returned home to his "usual occupations." If he was following chronological order in his subsequent comments, it would appear that he took steps to keep Constantine's attention on his request, for he writes next about a tract on Easter which he dedicated to the emperor, and of Constantine's request for Eusebius to prepare copies of Scripture for Constantinople's churches. He also is the logical source for information about the progress of conversions in Palestine which he says Constantine received with joy.[62] In any case, Eusebius could also have pressed his suit in person when he returned to Constantinople in the spring of 336 for the council summoned to hear charges against Bishop Marcellus of Ancyra. At this point, if not earlier, he received a reply in the form of a commission to deliver an oration at the closing ceremonies of the emperor's jubilee year on July 25.

This is the oration that survives as the *LC*. There is no reason to assume that the *LC* was the only, or even the most important, speech given on this occasion—there is, indeed, internal evidence that the audience might have been relatively small[63]—but the *LC* was a state oration, and as such it bears the marks of imperial support which make all such compositions at least semiofficial communications.[64] It contains numerous parallels with Constantine's Oration to the Saints, suggesting that the bishop mined that work diligently for topics that would please Constantine. Indeed, it may have been through the archives in Constantinople that he acquired his copy of that speech, a process that would explain why—as we saw in Chapter 8—he seems to have known so little about the circumstances in which it was delivered. Eusebius's remark at this point in the *VC* about a speaker who provoked Constantine's ire suggests that he took similar note of topics that would not win Constantine's favor.[65]

Eusebius does not say he returned to Caesarea after delivering the *LC,* and if the speech won Constantine's approval for his project, he is more likely to have stayed in Constantinople to carry out his design. Eusebius's narrative of the events of this period from July 336 to the emperor's death in May of the subsequent year contains a number of indications of autopsy which in turn provide an important key to the composition of the *VC*. Nor are these the only clues. In its present form, the *SC* is not entirely the speech that Eusebius promised, for it lacks a detailed description of the newly completed church, and it now appears that, after promising to append his description, Eusebius found that section more suitable for book III of the *VC* and thus deleted it from his speech. Since Eusebius expresses his intention of appending this speech in the fourth book of the *VC* (4.33), it follows that he wrote the fourth book before the third and that this is one of the passages left unrevised at his death. This is, in fact, only one of several indications that what is now book IV was the first one that Eusebius wrote, perhaps with a much smaller project in mind than the *VC* eventually became.[66]

There is another important conclusion to be drawn from this reconstruction of events. If it was the *LC* that won Constantine's approval for Eusebius's project, then there is all the more reason to believe that its account of his reign is the one that Constantine favored. This oration would have been Eusebius's chance to demonstrate to Constantine his qualifications for the project he envisioned. It was, in a manner of speaking, his grant application, a dry run for the *VC*. For both these reasons, the *LC* can serve as a control of sorts on the *VC*, because Eusebius would have been doubly certain to put into this speech only those sentiments that he believed would evoke Constantine's favor. In writing the *VC* after Constantine's death, Eusebius would not have felt such constraints. Wherever the *LC* and the *VC* cover the same ground, therefore, differences in tone or emphasis may indicate differences between subject and author.

The *LC* thus has the potential of resolving an important conundrum. It is clear to most readers that the *VC* is idealized, that Eusebius intended to tell the story not just of Constantine but of a paradigmatic Christian emperor, a pious Christian prince.[67] Less often overtly acknowledged is the obvious corollary that, if this is so, then even though there were obviously many points on which the emperor and his biographer agreed, in some ways the *VC* must be unreliable, reflecting Eusebius's agenda at least as much as, and perhaps more than, Constantine's own. On a priori grounds alone, this much can be readily conceded. The problem is, how can Constantine's program now be extricated with any confidence from this Eusebean matrix? How much is Constantine, and how much is Eusebius? This is the crux: How reliable is the bishop's depiction of Constantine and his interests? Some evidence can be extracted from careful scrutiny of the document itself, for despite all Eusebius's efforts, there are signs that Constantine's agenda was not identical to the impression given in the *VC*. There are, for instance, a few places in which Eusebius, amid all his praise, mildly rebuked his subject. These may be taken as indications of disagreement. Significantly, one of these passages concerned "the scandalous hypocrisy of those who crept into the Church, and assumed the name and character of Christians," gulling an emperor whose "purity of faith" led him "to credit the profession of these reputed Christians"—a seeming swipe at Constantine's low threshold for admission into the church.[68] At other points, as we have seen, contrary information peeps out from the edges of the curtain Eusebius has drawn—he gloats, for instance, that even the "self-styled philosophers" were forced to admit the truth of a speech Constantine gave to "his usual audience" shortly before his death, thereby indirectly letting us know that even at this late date non-Christians were part of the emperor's inner circle.[69]

Other differences emerge when the Constantinian documents in the *VC* are read without regard for the interpretative blanket in which Eusebius has wrapped them. As early as the new edition of the Church History, for instance, Eusebius began to connect the deliverance of the Christians from persecution in his day with the Hebrew Bible's narrative of the deliverance from bondage in Egypt. In this equation, Constantine took the part of Moses. Like the Hebrew prophet, Constantine was raised in the house of the enemy of God's people (in this case, Diocletian, not pharaoh), and like him, he received divine aid to free his people from their oppressor, in this case Maxentius, who like pharaoh before him drowned while trying to thwart God's will.[70] The analogy blossoms in the *VC*, which not only elaborates on the parallel between Constantine's victory at the Milvian Bridge and Moses' crossing of the Red Sea but in other sections depicts Constantine as praying like Moses in a tabernacle before battle and being protected like Moses from plots and enemies.[71]

There are obvious reasons why Eusebius should have turned to the Hebrew Bible for guidance on how to interpret Constantine's reign, for Christian Scripture did not contain many exempla useful for adapting to the novelty of a Christian emperor. Both Jesus's advice to "render unto Caesar the things that are Caesar's" and Paul's assertion that all rulers are from God implied a more passive relationship than was suitable for the conditions created by Constantine's conversion.[72] Moreover, in the first century Philo of Alexandria had already set up Moses as a model ruler, and Philo was an important influence on Christian thinkers in general, and Eusebius in particular.[73] But the

New Testament was not without other useful parallels, had Eusebius sought them. The Acts of the Apostles, for instance, contain the obvious parallel of Saint Paul, who like Constantine was converted by a vision experienced on the road and who saw himself as chosen to carry the faith to new peoples. There are numerous indications that this was the model that Constantine himself preferred. In his own oration, for instance, Constantine spoke of the salvation that awaits those—like himself and Paul—who find the truth at a mature age, and his self-description as "bishop of those outside" alluded to Paul both in image, as a ready parallel to the "apostle to the gentiles," and in vocabulary, echoing Paul's advice in I Corinthians to be judges of "those within," leaving to others judgment of "those without."[74] Like Paul, Constantine constantly depicted himself as a man summoned to his mission directly by God, and like the apostle he busied himself in writing epistles to unruly congregations. Paul's vision had given him charismatic authority on a par with the apostles, and it may have been with this precedent in mind that Constantine arranged for his remains to be placed in the middle of memorials to all the apostles in a church he had specially built for that purpose in Constantinople, thereby laying visual claim to the title by which he soon became known, *Isapostolos*.

Eusebius surely knew of this intention, for he heard the vision story himself, as he tells us, from the emperor's own lips, and he seems to have been present when Constantine disclosed his plans for the Church of the Apostles to house his remains.[75] His preference for the Moses analogy may be innocent enough, despite these parallels, but there were also practical reasons that made this analogy, as exalted as it was, preferable to that of the apostle. For one thing, Moses held a unique role in Jewish history; by definition, his position could not be replicated. For another, Moses himself enjoined his successors as rulers to serve the priests and carry out their wishes.[76] Moses, in other words, was a much safer model for a paradigmatic emperor than Paul, whose apostolic authority would only have complicated the relationship.

There is a similar difference between Constantine and Eusebius in Eusebius's narrative of the discovery of the Holy Sepulchre in Jerusalem. Where Eusebius's attention is fixed squarely on the tomb, Constantine's own letter, which the bishop reproduces at this point, speaks only of the cross. Similarly, Eusebius never mentions the one thing about Constantine's resting place, the Church of the Apostles, which immediately struck the eyes of subsequent observers: its cruciform shape.[77] Throughout the *VC*, his definition of the sign Constantine wrought in the aftermath of this vision experience is both innovative and problematic.[78] In all these instances, the simplest explanation is that this was the way Eusebius's mind worked. The Hebrew Bible was the most likely place to look for a model of the relationship between king and clergy, and as a man whose theology was shaped in the third century, Eusebius was still inclined to think of the cross as a subject to be avoided rather than as the object of veneration it soon became.[79]

Still, it remains noteworthy that all these variances run in the same direction, emphasizing the role of the clergy, restricting Constantine's independence of action, and setting a standard for admission to the Christian community which was both narrower and more exclusive than Constantine's own. The transparency of this deception undoubtedly underlies the anger with which Jacob Burckhardt and others since have responded to the *VC*, for in some sense the glibness is itself an insult to the intelligence.[80] Such half-truths readily generate suspicion that everything Eusebius wrote was a lie, leading to efforts such as Burckhardt's even to deny Constantine's own Christianity.

This underlying distrust of the *VC* enhances the significance of the *LC*. Because of the circumstances in which it was conceived and delivered, the *LC* stands as an important control on the *VC*, for no matter what else may be in doubt, one thing is certain: even if no one else had been in the room, Eusebius on this occasion would have taken Constantine's views into account when he described imperial belief and policy. When he wrote the *VC*, on the other hand, Constantine had already gone to a greater reward. Thus, even though the *VC* and the *LC* overlap in many ways, wherever the two vary, the evidence of the speech should be preferred to that of the biography.

Despite protests about the originality of his task in the prologue, the *LC* follows the general plan for an imperial encomium of this period, its ten chapters dividing fairly readily into sections on the significance of the occasion (1–3), what the emperor has done to deserve this sign of God's favor (4–6), and the emperor as an *eikon* of the divine (7–9), and ending with celebration of the peace and unity in which the empire resides (10). There are also differences from the general plan: Eusebius does not, for instance, dilate on the great deeds of the emperor's forebears—certainly unnecessary in the case of one who had ruled for so long. More significantly, Eusebius subordinates all the other stock imperial virtues to a celebration of the emperor's piety, to which he attributes the special closeness the emperor enjoys with his divine "friend" (φίλος). The reference unavoidably calls to mind the divine *comes,* or companion, who was a mandatory asset of successful emperors in the late empire.[81] With that political theory in mind, the general tenor of the oration—a celebration of the "Supreme Sovereign," carefully defined as "the One who is truly Supreme . . . the One who is above the Universe, the Highest of All, the Greatest, the Supreme Being, whose kingdom's throne is the vault of the heavens above, while the earth is footstool for His feet"[82]—takes on significance that extends beyond the boundaries of Christian thought. It is but one of many indications in this speech of Eusebius's familiarity with contemporary pagan thinking about kingship and the role of "the good king."[83]

The same language about divinity can be found in another royal oration that appears to have been delivered around the year 300 to none other than Diocletian himself. Here the orator describes God as "the Greatest Sovereign of the Universe, who is ever immortal, eternal, and holding power from eternity; the first fair Victor, from whom all victories are borne," as "the good and everlasting Light," and as "the wholly undefiled Father."[84] Even if the addressee was not the archpersecutor, the important point is that phrases that are recognizably Christian to a later audience belonged at this period to a wider vocabulary on which both Christians and pagans could draw.[85]

The similarity of language raises a question to which inevitably there will be more than one answer: Why did Eusebius use this terminology? Was he simply observing literary convention by using an outdated and meaningless vocabulary? Was he attempting to align Christian thinking with traditional belief? Or was he doing the opposite, confidently appropriating traditional terminology to the Christian cause, filling a traditional motif with what one scholar has described as an "aggressively Christian content"?[86] To debate the point is useless if another question is not answered first: What *type* of Christianity did Eusebius promote in this oration?

Early in the speech, Eusebius praises Constantine for having purged his empire of the "filth of godless error." It would seem that no better proof than this could be wanted of either Eusebius's aggressive style or Constantine's revolutionary intent. But what is this "godless error"? Eusebius proceeds to enumerate idol worship, the placating of demons, and licentious behavior—all traits that would have been as repugnant to learned pagans as to their Christian counterparts. Such pagans as these would even have nodded assent to Eusebius's praise of Constantine for rejecting blood sacrifice in favor of "the greatest sacrifice" of his own mind and soul, a sacrifice that even the anti-Christian Porphyry considered preferable to traditional blood offerings.[87] In other words, the oration only takes on an aggressive tone if we accept the Eusebian calculus, that monotheism equals monarchy, morality, and Christianity, whereas polytheism equals polyarchy, depravity, and paganism.

Once this stereotype is dismissed, an entirely different character emerges from Eusebius's words. For instance, at the outset of the oration, he defines the "Supreme Sovereign" as the One

> our triumphant sovereign himself praises to us, having fully perceived in Him the cause of his Empire; Him the God-loving Caesars, heirs to their father's learning, admit to be the source of all benefits; him the hosts of the army, the multitudinous peoples in cities and countrysides, the rulers of the lands in council worship, instructed by the great savior teacher; yes, even the entire species of mankind in general, people of every race, shape, and tongue, all in common alike and individually, though divided in their opinions on other matters, agree on this alone, calling on the One and Only God with an inbred logic, a self-taught and self-learned knowledge.[88]

Since Constantine's sons had Christian tutors, calling them "heirs to their father's learning" might seem another slap at paganism, but that would only be so if it is assumed that the Christian teaching they received was exclusive and intolerant of other belief. So it may indeed have been; but in the remainder of the passage, Eusebius signals otherwise, describing a broadly inclusive faith with a fairly low threshold for admission. For instance, he identifies Constantine's god with the god of the army and of the people, in fact, as the god of "the entire species of mankind" (πὰν ἀθρόως γένος ἀνθρώπων). Eusebius may have been engaging in nothing more than standard apologetic rhetoric, but in any sense but this the statement is pure fantasy. The "entire species of mankind" was a long way from universal Christian belief at this point, and the army in particular remained solidly pagan. When Eusebius elaborates on Constantine's religious instruction to his soldiers later in the oration, it is a scrupulously neutral "Heavenly Sovereign" whom he depicts the emperor teaching his soldiers to recognize as "giver of victory, savior, guardian, and rescuer."[89] What this passage in fact communicates, therefore, is a readiness to identify the Christian god with an older and broader framework of monotheistic belief.[90]

Even more striking is the "inbred logic" and "self-taught and self-learned knowledge" (λογισμοῖς ἐμφύτοις αὐτομαθέσι τε καὶ αὐτοδιδάκτοις ἐννοίαις) by which Eusebius depicts the peoples of the world calling on this deity. The language conforms to an apologetic conceit that characterized Christianity as "natural" religion. But at the same time it does not suggest a long and difficult course of tutelage and rigid doxology which is now thought to have set Christianity apart from traditional belief. It sounds, in fact, rather like the type of self-taught faith which Constantine in his letters, and Eusebius in the SC, present as the emperor's own.[91] If, in this age when it was so common, this passage did not seem to a pagan hearer to be an attempt to syncretize Christ with other forms of monotheistic belief, it must at least have signaled a Christian who recognized that, as the pagan Symmachus would later put it, there were many avenues to the same God.[92]

As the oration proceeds, even the Logos is defined as the one "voices of men learned in God have acclaimed in prophecy as supreme commander and chief high priest, prophet of the Father and carrier of great counsel, radiance of the paternal light and sole-begotten son, and by countless other titles."[93] All these titles have solid scriptural precedent, and in speaking of "countless other titles" Eusebius undoubtedly had in mind other Christian titles. But in the environment of the early fourth century, only other Christians would have been inclined to understand his words so narrowly.[94] It is significant, therefore, that

Eusebius never identifies Constantine's "friend" specifically as "Jesus" or "Christ"—words that, in fact, never appear anywhere in the speech. Instead, he is identified only as the "Logos,"[95] a term that had a thoroughly Christian theological identity by the fourth century but also an even longer history in pagan philosophy, where the Logos had long been recognized not only as a logical intermediary between God and man but, even more important for present purposes, as the principle specifically identified with rulership.[96] Of roughly 140 descriptive references to deity in the *LC,* fewer than 40 pertain in any way to the Second Person.[97] The remainder, more than two out of every three, deal with the First Person: God the Father, the Supreme Sovereign. Despite the neat hierarchy of God-Logos-Emperor celebrated by political theorists, it is actually this Being, not the Logos, who is most consistently identified as Constantine's God.[98]

In short, the language of the *LC* is universal and inclusive. The *SC* differs in tone and substance. From the first sentences, the tone becomes adversarial and defensive, as Eusebius addresses the charges of those "who in the blindness of their souls are ignorant of matters divine" and so are perplexed by the wealth and attention that Constantine has lavished on the Church of the Holy Sepulchre, finding it "a joke and frankly ridiculous" because they believe "that for so great a sovereign to bother himself with memorials to human corpses and tombs is unfitting and demeaning." The classical learning that Eusebius will display in the *LC* here is mocked as the "folly" that the philosopher pursues "with the conceit he calls wisdom."[99] Eusebius uses the mockery of this imaginary adversary to launch into an explanation of the role of the Son, which occupies the bulk of this speech. Only at the conclusion does he return to the specific topic of the Sepulchre, with a quick concession that his account may have been "superfluous and unnecessary" to an emperor who has "frequently received perception of the Savior's divinity through actual experience." After enumerating the items that he hopes the emperor will recount "should leisure permit," Eusebius ends with the triumphant Q.E.D. that this "trophy of His victory over death" was a project "entirely fitting and suitable for a victorious sovereign."[100]

Given the topic of this speech, it is not surprising that the *SC* should place greater emphasis on the Second Person than the *LC.* The two speeches are in a way parts of a whole, with the *LC* designed to discuss God the Father, the *SC* the Son. Together, they form the core of Eusebius's work *On the Theophany*, large parts of which correspond in both thought and wording to these speeches. The difference in subject by itself can explain the greater emphasis on the Second Person in the *SC* and the relative neglect of that Person in the *LC*, and it might simply be convenience that made the Father the subject of the state oration. But there are other differences that are not so easily explained. The *SC* is also decidedly more exclusivist in language than the *LC*, with Christ now referred to consistently as "our Savior" instead of the "common Savior" or "Savior of All" who will appear in the *LC*.[101] Where many names for God will be encouraged in that oration, here Eusebius takes pain to avoid any confusion, interjecting after the use of one of the circumlocutions with which the *LC* is peppered, "that is, specifically, the All-Holy Body of Christ." Now, indeed, Eusebius rules that it is a mistake to use such vague language. Where in the *LC* Constantine leads, guides, exhorts, and spares "even the godless," here all nations are "commanded" to "recognize this One alone as true."[102]

What are we to make of these differences? There are also similarities in the two speeches, and it is in the *SC* that Eusebius repeats his favored theme of the twin destiny of church and empire.[103] Moreover, Constantine listened to, and evidently enjoyed, both speeches, the *SC* as well as the *LC*. So it is reasonable to ask, do differences between the two really matter?

Constantine and Eusebius were not diametric opposites; there was significant overlap in their beliefs, as there is in all three of Eusebius's works that make up what might be called his Constantinian corpus. Both men believed that Constantine had been appointed by God, without need for human agency.[104] Eusebius's strong belief in the united destiny of empire and Christianity brought him to the conclusion that monarchy meant order, and Constantine in his own oration showed a similar orientation when he argued that a plurality of gods would mean both confusion and strife.[105] But while there were significant areas of agreement, the two men did not think identically on all issues, although thanks to the way Eusebius constructed the *VC*, it is easy to conclude that they did, that Eusebius was simply a channel for Constantine's thinking. The differences identified here all point in a certain direction: to limit the emperor's agenda to Christianity, and to control the definition of that Christianity. What was Eusebius up to?

The "Good King" Reborn

Ever since Norman Baynes, in a brief but influential 1934 article, called attention to the importance of the "political philosophy" of Eusebius's oration, the *LC* has been recognized as the basis of "that philosophy of the State which was consistently maintained throughout the millennium of Byzantine absolutism."[106] There is a similar consensus about the *VC*, that it was meant to portray the ideal of a Christian emperor as much as, if not more than, the life of its purported subject.[107] Less often acknowledged is the fact that the type of emperor outlined in these two works does not line up exactly. The emperor of the *LC* is a close friend and living image of the Divine Being, carrying out on earth a plan closely synchronized with the actions of his divine counterpart. Self-taught in the divine mysteries, he looks forward to eternal rule in the afterlife. The emperor of the *VC* is also appointed by God, and he also wars against the human counterparts of the demons. But he is constantly interacting with clergy and, to judge by the *VC*, spends the bulk of his career in service to the church. Lavishing his personal and fiscal resources with single-minded zeal on the triumph of his new faith, he cajoles, exhorts, berates, and, when necessary, chastises the bishops to achieve the goal of peace and unity. There is much similarity between theory and ideal, but in key ways there is also a disparity. Like images in a broken viewfinder, the two do not align exactly; they blur at the edges. At the point of disconnect, the edge where the images fail to fuse, stand the bishops.[108]

The answer to this puzzle lies in the nature of the "good king." Eusebius's debt to Hellenistic kingship theorists like Diotogenes and Ecphantus discussed in Chapter 4 is obvious. Like them, he assigns a celestial companion to the emperor, and his depiction of Constantine's rise to rule in the *VC* ("Thus then the God of all, the Supreme Governor of the whole universe, by his own will appointed Constantine, the descendant of so renowned a parent, to be prince and sovereign: so that, while others have been raised to this distinction by the election of their fellow-men, he is the only one to whose elevation no mortal may boast of having contributed")[109] could have been taken right out of their pages. But what does this similarity mean? Does it constitute a self-confident appropriation of the classical heritage, or an attempt to find a Christian role in the traditional structure, or something else entirely? It takes only a small shift in perspective for what may seem in retrospect "an aggressively Christian content" to become instead a reassuring confirmation of the existing order, a signal that Christians were reasonable people, educated with the proper values, people who could be dealt with.

One way to explain the contradictions in the way Eusebius represented Constantine in the *LC* and the *VC* is to see these works as part of a lifelong struggle on Eusebius's part to isolate the nature of the "good king" from its Hellenistic context—especially as that context had been appropriated and redefined by the senatorial order—and to redefine the concept in Christian terms. The task was harder than it now may seem, because the "good king" was one of those concepts that in any society become so well known and so well established that there no longer is any conscious connection between them and the value structure that produced them. In all likelihood, neither Eusebius nor his readers in the Greek East would have known what the phrase "senatorial values" meant. Like most traditional beliefs, the standard was accepted, rather than analyzed. Just as late-twentieth-century Americans judge their leaders according to principles that reflect the values and vision of eighteenth-century Boston merchants of whom they know little and care less, so Christians in the Roman Empire easily adopted Hellenized senatorial standards for a "good king" without asking how appropriate to their needs and situation those standards were. Yet as we saw in Chapter 2, the values that made up the concept of the "good king" as senators effectively defined them meant being good to the Senate, if for no other reason than that it was the Senate that would decide who was and was not a good king. This premise led to confusion and contradiction when Christians used the concept, because, as we saw with Lactantius, senatorial values conflicted in certain ways with Christian values.[110] In the most basic sense, senators could judge an emperor "good" without a care for how he treated Christians; in some cases, they could even think him "good" precisely because he mistreated Christians. Eusebius came to understand this conflict, and in the *VC* he defined a good ruler in terms of the church, not the Senate. In the deepest sense, this was the biggest and most important influence of that work.

Melito of Sardis illustrates the problem. The apology in which he made the case for a joint destiny of Rome and Christianity was written in response to a series of persecuting edicts that had left Christians at the mercy of "shameless informers and coveters of the property of others." In it, he begged the emperor to look into the injustices being perpetrated in his name, injustices "not fit to be executed even against barbarian enemies," and argued that only bad emperors, such as Nero and Domitian, had ever attacked the faith. The confusion with senatorial values is evident in the way Melito framed his case, for "shameless informers and coveters of the property of others" are precisely what senators had to fear under bad emperors. Good emperors, such as the one he addressed, exposed the falsehoods leveled against the faith and provided legal protections. In this argument, Melito obviously relied on the time-honored strategy of imperial panegyric to make his case, hoping that the emperor would use the face-saving device Melito provided him and revoke the decrees, rather than face the alternative of being assigned by history to the company of bad emperors. But what could Melito do if the man he conceded was a good emperor had indeed issued the edicts against which he protested and refused to rescind them? Not much, as his own answer to this conundrum indicates. "If these things are done by thy command," he wrote, "well and good. For a just ruler will never take unjust measures; and we indeed gladly accept the honor of such a death."[111]

Melito's apology shows that Christians in the second century had not yet worked through the problem of defining a "good emperor." Nor had they done so more than a century later, when Eusebius came to this same persecution in his Church History. The problem in this case was that the author of those edicts was a very good emperor, none other than Marcus Aurelius, the philosopher-king. By the fourth century, Marcus's reputation was secure, and evidently Eusebius did not want to challenge it. On the other hand, neither did he want to abandon the argument put forward by Melito that "good" emperors were good to Christianity. Thus, when he came to the circumstances of this persecution at the start of book V, Eusebius finessed the point by using two of Marcus's lesser-known names, "Antoninus Verus," to identify the author of the persecution, allowing the reader thereby to confuse Marcus Aurelius with his negligible co-ruler, Lucius Verus, even though by the time of this persecution Lucius had in fact been dead almost a decade.

The Church History was an early work, and Eusebius obviously had not yet come to grips with the need to provide a Christian version of the good king. His treatment of Marcus's persecution is only one of the strategies he adopted, and a particularly clumsy one at that. Typically, he followed the path of his predecessors in regarding neutrality, that is, the absence of hostile acts against Christians, as sufficient for a good emperor, and like them he was inclined to read anything more favorable as a sign of conversion, or at least "crypto-Christianity."[112] By the time Diocletian's persecution ended, his thinking had changed little. In editions of the Church History which were completed after the end of the persecution but before the war with Licinius which made Constantine sole emperor, Eusebius praised both Constantine and Licinius, whom at this point he knew only as the emperor responsible for the defeat of the hated Daza, as "God-beloved emperors, honored alike for their intelligence and their piety," as "advocates of peace and piety," beneficiaries of victory from "the one and only God of all."[113]

But a new criterion emerges in a speech Eusebius delivered no later than 315 in Tyre and subsequently incorporated into book X of the Church History. Here, Eusebius described how, in the aftermath of the persecution,

> the supreme rulers [i.e., Constantine and Licinius], conscious of the honor which they have received from Him, spit upon the faces of dead idols, trample upon the unhallowed rites of demons, make sport of the ancient delusion handed down from their fathers, and acknowledge only one God, the common benefactor of all, themselves included. And they confess Christ, the Son of God, universal King of all, and proclaim him Saviour on monuments, imperishably recording in imperial letters, in the midst of the city which rules over the earth, his righteous deeds and his victories over the impious.[114]

In this passage, Eusebius went far beyond any previous Christian writer in what he expected from a good emperor. No longer content, like Melito, with the mere absence of hostility, or even with a generalized goodwill to Christians, Eusebius raised the stakes, expecting Constantine and Licinius both to reject traditional rites and to confess Christ if they were to be "God-beloved emperors." Scholars have not missed the new tone, which they have quite naturally associated with the emergence of a new, more aggressive Christian spirit in the aftermath of the fall of the persecutors.[115] But even more it represents one further step in Eusebius's thinking about the nature of the good king. When he described how Constantine and Licinius "spit upon the faces of dead idols," trample "unhallowed rites," mock ancestral religion, and confess Christ, Eusebius spoke of actions that never would have won senatorial approval, such as had been required of good emperors in the past. Albeit unconsciously, Eusebius was, in fact, attempting to move away from a senatorial standard for judging the actions of good emperors.

In 315, Eusebius had moved far enough away from that standard to make favorable actions to Christianity a precondition for model behavior, and he had isolated specific actions, such as repudiating traditional religion, which would be more effective proofs of Christian belief than the general piety that all emperors were expected to possess. In another way, however, Eusebius remained wedded to traditional Christian ways of thinking about the good king. This was in his willingness to equate action with belief. The standard had already caused him problems in accounting for Constantine's first rival, Maxentius, for as we saw in Chapter 5, Maxentius's record with the Christian community of Rome was in fact quite favorable. In that case, however, Eusebius had used Maxentius's pact with the hated Daza to transform a relatively favorable record into a case of "feigned" support. Constantine's subsequent war with Licinius triggered another round of rethinking, for if now Licinius also had only feigned his hatred of paganism, then obviously all the criteria Eusebius had developed to this point still were not sufficient to ensure that the emperors he praised were in fact good Christians.

The *LC* was another attempt to define the good Christian king. To the extent that it redefined the emperor's divine comrade as the Christian god, it was successful in moving traditional thought closer to Christian standards, and in this sense it may even be called an aggressive and daring move. But there are numerous signs that Eusebius still felt constrained in this speech. The actions for which he praised Constantine and Licinius in 315, for instance, reappear in the *LC* almost word for word, but now they are performed by all converts, not specifically the emperor.[116] Indeed, very little of the hostility toward traditional practices which governs Constantine's actions in the *VC* is evident in the *LC,* and such as there is, is tempered and moderated. Eusebius uses a highly inclusive vocabulary to portray the emperor's Christianity; he allows a broader range of motives to explain both the confiscation of temple treasures and the razing of particular temples, and he describes the emperor's most visibly Christian activity, the construction of churches, as efforts to herald a sign rather than dedication to Christ. What is missing entirely from the *LC* yet present in abundance in the *VC* is the role of the clergy.

Eusebius's lifelong struggle to define a Christian good king is the context within which to understand the clericalism that Burckhardt rightly observed in the *VC.* The bishops are the new element in this work, playing a key role in the implementation of the emperor's plans from the time of his conversion to the moment of his death. Inevitably, despite Eusebius's warning that he intended to concentrate on "those circumstances only which have reference to his [Constantine's] religious character," both professional and casual readers cannot help but carry away the impression that dealing with the bishops was one of the most important items, perhaps *the* most important, on Constantine's agenda. The conclusion is not necessarily far from the truth. Constantine's efforts to establish a collegial relationship with the bishops comparable to that which emperors of the Principate enjoyed with the Senate, his self-characterization as "bishop of those outside," his constant flattering, cajoling, and wheedling to achieve his goals—all fit a pattern of shrewd political behavior. The distortion lies in what the *VC* leaves unsaid.

It is worthwhile to read Eusebius's entire disclaimer at this point. He writes,

> It is my intention, therefore, to pass over the greater part of the royal deeds of this thrice-blessed prince; as, for example, his conflicts and engagements in the field, his personal valor, his victories and successes against the enemy,

and the many triumphs he obtained: likewise his provisions for the interests of individuals, his legislative exactments for the social advantage of his subjects, and a multitude of other imperial labors which are fresh in the memory of all; the design of my present undertaking being to speak and write of those circumstances only which have reference to his religious character.[117]

Eusebius follows this passage with his notorious further disclaimer. "I shall select from the facts which have come to my knowledge," he writes, "such as are most suitable and worthy of lasting record." To the extent that they have written about this passage at all, scholars have either clucked at the bishop's disregard for scholarly objectivity or fixed on seeming contradictions—such as the disavowal of things military when such matters actually command a fair amount of attention—to suggest forgery or interpolation.

Lost in the smoke over this selective interest is the significance of what Eusebius had just written about his lack of interest in Constantine's "provisions for the interests of individuals, his legislative exactments for the social advantage of his subjects, and a multitude of other imperial labors which are fresh in the memory of all." What these words signal is that Eusebius has eliminated all those parts of Constantine's agenda which did not accord with his own. Yet the effect of the close identification between Constantine and Eusebius which the *VC* encourages in both tone and structure is that in doing so Eusebius was merely reflecting Constantine's own priorities. Now the question must be posed, is this wise?

The conclusion is difficult to avoid that the ideal emperor of the *VC* represents Constantine's own thinking less well than does the theoretical one of the *LC*, for the effect of Eusebius's changes, inevitably, was to exclude the entire social agenda reconstructed in the previous chapter, and also, by default, to magnify the importance of the bishops. Other problems with the *VC* fall into place with the premise that this distortion was intentional and was in fact a primary purpose of the *VC*. Eusebius is mocked, for instance, for his shallow treatment of the Council of Nicaea in the *VC*, where he concentrates on ceremony and ignores the theological issues. Yet what he shows is an emperor interacting with the bishops in a collegial fashion analogous to the way good emperors had always behaved with the Senate. Even more, by avoiding matters of substance, he minimizes the emperor's role in the resolution of such matters.

Again, there is good reason to believe that Constantine defined the relationship in similar ways. But there is a difference in nuance. Because there is nothing in the *VC* to show Constantine interacted with other bodies, particularly the Senate, in the same way, the message is conveyed that the bishops have now replaced the Senate in the role of imperial college. There is another important difference as well. The emperor of the Principate was collegial as a matter of deliberate choice; the ideal emperor of the *VC* is collegial as a matter of rule. Eusebius has, in fact, set up the bishops not only to take the place of the Senate in judging the good king but to act with an independence that the imperial Senate never had. This was his solution to the perennial problem of defining a Christian good king. The demand for action as proof of Christian faith had proved insufficient. Eusebius wanted a means to judge and, if necessary, condemn imperial conduct. He found this means in the bishops.

Eusebius's concern to introduce the bishops as the arbiters of imperial conduct explains his preference for the Hebrew Bible model of kingship exemplified by Moses to the more apostolic role that Constantine seems to have coveted, and this motive might explain as well both his peculiar treatment of Constantine's sign and his silence with regard to discovery of wood identified as being the true cross, for in both these cases the effect was to hedge what might have become an independent charismatic authority. A similar uneasiness might also underlie that care with which, as others have noticed, Eusebius bracketed his account of Constantine's vision, insisting that he would not have believed it himself had he not heard it from the emperor's own lips. Eusebius saw to it that bishops played a key role even at this defining moment of Constantine's rule. Whereas Constantine always depicted his relationship with God in solely personal terms and his knowledge of the divine as completely self-taught, in Eusebius's telling he is dependent on "those who were acquainted with the mysteries of His doctrines" even for understanding something as basic as what the sign meant. In this way, the bishops become mediators of the emperor's charismatic authority.[118]

Even with this modification, Constantine's vision gave him more authority over the bishops than Eusebius would have liked, but the situation was bearable, simply because by its very nature this authority was not such as Constantine could pass on to his successors. More than a dozen years after Constantine's death, Cyril of Jerusalem wrote Constantius II about the phenomenon of a cross that burned in the sky over the Holy City for a period of days, claiming it as a sign of "how far your zeal excels your forebear's piety."[119] Yet the report did Constantius precious little good in his efforts to impose his will on the bishops, for in the long run Constantine's prestige could not be passed on as Augustus's had been.

In redefining the role of the bishops, Eusebius was prescient, for this relationship between emperor and clergy lies at the core of the question of Christian coercion. Similarly prescient was his decision as early as 315 to light on hostile actions against the old ways in his speech at Tyre as the way to prove the benevolence of Constantine and Licinius, and it may not be accidental that twenty years later he generalized this conduct to all converts in his speech before Constantine.[120] As we will see in the next chapter, there is every reason to believe that here Eusebius was not innovating but reflecting an existing mood that supplies another piece for the puzzle.

Eusebius thus has an important part to play in the explanation of Constantine's agenda. It is not the part once assigned him by scholars and church historians who assumed that the author of the *VC* was what he intimated, a close confidant and adviser of the emperor. More sober recent judgments may have gone too far in reducing the number of his known contacts with Constantine to a handful, but they have performed the useful service of putting some distance between the historian and the life he records. The distance, in turn, opens the door to an understanding of the way Eusebius colored the *VC* with his own agenda. Thanks to Eusebius's lifelong struggle with the nature of the good king, his ideal emperor by default had no policy but a Christian one. Eusebius had succeeded in burying Constantine's agenda in his own fine print.

Eleven

Power Players

Athanasius sailed into exile with the tide on November 7, A.D. 335. For the next twenty months he would be in Gaul, far from his Egyptian base. There, incidentally, he would bring word of the ascetic practices that were now sweeping his native province and jump-start the trend to monasticism in the West. This would be the first of five exiles the bishop of Alexandria would endure during his long tenure. He would be banished again by Constantine's son, Constantius II, in 339 and 356; by Constantius's successor, Julian, in 362; and by Valens in 365—a total of seventeen years in all. In fact, the only Eastern emperor during this period who did not come to loggerheads with Athanasius was Jovian, presumably because he did not have the time: he died in 364 after less than eight months in office.

The same tide that carried Athanasius to distant shores swept Eusebius of Nicomedia to new heights of power and influence. In the spring of 336, Eusebius saw another detractor, the virulent Marcellus of Ancyra, deposed and sent into exile, and when Constantine became mortally ill in May 337 in a suburb of Nicomedia, to Eusebius fell the singular honor of baptizing the first Christian emperor. Churchmen in that age did not cultivate the healthy sense of irony which historians now develop so easily. Unable to accept the friend and champion of

Fig. 7. Constantine was not baptized until shortly before his death in 337, when he received the sacrament from Athanasius's enemy, Eusebius of Nicomedia. A later Western legend provided a more orthodox alternative in the person of Bishop Sylvester of Rome. This scene, from a series of frescoes in the eleventh-century Chapel of Saint Sylvester in the Church of the Quattro Coronati, Rome, illustrates a decisive contest between Sylvester and the chief rabbi in Rome. To the right, the rabbi strikes a bull dead by whispering the secret name of Jehovah in its ear, while Constantine and his mother, Helena, watch. In the broken portion on the left, Sylvester's hand can just be made out as he resurrects the bull in the name of Christ.

(Wilpert, *Röm. Mos.,* pl. 269)

the great heresiarch Arius in the role of Constantine's spiritual father, the Western church eventually found a more suitable candidate in the Roman bishop Sylvester, who did not become bishop of Rome until January 314—fifteen months after Constantine's victory at the Milvian Bridge and eleven months after he had left Rome for Milan and Gaul— thus leaving only two periods when both bishop and emperor were in Rome at the same time: three months in the summer of 315 and less than one month in the summer of 326. In this wonderful legend, Constantine comes into the faith not only at a time and place more to the liking of the Western church but also as the result of some memorable pyrotechnics, including a contest in the Coliseum between Sylvester and the chief rabbi of Rome, in which a bull is struck dead by the dreaded secret name of Jehovah, only to be resurrected by Sylvester in the name of Christ.[1] Such storytelling belongs to later ages, and it had no effect at all on Eusebius of Nicomedia, who soon established an ascendancy over Constantine's son and successor in the East, Constantius II. In 338 Eusebius was translated to Constantinople on the death of its bishop, Alexander, and in 339 he had the satisfaction of seeing Athanasius off to his second exile as well as his first.

Tides ebb, and tides flow. In 342, Eusebius of Nicomedia died, and with him died the best hope of producing a reformulated creed that would peacefully resolve the Arian controversy. Whatever his theological flaws, even the hostile accounts of his enemies leave little doubt that Eusebius was a consummate political player. As R. P. C. Hanson has put it, "They all detest him, but pay unwilling tribute to his ability."[2] Eusebius was a great manipulator, a master of what today would be called insider politics. Time and again he showed an ability to adapt to the different styles of political rulers, and after stumbling at Nicaea he never again let principle keep him from access to power. He excelled at putting together winning coalitions and so effectively mobilized the Eastern court against Athanasius that it remained hostile to Nicene orthodoxy until disaster brought in the firmly orthodox Theodosius I in 379. Had he lived, Eusebius would likely have negotiated the traps at the Council of Serdica in 343 with more grace than his successors showed, and he certainly would have kept the bishop of Alexandria well muffled and neutralized. From the time of Eusebius's death, Athanasius grew ever more defiant in his prose and outrageous in his reconstruction of events. Although he never became sufficiently strong to ignore the will of the emperor, Athanasius did win the battle of "the fine print." Dozens of books continue to be devoted to the career and theology of the bishop of Alexandria, his actions endlessly dissected and debated; the bishop of Nicomedia has been the subject of a single dissertation, published in Germany in 1903.[3]

While Athanasius and Eusebius of Nicomedia differ in style and theology, together they illustrate an important effect of the Age of Constantine. Whereas this period often is spoken of as the triumph of the church or heralded for the emergence of a church-state relationship, "the church," that is, the Christian community, had become a player long before the time of Constantine. What his reign produced was power players, in the persons of the bishops.[4] If players are individuals whose resources make their consent important to any deal, who are "in the loop," as one student of public policy defined them in Chapter 2, power players are the ones who use their resources in such a way as to gain maximum advantage for themselves and their constituents. Thanks to Constantine, bishops—particularly those of the great sees like Rome or Alexandria—had resources aplenty. The church historian Theodoret, writing in the fifth century, claims that Constantine ordered governors throughout the empire to provide subsidies for virgins, widows, and the clergy which were three times the amount in his own day, an amount that he indicates was still ample.[5] At a tense moment during their meeting with Constantine, Eusebius of Nicomedia mocked Athanasius for trying to portray himself to Constantine as a poor and humble cleric, replying that the bishop of Alexandria was in fact "a rich man, and powerful, and able to do anything."[6]

In insisting on his personal poverty, Athanasius was being conveniently obtuse. His resources as bishop, not his personal wealth, were the issue. For a sense of what those resources would be like, it is only necessary to consult the list of articles that a successor of Athanasius, Cyril, brought with him as bribes to the Council of Ephesus a century later—a king's ransom in linens and posh furnishings for prefects and chamberlains, not to mention twenty-five hundred pounds of gold to ease the burden of other court officials.[7] The fourth-century historian Ammianus Marcellinus, after observing the bishop of Rome's lifestyle, decided that men who won that office "will be secure for the future, being enriched by offerings from matrons, riding in carriages, dressing splendidly, and even feasting luxuriously, so that their entertainments surpass even royal banquets." Indeed, the great pagan aristocrat Praetextatus is supposed to have jokingly told Pope Damasus at midcentury that, if he could be bishop of Rome, he would become Christian on the spot.[8]

A longtime aristocrat like Praetextatus would not have been speaking merely of Damasus's finery and equipage—surely his own were just as grand, if not more. What his shrewd political eyes would have noticed was the clientele that the bishops' patronage resources commanded. In addition to the poor who were now attached to the church and the trains of priests and nuns that show up with alarming frequency in the pitched battles that Athanasius carefully chronicled for his supporters, this clientele included numerous stretcher bearers and grave diggers employed by the bishop—a large, physically fit corps as capable of filling stretchers as carrying them, with ready access to implements as useful in a street brawl as a hospital. In time of need, they doubled as a virtual paramilitary force.[9]

From the moment Constantine empowered them, bishops such as Athanasius and Eusebius of Nicomedia displayed a natural talent for effectively using all the resources at their disposal. Eusebius maneuvered himself into the capital city—first Nicomedia, then Constantinople—and used his proximity to the seat of power to leverage alliances with other bishops and dissident groups such as the Meletians to destroy the ascendancy Athanasius had gained at Nicaea. If Eusebius of Nicomedia became a master of insider politics, Athanasius was the bishop who realized Christianity's populist potential. Cut off from the corridors of power, the bishop of Alexandria developed a flair for outsider politics, appealing to new constituencies, developing new means for mobilizing support, and refining and maximizing the already considerable communications media at a bishop's disposal to enlarge and solidify his political base. Through a combination of writings and personal diplomacy, Athanasius formed lasting alliances with the bishop of Rome and with the solitaries who were spearheading the explosive growth of monastic communities in the Egyptian deserts. He thereby made up in numbers for what he lacked in access.

Athanasius was a gifted controversialist, able to rally the spirits of his flock during some of the darkest years the Nicene faith ever faced. With access to the emperor denied him, Athanasius learned to take his fight to a larger arena, broadening the numbers of participants and making firm allies out of diverse bystanders. In many ways, Christianity owes as large a debt to Athanasius for his political skills as for his firmly orthodox theology, for without his tenacity, his pugnaciousness, and, be it admitted, his ability to steer around the whole truth when the occasion demanded, the theological position he championed might well have been shouted down.

Bishops like Athanasius and Eusebius of Nicomedia soon demonstrated that their support was vital to keeping the peace. Eusebius of Caesarea probably had Athanasius (among others) in mind when he wrote in the *vita Constantini* that "in every city bishops were engaged in obstinate conflict with bishops, and people rising against people." In this same passage, Eusebius alluded to an incident that was still remembered half a century later, in which statues of the emperor himself evidently were defaced. "This state of things had little power to excite his anger," Eusebius wrote, "but rather caused in him sorrow of spirit; for he deeply deplored the folly thus exhibited by deranged men."[10] Sorrow, perhaps; but such events surely also made it known that henceforth emperors would ignore the bishops at their peril. No more than three decades later, the bishop of Bostra delivered the following warning to Constantine's nephew, Julian: "Although the Christians are a match for the Hellenes in numbers, they are restrained by our admonition that no one disturb the peace in any place." Less serene than Eusebius's ideal Constantine, Julian exclaimed in a letter reporting this communication that the "leaders of the Galilaeans," as he called the bishops, "leave no stone unturned, and have the audacity to incite the populace to disorder and revolt." Julian might, in this instance, have willfully misread a bishop's genuine desire to keep the peace. But he correctly saw that the power to keep peace is also the power to destroy peace. With patronage resources greatly enhanced by Constantine's redistributions, bishops stood atop a base of popular support that made them indispensable to the task of maintaining the delicate equilibrium necessary for urban tranquillity. No longer could an emperor ignore their concerns: that is what truly rankled Julian.[11]

This was surely an unintended consequence of Constantine's social program. The emperor could never have anticipated, much less intended, that the patronage resources he diverted to the bishops would allow them to develop political networks that would make them rivals to the local elites and even to the emperor himself. The real Constantine, as opposed to the ideal emperor of Eusebius's portrait, was scarcely more contained than his nephew later would be when Arius issued a similar threat (or at least what Constantine took to be a threat), claiming "we have the masses." In reply to "Ares Arius," Constantine threatened, "I myself, I said, shall advance, I who have been accustomed to end wars of senseless men." Constantine knew better, however, than to put his prestige on the line so casually, and before this letter ended, he was imploring Arius "to abound in piety toward Christ," which in Constantine's vocabulary always meant to be patient and endure. "I do not wish to fight," he wrote; "but fortified by Christ's faith, I desire you both to be cured and to heal others."[12]

There was reason for Constantine to be cautious, for Christians were never fully dependent on the resources he had placed at their disposal. What gave bishops their greatest power were certain intangible assets unique to their office, such as the longevity of their tenure—for life, under ordinary circumstances—which allowed them to forge a bond with their congregations which few local aristocrats and none of the annually rotated imperial governors could hope to match.[13] Even more important was the bishop's right and responsibility to expound on Scripture during the liturgy, an opportunity for the great orators who now blossomed in pulpits everywhere to exercise their control of "the fine print," interpreting events of the day in terms of the core messages of the faith. The bonds forged with their congregations by long years in their mutual roles—as teachers on the one hand, pupils on the other—gave bishops a natural edge in disputes with outsiders, just as (in twentieth-century terms) local fans provide a "home court advantage" for professional sports teams. In Alexandria, Athanasius and his successors demonstrated time and again their ability to mobilize constituents against ecclesiastical rivals, while in the West, Ambrose of Milan demonstrated the power of this bond even more vividly when his congregation repeatedly swarmed into the streets and occupied the churches in defense of their bishop during several months of tense negotiations with the imperial court in 385–86.[14]

Bishops thus differed from other types of officials with which the emperor dealt in not being primarily accountable to him. They had a power base in their local constituencies. Especially in the major sees election could be bitterly contested, with—as was already evident in the case of the Donatists—a significant, and not always loyal, opposition. The attention attracted by the racket from these contests, then and now, has been largely and deservedly negative. But it testifies to a vitality that stands in stark contrast to the increasingly arid and distant debates of the imperial Senate. Theological issues involved the entire

Christian community. Arius wrote popular songs that were sung—according to Athanasius—in taverns, and Gregory of Nyssa's account of popular involvement in theological issues in Constantinople has already been noticed (Chapter 8). Undoubtedly, much depended on the circles in which one moved. Had Gregory been not a bishop but a soldier-historian like Ammianus, he probably would have encountered similar passions about horse racing. Certainly, John Chrysostom's spirited attacks on theater and the games suggest that he would not have objected if his fellow Antiochenes had spent more time contemplating the mystery of the Trinity. Still, the point remains that the church now provided an outlet for popular activism such as had not existed since the end of the republic.[15]

Although untidy, this base of popular support is what made the bishops a potent political force, both on the imperial level and in their own cities, where they increasingly served as a powerful alternative to the local elites who formed the traditional ruling classes of the empire. Ammianus presents with disdain the riots that accompanied the selection of a bishop of Rome, and church historians view them with alarm. But like the theological controversies of the age, the congregation's role in their selection kept the leadership sensitive to changing conditions on a popular as well as theological level.[16] These congregations are what made the bishops power players, and it was as power players that bishops came increasingly to influence imperial policy during the course of the fourth century.

The relationship between the bishop and his congregation pertains directly to the growth of Christian coercion. Intolerance may underlie the use of coercion, at least in theory, but the connection is not as easy or as direct as it is usually depicted. Local studies have indicated that bishops were the critical factor in determining how a community responded to opportunities to coerce. Even after the decisive period of the late fourth century, the bishop of Chalcedon was able to send packing a monk intent on disrupting the Olympic games with the scornful rebuke, "As you are a monk, go and sit in your cell and keep quiet. This is my affair."[17] Earlier, when the imperial government still protected shrines and temples, some bishops became increasingly bold in their efforts to remove all vestiges of the old religion from their own districts. Bishop Marcellus of Apamea already began to test the imperial government's resolve during the prefecture of Cynegius by taking control of the destruction of his city's famous Temple of Zeus and leading forays against temples and shrines in the countryside. Marcellus met a grisly end—he was burned alive by pagan resisters— but his lead was followed by John Chrysostom, who, after he became bishop of Constantinople, organized the destruction of temples in Phoenicia, and Porphyry of Gaza, whose exploits are discussed below.[18] The names of two of Athanasius's successors in Alexandria are indelibly linked with two of the most spectacular acts of this age. Bishop Theophilus skillfully engineered the events that led to the siege of the Serapeum in 391, and in 415 Bishop Cyril provoked the particularly gruesome death of the philosopher Hypatia, whose only crime was to be caught in the middle of a power play between Cyril and the imperial prefect of the city.[19]

Ultimately, it was another bishop, Augustine of Hippo, who gave the church a theoretical justification for the practice of coercion. Drawing on Jesus' parable of the host whose guests were too busy to come to his banquet, Augustine turned what in the context of Luke's gospel seems to have been intended primarily as yet another example of God's different sense of "rich" and "poor," and perhaps secondarily as a warning to the Chosen People, into a proof text for coercive activity. When the host ordered his servants to "go out to the highways and hedges, and compel people to come in, that my house may be filled," Augustine explained, he meant by reference to the hedges to indicate those people who "are unwilling to be compelled." Alluding to the argument against coercion, Augustine told his flock that such people say "Let us come in of our own good will." But, he concluded, "This is not the Lord's order. 'Compel them.' saith he, 'to come in.' Let compulsion be found outside, the will will arise within."[20] He thus countered the longstanding Christian argument that true belief could not be compelled with the complacent sophism that

> no one is indeed to be compelled to embrace the faith against his will; but by the severity, or one might rather say, by the mercy of God, it is common for treachery to be chastised with the scourge of tribulation. Is it the case, because the best morals are chosen by freedom of will, that therefore the worst morals are not punished by integrity of law? . . . If any laws, there-

fore, have been enacted against you, you are not thereby forced to do well, but are only prevented from doing ill.[21]

Augustine's reasoning became definitive, at least for the Western church.

Because in the fourth century emperors became increasingly willing not only to support Christians but also to suppress traditional religion, it has been easy to make a prima facie case for inherent Christian intolerance as the cause of this coercion. Perhaps too easy. Christians did come to support the use against their enemies of the same force that once had been used against them, but not without reservations and misgivings. The shift in this ground is one of the most important consequences of the fourth century, but it was not inevitable, and "inherent intolerance" cannot fully account for it, for Christians had an equally inherent belief that true faith could not be coerced, as Augustine's need to address this charge shows. They also inherited as an article of faith the injunction that enemies must be endured and loved. This was the tradition Constantine had skillfully exploited to build his coalition. Before coercion could become a respectable alternative, this discourse had to be replaced by another equally powerful commandment—to resist Satan. The process by which this change occurred was not theological but political.

The Politics of Intolerance

Intolerance, the use by Christians of the coercive powers of the state to compel belief, is another tide that began to flow in this century. No sooner had Constantine died than, as we have seen, Eusebius of Caesarea proclaimed, with his usual hyperbole, that the first Christian emperor had ordered the destruction of the temples and an end to pagan sacrifices. His text itemizes only three such closures, and two of these clearly were as much for reasons of public morality as for religious intolerance.[22] Doubtless there were other temples and shrines that fell victim to vigilantism, and the power of legislation to create a climate, even when it cannot be enforced, should not be discounted. Even so, precious little remains to indicate that pagans found the reign of Constantine a revolutionary threat to their traditional beliefs.[23] Constantine's sons picked up Eusebius's cue, perhaps as he had intended they should. In 341, Constantius II ordered that "the madness of sacrifices shall be abolished," citing the authority of his late father in doing so.[24] In the same decade, Julius Firmicus Maternus, whose *Mathesis* (as we saw in Chapter 7) had earlier proclaimed the glories of astrology, now boldly urged Constantius and his brother Constans to take the offensive against paganism, declaiming that "the law of the Supreme Deity enjoins on you that your severity should be visited in every way on the crime of idolatry."[25] Later in the century, the emperor Gratian (367–83) touched off a decade-long struggle with the Senate in Rome by ordering the removal of the Altar of Victory, which had been set up by the first emperor, Augustus. With even greater consequence, Gratian abandoned another of Augustus's innovations, renouncing the title of pontifex maximus and thereby becoming the first emperor in almost four centuries to refuse the office that brought with it control of the Roman state religion.[26] The abandoned title eventually was picked up by the bishop of Rome, who uses it to this day.

Crucial changes occurred during the seventeen-year reign of Gratian's colleague, Theodosius I. In 379, with Theodosius firmly aboard, the emperors placed restrictions on the gatherings of sects deemed heretical. In the next year, Theodosius sealed the victory of Nicene orthodoxy in Constantinople by explicitly identifying "Catholic" Christianity as "that religion which the divine Peter the Apostle transmitted to the Romans . . . the religion that is followed by the Pontiff Damasus and by Peter, Bishop of Alexandria, a man of apostolic sanctity," and denouncing all other forms of Christianity as "demented and insane."[27] In 392, a comprehensive edict forbade all forms of sacrifice or divination, even in public temples, and the worship or veneration of gods or household idols. Other legislation stripped the old priesthoods of their public endowments and privileges and ultimately hastened the demise of the great religious festivals with which they were associated.[28]

The assaults were physical as well as verbal. At all times there had been Christians whose zeal for the faith had led them to assault pagan temples and shrines—the temptation was great enough for the bishops in Spain to stipulate that Christians killed during such incidents were not to receive the crown of martyrdom.[29] Whatever restraint such a judgment had imposed was removed during the four-year tenure of Theodosius I's prefect Maternus Cynegius (384–88), who not only turned a blind eye to such adventures but even put the power of his office behind them. The forces Cynegius unleashed continued to gain strength despite his untimely death. In 391, the Alexandrians—as ever, spoiling for a fight—rioted, and the agitated pagan population opted to make their stand on ground they deemed too sacred and too famous to be violated: the great temple of Serapis, a wonder of the ancient world. To their dismay, imperial troops sided with the Christian besiegers, and before the action was over the wonderful Serapeum lay in ruins. Even more daunting, instead of punishing the transgressors Theodosius held the pagans themselves responsible. For both reasons, the event marks a defining moment in the struggle between Christianity and traditional religion and culture.[30]

By the end of the fourth century, such events had left Christians and pagans staring at each other over a great divide. Eunapius of Sardis wrote a history with a markedly anti-Christian tone. Eunapius's work is now lost, but its outline may be glimpsed in the New History of Zosimus, who wrote about a century later and relied heavily on Eunapius for his account of the Age of Constantine, an emperor whom he cast as Caliban to the shining spirit of Julian's Ariel. The same effect occurred on the Christian side, as fifth-century church historians naturally read the Age of Constantine through the sharply polarized lens of their own day.[31] As always in the study of history, it is easy to look back on earlier events with knowledge of where they lead and see a much more linear development than would have been discernible at the time. Hence it was natural for subsequent church historians to assume that, if a world clearly divided between Christian and pagan resulted from Constantine's conversion, then this must have been what Constantine intended. Reformation polemicists added another layer of distortion by reading Constantine's policy through the light of their own sectarian battles and thereby positing coercion as a litmus test for the sincerity of that emperor's faith. Following this lead, modern scholars have customarily accepted repression as a natural by-product of Christians' refusal to recognize as legitimate the worship of any god but their own, and they therefore have rarely found need to look further for an explanation of this behavior.

The steady drumbeat of such events as the assaults of Cynegius and the destruction of the Serapeum encourages this sense of inevitability. But Constantine's success at building a stable consensus around the equally inherent Christian message of love and endurance shows that Christian rejection of other gods, while certainly a necessary part of the explanation for these coercive activities, is not by itself sufficient reason. Social and political factors run like an undercurrent through this century, and for understanding their tempo tides, not drums, are the better image—tides with their shifting sands, tides with their steady to and fro, tides with their countercurrents and power to erode. What they show, interspersed with the measures of suppression and coercion, are laws rescinding or scaling back the most extreme measures, and voices that continued to speak out against the use of force in matters of faith. A gentler rhythm also reveals a false note, whereby the coercive Christian has become the normative Christian.

The coercive Christian as normative is a modern construct—the worst sort of conceptual anachronism, one that has required every ounce of scholarly ingenuity to maintain. Synesius of Cyrene became bishop of Ptolemais in the Pentapolis of Egypt somewhere around 410. Because he was a student and friend of the philosopher Hypatia, whose brutal death he records, and because he accepted his bishopric only on the condition that it not interfere with his philosophical principles, Synesius was long considered no more than a Christian in name only, even though he was a bishop. But how could a Christian community have put an unbeliever in such an office? And if it did do so, what would that say about contemporary notions of acceptable Christian behavior? In the case of Synesius, the commonsense position has finally prevailed that a definition that calls into question the Christianity of a man deemed by his contemporaries suitable for a bishopric is probably a bit too restrictive.[32] There are others who might benefit from similar rethinking. Pegasius was bishop of Troy when the future emperor Julian, still keeping his pagan sentiments to himself, visited. Julian later described in a letter how Pegasius took great pride in the pagan monuments of his native place and even confided to him that he had only become bishop to protect them from harm. It may be too soon to do for Pegasius what others have done for Synesius—Pegasius did, after all, jump ship under Julian and accept one of the emperor's new priesthoods. But the fact remains that Pegasius was at one time

Christian enough to be acceptable to his flock as bishop, and his response to a leading question from Julian about sacrifices—"Is it not natural that they should worship a brave man who was their own citizen, just as we worship the martyrs?"—shows a broad-mindedness completely in tune with the type of Christianity Constantine advocated.[33]

Indirectly, Julian testifies in this letter to similar latitudinarian principles, for he wrote it to an unnamed pagan priest in defense of his decision to appoint Pegasius to one of his new priesthoods. The priest evidently had questioned the sincerity of a Christian bishop's newfound enthusiasm for the old gods, for the same reasons that Christians now question the sincerity of his Christianity, and Julian was driven to justify his action on the basis of these crypto-pagan memories. But in addition to reporting, and perhaps embroidering on, this encounter, Julian gave his correspondent another reason for not inquiring too nicely into the beliefs of newcomers. "If we drive away those who come to us of their own free will," he argued, "no one will be ready to heed when we summon."[34] There is an uncanny echo here of problems Christians faced in judging the sanctity of their clergy, and the letter at the very least shows that not all the ideologues were on the Christian side of this issue. It also shows Julian doing a little fancy footwork, conveniently ignoring the difference between admitting someone to the faith and putting that person in a position of leadership and trust. Most important of all, however, is the light it sheds on the activities of an emperor trying to build a broadly based, inclusive faith by noncoercive means. In a less peremptory way, his argument reflects the same motives that led Constantine to order Athanasius to "grant free admission to all who wish to enter the Church."[35] Here, as in so many ways, Julian proves the truest heir of the uncle he despised, providing through his commitment to a pragmatic faith that must be accepted voluntarily a faithful echo of Constantine's own sentiments.

But it is not necessary to argue the case for noncoercive Christianity on the basis of such dubious examples as Synesius and Pegasius, when abundant evidence survives in the writings of church fathers of unquestioned orthodoxy and sincerity. "I do not consider it good practice to coerce people instead of persuading them," Gregory of Nazianzen wrote. "Whatever is done against one's will, under the threat of force, is like an arrow artificially tied back, or a river dammed in on every side of its channel. Given the opportunity it rejects the restraining force. What is done willingly, on the other hand, is steadfast for all time. It is made fast by the unbreakable bonds of love."[36] Gregory wrote more than a half century after Lactantius, and almost two centuries after Tertullian, yet his words show that the Christian principle that true belief could not be forced was still intact. John Chrysostom, the future bishop of Constantinople, emphasized the Christian tradition of love when he addressed worshipers of the old gods in a homily delivered while he was still training for a career as a priest in his native Antioch. "Such is the character of our doctrine," he said to some imaginary pagan interlocutors. "What about yours? No one ever persecuted it, nor is it right for Christians to eradicate error by constraint and force, but to save humanity by persuasion and reason and gentleness. Hence no emperor of Christian persuasion enacted against you legislation such as was contrived against us by those who served demons."[37] John wrote these words around 380, a time when the process of Christian coercion is often depicted as well advanced; yet in his eyes it was still pagans, not Christians, who had to answer for coercive activity. Even later, no less a figure than Augustine of Hippo argued against the notion that anyone should be "violently coerced to communion by the force of any secular power."[38]

All these judgments should be read as proof of the staying power of the Constantinian consensus. But perhaps the best proof of all comes from the least likely source, Athanasius. For all his fierce advocacy of Nicene orthodoxy, the bishop of Alexandria still found it useful to belabor his enemies with the charge that they were using the pagans' weapon of persecution to enforce their views. It is "not the part of men who have confidence in what they believe, to force and compel the unwilling," he wrote, in a passage in which he deliberately contrasts the brute force of the Devil with the gentle love of the Savior: "and if they open to Him, He enters in, but if they delay and will not, He departs from them. For the truth is not preached with swords or with darts, nor by means of soldiers; but by persuasion and counsel."[39] Athanasius's use of this argument is telling. In characterizing his opponents as persecutors, Athanasius was using the traditional tactic of the underdog—clubbing them with their own rules, as Saul Alinsky would have said—for in Christian rhetoric, coercion was a tactic of the pagans.[40] Athanasius's use of the charge of "persecution" against his enemies confirms the potency of the Constantinian settlement, with its specific denial of coercion in matters of religion.

These words by such luminaries of the church put into perspective the temple closings and antipagan rhetoric of the middle decades of the century, because they indicate that such acts, although they draw the lion's share of modern attention, were at the time still capable of being read as isolated events rather than as clear signposts of an inevitable, life-and-death struggle. The Constantinian consensus, with its emphasis on patience and noncoercion, remained a legitimate and defensible Christian position long after coercive measures first began to be taken against non-Christian belief. Its success cautions against easy acceptance of the premise that Christian use of coercion was predetermined by that faith's intolerance. Thus, questions that did not need to be asked so long as inherent intolerance seemed a sufficient explanation for Christian coercion now demand attention: How did the coercive Christian become the normative Christian? If Constantine's tolerant and inclusive Christianity succeeded in building a coalition of Christians and pagans in favor of monotheism broadly defined, then why did a more coercive and intolerant form of Christianity come to assert itself by the century's end?

More important, for what reason did voices in favor of a more moderate approach become stilled? Why, for instance, did the group that on a priori grounds was most likely to maintain the Constantinian consensus—the converts who in Christian eyes seemed to be pouring into the church during this period—fail to prevent this drift into militant behavior?[41] For this last puzzle, violence is an attractive explanation, since its effect is often to drive all but the most partisan from the scene. But the confrontations that so readily catch the eye of observers mask subtler processes of opinion formation which, while more banal, are also potentially more informative. When viewed as a social rather than a religious or revolutionary process, the events of the post-Constantinian period reveal two important developments that have yet to receive the attention they deserve. On one side, the Christian community was increasingly destabilized by internal conflicts and the need to absorb new members; on the other, the anti-Christian agenda pursued by Constantine's nephew Julian during his brief but flamboyant rule, from 361 to 363, rekindled Christian fear of state-sponsored hostilities and created litmus tests that polarized opinion in new and dangerous ways. The effect of these twin changes was to make the militant message more credible.

Ascetic Politics

If bishops stand at the center of Christian coercion, monks must be placed in the forefront. The story of Christian coercion in these decades is punctuated by accounts of rampaging monks roving at will through town and countryside, systematically destroying shrines and monuments and terrorizing local populations. Libanius provided the classic treatment of this topic in a speech addressed to the emperor Theodosius, probably written in 386. Here, Libanius deplored the acts of monks who illegally "hasten to attack the temples with sticks and stones and bars of iron, and in some cases, disdaining these, with hands and feet." Deriding them as "renegades from the farms who claim to commune among the mountains with the creator of the universe," Libanius etched a frequently repeated portrait of the excesses of "this black-robed tribe, who eat more than elephants and, by the quantities of drink they consume, weary those that accompany their drinking with the singing of hymns, who hide these excesses under an artificially contrived pallor."[42] He is seconded by another pagan author, Eunapius, who railed against monks "who were men in appearance but led the lives of swine, and openly did and allowed countless unspeakable crimes." Such was their power, he complained, that "every man who wore a black robe and consented to behave in unseemly fashion in public, possessed the power of a tyrant."[43]

Whether Theodosius ever heard Libanius's words is uncertain, but it is clear that he was sensitive to their point. Two years later, he was in Milan when word was received of the burning of a synagogue in the Eastern frontier town of Callinicum and other shenanigans by monks in the neighborhood. According to Ambrose, the bishop of Milan, who recorded the event in a letter to his sister Marcellina, Theodosius's initial response to his plea in church for mercy was to say, "The monks commit many crimes."[44] In 390, Theodosius banned monks from the cities, restricting their movements to "desert places and desolate solitudes," and a Christian dialogue written around this time also found it necessary to address the problem of rogue monks.[45]

The prominence of these activities in the historical record, combined with the dramatic growth of the monastic movement during the course of the fourth century, has helped transform these desert solitaries into paradigmatic militants. The well-known judgments of Libanius and Eunapius seem amply confirmed by incidents like Callinicum and Theodosius's own comment about the crimes of the monks. But they need to be looked at more carefully before accepting their premise that the success of Christian coercion was due to nothing more than gangs and mob violence, with the monks playing the role of storm troopers for the Christian movement. Like the numbers of monks themselves, these accounts tend to be repeated uncritically.[46] Instances of localized violence during these decades are all too real.[47] But violence itself is not sufficient to explain the power the monks exercised, and too much concentration on their participation in such spectacles can be as misleading as an account of imperial power which limited itself to wars and armies. In both cases, a subtler but more pervasive source of authority needs to be defined.

Other voices speak of the deep respect the monks enjoyed in the Christian community, where their ascetic practices were equated with the philosophy of the ancient Greeks. "The opinions of these monks were always adopted by the people," according to the fifth-century church historian Sozomen, "and their testimony was universally received, because they were noted for their virtue and the philosophical tenor of their lives." Another fifth-century writer, Bishop Theodoret of Cyrrhus, justified his decision to write a history of the monks in his region by comparing his subjects not only to "the holy men of old" but also to "the athletes and pancratiasts who compete in the Olympic games" and the charioteers so idolized by late Roman society.[48]

It would be foolish to turn a blind eye to the terror and violence that organized bands of rampaging monks could spread, but too close a focus on such acts leads to a wrong diagnosis of the problem of coercion and forgoes an opportunity to gain an important insight into the process whereby militants take control of a movement. The larger question these acts of violence mask is, why was it tolerated? Here, for instance, is another account of armed bands:

> a strange group of men, perverse and violent, who professed continency . . . inspired by evil teachers of insolent boldness and lawless temerity, they spared neither their own people nor strangers, but, contrary to right and justice deprived men of their civil rights. . . . Many servants of God were even crippled by torture. Some had lime mixed with vinegar thrown in their eyes, and others were killed. As a result, [they] came to be hated even by their own people.[49]

This account has many parallels with those of Libanius and Eunapius, but unlike them it was not written by a pagan but a Christian, Possidius, the biographer of Augustine, and it does not deal with monks. It is, instead, his description of the Circumcellions, a group associated with the Donatists. In Possidius's eyes, these bands were every bit as disreputable and abhorrent as the monks were to Libanius and Eunapius. The point of reciting Possidius's account here is not to put one group over the other but to make clear that violence is just as easily condemned as condoned. It is partly a matter of which side the viewer is on, but the choice of that side itself can depend on whether violence appears wanton or part of a just cause—hence the importance of Possidius's final comment that, as a result of their excesses, the Circumcellions "came to be hated even by their own people."

The situation Possidius described was a reaction to efforts to bring about peace; it was then, according to Possidius, that "they who hated peace freely assailed the person who proposed it," and turned on those of their own who supported it. What Possidius described is the critical point so often lost on those who preach and study violence: to be effective, violent behavior has to be coupled with moral authority—if nowhere else, at least in the community on whose behalf the violent acts ostensibly are committed.[50] The violent activity associated with the monks requires a closer look at the links that tied them to the broader Christian community and also a more balanced understanding of the impression they made on the non-Christian community.

Scholars have long been aware of the prestige accorded to ascetic practices in late antiquity by pagans and Christians alike,[51] but the zeal with which the two sides contended for this distinction is far less frequently remarked. Traces of the contest survive in Libanius's attack on the "artificial pallor" of the monks in his oration to Theodosius. Libanius was the most accomplished orator of his day; his skill shows forth not merely in the cadences of his words but even more in the care he took to seek out his opponents' weak points, to turn their own rules against them when he could, to discredit them when he could not. The latter tactic is on display in his attack on the appetites of the monks, and his sneering reference to their "artificially contrived pallor" is a dead giveaway. It suggests that Libanius was aware that the monks had a reputation for abstinence and ascetic practices. In describing them as drunks and gluttons, he sought to undermine this reputation, but even he could not deny the emaciated look that they somehow managed to achieve despite their supposedly Rabelaisian appetites. By describing their appearance as "artificially contrived," Libanius sought to explain away the one glaring contradiction in his case, the physical evidence of the monks' regimen of self-denial. His comments, as well as those by Eunapius, should be read as attempts to undermine the prestige and authority of the desert fathers.[52]

More echoes redound from one of the most curious tracts to survive from this century, a satirical essay entitled *Misopogon,* or "The Beard-Hater," which the emperor Julian posted in Antioch before he marched off in the spring of 362 for what would prove to be his fatal invasion of Persia, reproaching the Antiochenes for the poor reception they had given him during his winter in their city. It is a whining, self-indulgent tract, and because Julian was angry at a predominantly Christian population for not taking to his revival of state-sponsored paganism, its thrust is often overlooked, for Julian chided the Antiochenes on precisely the grounds that they, though Christians, were not as ascetic as he, a pagan. Dissolute and fun-loving, they did not share Julian's zeal for a pious life, as evidenced by his austere habits, his aversion to popular entertainments, and, of course, his louse-ridden beard. In one striking passage, he adopts the voice of an Antiochene critic: "Would it not be better that the market place should be fragrant with myrrh when you walk there and that you should be followed by a troop of handsome boys at whom the citizens could stare, and by choruses of women like those that exhibit themselves every day in our city?" This, Julian replies, he will not do. "No, my temperament does not allow me to look wanton, casting my eyes in all directions in order that in your sight I may appear beautiful, not indeed in soul but in face."[53] The attack struck home. According to the church historian Socrates, Julian's reproaches left "an indelible stain" on the Antiochenes, and that stigma may be reflected in one of John Chrysostom's first sermons, in which he comforted fellow Christians with the thought that while in their city the now long-dead Julian had "dismissed generals and governors with contempt, but male and female prostitutes he made rise from the brothels in which they were prostituting themselves and form a cortege which he himself led around the streets of the entire city."[54]

In all likelihood, Julian's pretty boys and trains of temptresses were acolytes and nuns, and the people John considered to be whores were priestesses in Julian's revived pagan cults. But where the truth lies amid these accusations is beside the point. Julian and John were both trained in classical rhetoric, and both knew how to smear an opponent. Far more important is that both took it for granted that a reputation for asceticism would put their side in a good light and that accusations of licentious behavior would discredit their opponent. They were fighting for the same ground.

In this contest for bragging rights, Christians held a clear advantage. Pagans in late antiquity could be just as austere as Christians in their morality and as sincere in their commitment to asceticism, but unlike Christians they lacked the broad-based support networks that encouraged and contributed to such behavior. Christians reveled in the suffering of their monks, and they celebrated their acts of self-mortification just as fervently as an earlier age had commemorated the sacrifice of the martyrs.[55] Indeed, it was precisely the martyrs' role as exemplary Christians which these desert athletes inherited, their scorn for the things of this world and their willingness to make the ultimate sacrifice testifying to the strength of their commitment and putting the seal of purity on their faith just as surely as it had for those earlier spiritual warriors. By no coincidence, tales of the desert saints began to circulate during Constantine's reign, later to be set down in writing by, among others, bishops like Athanasius and Theodoret of Cyrrhus. Like the martyrologies that Christians listened to in church, these saints' lives simultaneously inspired Christians and validated their faith.

Moral authority, not random acts of violence, is what gave the monks their real power. As Norman Baynes once put it, "In the fifth century the voice of the monk was what the press is to-day, and with their religious slogans the monks produced the same effect as modern newspapers with their political war cries."[56] The significance of the monks, thus, is not that they perpetrated violence but that they helped legitimize it. As models of exemplary Christian behavior, they gave moral high ground to whichever side on which they stood, and we may suspect from the attacks of Libanius and Eunapius that they filled this role for not a few pagans as well. Yet as Constantine himself demonstrated, the martyrs were multifaceted figures, as much symbols of patience and forbearance as of riot and resistance. The monks, dedicated to the lives of desert solitaries, might just as readily have worn the mantle they inherited from the martyrs in the Constantinian fashion. What mobilized them instead on the side of violence? Given the exemplary nature of their role, the answer to this question can go far toward explaining the acceptance of coercion by the Christian community.

There can be no single answer to so large a question, but at least part of it seems to lie in an unintended consequence of internal conflicts. Athanasius and Eusebius of Nicomedia both seem to have contended for the favor of the monks, even though it was Athanasius who clearly won the battle of "the fine print." His Life of Antony, trumpeting his closeness to the revered founder of the desert movement, is filled with admonitions against the Arians and exhortations to obey their bishop, falling conveniently from the lips of Antony himself. The Life became, in turn, the paradigm for a new genre—hagiography, the writing of saints' lives—and so dominates the field that only in relatively recent times have scholars been able to prise alternative views of Antony and his movement from the record.[57]

Athanasius's alliance with the monks was so effective that on more than one occasion it allowed him to evade the reach of a hostile emperor, and his successors in Alexandria became famous for the uses to which they put these desert bands, even shipping them abroad when necessary to intimidate or overawe their opponents. In a political sense, the monks became a power base for the bishop of Alexandria, and it is important to remember when reading Athanasius's spirited writings that he did not pen them for modern historians, who chafe at their half-truths and inaccuracies, but to rally his followers. Some of them, in fact, seem to have been written for no other eyes but monks'.[58] Athanasius intended these writings to keep the cause alive and the faithful intact, and for all the years he was in exile they succeeded in doing precisely that—an enviable achievement. Read in this way, they reveal an intuitive grasp of the fundamentals of power politics—the importance of leaving no charge unanswered, of giving his supporters something to hang on to even when he was dead wrong. Where he could, Athanasius indicted the evidence; where he could not, he indicted the character of those who brought the charges. He knew instinctively that any offense was better than the best defense, and he accordingly met every charge with a broadside of counter-charges, scattering frequently outrageous claims like buckshot to ensure that his opponents would always have complaints to answer as well as to make. He spoke the truth, but not always the whole truth, especially if he did not expect his words to reach unfriendly ears.

In these forays, Athanasius made use of a rhetorical tradition that helps explain the subsequent posture of the monks, for he regularly, and quite literally, demonized his opponents, portraying them as agents of Satan. This was a technique that worked particularly well in the new genre of saint's life. Wrestling with demons was a particularly vital part of the desert saint's mental landscape, as the merest glance at the Life of Antony, or any other saint's life, will confirm. Antony set the pattern in Athanasius's Life, where the bulk of his training is spent wrestling with demons. The injunction to resist Satan lies at the core of Christian belief, residing alongside the equally important charge to "love thy enemy." In refusing to abjure Christ, the martyrs resisted Satan, and the monks were disposed to follow their example in this as in all other things.

Athanasius certainly did not invent this tradition, and he is by no means the only church father to make use of it. But by fusing this polemic with the ascetic life of the monk, he gave it a vitality that was uniquely suitable for the circumstances of the fourth century. Tapping into this tradition allowed Athanasius to undercut his opponents and deny them any right to a sympathetic or unbiased hearing—then as now, a far easier means of dealing with uncomfortable situations than the alternative of a reasoned give-and-take that more thoughtful forms of discourse would require. The effect of Athanasius's fiery rhetoric was to turn up the temperature of debate and thereby encourage what Guy Stroumsa has called the eristic impulse in Christian thought, the tendency that in these pages has been characterized by the injunction to resist Satan and all his acts.[59] Athanasius's writings thus become one example of the way the Constantinian consensus eventually was undermined.

The methods Athanasius used to win over the monks thus have a direct bearing on the question of Christian intolerance. But it is not the bearing that scholars usually have taken. According to the accepted view, pagans were the primary object of Christian intolerance. It is because of this view that so much of the debate over Constantine's Christianity has focused on the extent to which he did or did not persecute traditional belief. Yet like Constantine, Athanasius directed his most inflammatory rhetoric not at pagans but at other Christians— Christians he believed to be heretics. Here lies the first and most important key to the coercive turn Christianity took during the course of the fourth century: Christians first used both a rhetoric conducive to coercion and the tools of coercion itself not against pagans but against other Christians. Heresy, not paganism, was the first object of Christian intolerance. The pattern, once detected, is very regular: it was heresy that prompted Constantine to become involved in councils of bishops, and heresy was the one exception he ultimately made to his policy of noncoercion. Only subsequently did the rhetorical and political devices first used in the war against other Christians come to be used against non-Christians. When the prefect Cynegius turned the machinery of his office against the temples in the 380s, for instance, he used weapons devised for the battle against heretics to do so.[60] Heretics, it might be said, taught Christians the coercive habit.

Significantly, it was heretics, not pagans, who Augustine of Hippo says caused him to change from his original commitment to the traditional Christian position that true belief could not be coerced. "My first feeling about it," he explained to a Donatist correspondent who chided him for this reversal, "was that no one was to be forced into the unity of Christ, but that we should act by speaking, fight by debating, and prevail by our reasoning, for fear of making pretended Catholics out of those whom we knew as open heretics." But the results were too dramatic to be ignored: his own city of Hippo, once a Donatist strong-hold, had been "converted to Catholic unity by the fear of imperial laws," to such an extent that there were no longer any signs of its presence.[61]

Augustine is one of the few Christians from this period to have left a record of his thoughts about coercion, and it probably is no coincidence that he is also one of the few to have been confronted, in the Donatists, with opponents who were both entrenched and organized. The Donatists, moreover, were not heretics in the traditional sense, for their disagreement was over the definition of purity, not the definition of God. It was Augustine, with his keen sense of the significance of names and labels, who insisted on calling them such. A surviving lengthy exchange between him and the Donatist bishop Petilian explains why Augustine wrote so much about coercion, for Petilian was extremely effective in using core Christian texts to protest Catholic use of imperial forces against his sect. It was an expostulation from Petilian—"Far be it from our conscience to compel any one to embrace our faith"—which prompted Augustine's sophistic distinction, quoted above, between using force to compel belief and using it to punish wrongful conduct.[62]

Petilian's pamphlets, to which Augustine responded in a series of broadsides, are larded with quotations from Scripture which emphasize Christianity's irenic mission in Jesus' own words: "Blessed are the merciful," he shouts at Augustine; "Blessed are the peacemakers." And, most cutting of all, "Blessed are they which are persecuted for righteousness' sake; for theirs is the kingdom of heaven."[63] This is what made it imperative for Augustine to answer. Abstruse theological arguments could be ignored, but cases that were based on lessons familiar to every Christian demanded a response. The conflict between Augustine and Petilian was a fight for control of the moral high ground. Petilian saw an opening in the willingness of Catholics to use coercive force, and his response was to array the whole battery of Christian teaching about love and forbearance against them. The description of the Circumcellions by Augustine's biographer Possidius serves as a reminder that the Donatists were not entirely free of blame on this score themselves, and in other parts of his response Augustine was not slow to hurl the transgressions of Petilian's group back at him. But the real significance of their exchange is that it shows that it was Christians with variant beliefs who forced Augustine to come up with a theoretical justification for the use of force.

Even more, the fact that the exchange exists, and that it is centered on the meaning of core Christian texts, is a caution against making too easy an equation between Christian success and the violent behavior of the monks. Violence is not the whole story of Christian coercion—only the more visible part of a quieter process that results in the stilling of voices that might have spoken for moderation, but did not for fear of seeming less "zealous." It is the combination of the authority of the bishops and the force of the monks which accounts for the stilling of such voices, and heresy that accounts for the strengthening of both. But to pursue this process, sociology might be a better guide than either theology or anthropology, for an important aspect of the concern with heresy is rooted in the particular nature of the Christian community as a society—particular, that is, so far as religion in the ancient world was concerned.[64]

Destabilizing Conditions

At the turn of the fourth century, the Council of Elvira confidently ruled that those who perpetrated acts of violence against pagan temples would not be rewarded with the status of martyrs, on the grounds that "this is nowhere written in the Gospels and is never found being done by the apostles,"[65] and as we saw in Chapter 7, Constantine had been equally clear that he would not sanction such acts despite his personal attachment to the Christian faith. By the end of this century, as the aggressions of a Marcellus or Chrysostom in the East and the writings of Augustine in the West show, condemnation of such behavior was no longer quite so uniform. If it were not for the moderation shown in the earlier period, the coercive behavior adopted later might more easily be explained as an inevitable product of Christian intolerance. As it is, either the earlier situation must be dismissed as an aberration or the later one explained on the basis of changes that occurred during the half century that separates the reigns of Constantine and Theodosius.

An alternative theory holds that the goal of rulers like Constantine is not toleration but concord, that true toleration can only exist when there is no goal—as there was in Constantine's case—of eventually persuading the opposition to convert. In such cases, toleration is only a tactic, not a principle.[66] The distinction is a nice one but difficult to apply, for the principle of toleration also requires an interest in the outcome: indifference does not constitute toleration; toleration, rather, involves a principled commitment to abide, in the name of a higher principle, that which one despises. Toleration in this truest sense would be a rare thing to find at any time in history, and rarer still to find a population committed en masse to such a principle. Is there, in practice, a significant difference between a ruler who advocates toleration for itself and one who advocates toleration along with the wish that, at some happy time in an unspecified future, nonconformists will come to see the error of their ways? Such distinctions should not be used to deny Constantine's commitment to the principle that unity of belief, however desirable that might be, cannot be coerced.

It may well be that Constantine's moderation was motivated, at least in part, by the strength of potential opposition among the pagan elite. This opposition has long been posited, and for later periods of religious strife de facto toleration regularly occurred in such situations.[67] Thus, Constantine's concluding statement in the Edict to the Eastern Provincials—"I should, indeed, have advised this very thing [the destruction of the temples] to all men, if the violent opposition of wicked error were not immoderately embedded in some souls, to the detriment of our common salvation"—may be a candid admission of the limits of his ability to do otherwise as well as a rhetorical concession to Christian militants.[68] There is no reason to deny that such pragmatic concerns figured in Constantine's calculations; indeed, one aim of this book has been to demonstrate his political aptitude, and from that standpoint it would indeed be a miracle if he had ruled so long without possessing such basic political instincts. Constantine did treasure "the blessings of peace," and even Eusebius of Caesarea was careful, amid his chortling over the confiscation of temple treasures, to point out that this was a task for which the emperor deemed no military force would be necessary.[69] But expedient or no, the principle on which Constantine declined to use force—never more strenuously than when he was dealing particularly with a Christian audience—was that true belief could not be coerced.[70] He based his actions squarely on a core Christian principle: Jesus' order to "love thy enemy." In political terms, this was the truly revolutionary aspect of Christian belief, and the centrality of this commandment to Christian thought is precisely what makes the situation in the fourth century so urgently in need of careful and serious reevaluation.

Rodney Stark has put forward two "theoretical propositions" drawn from the workings of a market economy which readily apply to the religious situation of the fourth century. The first is: "The capacity of a single religious firm [i.e., a church] to monopolize a religious economy depends upon the degree to which the state uses coercive force to regulate the religious economy." The second, "To the degree that a religious economy is unregulated, it will tend to be very pluralistic."[71] The traditional argument of Christian intolerance, rewritten in terms of these propositions, would be restated as follows: "With the adoption of Christianity by Constantine, the Roman religious economy ceased to be unregulated; instead, the state assumed regulatory powers that in turn led to the suppression of pagan belief." In other words, these propositions would seem to vindicate the traditional interpretation. In fact, they do the opposite: they show the weakness of the traditional argument, for Diocletian was as much involved in regulating the religious economy as were Christian emperors after him. The change in the fourth century, thus, was not from unregulated paganism to coercive Christianity. Rather, it was that the Roman state, pagan or Christian, now defined its security explicitly in religious terms.

Stark's propositions clear the air, but they do not by themselves explain how, internally, militant Christians came first to dominate, and then to define, the Christian movement. Here is a principle with which to begin: Movements, even religious movements, need organization, and any organization can be taken over by those members who are more committed, more zealous, more ideologically focused than the rank and file—the activists and professional staffers.[72] To a degree, such a principle can explain how Christianity became more militant and more coercive as it became more powerful in the decades after Constantine. But to leave the topic at this point is to leave a larger question unanswered: If this is, indeed, what happened to the Christian movement, why was it the militant wing that prevailed? Love and forbearance are at least as central to the Christian message as the exclusivism that presumably fuels intolerance, and it is not as difficult as scholarship assumes to think of circumstances in which Christianity might have emerged from the fourth century in the hands of a tolerant and latitudinarian leadership, for a "big tent" type of mass movement is just as likely to be dominated by pragmatists as by ideologues. In Christianity, there was the additional factor of an equally strong pull in the central message to love one's enemies, making it just as likely that the most committed Christians would be those who were the most irenic. To explain why, instead, militants succeeded in gaining control of the Christian message, a different principle must be invoked.

It is a political truism that the more secure a community is, the more willing it will be to tolerate diversity and variant belief.[73] Constantine's success in asserting the irenic side of Christian teaching, then, rested at least in part on the relative security he established in the aftermath of Diocletian's intensely disruptive persecution. On this premise, the need now is to find destabilizing factors that allowed militants to reassert the equally potent Christian message to resist evil. Much more study needs to be done, but it may not be premature to put forth two developments that seem to have played a role. The first of these is a process of rethinking and redefinition of what it meant to be a Christian which took place at least partly as a result of the successes Christianity enjoyed in the aftermath of Constantine's conversion and which reinforced a significantly higher standard for model Christian performance than that emperor had wanted. A second, and related, development was the emperor Julian, who managed during his brief reign to resurrect Christian doubts about the stability of their new situation and to accelerate the polarization of Christians and pagans into two clearly identified, separate, and mutually hostile camps.

The relationship between these developments and their influence on the willingness of Christians to use coercion can only be sketched in the following pages. But with that sketch, it will then be possible to take a different perspective on the role of violence in these events. However incomplete, the discussion will have served its purpose if it shows that the change in Christian attitudes toward coercion in the fourth century was the result of a political rather than a theological dynamic. In a nutshell, what happened was not the inevitable result of innate Christian intolerance but rather was due to a particular set of circumstances which allowed Christian militants to reassert a rhetoric that Constantine had effectively stilled.

The place to begin, then, is with an easily ignored aspect of Christian identity. As we saw in Chapter 3, Christianity is an artificial community, in the sense that it does not define its membership according to criteria of race or ethnicity but by means of shared commitment to a certain set of beliefs. Such communities are artificial precisely because they do not have the inherited bonds of common ancestry which distinguish kin-based communities. Failure to take this difference into account easily leads to serious misdiagnosis. The image of tolerant pagans versus intolerant Christians, for instance, becomes far less stark once allowance is made for the different natures of the two communities. A kinship community will not normally have a great deal of interest in creeds or ideology, but it will frequently be deeply concerned with the purity of blood lines, endlessly inspecting genealogies and obsessed with female chastity. Conversely, a community that defines itself by commitment to a belief will be far less concerned with blood lines but obsessed with thought lines—the purity of members' attachment to their ideology or creed. Bedouin tribesmen will be every bit as zealous in defense of the virginity of a bride as will Christians in the defilement of doctrine. To compare the two types of communities without making this distinction necessarily skews the result. Purity of line is the factor that makes the two identical.

In communities based on ideological ties, success can itself be destabilizing, in the sense that there is little, if any, bar to prevent newcomers, attracted by the ideology of the host community, from overwhelming the original population. The number of newcomers in absolute terms is not as important as the impression they make. The effect is a sort of dissonance, in that the very goal theoretically sought—masses of new members—in practical terms proves disruptive and unsettling to the host community. In this sense, converts to Christianity in the fourth century were like immigrants to the United States in the nineteenth and twentieth centuries. In both cases, the newcomers raised questions of identity and loyalty which needed to be addressed and resolved.[74]

Although the internal struggles in Christianity during the fourth century have been long known and carefully studied, only in recent years have scholars come to appreciate how heretics and converts both had the similar effect of triggering a period of intense introspection, a period that resulted in a reinvention—and to a certain degree redefinition—of a less complicated past. One result of this process was a sharper delineation of Christian behavior, a stronger boundary between Christians and traditional society than had existed formerly, and with it a broadening of the number of activities that now became subject to Christian regulation. Collateral to the heresy debates was an increasing fear that a sizable number of converts were attracted as much by greater opportunities for the exercise of power which came with being Christian as by the message of repentance and salvation. Success, in other words, created a sense among many feeling Christians that their age had lost touch with the primitive faith of the church. The monastic movement and emphasis on ascetic practices which developed during this period represent one response to this felt need to regain touch with an earlier purity.[75] The dynamic relationship between heresy and conversion affected the progress of Christian thinking about the use of coercion.

Religious Migrants

Although artificial societies like the Christian community in most ways can be just as stable and durable as kin-based groups, they are less stable in one significant way: a birth requirement for membership places a natural check on the numbers of new members who will join a kin-based group in any generation, and it ensures a lengthy period of training and acculturation for those who do. But the size of an artificial group is, theoretically, limitless, and even the longest preliminary period of training and acculturation cannot come close in either quality or length of time to that provided by a kin group. In such communities, therefore, large numbers of newcomers are destabilizing under the best of conditions.[76] Reassuring evidence of the appeal and success of the message on the one hand, on the other the newcomers bring with them collateral habits and points of view that can clash with the values of the host community in inconvenient ways and create a sense of being overwhelmed by "foreign" and "subversive" elements. Just such an influx was one of the consequences of Constantine's policies. Constantine not only removed disincentives to conversion, but the favor and attention he showed the Christian community had the effect of making conversion fashionable, particularly among a leadership class whose antennae were always tuned to picking up what would and would not please those whose favors they sought. For reasons that are not difficult to imagine, the commitment of such converts was sometimes in doubt. No sooner had Constantine died than his biographer, Eusebius of Caesarea, began to complain about "the scandalous hypocrisy of those who crept into the Church, and assumed the name and character of Christians."[77] Later in the century, Augustine blamed the habits of his congregation in Hippo on the failure of bishops in the heady days of Constantine to enforce as strict a regimen on converts as they ought.[78]

There is reason to believe that the number of converts in the fourth century was not as great as either Christian comments or modern projections based on growth ratios would suggest.[79] But their absolute number is in this instance far less significant than the impression they made on the host community. The dissonance produced in Augustine by the difference between his ideal Christian norm and the reality he perceived around him typifies a complicated, and not entirely rational, process whereby over the course of the fourth century the very success of conversion increased pressure on converts on the one hand to demonstrate the sincerity of their conversion, and on congregations on the other to reconcile coercive measures with the traditional Christian principle that true belief can only be voluntary. Success also prompted considerable rethinking about the nature and meaning of Christian identity—about the boundaries of acceptable Christian behavior, as in Augustine's case, but also about exemplary Christian behavior, the behavior of overachievers. There is nothing like the quantity or quality of data needed to follow the process in detail, but two snapshots survive, taken at different points in the process, and these do allow at least some tentative observations.

The first is provided by Julius Firmicus Maternus, the same author whose treatise on astrology, *Mathesis,* mirrored Constantine's policies so faithfully (Chapter 6). About a decade later, Firmicus wrote *De errore profanarum religionum* (On the Error of Pagan Religions), in which he exhorted the emperors, Constantine's sons Constantius II and Constans, to destroy the temples, melt down the idols, and force pagans, if necessary, to abandon their ways, since it was better "that you free the unwilling than that you allow the willing to be ruined."[80] To bolster his case, Firmicus drew on a medical analogy well established in classical literature. Just as "those who are ill crave what is not good for them," Firmicus argued, so too, "there are those who refuse and reject [a religious cure] and are led by cupidity to desire their own death."[81] Christians were familiar with the medical analogy, but prior to Firmicus they had used it only for sick Christians, that is, heretics. Firmicus innovated not only by extending the analogy to cover non-Christians but also by combining it with the dire strictures of the Book of Exodus to create a powerful new argument, according to which, because of God's promise to destroy those who sacrifice "root and branch," "infected" pagans were a threat to others as well as themselves: "If the fearful penalty smote only the sacrilegious man, if the law's severity menaced only the sinner, he might well be confirmed in sacrilege by the rashness of his obstinate madness," Firmicus maintained; "but as it is, it menaces his line and posterity, and aims at leaving no portion of his most wicked seed, at seeing that no vestige of his unholy progeny shall remain."[82] In this way, Firmicus added the authority of the Hebrew Bible to the traditional community-based understanding of divine judgment which had provided the sanction for earlier persecutions of Christians (Chapter 3).

Christians were known to dabble in astrology despite the strictures of the church, but polytheistic references in *Mathesis* make it reasonably certain that Firmicus was still a pagan at the time he wrote that work, meaning that his conversion to Christianity must have occurred in the decade that separates these two books. In calling on the emperors to bring pagans to their senses by force, therefore, Firmicus might easily seem to be just one more proof that there is no zeal like a convert's, and thus his call for the suppression of variant belief apparently confirms the premise that Christian intolerance was the force that drove the coercive tide of this century. But chronology complicates the argument. Three laws against pagan practice survive from this period in the Theodosian Code. The first two are dated 341 and 343, the third either 346 or sometime in the mid-350s.[83] Firmicus certainly wrote after the first two of these laws, and probably after all three of them, which means that he was urging the emperors to take actions that were already under way. He was not blazing a trail, as is sometimes assumed, but following one that had been clearly laid out. Why?

The answer comes from similarities, rather than differences, between his two books. In both, for instance, Firmicus set a high standard of personal morality. In *Mathesis* he advised would-be astrologers to "be virtuous, honest, sober, content with modest food and goods, lest the desire of base fortune bring into disrepute the renown of this divine science," to live like priests, and never to give false witness, lend money at interest, or attend the games,[84] while in *De errore* he skewered the old gods for the example they set of licentiousness and immorality. In both books, thus, his moral sentiments accorded with those formally approved at court. More important, in both books he echoed what appeared to be prevailing imperial policy—for Constantine, a Divine Mind who protects the emperor; for his sons, the importance of suppressing pagan cult. It may be a mistake, therefore, to place overmuch weight on the vehemence and novelty of *De errore,* despite the change in tone, for Firmicus may well have written this book, like its predecessor, with no deeper purpose than the traditional one of members of his class: to curry favor with those who had patronage to dispense.

Firmicus seems, in other words, to be one of those new Christians brought into the faith by the opportunity for advancement. His path to conversion seems to have been precisely the one laid out by Constantine, through the celestial deities to perception of the Supreme Power and thence to Christ via the royal road of opportunity. But more had changed between the writing of these two books than Firmicus's religion. When he wrote the *Mathesis,* Firmicus addressed it in traditional fashion to a high-placed broker who he could hope would put his name in the emperor's ear. But much of the patronage that Romans like Firmicus coveted now flowed through the bishops, and the bishops, as we have seen, set a higher standard for converts than would have been sufficient for Constantine. *De errore,* then, would be the result of Firmicus's desire to demonstrate the sincerity of his conversion. Although it was addressed to the emperors, it was written, as was the *Mathesis,* for an intermediary, in this case his bishop.

There is an intriguing parallel with an author to whom Firmicus is frequently compared. Arnobius of Sicca wrote *Adversus nationes* (Against the Pagans) somewhere around the turn of the fourth century. Like Firmicus, he was a convert to Christianity, and like *De errore, Adversus nationes* is a vehement attack on paganism. Scholars have long seen a connection between the language of the two works, and it is fairly certain that Firmicus drew inspiration from the tract of his predecessor. Now the question is whether there is similarity on a deeper level as well. Like Firmicus, Arnobius had previously achieved distinction as an advocate for an alternative science, in his case not astrology but Neoplatonic philosophy. It has been argued that Arnobius wrote *Adversus nationes* not so much to attack paganism as to demonstrate to a doubting bishop that he had truly renounced Neoplatonism.[85] Arnobius converted before bishops had patronage to dispense. If there was need for him to provide some proof of his sincerity at a time when conversion to Christianity still had little promise of material benefits, then there certainly would have been a similar need for Firmicus to do so, for the seventh canon of the Council of Arles had obliged "those who wish to concern themselves with public affairs" to carry with them letters of commendation from their bishop.[86] It might therefore be best to read *De errore* as an exercise in self-exoneration, rather than as an expression of intolerance.

Still, the question remains why both Arnobius and Firmicus responded in the way they did. Each certainly had the skill and the capability to have provided a thoughtful demonstration of the similarities between their old and new beliefs, a reasoned exposition of the spiritual benefit they derived from Christianity which would also do justice to the values that had brought them to the faith. It thus becomes crucially important to the issue of coercion to understand why both instead responded with attacks instead of with love and understanding. Although the standard reason cannot be ruled out, neither should an important tactical consideration be ignored: it is always easier to prove a difference through contrast than through comparison, and the rhetorical training of the ancient curriculum would have equipped both men with a command of the forensic arsenal. Add to this rhetorical predisposition an atmosphere of suspicion and mistrust, and it is easy to see why for both men invective became the weapon of choice.

In other words, *De errore* may not reflect Christian intolerance so much as a confusion between zeal and aggression. Like Arnobius's *Adversus nationes, De errore* may thus reflect a defensive, rather than an offensive, tactic—then as now the best defense being a good offense. The aim in both cases was to prove that the author's old view had been abandoned, and attack was chosen as the means of doing so. In this instance, to renounce was to denounce.

Zeal provides the link to the second snapshot, which records events a little more than half a century after Firmicus wrote *De errore*. It occurs in the *Life of Porphyry, Bishop of Gaza,* the core of which appears to have been written by Porphyry's deacon, Mark, at some point after the bishop's death in 420.[87] Porphyry became bishop of Gaza in 395 and had to deal with a population that was not only still predominantly pagan but was, even at this late date, evidently not aware that it was supposed to be defeated. On his arrival, the residents of the neighboring villages filled the road to Gaza with thorns and brambles "and poured out filth, and made smoke of other evil-smelling things so that we were choked by the stench and went in peril of being blinded," according to Mark, who accompanied the new bishop.[88] Porphyry soon sent Mark on a mission to Constantinople, hoping to get the emperor, Arcadius, to order the demolition of Gaza's great temple of Marnas, a famous oracle. With the help of the bishop of Constantinople, Mark won the ear of Arcadius's chamberlain, Eutropius, and soon no less an official than Hilarius, the master of offices, was sent to Gaza with orders to overturn the idols. "But the temple of Marnas," Mark reports, "he suffered secretly to give oracles; for he received therefore a great sum of money."[89] What Mark attributes to corruption may in fact have been the emperor's bidding, for a later episode reveals that Arcadius did not share the bishop's zeal.

Frustrated by Hilarius's temporizing, Porphyry himself led a second embassy to the capital in the year 400. It was an uphill fight, because (Mark now admits) the emperor Arcadius himself was reluctant to disturb the peace of Gaza, whose pagan inhabitants paid good taxes.[90] Working through the empress, Eudoxia, Porphyry and his party devised an elaborate con, by which Arcadius was manipulated into consent through use of his newborn son, Theodosius II. By this time, Porphyry had learned that the choice of official to carry out the order was as important as the order itself, and this time he was determined to influence the selection. Mark writes, "But when the divine rescript was complete and signed, we besought the Lady [Empress Eudoxia] that the matter should be committed into the hands of some man among the nobles. And she bade [her chamberlain] Amantius seek out a man that was a zealous Christian, to whom it should be committed. For many of them which were in high places held the faith but in pretence; on whom the divine judgement came afterwards."[91] This time, the task was entrusted to Cynegius, "one of the consistory, an admirable man and fervent in the faith"—evidently the son of the prefect of that name who had rampaged through the East some fifteen years earlier.[92] With Cynegius in charge the great temple was indeed destroyed, an action that induced many of the pagans of Gaza to convert. But the reaction of Porphyry's congregation was mixed. While many rejoiced, Mark reports that "some of the believers also said unto the holy bishop that it behooved him to receive not those who came out of fear, but those whose purpose was good."[93] Evidently, enough traditional Christian sentiment persisted even at this late date for the new tactic to be unsettling to a number of Gaza's Christians. The reason for their complaint needs to be underlined. The congregation was not upset about the conversions, but about the means by which they had been accomplished—coercion. They were suffering a type of dissonance precisely because Christian teaching had been so clear and consistent up to this time in insisting that true belief could not be forced.

These anxieties were not new with Porphyry's congregation, nor were they by any means confined to it. Years earlier, the great pagan orator Libanius of Antioch had played on them in two separate orations. First, in a funeral oration for Julian, Libanius defended that emperor's efforts to revive paganism by pointing out that it rested on voluntarism. Julian, he claimed, "tried to win them [those who did not follow his example] by persuasion and refused the use of force" and "had a low opinion of those who had indulged in such practices [coercion], for they failed in their object, he thought, and he personally found no value in compulsion of this kind." Turning the medical analogy that was increasingly popular with Christian coercionists to his cause, Libanius explained:

Anyone suffering from a physical disease can be cured by putting him under restraint, but a false religious creed can never be eradicated by hacking and burning: even if a man's hand performs the sacrifice, his conscience reproaches him for it and condemns him for his bodily frailty attaching itself to the same objects of devotion as before. The result is a sort of illusion of change, not a real conversion of belief, and such people are either forgiven afterwards or, if put to death, are held in honour along with the gods they worship.[94]

A quarter century later, Libanius returned to this same theme when protesting attacks on pagan temples to the emperor Theodosius—the same speech cited in Chapter 7 for its conscious use of Christian arguments. Your advisers, Libanius warned Theodosius, may claim "that some other people have been converted by such measures and now share their religious beliefs." Do not be misled, he continued, for "they speak of conversions apparent, not real." "Their converts have not really been changed—they only say they have. This does not mean that they have exchanged one faith for another—only that this crew have been bamboozled. They go to their ceremonies, join their crowds, go everywhere where these do, but when they adopt an attitude of prayer, they either invoke no god at all or else they invoke the gods."[95] Libanius's choice of this rhetorical strategy was not random, nor should it be taken as mere coincidence that his addressee was a Christian emperor. He chose the argument deliberately, to force Christians to come to grips with, as he put it, "their very own rules."[96]

There are several layers of irony in the rhetoric of this period. Firmicus, now routinely cited as an example of Christianity's inherent intolerance, actually drew on pagan analogies to surgery and medicine for his argument, while Augustine, who blamed converts for practices to which he objected in his native church, readily accepted, and then refined for use by future Christian generations, the coercive tactics favored by pagan emperors. Role reversal thus is one of the processes of redefinition taking place during this period. It is reflected in the response that, according to Mark, Porphyry gave to his worried parishioners. "It is needful therefore, my children, that mankind be admonished by fear and threats and discipline," he said. "For even if they come doubting, time is able to soften their hearts, if Christ consent. But, that I may tell you yet another thing, even though they be not seen to be worthy of the faith, having been already in a state of evil, they that are born of them can be saved, by having converse with the good."[97] The new orthodoxy was born out of a decision fraught with perilous consequences: the end justifies the means.

The readings from these two snapshots are mixed. There are no signs that Firmicus was coerced to become a Christian, and despite his rhetoric there is every reason to believe that his calls for coercive action endorsed, rather than prompted, the laws of Constantius II and Constans. Porphyry, on the other hand, had to prod a reluctant emperor to act, and he only got his way by subterfuge. The success of his gambit alarmed as much as it pleased his congregation. Firmicus's zeal might have had an ulterior motive, but by the end of the century Porphyry had learned that success or failure of his plans depended on being provided with "a zealous Christian." Here is where the two portraits line up exactly: Firmicus seems to have urged coercive action in order to purge himself of suspicion, and Porphyry's biographer, Mark the deacon, clearly believed that less-than-zealous Christians were suspect. Both snapshots reflect the militant agenda; in both, people in the middle were getting squeezed.

Polarization

What the two snapshots reveal is a polarizing situation, one in which the broad middle ground on which most people like to stand shrinks to a thin line separating "right" from "wrong," "good" from "bad," "just" from "evil." Instead of a large gray area, there is only black or white, an either-or choice. When a situation becomes polarized, moderation makes one suspect. Thucydides had long ago described this scenario in his analysis of the degenerative effects of the war between Athens and Sparta, and his description remains a classic account of the effects of polarization. "In times of peace and prosperity," he wrote, "cities and individuals alike follow higher standards, because they are not forced into a situation where they have to do what they do not want to do. But war is a stern teacher; in depriving them of the power of easily satisfying their daily wants, it brings most people's minds down to the level of their actual circumstances." His account continues:

> To fit in with the change of events, words, too, had to change their usual meanings. What used to be described as a thoughtless act of aggression was now regarded as the courage one would expect to find in a party member; to think of the future and wait was merely another way of saying one was a coward; any idea of moderation was just an attempt to disguise one's unmanly character; ability to understand a question from all sides meant that one was totally unfitted for action. Fanatical enthusiasm was the mark of a real man, and to plot against an enemy behind his back was perfectly legitimate self-defence. Anyone who held violent opinions could always be trusted, and anyone who objected to them became a suspect. . . . If an opponent made a reasonable speech, the party in power, so far from giving it a generous reception, took every precaution to see that it had no practical effect.[98]

Thucydides' words are important in themselves, but they also caution against reading the polarization that occurred in the fourth century as unique, a product of Christianity's peculiar intolerance; they point instead to the more general effect of destabilizing conditions. As an organization, Christianity is neither more nor less intolerant than any other human organization, and neither more nor less vulnerable to the effects of destabilizing conditions and a polarizing discourse. The polarizing rhetoric of Christianity's internal battles helps to explain how moderate opinion became neutralized. Certainly Gregory of Nazianzen considered himself a victim of just such an environment, cast out from the bishopric of Constantinople "like ballast from an overloaded ship," because his "moderate sentiments proved a nuisance for the enemy."[99]

This is the point at which theology and sociology converge. The theological battles triggered by Arius resonated throughout the fourth century, producing ever more careful and sophisticated definitions of Christian belief. In a parallel process, conversions prompted new thinking about what it meant to be a Christian and a longing to reconnect with an unspoiled and innocent primitive church. The urge was already present in Eusebius's Church History, which blamed Diocletian's persecution on dissension and luxury, and in subsequent decades the monastic movement both inspired and was inspired by a sense of recommitment to the purer values of a simpler age. On both levels, the effect was to prompt new thinking about what was essential to Christianity, and the side effect was to raise and tighten the standard by which Christian performance was measured.[100]

Converts frequently became the pretext for instituting these reforms. When Augustine chided his parishioners for celebrating at gravesites like pagans, he may have been truly ignorant of this custom in the North African church and merely assumed it was new on the basis of his experience in Italy, which had different standards and traditions. But what is significant is that he defined the problem to his congregation as one that was created by converts, albeit converts of an earlier generation. Augustine's use of this pretext opens an important window onto the process whereby militants gained control of the definition of Christian values, for a by-product of this effort to establish ties with an idealized past was a reconstruction of that past as one of fortitude and resistance which resulted in a tightening of criteria, a raising of the threshold of Christian identity.

If Christians had to deal only with these internal disruptions, the outcome of this period of rethinking and redefinition might have been significantly different, for there is no reason to assume that a more militant, coercive church was the only possible, or even the most likely, result. But at just this time, a further, external development exacerbated the unsettled state of Christian affairs. In November 361, Constantine's nephew Julian, who had already risen in revolt, became emperor upon the death of his cousin Constantius II. He immediately launched an ambitious program to revive state-sponsored traditional religion. For the next nineteen months, Christians once again encountered an imperial government overtly hostile to their teachings and beliefs. Julian did not persecute, except in incidental ways—such as the torture Bishop Mark of Arethusa chose to endure rather than restore a temple he had destroyed.[101] But Julian did work to dismantle the state subsidies and privileges constructed by Constantine, while at the same time redirecting them to a new state religion consciously organized on a Christian model of hierarchical leadership and charitable practices. Articulate to a fault and highly educated in both Christian and traditional culture, Julian built his own "bully pulpit" from which he mercilessly lampooned Christians with uncomfortably accurate parodies.[102]

Christians were capable of bearing such affronts with dignity, and there were those among them who professed to be glad that state subsidies were ended, because Christianity was a faith that prospered in adversity.[103] But Julian took his campaign one step further, with a flamboyant revival of blood sacrifices, in which as many as one hundred cattle—the traditional hecatomb—were slaughtered at a time. By itself, the action was meaningless, no more than a schoolboy thumbing his nose at his teachers—even Julian's friends and sympathizers judged it a silly waste of meat.[104] But the symbolism could not have been more telling; in the political vernacular of the time, there was no more pointed way to signal an end to the Constantinian consensus than to revive a practice that for so many centuries had kept Christians from enjoying the fruits of public life. Julian's sacrifices were a calculated affront that symbolized not only the end of Constantine's compact with the bishops but also something darker, for no Christian could observe such services without calling to mind Diocletian, whose commitment to traditional religion sparked the terrorism that had ended a similar forty-year period of peace between Rome and Christianity.

The real heart of Constantine's compact with the bishops was not the patronage he provided; this served his interests as much as theirs and at most only sealed the compact. It was his commitment to remove such hindrances to full Christian participation in public life as blood sacrifices which lay at the heart of the compact—that, and the sense of security he managed to reinstate in a seriously traumatized community, quite possibly his greatest achievement. Although it is easy in retrospect to dismiss the brief reign of Julian as an aberration, and even to romanticize as heroic his efforts in a lost cause, he seems to have grasped the essence of his uncle's program better than any of his contemporaries. This insight accounts for the deep wounds he was able to inflict, despite a relatively short tenure. Christians at the time, moreover, had no assurance that another Julian was not in the offing, and they could plausibly fear that worse was yet to come. For those Christians who had never been comfortable with coexistence and who chafed under Constantinian restraints, Julian was a blessing, giving them a name and a face to attach to the amorphous enemy—in the words of Garth Fowden, "a single target to shoot at."[105] A quarter century after his death, Christians still spent as much time worrying about another Julian as they did rejoicing in the robust faith of Theodosius and his heirs.[106]

More significantly, Julian developed a litmus test that, for the first time, interposed ideology into the teaching of the classics. In June 362, Julian ruled that Christians were unfit to be teachers of the classical curriculum because they did not believe in the gods who inspired and filled out its pages.[107] As on all other issues, Christians had always been divided over their use of the classics. Tertullian uttered a classic cry in the second century, "What has Athens to do with Jerusalem?" But in the third century Origen had effectively argued that the classics were an important part of Christian education, if only so that the enemy might be refuted by his own weapons, and in the fourth Lactantius's systematic effort to reconcile Christianity with pagan thought shows that such efforts still were regarded favorably. The heresy battles of the fourth century subtly shifted this ground, with philosophy increasingly suspect as "the mother of heresy." But even as late as the middle of the century, as Robert Markus has observed, few Christians able to do so would have thought twice about sending their children to study the same curriculum as their pagan neighbors. Indeed, without the language, the looks, the innumerable coded signals that were absorbed unconsciously with classical *paideia,* Christian children simply would not have been able to compete in the elite culture of classical antiquity, as Julian knew full well.[108]

Julian did not, to be sure, prevent Christian children from attending the classes of pagan teachers, but this indulgence, if anything, only made the choice between God and Mammon even more evident to Christians already inclined to distrust traditional education. His regulations thus had the overall effect of driving a wedge between Christian belief and classical culture, thereby putting Christians steeped in this culture on the defensive in a way they had not been before.[109] It may be no coincidence that Basil of Caesarea subsequently wrote an elaborate justification for including the classics in Christian education. His treatise saved the classics for the Christian curriculum, but the mere need for such a work testifies to the degree of suspicion in which classical culture by then was held. Indeed, in his closing sentence, Basil warned his pupils to avoid the incurable sickness, "characteristic of the men of the present time," who intentionally avoided the help available from "those whose reasoning faculties are sound." Basil does not iden tify these lost souls, but in the context of his work Christians who were opposed to the use of the classics would be likely candidates.[110]

The effect of Julian's efforts was to polarize Christians and pagans, to remove the middle ground that traditional culture had previously provided, while at the same time lending credence to militant fears of a revival of persecution. Julian is by no means the entire answer to the puzzle of Christian coercion. But by acting out the heretofore unsub-stantiated fears of Christian militants, he gave credibility to their cause and in this sense strengthened the hand of those who insisted on extreme action. Hoping to revitalize traditional religion, he triggered dormant Christian insecurities and helped redefine both Christianity and paganism.

The Coercive Habit

Names locate: they fix a thing as good or bad, friend or foe. When something is given a name, that thing is also given an identity, and with identity, significance. Names can dignify; they can also debase. Julian knew a thing or two about the power of names, and he refused to dignify his opponents with their self-selected status of "Christians," a name that conceded a point about their founder's identity; instead, he regularly labeled them with the scornful toponymic *Galileans*. Chris-tians responded in kind. For centuries, they had chiefly used a generic denomination for the various beliefs of Greco-Roman antiquity, *Gen-tiles*. Borrowed from the Jews, the term signified "the nations," people who identified themselves by family or race, in contrast to the holy people united by their worship of God. In the period following Julian, a more derogatory term came into use, *paganus,* meaning liter-ally one who dwells in a *pagus*, or country district, with the additional, city-bred connotation of "hick" or "rube," now attached to followers of traditional religion because it was in those regions where its practice remained the strongest.[111] But once the term came into general use and became a label, it could be attached to all the miscellaneous baggage—real and imaginary—which Christians had collected to distinguish themselves from other beliefs. "Pagans" thus became not only idolaters and polytheists but also bloodthirsty worshipers of the infernal arts, slaves to passion and lust, necromancers and orgiasts. Their rites became by definition "superstitious"—evil and nefarious.[112] Thanks to this label, later ages needed no special justification for waves of persecution and pogrom.[113]

At the end of the century, middle-aged Christians and pagans alike lived in a world very different from the one in which they had grown up. Eunapius, author of a bitterly anti-Christian history, had learned from a Christian teacher, Chrysanthius, whom he continued to remember with great fondness. Even more instructive is the case of Victorinus, a celebrated pagan teacher who converted to Christianity and voluntarily relinquished his teaching post after Julian's ruling, even though the emperor personally promised to make an exception in his case. Victorinus's conversion was a principled one, and it came after many years of living comfortably with traditional beliefs that he felt were little different from those of his Christian students. Yet decades later, when Augustine looked back on this story, he could only picture it in battle terms, "as a dramatic renunciation of his pagan past and a painful break with the circle of his aristocratic friends." Robert Markus, who has observed this difference, concludes that "the image of a society neatly divided into 'Christian' and 'pagan' is the creation of late fourth-century Christians, and has been too readily taken at its face value by modern historians."[114]

Once thought of as the key to an ephemeral "pagan revival," Julian's actions now seem to have had the effect of reviving Christian fears and thereby strengthening the hand of rigorists and extremists. Ironically, Gibbon's last rationalist might be at least the proximate cause of the triumph of the intolerant Christianity that the philosophical historian so detested. The importance of Julian is that he brought into focus for the Christian community the weakness in the imperial system to which Tacitus centuries earlier had tried unsuccessfully to alert his fellow senators: How stable can a policy be when the whim of one man is sufficient to change it? Tacitus's voice went unheeded in part because by then senators were incapable of independent action. The difference in the fourth century was that the Christians, unlike the Senate, had the independence to resist.

It may be that in time the coercive forces in Christianity would have prevailed in any case, but it is possible now to identify conditions in the fourth century which made it easier for them to do so. Even though the outcome would still be the same, this shift in analysis means that, instead of taking coercion for granted as a natural outgrowth of Christian belief, attention can be paid to developments that allowed militants to gain the upper hand and thereby provide insight into how such transfers occur at other times and in other movements. Instead of seeing the coercion of the fourth century as the triumph of Christianity, in other words, it can be seen as the triumph of a particular kind of Christianity, a militant wing or faction.

That the theological battles of the fourth century were disruptive has always been evident, but a broader perspective shows how they were also destabilizing. This was Constantine's point in his letter to Arius and Alexander, and it has been confirmed in part by newer scholarship.[115] The conflict against heresy, however necessary, served to turn up the rhetoric and intensify Christian fear of "the enemy within." For the problem of coercion, the significance of the theological battles is that they began a process of polarization which was compounded by a simultaneous increase in the numbers of persons turning to Christianity. Suspicions about the sincerity of their commitment in turn encouraged converts like Firmicus Maternus to prove their faith by attacking their former belief. In these contests Christians shaped the tools, both rhetorical and physical, which a later generation would turn to use against paganism.

In this volatile situation, Julian—in so many ways Constantine's truest heir—set out to widen the gap his uncle had so skillfully narrowed, and he thereby strengthened the hand of those Christians who were already inclined to be suspicious of the pagan "other." It is the final irony in the study of this period: the man known to history as "the Apostate" is the surest guide to the goals and methods of the Constantinian consensus. As his argument to the pagan priest reveals, Julian adopted precisely the same latitudinarian standards that his uncle established for Christianity in his efforts to build a pagan analogue to the Christian movement. His negative actions are even more revealing.

Julian's flamboyant return to the practice of blood sacrifice and his efforts to deprive Christians of access to classical education reveal a keen understanding of the real heart of the Constantinian consensus, which was to remove obstacles to Christian participation in public life through creation of a religiously neutral public space.

As it had never been before, in the aftermath of Julian culture became a weapon for attacking moderates. It is this climate, rather than inherent Christian intolerance, which lies at the heart of the Christian turn to coercion, for it was "the peculiar ruthlessness of the insecure," in Peter Brown's striking phrase,[116] which gave credibility to the arguments of Christian militants. Instead of the fringe that Constantine had succeeded in making them, these militants now were able to cast themselves as "defenders of the faith." A subtler casualty of these events was a change in the climate of opinion. Revulsion at the excesses created by Diocletian's persecution had led to repudiation of the state as a means for enforcing belief. It is unlikely that Constantine thought of the repression of deviant Christian belief in the same light, since it was a policy that the bishops supported enthusiastically, but the unintended consequence of his decision to use the powers of the state to enforce orthodox belief was to erode the long-held Christian principle that belief could not be coerced, to restore the idea of the state as a means to create unity of belief. The polarizing rhetoric of the heresy debates, with its emphasis on the evil nature of opponents, helped restore coercion as a legitimate means of protecting the interests of the state.

Such are the social processes that contributed to the development of Christian coercion. But the story is still incomplete, for another perceptible difference between the Age of Constantine and his successors lies in the willingness of political authority to condone vigilante behavior. Where Constantine firmly closed the door on those Christians who were "saying the customs of the temples and the power of darkness have been taken away,"[117] little more than half a century later Theodosius I blinked in a celebrated confrontation over the burning of a synagogue on the Mesopotamian frontier and looked aside at the destruction of the Serapeum. Why this wavering resolve, with its predictable consequences? The nature of the relationship between firmness at the top and resolution at the bottom is uncertain and not easily calibrated. In this most delicate of all political dances, a single misstep can turn a noble desire to maintain the peace into the catalyst of revolution; but a different misstep can just as easily signal that restraints on vigilantism have been loosened.[118] This final dimension to the story of coercion is symbolized in the West by what has come down as a dramatic confrontation, resulting in victory for the independent moral authority of the church over the raw powers of the state. It occurred in Milan, when Ambrose was bishop and Theodosius I was emperor. But the issue, in fact, goes beyond the question of intolerance and is far older than the Christian religion; in it may be seen traces of the ancient political processes of legitimacy and patronage, and deepest of all the oldest rule of politics, "secure your political base." What it reveals, when all the layers of image and legend have been scoured clean, is the most enduring effect of the Age of Constantine: creation of a new source of imperial legitimacy, and with it a new constituency whose needs could no more be ignored than those of the imperial Senate in the Age of Augustus.

Twelve

Milan, 390

Visitors entering Room 13 of Vienna's Kunsthistorisches Museum, home of an impressive collection of works by the seventeenth-century Flemish master Peter Paul Rubens, cannot miss seeing a large canvas that hangs opposite the entryway. Its size alone, almost twelve feet by eight, is enough to attract attention. Even more, what engages the eye is the dramatic scene of men crowded around two central figures who stand confronting each other, evoking the curiosity that a good fight, or the prospect of one, always arouses. The two central figures on whom attention is focused stand on the steps of what evidently is a church; above, a cloud-strewn sky of lapis blue tells us that the event below is unfolding on Italian soil. Of these two figures, the one to the left obviously is a military man. Burly, with a round face and strong, black beard, he is clad in Roman armor and a cloak of imperial purple. Facing him, an equally strong and even more dominating figure, his flowing white beard, miter, and richly brocaded robe marking him just as obviously as a man of priestly office. It is this second figure who commands the eye, as much by his colors—gold and white amid predominant red, brown, and blue—as by his higher elevation on the stairs. Brows raised, his eyes implore the advancing officer. But his outstretched arm, gracefully but firmly placed to bar the way, does not waver as it restrains this powerful soldier's forward advance. No, it is the soldier's knee that is just beginning to crumble in involuntary genuflection, leaving the viewer in no doubt about the eventual outcome of this confrontation.

Recognition comes even before advancing close enough to read the title plate, both misleading and incomplete: "Emperor Theodosius Refused Entry into Milan Cathedral." Incomplete, because it leaves unidentified the figure who dominates the scene. This can be none other than the bishop of Milan, Ambrose, whose demand in A.D. 390 that Theodosius do penance for sanctioning the massacre of several thousand townsfolk in Thessalonica became a pivotal moment in the history of church and state in the West. The informal title of this work, "Ambrose and Theodosius," corrects the oversight. Misleading, in part, because of the way it depicts the major actors, here anachronistically displayed as emblems of church and state. In antiquity the emperor was the hieratic figure, a tradition that carried over into Christianity via the special role he assumed in regulating the church. In Eusebius's Tricennial Oration, it is the emperor who wears the rich brocades. A contemporary depiction of Theodosius on a silver plate shows him wearing the rich raiment and striking the beatific pose bestowed on Ambrose in Rubens' work, while a fifth-century mosaic of Ambrose in Milan's San Ambrogio Church shows a rather simple-looking man with hair and beard dark and short cropped in military fashion. Although crafted no more than fifty years after the bishop's death, the mosaic in the Chapel of St. Vittore in Ciel d'Oro is just as fanciful as the more imposing later renditions.[1] But it does show that the artist did not conceive of Ambrose in Old Testament dimensions. Rubens' portrait, thus, projects a seventeenth-century view. But there is a yet more important way in which the scene is misleading. Despite the vivid portrayal, the confrontation it depicts never occurred.

Like so many artists before him, Rubens took his inspiration from that medieval blockbuster Jacobus de Voragine's *Legenda aurea* (*Golden Legend*), a popularized narrative of the liturgical calendar written in the thirteenth century. There, under Ambrose's feast day, December 7, he would have read:

It is written in the *Tripartite History* that when the people of Thessalonica rebelled and slew certain officials, the Emperor Theodosius was so angry that he put all the citizens to the sword, to the number of about five thousand, without discerning the innocent from the guilty. But when later he came to Milan and wished to enter the church, Saint Ambrose met him at the door and enjoined him from entering, saying: "After such a crime, O Emperor, dost thou not see the enormity of thy presumption? Or is it that thine imperial estate blinds thee to thy sins? Thou art a ruler, Emperor, but like other men thou art the servant of God. How dost thou dare to lift hands to God that are yet stained with innocent blood? How dost thou dare to pray to God in His temple with the same lips that uttered an unjust and monstrous command? Withdraw, then, lest by a second sin thou aggravate the first. Accept the bonds which the Lord has placed upon thee, for they are the medicine that can cure thee!" And the emperor, weeping and groaning, retraced his steps to the palace.[2]

Theodosius did indeed do penance for the slaughter at Thessalonica—this much both Ambrose and his younger contemporary, Saint Augustine, confirm.[3] But neither say anything about access to the church being attempted and denied. Such confrontation as actually occurred, while equally significant, took place not on the steps of the cathedral but in carefully worded paragraphs that Ambrose sent the emperor from the prudent distance of his country estate, whence he had retired on receiving report of the tragedy. In this letter, Ambrose ever so gingerly raised the possibility of denying communion, reporting a dream in which he was "not allowed to offer the Holy Sacrifice" so long as Theodosius was in the church—and even considered these words so sensitive that he told the emperor he wrote them in his own hand (rather than dictating to secretaries) so that none but Theodosius would read them. But for the most part Ambrose drew inspiration from the hortatory tradition of courtly prose, urging Theodosius to listen not to his humble minister but to his own saintly conscience.

> I urge, I ask, I beg, I warn, for my grief is that you, who were a model of unheard-of piety, who had reached the apex of clemency, who would not allow the guilty to be in peril, are not now mourning that so many guiltless have perished. Although you waged battles most successfully, and were praiseworthy also in other respects, the apex of your deeds was always your

piety. The Devil envied you this, your most outstanding possession. Conquer him while you still have the means of doing so. . . . I among all other men, a debtor to your Piety, to whom I cannot be ungrateful, this piety which I discover in many emperors and match in only one, I, I say, have no charge of arrogance against you, but I do have one fear. I dare not offer the Holy Sacrifice if you intend to be present.[4]

Theodosius responded to this appeal by placing himself amid the penitents outside the cathedral, a self-inflicted punishment from which Ambrose relieved him, in what now appears to be a carefully crafted ceremony of damage control.[5] Shortly after this scene, Theodosius returned to Constantinople, and the incident might have been just one more page in the voluminous record of Ambrose's influence on the Western court had it not been embroidered into a more direct and dramatic confrontation, first by Ambrose himself, who used the fine print of his funeral oration for Theodosius to fix the scene as one of an emperor "who esteemed a reprover more than a flatterer," who "threw on the ground all the royal attire that he was wearing," and who "prayed for pardon with groans and with tears." The cue was taken up by Ambrose's biographer, Paulinus, and then by the church historians Sozomen and, especially, Theodoret about a half century later.[6] Their accounts interweave circumstances from an earlier encounter over destruction of a synagogue in the town of Callinicum, in far-off Mesopotamia. Here Ambrose did indeed boldly challenge the emperor, first with a letter that virtually threatened his order would not be obeyed, then with a confrontation at the altar which he described in a letter written subsequently to his sister, Marcellina. In this event, however, Ambrose's role was morally more ambiguous, since his aim was to dissuade Theodosius from punishing the rogue monks responsible for the fire and forcing the bishop of Callinicum to pay for rebuilding the synagogue. Indeed, the two encounters may well have been conflated by the later writers in order to eliminate such potentially compromising factors from what is otherwise an uplifting tale of Christian conscience confronting secular authority.

The event, then, is symbolic rather than real, and that is what makes the title of Rubens' painting prosaic as well as misleading. Rubens' version, completed probably in 1618, must be viewed next to a smaller copy produced two years later by his gifted pupil, Anthony Van Dyck—a feat that can only be accomplished with books, since the Van Dyck hangs some eight hundred miles away, in London's National Gallery.[7] Van Dyck's copy is, for him, unusually true to the original—as a rule, he preferred to find inspiration, rather than specific compositions, in his master's work. But there is a difference in overall impact. The Van Dyck is both more immediate and more confrontational, and closer inspection reveals changes in detail to explain the effect. The cathedral has shifted more into the scene, its dark stones obscuring most of that brilliant sky to call attention all the more relentlessly to the scene below. To the left, behind the emperor, the tips of weapons now intrude, just enough to emphasize the military might at his command. In the foreground, his chief retainer, presumably the army commander Timasius, is younger now; while he still stands defiantly with hand on hip, his posture has shifted subtly—shoulder raised, head flung back, palm open—the total effect somehow less military and more arrogant, even contemptuous of the priestly entourage he faces. There are similar touches on Ambrose's side. His little acolyte, now dark haired and in fuller figure, is more ethereal and angel-like, while the rest of the retinue (now including the unmistakable features of Antwerp's long-time burgomaster Nicholas Rockox) is both calmer and more determined than their counterparts in Rubens' original.

Finally, it is the faces that make the difference, the great portraitist emerging in this youthful work. Theodosius, though now beardless, is older, his face more wrinkled but also more patrician, more imperial (a bust of the emperor Galba is supposed to have been the inspiration). He looks up to the bishop from a tormented crouch, pain and anxiety both clearly visible in his features. In Ambrose, the changes are more subtle. He is frailer in body, and his face has lost the look of cherubic astonishment with which Rubens graced it, replaced by a leaner, more patriarchal visage. His eyes, sunken beneath a stern brow, promise eternal damnation. They, not the thin and stiffly outstretched arm, are what restrain Theodosius, who crumbles before them. Here, truly, is the triumph of the church, in all its spiritual dignity.

However many differences in the work of master and pupil, both stand in striking contrast to the fresco at the front of this book, showing Constantine sitting amid the bishops at Nicaea. Here the differences

Figs. 8–9. Ambrose and Theodosius: Two Views. The confrontation between Ambrose of Milan and Theodosius I came to be celebrated as a victory for the right of bishops to pass moral judgment on Roman emperors. Early in the seventeenth century, the great Flemish artist Peter Paul Rubens imagined the event in a painting that now hangs in Vienna's Kunsthistorisches Museum (fig. 8). A smaller copy by Rubens' pupil, Anthony Van Dyck, hangs in the National Gallery in London (fig. 9; *opposite*). Although they vary in detail, both paintings define a relationship between emperor and bishop which varies dramatically from the one symbolized by the image of Constantine at Nicaea in the frontispiece. (Kunsthistorisches Museum, Vienna)

are more than stylistic, and stunning in their implications. Where Theodosius stands in dread of a single bishop, Constantine sits in serene majesty amid a host of saints. Where the one supplicates, the other presides; where the one accepts, the other gives. In the compass of no more than a single lifetime, the relationship between bishop and emperor had been overturned—seemingly completely.[8]

This contrast brings out the real significance of the event depicted by Rubens and Van Dyck and the reason for musing on it here. It is a confrontation between armed might and moral strength, *potestas* and *auctoritas*. Its true title should be "Allegory of Church and State"; or, better, "Western Civilization," for truly what happened in this confrontation, whether it occurred on the steps of a cathedral or in the graceful periods of courtly rhetoric, was that at this moment the theoretical restraints on absolute power developed through centuries of ancient philosophy and rhetoric found both voice and teeth in the institution of the Christian bishop. Fittingly, then, a study that began with consideration of one conflict between an emperor and a bishop comes to an end with deliberation on another. Fittingly in another sense as well, for despite the obvious correlation between the shift in relative power of bishop and emperor portrayed in these two events and the growing use of force by Christians to compel adherence to their belief, the two events do not point to inherent intolerance as the explanation for that use of force but to older and deeper processes that justify thinking of Christian coercion as a political, rather than a theological, issue.

Emperor and Bishop

It is a pity that no Rubens ever felt inspired to translate to canvas that other confrontation some half century earlier with which this book began, in which another bishop "spoke painful words" to a Roman emperor, the confrontation between Athanasius and Constantine in 335. "The Lord will judge between me and you," we are told Athanasius said, "since you yourself agree with those who calumniate your humble servant." It is hard now to capture the effrontery in those words, spoken to an emperor brought by tradition and his own convictions to believe that he was the conduit between divine and mortal, the living voice of God on this earth. The two events seem made as a mirror image to each other, for just as Ambrose here brings a mighty emperor to his knees, then it was the patriarch who publicly humbled himself before the emperor to beseech an audience, and at that time the threat of divine judgment did not lead to remorse from the emperor but immediate exile for the bishop.

How would Rubens have captured this setting? It calls for a darker scene to be sure, with subtle shades of gray replacing the play of light and color in the Milan confrontation. A rotunda room, perhaps, an ironic echo of the Church of the Holy Apostles soon to be Constantine's burial sepulchre, the shadows of its circled columns the perfect lurking place for the accusers, watching with varying degrees of admiration, shock, and loathing as a radiant Athanasius, bathed in the light of God's own truth, asserts the spiritual authority of his office. Certainly that is how Athanasius would have painted it: "Angry as the emperor was, Pope Athanasius spoke painful words to him." Rubens would have had no interest in digging further. But what about Constantine— a tyrant red with apoplexy, caught in the moment of rising from his curule chair, borrowing the explosive personality of Valentinian, who later in the century would burst a blood vessel shouting at impertinent German emissaries? Risky. Constantine's image had suffered at the hands of the Reformers by Rubens' day, but he was still the first Christian emperor, a man who had felt God's touch. Constantine would need the sensitivities of a Van Dyck to capture the war of emotions which reigned at that moment in his heart, as he saw his cherished dream of unity and concord shatter against the adamant will of the bishop of Alexandria.

For this event the Flemish artists would have found a more complex story, and a less sure guide. Athanasius pops up here and there in Jacobus, always in circumstances that assume great prestige and respect. But the calendar Jacobus followed was laid down in Rome and consciously articulated to stress the primacy of the Holy See. Jacobus assigns no reading to the Alexandrian saint. Constantine, however, proliferates. He appears on a good half dozen separate days, always as the pious emperor who feared God. In addition, an inspiring account of his Vision of the Cross occurs on May 3, in the lengthy legend of his mother Helena's discovery of the true cross, and an equally uplifting description is given of his baptism, which the Roman calendar assigns with chronological insouciance to Pope Sylvester (December 31). How would Van Dyck have rendered a holy emperor and an impudent bishop? More important, would he have thought to juxtapose these two events so as to bring out the massive realignment that they signify, not just in the relative dignity of emperor and bishop, or even in the relative strength of Christianity and paganism, but most of all within Christianity itself, from a religion firmly grounded in the principle that true belief could not be coerced to one whose prelates freely interfered with the emperor's basic duty to provide security for all his subjects?

Perhaps it is just as well that this canvas lies unpainted by either of these great portraitists, for the two episodes with which this book begins and ends frame a problem at once too evanescent and too pedestrian for the artist's palette: not just the dramatic reversal in relative strength of emperor and bishop suggested by the very different outcomes of these two confrontations but also the complex series of events whereby a religion whose core values teach followers to love their enemies adopted for its own ends the same coercive powers under which it had itself suffered for three centuries; and, finally, the many layers of prejudice and assumption so encrusting the subject that they leave what on the surface appears to be but one explanation for these two very different processes. Yet surface impressions are often misleading.

It is the artist's special gift to find meaning in a moment, eternity in a gesture. Complex events do not lend themselves to such treatment; they require an eye for pattern rather than gesture, attention to shifts in the composition of each chronological layer. Such interpretation is the historian's art. It calls for a different temperament and different tools. The historian's palette holds not colors and brushes but solvents and scrapers. Where artists create their vision by adding shades of line and color, the historian's discoveries come through the patient peeling of layers of lamina. What historian, for instance, would not finish this imaginary painting without giving prominent space to another bishop, frail and scholarly, feverishly composing in the shadows a volume whose initial letters can just be made out: *Vita Constant . . .* ?

Eusebius of Caesarea writes nothing of this confrontation, although he was present, but his essay *De vita Constantini* put down the first of all the countless films with which historians have glossed this emperor's career over the ages—the first, and the hardest to peel off without removing the basic lines. For—not to belabor the image—Eusebius's influence lies more in the way he prepared the canvas than in the colors he used. While all those who would study this period must first come to grips with Eusebius, most have gone haring off in the wrong direction, taking issue with the accuracy of particular statements or the purity of Eusebius's motives. These are important topics, to be sure, but it is Eusebius's overall, guiding assumptions—blending Christian and monotheist, Constantine's goals and those of Christianity, Christianity and "the church"—which have had the most influence, for these so pervade his writing, have become such a predominant part of the subsequent mind-set, that they are as difficult to see as the transparent Italian air with which Rubens suffused his greatest works.

Christian Coercion

There is much Eusebius has to tell about the Age of Constantine—some willingly, some less so. It is possible to read Eusebius's *vita Constantini,* and even more his Tricennial Oration, as the beginning of an age-long struggle to define the role of the emperor in the church; it is also possible to see in the difference between these two works the first signs of resistance to the relatively low threshold for Christian identity which Constantine advocated, the tartness of Eusebius's comments about false Christians in the former work differing markedly from the expansive inclusiveness that he professed in Constantine's presence in the latter.[9]

Regarding the question of coercion, however, it is best to take leave of the bishop of Caesarea. Perhaps to protect the emperor from disgruntled militants, perhaps to capture his name for a separate agenda, Eusebius omitted non-Christian monotheists from Constantine's record and presented the emperor's police actions and confiscations of temple treasures—all actions with solid precedent in the acts of pagan emperors—as novelties that followed directly from Constantine's conversion, a frontal assault on all vestiges of traditional belief. In so doing, Eusebius overlaid Constantine's policies with a black-and-white definition of Christianity and paganism which only in recent decades has yielded to historical scrapers, revealing a vibrant and multicolored landscape, nourished by a universal revulsion at the excesses of Diocletian's persecution, all of which in turn make the moderate and inclusionist policy for Constantine outlined in these pages not only plausible but imperative. The success of this policy, in turn, gives renewed urgency to the search for an explanation for Christian coercion. For generations, the answer has seemed self-evident: intolerance is natural to Christianity, which teaches its believers to reject the existence of other gods. The answer is not so much wrong as inadequate, a relic of ancient hatreds. It confuses intolerance with exclusivism, and both with coercion, a separate process altogether, and it fails entirely to account for the great commandment of Christianity to return evil with good, hatred with love.

It is often wryly said that some topics are too important to be left to the social scientists. Perhaps intolerance is one of those, best left to the poets and tale spinners. The humorist Russell Baker once noted, for instance, that "when political sects have been too long in office they start believing they know what is good for you."[10] It would be nice if the whole problem of Christian intolerance were to boil down to nothing more than a religious variant of this political truism. But more needs to be explained. Why in one and the same group does intolerance at some times prevail, while at others it gives way to more latitudinarian sentiments? A novelist, Mary McCarthy, points the way to an answer. Musing over her childhood and the impact of her Catholic upbringing, McCarthy delineated "two distinct strains" in her background:

> There was the Catholicism I learned from my mother and from the simple parish priests and nuns in Minneapolis, which was, on the whole, a religion of beauty and goodness, however imperfectly realized. Then there was the Catholicism practiced in my grandmother McCarthy's parlor and in the home that was made for us down the street—a sour, baleful doctrine in which old hates and rancors had been stewing for generations, with ignorance proudly stirring the pot.[11]

With these few words, McCarthy calls to mind a simple truth easily overlooked in the abstract study of causality: mass movements are made up of people, as well as ideas. Her memories are the right place to begin thinking about Christian intolerance. Faiths are not intolerant;

people are intolerant. No matter the movement, no matter the ideology, the Grandmother McCarthys of this world are always there, sitting in their parlors, waiting for the right conditions to impose their baleful doctrines on their neighbors. But so, too, are the dedicated souls of McCarthy's "religion of beauty and goodness." Is it right to say that the one must prevail, the other fail? That one is more "Christian" than the other?

Hindsight is such a treacherous lens, luring more than one historian into disaster with the false clarity it affords. Certainly there is something in the notion that Christians were more rigid and unyielding in their beliefs than worshipers of the old gods. But such attitudes do not by themselves lead to coercion. When Jesus sent out the apostles, he told them to do no more than shake from their sandals the dust of towns that did not accept their teaching. Indeed, in the same commission, he warned his followers not to persecute but to expect persecution as their lot: "Behold, I send you out as sheep in the midst of wolves."[12] It is equally reasonable to say that there was always room for one more god in the ancient system; but to say this is not to say that the state religion of old Rome was "tolerant." If pagans did not preach compulsion, that was only because there was nothing to compel—the belief system shared by all peoples of their empire was polytheistic, with local variations only in the names of particular deities and the specifics of particular practices.[13] All but the Jews were easily able to find a way to express fealty to Rome in the existing pattern of their worship, and the Jews shared with pagans a tradition of blood sacrifice which allowed them the option to honor Rome in a way that Christians could not. Once Caesar had worked out a compromise whereby Jews pledged to sacrifice to their deity on behalf of Rome, they could safely be regarded as just another nationality in the Roman system, and they remained so even after destruction of the temple in the year 70. Christianity, as an artificial community that defined kinship on the basis of belief, attracted a more heterogeneous membership and in so doing threatened the established order.

Power, not theology, is the constant. By reminding us that intolerance is a human trait that will show up in any movement large enough to attract more than one type of human being, McCarthy's two types of Catholicism bring to the fore the real challenge of studying

Christian coercion, which is to identify the conditions that allow the views of those among us stewing with "old hates and rancors" to prevail. That is the challenge: to isolate the conditions that nourish this type of human behavior and allow it to prevail.

Alternative Histories

Here is an "if" history question: suppose there had been no persecutions. What would have been the effect on the Christian movement? The apologists, we may assume, would still have emerged as spokesmen for Christian beliefs, for even without the need to appeal to emperors for toleration, the urge to spread the good news of Christ's resurrection still would have led to outreach and efforts to make the Christian message coherent and attractive to the dominant culture. The Christian communities also would still likely have organized themselves along the same lines and created the same networks of interdependence, since all these arose to meet needs little related to the attitude of Roman government, though it might be expected that the powers of the bishops would have been less extensive and the ties between the different local communities looser without the need to unite against an external threat. The biggest difference would have been in the role of the martyrs. Presumably, the urge to bear witness and to replicate Christ's agony would still have called forth individuals with the ability to make a spectacular effort of commitment, but if for no other reason than that opportunities to testify would have been fewer, this energy would have to have been channeled into different forms of expression, less disruptive and confrontational than the show trials of the second and third centuries. Perhaps it would have gone into the forms of monachism which came into vogue with the end of persecution after Constantine.

What about coercion? If the scars carved into the Christian psyche by living three centuries in the shadow of pogrom were absent, might coercion have been a less likely outcome of Christian rulership? Like all "if" history questions, the aim of this one is not to create an imaginary universe, or to pose questions impossible to resolve, but to direct attention to alternative ways of formulating traditional questions. The direction of this "if" history question is to consider the subject of

Christian coercion in the broader context of the Roman state and the Christian community. What it points to is the significance of Constantine's choice of an inclusive and noncoercive Christianity. Without the success of this policy, it would be an easy matter to turn the question of Christian coercion into a variant of the heredity-versus-environment argument: Christians might not have been inherently coercive, but the paranoia induced by centuries of oppression created in them a predisposition toward militant action, leaving them thirsting for revenge, their voices (in Arnaldo Momigliano's memorable phrase) "shrill with implacable hatred."[14] But the success of Constantine's actions shows that despite all the persecutions of the preceding centuries, the tradition of love and forbearance continued to exert a powerful hold over the Christian psyche in the early fourth century.

So what this "if" history question primarily reveals is the importance of the period of roughly fifty years which separates the two events with which this book opens and closes. The previous chapter explored some of the changes during this dynamic half century which help explain why Christians abandoned a longstanding commitment to the principle that true belief cannot be compelled, and it offered an explanation of the turn to coercion based on social, political, and institutional factors rather than inherent predisposition: episcopal rivalries, the destabilizing effects of rapid growth, and, finally, Julian's calculated effort to undermine the Constantinian consensus, which only fed Christian fears of attack from within and without and thereby strengthened the hand of Christian militants. But, while shifting the focus from theology to organization, that chapter still leaves attention where it has always been: on Christianity as the sole determinant in a tragic and now only slightly more edifying tale. This study is no apologia for Christian belief or behavior; even with the more general conditions exposed by attention to the dynamics of groups and movements, there remains much in these pages for Christians to confront and ponder. But is it still possible for even the most jaundiced player of the blame game blithely to argue that the Greco-Roman world knew nothing of intolerance before Christianity appeared in its midst, that this was the new thing Christian faith brought? The story of Ambrose and Theodosius may yet be most misleading in its Christian dimension, for where on the surface there would seem to be only more evidence of the steady progress of intolerance over compromise, of rigid bishop over pliant emperor, of church over state, the most important message of this story lies beneath the confrontation that meant so much to later ages.

Let us consider another, though less conscious, attempt at "if" history: What if the Roman Empire had converted to Christianity a century and a half earlier, under Marcus Aurelius instead of under Constantine? This is precisely the question John Stuart Mill posed for himself in a statement used as an epigraph to this book. "It is a bitter thought," Mill wrote, "how different a thing the Christianity of the world might have been, if the Christian faith had been adopted as the religion of the empire under the auspices of Marcus Aurelius instead of those of Constantine."[15] The statement comes from Mill's classic defense of the rights of the individual, *On Liberty,* published in 1859, the heyday of Victorian liberalism. Mill himself was both a product and a shining light of that complex mixture of faith and doubt which constituted Victorian optimism. The son of an ardent Benthamite, Mill was taught to subject all aspects of human activity to the rigid criteria of utilitarianism, an education that led him, in 1826, to an almost complete mental and emotional breakdown. The man who emerged from that moment of profound crisis became one of the most vigorous and lucid advocates for the freedom of speech and action in the history of Western thought.

At the point in his argument where he invoked the philosopher-king, Mill was building the case that liberty of thought and speech must be extended even to beliefs that the wisest minds of the day condemn. What ruler, he asks, was ever wiser than Marcus Aurelius, the philosopher-king? Yet Marcus deemed Christianity both immoral and blasphemous, as indeed it was according to the established opinion of his day, and so condoned the persecution of Christians. This is the point at which Mill gives voice to his "bitter thought." In choosing Marcus Aurelius as his optimal champion of Christian belief, Mill was thus able to score two points at once, simultaneously forgiving Marcus for the torture of innocents while also holding him up as a shining light of what Christianity might have been.

Mill's thoughts about Constantine must be inferred, because unlike Marcus Constantine does not figure into the preceding paragraphs, and Mill has nothing to say about the first Christian emperor after this one comment. Obviously, Mill meant him as a contrast to the philosopher-king, and a negative one at that. But in what way? The only hint lies a few pages earlier, where Mill refers to the Roman Catholic Church as "the most intolerant of churches."[16] Presumably, in his mind, Constantine played a part in this outcome, whereas Aurelius might have prevented it.

In making this decision, Mill was acting on the most informed opinion of his day. A few years later, his younger contemporary Matthew Arnold published an influential essay on Marcus Aurelius, "the ruler of the grandest of empires and . . . one of the best of men," in which he echoed Mill's thought.[17] A friend of Thomas Carlyle's, Mill was familiar with the then fashionable theory of the Great Man, the individual whose will was so attuned to the spirit of the age that he single-handedly made history turn. Mill also certainly carried in his head Gibbon's picture of decline and fall, according to which the philosopher-emperor had presided over "the period in the history of the world, during which the condition of the human race was most happy and prosperous," whereas Constantine, by contrast, was thrown up during an age of barbarism and superstition which destroyed the glory and grandeur of classical civilization.[18]

Personality made it an easy image to project. Where Marcus struggled to keep even the most sensitive human emotions under the strict control of his philosophy, Constantine gave vent to rage and violence even in his legislation. Christianity, moreover, had been a negligible religion when the empire was at its height and only became the dominant religion after a century of upheaval and decline, during which newer races and cruder classes came into their own; with such a correlation, it was a simple matter to identify the one as the cause of the other, especially since by the nineteenth century Christianity had been identified as the prime obstacle to the science in which enlightened gentlemen so fervently believed. Nor was there any reason to doubt that coercion was inevitable once Christianity gained the upper hand, given the intolerance of other beliefs which lay at the core of its being. All of this was part and parcel of the reinventing of the ancient world which took place with the Enlightenment. In his little foray into "if" history, therefore, Mill could plausibly believe that the conversion of a persecuting emperor would have resulted in a more reasonable and established Christianity than the one recognized by an emperor who renounced persecution as a tool of religious policy. The ease with which so systematic a thinker as Mill could put forward such a patently contradictory thesis testifies to the strength of Gibbon's blame-the-victim analysis.

This is not a premise that our age can take too seriously; another work, published in the same year as *On Liberty,* explains why. Charles Darwin's *Origin of Species* set off fireworks with its implications that a biblical understanding of life was insufficient. The echoes of that conflict still resonate, but beneath the smoke and bluster it raised is the primary point of Darwin's study, which is that species evolve gradually, over time. Along with the social sciences that developed during this same period, Darwin's concept of evolution helped to ground the modern psyche in the premise of a world that is constantly changing, though in ways that often are perceptible only over long periods.[19] Sudden, violent revolutions, the product of a single Great Man, are less congenial to the post-Darwinian age than is the concept of change that moves like glaciers, imperceptibly over centuries. Understanding change as the product of events of such long duration, longer sometimes than the lifetimes of entire species, our age finds it difficult to make so much depend on a single individual and equally difficult to adopt the static definitions of those rigid and unchanging Christians and pagans who peopled Gibbon's imagination. Gibbon's concept of a single, normative Christian opposed to a single, normative pagan allowed him to picture Christianity as an eternally foreign substance, a virus implanted in the Roman Empire which could grow robust only at the expense of its host. To post-Darwin eyes, Christians and pagans seem more in flux, constantly interacting, learning from each other, both changing and being changed by broader forces, including a growth in other-worldly concerns which was well under way during the high empire, forces of which Christianity was as much a product as a cause. To such eyes, the clash between Ambrose and Theodosius cannot seem more than part of a very long tale.

Those who study other periods of religious strife have also had to come to grips with the problem of intolerance. To Reformation scholars, it once seemed self-evident that Protestants were the tolerant side, because of the Protestant emphasis on the importance of individual judgment. Although the reason differs from the one Gibbon gave for polytheists, it smacks of the same theoretical and a priori reasoning, and like Gibbon's it flies in the face of abundant counterevidence. Far more decisive than sect, it now appears, was size: regardless of denomination, Catholic or Protestant, wherever a group was sufficiently dominant enough to do so, it sought to impose its will by force—a phenomenon so consistent that at least one scholar has labeled toleration in this period a "loser's creed."[20] There was something to Augustine's reasoning, therefore, when he scoffed at a correspondent's plea for moderation with the gibe, "You say you do not wish to act cruelly; I think you are not able. You are so few in number that you would not dare to act against opponents who are more numerous than you, even if you wished."[21] But explanations based on such calculations ignore the importance people attach to a just cause, their need to feel their leaders are "playing by the rules." Augustine himself put it best in his oft-quoted question, "Without justice, what are governments except great robberies?"[22]

To avoid these pitfalls, Peter Kaufman has ignored traditional denominational categories and divided the religious strategies of the Reformers along the lines of what he calls "redeeming politics," the sense that salvation is a community responsibility.[23] This view of the state as the instrument of a divine plan is what another Reformation scholar, Bob Scribner, had in mind when he wrote of a "moralised universe" that underlay sixteenth-century persecutions, "the view that individual or collective deviance could call down divine punishment on the community as a whole."[24] Kaufman aptly dubs this political theology "Constantine's shadow," in recognition of the example set by the first Christian emperor. Such are the insights that can flow from peeping around the chronological boundaries that normally separate the scholarship of one period from that of another. In identifying a concept that had its origins long before the Reformation, and was largely untouched by it, Kaufman allows a more nuanced understanding of the problem of coercion than was possible using the old categories of "Catholic" and "Protestant." But if he had peeped further, Kaufman would have seen that Constantine labored as much under this particular shadow as did his successors. The idea of the state as a religious community does not originate in the fourth century; its reach is much further, as far back as the origins of the ancient state in the cult of the gods. It is the reason no ancient state could easily separate religious from political issues.

Still, this widespread belief, shared by pagans and Christians alike in that age, that divinity was active in human affairs, that god or the gods intervened regularly in the day-to-day operation of ordinary life, is the place to begin an explanation of Christian use of coercion in the fourth century, for it constitutes the deepest of underlying causes and the biggest break between modern and ancient thinking. The ancient state was built on the premise that organized human activity was needed to ensure that this potent force remained benevolent to the community. Intellectually and in the abstract, this distinction is easy enough to grasp, but it is just as easy to forget when assessing particular developments.

A case in point is the desert solitaries of this period of Christian history who formed the backbone of the burgeoning movement into monastic life. A few years after Mill and Darwin, a twenty-seven-year-old prodigy, William Lecky, published *The Rise and Influence of Rationalism in Europe,* in which he held up the "merciless fanaticism" of the desert monks as the antithesis to everything rational:

> Abandoning every tie of home and friendship, discarding all the luxuries and most of what are deemed the necessaries of life, scourging and macerating their bodies, living in filth and loneliness and desolation, wandering half-starved and half-naked through the deserts with the wild beasts for their only companions, the early monks almost extinguished every natural sentiment, and emancipated themselves as far as possible from the conditions of humanity. . . . They had learned to embrace misery with a passionate love. They enjoyed a ghastly pleasure in multiplying forms of loathsome penance, and in trampling upon every natural desire.[25]

The monks and holy men who populate the landscape of the late Roman world were, in Lecky's view, living proof of how far Rome had fallen from its classical pinnacle and thus proof as well of the role of Christianity in that decline. Lecky's judgments resonated with his age. *Rationalism* was an instant best-seller, reprinted twenty times over the course of the subsequent half century. In more prosaic form, his thinking survives in those textbooks still being written which blame Christianity and the monastic movement for draining money, manpower, and imperial energies at a time when all three were desperately needed to shore up defenses against barbarian invaders. The premise behind such reasoning is that religion is nice but God alone does not win wars; so "praise the Lord and pass the ammunition." But does this premise hold for an age that believed God did win wars, and thought it had the evidence to prove it?

Daniel the Stylite

Daniel the Stylite (409–93) was one of those solitaries whom Lecky had in mind. Living more than thirty years confined within the space of a small platform, perched atop a pillar some sixty feet off the ground on which he stood day and night, his body oozing with sores and broken by neglect, Daniel easily seems to embody the sad decay brought on by that scorn for all things physical which Christianity engendered. Moreover, his life, written shortly after his death by one of his disciples, includes an account that, on the surface, confirms these modern assessments. It is the story of Titus, a Gallic general of the emperor Leo (457–74) who, when sent to Daniel on some mission, was so impressed by what he saw that he resigned his commission and opted to stay with the saint. In desperation, Leo begged Daniel to return an officer whose presence on the front lines was badly needed, but Daniel was deaf to this plea, and Titus died soon after while striving to emulate the saint, having jury-rigged a device that would allow him to hang suspended by his armpits from a ceiling beam and trying to live on a diet of three figs a day until "it pleased the Lord to call him while he was at prayer."[26] Thus, on one level, the story of Titus is that of an important and useful officer whose life was needlessly wasted in the pursuit of "merciless fanaticism."

Below the surface is a different and far more insightful story. The Christian community defined itself by its holy men. Where Lecky saw a community mired in superstition and fanaticism, contemporaries saw individuals who had shaped themselves by dint of a lifetime of self-denial into conduits for the divine, models of Christian indifference to the physical realm, living icons who could deliver God's judgment with instant, and sometimes fearful, authority. Much insight can be gained by comparing holy men like Daniel with Plato's philosopher-king—an exercise that would have revolted and bewildered Lecky's generation. Yet for all their apparent differences, holy men spurned material needs, just as the philosopher-king was supposed to do; they devoted themselves to a long and arduous training process, and they had learned to order their lives according to eternal principles rather than passing fashions. Like philosopher-kings, they sacrificed their personal good, which consisted in contemplating divine mysteries, in order to help fellow dwellers in this mortal cave. Indeed, the only difference between the two is that a Christian philosopher-king came to these eternal verities through spiritual, rather than rational, discipline. A defining difference to Lecky, and perhaps also to us; but what contemporaries saw as they raised their eyes reverently to Daniel, begging him to spare them time from his heavenly vigil, was a living beacon to the unchanging verities of the stars.

Titus clearly was an ambitious officer, upwardly mobile, an overachiever. What he observed in Daniel was great spirituality, to be sure, but also great power, a power such as made even the emperor's pale in comparison. It was a power that drew people from throughout the Eastern provinces and beyond to seek aid, counsel, and advice from a man who had proved his superiority to the needs of this world, and in so doing had brought himself that much closer to the unseen power of the universe. Titus spent his time with Daniel spying on the saint to discover his secret and trying to outdo him in spectacular acts of self-mortification. He died because he was too impatient to follow the saint's surprisingly rational advice to proceed gradually and not push his body beyond what it was prepared to endure.

Although a modern story would end with Leo's complaint that he needed Titus in the army, the point in Daniel's Life is not the emperor's request but Daniel's reply:

> And the holy man sent a letter of counsel by them to the Emperor, beseeching him and saying, "You yourself need no human aid; for owing to your perfect faith in God you have God as your everlasting defender; do not therefore covet a man who to-day is and tomorrow is not; for the Lord doeth all things according to His will. Therefore, dedicate thy servant to God Who

is able to send your Piety in his stead another still braver and more useful; without your approval I never wished to do anything."

Leo, the story continues, "was satisfied and sent and thanked the holy man and said, 'To crown all your good deeds there yet remained this good thing for you to do. Let the man, then, remain under your authority, and may God accept his good purpose.'" To a modern ear, these words may seem to confirm the skewed priorities of a superstitious age. But Leo held the Eastern empire together at a time when the West was crumbling, and both he and his contemporaries attributed his success to the reverence he paid holy men like Daniel.

Modern scholars have developed yet a third way of seeing these holy men. Shunning both Lecky's cultural absolutes and contemporaries' fixation on those dramatic moments when holy men confronted the demons, this scholarship has focused on the ability of these individuals to act as mediators of those conflicts large and small which punctuated the routine of late antique life, and to do so precisely because of their regimen of self-denial, which proved their indifference not only to physical needs but even more to considerations of pride, prestige, and power. This indifference immediately set holy men apart in a society where influence peddling had been developed into a high art form. It has even been suggested that the glue holy men provided for the fabric of a society increasingly dominated by *potentiores*— "malefactors of great wealth," to use a more recent phrase—helped hold the Eastern empire together as the provinces in the West crumbled, giving a suitably social scientific explanation for what the ancients, as Leo's response to Daniel shows, already knew.[27]

Because divine support was deemed crucial to success, the potential for religious issues to drive policy was always present in the ancient world. Augustus assiduously cultivated the goodwill of the gods, particularly Apollo, and even in Gibbon's celebrated Golden Age imperial ideology was ready to attribute military success as much to the piety as the military prowess of the emperor.[28] As the importance of the emperor's ties to a potent deity increased in the third century, it followed that maintaining the goodwill of that deity constituted a matter of what today would be called national security—a form of thinking which helps explain the outbreak of empirewide persecutions of Christians in that century. When emperors became Christian, they continued to be exalted, hieratic figures with an acknowledged right, and duty, to involve themselves in religious matters, and they continued to need an institutional arena for enacting those rituals of mutual affirmation and support by which emperor and elites projected the legitimacy of their privilege to army and people. Continuities with the past, therefore, are as much a part of the explanation of Christian coercion as the changes wrought by Constantine.

By showing continuities that underlie the premodern worldview, this understanding of the way prayer could be an important part of "national security" helps avoid many of the mistakes that flow from a division of the world into "Christian" and "pagan" or "Protestant" and "Catholic." But simply because this worldview was so prevalent and so long-lasting, it is of little help in understanding why and how those individuals of an intolerant temperament, the Grandmother McCarthys with their "hates and rancors," are able to prevail at some times, while at others they are silenced. There is a need, in other words, to move from the theoretical plane onto the practical. In attempting to do just this for the Reformation, Scribner has called attention to the role labels play in giving an identity to variant beliefs, thereby stigmatizing those who hold them with a different identity, a sense of being "the other." Once such labels are created, he explains, "they remain present as a cultural fund to be drawn upon—they can be disseminated, appropriated, internalised, modified, even mutated—and so are available for mobilisation at any given moment when they might be thought appropriate."[29] Thus, while in most periods a commonsense toleration prevails among the citizen body—what Scribner calls a "tolerance of practical rationality" and what Alan Wardman earlier called "the habit of compromise"—these same citizens can be transformed into a persecuting mob when the right leader hits on the right message to turn long-dormant fears against a particular group or set of beliefs.[30] This being the role of labels, it is worthy of notice that the label of *pagan,* with all the pejorative connotations it now enjoys, came into use precisely during the period of the late fourth century when the process of Christian redefinition was already breaking down the Constantinian consensus and replacing it with notions of a hostile gulf that separated two warring armies.

Religion and Politics

The effect of these random considerations is to reveal deeper layers in the portrait of Ambrose and Theodosius than could be touched by the artist's brush, layers made of that complex interplay between leaders and community which constitutes the sphere customarily known as "politics." Here is where the taboo against political interpretations of fourth-century Christianity, erected in the wake of Burckhardt's man-handling of the first Christian emperor, has had its most baleful effect, for whereas intolerance may be a theological problem, coercion is a political one. To confuse the two is to treat political symptoms with theological remedies.

There is another quotation at the front of this book, from a man whose name rarely is found in close proximity to John Stuart Mill's. Assessing the momentous changes that accompanied the breath-takingly swift collapse of the Soviet Union in 1991, former president Richard M. Nixon coolly advised his readers that "revolutionary up-heavals may change how the world looks but seldom change the way the world works."[31] Mr. Nixon was writing to justify the safely unim-aginative steps taken during his own presidency, but his words nev-ertheless serve as a reminder that there are rules of political behavior which underlie, and survive, periods of momentous change, such as occurred in the sudden collapse of Soviet communism or, fifteen cen-turies earlier, the change from paganism to Christianity in the Roman Empire. Although these mundane political realities are easily forgotten in the excitement and tumult of the immediate moment, the long view encouraged by Mr. Nixon's statement brings out their continued im-portance. In both periods, despite changes in rhetoric and style, the political game continued to be played, and political skills continued to influence the outcomes of winners and losers.

In the case of the Roman Empire, the continuities that underlie the shift from pagan to Christian emperors were the twin demands of legitimacy and patronage. As had emperors in the first century, so emperors in the fourth sought to make their subjects, and particularly the armies, believe that they ruled in accordance with some principle greater than armed might, to make them, in Xenophon's useful phrase, "all willing to be his subjects."[32] In addition to willing subjects, fourth-century emperors continued to need willing subordinates, governors and civic elites, to carry out the imperial will. In return, these subordinates received patronage in all its manifold forms, from the basic promise of resources and fiscal gain to the more intangible guarantees of access and preferment, all adding up to a comfortable sense of protected interest. At this level, what the change from paganism to Christianity, symbolized in the confrontation between Ambrose and Theodosius, represents is the arrival of a new player in an age-old game. Access and influence, patronage and prestige—these are the constants in the game of empire.

These continuities in political behavior and priorities provide a context for the confrontations that begin and end this book, between Constantine and Athanasius in 335, and Ambrose and Theodosius in 388 and 390. These confrontations, in turn, help identify social and political factors in the escalating use of coercion by a Christian government. By looking forward to this century rather than backward, it has been possible to uncover two neglected aspects of Roman government and the early church. The first is the nature of the emperor as head of a state that was also a religious institution; the second is a Christian tradition, based on the central injunction to return hate with love, that true belief cannot be coerced. This is the tradition Constantine adopted and used to create a consensus of Christian and pagan elite centered on the principle of a broadly inclusionist public religion that would avoid those aspects of state cult, such as blood sacrifice, which had previously restricted Christian participation in government. The consensus proved remarkably resilient, outlasting the more strident postures adopted by both his son Constantius II and his nephew Julian. Given the success of this policy, it becomes a matter of urgent concern to explain why, eventually, it failed.

The reason, or at least part of it, lies in a change that occurred in the relative strength of emperor and bishop between the time of these two confrontations. On the surface, the change is revolutionary; underneath, it represents emergence of a new center of interest and support, a new nexus of legitimacy and patronage, centered on the Christian bishop.

Constantine had found a charismatic role for himself with his vision experience, a story that from Eusebius's account we may conclude he took an active role in circulating. By such methods, Constantine had been able to negotiate a role for himself analogous to that of the bishops as a mediator of the divine will. Constantine's efforts to give the emperor's traditionally sacrosanct role a Christian cast through such neologisms as "bishop of those outside" and his carefully cultivated image of divine selection won for him a status eventually recognized by the title of *Isapostolos,* "equal to the Apostles." Like Augustus before him, Constantine knew that this *auctoritas* was far more important and effective than any constitutional niceties. But unlike Augustus, Constantine never found a way to transmit his personal standing intact to his successors.

The reason for this failure was the bishops. In Constantine's scheme—which is not likely to have been any more consciously thought out than Augustus's—the bishops clearly were designated to play the legitimating role that had been assigned in the Principate to the Senate, and Constantine followed his predecessor's rule book page by page in the resources and courtesies that he lavished on this new order. Like the senators before them, the bishops now made the standards of their order the criteria for a "good king." This is, on one level, what changed. As T. D. Barnes has put it, orthodoxy became one of the imperial virtues—the point Ammianus missed when he complained about the privileges of the bishops.[33] But where imperial senators were prepared by both experience and preference to play their role as imperial guarantors to the hilt and without complaint, Christian bishops developed out of an alternative tradition, independent of both empire and emperor, secure in a local power—their congregations—which imperial senators lacked. Even Constantine, as we saw in Chapter 9, became increasingly dependent on bishops to carry out his social agenda.

This growing strength of the bishops was an unintended consequence of Constantine's policies. Constantine himself could never have imagined a situation such as that in which Theodosius found himself. But Constantine's position, by definition, was unique. It could not pass down to his successors. Instead, the church, through its bishops, assumed the role of legitimator which had been played by the Senate during the Principate. The change meant that emperors now had to minister to the priorities and interests of the bishops at least as zealously as they had once done for the Senate, and they had to find a common ground on which to meet as equals, just as emperors of the Principate had done in continuing to hold senatorial offices such as the consulship. Naturally, these priorities became increasingly religious. Mr. Nixon was right to think of such change as a gradual process, for certainly in the case of the Roman Empire the credibility of the Senate had been waning, and the need for a religious sanction waxing, long before the birth of Constantine, much less Theodosius. This is a pattern that continued unaffected by the superficial change from senator to bishop.

Christianity was not responsible for this change. But before Christianity came into association with the government, the divine had no institutional base such as the civic elites had in the Senate. Roman religion was administered by the same elites that held control of other civic offices. This identity of interest, a strength in the heyday of classical culture, made it impossible for priests of the ancient cults to assert an independent authority when, in the late empire, emperors based their rule on more overtly religious lines. But alienation from the public life of the empire had forced Christians to develop leadership networks that were independent of the traditional civic ties. The bishops, with their tradition of coordinated decision making, had such institutional stability, and in addition their control of patronage and the pulpit gave them a power base from which to act more independently than the imperial Senate ever could. Their skill and experience in public discourse, and their increasing mastery of administration and ceremony, all play a part in the dominance Ambrose was able to assert over Theodosius. Had not Ambrose demonstrated his hold over the people of Milan so effectively in previous encounters with an Arian court, his success with Theodosius would have been far less likely.

However restrained Ambrose's treatment of Theodosius may seem when compared with the embellished version that later prevailed, it is nonetheless a rebuke that a senator could never have delivered, even at the height of the Principate. When he confronted Theodosius over Callinicum's synagogue, Ambrose deliberately and self-consciously assumed the mantle of the holy man. His sermon that week, which he repeated in Epistle 41 for the benefit of his sister (and posterity), dwelt on the duty of the prophet to chastise misdeeds and ended with the example of King David yielding to the prophet Nathan—while managing to observe in the process that Christ's healing oil is owned by the church, not the synagogue. Theodosius got the point. "When I came down from the pulpit," Ambrose told his sister, "he said to me: 'You spoke about me.'"[34]

This was unique in bishops, their ability to absorb every aspect of Christian prestige and authority into their own person, be it that of the apologist, the martyr, or the prophet. In this case, Ambrose needed all these powers and more to prevail. Earlier, he had tried to intervene in a more traditional fashion, with a behind-the-scenes letter cast in the familiar cadences of imperial panegyric. Invoking the model of "the good king," Ambrose began that letter gingerly, reminding Theodosius that a good emperor will not rest his authority solely on military strength: "For this is the difference between good and bad princes, that the good love liberty, the bad slavery." As he warmed to his subject, however, Ambrose became more and more heavy handed. Playing on the constant reluctance of Roman emperors to commit their prestige in situations in which the outcome was not certain, he hinted that both the bishop of Callinicum and Theodosius's own local representative might balk at such an order, and he even presumed to warn that God might no longer aid the emperor on the field of battle.[35] These appeals to standard classical models of political suasion got Ambrose nowhere; Theodosius did not even deign to reply. Only when the bishop confronted him in church with the full array of exempla from the Hebrew Bible did the emperor give way.

Yet Athanasius, like Ambrose, had also tried to don the mantle of the holy man—"The Lord will judge between me and you"—and all it got him was an excursion to Gaul. Why the different outcomes? The most obvious answer is in the setting of the two events, the palace in the one instance, the church in the other. Whereas Ambrose had all the levers of a Christian liturgy at his disposal when he confronted Theodosius, Athanasius had to deal with Constantine in a venue where every advantage accrued to the emperor. Indeed, it is not known whether Constantine ever attended services in a church. The odds are against it. Unbaptized, he would not even have been able to attend for the entire service, much less assume the privileged position to which his rank and office—emperor and pontifex maximus—entitled him.

In the *vita Constantini*, Eusebius depicts the emperor poring over Scripture and the imperial palace as so filled with theological discourse as to be indistinguishable from a church. Presumably, these efforts helped supply the loss.[36]

In church, Ambrose was able to use the added leverage of public ceremony, confronting the emperor during mass and refusing to proceed with the Eucharist until he responded. Tense moments followed, for Theodosius was not inclined to reverse his decision. "The monks commit many crimes," Ambrose quotes him as saying during their confrontation, a remark for which the bishop evidently had no response. Fortunately for him, Timasius jumped in at that moment with further criticisms, giving Ambrose an opportunity to deflect the point: "I answered him: 'With the Emperor I deal as is fitting, because I know that he has the fear of God, but with you, who speak so roughly, one must deal otherwise.'"[37] There is no telling how long the standoff might have gone on if the setting had been different. But here Ambrose had the upper hand. Even if the congregation had no idea what was happening, it would have been obvious that the flow of the mass had been interrupted, and the longer Theodosius sat silent, the more awkward and obvious the interruption became. At last, the emperor yielded.

The confrontation between Ambrose and Theodosius was not so much a turning point as a validation of a process that began with Constantine's decision to use the coercive powers of the state to protect the interests of one Christian party against another. The ultimate effect of Ambrose's ability to prevail on Theodosius over the burning of Callinicum's synagogue was that it sent forth a signal of indecision at the highest levels which in turn created openings for those Christians who burned to use such extreme measures. Marcus Aurelius and Constantine, each in his way, had signaled a firmness of intent—Aurelius, that he would not tolerate the challenge to traditional belief posed by Christianity; Constantine, that despite his personal adoption of Christianity all beliefs would be tolerated. Theodosius went further than Constantine, making Christianity the only official religion of the empire and disestablishing all others. But, as his initial decision to punish the perpetrators in Callinicum shows, Theodosius had not abandoned his duty as emperor to preserve the peace and protect the property of all Romans, Christian or not. When he gave in to Ambrose in 388, Theodosius signaled a weakening of will, captured so beautifully by the portraitists in the crumbling of a knee.

It is no longer possible, at this remove, to decide how much choice Theodosius had. His regime had been punctuated by instability, both foreign and domestic; too many acts of civil disobedience, of the sort Ambrose evoked in his warnings over Callinicum, and the aura of omnipotence which girded the power of the Roman emperor would surely have collapsed. It may be that what now seems like a bald threat from Ambrose was meant at the time as a piece of serious counsel: Could the emperor afford another bout of domestic turbulence? Ambrose told his sister that the emperor remained silent for some time after the bishop approached him from the pulpit.

> Then, after standing for some time, I said to the Emperor: "Let me offer [the Eucharist] for you without anxiety, set my mind at ease." As he continued sitting and nodded, but did not give an open promise, and I remained standing, he said that he would amend the edict. I went on at once to say that he must end the whole investigation, lest the Count should use the opportunity of the investigation to do any injury to the Christians. He promised that it should be so. I said to him, "I act on your promise," and repeated, "I act on your promise." "Act," he said, "on my promise." And so I went to the altar, whither I should not have gone unless he had given me a distinct promise.[38]

It seems likely that Theodosius was weighing precisely these calculations as he sat before the waiting Ambrose. In the end, he decided that he needed the bishop more than he needed the Constantinian consensus. Why?

Another question must be asked first: Why did Ambrose intervene? Callinicum was as far from his immediate affairs as it was from Theodosius's, and Ambrose was not even in Milan when he learned of the emperor's decision but Aquileia. It would have been an easy matter for him to duck. Why, then? The question would be easier to answer if it were known who brought the news to Ambrose and for what reason. Here is where Mr. Nixon's advice becomes particularly useful. Turn away from Christianity's theological novelties and thoughts of coercion which follow in its train, and it is still possible to see under the layers of gloss the old and familiar outlines of patronage. As Eusebius of Nicomedia showed when he used his access to the court to support, and win the support of, the Meletians, the bishop in whatever city the emperor happened to reside could be a powerful patron.[39]

Even a bishop at odds with the court was still the obvious point of entry for bishops from the hinterlands seeking imperial support, as the *Life* of Bishop Porphyry of Gaza—the same Bishop Porphyry whose desire for "zealous Christians" figured into the previous chapter— shows. When Porphyry determined to journey to the capital and gain the emperor's permission to destroy the great temple that was Gaza's pride and joy, his first call was on the bishop, John Chrysostom, who was able to gain them immediate access to the empress, even though (as he candidly told his guests) he was not on good terms with the imperial family.[40] The episode is thus testimony to the asset that a bishop in residence could be, even when alienated from the imperial party. So it would have been natural for any emissaries from the bishop of Callinicum to call on Ambrose for support. However sincere his concern for the priority of the church might have been, Ambrose would not have been unmindful either of the opportunity to confer a benefit and enlist new allies or of the effect on his episcopal rivals of a timely demonstration of his sway over the emperor. Thus, even in so blatant a case of coercion as this, familiar exchanges and local contingencies can offer as much of an explanation for Ambrose's willingness to get involved in such distant problems as the assumption that he was driven to do so by intolerant zeal.

Despite Ambrose's evident satisfaction with the outcome of the confrontation over Callinicum as he recounted the event to his sister, it appears that Theodosius was displeased with the bishop and proceeded to deny him that access on which his patronage depended.[41] It took the Thessalonica affair to bring him back into the emperor's good graces.

The scenario that unfolded in the summer of 390 in that Macedonian city, strategically situated on the major road connecting the Eastern and Western halves of the empire, is difficult to imagine happening at any time other than the late Roman Empire. Chariot races were the megasport of the day, and winning charioteers had a celebrity status that eventually was incorporated into the emperor's own aura.[42] One of Thessalonica's leading drivers offended the Gothic commander of the city's garrison and was taken into custody, apparently at a time when his skills were needed in a set of crucial games [43] Enraged, his followers lynched the general, Butheric. Reprisals were a foregone conclusion: the emperor's prestige, and the continued loyalty of his troops, required no less. But Butheric's troops went far beyond what was expected, indiscriminately slaughtering upwards of five thousand people, innocent and guilty alike. Heart-rending stories circulated in the aftermath: of the father forced to choose which of his two sons' lives to save with his own; of the slave who gave up his own life to save his master; of visitors who lost their lives for no other reason than being in the wrong place at the wrong time.[44]

The disaster at Thessalonica stands in direct contrast to the peaceful resolution of a similarly serious situation in Antioch only a few years earlier. In 387, announcement of a new tax sent the citizens of that city on a rampage. Before order was restored, the houses of several important officials had been burned to the ground and, far more seriously, statues of the emperor overturned and defaced, a treasonable offense. The city fathers, remembering how Diocletian had decimated their ranks after an earlier disturbance, fled to their country estates, and all who had the means to follow their example did likewise. The rest of the citizenry had no choice but to await in trembling the result of embassies sent to assuage Theodosius's righteous anger. On this occasion, Theodosius listened to the soothing words of city officials and Antioch's bishop, Flavian, and put aside his wrath.[45]

This sort of gesture was grist for the ancient propaganda mill. In the aftermath of Theodosius's favorable decision, public orators made certain that Antioch's penitent citizens appreciated their emperor's clemency and restraint, using the tools of their trade to compare Theodosius to revered predecessors. Interestingly, in light of John Stuart Mill's judgment, both Christian and pagan orators chose Constantine as their exemplar. The young priest and future bishop John Chrysostom described how that emperor reacted in a similar situation— most likely the same one to which Eusebius alluded in the *vita Constantini*.[46] When his advisers warned that the imperial image could not be defaced with impunity, Constantine, according to Chrysostom, merely smiled and replied, "I am quite unable to perceive any wound inflicted upon my face. The head appears sound, and the face also quite sound." Chrysostom's teacher, the rhetor Libanius, added to the story, telling how Constantine responded to advice from two of his brothers, the one counseling military action, the other urging him simply to ignore the offense. Constantine agreed with the latter, Libanius said, and told the other that harsh advice "was of little use to an emperor."[47] The effect of these stories was clear. By virtue of his similar moderation, Theodosius had lived up to the example of Constantine and proved that he was worthy to rule.

This is the way the system was supposed to work, with punishment restricted to the ringleaders and the sentences of other participants, after a show of true repentance, tempered by the mercy of divine majesty. Such voluntary restraint of a coercive power that was all too real was both prestigious and economical. It allowed the emperor to maintain and even enhance his dignity without having to rely on the soldiery and thereby maintained the civic covenant established by Augustus centuries earlier. On occasions such as this, the late antique world came together in a great ceremonial recommitment by ruler and ruled alike to a system of justice and order.

At Thessalonica, things had gone terribly wrong. It would have been one thing if the slaughter of citizens had been a spontaneous act on the part of the soldiers. But as in the case of Antioch, some weeks elapsed between riot and reprisal, during which time messages passed between the court, now in Milan, and the officials on the scene. This time, however, clemency was not the result. It is hard now to know exactly what caused the sterner response. It is conceivable that the moderation shown earlier at Antioch worked against the citizens of Thessalonica, convincing the emperor that a more forceful example had to be set. But it is even more likely that Theodosius had less flexibility than on the earlier occasion. For one thing, he was now in the West and therefore unable to take personal charge of the situation. For another, this time the injury was not done to him personally but to the commander of troops whose loyalty no emperor could safely alienate.

Theodosius was trapped between two vital constituencies: the military, which he needed for the defense of emperor and empire alike, and the civic elites, whose cooperation was essential to the smooth running of the state. Successful emperors were those, like Augustus, who found a way to reconcile these two constituencies while at the same time using the one as a check on the other. But in certain key ways the interests of the two were incompatible. Soldiers had little respect for an emperor who shrank from the use of force, while the elites expected emperors to keep in check the blatant display of raw power. The real threat of the Thessalonica affair was that it had brought to the fore the basic opposition of the two sides, forcing Theodosius into the impossible situation of having to choose between two equally vital interests. It is the sense of those who have studied this event carefully that the troops in Thessalonica vastly exceeded Theodosius's orders and went on a rampage of their own making. Even if true, Theodosius did not have the option of saying so and thereby deflecting blame onto the troops. He dare not. In addition to being serene, the emperor also had to be perceived as omnipotent. Better that whatever the troops did they did by his order than to admit that he was unable to control them.

Events subsequent to the massacre have the smell of damage control. Word came from the court that Theodosius had sent a counterorder when his rage over the actions of the mob had abated, but it had arrived too late to prevent the slaughter. It was plausible, given ancient assumptions about imperial anger,[48] and the topos of order and counterorder had the comfortable familiarity needed to give the event a suitably tragic spin. But in this case, the well-planned exercise in deniability was insufficient. Even a law in which the emperor committed himself in the future to obey a thirty-day cooling-off period failed to restore confidence.[49] The slaughter had been too great and too indiscriminate, the display of animal ferocity too repulsive.

Why was this event so different? Years earlier, the same John Chrysostom who had praised Theodosius's moderation so ably after the resolution of the "Riot of the Statues" published a youthful essay in which he compared the virtues of a king with those of a monk—the essay already reviewed in Chapter 2 for its striking combination of new and old in the description of kingship. Distilling centuries of classical thought into a few phrases, Chrysostom described the true king as one "who truly rules over anger and envy and pleasure, who commands all things under the laws of God, who keeps his mind free, and who does not allow the power of the pleasures to dominate his soul." Such a one,

Chrysostom wrote, "I would gladly see ruling peoples and earth and sea and cities and peoples and soldiers. For the person who has put the reasoning power of his soul in charge of his passions also will more easily rule over men as well with the divine laws, so that he will be to the ruled as a father, frequenting the cities with all kindness." But an unworthy king, Chrysostom warned, "is enslaved to anger and to the love of power and pleasures." This person "will appear quite ridiculous to his subjects, since he wears a crown of gems and gold but is not crowned with moderation," and "will not even know how to administer his command." How, Chrysostom asked, could a person unable to rule himself "guide others rightly by the laws?"[50] The sentiment accords precisely with that uttered by another Chrysostom more than two centuries earlier.[51] Christians and pagans had no dispute on this point. An emperor must allow his anger, however righteous, to be assuaged. In the Thessalonica affair, Theodosius had failed to do so, and classical political theory allowed only one conclusion to be drawn. Henceforth, he would be known as a rogue emperor, unpredictable and unreliable.

It was in this context that the letter from Ambrose discussed at the start of this chapter arrived. Its tone indicates that the bishop had learned from his mishandling of the Callinicum matter. Gone is the presumptuousness, the high-handed indifference to imperial etiquette, the unseemly self-satisfaction. This time, Ambrose was the soul of discretion. Instead of remonstrating with the emperor like a prophet, he pleaded with him like a pastor, appealing to his own conscience and sense of right and suggesting a public display of remorse in the rite of penance. The change, from a discourse of power to one of personal salvation, made all the difference. With it, Ambrose offered a lifeline, carefully orchestrated to spare the emperor all but the bare minimum of disgrace. For an emperor to do such a thing, of course, was unprecedented, and that is precisely why it worked. By focusing on the emperor's remorse, the scene deflected attention from a political disaster of the highest magnitude. In the words of a recent biographer, the bishop "turned the catastrophe into a public relations triumph for the emperor."[52]

Far from separating the interests of church and state, Ambrose's handling of the Thessalonica affair brought the two together more tightly than ever before. At just the moment when the delicate courtesies and elegant rituals that for centuries had sustained the game of empire failed in their basic purpose of reconciling the ruled to their ruler, Ambrose showed how the healing embrace of the church could still provide the emperor with "willing subjects." When he wrote to the emperor about Callinicum, Ambrose had asked, "Which, then, is of greater importance, the show of discipline or the cause of religion?" His own answer was, "It is needful that judgment should yield to religion." This was a novel and audacious claim, advising Theodosius in effect that he could safely ignore the interests of any other constituency, and even of public order, so long as he had the support of the bishops. Ambrose used language suitable to courtly prose: "Priests are the calmers of disturbances, and anxious for peace," he wrote, "except when even they are moved by some offense against God, or insult to the Church."[53] The same claim in even more veiled terms had irked Constantine and sent Julian into a fit of self-righteous indignation. It is an important sign of changed circumstances that on this occasion Theodosius heard Ambrose out. Translated into blunter prose, what Ambrose proposed was a deal: the bishops would now assume the traditional duties of the civic elites in keeping the peace, and in return the emperor would protect their vital interests, just as previously he had protected those of the civic elites. This was an offer no emperor could pass up without careful consideration, for if bishops really could do the job of controlling urban violence, then it stood to reason they could unleash those same mobs as well.

As Peter Brown has shown, the potential for cities to erupt into precisely the type of violence which occurred in Antioch in 387 and Thessalonica in 390 was a constant worry for the emperors.[54] This is what made the civic elites such an important constituency. The emperor was not all-powerful; he relied on local support. According to the unwritten rules of the game of empire, the elites undertook to maintain order in their cities in return for the emperor's guarantee to safeguard their interests. Failure to keep up their part of the bargain, rather than any complicity in the actual event, is what moved Diocletian to exact a punishment that still made Antioch's city fathers tremble in 387. Yet as the spokesman for those interests had to admit, there were times when even the city fathers lost control. "The city councillors," Libanius explained in the aftermath of the riot of 387, "so far from participating in or witnessing such behaviour, went to ground wherever they could and tried to save their own skins, for they were afraid that if they appeared on the scene, they would be lynched."[55] Under these conditions, a promise that bishops could do a better job had real meaning, and by throwing Theodosius a lifeline for Thessalonica, Ambrose made good on that promise. He showed that Christian ceremonial could provide what the most eloquent panegyrists could not—credibility. The compact with the restraining forces of moral suasion was intact, harmony was restored.

Gauging Intolerance

Maybe the fifth-century historians had it right after all when they conflated Callinicum with Thessalonica. Separately, the two events that make up the legend of Ambrose and Theodosius are contradictory in both content and result. Only when they are put together do they have a story to tell. Unfortunately, the ancients put them together indifferently, and the result was a botched job. It was for Callinicum, not Thessalonica, that Ambrose showed the sternness captured by Rubens and Van Dyck, and his victory did nothing to enhance his stature or prestige, either then or now. Thessalonica was a nobler cause, but there was no confrontation: penance served the emperor's plans as much as the bishop's. Mingled, the two events speak powerfully for the struggle between church and state which has been one of Christianity's lasting marks on Western civilization; but together they also hopelessly muddle the examination of Christian coercion. Coercion had nothing to do with the confrontation over Thessalonica, and even in the case of Callinicum the use of force to compel belief was not uppermost in the mind of either Ambrose or Theodosius. Even here, the issue was not faith but power.

The historian's palette was made for scenes such as this, scenes of ambiguity and failure. Its scrapers and solvents have revealed the separate layers to the story of Ambrose and Theodosius and something much older underlying both—ancient ideas about the nature of the state, the role of the ruler, and the process of resource distribution. Three elements thus unite the events at the start and end of this book, the events in Constantinople and Milan: the position of the emperor at the top of a pyramid of resource distribution; the role of intermediaries, patrons, as brokers of those resources; and the presence of the Christian bishop, a superficial novelty whose position in these proceedings is now more clearly identified. Bishops had become the new brokers.

With the two incidents reassembled more carefully, the final piece in the puzzle of Christian coercion falls into place.

Although Christianity as a monotheistic faith was certainly exclusive, the great commandment to "love thy enemy" sufficiently neutralized the potential for hatred to make it no more prone to coercion than any other belief system. Then as now the apologetic impulse could make Christians eager to find common ground with nonbelievers. It was Christian apologists who articulated more clearly than anyone else in the first three centuries of this era the principle that true belief cannot be coerced. In the fourth century, they abandoned, or at least modified, that principle. Thus, the easiest answer for the change in Christian thinking about coercion during the course of that century is not intolerance but power: toleration is a "loser's creed." Certainly, it would be an easy matter to show that Christians and pagans alike only argued for toleration while they were weak and that the pagans were borrowing Christian arguments when they did so.[56] But this answer by itself is insufficient: it undervalues the impact of ignoring one's own rules. A better and more basic explanation lies in a belief deeply embedded in ancient thinking about the nature of the state, an underlying belief that took the longest period of time to change. This was the idea that the state was a religious institution, and with it the belief that divine support was crucial to success in this world. Such belief makes maintenance of the goodwill of divinity a primary function of leadership and thereby blurs the distinction between religious and secular which characterizes modern thinking. On this view, the Christian turn to coercion in the decades following Constantine would be a matter of the Christian state taking steps to ensure the benevolence of the new deity just as the pagan state had done before, ensuring what today would be called "national security."

There is something in both these options, and they both have the advantage of moving away from the notion that what happened in the fourth century was unique. But like other general explanations, they cannot account for variety, and they continue to point in the wrong direction, to the clash between Christians and pagans. Rather than rely on either of them to explain events of the fourth century, it is better to turn to the traits Christianity exhibits as a mass movement. Like all other mass movements, Christianity had to find room for variety in order to grow. Its core message contains internal contradictions, chief among which are the two injunctions to love even enemies and yet to resist Satan. In other mass movements, the messages will express themselves differently, but in the most general sense they will be the same: a message that is essentially expansionist and inclusive, twinned with a message that is the opposite, hostile and exclusive. These contradictions gave the Christian movement sufficient flexibility to meet changing circumstances; they allowed it to survive and adapt. But they also created a critical need for interpretation, a need to explain not only Scripture but also how the lessons of Scripture applied to everyday life. Because most day-to-day situations are ambiguous, Christians constantly needed to know if one should be embraced or resisted. They needed prestigious members of their community to put these ambiguities into context.

Because of these multiple messages, the opportunity was always present for different subgroups to seize control of the larger body by seizing control of the message. Constantine successfully advocated the irenic message. To be sure, he was aided by general revulsion at the excesses of Diocletian's persecution. But his own constant labors to develop a tolerant consensus should not go unappreciated. By constant stroking and soothing ministrations, Constantine convinced wary Christians that the peaceful balance of the late third century could be restored and that the Roman government could be trusted to preserve and advance Christian interests.

Ironically, Constantine's great success was also, ultimately, his undoing. The number of new Christians who entered the church in response to the emperor's "carrot-without-the-stick" approach was a destabilizing new factor in a community divided as never before by the fear of internal subversion. Christian rhetoric heated up in this internal debate and brought the eristic side of the core message to the fore. Enemies became demonized, literally, as agents of Satan. Because Roman emperors traditionally were responsible for proper worship, Constantine was vulnerable to demands that he protect the flock from "the enemy within." Thus, it was an internal issue, heresy, not a longing for revenge against pagans, which first brought the coercive mechanisms of the state into play and which contributed to the sort of polarizing discourse required to advance the militant agenda.

At a moment when the twin shocks of heresy and growth were already creating fissures, Julian came to the throne with an agenda not merely to withdraw resources from Christian bishops but also to isolate Christianity itself at the margins of classical culture. Julian's ill-starred rule provided militants with a credible external threat. By making culture for the first time a litmus test for sincere belief, in all likelihood deliberately to strengthen the hand of those Christians who always found Greco-Roman learning suspect, and by his flamboyant revival of blood sacrifice, Julian drove a wedge into the Constantinian consensus, forcing Christians and pagans alike to take sides.

These were the elements underlying the confrontations between Ambrose and Theodosius. His predecessors had struggled to restore the equilibrium that Julian had upset, but Theodosius's reign constituted one surrender after another of those principles. The Callinicum incident revealed the new role of the bishop as a broker in the age-old game of patronage and favor. With Thessalonica, however, Ambrose demonstrated the superiority of the Christian rite of reconciliation to all the delicate rituals and elegant phrases that for centuries had constituted the rules of empire. Henceforth, emperors needed the bishops as a backdrop for the ceremonies that legitimated their rule.

Thessalonica did more: it validated the decision on Callinicum. This is why the two incidents must be seen together, for it is only when combined that their full force can be felt. When Theodosius gave in to Ambrose over the Callinicum affair, he almost certainly did so without realizing the mischievous consequences of his decision—Ambrose had done well to emphasize how distant, isolated, and unimportant Callinicum was. His failure to act decisively is the important missing part of the puzzle of Christian coercion. The relationship between leaders and followers in any society is more complex than the simple model of orders given and obeyed will allow. But in the matter of militancy it seems clear that signals from the top can be decisive.

Constantine had effectively squelched militant behavior when he took over the Eastern provinces, both by firmly articulating the principle that "it is one thing to undertake the contest for immortality voluntarily, another to compel it with punishment,"[57] and by being equally firm with any who stepped over the bounds of that principle, whether political ally or no. On the Callinicum affair, Theodosius may not have caved in as completely as Ambrose would have us believe, but it is evident that this is one of many mixed signals that came from his court, and it may in the end have been the decisive one. Whatever the forces that drive militants to act, mixed signals from the top can only encourage them. The difference between Constantine's principled firmness and Theodosius's fuzzy waffling helps explain why, despite Mill's judgment, Constantine by this time was remembered not for his rages but as a model of forbearance.

This sketch of the process whereby militants gained the upper hand in the Christian community is certainly incomplete. But the elements of a community hardened first by conflict with heretics and then by perceived abuse of imperial power—in this case, not just Julian but also Valentinian II and his mother—are certainly present in Ambrose's profile.[58] What his confrontations with Theodosius add to the picture is an understanding of the symbiosis that had developed between the Christian bishops and the traditional functions of Roman rulership. Here is where the underlying constants suggested by Mr. Nixon's comment come into play, for the greatest constant in this whole complicated story emerges when bishops replace senators as a core constituency, as keepers of the peace. It is a natural, and unsurprising, effect of this transfer that emperors should henceforth guard Christian interests as zealously as in the past they had guarded those of their previous partners in empire, the Senate.

·   This has not been a cheerful story, and it does not have a happy ending. However, it does have a note of hope, which is this: the first stage to the successful resolution of a problem is to define that problem properly. Previous diagnoses of the problem of Christian coercion in the fourth century have defined it as a congenital condition, innate to the faith. With such a diagnosis, the prognosis must be hopeless. But if the diagnosis offered here is correct, then the phenomenon no longer needs to be privileged in this way, set apart as unique and inevitable. It becomes part of the great dialogue that the study of history encourages between past and present. Whether history itself contains lessons or not, those who study history will draw lessons from it, and those lessons will influence not merely the way we shape our past but also the way we define our present and anticipate our future. The lesson of the fourth century is not that Christianity is intolerant and there is nothing to be done about it; it is that there are persons in every mass movement who are willing to coexist with variant belief and others who see such nonbelievers as outsiders and as a threat that must be neutralized. If Christian coercion can be understood as a phenomenon of human organization, then it is possible to hope that the circumstances that caused one view to prevail over the other in the fourth century may be identified, classified, and used to understand these same phenomena when they recur in other periods.

Appendix

The First Sirmondian Constitution

IMP. CONSTANTINVS A. AD ABLABIVM P(RAEFECTVM) P(RAETORI)O. [Satis mirati sumus gravitatem tuam, quae plena iustitiae ac probae] religionis est, clementiam nostram sciscitari voluisse, quid de sententiis episcoporum vel ante moderatio nostra censuerit vel nunc servari cupiamus, Ablabi, parens karissime atque amantissime. Itaque quia a nobis instrui voluisti, olim promulgatae legis ordinem salubri rursus imperio propagamus. Sanximus namque, sicut edicti nostri forma declarat, sententias episcoporum quolibet genere latas sine aliqua aetatis discretione inviolatas semper incorruptasque servari; scilicet ut pro sanctis semper ac venerabilibus habeantur, quidquid episcoporum fuerit sententia terminatum. Sive itaque inter minores sive inter maiores ab episcopis fuerit iudicatum, apud vos, qui iudiciorum summam tenetis, et apud ceteros omnes iudices ad exsecutionem volumus pertinere. Quicumque itaque litem habens, sive possessor sive petitor vel inter initia litis vel decursis temporum curriculis, sive cum negotium peroratur, sive cum iam coeperit promi sententia, iudicium elegerit sacrosanctae legis antistitis, ilico sine aliqua dubitatione, etiamsi alia pars refragatur, ad episcopum personae litigantium dirigantur. Multa enim, quae in iudicio captiosa praescriptionis vincula promi non patiuntur, investigat et publicat sacrosanctae religionis auctoritas. Omnes itaque causae, quae vel praetorio iure vel civili tractantur,

485

episcoporum sententiis terminatae perpetuo stabilitatis iure firmentur, nec liceat ulterius retractari negotium, quod episcoporum sententia deciderit. Testimonium etiam ab uno licet episcopo perhibitum omnis iudex indubitanter accipiat nec alius audiatur testis, cum testimonium episcopi a qualibet parte fuerit repromissum. Illud est enim veritatis auctoritate firmatum, illud incorruptum, quod a sacrosancto homine conscientia mentis inlibatae protulerit. Hoc nos edicto salubri aliquando censuimus, hoc perpetua lege firmamus, malitiosa litium semina conprimentes, ut miseri homines longis ac paene perpetuis actionum laqueis implicati ab improbis petitionibus vel a cupiditate praepostera maturo fine discedant. Quidquid itaque de sententiis episcoporum clementia nostra censuerat et iam hac sumus lege conplexi, gravitatem tuam et ceteros pro utilitate omnium latum in perpetuum observare convenit. DATA III NONAS MAIAS CONSTANTINOPOLI [DALMATIO ET ZE-NOFILO CONSS.] (May 5, 333)

Emperor Constantine Augustus to Ablabius, Praetorian Prefect.

We are not a little surprised, Ablabius, dearest and most beloved parent, that Your Gravity, who is full of justice and proper reverence, has wished to inquire of Our Clemency, either what Our Moderation previously advised regarding judgment by bishops or what we now desire to be observed. Thus, since you have wished to be instructed by us, we issue again the order of the law formerly promulgated for the imperial benefit. We ordain, therefore, just as the appearance of our edict revealed, that the judgment of bishops issued any where or way without any distinction of age be preserved inviolate and uncorrupted; that is to say, that whatever judgment shall have been determined by the bishops be held ever sacred and venerable. Whether, therefore, judgment has been given by bishops between minors or between adults, we wish it to be suitable for execution by you, who hold the highest court, and by all the other judges. Whoever, therefore, having a suit, whether defendant or plaintiff, either during the start of the suit or after the allotted time has run out, when closing arguments are being made or when sentence is about to be pronounced, should choose the court of the high priest of the sacrosanct law, instantly, without any hesitation, even if the other party is opposed, let the parties to the suit be directed to the bishop. For many things which in a court of law the captious bonds of legal objection do not allow to be brought forth, the esteem (*auctoritas*) of the sacrosanct religion finds out and makes known. Therefore, all cases which are conducted either by praetorian or by civil law, upon being settled by the judgment of bishops shall be confirmed by a law of perpetual standing, nor is it permitted that a matter which the judgment of bishops shall have decided may be appealed further. Furthermore, it is permitted that every judge may accept without doubt testimony by a single bishop, nor should any other witness be heard when testimony by a bishop may have been pledged by whichever party. That is truly confirmed by the authority of truthfulness, that is incorrupted, which the recollection of unimpaired memory shall have brought forth from a sacrosanct man. This we once decreed in a salutary edict, this we reinforce with a perpetual law, curtailing the wicked seeds of litigation so that wretched men, entangled in the long and nearly endless snares of legal procedure may have a timely release from mischievous pleadings or absurd love of disputation. Whatever, therefore, that Our Clemency has advised regarding the judgments of bishops and that we have now encompassed in this law, it behooves Your Gravity and the others to observe in perpetuity for the advantage of all sides. Given in Constantinople on the third day before the nones of May, Dalmatius and Zenofilus being consuls [May 5, A.D. 333].

(Ed. Mommsen I:2, 907–8)

Notes

1. George Skelton, "Capital Journal: What Really Matters in Sacramento," *Los Angeles Times*, Feb. 18, 1993, A3.
2. Michael Schrage, "Innovation," *Los Angeles Times*, Feb. 25, 1993, D2.
3. Matt. 18:20.
4. Gibbon (1909–14) 2: 2.

Chapter One. Constantinople, A.D. 335

1. From Constantine's "Letter to the Bishops at Tyre," in Athan., *Apol. sec.* 86. On Constantine's age, see Chapter 2 below, n. 3.
2. Eus., *VC* 4.42.
3. Soc., *HE* 1.29; cf. Soz., *HE* 2.25.8. Athanasius tells the story of Arsenius in his Apology against the Arians in a way that suggests it was all settled before the Council of Tyre met. It is possible to read his narrative in a way that would have the discovery of Arsenius occur at the time of the council (he says that the fugitive bishop was discovered hiding in Tyre after going there to see how the trial would come out). But since Athanasius says nothing about showing Arsenius's hands to the council, the incident was most likely embroidered. Arnold (1991) 156 accepts the story as genuine.
4. On Athanasius's flight from Tyre, see Peeters (1944); Barnes (1981) 240 put the arrival of the pursuing bishops "only a few hours" after Constantine dispatched his letter; Arnold (1991) 165 argues that Athanasius actu-

ally was taken from Tyre under "protective custody." On the complicated chronology of this episode, see Drake (1987) and Chapter 9 below.

5. Epiph., *Pan.* 69.9.5.

6. Walter (1970) 13–15 and figs. 17, 38, 46, 49, 59. A handsome modern version of this scene may be viewed in a 1986 icon of "The Seven Ecumenical Councils" in the Russian Orthodox Church of the Holy Fathers of the Seven Oecumenical Councils in New York City.

7. Eus., *VC* 1.27.

8. Here and elsewhere I use the traditional term *pagan,* despite its negative connotations, to refer collectively to all non-Christian beliefs in the ancient world. I do so reluctantly, and simply because scholars have yet to come up with a suitable alternative. *Polytheists,* as preferred by anthropologists, is more neutral in one sense but more misleading in others, since it excludes by definition a significant class of non-Christian monotheists and thereby plays directly into the hands of apologists who tried to eliminate such middle ground by defining the choice as one between monotheism and polytheism (see Chapters 4 and 10 below). For a good discussion of the term, see Chuvin (1990) ch. 1.

9. On the foundation of Constantinople: Frolow (1944); Dagron (1974); La Rocca (1992–93). On the Sunday law (*CTh* 2.8.1) and its effect, see Salzman (1990). For other legal privileges, see *CTh* 16.5.1; Rabello (1970); Dupont (1967); and below, Chapter 9.

10. On the motif of "a new Constantine," see Magdalino (1994). On the Constantine legend: Gerland (1927); Linder (1975); Winkelmann (1978); Kazhdan (1987); Salmon (1990); Grünewald (1992–93); Lieu & Montserrat (1998). On the "Donations of Constantine": Maffei (1964); Pohlkamp (1988).

11. The problem is exhaustively reviewed in Arnold (1991) 103–73. See further Martin (1996) 348–87.

12. Burckhardt (1949) 262–63, 292. For a survey of Protestant views of Constantine's effect on Christianity, see Williams (1998).

13. Seeck (1921) 1: 472 (at n. 56,8).

14. Eus., *VC* 1.26–27.

15. Burckhardt (1949) 283.

16. Conversion as a sudden spiritual awakening was given its classic description by Nock (1933) 7–8: "a passion of willingness and acquiescence, which removes the feeling of anxiety, a sense of perceiving truths not known before, a sense of clean and beautiful newness within and without and an ecstasy of happiness; these emotions are sometimes, and in fact often, accompanied by hallucinatory or quasi-hallucinatory phenomena." Nock drew on another classic work, James (1902), but in these lectures James (as did Nock himself) also saw conversion as a process that could be "gradual or sudden" (see Lec. 9, "Conversion"), and more recent scholar-

ship recognizes a longer conversion process than stressed in the classic model. See Chapter 5 below.

17. Sian Phillips ("Livia"), *TV Times, Los Angeles Times,* Nov. 6, 1977, 3.
18. Baynes (1972).
19. Baynes (1972) 19.
20. Viz. Alföldi (1948). The entire question is now reviewed in Girardet (1998).
21. "The inflexible, and, if we may use the expression, the intolerant zeal of the Christians, derived, it is true, from the Jewish religion." In the famous fifteenth chapter: Gibbon (1909–14) 2: 3. By the end of that chapter (2: 57), Gibbon had switched to the phrase "exclusive zeal." Gibbon scrupulously excluded divine will as a factor, to the consternation of the Established clergy. His other causes were: (2) "the doctrine of a future life"; (3) "the miraculous powers ascribed to the primitive church"; (4) "the pure and austere morals of the Christians"; and (5) "the union and discipline of the Christian republic, which gradually formed an independent and increasing state in the heart of the Roman empire."
22. Gibbon (1909–14) 1: 33.
23. Stark (1996) 206: "History suggests that when non-exclusive faiths are challenged by exclusive competitors, in a relatively unregulated market, the exclusive firms win." Paganism is defined as tolerant behavior in O'Donnell (1977). A similar view is reflected in Bowersock (1990) 6: "Polytheism is by definition tolerant and accommodating."
24. Ch. 71. Gibbon (1909–14) 7: 320.
25. "On Toleration. In Connection with the Death of Jean Calas." In Voltaire (1912) 42.
26. Gibbon (1909–14) 2: 103.
27. Gibbon (1909–14) 1: 31; 2: 87.
28. "The Martyrdom of Fructuosus" (A.D. 259), in *Act. Mart.* 179. The governor, Aemilianus, evidently had a sardonic sense of humor. Just before this exchange, he said to Fructuosus, "Do you know that the gods exist?" When the bishop answered, "No, I do not," the governor replied, "You will know later." Fructuosus and his companions were sentenced to be burned alive.
29. Garnsey (1984) 16 calls the assertion that true belief must be voluntary in Tert., *Apol.* 25.4 a groundbreaking expression of religious freedom as "a general principle, an attribute of individuals, not of an ethnos or polis." For discussion of "the Enlightenment stereotype" and its limitations, see Laursen & Nederman (1998) 1–8.
30. See, e.g., Kee (1982). Far more sophisticated, but based on the same dichotomy, is Grünewald (1990).
31. Baynes (1972) 3.
32. For an excellent discussion, see the classic study of the 1962 Cuban

missile crisis by Allison (1971). For further illustration of the way this and other models influence historical study, see Davidson & Lytle (1986) ch. 12.

33. Syme (1939) 7.
34. Millar (1977) xi.
35. Barnes (1981); Lane Fox (1987).
36. Liebeschuetz (1979); Wardman (1982); Price (1984); Beard & North (1990); Fishwick (1987–91).
37. Alinsky (1972) 113.
38. Henry (1985) 125. See also the perceptive comment by Momigliano (1990) 152: "Those who accept the notion of the Church as a divine institution which is different from the other institutions have to face the difficulty that Church history reveals only too obviously a continuous mixture of political and religious aspects. . . . By contrast the historians of the Church as a worldly institution have to reckon with the difficulty of describing without the help of a belief what has existed through the help of a belief."
39. Alinsky (1972) 119. On the failure to distinguish political and theological issues, see Bagnall (1993) 305.
40. Brown (1963), 283–305; Brown (1995) ch. 2; Fowden (1978).
41. Wardman (1982) 148.

Chapter Two. The Game of Empire

1. See Beard & North (1990); Szemler (1972); Feeney (1998).
2. With the rise of late antiquity as a field of inquiry, Western scholars have become far more sophisticated in their treatment of the role of the Roman emperor in the church than was once the case. For two thoughtful statements, see Chesnut (1986) 162; Fowden (1993) 112.
3. Estimates of Constantine's age have varied widely. Taking their lead from panegyrists who celebrated the emperor's youth and vigor (e.g., *Pan. Lat.* VI [VII].17.1) and from certain comments by Constantine himself, historians once concluded that he must have been in his mid-twenties at the time of his conversion in 312, placing his birth as late as 390. However, these comments do not need to be taken literally, since the motif of "the youthful ruler" was a popular one, and Constantine himself had reason to minimize his age during the years of the Great Persecution. His biographer Eusebius states (*VC* 1.5) that the emperor reigned more than thirty years and lived twice as long as he reigned, a chronology that is roughly shared by other ancient sources. This would push his birth date to the early 270s. See Barnes (1982) 39–40.
4. Hume (1875) 1: 110.

5. On Augustus's "beau geste," Jones (1951); Lacey (1974). More generally: Millar & Segal (1984); Raaflaub & Toher (1990); Wallace-Hadrill (1993).
6. Augustus, *Res Gestae* 34.3.
7. Pope Gelasius I (492–96) in his statement of the doctrine of the "two powers" in a letter to the emperor Anastasius: "Indeed, August Emperor, two forces rule this world—the sacred authority [*auctoritas*] of the bishops and the royal power [*potestas*]," Gel., *Ep. VIII*, PL 59, col. 42: Duo quippe sunt, imperator Auguste, quibus principaliter mundus hic regitur: auctoritas sacra [*al.* sacrata] pontificum, et regalis potestas.
8. Ulpian in Just., *Dig.* 1.4.1. On kingship theory, see Goodenough (1928); Straub (1939); Ensslin (1943); Steinwenter (1946); Béranger (1953); Taeger (1957); Dvornik (1966); Dagron (1967); Martin (1982); Chesnut (1978); Small (1996).
9. Wallace-Hadrill (1982); Fergus Millar (1984a) questioned the importance of patronage to the republican political system; see also Millar (1998).
10. See below, n. 44 and Chapter 4, n. 7.
11. On patronage: Saller (1982); Wallace-Hadrill (1989); Lendon (1998).
12. Dowling (1972) 393.
13. Smith (1988) xiii.
14. Dio 52.4.1.
15. Agrippa speaks from 52.1–13, Maecenas from 52.14–40. For the quoted passage, see 52.14.2.
16. Dio 52.40.1–2.
17. Xen., *Cyr.* 3.1.20.
18. Xen., *Cyr.* 1.1.3. The statement was used as a starting point by Charlesworth (1937), a pathbreaking study. Wallace-Hadrill (1981) has demonstrated that the imperial virtues were more fluid than Charlesworth thought.
19. Xen., *Cyr.* 7.5.37–57.
20. MacMullen (1974) 88–89. On the size of the Roman population: Lo Cascio (1994).
21. Kaster (1988) ch. 1; Brown (1992) ch. 2.
22. Xen., *Cyr.* 8.1.37–40.
23. Dio 52.35.1–2.
24. Dio 52.38.1.
25. Wallace-Hadrill (1982) 36: "The Principate was established by an act of denial (*recusatio*), ritually perpetuated from reign to reign."
26. Plin. Iun., *Pan.* 2.3–4.
27. Dio 52.39.2–4.
28. Plin., *NH* 6.24.89.
29. Tac., *Ger.* 44.
30. Dio 52.27.3. For Tacitus's comment, see text at n. 29 above.

31. Tac., *Hist.* I.4: evulgato imperii arcano posse principem alibi quam Romae fieri.
32. Gibbon's halcyon picture of the second century in ch. 3 is justly famous and a hallmark of his work: "If a man were called to fix the period in the history of the world, during which the condition of the human race was most happy and prosperous, he would, without hesitation, name that which elapsed from the death of Domitian to the accession of Commodus. The vast extent of the Roman Empire was governed by absolute power, under the firm but gentle hand of four successive emperors, whose character and authority commanded involuntary respect. The forms of the civil administration were carefully preserved by Nerva, Trajan, Hadrian, and the Antonines, who delighted in the image of liberty, and were pleased with considering themselves as the accountable ministers of the laws." Gibbon (1909–14) 1: 85 f.
33. Aur. Vict., *Caes.* 39. For Diocletian's name, see Lact., *DMP* 9.
34. Millar (1977) 350 identifies the end of the second century and beginning of the third as "the period in which the emperor finally emerged from what remained of the senatorial context, and could be seen as an independent monarchy."
35. MacMullen (1986) 215. See Tocqueville (1835–40) pt. 1, ch. 14, "General tendency of the laws under the rule of the American Democracy, and habits of those who apply them."
36. Sickle (1939); Chastagnol (1970); Talbert (1984).
37. Gibbon (1909–14) 1: 86.
38. Burckhardt (1949) 32 refers to generals as "a kind of Senate in arms." Cf. for the republic Brunt (1971) 117: "the effective popular instrument was the army."
39. *Gesta Senatus Urbis Romae,* tr. Pharr (1952) 3–7.
40. On acclamations: Roueché (1984). On the importance of ceremonial in general, MacCormack (1981), Cannadine & Price (1987).
41. Brown (1992) ch. 1; see also Heather (1994).
42. Xen., *Cyr.* 8.2.4.
43. Dio 53.19.2–3. Julius Caesar had ordered the proceedings of the Senate to be published for the first time during his consulate in 59 B.C., a move that was widely seen as a means of exerting public pressure on that body. Significantly, Augustus canceled the publication. See Suet., *Aug.* 36.
44. Dio 52.3. For the estimated number of open appointments, see Saller (1982) 50; Hopkins (1980) 121 estimates that there were no more than 150 administrative positions in the entire empire in the second century A.D. Lendon (1998) 3 estimates 30,000 civilian officials in the empire at its most bureaucratic stage. See also Chapter 4 below, n. 5.
45. Taft (1925) 66.
46. Tac., *Ann.* I.47.

47. Tac., *Ann.* I.35.
48. Brown (1992) 50: "So much alert attention to deportment betrays a fact almost too big to be seen. We are in a world characterized by a chilling absence of legal restraints on violence in the exercise of power."
49. Diotogenes apud Stobaeus II.7.61. On the problem of date, see Chesnut (1986) 144–45.
50. Xen., *Cyr.* 1.1.3; see n. 18 above.
51. A striking example of the different perspective is the conclusion drawn by Millar (1984b) 58. For more extensive, and equally insightful, studies, see Zanker (1988); Nicolet (1991). For Augustus's boast, see Suet., *Aug.* 28.3.
52. For a useful survey of the argument, see Levick (1982). On local influences, Harl (1996). Ando (forthcoming) demonstrates the skill with which provincials used imperial propaganda to manipulate the system.
53. Plin., *NH* 6.24.84.
54. Cosmas, *Chr. Top.* 11.338.
55. Millar (1977) 6.
56. Millar (1977) 6: "If we follow our evidence, we might almost come to believe that the primary role of the emperor was to listen to speeches in Greek."
57. For a good overview of the rules for panegyrics, see the introductory discussion by Russell and Wilson in Men. Rhet., *Peri epideik.* Also useful are Maguinness (1932); Straub (1939); Previale (1949–50); MacCormack (1975) and (1976); Kennedy (1983); Schmitz (1997).
58. Dio Chr., *First Discourse on Kingship,* 36. On Dio: Jones (1979).
59. On Themistius, see *PLRE* 1: 889–94; Dagron (1967); Vanderspoel (1995).
60. Them., *Or.* 1.11, tr. Downey (1958) 61.
61. Dio Chr., *Second Discourse on Kingship* 75.
62. Dio Chr., *Third Discourse on Kingship* 2.
63. Dio Chr., *First Discourse on Kingship* 20, *Second Discourse on Kingship* 77.
64. Dio Chr., *Third Discourse on Kingship* 60.
65. Plin. Iun., *Pan.* 53.5.
66. Joh. Chry., *Comp.* 2–3.
67. Seston (1947); Straub (1957); Caron (1975); Decker & Dupuis-Masay (1980).

Chapter Three. The Church Becomes a Player

1. Epistle of James 2:2–4.
2. The widely used estimate of 7–10 percent of the population in 312 was made on the basis of an extensive survey of all the literary evidence by Harnack (1904–5) 2: 387, n. 1. Using an estimate of 1,000 Christians in the year 40 and a projected growth of 3.42 percent a year, or 40 percent per decade, Stark (1996) ch. 1 calculated a Christian population of 6.3

million in 300, roughly 10.5 percent of an estimated total population of 60 million. Cf. similar numbers in Hopkins (1998) 192.

3. Gibbon (1909–14) 2: 57: "exclusive zeal."
4. Brown (1995) 16–17.
5. As observed by George (1997) 71.
6. Gibbon (1909–14) ch. 15, 2: 57. Sulpicius Severus is cited in ch. 16 at 2: 111.
7. Bayat (1998) 138–41. Cf. the conclusion of Stark (1996) 208: "The early church was a mass movement in the fullest sense and not simply the creation of an elite."
8. This discussion is based loosely on Stark (1987).
9. *Letter to Diognetus* 5.5, tr. in Richardson (1953): 216–17 (slightly altered). Stark (1996) 213 cites Christianity's lack of traditional ethnic criteria as a prime reason for the success of the movement.
10. Stark (1996) ch. 5.
11. See, e.g., Deutsch (1973) 823; Stark (1996) 20.
12. Origen, *c. Cels.* 3.10–11.
13. Matt. 22:18–22.
14. Mark 9:38–40.
15. Luke 18:18–25.
16. On the date of the *HE,* see, with discussion of earlier scholarship, Louth (1990); Burgess (1997). On Eusebius, see further Chapter 10 below.
17. Stark (1987) 13, 23. I am indebted to the insights of Stroumsa (1993). See also White (1993b) 32.
18. Stark (1987) 26–27. See also Hefner (1993) 30.
19. Gen. 18:23–25.
20. Matt. 24:38–41.
21. John 13:34–35.
22. Luke 6:32–36. Cf. Matt. 5:43–49.
23. I Cor. 14:2, 9.
24. Stark (1987) 21 stresses on the importance of achieving a critical mass of followers by the end of the first generation if a new faith is to survive the "crisis of confidence" which comes with the passing of the first generation. Failing this, he argues, survivors "will lose hope and turn the movement inward—adopt a new rhetoric that de-emphasizes growth and conversion."
25. Celsus's work, the *Alethe Logos* (or True Account), only survives in passages quoted more than half a century later in a rebuttal by the Christian Origen. For the passage cited, see Orig., *c. Cels.* 3.59.
26. Lucian, *obit. Per.* 13.
27. Min. Fel., *Oct.* ch. 9.
28. Tac., *Ann.* 15.43–45.
29. Tac., *Ann.* 15.45.

30. Plin. Iun., *Ep.* X.96, tr. Stockton (1975) 203–4.
31. Min. Fel., *Oct.* 8–9. Cf. the account of the persecution at Lyons around 180, where Christians are accused "of Thyestean banquets and Oedipodean intercourse," Eus., *HE* 5.1.14.
32. Min. Fel., *Oct.* 9.
33. Acts 19:23–41.
34. Christians used the Greek word *ekklesia*, meaning "assembly," to denote their community (a use that survives in the modern English adjective *ecclesiastical*). The word *church* derives from the Greek *kuriakos oikos*, meaning "the Lord's house."
35. See Price (1984); Beard & North (1990).
36. Tert., *Apol.* 40.
37. As Lane Fox (1987) 314. For Gibbon's five causes, see Chapter 1 above, n. 21.
38. Stark (1987) 13. For the concept of the religious marketplace, see North (1992) 178–79; Stark (1996) ch. 9.
39. Lane Fox (1987) makes a vigorous case for the continued vitality of paganism; see also MacMullen (1981). Ferguson (1970) is still a useful survey. More recently, Feeney (1998).
40. Theologians use the term *henotheism* (from the Greek word for "one," *henos*) to distinguish this type of monotheism from the Judaeo-Christian variety, on the grounds that, unlike true monotheists, henotheists do not deny the existence of other gods. In this rigorous sense most Christians of the time would have to be termed henotheists as well, since they did not deny the existence of the pagan gods but thought of them instead as evil rather than good. More important, Christians and pagans alike conceived of deity as operative in human affairs on a day-to-day basis.
41. "The Martyrdom of Pionius the Presbyter and His Companions," *Act. Mart.* 157 f.
42. Alinsky (1972) xviii.
43. Greg. I, *Ep.* XI.56 (A.D. 601); John Paul II, "Becoming Christians Won't Betray Their Faith, Pope Tells Voodooists," *Los Angeles Times,* Feb. 5, 1993, A12.
44. Nock (1933) 241. "Sun of righteousness": Mal. 4:2; the "Sun of salvation" derives from numerous associations of God with light and salvation, esp. in Psalms (e.g., Ps. 26); see Dölger (1920) 381; see further, Dölger (1918).
45. Mark 9:42–43. Luke 9:49 has the first part only; Matt. 18:6–9 the second, in a different context .
46. Hefner (1993) 11 (drawing on the work of Max Weber). On the hardening of Christian attitudes toward philosophy in the fourth century, see Fowden (1986) 208–9.
47. Eus, *HE* 5.1.23.
48. *Act. Mart.* 163.

49. Mar. Aur., *Med.* 11.3; the Loeb editor (p. 384) thought the specific reference to Christians in this passage a possible gloss, although he conceded that the general reference to Christians remained likely.
50. Quoted in Orig., *c. Cels.* 8.39.
51. Eus., *HE* 5.1.38–39, 60.
52. *Act. Mart.* 159. Aristides was an Athenian statesman of the fourth century B.C. whose name became synonymous with unflinching honesty. Anarchus of Abdera was a philosopher who was tortured to death by the tyrant of Cyprus in the third century B.C.
53. John 14:17. The passage from Acts is 2:2–3.
54. Hefner (1993) 30.
55. Acts 6:3. Cf. I Tim. 3.1–13.
56. Gordon (1990).
57. Gibbon (1909–14) ch. 15, 2: 58.
58. Stoops (1993) 143–57; cf. Bobertz (1988).
59. On the importance of communication, Riddle (1931) 104–5; Clark (1993); Tilley (1990).
60. His letter is reproduced in Eus., *HE* 7.22; the passage quoted occurs as *HE* 7.22.8.
61. Const., *OC* 11.5, 15.1.
62. Harnack (1904–5) 2: 453 estimated there were about thirteen hundred to sixteen hundred bishops in the empire in 312. On the Christian population, see n. 2 above.

Chapter Four. The Old Guard Changes

1. On Gallienus's actions, see Eus., *HE* 7.13.1–2. Lact., *DMP* 13.1 gives the date of Diocletian's first edict as February 24, 303. The fourth edict was issued by early 304. See Corcoran (1996) 179–82.
2. Eus., *HE* 8.1.1.
3. Lact., *DMP* 2–5. Lactantius dwells with loving detail on Valerian's fate in captivity, where he was forced to spend the rest of his days as the Persian king's footrest. After his death his hide was tanned and stuffed and put on display in the palace.
4. Lact., *DMP* 7. For Lactantius's account of the origin of Diocletian's persecution, see *DMP* 10–11.
5. Heather (1994) 18. For estimates for earlier periods, see Chapter 2 above, n. 44.
6. On Pliny's appointment, see Millar (1977) 325–26. See further Chapter 3 above, at n. 30.
7. In the twelfth century, southern China had 4,000 officials deployed in 1,000 units, or about 1 for every 15,000 inhabitants: Hopkins (1980) 121.

In 1985, the United States Congress alone had a staff of more than 24,000: Smith (1988) 281.

8. Lact., *DMP* 22 (Creed tr., with minor modifications).
9. Aur. Vict., *Caes.* 39–40.
10. Dio 77.15.2. On the Severans: Birley (1989); Grant (1996). On Marcus's policy: Wallace-Hadrill (1982) 46.
11. *IIA* III: 16–55. On this work see Syme (1971); Barnes (1978); Paschoud (1988).
12. The text of the edict and a translation by E. Graser are in Frank (1933–40) 5: 305–421. The translation here is as adapted in Lewis & Reinhold (1955) 2: 465. Corcoran (1996) 207–13 has a good discussion of the rhetoric of the preamble, which he calls "the most striking example of the high rhetoric of late imperial pronouncements" (207). See also his fuller discussion of the edict, 205–33.
13. Lact., *DMP* 7.2–3.
14. Xen., *Cyr.* 8.1.14–15.
15. Braudel (1973) 1: 355. His chapter on distance, which is introduced by this epigram, may be profitably read alongside the calculations in Mac-Mullen (1976), esp. chs. 3, 8, and 9.
16. Ammianus 16.10.9–11. Cf. his judgment on Constantius at 21.16.7. This scene is now a locus classicus for studies of ceremony in late antiquity: MacCormack (1981) 40–43.
17. Xen., *Cyr.* 8.1.41. The connection between these passages was previously noticed by A. Wallace-Hadrill (1982) 33; cf. Matthews (1989) 233.
18. On acclamations, see above, Chapter 2, n. 40.
19. Dio Chr., *First Discourse on Kingship,* 79–80.
20. Diotogenes II.7.61–62. On the date and authenticity of these works, see Delatte (1942); Burkert (1972).
21. Ecphantus II.7.65, 64. For the oration, see *Corp. Herm.* XVIII.8, tr. Barker (1956) 374–75. For a useful survey of the Hellenistic roots of this ideology, see Chesnut (1978).
22. Eus., *LC* 5.4, 6–7.
23. Julian, *Caes.* 335B. Dvornik (1955); Bowersock (1982a); Athanassiadi (1992); Bradbury (1995).
24. "The Code of Hammurabi," Prologue, tr. T. Meek in Pritchard (1969) 164. For an argument connecting Hellenistic ruler worship with precedents in the ancient Near East, see McEwan (1934). On ruler cult, see Cerfaux & Tondrian (1957); Small (1996).
25. On Roman cult: Millar (1972); Price (1980) and (1984).
26. *Corp. Herm.* 24.1–3, tr. Scott (1924) 1: 495 f.
27. Suetonius, *Vita Tiberii* 27, in idem, *De vita Caesarum*, text and tr. J. C. Rolfe, *The Lives of the Caesars* (Cambridge, Mass., 1913), 1: 334.
28. Nock (1947) 104.

29. *FHG* 4: 197; Nock (1930) 263–64.
30. Ecphantus II.7.64.
31. Dölger (1920); Dölger (1918). Halsbergh (1972). For Christus-Helios, see Chapter 4, fig. 2, and Toynbee & Ward-Perkins (1958) 72 f., 116 f. See also below, Chapter 10, n. 85.
32. Lucian, *obit. Per.* 12–13. For Paul, I Cor. 1:2. Lucian's comment serves to confirm the roughly contemporary claim of Justin Martyr that it was the responsibility of bishops to care for orphans and widows, those in need, those in prison, and "those foreigners dwelling among us." Just. Mart., 1 *Apol.* 67.7.
33. Lucian, *obit. Per.* 13.
34. From Eus., *HE* 7.22.1–10.
35. Stark (1993) 170 f.
36. Bobertz (1992).
37. *Acta Petri* 30. Cf. Stoops (1993) 152: "The story of Chryse . . . is designed to show definitively that those who are patrons on the material level are not suited to be spiritual leaders and should not receive honor or authority within the community." According to Suetonius, the emperor Vespasian drew a similar distinction between source and efficacy when his son Titus complained about a new tax on public toilets: "He [Vespasian] held a piece of money from the first payment to his son's nose, asking whether its odour was offensive to him. When Titus said 'No,' he replied, 'Yet it comes from urine.'" Suet., *Vesp.* 23.3.
38. Letter of Bishop Cornelius of Rome, in Eus., *HE* 6.43.11.
39. Stark (1993) 160.
40. Stark (1993) 161 points out the effects on traditional communities of the disasters of the third century. Stoops (1993) 146 notes the disruptive effect of conversion even in the more peaceful second century. On religious developments, see Nock (1947); Liebeschuetz (1979) 307; Martin (1991). On pagan monotheism, see now Athanassiadi & Frede (1999).
41. The classic treatment is Dodds (1965). On Aristides, see Behr (1968); on Fronto, Champlin (1980). In general, Lane Fox (1987) pt. 1.
42. Apul., *Metam.* 11.1–6. See Nock (1933) ch. 9.
43. Apul., *Metam.* 11.4.
44. In addition to the story of Peregrinus (above, n. 32), his exposé of *Alexander, the False Prophet* is best known. Translations are readily available in the series of Loeb Classical Texts or Casson (1962). See also n. 41 above.
45. Bowersock (1990) 26. The classic work on Julian remains Bidez (1930); see also Nulle (1959) and (1961). On Eunapius, see Breebaart (1979); Penella (1990).
46. See the inscriptions quoted in Lane Fox (1987) ch. 5. See further Robinson (1993).
47. Plin. Iun., *Ep.* X.96, tr. Stockton (1975) 204.

48. In response to Pliny's report of anonymous denunciations, Trajan wrote, "Pamphlets circulated anonymously . . . create the worst sort of precedent and are quite out of keeping with the spirit of our age" (Sine auctore vero propositi libelli . . . et pessimi exempli nec nostri saeculi est: Plin. Iun., *Ep.* X.97). In describing his encounter with Athanasius to the bishops at Tyre in 335, Constantine wrote that he granted the request for a hearing because "this seemed reasonable to me and fitting to the times" (τοῖς καιροῖς πρέπον): Athan., *Apol. sec.* 86.9.

49. Dio 52.36.1–2.

50. Eus., *HE* 8.1.

51. Lact., *DMP* 42.

52. Lact., *DMP* 33–35. On the edict, see further below.

53. Lact., *DMP* 11.

54. Lact., *DMP* 29.

55. *Mos. et Rom. coll.* 15.3, with modifications from Stevenson (1957) 283. The document has been dated as early as 297, but Barnes (1981) 20 dates it to 302; Corcoran (1996) 135–36 presents the case for alternative dates but finds 302 "by far the most likely."

56. Lact., *DMP* 10.1–4.

57. Barnes (1981) 18 places the event in 299. Davies (1989) argues for 302.

58. In Constantine's Edict to the Eastern Provincials, Eus., *VC* 2.50.

59. Lact., *DMP* 11.7.

60. Eus., *PE* 4.135D–136A.

61. Lact., *DI* 5.2.3.

62. Eus., *c. Hier.* Hägg (1992) has challenged the traditional identification of the author of this tract with Eusebius of Caesarea. For Hierocles, see Barnes (1976b).

63. Digeser (1998) includes a review of earlier scholarship.

64. Lact., *DI* 5.2.

65. Lact., *DMP* 34.1–2. Creed notes that in a Greek translation published in Eus., *HE* 8.17, the Latin that he translates "such self-will," *tanta voluntas,* is rendered *pleonexia,* "greed," or a "seeking-to-have-more," a term that calls to mind Diocletian's attitude in the Edict on Prices. See Corcoran (1996) 208–11.

66. There is disagreement over the extent of Neoplatonist involvement in the Great Persecution. Wallis (1972) 102, n. 1, concluded that "Neoplatonists do not seem to have encouraged persecution of the Christians." Liebeschuetz (1979) 235 thought the Neoplatonist movement "became self-consciously pagan and hostile to Christianity." Cf. idem 247. See also Millar (1977) 573; Lane Fox (1987) 592–95.

67. Fowden (1993) 3: "The defining characteristic of late antiquity . . . was its conviction that knowledge of the One God both justifies the exercise of imperial power and makes it more effective."

68. At the end of the second century, Celsus tied expressions of loyalty to blood sacrifice. Orig., *c. Cels.* 8.63. As Alföldi (1948) 9–10 noted, the effect of Gallienus's edict was that the empire now gave up the requirement "to prove and express" loyalty by sacrifice to gods. Cf. Frend (1967) 207: "Seventy years later, when Origen wrote his reply, Celsus could not have argued convincingly on these lines."

69. Eus., *HE* 8.1.2. Eusebius does not say which emperor was responsible for loosening the obligation to sacrifice, and some scholars think the change was introduced by Diocletian. But the context of Eusebius's remarks is the effect of Galerius's changes, indicating that he at least saw the relaxation as a product of the period in general, if not of Gallienus in particular. Government service appears to have been an avenue for Christian mobility even in the Principate. See Finn (1982).

70. Eus., *VC* 2.51.

71. Lact., *DI* 5.23; cf. 5.13.11. Const., *OC* 22; Athan., *Hist. Ar.* 64; cf. Ste. Croix (1954) 100.

72. Burckhardt (1949) 268: After 311 "the Christians returning home from prisons and mines were joyfully welcomed even by the pagan population, so weary had men grown of horrors." Cf. MacMullen (1969) 25–30; Barnes (1991) 237.

73. Eus., *DE* 8.5. Cf. Eus., *HE* 9.1.11, where Eusebius describes the welcome given returning Christians by their pagan neighbors. Cf. Lact., *DI* 5.13.11 (pagan revulsion at cruelty), Athan., *Hist. Ar.* 64 (pagans shelter Christians). Barnes (1976a) 416 argued that "tyrannus" in Eusebius "denotes a legitimate emperor who persecuted the Christians."

74. Schattschneider (1960) 2–3. Cf. Deutsch (1973) 398.

75. Lact., *DMP* 34.3–5.

Chapter Five. In Search of a Vision

1. Eus., *VC* 2.28. For the date, see Barnes (1981) 377, n. 12.

2. Eus., *VC* 4.9. Jones (1962) 171–72 thought the letter convinced Shapur that Christians in his realm could not be trusted; Barnes (1981) 258 describes it as "polite and personal."

3. Eusebius's reference (*VC* 1.12) to Constantine's youth at the time of the persecution at one time added fuel to arguments against the authenticity of that work. Similarly, Constantine refers to himself in the Edict to the Eastern Provincials as still young while with Diocletian: Eus., *VC* 2.51. Jones (1954) drained much of the force from this criticism with the technical point that, in Roman usage, *puer* could apply to any man under the age of thirty, and even more with his demonstration that the Constantinian documents in the *VC* were genuine. Ison (1987) attributed such language to court rhetoric. He is aided by *Pan. Lat.* VI.17.1, which com-

pares Constantine to the youthful Alexander. Elliott (1997) 84 suggests the more sinister motive of masking the emperor's complicity in the persecution. See also Chapter 2 above, n. 3.

4. Eus., *PE* 4.10–19 uses the argument against blood sacrifice of the Neoplatonist and anti-Christian Porphyry to justify Christian practice. On changing pagan practice, see further Bradbury (1995); Bagnall (1993) 262; and Chapter 6 below, n. 20.

5. *Pan. Lat.* VIII.3–4.

6. Lact., *DMP* 19.1–5.

7. Barnes (1981) 75 inferred Constantine's service in Persia from his reference to Babylon at *OC* 16. According to Lactantius (*DMP* 18.10), Constantine rose to the rank of *tribunis ordinis primi* in Diocletian's *comitatus*, and he was probably in this rank when Eusebius first saw him riding at Diocletian's side, *VC* 1.19. The date was probably 296 or 297, when Diocletian marched through Palestine to put down a usurper in Alexandria. Barnes (1981) 17.

8. As often in Roman dynastic arrangements, Maxentius's relationship to Constantine is convoluted. It is usual to refer to the two as brothers-in-law, because Maxentius's sister Fausta married Constantine in 307. But since Constantine's father, Constantius I, put aside his mother, Helena, when he was elevated to Caesar in 293 to wed Maximian's daughter, Theodora, who was Maxentius's half sister, Maxentius was brother-in-law to the father as well as the son, and uncle to the latter as well.

9. *Eudoxia* 6–13.

10. Details of the progress of the persecution continue to be debated, but the general outline is clear. See Barnes (1981) ch. 2; Liebeschuetz (1979) 245–52; Kolb (1988); Davies (1989); Portmann (1990); Woods (1992); Brock (1994).

11. The case for propaganda has been vigorously restated by Grünewald (1990). See the sober comments by Nixon (1993). See also Nixon & Rodgers (1994) 26–33.

12. See, e.g., MacCormack (1976) 155; Matthews (1989) 247–49.

13. *Pan. Lat.* VI (VII) 14.3. See Nixon (1993).

14. See now the excellent treatment in Smith (1997).

15. Delbrueck (1933); Bruun (1976).

16. Sutherland (1967) 110–11.

17. Lact., *DMP* 24.9.

18. Eus., *HE* 9.5.

19. Nicholson (1994).

20. Pincherle (1929); Schoenebeck (1939); Pezzela (1967); Decker (1968).

21. *Lib. Pont.*, s.v. Eusebius (32), Miltiades (33). See Salvatorelli (1928) 297–98; Grégoire (1930) 212; Frend (1967) 388–89; Decker (1968) 515.

22. Eus., *HE* 8.14.1.

23. Const., *OC* 22.
24. Eus., *HE* 8.14.7.
25. By Roman inclusive reckoning, which counted the first year, in this case 306, as well as the last, 310. Thus, 306 to 310 equals five years, instead of four.
26. *Pan. Lat.* VI (VII) 23.1–2.
27. *Pan. Lat.* VI (VII) 3.3–4.
28. *Pan. Lat.* VI (VII) 14.1.
29. *Pan. Lat.* VI (VII).
30. *Pan. Lat.* VI (VII) 16.5, 16.1.
31. *Pan. Lat.* VI (VII) 15.4.
32. *Pan. Lat.* VI (VII) 16.2
33. Eus., *VC* 1.27.
34. Eus., *VC* 1.29–32.
35. Lact., *DMP* 44.3–5. On the date of the *DMP,* see Barnes (1973).
36. See MacMullen (1968). On dreams in antiquity, see Hanson (1981); Price (1987); Miller (1994).
37. *Pan. Lat.* XII (IX) 2.5, mente diuina; 4.1, diuinum numen; 11.4, diuino . . . instinctu; 13.2, deus ille mundi creator et dominus; 26.1: summe rerum sator.
38. For the arch: l'Orange & Gerkan (1939); Pierce (1989); Hall (1998).
39. *Pan. Lat.* VI (VII) 21.4–6.
40. Most strenuously by Grégoire in (1930) and (1939); see also Seston (1936); Orgels (1948); Galletier (1950); Paschoud (1971): Bleckmann (1992). For the coins, see Bruun (1958) and (1962); Alföldi (1964). For the arch, see n. 38 above.
41. Béranger (1970); Liebeschuetz (1981); Müller-Rettig (1990); Rodgers (1980) argues that the passage does not say that Constantine saw his features on the god Apollo, but on the first of the emperors, Augustus. On the meaning of neutral pagan language, see Jones (1962) 83; cf. Barnes (1981) 48: "the dead weight of iconographic tradition."
42. Jones (1962) 85; Barnes (1981) 306, n. 148. DiMaio (1988) is an attempt to revive this explanation.
43. *Pan. Lat.* XII (IX) 26.1–2. Nixon and Rodgers translate *summe rerum sator* at 2.5 as "supreme creator of things."
44. Eus., *LC* 6.2; cf. *LC* 10.7. Similar sentiments were voiced by Constantine's pagan orators. See *Pan. Lat.* VI (VII) 21.4; *Pan. Lat.* IV (X) 2.5–6. At *VC* 4.67, Eusebius describes Constantine's body as continuing to receive courtiers "as though he were still alive." On Eusebius's speech, see also Chapter 10 below.
45. Const., *OC* 11.1–2. On this speech, see further Chapter 9.
46. Eus., *VC* 2.28.
47. Eus., *VC* 4.20. For the Sunday law, *CTh* 2.8.1.

48. *Pan. Lat.* VI (VII) 3.1.
49. *Pan. Lat.* VI (VII) 7.3–5.
50. Eus., *VC* 1.27.
51. Nock (1933) 266, 7–8. James' classic discussion of the psychology of conversion in his Gifford Lectures at the University of Edinburgh in 1901–2 appears as chs. 9 and 10 of James (1902). See also Chapter 1 above, n. 16.
52. Eus., *VC* 2.12.
53. White (1993c); see also Stark (1993); Hefner (1993); Rambo (1993). See also the various essays in Needleman & Baker (1979). On the need of Christian converts to learn a new history, see Momigliano (1963b) 82–83. The description of "biographical reconstruction" is in Segal (1990) 74.
54. *Pan. Lat.* VI (VII) 14.3. Goodenough (1953) 434: Helios "was the one God whom all religions recognized as behind their particular saviors." See also Chapter 4 above, n. 31.
55. *VC* 3.34.

Chapter Six. Building a Coalition

1. Lact., *DMP* 48.2–12; cf. Eus., *HE* 10.5.2–14. See Anastos (1967) and (1979).
2. Lact., *DMP* 48.2.
3. Lact., *DMP* 48.11.
4. Lact., *DMP* 48.2–3.
5. Lact., *DMP* 46.1–7.
6. Lact., *DMP* 50.7.
7. Eus., *HE* 9.9.1. Eusebius's account of the war between Constantine and Licinius is in Eus., *VC* 2.1–19.
8. Jones (1962) 82–83.
9. Elliott (1987) and (1997) ch. 4 questions Eusebius's account and argues that Constantine was born a Christian.
10. Smith (1988) 507.
11. Deutsch (1973) 360.
12. Constantine's views may be seen in his letter to the principals in the Arian controversy, Eus., *VC* 2.64–72. On this controversy, see Chapter 7 below.
13. Constantine's Edict to the Eastern Provincials is at Eus., *VC* 2.48–60 (for the passages cited, see 2.49, 53, 54).
14. Edict to the Palestinians, Eus., *VC* 2.24–42 (for the passage cited, see 2.27).
15. Alföldi (1932); Kraft (1954–55); Bruun (1962).
16. Eus., *VC* 1.31.
17. Lact., *DMP* 44.5: Commonitus est in quiete Constantinus, ut caeleste signum dei notaret in scutis atque ita proelium committeret. Fecit ut

iussus est et transversa X littera, summo capite circumflexo, Christum in scutis notat.

18. Bruun (1966) 61; Alföldi (1964); Bruun (1992). for the solar disk, see Gardthausen (1924) 98–102. See further Black (1970).
19. Eus., *VC* 1.29–32.
20. On changes in the importance of blood sacrifice, see Bradbury (1995); cf. Nilsson (1945) 65: "Animal sacrifice was not the dominating rite" in late antiquity. See also Bagnall (1993) 262–68. Cf. Chapter 5 above, n. 4.
21. Saint Paul speaks of "the breadth and length and height and depth of Christ's love" at Eph. 3:18. MacMullen (1984) 21; Wardman (1982) 136.
22. See Grabar (1967) 177 (Isis-Horus); Grabar (1968) 28–29 (Good Shepherd), 80 (Christus-Helios); Bahat (1990) 74 (Christian Orpheus).
23. Momigliano (1963b) 79.
24. For this treatment of Lactantius, see Digeser (1998) and Digeser (1999).
25. Jer., *vir. Ill.*
26. Lact., *DI* I.1.
27. Digeser (1994).
28. Lact., *DI* 5.1.
29. Digeser (1999) ch. 5.
30. Lact., *DI* 5.13. For the story of Mucius Scaevola, see Livy, 2.12–13; and for Marcus Regulus, Livy, 18 *periocha,* and Horace, *Carm.* 3.5.
31. Schattschneider (1960) 2–3 (see Chapter 4 above, at n. 74).
32. In Orig., *c. Cels.* III.44.
33. Lact., *DI* 5.1. The quotation is from Virgil, *Bucol.* X.8.
34. Lact., *DI* 5.19. Vanderspoel (1990) 182 likens the Neoplatonist Porphyry's efforts to assemble and elucidate pagan oracles to "compiling Scripture (or divine revelation) for the religious elements in Neoplatonism." Cf. Wallis (1972) 105; Potter (1994) 49, 95. See further Chapter 3, n. 44. Lim (1995) documents the increasing tendency to appeal to authority in late antiquity.
35. Lact., *DI* 5.20.
36. Garnsey (1984) 16 notes that Christians were the first to argue for freedom of religion as a general principle.
37. Lact., *DI* 5.19.
38. Lact., *DMP* 48.2–3.
39. Frend (1952); Girardet (1975); Barnes (1982) ch. 15; Girardet (1989).
40. Optatus 3.3: quid est imperatori cum ecclesia?
41. Eus., *HE* 10.5.15–17. For a reading of this correspondence as proof of Constantine's orthodoxy, see Elliott (1997) ch. 5.
42. Eus., *HE* 10.6.1. On Constantine's monetary reforms and the fate of the *follis,* see Chastagnol (1982) 356–59.
43. Eus., *HE* 10.7.2.

44. Jones (1964) 1: 440 provides figures that indicate a *follis* was worth 3 *solidi*, at a time when 4 *solidi* paid for a year's rations for a common soldier (1: 447).
45. Eus., *HE* 10.7.1–2.
46. Optatus, 1.22. Anulinus's letter is quoted by Augustine, *Ep.* 88.2.
47. Using terms defined by Schattschneider (1960) 40, 82.
48. Eus., *HE* 7.29–30. Millar (1971).
49. Optatus, Appx. 7: Quid potius agi a me pro instituto meo ipsiusque principis munere oporteat . . . ? (my tr.).
50. *Pan. Lat.* IV (X).5.2: "But you bring it to pass, greatest of rulers, that things which had previously been shut away are seen to lie open, you who desire as much to be seen in your entirety as the rest were reluctant." See *CTh.* 1.16.6, 1.16.7, 9.1.4, and Chapter 9 below.
51. Constantine's letter: Eus., *HE* 10.6. Aug., *c. litt. Petil.* 1.4.7, 1.5.10, 1.8.13 refers to Donatist attacks on Ossius.
52. Eus., *HE* 10.5.18–20.
53. Eus., *HE* 7.31.1.
54. In a subsequent letter to the vicar of Africa, Constantine reported that the Donatists alleged to him "that the whole case had not been heard, and that the same bishops had rather locked themselves up in a certain place and reached the verdict most amenable to themselves." Optatus, Appx. 3. See further Pietri (1976) 1: 60–66.
55. Eus., *HE* 10.5.19–20.
56. Barnes (1982) 71.
57. See the letter of bishops at Arles to Pope Silvester of Rome (Miltiades having died in the interim) in Optatus, Appx. 4. The letter regrets his absence in language that could be taken to mean either he had chosen not to attend or he had been excluded. As a rule, bishops of Rome did not attend councils elsewhere as a way of protecting their primacy.
58. Optatus, Appx. 5.
59. Optatus, Appx. 7.
60. Letter to Celsus (Optatus, Appx. 7). Constantine had already characterized the Donatists as "officers of the devil" in his letter to the Catholic bishops after the council of Arles (Optatus, Appx. 5); in his letter of 330 to the Numidian bishops (Optatus, Appx. 10), he argues that "there is no doubt that heresy and schism proceed from the devil."
61. "Constantine Augustus to all the bishops throughout Africa and to the people of the Catholic Church." Optatus, Appx. 9.
62. Optatus, Appx. 10.
63. Barnes (1981) 254.
64. See, e.g., Eus., *LC* 1.1. ("Highest of All"); 1.3, 2.5, 5.5, 5.8 ("Supreme Sovereign"); 10.2 ("Universal Creator"). See further Chapter 10 below.

65. Eus., *LC* 9.5: νέου τινὸς ἐπιφανέντος. At *LC* 4.2, Eusebius speaks of the Logos "coming into contact with mortals." On this speech, see further Chapter 10 below.
66. Solar imagery: *LC* 3.4; longevity of rule: *LC* 2.1 and *VC* 1.5; divine selection: *LC* 3.1, 7.12, and *VC* 1.24. See further Goodenough (1928); Baynes (1934); Chesnut (1978); and Chapter 10 below.
67. See, e.g., Barker (1956) 460: "Along with Eusebius of Caesarea, he [Lactantius] became the apologist and prophet of the new Christian Empire; and it has been said that the two were the Virgil and Horace of Constantine, founding a political ideology in support of his government as their predecessors had done for the government of Augustus."
68. Eus., *HE* 8.1.2; at *DI* 5.1, Lactantius gives as one reason for his work the fact that "very many are wavering, especially those who have had some acquaintance with literature"; for the church of Nicomedia, see Lact., *DMP* 14.3.
69. Stark & Bainbridge (1985) 99–125.
70. The groundbreaking article was Meigne (1975). His arguments were further refined by Suberbiola (1987), who argued for five councils, dating from 298 to 396. Of the ten canons discussed here, Suberbiola places five (2–4, 59, and 60) in either 298 or 309; he assigns the remaining five (40, 41, 55–57) to councils that would have met at midcentury: see his Appx. 2. The most recent edition of the canons is in Martinez & Rodriguez (1987): 233–68; they are most readily available in Hefele-Leclercq (1973) vol. 1, pt. 1: 212–64.
71. For the theory, see Stark & Bainbridge (1985) 99–125.
72. "Si quis idola fregerit et ibidem fuerit occisus, quatenus in Evangelio scriptum non est neque invenietur sub apostolis unquam factum, placuit in numero eum non recipi martyrum." Hefele-Leclercq (1973) vol. 1, pt. 1: 163. Lane Fox (1987) 664 has argued for a date later in Constantine's reign, on the grounds that Christians were not in a position to attack temples earlier; Suberbiola (1987) 46–47 assigns it to a first council that he places in 298.
73. Lact., *DMP* 11.5.
74. See Chapter 2.
75. Eus., *VC* 1.44.
76. Eus., *VC* 4.24.
77. Seston (1947); Straub (1967); Caron (1975); Decker & Dupuis-Masay (1980).
78. Eus., *VC* 1.44.
79. For the letter to Aelafius, see Optatus, Appx. 3; to the bishops (my tr.), idem, Appx. 5.
80. As observed by Alinsky (1972) 133. Jesus' statement is at Luke 11:23.
81. Alinsky (1972) 152.

82. Stark & Bainbridge (1985) 104–7, 123. Rubin (1970) 125 may offer a hip, secular insight into the Donatist attitude in his account of radical thinking in the 1960s: "Satisfy our demands, and we got twelve more. The more demands you satisfy, the more we got. . . . Demonstrators are never 'reasonable.' We always put our demands forward in such an obnoxious manner that the power structure can never satisfy us and remain the power structure. Then, we scream, righteously angry, when our demands are not met. . . . Goals are irrelevant. The tactics, the actions, are critical."

83. Refuted by Jones (1959).

84. Hofstadter (1965a) 39; Stroumsa (1994). See also n. 71 above.

85. The canon reads: "Ut qui in pace arma projiciunt excommunicentur. De his qui arma projiciunt in pace, placuit abstineri eos a communione." The subject could be gladiators rather than soldiers, since canons 4 and 5 deal with charioteers and theater personnel. See Hefele-LeClercq (1973) vol. 1, pt. 1: 186.

Chapter Seven. Consensus Politics

1. Millar (1977) 591, n. 7, suggested that *CTh* 1.27.1, a law attributed to Constantine which gave judicial powers to bishops, might actually have been issued by Licinius. See further Corcoran (1993). Barnes (1981) 68 f. notes the effect of Constantinian propaganda on Licinius's reputation. On *CTh* 1.27.1, see further Chapter 9 below, n. 18. On Christian population, see Chapter 3 above, n. 2.

2. Eus., *VC* 2.2.

3. Constantine's letter, dated A.D. 325, is included as an addendum to Gel., *HE* (= Opitz, *Urk.* 27: 10.1–11.4), tr. Stevenson (1957) 372–73 (slightly modified).

4. For a chronology of the controversy and discussion of the issues, see Hanson (1988).

5. Hunt (1982) ch. 2; Wilken (1992b). On the Helena legend, see also Chapter 9 below. On the executions of Crispus and Fausta, see Austin (1980); Pohlsander (1984); Woods (1998).

6. Julian, *Caes.* 336AB. See further Seston (1936); Paschoud (1971); Pohlsander (1984); Woods (1998). Burckhardt (1949) 284 connected the incident with "sultanism." Helena's pilgrimage: Drijvers (1992), ch. 5.

7. Gregg & Groh (1981); Hanson (1988) 145; Wiles (1962). See further Gregg (1985); Williams (1987); Barnes & Williams (1993); Wiles (1996). Chadwick (1998) provides a lucid overview.

8. Soz., *HE* 1.6.

9. Eus., *VC* 2.69.

10. Eus., *VC* 2.71.

11. Constantine's "Letter to Arius and Alexander" is in Eus., *VC* 2.64–72.

12. Eusebius customarily divided his works into chapters, but textual difficulties suggest that some, if not all, of the headings for the *VC* were written by another. See Winkelmann (1975) xlvi–xlix.
13. Eus., *VC* 2.48–60.
14. Eus., *VC* 2.48–54.
15. Eus., *VC* 2.56.1 (my tr.).
16. Eus., *VC* 2.59.
17. Eus., *VC* 2.65 (my tr.).
18. Bloch (1945) is an effective representation of this view. See also the chapters by Bloch and others in Momigliano (1963a).
19. Momigliano (1963b) 94: "The opposition to Christianity can be guessed rather than demonstrated in the majority of the pagan students of history."
20. Brown (1961) 9–10.
21. Winkelmann (1961) 250.
22. Brown (1995) 47. On the Calendar of 354 as an expression of a common cultural heritage, see Salzman (1990). For funerary art, and in general, Elsner (1998), Brown (1998).
23. Eus., *VC* 4.55.
24. On Sopater, see Eun., *Vit. Soph.* 463–64. For the foundation stories, Dagron (1974) 37–45; La Rocca (1992–93).
25. Firm. Mat., *Math.* 4.Pr.1–3.
26. The work can be dated on the basis of internal evidence to c. 336. See Mommsen (1894).
27. See, e.g., *Math.* 1.5.6, 1.5.10, 2.30.5, 3.1.9, 4.1.3.
28. Firm. Mat., *Math.* 1.10.14.
29. Firm. Mat., *Math.* 5.Pr.3.
30. Firm. Mat., *Math.* 1.Pr.7–8 refers to Lollianus's appointment as governor of the East by Constantine and addresses him as "Proconsul and designated consul ordinarius." Lollianus did not actually become consul until 355. *PLRE* 1: 512–14.
31. Lib., *Or.* 30.26.
32. Them., *Or.* V, 67B, 68A. Tr. Barker (1956) 378–79. For Themistius, see Vanderspoel (1995). For toleration in Themistius, Daly (1971). However, Brown (1995) 37 points out that the circumstances behind Themistius's speeches must not be ignored: he often sought simply to put an acceptable face on a failed policy.
33. Symm., *Rel.* III.10: "uno itinere non potest perveniri ad tam grande secretum."
34. Garnsey (1984) 21; see also Ando (1996) 186–89.
35. Lib., *Or.* 30.29. Cf. the useful comments on rhetorical training in French (1998) 469–70.
36. Alinsky (1972) 152; Deutsch (1973) 398.
37. Winkelmann (1961) 250: "Er war ein ertragbares Übel." Conversely, Bar-

nes (1981) 210: "A change so sudden, so fundamental, so total shocked pagans."
38. Barnes (1981) 213. See also Logan (1992). The letter of the Council of Antioch survives only in a Syriac version that was translated back into Greek by Edouard Schwartz. See Opitz, *Urk.* 18.
39. "Letter to the Church of Nicomedia," in Gel., *HE* 3, Suppl 1 (= Opitz, *Urk.* 27), tr. Stevenson (1957) 373.
40. Millar (1977) 595.
41. Eus., *VC* 3.10.
42. Millar (1977) 203–6.
43. Eus., *VC* 3.12.
44. Eus., *VC* 3.12.
45. Eus., *VC* 3.13 (Richardson tr. slightly modified).
46. Quoted in Theod., *HE* I.6.
47. Athanasius appended Eusebius's letter to his *De decr.* 33.1–17 (= Opitz, *Urk.* 22). The passage quoted is at 33.7 Newman-Robertson tr., slightly modified.
48. Barnes (1981) 216.
49. Athan., *De decr.* 19.
50. Soc., *HE* 1.23.
51. Eus., *VC* 3.6.
52. Piganiol (1932) 226.
53. Eutr., *Brev.* 10.7. For Eutropius's career, see *PLRE* 1: 317.
54. So Young (1983) 76: "[Athanasius's] apologetic works take the form of dossiers of relevant documents. . . . Yet their objective appearance is deceptive to the extent that the documents were carefully selected to support Athanasius' case." Barnes (1993) is a careful, albeit polemical, study.
55. Soz., *HE* 2.16
56. Soc., *HE* 1.26.
57. Gel., *HE* 3.15.1–5 (= Opitz, *Urk.* 32), tr. Coleman-Norton (1966) 1: 202.
58. Soc., *HE* 1.6.
59. Barnes (1981) 228.
60. Athan., *Apol. sec.* 6 steadfastly denies the charges. Bell (1924) 38–77 offers a detailed account of the pursuit and beating of Meletian monks in 335, based on London Papyrus 1914. Arnold (1991) 71–89 challenges Bell's interpretation of these events. See further Martin (1996) chs. 5–6.
61. Soc., *HE* 1.9 (= Opitz, *Urk.* 23.6–7).
62. Athan., *Apol. sec.* 11–12.
63. Athan, *Apol. sec.* 60–61. Barnes (1981) 232.
64. Soc., *HE* 1.9.30 (= Opitz, *Urk.* 33); for the date, Barnes (1981) 233.
65. Barnes (1981) 234. For the story of Arsenius, see Chapter 1 above.
66. Eus., *VC* 4.42.
67. Athan., *De decr.* 33.10.

68. Athan., *De decr.* 33.16.
69. Eus., *VC* 3.13.
70. Letter to the Church of Nicomedia, in Gel., *HE* 3, Suppl 1 (= Opitz, *Urk.* 27: 14), tr. Stevenson (1957) 373.
71. Athan., *Or. Ar.* 59; cf. Soz., *HE* 2.22.
72. Williams (1951) argued that Arians were theologically more inclined to compromise with the emperor than were orthodox Christians. Chesnut (1986) 159 summarizes the objections to this position.
73. See, e.g., Athan., *De decr.* 38.
74. Constantine quotes from Arius's letter in his own response, preserved in Gel., *HE* 3.19.5 (= Opitz, *Urk.* 34); for the date: Barnes (1981) 232.
75. Soc., *HE* 1.9.30 (= Opitz, *Urk.* 33).
76. Soc., *HE* 1.10 (Zenos tr., with slight emendation). Acesius's scriptural reference is to John 5:15. Socrates identifies the priest who told him the story at *HE* 2.38.
77. Soz., *HE* 1.18. See further Lim (1995) 191–213.
78. Novatians were included in the Edict against the Heretics in Eus., *VC* 3.64, but in *CTh* 16.5.2, dated 326, Constantine specifically exempted the sect from the order to surrender their churches. Soz., *HE* 1.14.9–11 tells how Constantine acceded to the request of a Novatian holy man, Eutychian, that an accused officer be released.
79. "However many he saw responsive to a superior sentiment and endowed with a sound and like-minded character he received eagerly, showing that he himself rejoiced in the mutual agreement of all. But those who stayed unyielding he turned away from." Eus., *VC* 1.44. Eusebius may be speaking specifically of the Council of Arles in this passage, but the statement holds true for every period of Constantine's career. For instance, Eusebius's summary of Constantine's remarks to the bishops following the Council of Nicaea, at *VC* 3.21, has the emperor exhorting them "above all else to honor mutual harmony" (πάντων περὶ πολλοῦ τιμωμένων τὴν σύμφωνον ἁρμονίαν). A decade later, Eusebius says at *VC* 4.41, Constantine urged the bishops at the Council of Tyre "to conduct themselves with concord and harmony" (σὺν ὁμονοίᾳ καὶ συμφωνίᾳ τῇ πάσῃ ἔχεσθαι).

Chapter Eight. Controlling the Message

1. Vincent (1913); Brooks (1921); Neri (1971); Kartsonis (1986). On the festival, Black (1954); Emonds (1956).
2. Eus., *VC* 3.25–40.
3. Drake (1984). Walker (1990) suggests rivalry with the bishop of Jerusalem as a reason for Eusebius's reticence.

4. *Itin. Eger.* 37.2.
5. On the rise of pilgrimage, see Hunt (1982); Wilken (1992b). On Egeria, Sivan (1988). For the date of her pilgrimage, Devos (1967).
6. Eusebius discusses Helena's pilgrimage at *VC* 3.41–44. Gibbon (1909– 14) 2: 481, n. 66. I argued for the likelihood of debris that was identified as that of the cross in Drake (1985a). Taylor (1993) ch. 6 reviews more recent archaeological data. Hunt (1997) remains skeptical in a judicious review of the evidence.
7. Constantine "outfitted with many and abundant distinctions an enormous house of prayer and temple sacred to the Saving Sign, and he honored a memorial full of eternal significance and the Great Savior's own trophies over death with ornaments beyond all description." Eus., *LC* 9.16. On this passage see Drake (1976) 171, n. 25. See also preceding note and Chapter 10 below, n. 79.
8. On Constantine's buildings: Alexander (1971–73); Armstrong (1974); Krautheimer (1983); Odahl (1995). On Augustus, see Chapter 2 above, at n. 51.
9. So Liebeschuetz (1979) 292: "Constantine certainly did not realize the full significance of his change of religious allegiance. The fact is, the Church could never be simply the religious department of the *respublica*, as the old religion had been. The Church had its own officers, the clergy, who were absolutely distinct from the officers of the state."
10. Eus., *VC* 1.32, 3.1, 4.17, 4.22, 4.29, 4.52; cf. 1.17 (regarding Constantius I), and see Chapter 10 below.
11. See, e.g., Deut. 17.18–19: "And when he [the king] sits on the throne of his kingdom, he shall write for himself in a book a copy of this law, from that which is in charge of the Levitical priests; and it shall be with him, and he shall read in it all the days of his life, that he may learn to fear the Lord his God, by keeping all the words of this law and these statutes, and doing them." I am grateful to Professor Jeff Tigay for calling my attention to this motif. See also Leach (1973); Chesnut (1986) 130–31. On the treatment of Constantine in the *VC*, see further Chapter 10 below.
12. Eus., *VC* 4.29.
13. Burckhardt (1949) 300–301.
14. On speech making as part of the emperor's role, see Millar (1977) 206: "It is vital to remember this irreducibly personal activity of oratory, the frequency with which it was required and its significance to the audience as an indication of the emperor's personal culture, or lack of it." See also Chapter 2 above. For late antiquity, Brown (1992) chs. 1–2. On Valens' limited command of Greek, see Sugars (1997) 231–32.
15. Eus., *VC* 4.29. For Augustus's cultural activities, see Suet., *Aug.* 84–89.
16. Eun., *vit. Soph.* 462.

17. See, with examples, Wilken (1983) 120.
18. Eus., *LC* 5.5. For his attitude toward finery, see *LC* 5.6. On the role of panegyric, see Chapter 2 above.
19. Dio Chr., *Fourth Discourse on Kingship* 124.
20. Dio Chr., *First Discourse on Kingship* 33.
21. Dio Chr., *Fourth Discourse on Kingship* 124.
22. Ecphantus II.7.64.
23. Dio Chr., *First Discourse on Kingship* 25.
24. Dio Chr., *Third Discourse on Kingship* 86–87, 89.
25. *CTh* 1.16.6.1.
26. *CTh* 9.1.4.
27. Gibbon (1909–14) 2: 230; Burckhardt (1949) 339; Pharr (1952) 224, n. 15.
28. *CTh* 1.16.6.1. As Cameron (1976) 241 has remarked, "Constantine shared, it seems, the simple conviction of many modern admirers of the Antioch claque and its successors the Blues and Greens, that, though such public expressions of approval and disapproval could hardly be expected to be spontaneous, it was nevertheless easy enough to tell which were genuine and which the work of private supporters."
29. Const., *OC* 8.1–2.
30. Ulpian in Just., *Dig.* 1.4.1. On this ruling, see Chapter 2 above, n. 8.
31. Extensive quotations from Hierocles' Life survive in Eus., *c. Hier.* See further Chapter 4 above, n. 62, and Frend (1987). For Porphyry, see Digeser (1999) ch. 4. For Daza's efforts, Eus., *HE* 9.2–7; see also Teall (1967) 23; Nicholson (1994).
32. On the rich variety of Constantine's coinage, see Schoenebeck (1939) 49. Smith (1997) 185 refers to Constantine as "the master image-manipulator of the period."
33. Burckhardt (1949) 300–301. MacMullen (1966) called attention to the importance of Christian rhetoric; see also MacMullen (1989). Cameron (1991) 79 refers to preaching as "the hidden iceberg of Christian discourse"; cf. Liebeschuetz (1979) 292: "The weekly services, sermons, the discipline of penance, and religious instruction offered the clergy means of indoctrination which had no precedent."
34. Jer., *Ep.* 52.8. Cf. Spira (1989) 141; Wilken (1983) 105–6, and preceding note.
35. Baynes (1972) 83, n. 57. On Baynes, see further Chapter 1 above.
36. "The first was to unite the inclination of all peoples regarding divine matters into a single sustaining habit; second, I was eager to restore and rejoin the body of our common empire which had been stricken as if with a terrible wound. The former I planned to provide for through the hidden eye of the mind; the latter I attempted to correct by the power of military

arms, knowing that if I were to establish through my prayers a common agreement among all the servants of god, the conduct of public affairs would enjoy a change concurrent with the pious sentiments of all." Eus., *VC* 2.65 (my tr.). See Chapter 7, n. 17.

37. Dörries (1960) 25–26, 45; Barnes (1981) 210–11. A key part of Barnes' argument is Eusebius's assertion that Constantine banned pagan sacrifice. Placing this ban prior to the edict, Barnes concludes that failure to mention sacrifice in the latter proves that the ban was still in force: see Barnes (1984).
38. Eus., *VC* 2.60.1, 2.59.1 (my tr.).
39. Eus., *VC* 2.60.2 (my tr.).
40. Scribner (1996) 32–47 catalogued nine types of toleration during the Reformation. Constantine's indication that he would have enforced conformity had he had the resources would fall under category seven, "toleration by dint of too few resources to enforce wider conformity," which Scribner defines as "the practical compromise accepted by a ruler faced with widespread disaffection of noble elites who could not be coerced without danger of serious upheaval" (37). Turchetti (1991) has attempted to distinguish between toleration as a goal in itself and toleration as an interim strategy for early modern French rulers, arguing that the latter should be identified as a policy of "concord" rather than toleration. But attempting to factor motivation into tolerant actions, while useful for some analyses, can be misleading in others, since true toleration only applies to practices that the tolerator finds distasteful or abhorrent to begin with. See Razavi & Ambuel (1997) vii–xii. See further below, n. 79, and Chapter 11.
41. Baynes (1972) 6. See also n. 35 above.
42. See Chapter 6, text at n. 58.
43. On flexibility, see Chapter 3 above; for coercion, see Chapter 1.
44. Greg. Nys., *de deitate* 121.7–12, tr. Jones (1964) 2: 964. On this passage, see Lim (1995) 149–50.
45. Rom. 13:1–2.
46. Elliott (1997) 84 attributes the emphasis in Constantinian propaganda on the emperor's youth to his vulnerability to a charge of being an accessory to Diocletian's persecution.
47. Eus., *VC* 4.29, 4.48.
48. Eus., *VC* 2.65 (letter to Arius and Alexander), "I make that god who is the helpmate of my endeavors and savior of all my witness"; cf. Eus., *VC* 2.28 (Edict to the Palestinians): "And now, with such a mass of impiety oppressing the human race, and the commonwealth in danger of being utterly destroyed, as if by the agency of some pestilential disease . . . what was the relief, and what the remedy which the Divinity devised for these evils?

. . . I myself, then was the instrument whose services he chose, and esteemed suited for the accomplishment of his will."

49. E.g., Eus., *VC* 2.24–42 (Edict to the Palestinians).
50. Eus., *VC* 4.29.
51. Eus., *VC* 4.29.1–2: προσήκειν ἡγούμενος ἑαυτῷ λόγῳ παιδευτικῷ τῶν ἀρχομένων κρατεῖν λογικήν τε τὴν σύμπασαν καταστήσασθαι βασιλείαν. For Xenophon, see *Cyr.* 1.1.3 and Chapter 2 above.
52. Drake (1995).
53. Eus., *VC* 4.29.
54. Eus., *VC* 4.32.
55. Barnes (1981) 74.
56. Lane Fox (1987) 651. On the translation, Eus., *VC* 4.32.
57. The philological argument is summarized by Lane Fox (1987) 629–30. Fisher (1982) focused on translation technique; see also Brock (1979). Ison (1985) 31–67 posits separate translators for the poem and commentary, in the latter of which he finds clear references to the Latin text.
58. Const., *OC* 2.1–2.
59. Const., *OC* 1: "That light which far outshines the day and sun, first pledge of resurrection, and renovation of bodies long since dissolved, the divine token of promise, the path which leads to everlasting life—in a word, the day of the Passion—is arrived."
60. Const., *OC* 1.1.
61. Arguing for a date in 324 or 325 are Mazzarino (1974) 88–150; Decker (1978) 85; Ison (1985) 210; Lane Fox (1987) 643. Barnes originally opted for 317, subsequently settled on any Good Friday between 321 and 324, then pronounced himself "no longer convinced that the exact year and place can be conclusively established": Barnes (1982) 69, n. 99. See also Drake (1985b).
62. Eus., *VC* 4.32.
63. In the sixth century a career bureaucrat, John Lydus, indicated that such a dossier existed in his own day. Lyd., *De mag.* II.30, III.33. On Eusebius's plans to write the *vita Constantini,* see Drake (1988); see further Chapter 10 below.
64. Eus., *VC* 4.29. See above, at n. 12.
65. Barnes (1976a) 418 ff.
66. Const., *OC* 1.1. The nickname was coined by Schwartz (1907) 1427.
67. Const., *OC* 5.1
68. Const., *OC* 11.2
69. Const., *OC* 25.5; cf. 20.10.
70. Goodenough (1928); Baynes (1934); Drake (1976) ch. 4. Eus., *LC* 2 depicts emperor and Logos acting as agents of the Supreme God in their respective spheres. See further Chapter 1 above and Chapter 10 below.

71. Const., *OC* 11.1. Barnes (1981) 75 takes this passage as reference to Constantine's own conversion. Elliott (1987) 432–33 challenges this interpretation. Doubt was first cast on the authorship of this oration by Rossignol (1845). For a survey of the arguments, see Baynes (1972) 56, n. 19. Almost all recent scholars stipulate authenticity: see Mazzarino (1974) 103–9; Barnes (1981) 74; Lane Fox (1987) 627 ff.
72. Const., *OC* 3.2–3, 5.
73. Const., *OC* 11.1.
74. Const., *OC* 11.4
75. Const., *OC* 11.5–6.
76. Eus., *VC* 2.56.1, 2.59.1.
77. Eus., *VC* 2.56.2. See Barnes (1984); Barnes (1986b) 49. See text above at n. 39.
78. Const., *OC* 11.7, 11.6.
79. A point made by Digeser (1999) ch. 5. Digeser draws on Turchetti to make a further distinction between a policy of toleration and a policy of concord. The distinction may be artificial, since much of what Turchetti identifies as a "policy of concord" on closer inspection appears to be no more than a euphemism for classic intolerance; but it is in any case a finer distinction that needs to be made for this argument. See further n. 40 above.
80. Const., *OC* 11.7. See Drake (1989).
81. Const., *OC* 1.4.
82. Const., *OC* 13 (my tr.).
83. See Chapter 7 above, text at n. 76.
84. Brown (1998) 642.
85. On this rhetorical device, see Chapter 2 above.
86. Const., *OC* 15.4.
87. See, e.g., Plato, *Apol.* 28d.
88. Const., *OC* 11.7.
89. Const., *OC* 11.7, 13.1 (πρὸς τὸ βεβαιοῦσθαι τὴν καθ᾽ ἑκάστου πίστιν, 171.32–33).
90. In the case of the Jews, scholars have reached opposite conclusions, depending on whether they heed Constantine's rhetoric or his actions. Thus, Hollerich (1992) 594 cites Constantine's characterization of the Jews as "a hostile, nefarious sect" in *CTh* 16.8.1, and Parkes (1964) 767 calls attention to his "deliberately offensive" language." Conversely, Fowden (1993) 87 cites the "relatively tolerant attitude" displayed in *CTh* 16.8.2. In the same way, Constantine's complaint to the bishops at Arles in 314 about the Donatists (see Chapter 6 above, at n. 59) is widely quoted as an example of his piety; much less often is it noted that he proceeded to hear their appeal anyway.
91. Eus., *VC* 4.61–63. See now Yarnold (1993). Schwartz (1908) 3099 called

attention to the importance of Drepanum's spa. On the location of Constantine's deathbed, see Woods (1997). See also Fowden (1994b).

92. Eus., *VC* 4.58–60.

Chapter Nine. Controlling the Agenda

1. See Chapter 1 above.
2. Elliott (1997) 297 argues that the bishops never returned to Tyre. The chronology of this period is admittedly vexing; but it is difficult to understand how, if the council had completed its deliberations in late August, Constantine could still have been ignorant of its decision in November, as he claims to be in his "Letter to the Bishops at Tyre" (Athan., *Apol. sec.* 86). Elliott considers this letter a forgery.
3. Porphyry of Gaza's mission to Constantinople (see Chapter 11) sailed about the same time of year (September 23) and made it to Constantinople in twenty days (*vit. Por.* 34). If Athanasius had used the same transport with which he fled Tyre, it would have taken no more than two days' sail to reach Tarsus. The modern Turkish highway E90, which roughly parallels the ancient Roman road, stretches approximately 445 kilometers between Tarsus and Ankara. Land travelers not using the public post did well to make 20 kilometers a day, meaning Athanasius would have arrived in ancient Ancyra in twenty-two to twenty-three days. From Ancyra, he had a choice of routes to Constantinople, a distance of 400–450 kilometers, or twenty to twenty-three days. I am grateful to my colleague Frank Frost for advice about the mechanics of ancient travel. See also Jones (1964) 2: 842. On the *Life of Porphyry,* see Chapter 11 below, n. 87.
4. Athan., *Apol. sec.* 86.2–12.
5. The *Festal Index* for 335–36 says that Athanasius arrived in Constantinople on ii Athyr (October 30). Assuming the encounter in the street took place on the same day and Constantine dispatched his letter immediately, there still would have been no more than one week for the bishops to receive it in Tyre and then travel to Constantinople. See Drake (1987).
6. Seeck (1921) 4: 57; Orlandi (1975); Barnes (1993) 28–29.
7. Peeters (1945); Arnold (1991) 167 argues that "Athanasius's narrative simply compresses events past the point of chronological accuracy."
8. Epiph., *Pan.* 69.9.4–6.
9. The closest in wording to Athanasius's claim is Sarah's bitter demand to Abraham, Gen. 16:5, but David's similar claim to vindication in his struggle with Saul (I Sam. 24:12) was more apropos. It would have been all the more infuriating if Athanasius had meant to echo Saint Paul's frequent cries for judgment, for Constantine had already staked out his own claim to that saint's mantle (see Chapter 10 below). See Eus., *VC* 4.29.1 for the claim that "he sometimes passed sleepless nights in furnish-

ing his mind with Divine knowledge"; cf. Eus., *VC* 4.17: "He modeled as it were his very palace into a church of God . . . and devoted himself to the study of those divinely inspired oracles."

10. Ammianus 22.5.4.
11. Ammianus 21.16.18.
12. Frakes (1991) ch. 5. Barnes (1993) 166 attributes this neglect to "a deep and insidious bias."
13. As John Matthews (1989) observed, "It was a sign of his [Gallus Caesar's] final humiliation when he was conveyed to Pola in a private carriage, wearing none of the imperial insignia" (264). On the *cursus publicus,* see Jones (1964) 2: 830–34; Ramsay (1925).
14. Compare the representations of Christ as the Good Shepherd in the third-century catacombs of Priscilla and Callistus in Rome and the early-fourth-century cathedral of Bishop Theodore in Aquileia with the painting of Christ between Saints Peter and Paul in the catacomb of Pietro e Marcellino or the mosaic of Christ enthroned among the apostles in the Church of Sta. Pudenziana, Rome, both late fourth century. See also Christ sitting in judgment among the angels on the nave wall of S. Apollinare Nuovo, Ravenna, c. A.D. 520: Huyghe (1963) 24, 26; Grabar (1968) 29–30, 212–13; Capeti (n.d.) 19, 22. See also Shepherd (1967); Pelikan (1985) ch. 4.
15. Mark 9:43. Cf. Liebeschuetz (1979) 292: "Clerical immunities and the coercion of religious dissent were areas where the interest of clergy and administration potentially and actually diverged."
16. Theodosius's instructions, which appear as *CTh* 1.5 (March 26, 429), were also read into the minutes of the Senate meeting, December 25, 438. These minutes form a preamble to the code. The minutes record forty-three different acclamations that the senators shouted in sequence, as well as various others shouted during the course of the meeting. According to Pharr (1952) 5, n. 50, the word translated as "repeated" (*dictum*) "may mean shouted . . . in concert, or shouted by . . . different Senators."
17. On the emperor's law-giving activities, see Millar (1977) ch. 5. See also Turpin (1991).
18. *CTh* 1.27.1. The subscription has been corrupted, putting date and authorship in doubt. Corcoran (1996) 284–85 argues for Licinius as the author. See also Chapter 7 above, n. 1. For the 316 law, see *CJ* 1.13.1.
19. *CS* 1. The complete text and translation of this law is in the appendix to this volume.
20. Selb (1967) 176.
21. "If the number of 'witnesses' is not mentioned, two are enough, since the plural is satisfied by two." Ulpian in Just., *Dig.* 22.5.12. Deut. 19:15 specifies "only on the evidence of two witnesses, or of three witnesses, shall a charge be sustained." Jesus affirms the principle at Matt. 18:16:

"Take one or two others along with you, that every word may be confirmed by the evidence of two or three witnesses." Saint Paul urged Christians to settle their disputes within the community (I Cor. 6), but his complaint against Christians who do otherwise ("Does he dare go to law before the unrighteous instead of the saints?") indicates that the decision to do so was voluntary. Paul also specifies that Christians should not resolve disputes with non-Christians: "For what have I to do with judging outsiders? Is it not those inside the church whom you are to judge? God judges those outside" (I Cor. 5:12–13).

22. See, e.g., Shepherd (1968) 26: "Perhaps the most revolutionary act in establishing the Church was the legal recognition of episcopal courts in matters of civil litigation." Gaudemet (1947) 32: "Il n'est pas, dans toute l'oeuvre législative de Constantin, disposition plus célèbre que les deux constitutions qui sanctionnent le pouvoir juridictionnel de l'évêque."

23. Sirmond published the collection as an appendix to his edition of the *Theodosian Code* (Paris, 1631). It has been kept in this position by subsequent editors. See further Sclb (1967); Vessey (1993).

24. *CTh* 16.9.1; on this law, cf. Eus., *VC* 4.27.

25. Ammianus 30.4.8–9.

26. On gold, see Const., *OC* 8.1–2, and Chapter 7 above; on appeals, see below.

27. Jones (1964) 1: 482, 502; examples 1: 492 f, 578 f.

28. Optatus, Appx. 5: "Sicut in causis gentilium fieri solet, appellationem interposuerunt. Equidem gentes minora interdum iudicia refugientes ubi iustitia cito deprehendi potest, magis ad maiora iudicia auctoritate interposita, ad appellationem se conferre sunt solitae."

29. *CTh* 9.32.36.

30. *CTh* 11.36.2 (315).

31. *CTh* 11.36.1 (A.D. 314): "Just as aid must not be denied to those litigants who appeal justly, so it is not fitting that those persons against whom judgment has justly been rendered should uselessly, by appeal, delay proceedings that are properly conducted." For a ban on appeals, see *CTh* 11.36.2 (A.D. 315): "If any person should appeal from an interlocutory decision or from an execution in a case that has been previously decided and should hastily request a trial in another audience hall, he shall be punished by the penalty of thirty folles."

32. *CTh* 1.5.1. Order to appeal: *CTh* 11.34.1 (331); order to forward cases for review: *CTh* 1.16.3 (319).

33. Const., *OC* 25.5: καὶ τῶν μετὰ δικαιοσύνης συμβολαίων. Cf. *OC* 13 (trial before the holy court at the last judgment), *OC* 23 (services and benefits).

34. Given Aug. 1: *CTh* 2.26.3 (boundary disputes), 3.30.4 (property of minors), 4.5.1 (property in litigation). Given Aug. 1, posted Sept. 1: *CTh*

11.30.16 (procedure for appeals); 11.30.17 (failure to appeal); 11.34.1 (failure to appeal through fear). Posted Oct. 1: *CJ* 3.13.4 (appeals). Posted Nov. 1: *CTh* 1.16.6 (public trials). As further indication of Constantine's agenda during this period, *CJ* 3.19.2, dated in late July, set a time limit on delay of trials.

35. Rights of minors: *CTh* 3.30.6; malfeasance: *CTh* 8.1.3–4.
36. *CTh* 1.16.7, dated as given in Constantinople, Nov. 1, 331.
37. Eus., *VC* 4.29.4
38. Leontius, *vit. Joh.* 4
39. A judiciary oriented toward rank was, of course, nothing new: Roman justice always took class distinctions into account, and writers on earlier periods simply took it for granted. See, e.g., Tac., *Ann.* 1.75.1–2 on Tiberius, and Garnsey (1970); Ste. Croix (1981) 366–67.
40. Aug., *Conf.* 6.10. On this passage, see also Ste. Croix (1981) 366–67.
41. Mark 12:38–40 (New English Bible). On Lenin: Wolfe (1948) 87.
42. Phil., *Vit. Soph.* 559–61. After the governor agreed to forward the Athenians' complaints to the emperor (a decision Philostratus attributes to their pique with Herodes), Herodes tried to detain his opponents in Athens with a countercharge of conspiracy, and they were only able to get to the emperor by stealing out of the city. For a reading of this trial as forcing Marcus to choose between the conflicting values of friendship and justice, see Brown (1992) 48–49.
43. Ammianus 27.11.3–4. On Probus, see *PLRE* 1: 736–40.
44. *CTh* 1.16.4.
45. *CTh* 9.1.4.
46. Aug., *Conf.* 6.10 (16) and text at n. 40 above; on Alypius's inability thereafter to "sell his counsel," *Conf.* 7.6 (13).
47. Cf. Jones (1964) 1: 504.
48. On sources and authorship of the *HA,* see Chapter 4 above, n. 11.
49. *HA* Aurelian 43.1–5.
50. Lib., *Or.* 30.48–49.
51. So Constantine wrote to the bishops at the Council of Arles in 314: "For I tell you, as is the truth, that the judgment of the priests should be regarded as if God himself were in the judge's seat." Optatus, Appx. 5. Everything he wrote in that letter need not be taken at face value (see Chapter 6 above, at n. 59), but if nothing else this statement shows that cajoling the bishops was certainly on his agenda. Cf. Eus., *VC* 1.32 (Constantine includes "the priests of God" among his counselors), 2.69 (urging the bishops to regard him as "a fellow servant"), 4.27 ("he rated the priests of God at a higher value than any judge whatever").
52. Theodosius's law, see *CTh* 11.39.8 (June 29, 381); Justinian's view was expressed in *Novel* 123.7 (A.D. 546), in *CJ,* vol. 3. For the Hindu principle, see Scott (1932) 13: 49, note.

53. Gibbon (1909–14) 2: 111. The citation is from Sulp. Sev., *Chron.* 2.32 (referring to Valerian's persecution).
54. Ammianus 27.3.14–15. Gilliard (1984) established that few senators in the fourth century came from the senatorial class. See also Rousselle (1997). Cf. Chadwick (1980) 11: "In general the bishop was a figure that people wanted to like, and of whom they hoped that their expectations would be realized."
55. Julian, *Ep.* 20, 453a.
56. Julian, *Ep.* 22, 430D–431A.
57. Julian, *Ep. Pr.* 305C.
58. Julian, *Ep.* 22, 430C.
59. See the record of Constantine's donations in the *Lib. Pont.* under Pope Silvester (34). Eusebius discusses Constantine's benefactions and provision for the poor throughout the *vita Constantini*. See, e.g., at *VC* 1.42–43; 2.21, 45–46; 3.48, 50; 4.39. See also the provisions for return of property and inheritances in Constantine's Edict to the Palestinians, Eus., *VC* 2.35–41.
60. Lact, *DI* 6.12. On corruption, *DI* 5.9.
61. Const., *OC* 2.1–2.
62. *CTh* 16.2.6. The law bears a date in 326, but it has been redated to 329. For tax evasion as Constantine's motive, see Jones (1964) 1: 89.
63. Julian, *Ep. Pr.* 305AB.
64. Greg. Naz., *De se ipso* ll.155–66: "Some of them are the offspring of tribute-mongers, whose only concern is falsification of accounts. Some come straight from the tax booth and the sort of statutes you get there: some from the plough, with their sunburn still fresh: some again from day-long exertions with the mattock and the hoe: some have just left the galleys or the army. They are still redolent of the bilge water, or exhibit the brand on their bodies; but they have blossomed into captains of the people, and generals resolved not to yield an inch. Then there are those who, as yet, have not washed the soot of their fiery occupations from their persons, slave material who ought to be in the mills."
65. See, e.g., Jones (1964) 1: 480; Selb (1967) 193. McLynn (1994) 269 argues that the law remained in force but in practical terms was a dead letter "except for the few bishops sufficiently confident to invoke it." Libanius, *Or.* 30.11 complains of rampaging monks who were able to avoid charges by appealing to the bishop's court, but such appeals do not indicate that *CS* 1 remained in force, since they would have fallen under the same right of *praescriptio fori* which allowed soldiers to appeal to military courts.
66. *CTh* 1.22.2.
67. *CTh* 11.39.3.
68. See his letter to the congregation of Nicomedia denouncing Eusebius:

Gel., *HE* 3, Suppl 1 (= Opitz, *Urk*. 27), and his response to Arius's demand for reinstatement: Gel., *HE* 3.19 (= Opitz, *Urk*. 34). On both of these letters, see further Chapter 7 above.

69. See, e.g., Aug., *de op. monach*. 37. Augustine's biographer, Possidius, describes Augustine's diligence in hearing cases and the role he played as intercessor with the authorities: Possid., *v. Aug*. 19–20. Young (1983) 171 points out that "one of the things [Synesius] dreaded about becoming a bishop was being overwhelmed by the enormous burden of arbitration in local disputes and of correspondence on behalf of individuals seeking the righting of wrongs or personal advancement" (citing *Epp*. 105 and 57). See also Chadwick (1980) 8; Lamoreaux (1995) 143–46.

70. Eus., *VC* 2.71.
71. Gibbon (1909–14) 2: 2. See also Chapter 1 above.
72. Eus., *VC* 3.64–65.
73. Eus., *VC* 2.71. See *OC* 15.4, and for Constantine's letter to the bishops of North Africa, Optatus, Appx. 9. See further Chapter 6 above.
74. As observed for a later period of religious strife by Scribner (1996) 11–15.
75. Eus., *VC* 3.66.
76. Eus., *VC* 4.27.
77. Eus., *VC* 2.71.
78 Smith (1988) 279.

Chapter Ten. The Fine Print

1. Eusebius's presidency has been contested, primarily on the grounds that Athanasius subsequently identified the imperial count Dionysius as in charge (Athan., *Apol. sec.* 28). The claim must be balanced against Athanasius's very strong need to create doubt as to the legitimacy of the council that ordered his deposition. See Barnes (1993) 169.
2. Eus., *HE* 3.28 cites Dionysius of Alexandria, who died in 365, as being bishop during his own lifetime, and at *HE* 7.26, after completing a discussion of Dionysius and before moving on to Paul of Samosata, who became bishop of Antioch sometime between 257 and 260, Eusebius writes that he had now come to events of his own day.
3. I follow here the dating for The Chronicle and Church History proposed by Burgess (1997), which demolishes arguments for dating these works prior to the Great Persecution. An earlier step in the same direction was taken by Louth (1990).
4. Momigliano (1990) 140.
5. Eus., *HE* 1.1.
6. Markus (1975) 15 and passim.
7. Eus., *HE* 1.1.4. Cf. Momigliano (1990) 141: "In the simplicity of its structure and in the matter of its documentation the Ecclesiastical Histo-

ry of Eusebius was one of the most authoritative prototypes ever created
by ancient thought: indeed it was the last model elaborated by ancient
historians for the benefit of later generations—if we except the Life of
Antony by Athanasius, which became a model for later hagiography."

8. Warmington (1998) 266.
9. Burckhardt (1949) 283. On accuracy: Barnes (1981) 141. See also Chapter 1 above.
10. Barnes (1981) 141.
11. Smith (1988) 80.
12. Momigliano (1963b) 85. Cf. Adler (1990) 498: "Christian scholars rarely studied the past strictly as an exercise in antiquarianism." Or, as Stevenson (1929) 35 put it, "Though Eusebius attempted so many branches of literature, we may be sure that his main interest was in Apologetics, not in Chronology or History for its own sake." On Eusebius's language, Smith (1989) chs. 3–4. On Eusebius's use of documents, Adler (1992) esp. 479: "The personality of the author that is revealed throughout the Chronicle is that of a writer both acutely aware of the difficulties attending the use of historical documents, and one entirely satisfied to live within the constraints imposed by them."
13. Aug., *civ. Dei*, bk. 1. See further Chesnut (1992). On Constantius I's good fortune and death: Eus., *VC* 1.18; Cynegius: *PLRE* 1: 235–36.
14. Cameron (1991) 58.
15. "The gravest of the ecclesiastical historians, Eusebius himself, indirectly confesses that he has related whatever might redound to the glory, and that he has suppressed all that could tend to the disgrace, of religion." Gibbon (1909–14) 2: 144. On his methods, Gustafsson (1961).
16. Eus., *HE* 5.5.1–5; Dio 72.8; for the relief, see Caprino (1955) tav. 12, fig. 24.
17. Momigliano (1963b) 85.
18. Eus., *HE* 8.1.7–8. The quotation is from Lam. 2:1–2.
19. On ancient historiography: Momigliano (1963b); Boer (1968); McDonald (1975); Chesnut (1975); Ruggini (1977); Wiseman (1981); Croke & Emmett (1983); Fornara (1983). On Eusebius: Lawlor (1912); Laqueur (1929); Eger (1939); Downey (1965); Grant (1980); Trompf (1983); Cameron (1983).
20. Eus., *HE* 8.1.8.
21. Eus., *HE* 8.1.8.
22. Bauer (1971). See also the judicious discussion by Williams (1989b).
23. Orig., *c. Cels.* 3.10–11. Another way to appreciate Eusebius's perspective is to compare it with Hopkins' conclusion (1998) 196, 212–13 that until the end of the second century Christianity was both too small and too isolated to produce a literate leader for each Christian community.
24. Eus., *HE* 4.26.7–8.

25. Origen, *c. Cels.* 2.30.
26. Eus., *SC* 16.5–6. On the significance of Eusebius's pairing, see Peterson (1935) 75; Baynes (1934).
27. Fowden (1982).
28. For instance, Barnes (1981) 254–55 justifies his reading of the *LC* as "aggressively Christian" in part on Eusebius's claim that "in place of polytheism, Constantine has established monotheism."
29. Eus., *PE* I.4 (10d).
30. Chesnut (1986) 136.
31. Eus., *LC* 7.10. Cf. Eusebius's comment on Ps. 78: "We who were not worthy to suffer unto death, and shed our blood for God's sake, yet being the sons of them who suffered thus, dignified by the virtue of our fathers, pray that through them we may obtain mercy." See Wallace-Hadrill (1960) 16.
32. The original remark, "There is less in this than meets the eye," was made by a young Tallulah Bankhead to the drama critic Alexander Woollcott at a pretentiously staged revival of Maeterlinck's "Aglavaine & Selysette." Woollcott (1922) 86.
33. Millar (1977) 205.
34. Eus., *VC* 1.11. Soc., *HE* 1.23. Doubts about the *VC* were expressed as early as the seventeenth century, but the most vigorous advocate in the modern debate was Grégoire (1938); the argument was significantly undermined by the discovery of a fourth-century papyrus that confirmed the accuracy of the Edict to the Palestinians in *VC* 2.24–42. See Jones (1954). See also Winkelmann (1962). On Burckhardt, see Chapter 1 above.
35. Eus., *VC* 1.6–7. A contemporary handbook surviving under the name of Menander Rhetor provides instruction for imperial orations: Men. Rhet., *Peri epideik.* 368–77.
36. μόνα τὰ πρὸς τὸν θεοφιλῆ συντείνοντα βίον λέγειν τε καὶ γράφειν: Eus., *VC* 1.11. Another famous sticking point—Eusebius's stated intent at *VC* 1.23 to ignore the fate of the persecutors which he in fact proceeds to discuss—has been resolved by Hall (1993) 242–43, demonstrating that Eusebius wrote with the fuller account of *HE* 8.13 in mind.
37. See, e.g., Richardson (1890) 505, n. 1: "Like very many other things which Eusebius tells of Constantine, that which was entirely customary with other emperors as well as Constantine has the appearance of being peculiar to him." Straub (1939) 111; Frend (1967) 168.
38. Duchesne (1910) 191. On the importance of rhetorical silences, see Hedrick (forthcoming), esp. introduction and ch. 5.
39. Eus., *VC* 1.27–29. For Eusebius's account, see text in Chapter 1 at n. 14 and in Chapter 5 at n. 34.
40. See Chapter 5 above and Elliott (1997) ch. 4.

41. Eus., *VC* 1.28.
42. Eus., *VC* 1.10.2.
43. At *VC* 3.24, Eusebius refers to the large number of Constantine's letters of various types, and at *VC* 3.59 he speaks of other letters that he could have included.
44. Quasten (1950) 3: 310: "his [Constantine's] chief theological adviser"; Gillman (1961) 198: "the Emperor's confidant and advisor"; Momigliano (1963b) 85: "the shrewd and worldly adviser of the Emperor Constantine"; Frend (1968) 27: "the architect of Constantine's religious policy in the final period of his reign"; Lewy (1983) 73: "the head of the victorious church at the time of Constantine."
45. Pecock's observation (in *The Repression or over much blaming of the Clergy* 3.12) is cited in Webb (1981) 97. Gibbon (1909–14), 2: 136; cf. 2: 148, 222.
46. Eus., *VC* 3.60.
47. See, e.g., Eus., *VC* 2.45, 2.60. 4.7, 4.33. See further, Drake (1988) 26 and nn. 42–43 above. For Constantine's letters: Eus., *VC* 4.34, 35.
48. So the author of a handbook that survives from the period advised his students on the subject of signs and portents of their subject's greatness: "If there is anything like this in connection with the emperor, work it up; if it is possible to invent, and to do this convincingly, do not hesitate; the subject permits this, because the audience has no choice but to accept the encomium without examination." Men. Rhet., *Peri epideik.* 371.10–14. On the pretense of familiarity, Cameron (1983) 84.
49. Warmington (1985) 94; cf. Barnes (1989) 111–12.
50. Barnes (1981) 266.
51. Warmington (1988).
52. Eus., *VC* 2.23 and 2.47, referring to the Edict to the Palestinians and the Edict to the Eastern Provincials, respectively.
53. For the process of imperial decision making, see Millar (1977) 203–72.
54. Eus., *VC* 2.47 describes the Edict to the Eastern Provincials as αὐτό-γραφον οὖσαν αὐτοῦ, which Richardson translates, "which is in his own handwriting." The phrase could also mean "bearing his own signature." Eusebius uses similar language at *VC* 3.16: δι' οἰκείου παρεδίδου γράμματος (regarding Constantine's letter on the decisions at Nicaea); 3.23: δι' οἰκείας ἐπέστελλε γραφῆς (regarding his letter to the Egyptians); and 4.8: τοῦτο τὸ βασιλέως ἰδιόγραφον γράμμα (regarding his letter to Shapur). For a discussion: Turpin (1991). For the inscription, Millar (1977) 247.
55. Barnes (1989) 112.
56. So the concluding words of the *SC* (Eus., *SC* 18.2): "impressing on the Heavenly Logos of God the imperial seal [βασιλικοῖς χαρακτῆρσιν ἐκτυπούμενος] as victor and triumphator, and in clear-cut and unam-

biguous terms making unto all peoples, by deed as well as by word, a pious and devout confession."

57. Drake (1976) ch. 3.
58. Barnes (1981) 271.
59. Eus., *VC* 4.33.1.
60. Eus., *VC* 4.46.
61. Eus., *SC* 11.7, 18.1–3.
62. Eus., *VC* 4.34–36. On the copies, see Robbins (1989).
63. In the prologue, Eusebius contrasts his audience of initiates worthy of admission to "the sanctuary of the holy palace" with the vulgar masses outside and refers to others "contesting the same route with me." See Drake (1976) 83, with notes.
64. See Chapter 5, text at n. 12.
65. Eus., *VC* 4.48. In the introduction to his 1902 edition of the *VC* (p. C), Ivar Heikel took note of various similarities between that work and the *OC*.
66. See further Drake (1988).
67. See n. 107 below.
68. Eus., *VC* 4.54. Spiegl (1971).
69. Eus., *VC* 4.55.
70. Eus., *HE* 9.9.4–8. On the Moses analogy, see Becker (1910); Dvornik (1955) 2: 644; Chesnut (1986) 134; Hollerich (1989); Rapp (1998).
71. Eus., *VC* 1.12 (raised in palace); 1.38 (Maxentius drowns like pharaoh); 2.11 (Licinius hardened his heart like pharaoh); 2.12, 12.14 (Constantine prays in tabernacle).
72. Matt. 22:18–22; Rom. 13:1–2.
73. Dvornik (1966) 2: 644.
74. I Cor. 5:12–13. Const., *OC* 11.1. Elliott (1987) 432–33 argues against taking this passage as a personal reference.
75. For Constantine's testimony, Eus., *VC* 1.28; on the Church of the Apostles, Eus., *VC* 4.60, and Drake (1988) 32–33. For Constantine and Paul, see Montgomery (1968); Coleman (1914) 138–39 found the parallel so obvious that its absence proved, to him, that the vision story was a fabrication.
76. Deut. 17:18–19; cf. Chapter 8 above, n. 11.
77. Drake (1985a); Hunt (1997) cautions against overconcentration on the issue of the cross. See Chapter 8 above, n. 6.
78. Gillman (1961); Storch (1970); Gunton (1985).
79. So Stevenson (1929) 136: "He really belonged to the third century, not to the fourth." Cf. Ward-Perkins (1966) 36.
80. Burckhardt (1949) 260–61 followed his famous conclusion about Eusebius's honesty with the observation that "he speaks of the man but really means a cause, and that cause is the hierarchy."

81. Eus., *LC* 2.2, 2.4. See Chapter 4 above, text at n. 28.
82. Eus., *LC* 1.1: μέγαν δ᾽ ἐγὼ βασιλέα καλῶ τὸν ἀληθῶς μέγαν . . . τὸν ἐπέκεινα τῶν ὅλων, τὸν πάντων ἀνώτατον, τον ὑπέρτατον, τὸν ὑπερμεγέθη, οὗ θρόνοι μὲν τῆς βασιλείας ἁψῖδες οὐράνιοι, γῆ δ᾽ ὑποπόδιον αὐτοῦ τῶν ποδῶν. Cf. Isa. 66:1.
83. Goodenough (1928); Chesnut (1986) 141–74. See also n. 107 below.
84. *Corp. Herm.* XVIII. See esp. Frag. 9: τὸν μέγιστον βασιλέα τῶν ὅλων θεόν, ὅς ἀθάνατος μέν ἐστι διαπαντός. ἀΐδιός τε καὶ ἐξ ἀιδίου τὸ κράτος ἔχων, καλλίνικος πρῶτος. ἀφ᾽ οὗ πᾶσαι αἱ νῖκαι εἰς τοὺς ἐξῆς φέρονται. . . . Frag. 14: ἀγαθὸς ὑπάρχων καὶ ἀειφεγγής. . . . Frag. 12: πανακηράτῳ . . . πατρί. See also Frag. 8: τὸν ὕπατον βασιλέα τῶν ὅλων. Frag. 10: τοῦ κρείττονος θεοῦ, and cf. Frags. 2, 6, 7, 22. Nock & Festugière (1954) 2: 242 dated this speech to c. A.D. 300. Despite similarities with Christian terminology, they concluded (1: v) that the *Corpus* bears "nulle marque évidente ni de christianisme ni de néoplatonisme."
85. See, with examples, Battifol (1914) 188–201. Particularly strong is the similarity between Christian and pagan solar symbolism. As Baynes (1972) 102 observed, "The worship of the Unconquered Sun of paganism may have formed for many the bridge by which they passed into the Christian Church." The same state of flux has been observed in the art of this period. See, for instance, Schoenebeck (1939) 25 f. and the striking "Christus-Helios" mosaic from the Tomb of the Julii, which shows Christ driving the chariot of the Sun, in Toynbee & Ward-Perkins (1958) 72 f., 116 f. See also figs. 1 and 2 in Chapter 4. On the development of Christian solar symbolism, see Usener (1905); Dölger (1920).
86. Barnes (1981) 254. Writing of panegyric later in the century, Cameron (1970) 199 points out that pagan imagery was used by Christian rhetors because it "had long since become merely decorative."
87. Eus., *LC* 2.5. Porphyry accepted blood sacrifice but described it as inferior to the sacrifice of pure thoughts (Porph., *De abst.* 1.57, 2.34). On the debate over whether Constantine banned all blood sacrifice, see Errington (1988); Bradbury (1994); and above, Chapter 5, n. 4, and Chapter 6, n. 20. On philosophical objections to sacrifice, see further Nock (1933) 224–25; Simmons (1995) 304–18.
88. Eus., *LC* 1.3.
89. νίκης δοτῆρα σωτῆρα φύλακά τε καὶ βοηθόν, Eus., *LC* 9.10. Cf. *CTh.* 7.20.2, in which Constantine is given a pagan salute by his troops. Seeck (1919) 176 dated this law to 326; Barnes (1981) 309, n. 42 (cf. Barnes [1982] 69, n. 102), has attempted to redate it to 307.
90. For estimates of the size of the Christian population in the early fourth century, see Chapter 3 above, n. 2. See also Gaudemet (1958) 88; Lane Fox (1987) 592.

91. Eus., *LC* 1.3; cf. *SC* 11.1: the speech is "not intended to initiate you, who have been instructed by God." At the outset of his Edict to the Eastern Provincials (Eus., *VC* 2.48), Constantine describes knowledge of God as the product of reason, vision, and virtue, and in the *OC* (11.1) he describes his own education as not owing to human knowledge.

92. Symm., *Rel.* 10: "Vno itinere non potest peruenire ad tam grande secretum."

93. Eus., *LC* 3.6.

94. Jesus appears frequently in the Gospels as προφήτης, although not as προφήτης τοῦ πατρός: Bauer (1957) 731. "Supreme commander" (ἀρχιστράτηγος) occurs in Dan. 8:11, and "chief high priest" (ἀρχιερεὺς μέγας) in I Macc. 13:42. For ἀπαύγασμα, see Heb. 1:3; and for βουλῆς ἄγγελος, Isa. 9:5.

95. Fourteen times: Eus., *LC* 1.6 (twice), 2.1, 2.2, 2.4 (twice), 3.5 (four times), 4.2 (twice), 6.9, 6.19. Logos and Soter are Eusebius's two most common expressions for the Second Person in this oration. See n. 97 below.

96. On the complicated development of the concept, see Leisegang (1926), esp. secs. 4–5. Plut., *Ad princ. inerud.* 1 (*Moralia* 779F) links an abstract, though not clearly divine, Logos with the ruler: "when philosophical reason derived from philosophy has been established as the ruler's coadjutor and guardian" (ὁ δ᾽ ἐκ φιλοσοφίας τῷ ἄρχοντι πάρεδρος καὶ φύλαξ ἐκατοικισθεὶς λόγος). Additional references in Baynes (1934) 169 f. Theologically, there is a significant distinction between the Christian Logos and the pagan concept, in that the former was not thought to be innate in the ruler. But what is significant politically is the way that, through the term φίλος, Eusebius ties the Logos to the prevailing concept of an imperial *comes* (see above, n. 81).

97. "Logos" fourteen times, "Savior" sixteen times. See nn. 96 and 102. Remaining references are phrases such as "Governor of this entire cosmos" (1.6) or "great high priest of the great God" (1.6, 3.5).

98. As Eusebius professes at the outset, Πανήγυρις μὲν αὕτη βασιλέως μεγάλου (1.1). The hierarchy God-Logos-Emperor is established at 1.6, but at 3.1 it is God, not the Logos, who guarantees the emperor's reign, God, not the Logos, who at 7.12 chooses and appoints the emperor and, at 6.21, reveals to Constantine "His own Saving Sign." Despite the theory, then, in practice Constantine appears as much coordinate with as subordinate to the Logos. Thus at 7.13, he is described as "the prefect of the Supreme Sovereign" (οἷα μεγάλου βασιλέως ὕπαρχος)—the exact phrase used for the Logos at 3.6—and is pictured combating the visible enemies of God as the Soter combats the invisible ones.

99. Eus., *SC* 11.3, 4.

100. Eus., *SC* 18.1–3.

101. "Our Savior," Eus., *SC* 16.3, 4, 5; 17.8, 12, 13. Sixteen of the roughly forty references to the Second Person in the *LC* are to the Savior: 1.3, 2.2 (twice), 2.3, 2.4, 2.5, 6.9, 7.12, 7.13, 8.8, 9.4, 9.10, 9.11, 9.16, 9.19, 10.6. On Soter as a Hellenistic concept, see, with references, Goodenough (1928) 85, 98; Nock (1951); Chesnut (1978).
102. Eus., *SC* 16.3, 11.17. 16.9; cf. Eus., *LC* 7.12.
103. Eus., *SC* 16.5: "But two great powers—the Roman Empire, which became a monarchy at that time, and the teaching of Christ—proceeding as if from a single starting point, at once tamed and reconciled all to friendship. Thus each blossomed at the same time and place as the other."
104. Eus., *VC* 1.24: "Thus then the God of all, the Supreme Governor of the whole universe, by his own will appointed Constantine, the descendant of so renowned a parent, to be prince and sovereign: so that, while others have been raised to this distinction by the election of their fellow-men, he is the only one to whose elevation no mortal may boast of having contributed."
105. Const., *OC* 3; see Chapter 8, text at n. 72.
106. Baynes (1934) 168. Cf. Cranz (1952) 47.
107. See, e.g., Greenslade (1954) 11; Winkelmann (1961) 242; Farina (1966) 22 and passim; Chesnut (1986) 124–25.
108. Seston (1947) 129–30 challenged Eusebian authorship of the *VC* on the basis of the difference between the role of emperor and bishops in this work and the *LC*. See also Burckhardt in n. 80 above.
109. Eus., *VC* 1.24.
110. See Chapter 4 above.
111. Eus., *HE* 4.26.5–9.
112. As observed by Aland (1968) 124: "Each of these [emperors who do not persecute] immediately becomes a protector of the Church. Occasionally, they even elevate him to the position of a secret Christian." For Eusebius's own use of this standard, see M. Smith (1989) 110–28. Eusebius's acceptance of Melito's joint destiny of Rome and Christianity is ignored by Tabbernee (1997), an otherwise excellent study.
113. Eus., *HE* 9.9.1, 23; 9.10.2.
114. Eus., *HE* 10.4.16. On this speech, see C. Smith (1989). Tabbernee (1997) 330–32.
115. Momigliano (1963b) 80; Chesnut (1986) 134.
116. Eus., *LC* 10.2: "And so all who are being converted to the Higher Power now spit on the faces of the dead idols, trample under the rightless rites of the demons, and ridicule the dated delusions of their forefathers."
117. Eus., *VC* 1.11.
118. Cf. Const., *OC* 11.1, with Eus., *VC* 1.32.
119. Cyril, *Ad Con.* 3.

120. Cf. Eus., *HE* 10.4.16, and Eus., *LC* 10.2. See also text above at nn. 114 and 116.

Chapter Eleven. Power Players

1. Yarnold (1993) traces the beginning of the legend to "the third quarter of the fifth century." For the legend of Sylvester see Jac., *Leg. Aur* (Dec. 31); Ehrhardt (1959–60); Loenertz (1975); Linder (1976); Pohlkamp (1992); Fowden (1994a). For the dates, see Barnes (1982) 72, 77. On Constantine's last days, see above, Chapter 8, n. 91.
2. Hanson (1988) 29.
3. Lichtenstein (1903). In a five-year period (1990–95), the following books appeared on Athanasius: Kannengiesser (1990); Rubenson (1990); Arnold (1991); Barnes (1993); Vivian (1994); Brakke (1995).
4. On the bishops, see Chadwick (1980); Wardman (1982) ch. 6; Lizzi (1987) and (1989); Bowersock (1986).
5. Theod., *HE* I.10. Cf. Jones (1964) 2: 898–99.
6. Athan., *Apol. sec.* 9.
7. Cyril's benefactions are detailed in a letter of his archdeacon Epiphanius to the bishop of Constantinople: *ACO* I.iv.ii: 224–25. Cf. Jones (1964) 1: 346.
8. Ammianus 27.3.14. Praetextatus's jest is reported by Jer., *c. Joannem* 8: "Miserabilis Praetextatus, qui designatus consul est mortuus. Homo sacrilegus, et idolorum cultor, solebat ludens beato papae Damaso dicere, Facite me Romanae urbis episcopum, et ero protinus Christianus."
9. It was part of Athanasius's genius to depict virgins and priests as innocent victims of the excessive force used by his opponents. Other evidence suggests that his supporters were not always passive victims. Soz., *HE* 2.31 reports that after exiling Athanasius Constantine had to order "the clergy and the holy virgins to remain quiet," and also that the emperor referred to the bishop in letters both to the clergy and to the hermit Antony as "an exciter of sedition . . . contumelious and arrogant and the cause of dissension and sedition." Some sense of the resources Athanasius and other bishops had at their disposal can be gleaned from *CTh* 16.2.42 of 416, restricting the number of attendants (*parobolani*) in Alexandria to 500 (the limit was raised in 418 to 600 in *CTh* 16.2.43). See also *CTh* 9.40.16 of 398, regulating "the audacity of the clerics and monks" and 16.3.1 of 390 denying monks access to cities (revoked two years later in 16.3.2). On the capacity of this force for violence, and the support bishops drew from the poor, see Brown (1992) 89–103.
10. Eus., *VC* 2.4.

11. Julian, *Ep.* 41, 437cd; cf. Soz., *HE* 5.15. On urban peace, see Brown (1992) ch. 3.
12. Gelasius, *HE* 3.19 (= Opitz, *Urk.* 34), tr. Coleman-Norton (1966) 1: 186.
13. Fowden (1978) 58 calculated that Egypt had twenty-five different praetorian prefects during Athanasius's tenure as bishop—an average of less than two years each to Athanasius's forty-five.
14. For a sophisticated reinterpretation of Ambrose's conflict with the court, see McLynn (1994) ch. 4. On the powers of the bishop in general, see Fowden (1978) 57 and n. 4 above; of the bishop of Alexandria in particular, n. 9.
15. As observed by Mann (1986) 325. For Arius's popular songs, see Athanasius, *De syn.* 15, *Or. Ar.* I.4. On elections, Gryson (1979) and (1980). For Gregory's description of Constantinople, see Chapter 8 above, at n. 44. For a sample of the pleasures that tempted Chrysostom's congregation in Antioch, see, e.g., his *Address on Vainglory,* conveniently translated in Laistner (1951) 85–122.
16. Ammianus 27.3.12–15. Soc., *HE* 4.29. On reaction against, and efforts to contain, public disorder in the fourth century, see Lim (1995) ch. 7 and passim. Wilson (1987) 44 discusses the danger religious movements face of ossifying through failure to respond to changed circumstances. On the importance of theology, see Chapter 3 above, at n. 18.
17. Brown (1995) 51. As an example of both the influence of local clergy and the elasticity of the Christian message, attention may be called to the British priest who encouraged his parishioners to shoplift from a local supermarket for assertedly destroying community life with the observation, "Jesus said love your neighbor; he didn't say love Marks & Spencers." *Los Angeles Times,* Mar. 16, 1997, A6.
18. For Marcellus: Soz., *HE* 7.15.12 ff., and Fowden (1978) 65. On p. 64, Fowden discounts the claim of Theod., *HE* 5.21, that Marcellus was "the first bishop . . . to use the law as a weapon."
19. Soc., *HE* 7.15; Brown (1992) 116.
20. Aug., *Ser.* 112 (62). The passage is Luke 14:23. Augustine makes the same argument in *Ep.* 93, To Vincentius. See further on this topic Markus (1970) 133–53.
21. Aug., *c. litt. Petil.* 2.84.
22. *VC* 3.54 announces "Destruction of Idol Temples and Images Everywhere"; 3.55, 56, and 58 specify destruction of two Venus temples—obviously on moral more than religious grounds—and a temple of Asclepius at Aegae in Asia Minor. Lane Fox (1987) 671 speculates that the action against the Asclepius temple, as well as an assault on the priest of Apollo at Didyma, resulted from association with the recent persecution.

23. On the intent of fourth-century legislation, see Bradbury (1994) 133–39; cf. Brown (1998) 638: "The laws were frankly intended to terrorize the emperor's subjects on matters of religion." Opinions differ as to the extent of pagan reaction to Constantine's laws: see Chapter 7 above, n. 37.

24. *CTh* 16.10.2.

25. Firm. Mat., *Err.* 29.1.

26. Cameron (1968). See also McLynn (1994) ch. 3.

27. *CTh* 16.1.2. The 379 law, *CTh* 16.5.5, annuls a rescript issued earlier which does not survive but presumably is the law permitting free exercise of religion mentioned by Soz., *HE* 7.1.

28. *CTh* 16.10.14. For a readable account, see Chuvin (1990) 57–72.

29. See Chapter 6 above.

30. Law of 392: *CTh* 16.10.12. On Cynegius, see Matthews (1967).

31. Markus (1990).

32. Cameron & Long (1992) 19–28, with discussion of date and bibliography. Cf. Young (1983) 177: "To state whether one thinks Synesius was really a Christian or not, says more about one's own understanding of Christianity than about Synesius himself."

33. Julian, *Ep.* 19. See Chuvin (1990) 42: "What Pegasius' attitude clearly demonstrates is the proximity of beliefs among a number of cultivated minds."

34. Julian, *Ep.* 19.

35. Athan., *Apol. sec.* 59. See above, Chapter 7, n. 74.

36. Greg. Naz., *De vita* 1293–1302.

37. Joh. Chry., *Bab.* 13.

38. Aug., *Retr.* 129.

39. Athan., *Hist. Ar.* 33; see also 66–67.

40. Alinsky (1972) 152. Cf. Chapter 7 above, text at n. 36.

41. Stark (1996) 8–10 has produced (admittedly theoretical) growth projections that show Christians becoming the majority religion by the middle of the fourth century. Conversely, Brown (1995) 23–24 cautions against uncritically accepting claims of "crowds of the heathen" entering the church. For present purposes, the actual number of converts during this period is less significant than the perception by Christians in the fourth century that this number was both large and of questionable loyalty.

42. Lib., *Or.* 30.48. For the date, see Norman's introductory note in the Loeb edition, 2: 97.

43. Eun., *Vit. Soph.* 472.

44. Ambr., *Ep.* 41.27. Ambrose's account of the incident leaves much to be desired. See McLynn (1994) 303–8 and Chapter 12 below.

45. *Cons. Zacch.* 3.3, "Quae instituta monachorum, uel quare a multis odio

habeantur." The editors suggest that a prime objective of the dialogue was to refute antimonastic sentiment: see 1: 30. Theodosius's ban, *CTh* 10.3.1, was repealed less than two years later, in *CTh* 10.3.2.

46. Bagnall (1993) 301.

47. Brown (1963); Fowden (1978); Markus (1981); MacMullen (1984) ch. 10; Van Dam (1985); Gaudemet (1990); Frend (1990); Lizzi (1990); Padovese (1992); Gentili (1992); Brown (1998).

48. Soz., *HE* IV.10; Theod., *Hist. monach.* Prol. 2–3.

49. Possid., *v. Aug.* 10.

50. A convenient, though by no means most reputable, example is the judg-ment of 1960s activist Jerry Rubin (1970) 66 on the civil rights move-ment: "The Peace Movement was too . . . polite. Martin Luther King was only as powerful as the black man standing behind him with a molotov cocktail." Such thinking begs the question of whether such violence would have had any effect without the enormous prestige won by the preacher of nonviolence. Cf. Smelser (1962) 261: "Were it only a matter of force, it is probable that all expressions of hostility could be put down easily."

51. See, e.g., Markus (1974); Brown (1995) ch. 2.

52. Wilken (1983) 120 on the popularity of drunkenness as a rhetorical theme. On the importance of appearance, see Shaw (1998).

53. Julian, *Mis.* 350D–351A .

54. Joh. Chry., *Bab.* 77. Soc., *HE* 3.17.

55. Christian regard for the monks corresponds to Mary Douglas's character-ization of "strong group" behavior. Douglas assigns hermits an important role in such groups as "a perennial source of metaphors of radical social change." Douglas (1982) 221, 234. Fowden (1982) offers a good treat-ment of the role of pagan ascetics.

56. Baynes (1926) 148. Cf. Mosca (1939) 434: "In general, in every society, circumstances being equal, success is reserved for individuals who pos-sess in eminent degree the endowments which, in that society at that particular time, are most widely diffused and most highly esteemed."

57. Gregg & Groh (1981) 137: "There are good reasons to believe that the Antony 'project' was undertaken for the express purpose of combating attempts by the Arians to enlist the monks in support of their cause." See also Brakke (1995) ch. 4. Cf. Rubenson (1990); Goehring (1992); Goehring (1997). Barnes (1986a) cast doubt on Athanasian authorship of the Life of Antony.

58. In *Ep.* 54.5, to Serapion, Athanasius recommends the history of Arianism which he wrote for the monks but also cautions Serapion not to give copies to anyone or make one for himself, "lest what is imperfectly expressed through infirmity or the obscurity of language, do hurt to the reader." Cf. Young (1983) 76.

59. Stroumsa (1994); cf. Drake (1996).
60. Fowden (1978) 62–63. As Cameron (1977) 21 noted: "It is significant, and typical, that, once a Christian, Victorinus should have turned his pen against heresy rather than paganism."
61. Aug., *Ep.* 93 To Vincentius.
62. Aug., *c. litt. Petil.* 2.84.
63. Aug., *c. litt. Petil.* 2.63–72.
64. Walsh (1986) 179–82.
65. Hefele-Leclercq (1973) I, 1: 163. See Chapter 6 above, at n. 73.
66. Turchetti (1991) distinguishes between policies of "toleration" and "concordance" in early modern European monarchies, defining the latter as the traditional Christian policy of religious unity. I find it difficult to distinguish between what Turchetti calls "concordance" and what less sympathetic writers have traditionally called "intolerance." The difficulties in this article are smoothed over in Laursen & Nederman (1996) 9–10, where the distinction is turned into a difference between commitment to the idea of diversity as a permanent condition and ad hoc situations that do not abandon the long-term goal of religious unity. The latter would then correspond to situations that produced de facto toleration, as identified by Scribner (1996) 35–38. But see also Burgess (1996). See also above, Chapter 8, n 40.
67. Baynes (1972) 19, Alfoldi (1948) 30, 82. Scribner (1996) 35–38 cites the "balance of contending groups" and "toleration by dint of too few resources to enforce wider conformity" as two of the nine ways that religious toleration manifested itself during the Reformation. Two of his other conditions, however—popular willingness to accept differences, or what he calls "the tolerance of practical rationality," and "de facto toleration by virtue of pastoral latitudinarianism"—may equally apply. See above, Chapter 8, n. 40.
68. Eus., *VC* 2.60.2 (my tr.). See also Chapter 8 above, text at n. 39.
69. Eus., *LC* 8.3; cf. *VC* 3.54.5 and Chapter 10 above, text following n. 116.
70. See, e.g., his use of Jesus' example at Const., *OC* 15.3–4, and the argument for diversity at *OC* 13; see also his argument to the Numidian bishops in 330 urging toleration as a form of martyrdom (Optatus, ed. Maier, II, 67–80). See further above, Chapters 6 and 8.
71. Stark (1996) 194.
72. The principle is stated by Mosca (1939) 53. It was already known to Gibbon (1909–14) 2: 57, who attributed to Christian zeal "that irresistible weight which even a small band of well-trained and intrepid volunteers has so often possessed over an undisciplined multitude, ignorant of the subject, and careless of the event of the war." Cf. Brinton (1965) 157 and, for the principle applied to contemporary politics, Hofstadter (1965c), esp. 138.

73. Khashan (1992) 23–31 is a discussion of theories of minority group behavior in the context of a contemporary political issue which can be useful for understanding other periods of history. See, e.g., 29: "It suits the leaders of ethnic and religious groups . . . to advance the level of hatred among their group members against other groups, in a bid to sustain (or even augment) their influence and status within the community." In another context, Hofstadter (1965a) 15 n. observed, "The ecumenicism of hatred is a great breaker-down of precise intellectual discriminations."

74. Hopkins (1998) 220–21 estimates on the basis of a conversion rate of 3.4 percent per annum in its first three centuries that at any given time two-fifths of all adult Christians would have become members during the previous ten years, a rate that "put a tremendous strain on the absorptive and instructional capacity of older members." For this reason, he concludes, "Christianity was a religion which, because of the rapidity of its expansion, always had to be questioning its members about the nature and degree of their adherence." A classic liberal analysis of massive immigration on the United States in the twentieth century is Hofstadter (1965a). Hofstadter's methods have been criticized, but his key insight remains useful. See Drake (1998).

75. Markus (1980); Markus (1990) ch. 2. See also Ando (1996).

76. So White (1993b) 32.

77. Eus., *VC* 4.54.

78. Aug,, *Ep.* 29.8–9; cf. Brown (1995) 23–24. See also Chapter 7 above.

79. See n. 41 above.

80. Firm. Mat., *Err.* 16.4: "melius est ut liberetis inuitos quam ut uolentibus concedatis exitium."

81. Firm. Mat., *Err.* 16.5: "Aegrotantes contraria delectant; 16.4: Nolunt quidam et repugnant et exitium suum prona cupiditate desiderant."

82. Firm. Mat., *Err.* 28.10. The reference is to Exod. 22:20.

83. *CTh* 16.10.2 (341); 16.10.3 (343), 16.10.4 (probably 346). See the discussion by Turcan in his edition of Firm. Mat., *Err.* 19, 25–6.

84. Firm. Mat., *Math.* 2.30.2, 2.30.12. Cf. 2.30.1–2, 8–9.

85. Simmons (1995) 46 calls attention to Jerome's identification of Arnobius as a Neoplatonic philosopher whose bishop initially doubted the sincerity of his conversion.

86. Hefele-Leclercq (1973) I, 1: 187. See the conclusion of Chapter 6 above.

87. The *Life* suffers from interpolation: see MacMullen (1997) 174, n. 68. But even though its account may not be accurate in detail, it seems safe to use as a representation of what Christians in late antiquity considered plausible behavior: see Kelly (1995) 168–70.

88. *vit. Por.* 17. As in the instance of Paul and the silversmiths of Ephesus (Chapter 3 above, text at n. 33), readers need always to remember that

Christian writers of these centuries took it for granted that pagans, unlike themselves, were incapable of being motivated by true religious sentiment.

89. *vit. Por.* 27.
90. *vit. Por.* 41.
91. *vit. Por.* 50–51.
92. For Cynegius, see *PLRE* 2: 331.
93. *vit. Por.* 72–73.
94. Lib., *Or.* 18.121–22.
95. Lib., *Or.* 30.28.
96. See Chapter 7 above, at n. 35.
97. *vit. Por.* 73.
98. Thucy. 3.82–83.
99. Greg. Naz., *De se ipso* II, 146–48.
100. See Brown (1988); Markus (1990) 90; Wortley (1992); Elm (1994). On Eusebius, see Markus (1975) 17 and Chapter 10 above.
101. Soz., *HE* 5.5. Fowden (1978) 60.
102. Most famously in his tract *Against the Galilaeans* (tr. W. C. Wright, *Julian* [Loeb Classical Library] 3: 318–427). See further on Julian Bidez (1930), Malley (1978); Wilken (1979); Meredith (1980), Smith (1995).
103. So John Chrysostom, advising parents not to oppose their sons' becoming monks for fear that the emperors might again become pagan: "For our status is not like that of the Greeks. It does not depend on the opinions of rulers, but it stands upon its own strength and is more apparent the more it is attacked." Joh. Chry., *Adv. oppug.* 2.9.
104. Ammianus 22.12.6–7.
105. Fowden (1993) 56; on the basis of Julian's philosophy, Smith (1995) 220 comes to the same conclusion: "The failure of Julian's cultural programme was uniquely harmful to the pagan cause, because his universalized theory of paganism at last presented the Christians with just the thing they had lacked till then—an all-embracing version of paganism on which they could focus their attack." See also Chesnut (1986) 235: "Julian, the pagan persecutor, was naturally the arch example of a bad emperor. Julian could be held out as proof that the Christians could not live in safety unless there were a Christian emperor on the throne."
106. Wilken (1983) 128. Cf. the perceptive remark of Wardman (1982) 152: "It seems likely that Julian gave considerable offence to all, not by taking religion seriously, since the other emperors did this, but by making it an obtrusive issue yet again in the manner of those who had persecuted the Christians." On Julian in later scholarship, see Nulle (1959); Braun & Richer (1978) and (1981); Penella (1993).
107. Julian, *Ep.* 36. Ammianus 22.10.7, 25.4.20.
108. Markus (1974).

109. Markus (1974) 4; Fowden (1986) 209 notes, with examples, an increasing tendency to identify heresy with classical thought.
110. On Basil, see Fortin (1981); Rousseau (1994).
111. Chuvin (1990) 9 notes with favor Godefroy's early seventeenth-century proposal to identify pagans as "people of the place."
112. Salzman (1987), Hunt (1993).
113. So Scribner (1996) 41: "Once the identity of outsiders had been established in common discourse, they became natural suspects and potential objects of fear or hostility; they were thus available as scapegoats at times of anxiety. . . . Stigmatisation became more intense when it was linked to a process of diagnosis and explanation: that is, when a particular group could be associated in a causal manner with a specific threat or problem."
114. Markus (1990) 28–29.
115. Lim (1995) 24–30 attributes a negative attitude toward public debate in late antiquity to instability produced by the disruptions of the third century. For Constantine's letter, see Eus., *VC* 2.64–72, and Chapter 7 above, at nn. 9–11.
116. Brown (1992) 116.
117. In the Edict to the Eastern Provincials, Eus. *VC* 2.60.2. See above, Chapter 8, at n. 39.
118. So Brinton (1965) 53: "The line in actual practice of government between force and persuasion is a subtle one, not to be drawn by formulas, by 'science' or textbooks, but by men skilled in the art of ruling. One of the best signs of the unfitness of the ruling class to rule is the absence of this skill among its members. And this absence is recorded in history in the accumulated minor disturbances and discontents which precede revolution."

Chapter Twelve. Milan, 390

1. For Ambrose's mosaic, see Wilpert (1924) 3: 84, 1. See also the discussion in McLynn (1994) xviii. For Constantine's raiments, Eus., *LC* V.4, 6. The missorium of Theodosius, in the Academia de la Historia, Madrid, is depicted in Bianchi Bandinelli (1971) 358.
2. Jac., *Leg. Aur.* (Dec. 7).
3. Ambr., *Obit.* 34; Aug., *civ. dei* 5.26.
4. *Ep.* 51 (3).
5. McLynn (1994) 315–30.
6. Paulinus, *vit. Amb.* 7 (22–24); Soz., *HE* 7.25; Theod., *HE* 5.17. Ambr., *Obit.* 34.
7. For an excellent discussion, on which I have relied heavily in these pages,

see Barnes (1990) 17–25. For a specific comparison of these two paintings, Wheelock (1990) 100–102.

8. On this icon, see Chapter 1 above, text at n. 6.
9. Cf. Eus., *VC* 4.54 and *LC* 1.3. See also Chapter 10 above, at nn. 68 and 88.
10. Baker (1992).
11. McCarthy (1957) 21.
12. Matt. 10: 14, 16.
13. A point made by Garnsey (1984). Similarly Remer (1998) 74 argues that without the Christian distinction between church and state "it is doubtful that Locke and Jefferson could have developed their arguments for religious liberty." See also Chapter 2 above.
14. Momigliano (1963b) 79 (referring to Lact., *DMP*).
15. Mill (1977) 237.
16. Mill (1977) 232.
17. "Who will not venture to affirm that, by the alliance of Christianity with the virtue and excellence of men like the Antonines,—of the best product of Greek and Roman civilisation, while Greek and Roman civilisation had yet life and power,—Christianity and the world, as well as the Antonines themselves, would not have been gainers?" Arnold (1865) 355, 362.
18. Gibbon (1909–14) 1: 85 f. Gibbon's description of the fall of Rome as "the triumph of barbarism and religion" is at 7: 320. Carlyle's lectures were delivered in 1840 and printed in Carlyle (1841). On the importance of Rome to Victorian England, see Vance (1997).
19. Darwin (1859). His ideas about human evolution were worked out more explicitly in Darwin (1871). On the impact of the theory of evolution, see Bowler (1984).
20. Pettegree (1996) 198: "In the early modern period it [toleration] was only ever a loser's creed." For a review, and critique, of standard accounts of toleration, see Laursen & Nederman (1998) 1–10.
21. Aug., *Ep.* 93, To Vincentius.
22. "Remota itaque iustitia quid sunt regna nisi magna latrocinia?" Aug., *civ. dei* IV.4.
23. Kaufman (1990) 5 and passim.
24. Scribner (1996) 43.
25. Lecky (1865) 2: 34–35.
26. *vit. Dan.* 60–63.
27. Frend (1972).
28. For Augustus and Apollo, see: Gagé (1955); Lambrechts (1953); Wilhelm (1986). For Marcus Aurelius's piety as a cause of victory, see Chapter 10 above, n. 16.
29. Scribner (1996) 44–45; see also 32–33.
30. Wardman (1982) 36; Scribner (1996) 38.

31. Nixon (1992) 21.
32. Xen., *Cyr.* 1.1.3
33. Barnes (1993) 174: "By the end of the fourth century Christian orthodoxy had been added to the traditional list of virtues required in a legitimate emperor." For Ammianus see 21.16.18 and Chapter 9 above, at nn. 11–12.
34. Ambr., *Ep.* 41.
35. Ambr., *Ep.* 40.
36. Eus., *VC* 4.17, 29.
37. Ambr., *Ep.* 41.27.
38. Ambr., *Ep.* 41.28.
39. Soc., *HE* 1.6. See also Chapter 7 above, at n. 61.
40. *vit. Por.* 33–54. The *Life* contains material interpolated from later periods, but this passage seems secure. See Chapter 11, n. 87, and Kelly (1995) 168–70.
41. For this and what follows I rely heavily on the reconstruction of events proposed in McLynn (1994) 298–309.
42. Cameron (1973) 248–52; cf. Cameron (1976) 181–82.
43. Soz., *HE* 7.25. I follow the reconstruction of events in McLynn (1994) 315–23.
44. Soz., *HE* 7.25.
45. McLynn (1994) 318–23; Brown (1992) 105–7. See also French (1998).
46. Eus., *VC* 3.4. See above, p. 398.
47. Joh. Chry., *Statuis* XXI.11; Lib., *Or.* 19.19; cf. *Or.* 20.24, where the two brothers are identified as Hannibalianus and Julius Constantius, the hawk and the dove, respectively. This positive use of Constantine takes on all the greater significance in light of Libanius's general tendency to treat Constantine negatively in his later works. See Wiemer (1994); Malosse (1997).
48. Brown (1992) 55: "Anger was a passion of the soul that the upright man could regret. Anger might be cooled. . . . In this way, emphasis on anger formed part of the late Roman language of amnesty."
49. *CTh* 9.40.13. On the date of this law, see McLynn (1994) 322.
50. Joh. Chry., *Comp.* 2.
51. See Chapter 2, at n. 66.
52. McLynn (1994) 323.
53. *Ep.* 40.6, 11.
54. Brown (1992) ch. 3.
55. Lib., *Or.* 19.32.
56. Garnsey (1984) 21; Ando (1996). See also Chapter 7 above, at n. 35.
57. Eus., *VC* 2.60.1 (my tr.). On the significance of indecision, see Smelser (1962) 308–10.
58. McLynn (1994) chs. 4–5.

Works Cited

PRIMARY SOURCES

Unless otherwise indicated in the notes, all translations are from the versions cited below. (All quotations from the Holy Bible are from the Revised Standard Version.)

ACO	*Acta conciliorum oecumenicorum.* Ed. E. Schwartz. Berlin, 1925–26.
Act. Mart.	*The Acts of the Christian Martyrs.* Ed. and tr. H. Musurillo. Oxford, 1972.
Acta Petri	*Les Actes de Pierre.* Ed. L. Vouaux. Paris 1922. Tr. G. C. Stead, "The Acts of Peter." In *New Testament Apocrypha,* ed. W. Schneemelcher, Eng. tr. ed. R. McL. Wilson, 2 vols., 2: 276–321. Philadelphia, 1964.
Ambr., *Ep.*	*Sancti Ambrosi opera, X: Epistulae et acta.* Ed. M. Zelzer & L. Krestan. Corpus Scriptorum Ecclesiasticorum Latinorum, vol. 82, t. 1–4. Vienna, 1990–96. Tr. H. de Romestin et al., *Ambrose: Select Works and Letters.* In *A Select Library of Nicene and Post-Nicene Fathers of the Christian Church,* ed. P. Schaff & H. Wace, ser. 2, 10: 411–73. New York, 1898.
Ambr., *Obit.*	Sancti Ambrosii. *De obitu Theodosii oratio.* In *Opera omnia,* ed. D. A. B. Caillau. 2d ed. VIII: 117–39. Paris, 1842.

Tr. Roy J. Deferrari, "On Emperor Theodosius." In L. McCauley et al., *Funeral Orations by St. Gregory Nazianzen and St. Ambrose,* Fathers of the Church, 22: 307–32. Washington, D.C., 1953.

Ammianus   Ammianus Marcellinus. *Rerum Gestarum Libri qui supersunt.* Text and tr. John C. Rolfe. 3 vols. Loeb Classical Library. Cambridge, Mass., 1935–40; vols. 1, 3 rev. 1950–52.

Apul., *Metam.*   Apuleius. *Metamorphoses.* Ed. R. Helm. Berlin, 1961. Tr. R. Graves, *The Golden Ass.* New York, 1951.

Athan., *Apol. sec.*   Athanasius. *Apologia secunda (contra Arianos).* Ed. H. G. Opitz, *Athanasius Werke,* II, 2: 87–168. Berlin, 1938.
Tr. A. Robertson, *Apology.* In *A Select Library of Nicene and Post-Nicene Fathers of the Christian Church,* ed. P. Schaff & H. Wace, ser. 2, 4: 100–47. New York, 1891.

Athan., *De decr.*   Athanasius. *De decretis Nicaenae synodi.* Ed. H. G. Opitz, *Athanasius Werke,* II, 1: 1–45. Berlin, 1936.
Tr. Henry Cardinal Newman, rev. by A. Robertson, *Defense of the Nicene Council.* In *A Select Library of Nicene and Post-Nicene Fathers of the Christian Church,* ed. P. Schaff & H. Wace, ser. 2, 4: 73–76, 149–72. New York, 1891.

Athan., *De syn.*   Athanasius. *De synodis.* Ed. H. G. Opitz, *Athanasius Werke,* II, 1: 231–40. Berlin, 1936.
Tr. Henry Cardinal Newman, rev. by A. Robertson, *On the Councils of Ariminum and Seleucia.* In *A Select Library of Nicene and Post-Nicene Fathers of the Christian Church,* ed. P. Schaff & H. Wace, ser. 2, 4: 451–80. New York, 1891.

Athan., *Ep.*   Athanasius. *Epistulae.* PG 26: 529–648b.
Tr. A. Robertson, *Letters of St. Athanasius.* In *A Select Library of Nicene and Post-Nicene Fathers of the Christian Church,* ed. P. Schaff & H. Wace, ser. 2, 4: 506–81. New York, 1891.

Athan., *Hist. Ar.*   Athanasius. *Historia Arianorum ad Monachos.* Ed. H. G. Opitz, *Athanasius Werke,* II, 1: 183–230. Berlin, 1936.
Tr. A. Robertson, *Arian History.* In *A Select Library of Nicene and Post-Nicene Fathers of the Christian Church,*

ed. P. Schaff & H. Wace, ser. 2, 4: 266–302. New York, 1891.

Athan., *Or. Ar.*   Athanasius. *Orationes contra Arianos.* PG 26: 11–526. Tr. A. Robertson, *Against the Arians.* In *A Select Library of Nicene and Post-Nicene Fathers of the Christian Church,* ed. P. Schaff & H. Wace, ser. 2, 4: 303–447. New York, 1891.

Aug., *Conf.*   Augustine. *Confessiones.* Ed. J. J. O'Donnell. 3 vols. Oxford, 1992. Tr. V. J. Bourke, *Confessions.* Fathers of the Church, vol. 21. New York, 1953.

Aug., *c. litt. Petil.*   Augustine. *contra litteras Petiliani.* Ed. M. Petschenig, *Scripta contra Donatistas II.* Corpus Scriptorum Ecclesiasticorum Latinorum 52: 1–227. Vienna, 1909. Tr. J. R. King & C. D. Hartranft, *Answer to Letters of Petilian, Bishop of Cirta.* In *A Select Library of Nicene and Post-Nicene Fathers of the Christian Church,* ed. P. Schaff, ser. 1, 4: 519–629. New York, 1887.

Aug., *civ dei*   Augustine of Hippo. *De civitate Dei.* Ed. B. Dombart & A. Kalb. 2 vols. Corpus Christianorum Series Latina, vols. 47–48. Turnhout, Belgium, 1955. Tr. M. Dods, *City of God.* In *A Select Library of Nicene and Post-Nicene Fathers of the Christian Church,* ed. P. Schaff, ser. 1, 2: 1–511. New York, 1886.

Aug., *de op. monach.*   S. Aureli Augustini Hipponiensis episcopi. *de opere monachorum.* Ed. J. Zycha, Corpus Scriptorum Ecclesiasticorum Latinorum 41: 529–96. Vienna, 1900. Tr. H. Browne, *Of the Work of Monks.* In *A Select Library of Nicene and Post-Nicene Fathers of the Christian Church,* ed. P. Schaff, ser. 1, 3: 503–24. New York, 1887.

Aug., *Ep.*   S. Aureli Augustini Hipponiensis episcopi. *Epistulae,* ed. Al. Golbacher, Corpus Scriptorum Ecclesiasticorum Latinorum, vols. 34–35, 44, 57–58. Vienna, 1895–1923. Tr. W. Parsons, *St. Augustine Letters,* 5 vols. Fathers of the Church, vols. 12, 18, 20, 30, 32. New York, 1951–56.

Aug., *Retr.*   Sancti Aureli Augustini. *Retractationum,* libri duo. Ed.

P. Knoll, Corpus Scriptorum Ecclesiasticorum Latinorum, vol. 36. Vienna, 1902.
Tr. M. I. Bogan, *The Retractations.* Fathers of the Church, vol. 60. Washington, D.C., 1968.

Aug., *Ser.*   Sancti Aureli Augustini. *Sermones de Scripturis.* PL 38. Tr. R. G. MacMullen, "Sermons on Selected Lessons of the New Testament." In *A Select Library of Nicene and Post-Nicene Fathers of the Christian Church,* ed. P. Schaff, ser. 1, 6: 237–545. New York, 1887.

Augustus, *Res*   *Res Gestae Divi Augusti. The Achievements of the Divine*
Gestae   *Augustus.* Ed. V. Ehrenberg & A. H. M. Jones. Tr. P. A. Brunt & J. M. Moore. Oxford, 1967.

Aur. Vict., *Caes.*   Sextus Aurelius Victor. *De Caesaribus.* Ed. Fr. Pichlmayr, R. Gruendel. Leipzig, 1970. Tr. H. W. Bird, *Liber de Caesaribus of Sextus Aurelius Victor.* Translated Texts for Historians, 17. Liverpool, 1994.

CJ   *Corpus iuris civilis.* Ed. T. Mommsen, P. Krüger, R. Scholl, & G. Kroll. 13th ed. 3 vols. Berlin, 1920–28; repr., Dublin, 1968–73. Tr. S. P. Scott, *The Civil Law.* 17 vols. repr. in 7. New York, 1973 (orig. pub. 1932).

Const., *OC*   *Oratio Constantini ad sanctum coetum.* Ed. I. A. Heikel, *Eusebius Werke,* I, Die griechischen christlichen Schriftsteller der ersten Jahrhunderte, 7: 154–92. Leipzig, 1902. Anonymous Bagster tr. revised by E. C. Richardson, "The Oration of the Emperor Constantine which he addressed 'To the Assembly of the Saints.'" In *A Select Library of Nicene and Post-Nicene Fathers of the Christian Church,* ed. P. Schaff & H. Wace, ser. 2, 1: 561–80. New York, 1890.

Cons. Zacch.   *Consultationes Zacchaei christiani et Apollonii philosophi.* Ed. and tr. J. L. Feiertag & W. Steinmann, *Questions d'un Païen à un Chrétien.* Sources chrétiennes, 401–2. Paris, 1994.

Corp. Herm.   A. D. Nock & A.-J. Festugière, eds. *Corpus Hermeticus.* 4 vols. Paris, 1954–60.

Tr. Brian Copenhaver, *Hermetica: The Greek Corpus Hermeticum and the Latin Asclepius.* Cambridge, 1992.

Cosmas, *Chr. Top.*   *The Christian Topography of Cosmas, an Egyptian Monk.* Ed. and tr. J. W. McCrindle. New York, 1897; repr., 1967.

CS   *Constitutiones Sirmondianae.* In *Theodosiani libri XVI cum Constitutionibus Sirmondianis et Leges novellae ad Theodosianum pertinentes.* Ed. Th. Mommsen & P. Meyer. 3 vols. 3d ed. 1, 2: 907–21. Berlin, 1962.

CTh   *Theodosiani libri XVI cum Constitutionibus Sirmondianis et Leges novellae ad Theodosianum pertinentes.* Ed. Th. Mommsen & P. Meyer. 3 vols. 3d ed. Berlin, 1962.
Tr. Clyde Pharr et al., *The Theodosian Code and Novels and the Sirmondian Constitutions.* Princeton, 1952; repr., 1969.

Cyril, *Ad Con.*   Cyril of Jerusalem. *Epistula ad Constantium imperatorem.* Ed. E. Bihain, "L'épitre de Cyrille de Jérusalem à Constance sur la vision de la Croix. Tradition manuscrite et édition critique." *Byzantion* 43 (1993): 264–96.
Tr. L. McCauley & A. Stephenson, *The Works of S. Cyril of Jerusalem.* Fathers of the Church, 64: 231–35. Washington, D.C., 1970.

Did. Apos.   *Didascalia et Constitutiones apostolorum.* Ed. F. X. Funk. 2 vols. Paderborn, Germany, 1905.
Tr. R. Hugh Connolly, *Didascalia apostolorum.* Oxford, 1929; repr., 1969.

Dio   Dio Cassius. *Dio's Roman History.* Text and tr. Earnest Cary. 9 vols. Loeb Classical Library. London, 1914–27.

Dio Chr.   Dio Chrysostom. *Discourses.* 5 vols. Text and tr. J. W. Cohoon & H. Lamar Crosby. Loeb Classical Library. Cambridge, Mass., 1932–51.

Diotogenes   Diotogenes "the Pythagorean." *Peri basileias.* In Stobaeus, *Anthologiam* II.7.61–2. Ed. O. Hense, 4: 263–70. Berlin, 1909.
Tr. E. Barker, *From Alexander to Constantine: Passages and Documents Illustrating the History of Social and Political Ideas, 336 B.C.–A.D. 337,* 363–67. Oxford, 1956.

Works Cited

Ecphantus | Ecphantus "the Pythagorean." *Peri basileias*. In Stobaeus, *Anthologiam* II.7.64–6. Ed. O. Hense, 4: 271–79. Berlin, 1909.
Tr. E. Barker, *From Alexander to Constantine: Passages and Documents Illustrating the History of Social and Political Ideas, 336 B.C.–A.D. 337,* 367–72. Oxford, 1956.

Epiph., *Pan.* | Epiphanius. *Panarion.* Ed. Karl Holl. Die griechischen christlichen Schriftsteller der ersten Jahrhunderte, 25, 31, 37. Leipzig: J. C. Hinrich, 1915–33. Vol. 2: Haereses XXXIV–LXIV, 2d ed. by Jurgen Dummer. Berlin, 1980.
Tr. P. Amidon, *Panarion*. Oxford, 1990.

Eudoxia | *Eudoxia and the Holy Sepulchre: A Constantinian Legend in Coptic.* Ed. T. Orlandi, tr. B. Pearson. Testi e documenti per lo studio dell' Antichità 67. Milan, 1980.

Eun., *Vit. Soph.* | Eunapius of Sardis. *Lives of the Philosophers and Sophists.* Text and tr. in W. C. Wright, *Philostratus and Eunapius.* Loeb Classical Library, 342–563. Cambridge, Mass., 1921.

Eus., *c. Hier.* | Eusebius of Caesarea. *Contra Hieroclem.* Text and tr. F. C. Conybeare, *Philostratus, The Life of Apollonius of Tyana, the Epistles of Apollonius and the Treatise of Eusebius.* 2 vols. Loeb Classical Library, 2: 484–605. London, 1912.

Eus., *DE* | Eusebius of Caesarea. *Demonstratio Evangelica.* Ed. I. Heikel, *Eusebius Werke,* VI. Die griechischen christlichen Schriftsteller der ersten Jahrhunderte, 23. Leipzig, 1913.
Tr. W. J. Ferrar, *The Proof of the Gospel.* 2 vols. in 1. London, 1920; repr., Grand Rapids, Mich., 1981.

Eus., *HE* | Eusebius of Caesarea. *Historia ecclesiastica.* Ed. E. Schwartz, *Die Kirchengeschichte,* 3 vols. Die griechischen christlichen Schriftsteller der ersten Jahrhunderte, 9. Leipzig, 1903–9.
Tr. A. C. McGiffert, "The Church History of Eusebius." In *A Select Library of Nicene and Post-Nicene Fathers of the Christian Church,* ed. P. Schaff & H. Wace, ser. 2, 1: 1–403. New York, 1890.

Eus., *LC* | Eusebius of Caesarea. *Laus Constantini.* Ed. I. A.

Heikel, *Eusebius Werke,* I, Die griechischen christlichen Schriftsteller der ersten Jahrhunderte, 7: 195–223. Leipzig, 1902.
Tr. H. A. Drake, *In Praise of Constantine: A Historical Study and New Translation of Eusebius' Tricennial Orations,* 83–102. Berkeley, 1976; repr., 1978.

Eus., *PE* Eusebius of Caesarea. *Praeparatio Evangelica.* Ed. K. Mras, *Eusebius Werke,* VIII: 1–2, Die griechischen christlichen Schriftsteller der ersten Jahrhunderte, 43. Berlin, 1954–56.
Tr. E. H. Gifford, *Preparation for the Gospel.* 2 vols. Oxford, 1903; repr., Grand Rapids, Mich., 1981.

Eus., *SC* Eusebius of Caesarea. *De sepulchro Christi* (chs. XI–XVIII of printed text of the *LC*). Ed. I. A. Heikel, *Eusebius Werke,* I, Die griechischen christlichen Schriftsteller der ersten Jahrhunderte, 7: 223–59. Leipzig, 1902.
Tr. H. A. Drake, *In Praise of Constantine: A Historical Study and New Translation of Eusebius' Tricennial Orations,* 103–27. Berkeley, 1976; repr. 1978.

Eus., *VC* Eusebius of Caesarea. *De vita Constantini.* Ed. F. Winkelmann, *Über das Leben des Kaisers Konstantins. Eusebius Werke,* I, 1. Die griechischen christlichen Schriftsteller der ersten Jahrhunderte. Berlin, 1975.
Tr. E. C. Richardson, *The Life of Constantine.* In *A Select Library of Nicene and Post-Nicene Fathers of the Christian Church,* ed. P. Schaff & H. Wace, ser. 2, 1: 471–559. New York, 1890.

Eutr., *Brev.* Eutropius. *Breviarium ab urbe condita.* Ed. C. Santini. Leipzig, 1979.
Tr. H. W. Bird. Translated Texts for Historians, 14. Liverpool, 1993.

Exc. Val. *Excerpta Valesiana.* Text and tr. John C. Rolfe. In vol. 3 of Ammianus Marcellinus. Loeb Classical Library. Cambridge, Mass., 1939; rev. 1952.

Festal Index *Histoire 'Acéphale' et Index syriaque des lettres festales d'Athanase d'Alexandrie.* Ed. A. Martin & M. Albert. Paris, 1985.
Tr. A. Robertson, "Letters of Athanasius." In *A Select Library of Nicene and Post-Nicene Fathers of the Christian*

	Church, ed. P. Schaff & H. Wace, ser. 2, 4: 506–53. New York, 1891.
Firm. Mat., *Err.*	Firmicus Maternus. *De errore profanarum religionum.* Ed. and tr. R. Turcan. Budé ed. Paris, 1982. Tr. C. Forbes, *The Error of the Pagan Religions.* Ancient Christian Writers. New York, 1970.
Firm. Mat., *Math.*	Firmicus Maternus. *Mathesis.* Ed. and tr. P. Monat. Budé ed. 2 vols. Paris, 1992–94. Tr. J. R. Bram, *Ancient Astrology: Theory and Practice.* Park Ridge, N.J., 1975.
FHG	K. & T. Muller. *Fragmenta historicorum graecorum.* Scriptorum graecorum bibliotheca. 5 vols. Paris, 1853–1938.
Gel., *Ep.*	Gelasius Papa I, *Epistolae et Decreta,* PL 59: 13–102.
Gel., *HE*	Gelazius of Cyzicus. *Historia Ecclesiastica.* Ed. G. Loeschcke & M. Heinemann. Leipzig, 1918.
Greg. I, *Ep.*	P. Ewald & L. Hartman, eds. *Gregorii I Papae Registrum epistolarum.* 2 vols. Vienna, 1899.
Greg. Naz., *De se ipso*	Gregory Nazianzen. *De se ipso et de episcopis.* PG 37: 1166–1227. Tr. D. M. Meehan, "Concerning Himself and the Bishops." In *Gregory Nazianzen, Three Poems.* Fathers of the Church, 75: 49–74. Washington, D.C., 1987.
Greg. Naz., *De vita*	Gregory Nazianzen. *De vita sua.* Ed. C. Jungck. Heidelberg, 1974. Tr. D. M. Meehan, "Concerning His Own Life." In *Gregory Nazianzen, Three Poems.* Fathers of the Church, 75: 75–130. Washington, D.C., 1987.
Greg. Nys., *de deitate*	Gregory of Nyssa. *De deitate Filii et Spiritus Sancti.* Ed. E. Rhein et al., *Gregorii Nysseni Sermones, pars III.* Gregorii Nysseni Opera 10, 2: 117–44. Leiden, 1996.
HA	[*Scriptores*] *Historiae Augustae.* Text and tr. D. Magie. 3 vols. Loeb Classical Library. Cambridge, Mass., 1921–32.
Horace, *Carm.*	Horace. *Carmina.* Ed. C. E. Bennett & J. C. Rolfe in *Horace: The Complete Works.* Boston, 1934.
Itin. Eger.	*Itinerarium Egeriae.* Ed. Aet. Franceschini & R. Weber,

Fathers of the Christian Church, ed. P. Schaff, ser. 1, 9: 317–489. New York, 1889.

Julian, *Caes.* Julian. *Caesares.* Text and tr. W. C. Wright, *The Works of the Emperor Julian.* 3 vols. Loeb Classical Library, 2: 344–415. Cambridge, Mass., 1913–23.

Julian, *Ep.* Julian. *Letters.* Text and tr. W. C. Wright, *The Works of the Emperor Julian.* 3 vols. Loeb Classical Library, 3: 2– 303. Cambridge, Mass., 1913–23.

Julian, *Ep. Pr.* Julian. "Fragment of a Letter to a Priest." Text and tr. W. C. Wright, *The Works of the Emperor Julian.* 3 vols. Loeb Classical Library, 2: 296–339. Cambridge, Mass., 1913–23.

Julian, *Mis.* Julian. *Misopogon.* Text and tr. W. C. Wright, *The Works of the Emperor Julian.* 3 vols. Loeb Classical Library, 2: 420–511. Cambridge, Mass., 1913–23.

Just., *Dig.* Justinian. *Digesta.* In *Corpus iuris civilis,* vol. 1, ed. T. Mommsen, P. Krüger, R. Scholl, & G. Kroll. 13th ed. 3 vols. Berlin, 1920–28; repr., Dublin, 1968–73. Tr. Alan Watson, ed., *The Digest of Justinian.* 2 vols. Philadelphia, 1998.

Just. Mart., *Apol.* Iustini Martyris. *Apologiae pro Christianis.* Ed. M. Marcovich. Patristische Texte und Studien, 38. Berlin, 1994.

Lact., *DI* L. Caeli Firmiani Lactanti. *Divinae institutiones et epitome divinarum institutionum.* Ed. S. Brandt. *Opera omnia,* I, 2: 274–761. *Corpus Scripturum Ecclesiasticorum Latinorum* 19. Vienna, 1890; repr., New York, 1965. Tr. Mary Francis McDonald, *Lactantius, The Divine Institutes, Books I–VII.* Washington, D.C., 1964.

Lact., *DMP* L. Caelius Firmianus Lactantius. *De mortibus persecutorum.* Ed. and tr. J. L. Creed. Oxford Early Christian Texts. Oxford, 1984.

Leontius, *vit. Joh.* Leontius Neopolitanus. *Vita Iohannis Eleemosynarii.* Ed. A. J. Festugière & L. Rydén, *Léontios de Néapolis. Vie de Syméon le Fou et Vie de Jean de Chypre.* Biblioth. archéolog. et histor. 95: 343–437. Paris, 1974. Tr. E. Dawes & N. H. Baynes, "Life of St. John the

Almsgiver." In *Three Byzantine Saints*, 199–262. Oxford, 1948.

Lib., *Or.* Libanius. *Orations*. Ed. and tr. A. F. Norman, *Libanius Selected Works*. 2 vols. Loeb Classical Library, 451–52. Cambridge, Mass., 1969–1977.

Lib. Pont. *Liber Pontificalis*. Ed. L. Duchesne. 3 vols. Paris, 1892–1956.
Tr. R. Davis, *The Book of Pontiffs*. Translated Texts for Historians, 5. Liverpool, 1989.

Livy Titus Livius. *Ab urbe condita*. Text and tr. B. O. Foster et al. 14 vols. Loeb Classical Library. Cambridge, Mass., 1919–59.

Lucian, *obit. Per.* Lucian. *De obitu Peregrini*. Text and tr. A. M. Harmon, *Lucian*. 8 vols. Loeb Classical Library, 5: 2–51. Cambridge, Mass., 1913; repr., 1947–67.

Lyd., *De mag.* Ioannes Lydus. *On Powers, or The Magistracies of the Roman State*. Ed. and tr. A. C. Bandy, American Philosophical Society, Memoirs 149. Philadelphia, 1983.

Mar. Aur., *Med.* *The Communings with Himself of Marcus Aurelius Antoninus, Emperor of Rome, together with his speeches and sayings*. Text and tr. C. R. Haines. Loeb Classical Library. Rev. ed. Cambridge, Mass., 1930.

Men. Rhet., *Peri epideik.* Menander Rhetor. *Peri epideiktikon*. Ed. and tr. D. A. Russell & N. G. Wilson, *Menander Rhetor*, 76–95. Oxford, 1981.

Min. Fel., *Oct.* Minucius Felix. *Octavius*. Ed. B. Kytzler. Leipzig, 1982. Tr. R. E. Wallis, *The Octavius*. In *The Ante-Nicene Fathers*, ed. A. Roberts, J. Donaldson, & A. C. Coxe, 4: 173–98. New York, 1885.

Mos. et Rom. coll. *Mosaicarum et Romanarum legum collatio*. Ed. and tr. M. Hyamson. London, 1913.

Opitz, *Urk.* H. G. Opitz. *Urkunden zur Geschichte des Arianischen Streites, 318–328. Athanasius Werke*, III: 1. Berlin, 1934.

Optatus S. Optati Milevitani. *Libri VII*. Ed. J.-L. Maier, *Le dossier du Donatisme*, 2 vols. TU 134, 135. Berlin, 1987–89.

	Tr. M. Edwards, *Optatus: Against the Donatists.* Translated Texts for Historians, 27. Liverpool, 1997.
Origen, *c. Cels.*	Origen. *Contra Celsum.* Ed. M. Borret. Sources chrétiennes no. 132. Paris, 1967–69. Tr. H. Chadwick, *Origen, Contra Celsum.* Oxford, 1953.
Pan. Lat.	*XII Panegyrici Latini.* Ed. R. A. B. Mynors. Oxford, 1964. Tr. C. E. V. Nixon & B. Rodgers, *In Praise of Later Roman Emperors.* Berkeley, 1994.
Paulinus, *vit. Amb.*	Paulinus Milanensis. *De vita Ambrosii.* Ed. A. A. R. Bastiaensen, *Vite dei Santi dal secolo III al secolo VI,* iii: 51–124. Milan, 1975. Tr. John A. Lacy, In *Early Christian Biographies,* ed. Roy J. Deferrari. Fathers of the Church, 15: 33–66. Washington, D.C., 1952; repr., 1964.
PG	J.-P. Migne, ed. *Patrologia cursus completus. Series graeca.* 161 vols. in 166. Paris, 1857–66.
Phil., *Vit. Soph.*	Philostratus. *Lives of the Sophists.* Text and tr. W. C. Wright, *Philostratus and Eunapius.* Loeb Classical Library, 2–315. Cambridge, Mass., 1921.
PL	J.-P. Migne, ed. *Patrologiae cursus completus. Series latina.* 222 vols. Paris, 1844–1902.
Plin. Iun., *Ep.*	Pliny the Younger. *Letters and Panegyricus.* 2 vols. Text and tr. B. Radice. Loeb Classical Library. Cambridge, Mass., 1969–75.
Plin. Iun., *Pan.*	Pliny the Younger. *Panegyricus . . . Traiano.* In *Letters and Panegyricus.* 2 vols. Text and tr. B. Radice. Loeb Classical Library, 2: 317–547. Cambridge, Mass., 1969–75.
Plin., *NH*	Pliny the Elder. *Natural History.* Text and tr. H. Rackham, W. H .S. Jones, & D. E. Eichholz. 10 vols. Loeb Classical Library. Cambridge, Mass., 1938–63.
Plut., *Ad princ. inerud.*	Plutarch. "To an Uneducated Ruler." Text and tr. H. N. Fowler, Plutarch's *Moralia.* 15 vols. Loeb Classical Library, 10: 52–71. Cambridge, Mass., 1936.

Porph., *De abst.* Porphyry. *De abstinentia.* Ed. M. Patillon & J. Bouffartigue, *De l'abstinence.* 3 vols. Paris, 1977–95.

Possid., *v. Aug.* Possidius. *vita Sancti Aurelii Augustini.* PL 32: 33–378. Tr. Sister Mary Magdeleine Muller & Roy J. Deferrari, "Life of St. Augustine." In *Early Christian Biographies,* ed. Roy J. Deferrari. Fathers of the Church, 15: 73–124. Washington, D.C., 1952; repr., 1964.

Soc., *HE* Socrates Scholasticus. *Historia Ecclesiastica.* Ed. R. Hussey. Oxford, 1853.
Tr. A. C. Zenos, *The Ecclesiastical History of Socrates Scholasticus.* In *A Select Library of Nicene and Post-Nicene Fathers of the Christian Church,* ed. P. Schaff & H. Wace, ser. 2, 2: 1–178. New York, 1890; repr., Grand Rapids, Mich., 1957.

Soz., *HE* Salaminius Hermias Sozomen. *Historia Ecclesiastica.* 2d ed. J. Bidez & G. C. Hansen, Die griechischen christlichen Schriftsteller der ersten Jahrhunderte, 50. Berlin, 1960.
Tr. C. Hartranft, *The Ecclesiastical History of Sozomen.* In *A Select Library of Nicene and Post-Nicene Fathers of the Christian Church,* ed. P. Schaff and H. Wace, ser. 2, 2: 179–427. New York, 1890.

Suet., *Aug.* Suetonius. *Divus Augustus.* In idem, *De vita Caesarum.* Text and tr. J. C. Rolfe, *The Lives of the Caesars.* 2 vols. Loeb Classical Library, 1: 122–287. Cambridge, Mass., 1913.

Suet., *Vesp.* Suetonius. *Divus Vespasianus.* In idem, *De vita Caesarum.* Text and tr. J. C. Rolfe, *The Lives of the Caesars.* 2 vols. Loeb Classical Library, 2: 280–321. Cambridge, Mass., 1913.

Sulp. Sev., *Chron.* Sulpicius Severus. *Chronicorum.* Ed. C. Halm, Corpus Scriptorum Ecclesiasticorum Latinorum, 1: 3–105. Vienna, 1866.
Tr. A. Roberts, *The Sacred History of Sulpitius Severus.* In *A Select Library of Nicene and Post-Nicene Fathers of the Christian Church,* ed. P. Schaff & H. Wace, ser. 2, 11: 71–122. New York, 1894.

Symm., *Rel.* Symmachus. *Relationes.* Ed. G. Meyer. Leipzig, 1872.

Tr. R. H. Barrow, *Prefect and Emperor: The* Relationes *of Symmachus, A. D. 384.* Oxford, 1973.

Tac., *Ann.* Tacitus. *Annals.* Ed. and tr. J. Jackson. 3 vols. Loeb Classical Library. Cambridge, Mass., 1931–37.

Tac., *Ger.* Tacitus. *Germania.* Text and tr. M. Hutton, rev. by E. H. Warmington. Loeb Classical Library. Cambridge, Mass., 1980.

Tac., *Hist.* Tacitus. *Historiarum libri qui supersunt.* Ed. C. & W. Heraeus; besorgt von Wilhelm Heraeus. Leipzig, 1899–1904.

Tert., *Apol.* Tertullian. *Apologeticum.* Ed. E. Dekkers. Corpus Christianorum Series Latina, I: 77–171. Turnhout, Belgium, 1954.
Tr. S. Thelwall, *The Apology.* In *The Ante-Nicene Fathers,* ed. A. Roberts & J. Donaldson, 3: 17–55. New York, 1890.

Them., *Or.* *Themistii orationes quae supersunt.* Ed. H. Schenkl, G. Downey. 3 vols. Leipzig, 1965–74.

Theod., *HE* Theodoret of Cyrrhus. *Historia Ecclesiastica,* 2d ed. by F. Scheidweiler & L. Parmentier. Die griechischen christlichen Schriftsteller der ersten Jahrhunderte, 44 (19). Berlin, 1954.
Tr. B. Jackson, *The Ecclesiastical History of Theodoret.* In *A Select Library of Nicene and Post-Nicene Fathers of the Christian Church,* ed. P. Schaff & H. Wace, ser. 2, 3: 1–159. New York, 1892.

Theod., *Hist. monach.* Theodoret. *Philotheos Historia.* Ed. P. Canivet & A. Leroy-Molinghen. 2 vols. Paris, 1977–79.
Tr. R. M. Price, *A History of the Monks of Syria.* Kalamazoo, Mich., 1985.

Thucy. Thucydides. *Historiae.* Ed. H. S. Jones & J. E. Powell. 2d ed., rev. 2 vols. Oxford, 1942–63.
Tr. R. Warner, *The Peloponnesian War.* Baltimore, 1954.

Virg., *Bucol.* Virgil. *Bucolics and Georgics.* Ed. T. E. Page. London, 1898; repr., 1965.
Tr. B. H. Fowler, *Vergil's Eclogues.* Chapel Hill, 1997.

vit. Dan. *vita S. Danielis Stylitae. Analecta Bollandiana* 32 (1913): 121–229.

	Tr. E. Dawes & N. H. Baynes, *Three Byzantine Saints*, 1– 84. Oxford 1948.
vit. Por.	Marcus Diaconus. *Vie de Porphyre, éveque de Gaza.* Ed. H. Grégoire & M.-A. Kugener. Paris, 1930. Tr. G. F. Hill, *The Life of Porphyry, Bishop of Gaza.* Oxford, 1913.
Xen., *Cyr.*	Xenophon. *Cyropaedia.* Ed. and tr. W. Miller. 2 vols. Loeb Classical Library. London, 1914.

SECONDARY WORKS

AJP	*American Journal of Philology*
ANRW	*Aufstieg und Niedergang der römischen Welt: Geschichte und Kultur Roms im Spiegel der neueren Forschung.* Ed. H. Temporini & W. Haase. Berlin, 1972–.
CAH	*The Cambridge Ancient History*
CJ	*Classical Journal*
CP	*Classical Philology*
DOP	*Dumbarton Oaks Papers*
GRBS	*Greek, Roman and Byzantine Studies*
HTR	*Harvard Theological Review*
JECS	*Journal of Early Christian Studies*
JEH	*Journal of Ecclesiastical History*
JHS	*Journal of Hellenic Studies*
JRS	*Journal of Roman Studies*
JTS	*Journal of Theological Studies*
PLRE	*Prosopography of the Later Roman Empire.* Ed A. H. M. Jones, J. R. Martindale, & J. Morris. 3 vols. in 4. Cambridge, 1971–92.
RE	*Paulys realencyclopadie der classischen altertumswissenschaft.* Neue bearbeitung unter mitwirkung zahlreicher fachgenossen. 24 vols. 1957–90.
RHE	*Revue d'Histoire Écclesiastique*
YCS	*Yale Classical Studies*

Adler (1990)   W. Adler. "The Origins of the Proto-Heresies: Fragments from a Chronicle in the First Book of Epiphanius' *Panarion.*" *JTS* 41: 472–501.

Adler (1992)   W. Adler. "Eusebius' Chronicle and Its Legacy." In Attridge & Hata (1992): 467–91.

Aland (1968)   K. Aland. "The Relation between Church and State in Early Times: A Reinterpretation." *JTS*, n.s., 19: 115–27.

Alexander (1971–73)   S. Spain Alexander. "Studies in Constantinian Church Architecture." *Riv di Archeologia Cristiana* 47: 281–330; cont'd. 49: 33–44.

Alföldi (1932)   A. Alföldi. "The Helmet of Constantine with the Christian Monogram." *JRS* 22: 9–32.

Alföldi (1948)   A. Alföldi. *The Conversion of Constantine and Pagan Rome.* Tr. H. Mattingly. Oxford.

Alföldi (1964)   M. Alföldi. "Die Sol Comes-Münze vom Jahre 325, Neues zur Bekehrung Constantins." *Mullus, Festschr. Th. Klauser.* JAC, ergbd 1: 10–16.

Alinsky (1972)   S. Alinsky. *Rules for Radicals: A Practical Primer for Realistic Radicals.* New York.

Allison (1971)   G. Allison. *Essence of Decision: Explaining the Cuban Missile Crisis.* Boston.

Anastos (1967)   M. Anastos. "The Edict of Milan (313): A Defense of Its Traditional Authorship and Designation." *Rev des Études Byzantins (Mél. V Grumel, II)* 35: 13–41.

Anastos (1979)   M. Anastos. "Complementary Note to 'The Edict of Milan.'" In idem, *Studies in Byzantine Intellectual History,* 1–7. London.

Ando (1996)   C. Ando. "Pagan Apologetics and Christian Intolerance in the Ages of Themistius and Augustine." *JECS* 4: 171–207.

Ando (forthcoming)   C. Ando. *Communis patria.* Berkeley.

Armstrong (1974)   G. Armstrong. "Constantine's Churches: Symbol and Structure." *Journal of the Society of Architectural Historians* 33: 5–16.

Arnold (1865) M. Arnold. "Marcus Aurelius." In *Essays in Criticism,* 1st ser., 344–79. London.

Arnold (1991) D. W. H. Arnold. *The Early Episcopal Career of Athanasius of Alexandria.* Christianity and Judaism in Late Antiquity, vol. 6. Notre Dame, Ind.

Athanassiadi (1992) P. Athanassiadi. *Julian: An Intellectual Biography.* London.

Athanassiadi & Frede (1999) P. Athanassiadi & M. Frede, eds. *Pagan Monotheism in Late Antiquity.* Oxford.

Attridge & Hata (1992) H. Attridge & G. Hata, eds. *Eusebius, Christianity, and Judaism.* Detroit.

Austin (1980) N. J. E. Austin. "Constantine and Crispus, A.D. 326." *Acta Classica* 23: 133–38.

Ayres & Jones (1998) L. Ayres and G. Jones, eds. *Christian Origins: Theology, Rhetoric, and Community.* London.

Bagnall (1993) R. Bagnall *Egypt in Late Antiquity.* Princeton.

Bahat (1990) D. Bahat. *The Illustrated Atlas of Jerusalem.* Tr. H. Rubenstein. New York.

Baker (1992) R. Baker. "Time for a Change." *New York Times,* Saturday, May 30, 19.

Barker (1956) E. Barker. *From Alexander to Constantine: Passages and Documents Illustrating the History of Social and Political Ideas, 336 B.C.–A.D. 337.* Oxford.

Barnes (1973) T. D. Barnes. "Lactantius and Constantine." *JRS* 63: 29–46.

Barnes (1976a) T. D. Barnes. "The Emperor Constantine's Good Friday Sermon." *JTS,* n.s., 27: 414–23.

Barnes (1976b) T. D. Barnes. "Sossianus Hierocles and the Antecedents of the 'Great Persecution.'" *Harvard Studies in Classical Philology* 80: 239–52.

Barnes (1978) T. D. Barnes. *The Sources of the Historia Augusta.* Col. Latomus 155. Brussels.

Barnes (1981) T. D. Barnes. *Constantine and Eusebius.* Cambridge, Mass.

Barnes (1982)   T. D. Barnes. *The New Empire of Diocletian and Constantine.* Cambridge, Mass.

Barnes (1984)   T. D. Barnes. "Constantine's Prohibition of Pagan Sacrifice." *AJP* 105: 69–72.

Barnes (1986a)   T. D. Barnes. "Angel of Light or Mystic Initiate? The Problem of the Life of Antony." *JTS,* n.s., 37: 353–68.

Barnes (1986b)   T. D. Barnes. "The Constantinian Reformation." *The Crake Lectures, 1984* (Sackville, New Brunswick), 39–57.

Barnes (1989)   T. D. Barnes. "Panegyric, History, and Hagiography in Eusebius' Life of Constantine." In Williams (1989a), 94–123.

Barnes (1990)   S. J. Barnes. "The Young Van Dyck and Rubens." In Wheelock (1990), 17–25.

Barnes (1991)   T. D. Barnes. "Pagan Perceptions of Christianity." In *Early Christianity. Origins and Evolution to A.D. 600: In Honor of W. H. C. Frend,* ed. I. Hazlett, 231–43. London.

Barnes (1993)   T. D. Barnes. *Athanasius and Constantius: Theology and Politics in the Constantinian Empire.* Cambridge, Mass.

Barnes & Williams (1993)   M. R. Barnes & D. H. Williams, eds. *Arianism after Arius: Essays on the Development of the Fourth Century Trinitarian Conflicts.* Edinburgh.

Battifol (1914)   P. Battifol. *La paix constantinienne et le catholicisme.* 2d ed. Paris.

Bauer (1957)   W. Bauer. *A Greek-English Lexicon of the New Testament and Other Early Christian Literature.* 4th ed., tr. Wm. Arndt & F. Gingrich. Chicago.

Bauer (1971)   W. Bauer. *Orthodoxy and Heresy in Earliest Christianity.* Translated by a team from the Philadelphia Seminar on Christian Origins, and edited by R. A. Kraft & G. Krodel. Philadelphia.

Bayat (1998)   A. Bayat. "Revolution without Movement, Movement without Revolution: Comparing Islamic Activism in Iran and Egypt." *Comparative Studies in Society and History* 40, 1: 136–69.

Baynes (1926) N. H. Baynes. "Alexandria and Constantinople: A Study in Ecclesiastical Diplomacy." *Journal of Egyptian Archaeology* 12: 145–56.

Baynes (1934) N. H. Baynes. "Eusebius and the Christian Empire." *Annuaire de l'Institut de Philologie et d'Histoire Orientale (Mélanges Bidez)* 2: 13–18; repr. in idem, *Byzantine Studies and Other Essays,* 168–72. London, 1955. Citations are to pages of the reprint.

Baynes (1972) N. H. Baynes. *Constantine the Great and the Christian Church.* 2d ed. with introduction by H. Chadwick, London; orig. pub. as the Raleigh Lecture of 1929 in *Proceedings of the British Academy* 15 (1929): 341–442; issued separately in 1931.

Beard & North (1990) M. Beard & J. North, eds. *Pagan Priests: Religion and Power in the Ancient World.* Ithaca, N.Y.

Becker (1910) E. Becker. "Konstantin der Grosse, der 'neue Moses': Die Schlacht am Pons Milvius und die Katastrophe am Schilfmeer." *Zeitschrift für Kirchengeschichte* 31: 161–71.

Beggs (1998) M. R. Beggs. "From Kingdom to Nation: The Transformation of a Metaphor in Eusebius' Historia Ecclesiastica." Ph.D. diss., Univ. Notre Dame.

Behr (1968) C. A. Behr. *Aelius Aristides and the Sacred Tales.* Amsterdam.

Bell (1924) H. I. Bell. *Jews and Christians in Egypt.* Oxford.

Béranger (1953) J. Béranger. *Recherches sur l'aspect idéologique du principat.* Schweizerische Beiträge zur Altertumswissenschaft 6. Basel.

Béranger (1970) J. Béranger. "L'expression de la divinité dans les Panegyriques latins." *Museum Helveticum* 27: 242–54.

Bianchi Bandinelli (1971) R. Bianchi Bandinelli. *Rome, the Late Empire: Roman Art A. D. 200–400.* Tr. Peter Green. New York.

Bidez (1930) J. Bidez. *La vie de Julien.* Paris.

Binns (1974) J. W. Binns, ed. *Latin Literature of the Fourth Century.* London.

Birley (1989)   A. R. Birley. *Septimius Severus, the African Emperor.* Rev. ed. New Haven.

Black (1954)   M. Black. "The Festival of Encaenia Ecclesiae in the Ancient Church with Special Reference to Palestine and Syria." *JEH* 5: 78–85.

Black (1970)   M. Black. "The Chi-Rho Sign—Christogram and/or Staurogram?" In *Apostolic History and the Gospel: Biblical and Historical Essays Presented to F. F. Bruce,* ed. W. Gasque & R. Martin, 319–27. Grand Rapids, Mich.

Bleckmann (1992)   B. Bleckmann. "Pagane Visionen Konstantins in der Chronik des Johannes Zonaras." In Bonamente & Fusco (1992–93), 1: 151–70.

Bloch (1945)   H. Bloch. "A New Document of the Last Pagan Revival in the West." *HTR* 38: 199–244.

Blumenthal & Markus (1981)   H. Blumenthal & R. A. Markus, eds. *Neoplatonism and Early Christian Thought.* London.

Bobertz (1988)   C. Bobertz. "Cyprian of Carthage as Patron: A Social Historical Study of the Role of Bishop in the Ancient Christian Community of North Africa." Ph.D. diss., Yale Univ.

Bobertz (1992)   C. Bobertz. "The Development of Episcopal Order." In Attridge & Hata (1992), 183–211.

Boer (1968)   W. den Boer. "Graeco-Roman Historiography in Its Relation to Biblical and Modern Thinking." *History and Theory* 9, 1: 60–75.

Bonamente & Fusco (1992–93)   G. Bonamente & F. Fusco, eds. *Costantino Il Grande: Dall'Antichità all' Umanesimo.* Colloquio sul Cristianesimo nel mondo antico, Macerata, 18–20 Dicembre 1990. 2 vols. Macerata.

Bonamente & Nestori (1988)   G. Bonamente & A. Nestori, eds. *I Cristiani e l'Impero nel IV secolo. . . .* Macopàta.

Bowersock (1982a)   G. Bowersock. "The Emperor Julian on His Predecessors." *YCS* 27: 159–72.

Bowersock (1982b)   G. Bowersock. "The Imperial Cult: Perceptions and Persistence." In Meyers & Sanders (1982), 171–82.

Bowersock (1986)   G. Bowersock. "From Emperor to Bishop: The Self-

Conscious Transformation of Political Power in the Fourth Century A.D." *CP* 81: 298–307.

Bowersock (1990) G. Bowersock. *Hellenism in Late Antiquity.* Ann Arbor, Mich.

Bowler (1984) P. Bowler. *Evolution: The History of an Idea.* Berkeley.

Bradbury (1994) S. Bradbury. "Constantine and the Problem of Anti-Pagan Legislation in the Fourth Century." *CP* 89: 120–39.

Bradbury (1995) S. Bradbury. "Julian's Pagan Revival and the Decline of Blood Sacrifice." *Phoenix* 49: 331–56.

Brakke (1995) D. Brakke. *Athanasius and the Politics of Asceticism.* Oxford.

Braner (1968) J. C. Braner, ed. *The Impact of the Church upon Its Culture: Reappraisals of the History of Christianity.* Essays in Divinity, II. Chicago.

Braudel (1973) F. Braudel. *The Mediterranean and the Medieval World in the Age of Philip II.* Eng. tr. S. Reynolds. 2 vols. New York.

Braun & Richer (1978) R. Braun & J. Richer, eds. *l'Empereur Julien : De l'histoire à la légende (331–1715).* Paris.

Braun & Richer (1981) R. Braun & J. Richer, eds. *L'Empereur Julien: De la légende au myth (De Voltaire à nos jours).* Paris.

Breebaart (1979) A. B. Breebaart. "Eunapius of Sardis and the Writing of History." *Mnemosyne* 32: 360–75.

Brinton (1965) C. Brinton. *The Anatomy of Revolution.* Rev. ed. New York.

Brock (1979) S. Brock. "Aspects of Translation Technique in Antiquity." *GRBS* 20: 69–87.

Brock (1994) P. Brock. "Why Did St. Maximilian Refuse to Serve in the Roman Army?" *JEH* 45: 195–209.

Bromley & Hammond (1987) D. Bromley & P. Hammond, eds. *The Future of New Religious Movements.* Macon, Ga.

Brooks (1921) N. C. Brooks. *The Sepulchre of Christ in Art and Liturgy, with Special Reference to the Liturgic Drama.* Univ. Illinois Studies in Language and Literature, 7:2. Urbana.

Brown (1961)   P. R. L. Brown. "Aspects of the Christianization of the Roman Aristocracy." *JRS* 51: 1–11.

Brown (1963)   P. R. L. Brown. "Religious Coercion in the Later Roman Empire: The Case of North Africa." *History* 48: 283–305.

Brown (1964)   P. R. L. Brown. "St. Augustine's Attitude to Religious Coercion." *JRS* 54: 107–16.

Brown (1988)   P. R. L. Brown. *The Body and Society: Men, Women, and Sexual Renunciation in Early Christianity.* New York.

Brown (1992)   P. R. L. Brown. *Power and Persuasion in Late Antiquity: Towards a Christian Empire.* Madison, Wis.

Brown (1995)   P. R. L. Brown. *Authority and the Sacred: Aspects of the Christianisation of the Roman World.* Cambridge.

Brown (1998)   P. R. L. Brown. "Christianization and Religious Conflict." *CAH* 13: 632–64.

Brunt (1971)   P. A. Brunt. *Social Conflicts in the Roman Republic.* New York.

Bruun (1958)   P. Bruun. "The Disappearance of Sol from the Coins of Constantine." *Arctos,* n.s., 2: 15–37.

Bruun (1962)   P. Bruun. "The Christian Signs on the Coins of Constantine." *Arctos,* n.s., 3: 5–35

Bruun (1966)   P. Bruun, ed. *Roman Imperial Coinage,* vol. 7. London.

Bruun (1976)   P. Bruun. "Portrait of a Conspirator: Constantine's Break with the Tetrarchy." *Arctos,* n.s., 10: 5–25.

Bruun (1992)   P. Bruun. "Una permanenza del Sol invictus di Costantino nell' arte cristiana." In Bonamente & Fusco (1992–93), 1: 219–30.

Burckhardt (1949)   J. Burckhardt. *Die Zeit Konstantins des Grossen.* Leipzig, 1880, 2d ed. Tr. M. Hadas, *The Age of Constantine the Great.* New York. Citations are to pages of the English translation.

Burgess (1996)   G. Burgess. "Thomas Hobbes: Religious Toleration or Religious Indifference?" In Laursen & Nederman (1996), 139–61.

Burgess (1997)   R. W. Burgess. "The Dates and Editions of Eusebius'

Chronici canones and *Historia Ecclesiastica.*" *JTS,* n.s., 48: 471–504.

Burkert (1972)   W. Burkert et al. *Pseudepigrapha I.* Fond. Hardt, Entretiens sur l'Antiquité classique 18. Geneva.

Cameron (1968)   A. Cameron. "Gratian's Repudiation of the Pontifical Robe." *JRS* 58: 96–102.

Cameron (1970)   A. Cameron. *Claudian: Poetry and Propaganda at the Court of Honorius.* Oxford.

Cameron (1973)   A. Cameron. *Porphyrius the Charioteer.* Oxford.

Cameron (1976)   A. Cameron. *Circus Factions: Blues and Greens at Rome and Byzantium.* Oxford.

Cameron (1977)   A. Cameron. "Paganism and Literature in Late Fourth Century Rome." In *Christianisme et formes littéraires de l'antiquité tardive en Occident,* ed. M. Fuhrmann, 23: 31–40. Fondation Hardt, Entretiens sur l'antiquité classique. Geneva.

Cameron (1983)   Averil Cameron. "Eusebius of Caesarea and the Rethinking of History." In *Tria Corda: Scritti in onore di Arnaldo Momigliano,* ed. E. Gabba, Bib di Athenaeum, 1: 71–88. Como.

Cameron (1991)   Averil Cameron. *Christianity and the Rhetoric of Empire: The Development of Christian Discourse.* Berkeley.

Cameron & Long (1992)   A. Cameron & J. Long. *Barbarians and Politics at the Court of Arcadius.* Berkeley.

Cannadine & Price (1987)   D. Cannadine & S. Price, eds. *Rituals of Royalty: Power and Ceremonial in Traditional Societies.* Cambridge.

Capeti (n.d.)   S. Capeti. *Mosaici di Ravenna.* 2d ed. Milan.

Caprino (1955)   C. Caprino et al. *La colonna di Marco Aurelio.* Studi e materiali del Museo dell' Impero romano. Rome.

Carlyle (1841)   T. Carlyle. *On Heroes, Hero-Worship, and the Heroic in History.* London.

Caron (1975)   P. G. Caron. "Constantin le Grand ἐπίσκοπος τῶν ἐκτός de l'église romaine." *Rev International des droits de l'antiquité* 22: 179–88.

Casson (1962)   L. Casson, tr. *Selected Satires of Lucian.* Chicago.

Cerfaux & Tondrian (1957)   L. Cerfaux & J. Tondrian. *Un concurrent du christianisme, le culte des souverains dans la civilisation gréco-romaine.* Tournai.

Chadwick (1980)   H. Chadwick. *The Role of the Christian Bishop in Ancient Society.* Center for Hermeneutical Studies, Berkeley, Protocol of the Thirty-fifth Colloquy: February 25, 1979, ed. E. C. Hobbs & W. Wuellner. Berkeley.

Chadwick (1998)   H. Chadwick. "Orthodoxy and Heresy from the Death of Constantine to the Eve of the First Council of Ephesus." *CAH* 13: 561–600.

Champlin (1980)   E. Champlin. *Fronto and Antonine Rome.* Harvard.

Charlesworth (1937)   M. Charlesworth. "The Virtues of a Roman Emperor: Propaganda and the Creation of Belief." *Proceedings Brit. Acad.* 23: 105–33.

Chastagnol (1970)   A. Chastagnol. "L'évolution de l'ordre sénatorial aux IIIe et IVe siècles." *Revue Historique* 244: 305–14.

Chastagnol (1982)   A. Chastagnol. *l'Evolution politique, sociale et économique du monde romain de Diocletian à Julien.* Paris.

Chesnut (1975)   G. Chesnut. "The Pattern of the Past: Augustine's Debate with Eusebius and Sallust." In *Our Common History as Christians: Essays in Honor of Albert C. Outler,* ed. J. Deschner et al., 69–95. New York.

Chesnut (1978)   G. Chesnut. "The Ruler and the Logos in Neopythagorean, Middle Platonic, and Late Stoic Political Philosophy." *ANRW* 2, 16, 2: 1310–32.

Chesnut (1986)   G. Chesnut. *The First Christian Histories: Eusebius, Socrates, Sozomen, Theodoret, and Evagrius,* 2d ed. Macon, Ga.

Chesnut (1992)   G. Chesnut. "Eusebius, Augustine, Orosius, and the Later Patristic and Medieval Christian Historians." In Attridge & Hata (1992): 687–713.

Chuvin (1990)   P. Chuvin. *A Chronicle of the Last Pagans.* Tr. B. A. Archer. Cambridge, Mass.

Clark (1993)   E. Clark. "Elite Networks and Heresy Accusations: Towards a Social Description of the Origenist Controversy." In White (1993a), 79–117.

Coleman (1914)   C. Bush Coleman. *Constantine the Great and Christianity,* Columbia Studies 60, 1. New York.

Coleman-Norton (1966)   P. R. Coleman-Norton. *Roman State and Christian Church: A Collection of Legal Documents to A.D. 535.* 3 vols. London.

Corcoran (1993)   S. Corcoran. "Hidden from History: The Legislation of Licinius." In Harries & Wood (1993), 97–119.

Corcoran (1996)   S. Corcoran. *The Empire of the Tetrarchs: Imperial Pronouncements and Government, A.D. 284–324.* New York.

Cranz (1952)   F. E. Cranz. "Kingdom and Polity in Eusebius of Caesarea." *HTR* 45: 47–66.

Croke & Emmett (1983)   B. Croke & A. Emmett. "Historiography in Late Antiquity: An Overview." In *History and Historians in Late Antiquity,* ed. idem, 1–12. Sydney.

Dagron (1967)   G. Dagron. *L'Empire romain d'Orient et les traditions politiques de l'Hellenisme: le témoignage de Themistios.* Centre de Recherche d'histoire et civilization byzantines, Travaux et Mémoires 3: 1–242.

Dagron (1974)   G. Dagron. *Naissance d'une capitale: Constantinople et ses institutions de 330 à 451.* Bib Byzantin, Études 7. Paris.

Daly (1971)   L. J. Daly. "Themistius' Plea for Religious Tolerance." *GRBS* 12: 65–79.

Darwin (1859)   C. Darwin. *On the Origin of Species by Means of Natural Selection, or, The Preservation of Favoured Races in the Struggle for Life.* London.

Darwin (1871)   C. Darwin. *The Descent of Man.* London.

Davidson & Lytle (1986)   J. Davidson & M. Lytle. *After the Fact: The Art of Historical Detection,* 2d ed. New York.

Davies (1989)   P. S. Davies. "The Origin and Purpose of the Persecution of 303." *JTS,* n.s., 42: 66–94.

Decker (1968)   D. de Decker. "La politique religieuse de Maxence." *Byzantion* 38: 472–562.

Decker (1978)   D. de Decker. "Le 'Discours à l'assemblée des saints' attribué à Constantin et l'oeuvre de Lactance." In Fontaine & Perrin (1978), 75–87.

Decker & Dupuis-Masay (1980) — D. de Decker & G. Dupuis-Masay. "L'‘épiscopat’ de l'empereur Constantin." *Byzantion* 50: 118–57.

Deichmann (1958) — W. Deichmann. *Frühchristliche Bauten und Mosaiken von Ravenna.* 2d ed. Wiesbaden.

Delatte (1942) — L. Delatte. *Les Traités de la Royauté d'Ecphante, Diotogène et Sthénidas.* Bibliothèque de la Faculté de Philosophie et Lettres de l'Université de Liège, Fasc. XCVII. Liège.

Delbrueck (1933) — R. Delbrueck. *Spätantike Kaiserporträts von Constantinus Magnus bis zum Ende des Westreichs.* Berlin.

Deutsch (1973) — M. Deutsch. *The Resolution of Conflict: Constructive and Destructive Processes.* New Haven.

Devos (1967) — P. Devos. "La date du voyage d'Égérie." *Analecta Bollandiana* 85: 165–94.

Digeser (1994) — E. Digeser. "Lactantius and Constantine's Letter to Arles: Dating the *Divine Institutes.*" *JECS* 2: 33–52.

Digeser (1998) — E. Digeser. "Lactantius, Porphyry, and the Debate over Religious Toleration." *JRS* 88: 129–46.

Digeser (1999) — E. Digeser. *Lactantius and Rome: Church, State, and Tolerance in Late Antiquity.* Ithaca, N.Y.

DiMaio (1988) — M. DiMaio et al. "*Ambiguitas Constantiniana:* The *caeleste signum Dei* of Constantine the Great." *Byzantion* 58: 333–60.

Dodds (1965) — E. R. Dodds. *Pagan and Christian in an Age of Anxiety: Some Aspects of Religious Experience from Marcus Aurelius to Constantine.* Cambridge.

Dölger (1918) — F. J. Dölger. *Die Sonne der Gerechtigkeit und der Schwarze, eine religions-geschichtliche Studie zum Taufgelöbnis.* Liturgiegeschichtliche Forschungen, vol. 2. Münster.

Dölger (1920) — F. J. Dölger. *Sol Salutis, Gebet und Gesang im christlichen Altertum.* Liturgiegeschichtliche Forschungen, vols. 4–5. Münster.

Dörries (1954) — H. Dörries. *Das Selbstzeugnis Kaiser Konstantins.* Akad.

Wiss., Göttingen, Phil.-Hist. Kl., Abhandlungen, ser. 3, 34. Göttingen.

Dörries (1960)   H. Dörries. *Constantine and Religious Liberty.* Tr. R. Bainton. New Haven.

Dörries (1972)   H. Dörries. *Constantine the Great.* Tr. R. Bainton. New York.

Douglas (1982)   M. Douglas. "Cultural Bias." Royal Anthropological Institute, Occasional Paper 35 (1978); repr. in idem, *In the Active Voice,* 183–254. London. Citations are to pages of the reprint.

Dowling (1972)   R. E. Dowling. "Pressure Group Theory: Its Methodological Range." In *Questioning the Past: A Selection of Papers in History and Government,* ed. D. P. Crook, 383–99. St. Lucia, Queensland.

Downey (1958)   G. Downey. "Themistius' First Oration." *GRBS* 1: 49–69.

Downey (1965)   G. Downey. "The Perspective of the Early Church Historians." *GRBS* 6: 57–70.

Drake (1976)   H. A. Drake. *In Praise of Constantine: A Historical Study and New Translation of Eusebius' Tricennial Orations.* Berkeley.

Drake (1984)   H. A. Drake. "The Return of the Holy Sepulchre." *Catholic Historical Review* 70: 263–67.

Drake (1985a)   H. A. Drake. "Eusebius on the True Cross." *JEH* 36: 1–22.

Drake (1985b)   H. A. Drake. "Suggestions of Date in Constantine's 'Oration to the Saints.'" *AJP* 106: 335–49.

Drake (1987)   H. A. Drake. "Athanasius' First Exile." *Greek, Roman and Byzantine Studies* 27: 193–204.

Drake (1988)   H. A. Drake. "What Eusebius Knew: The Genesis of the Vita Constantini," *CP* 83: 20–38.

Drake (1989)   H. A. Drake. "Policy and Belief in Constantine's 'Oration to the Saints.'" *Studia Patristica* 19: 43–51.

Drake (1995)   H. A. Drake. "Constantine and Consensus." *Church History* 64: 1–15.

Drake (1996)   H. A. Drake. "Lambs Into Lions: Explaining Early Christian Intolerance." *Past and Present*, no. 153: 3–36.

Drake (1998)   H. A. Drake. "Fourth Century Christianity and 'the Paranoid Style.'" In Hillard (1998), 2: 357–68.

Drijvers (1992)   J. Drijvers. *Helena Augusta: The Mother of Constantine the Great and the Legend of Her Finding of the True Cross.* Leiden.

Duchesne (1910)   L. Duchesne. *Histoire ancienne de l'Église.* 4th ed. 3 vols. Paris.

Dugmore & Duggan   C. W. Dugmore & C. Duggan, eds. *Studies in Church
(1964)   History.* 2 vols. London.

Dupont (1967)   C. Dupont. "Les privilèges des clercs sous Constantin." *RHE* 62: 729–52.

Dvornik (1955)   F. Dvornik. "The Emperor Julian's 'Reactionary' Ideas on Kingship." In *Late Classical and Medieval Studies in Honor of A. M. Friend Jr.,* ed. K. Weitzmann, 71–81. Princeton.

Dvornik (1966)   F. Dvornik. *Early Christian and Byzantine Political Philosophy,* 2 vols. Washington, D.C.

Eger (1939)   H. Eger. "Kaiser und Kirche in d. Geschichtstheologie Eusebs von Caesarea." *Zeitschrift für die Neutestamentliche Wissenschaft* 38: 97–115.

Ehrhardt (1959–60)   A. Ehrhardt. "Constantine, Rome, and the Rabbis." *Bulletin of the John Rylands Library* 42: 288–312.

Elliott (1987)   T. G. Elliott. "Constantine's Conversion: Do We Really Need It?" *Phoenix* 41: 420–38.

Elliott (1997)   T. G. Elliott. *The Christianity of Constantine the Great.* Scranton, Pa.

Elm (1994)   S. Elm. *"Virgins of God": The Making of Asceticism in Late Antiquity.* Oxford.

Elsner (1998)   J. Elsner. "Art and Architecture." *CAH* 13: 736–61.

Emonds (1956)   H. Emonds. "Enkainia—Weihe und Weihegedächtnis." In *Enkainia, Gesammelte Arbeiten zum 800-jährigen Weihegedachtnis der Abteikirche Maria Laac,* 30–57. Dusseldorf.

Ensslin (1943)   W. Ensslin. *Gottkaiser und Kaiser von Gottes Gnaden.* Bayer. Akad. Wiss., Sitzungsber., Phil.-Hist. Abteilung, Heft 6. Munich.

Errington (1988)   R. M. Errington. "Constantine and the Pagans." *GRBS* 29: 309–18.

Farina (1966)   R. Farina. *L'Impero e l'Imperatore cristiano in Eusebio di Cesarea, la prima teologia politica del Cristianesimo.* Bibl Theol Salesesiana, ser. 1: Fontes, vol. 2. Zürich.

Feeney (1998)   D. Feeney. *Literature and Religion at Rome: Cultures, Contexts, and Beliefs.* Cambridge.

Ferguson (1970)   J. Ferguson. *The Religions of the Roman Empire.* London.

Finn (1982)   T. M. Finn. "Social Mobility, Imperial Civil Service, and the Spread of Early Christianity." *Studia Patristica* 17, 1: 31–7.

Fisher (1982)   E. Fisher. "Greek Translations of Latin Literature in the Fourth Century A.D." *YCS* 27: 173–215.

Fishwick (1987–91) D. Fishwick. *The Imperial Cult in the Latin West: Studies in the Ruler Cult of the Western Provinces of the Roman Empire,* 2 vols. Leiden.

Fontaine & Perrin (1978)   J. Fontaine & M. Perrin, eds. *Lactance et son temps: Recherches actuelles.* Théologie Historique, vol. 48. Paris.

Fornara (1983)   C. W. Fornara. *The Nature of History in Ancient Greece and Rome.* Berkeley.

Fortin (1981)   E. L. Fortin. "Christianity and Hellenism in Basil the Great's Address Ad Adulescentes." In Blumenthal & Markus (1981), 189–203.

Fowden (1978)   G. Fowden. "Bishops and Temples in the Eastern Roman Empire, A.D. 320–435." *JTS,* ser. 2, 29: 53–78.

Fowden (1982)   G. Fowden. "The Pagan Holy Man in Late Antique Society." *JHS* 102: 33–59.

Fowden (1986)   G. Fowden. *The Egyptian Hermes: A Historical Approach to the Late Pagan Mind.* Cambridge.

Fowden (1993)   G. Fowden. *Empire to Commonwealth: Consequences of Monotheism in Late Antiquity.* Princeton.

Fowden (1994a)   G. Fowden. "Constantine, Silvester, and the Church of
                    S. Polyeuctus in Constantinople." *Journal of Roman Ar-
                    chaeology* 7: 274–84.

Fowden (1994b)   G. Fowden. "The Last Days of Constantine: Opposi-
                    tional Versions and Their Influence." *JRS* 84: 146–70.

Frakes (1991)   R. M. Frakes. "Audience and Meaning in the Res Ges-
                    tae of Ammianus Marcellinus." Ph.D. diss., Univ. Cali-
                    fornia, Santa Barbara.

Frank (1933–40)   T. Frank, ed. *An Economic Survey of Ancient Rome.* 6
                    vols. Baltimore.

French (1998)   D. French. "Rhetoric and the Rebellion of A.D. 387 in
                    Antioch." *Historia* 47: 468–84.

Frend (1952)   W. H. C. Frend. *The Donatist Church: A Movement of
                    Protest in Roman North Africa.* Oxford.

Frend (1967)   W. H. C. Frend. *Martyrdom and Persecution in the Early
                    Church: A Study of a Conflict from the Maccabees to Dona-
                    tus.* New York.

Frend (1968)   W. H. C. Frend. "The Roman Empire in Eastern and
                    Western Historiography." *Proceedings of the Cambridge
                    Philological Society,* n.s., 14, 194: 19–32.

Frend (1972)   W. H. C. Frend. "The Monks and the Survival of the
                    East Roman Empire in the Fifth Century." *Past and
                    Present,* no. 54: 3–24.

Frend (1987)   W. H. C. Frend. "Prelude to the Great Persecution: The
                    Propaganda War." *JEH* 38: 1–18.

Frend (1990)   W. H. C. Frend. "Monks and the End of Greco-Roman
                    Paganism in Syria and Egypt." *Cristianesimo nella storia*
                    11: 469–84.

Frezza (1989)   P. Frezza. "L'Esperienza della Tolleranza religiosa fra
                    Pagani e Cristiani dal IV al V sec. D.C. nell' Oriente
                    ellenistico." *Studia et Documenta Historiae et Iuris* 55:
                    41–97.

Frolow (1944)   A. Frolow. "La dédicace de Constantinople dans la tra-
                    dition byzantine." *Revue de l'Histoire des Religions* 127:
                    61–127.

Gagé (1955)   J. Gagé. *Apollon Romain, Essai sur le Culte d'Apollon et le*

Développement du "ritus Graecus" à Rome des Origines à Auguste. Bibl des Écoles franç d'Ath et de Rome, fasc 182. Paris.

Galletier (1950)   E. Galletier. "La mort de Maximien d'après le Panégyrique de 310 et la vision de Constantin au temple d'Apollon." *Revue des Études Anciennes* 52: 288–99.

Gardthausen (1924)   V. Gardthausen. *Das Alte Monogramm.* Leipzig.

Garnsey (1970)   P. Garnsey. *Social Status and Legal Privilege in the Roman Empire.* Oxford.

Garnsey (1984)   P. Garnsey. "Religious Toleration in Classical Antiquity." In Shiels (1984), 1–27.

Gaudemet (1947)   J. Gaudemet. "La Législation religieuse de Constantin." *Revue d'Histoire et de l'Église de France* 33: 25–61.

Gaudemet (1958)   J. Gaudemet. *L'Église dans l'Empire romain (IVe–Ve s.).* Histoire du Droit et des Institutions de l'Église en Occident, 3. Paris.

Gaudemet (1990)   J. Gaudemet. "La législation anti-paienne de Constantin à Justinien." *Cristianesimo nella storia* 11: 449–68.

Gentili (1992)   S. Gentili. "Politics and Christianity in Aquileia in the Fourth Century A. D." *L'Antiquité Classique* 61: 192–208.

George (1997)   E. C. George. "Kierkegaard and Tolerance." In Razavi & D. Ambuel (1997), 70–80.

Gerland (1927)   E. Gerland. *Konstantin der Grosse in Geschichte und Sage.* Byzantinische-Neugriechischen Jahrbücher, Beiheft 23. Texte und Forschungen zur Byzantinisch-Neugriechischen Philologie. Athens.

Gibbon (1909–14)   E. Gibbon. *The Decline and Fall of the Roman Empire.* Ed. J. Bury. 7 vols. London.

Gilliard (1984)   F. Gilliard. "Senatorial Bishops in the Fourth Century." *HTR* 77: 153–75.

Gillman (1961)   I. Gillman. "Constantine the Great in the Light of the Christus Victor Concept." *Journal of Religious History* 1: 197–204.

Girardet (1975)   K. M. Girardet. *Kaisergericht und Bischofsgericht. Studien zu den Anfängen des Donatistenstreites (313–315) und*

	zum Prozess des Athanasius von Alexandrien (328–346). Antiquitas, ser. 1, vol. 21. Bonn.
Girardet (1989)	K. M. Girardet. "Die Petition der Donatisten an Kaiser Konstantin (Frühjahr 313)—historische Voraussetzungen und Folgen." *Chiron* 19: 185–206.
Girardet (1998)	K. M. Girardet. "Die Konstantinische Wende und ihre Bedeutung für das Reich. Althistorische Überlegungen zu den geistigen Grundlagen der Religionspolitik Konstantins d. Gr." In *Die Konstantinische Wende,* ed. E. Mühlenberg, 9–122; bibliography in idem, 236–50. Güterslohe.
Goehring (1992)	J. Goehring. "The Origins of Monasticism." In Attridge & Hata (1992): 235–55.
Goehring (1997)	J. Goehring. "Monastic Diversity and Ideological Boundaries in Fourth-Century Christian Egypt." *JECS* 5: 61–84.
Goodenough (1928)	E. R. Goodenough. "The Political Philosophy of Hellenistic Kingship." *YCS* 1: 55–102.
Goodenough (1953)	E. R. Goodenough. "Religious Aspirations." In *The Age of Diocletian: A Symposium,* 37–48. New York.
Gordon (1990)	R. Gordon. "Religion in the Roman Empire: The Civic Compromise and Its Limits." In Beard & North (1990), 235–55.
Grabar (1967)	A. Grabar. *The Golden Age of Justinian.* Tr. S. Gilbert & J. Emmons. New York.
Grabar (1968)	A. Grabar. *Early Christian Art (A.D. 200–395).* Tr. S. Gilbert & J. Emmons. New York.
Grant (1980)	R. M. Grant. *Eusebius as Church Historian.* Oxford.
Grant (1996)	M. Grant. *The Severans: The Changed Roman Empire.* New York.
Greenslade (1954)	S. L. Greenslade. *Church and State from Constantine to Theodosius.* London.
Gregg (1985)	R. C. Gregg. *Arianism: Historical and Theological Reassessments. Papers from the Ninth International Conference on Patristic Studies, Oxford, September 5–10, 1983.* Philadelphia.

Gregg & Groh (1981)	R. C. Gregg & D. E. Groh. *Early Arianism: A View of Salvation*. Philadelphia.
Grégoire (1930)	H. Grégoire. "La 'conversion' de Constantin." *Revue de l'Université de Bruxelles* 36: 231–72.
Grégoire (1938)	H. Grégoire. "Eusèbe n'est pas l'auteur de la 'Vita Constantini' dans sa forme actuelle, et Constantin ne s'est pas 'converti' en 312." *Byzantion* 13: 561–83.
Grégoire (1939)	II. Grégoire. "La vision de Constantin 'liquidée.'" *Byzantion* 14: 341–51.
Grell & Scribner (1996)	Ole Peter Grell & Bob Scribner, eds. *Tolerance and Intolerance in the European Reformation*. Cambridge.
Grünewald (1990)	Thomas Grünewald. *Constantinus Maximus Augustus: Herrschaftspropaganda in der zeitgenossischen Überlieferung*. Historia Einzelschriften, 64. Stuttgart.
Grünewald (1992–3)	Thomas Grünewald. "Constantinus novus: Zum Constantin-Bild des Mittelalters." In Bonamente & Fusco (1992–93), 1: 461–85.
Gryson (1979)	R. Gryson. "Les élections épiscopales en Orient au IVe siècle." *RHE* 74: 301–45.
Gryson (1980)	R. Gryson. "Les élections episcopales en Occident au IVe siècle." *RHE* 75: 257–83.
Gunton (1985)	C. Gunton. "Christus Victor Revisited: A Study in Metaphor and the Transformation of Meaning." *JTS*, n.s., 36: 129–45.
Gustafsson (1961)	B. Gustafsson. "Eusebius's Principles in Handling His Sources, as Found in His Church History, Bks. I–VII." *Studia Patristica* 4, 2(TU 79): 429–41.
Hägg (1992)	T. Hägg. "Hierocles the Lover of Truth and Eusebius the Sophist." *Symbolae Osloenses* 67: 138–50.
Hall (1993)	S. G. Hall. "Eusebian and Other Sources in Vita Constantini I." In *Logos. Festschrift für Luise Abramowski*, ed. H. Brennecke et al., 239–63. Berlin.
Hall (1998)	L. J. Hall. "Cicero's *instinctu divino* and Constantine's *instinctu divinitatis*: The Evidence of the Arch of Constantine for the Senatorial View of the 'Vision' of Constantine." *JECS* 6: 647–71.

Works Cited

Halsbergh (1972)	G. H. Halsbergh. *The Cult of Sol Invictus.* Leiden.
Hanson (1981)	J. Hanson. "Dreams and Visions in the Graeco-Roman World and Early Christianity." *ANRW* 2, 23, 2: 1395–1427.
Hanson (1988)	R. P. C. Hanson. *The Search for the Christian Doctrine of God: The Arian Controversy, 318–381.* Edinburgh.
Harl (1996)	K. Harl. *Coinage in the Roman Economy.* Baltimore.
Harnack (1904–5)	A. von Harnack. *Die Mission und Ausbreitung des Christentums in den ersten drei Jahrhunderten.* 2d ed. Tr. J. Moffatt, *The Expansion of Christianity in the First Three Centuries.* New York.
Harries & Wood (1993)	Jill Harries & Ian Wood, eds. *The Theodosian Code: Studies in the Imperial Law of Late Antiquity.* London.
Heather (1994)	P. Heather. "New Men for New Constantines: Creating an Imperial Elite in the Eastern Mediterranean." In Magdalino (1994), 11–33.
Hedrick (forthcoming)	C. Hedrick. *History and Silence: Purge and Rehabilitation in Late Antiquity.* Austin.
Hefele-Leclercq (1973)	Karl J. Hefele. *Histoire des conciles.* Tr. and rev. H. Leclercq. 11 vols. in 21. Paris.
Hefner (1993)	R. Hefner. "World Building and the Rationality of Conversion." In *Conversion to Christianity: Historical and Anthropological Perspectives on a Great Transformation,* ed. idem, 3–44. Berkeley.
Henry (1985)	P. Henry. "Why Is Contemporary Scholarship So Enamored of Ancient Heretics?" *Studia Patristica* 17, 1: 123–6.
Herrin (1987)	J. Herrin. *The Formation of Christendom.* Princeton.
Hillard (1998)	T. Hillard et al., eds. *Ancient History in a Modern University.* 2 vols. N.S.W., Australia.
Hofstadter (1965a)	R. Hofstadter. "The Paranoid Style in American Politics." In Hofstadter (1965b), 3–40.
Hofstadter (1965b)	R. Hofstadter. *The Paranoid Style in American Politics and Other Essays.* New York.

Hofstadter (1965c)   R. Hofstadter. "Goldwater and Pseudo-Conservative Politics." In Hofstadter (1965b), 93–141.

Hollerich (1989)   M. Hollerich. "Myth and History in Eusebius's De vita Constantini: Vit. Const. 1.12 in its Contemporary Setting." *HTR* 82: 421–45.

Hollerich (1992)   M. Hollerich. "Eusebius as a Polemical Interpreter of Scripture." In Attridge & Hata (1992), 585–615.

Hopkins (1980)   K. Hopkins. "Taxes and Trade in the Roman Empire (200 B.C.–A.D. 400)." *JRS* 70: 101–25.

Hopkins (1998)   K. Hopkins. "Christian Number and Its Implications." *JECS* 6: 184–226.

Hume (1875)   David Hume. "Of the First Principles of Government." In *Essays Moral, Political, and Literary by David Hume,* ed. T. H. Green & T. H. Grose, 2 vols., 1: 109–13. London.

Hunt (1982)   D. Hunt. *Holy Land Pilgrimage in the Later Roman Empire, A.D. 312–460.* Oxford.

Hunt (1993)   D. Hunt. "Christianising the Roman Empire: The Evidence of the Code." In Harries & Wood (1993), 143–58.

Hunt (1997)   D. Hunt. "Constantine and Jerusalem." *JEH* 48: 405–24.

Huyghe (1963)   R. Huyghe, ed. *Larousse Encyclopedia of Byzantine and Medieval Art.* Hamlyn, England.

Irshai (1996)   O. Irshai. "Cyril of Jerusalem: The Apparition of the Cross and the Jews." In *Contra Iudaeos: Ancient and Medieval Polemics between Christians and Jews: Texts and Studies in Medieval and Early Modern Judaism,* ed. O. Limor & G. Stroumsa, 10: 85–194. Tübingen.

Ison (1985)   D. Ison. "The Constantinian Oration to the Saints—Authorship and Background." Ph.D. diss., Univ. London.

Ison (1987)   D. Ison. "PAIS THEOU in the Age of Constantine." *JTS,* n.s., 38: 412–19.

James (1902)   William James. *The Varieties of Religious Experience: A Study in Human Nature.* New York.

Jones (1951)   A. H. M. Jones. "The Imperium of Augustus." *JRS* 41: 112–19.

Jones (1954)   A. H. M. Jones. "Notes on the Genuineness of the Constantinian Documents in Eusebius's Life of Constantine." *JEH* 5: 194–200.

Jones (1959)   A. H. M. Jones. "Were Ancient Heresies National or Social Movements in Disguise?" *JTS*, n.s., 10: 280–97. (Repr. as *Were Ancient Heresies Disguised Social Movements?* Philadelphia, 1966.)

Jones (1962)   A. H. M. Jones. *Constantine and the Conversion of Europe.* Rev. ed. New York.

Jones (1964)   A. H. M. Jones. *The Later Roman Empire: A Social, Economic, and Administrative Survey.* 2 vols. Norman, Okla.

Jones (1979)   C. P. Jones. *The Roman World of Dio Chrysostom.* Cambridge.

Kannengiesser   C. Kannengiesser. *Le Verbe de Dieu selon Athanase d'Al-*
(1990)   *exandrie.* Tournai.

Kartsonis (1986)   A. Kartsonis. *Anastasis: The Making of an Image.* Princeton.

Kaster (1988)   R. Kaster. *Guardians of Language: The Grammarian and Society in Late Antiquity.* Berkeley.

Kaufman (1990)   P. Kaufman. *Redeeming Politics.* Princeton.

Kazhdan (1987)   A. Kazhdan, "'Constantin imaginaire': Byzantine Legends of the Ninth Century about Constantine the Great." *Byzantion* 57: 196–250.

Kee (1982)   Alistair Kee. *Constantine versus Christ: The Triumph of Ideology.* London.

Kelly (1995)   J. N. D. Kelly. *Golden Mouth: The Story of John Chrysostom—Ascetic, Preacher, Bishop.* Ithaca, N.Y.

Kennedy (1983)   G. Kennedy. *Greek Rhetoric under Christian Emperors.* A History of Rhetoric, vol. 3. Princeton.

Khashan (1992)   H. Khashan. *Inside the Lebanese Confessional Mind.* Lanham, Md.

Kolb (1988) F. Kolb. "L'ideologia tetrarchica e la politica religiosa di Diocleziano." In Bonamente & Nestori (1988), 17–44.

Kraft (1954–55) K. Kraft. "Das Silbermedallion Constantins des Grossen mit dem Christus-monogramm auf der Helm." *Jahrbuch für Numismatik und Geldgeschichte* 5–6: 151–78.

Krautheimer (1983) R. Krautheimer. *Three Christian Capitals: Topography and Politics.* Berkeley.

Lacey (1974) W. K. Lacey. "Octavian in the Senate, January 27 B.C." *JRS* 64: 176–84.

Laistner (1951) M. L. W. Laistner. *Christianity and Pagan Culture in the Later Roman Empire.* Ithaca, N.Y.

Lambrechts (1953) P. Lambrechts. "La politique 'apollonienne' d'Auguste et le culte impérial." *La nouvelle Clio* 4/5: 65–82.

Lamoreaux (1995) J. Lamoreaux. "Episcopal Courts in Late Antiquity." *JECS* 3: 143–67.

Lane Fox (1987) Robin Lane Fox. *Pagans and Christians: Religion and the Religious Life from the Second to the Fourth Century A.D.* New York.

Laqueur (1929) R. Laqueur. *Eusebius als Historiker seiner Zeit.* Arbeiten zur Kirchengeschichte, no. 11. Berlin.

La Rocca (1992–93) E. La Rocca. "La fondazione di Costantinopoli." Bonamente & Fusco (1992–93), 2: 553–83.

Laursen & Nederman (1996) C. Laursen & C. Nederman, eds. *Difference and Dissent: Theories of Tolerance in Medieval and Early Modern Europe.* Lanham, Md.

Laursen & Nederman (1998) C. Laursen & C. Nederman, eds. *Beyond the Persecuting Society: Religious Toleration before the Enlightenment.* Philadelphia.

Lawlor (1912) H. J. Lawlor. *Eusebiana: Essays on the Ecclesiastical History of Eusebius, Bishop of Caesarea.* Oxford.

Leach (1973) E. Leach. "Melchisedech and the Emperor: Icons of Subversion and Orthodoxy." *Proceedings of the Royal Anthropological Institute, 1972* (London): 5–14.

Lecky (1865) W. E. H. Lecky. *The Rise of Rationalism in Europe.* 2 vols.

	London. Repr., New York, 1955. Citations are to pages of the reprint.
Leisegang (1926)	H. Leisegang. "Logos." *RE* 13, 1: 1035–81.
Lendon (1998)	J. E. Lendon. *Empire of Honour: The Art of Government in the Roman World.* Oxford.
Levick (1982)	B. Levick. "Propaganda and the Imperial Coinage." *Antichthon* 16: 104–16.
Lewis & Reinhold (1955)	N. Lewis & M. Reinhold, eds. *Roman Civilization.* 1st ed. 2 vols. New York.
Lewy (1983)	Y. Lewy. "Julian the Apostate and the Building of the Temple." *Jerusalem Cathedra* 3: 70–96. (Original Hebrew version published in *Zion* 6 [1941].)
Lichtenstein (1903)	A. Lichtenstein. *Eusebius von Nikomedien. Versuch einer Darstellung seiner Persönlichkeit und seines Lebens unter besonderer Berücksichtigung seiner Führerschaft im arianischen Streit.* Halle.
Liebeschuetz (1979)	J. H. W. G. Liebeschuetz. *Continuity and Change in Roman Religion.* Oxford.
Liebeschuetz (1981)	J. H. W. G. Liebeschuetz. "Religion in the Panegyrici Latini." In *Überlieferungsgeschichtliche Untersuchungen,* ed. F. Paschke et al., Texte und Untersuchungen, vol. 125, 389–98. Berlin.
Lieu & Montserrat (1998)	S. Lieu & D. Montserrat, eds. *Constantine: History, Historiography, and Legend.* London.
Lim (1995)	R. Lim. *Public Disputation, Power, and Social Order in Late Antiquity.* Berkeley.
Linder (1975)	A. Linder. "The Myth of Constantine the Great in the West: Sources and Hagiographic Commemoration." *Studi Medievali,* ser. 3, 16: 43–95.
Linder (1976)	A. Linder. "Ecclesia and Synagogue in the Medieval Myth of Constantine the Great." *Revue Belge du Philologie et d'Histoire* 54: 1019–60.
Lizzi (1987)	R. Lizzi. *Il potere episcopale nell' oriente romano: Rappresentazione ideologica e realtà politica (IV–V sec. d. C.)* Rome.

Lizzi (1989)   R. Lizzi. *Vescovi e strutture Ecclesiastiche nella Citta Tar-doantica: L'Italia Annonaria nel IV–V secolo d.C.* Biblioteca di Athenaeum 9. Como.

Lizzi (1990)   R. Lizzi. "Ambrose's Contemporaries and the Christianization of Northern Italy." *JRS* 80: 156–73.

Lo Cascio (1994)   E. Lo Cascio. "The Size of the Roman Population: Beloch and the Meaning of the Augustan Census Figures." *JRS* 84: 23–40.

Loenertz (1975)   R. J. Loenertz. "Actus Sylvestri: Genèse d'une légende." *RHE* 70: 426–39.

Logan (1992)   A. H. B. Logan. "Marcellus of Ancyra and the Councils of A.D. 325: Antioch, Ancyra and Nicaea." *JTS*, ser. 2, 43: 428–46.

l'Orange & Gerkan (1939)   H. P. l'Orange & A. von Gerkan. *Der Spätantike Bildschmuck des Konstantinsbogens.* Studien zur spätantiken Kunstgeschichte, 10. Berlin.

Louth (1990)   A. Louth. "The Date of Eusebius' Historia Ecclesiastica." *JTS*, n.s., 41: 111–23.

MacCormack (1975)   S. MacCormack. "Latin Prose Panegyric." In *Empire and Aftermath: Silver Latin II*, ed. T. Dorey, 143–205. London.

MacCormack (1976)   S. MacCormack. "Latin Prose Panegyrics: Tradition and Discontinuity in the Late Roman Empire." *Rev des Études Augustiniennes* 22: 29–77.

MacCormack (1981)   S. MacCormack. *Art and Ceremony in Late Antiquity.* Berkeley.

MacMullen (1966)   R. MacMullen. "A Note on Sermo Humilis." *JTS*, n.s., 17: 108–12.

MacMullen (1968)   R. MacMullen. "Constantine and the Miraculous." *GRBS* 9: 81–96.

MacMullen (1969)   R. MacMullen. *Constantine.* New York.

MacMullen (1974)   R. MacMullen. *Roman Social Relations, 50 B.C. to A.D. 284.* New Haven.

MacMullen (1976)   R. MacMullen. *Roman Government's Response to Crisis, A.D. 235–337.* New Haven.

MacMullen (1981)   R. MacMullen. *Paganism in the Roman Empire*. New Haven.

MacMullen (1984)   R. MacMullen. *Christianizing the Roman Empire: A.D. 100–400*. New Haven.

MacMullen (1986)   R. MacMullen. "Judicial Savagery in the Roman Empire." *Chiron* 16: 147–66; repr. in idem, *Changes in the Roman Empire*, 204–17. Princeton, 1990. Citations are to pages of the reprint.

MacMullen (1989)   R. MacMullen. "The Preacher's Audience (A.D. 350–400)." *JTS*, n.s., 40: 503–11.

MacMullen (1997)   R. MacMullen. *Christianity and Paganism in the Fourth to Eighth Centuries*. New Haven.

Maffei (1964)   D. Maffei. *La donazione di Costantino nei giuristi medievali*. Milan.

Magdalino (1994)   P. Magdalino, ed. *New Constantines: The Rhythm of Imperial Renewal in the East from Constantine the Great to Michael Palaiologos*. Society for the Promotion of Byzantine Studies, Publications, vol. 2. Leiden.

Maguinness (1932)   W. S. Maguinness. "Some Methods of the Latin Panegyrists." *Hermathena* 47: 42–61.

Malley (1978)   W. J. Malley. *Hellenism and Christianity: The Conflict between Hellenic and Christian Wisdom in the Contra Galilaeos of Julian the Apostate and the Contra Julianum of St. Cyril of Alexandria*. Analecta Gregoriana 110; Fac Theologiae Sectio B, ser. 68. Rome.

Malosse (1997)   J.-P. Malosse. "Libanius on Constantine Again." *Classical Quarterly* 47: 519–24.

Mann (1986)   M. Mann. *A History of Power from the Beginning to A.D. 1760*. Sources of Social Power, vol. 1. Cambridge.

Markus (1970)   R. A. Markus. *Saeculum: History and Society in the Theology of St. Augustine*. Cambridge.

Markus (1974)   R. A. Markus. "Paganism, Christianity, and the Latin Classics in the Fourth Century." In Binns (1974), 1–21.

Markus (1975)   R. A. Markus. "Church History and Early Church Historians." In *The Materials, Sources, and Methods of Ecclesiastical History,* ed. D. Baker, Studies in Church History 11, 1–17. Oxford.

Markus (1980)   R. A. Markus. "The Problem of Self-Definition: From Sect to Church." In Sanders (1980), 1–15.

Markus (1981)   R. A. Markus. "Christianity and Dissent in Roman North Africa: Changing Perspectives in Recent Work." In *Schism, Heresy, and Religious Protest,* ed. D. Baker, Studies in Church History 9, 21–36. Oxford.

Markus (1990)   R. A. Markus. *The End of Ancient Christianity.* Cambridge.

Martin (1982)   J.-P. Martin. *Providentia deorum: Recherches sur certains aspects religieux du Pouvoir impérial romain.* Coll. de l'École française de Rome, 61. Rome.

Martin (1991)   L. H. Martin. "The Pagan Religious Background." In *Early Christianity: Origins and Evolution to A.D. 600,* ed. I. Hazlett, 52–64. Nashville.

Martin (1996)   A. Martin. *Athanase d'Alexandrie et l'Eglise d'Egypte au IVe siècle (328–373).* Collection de l'École française de Rome 216. Rome, 1996.

Martinez &   G. Martinez Diez & F. Rodriguez, eds. *La coleccion*
Rodriguez (1987) *canonica Hispana, IV: Concilios Galos, concilios hispanos: primera parte.* Madrid.

Matthews (1967)   J. Matthews. "A Pious Supporter of Theodosius I: Maternus Cynegius." *JTS,* n.s., 18: 438–46.

Matthews (1989)   J. Matthews. *The Roman Empire of Ammianus.* London.

Mazzarino (1974)   S. Mazzarino. *Antico, tardantico ed era costantiniana.* Storia e civiltà, 13. Bari.

McCarthy (1957)   M. McCarthy. *Memories of a Catholic Girlhood.* New York.

McDonald (1975)   A. H. McDonald. "Theme and Style in Roman Historiography." *JRS* 65: 1–10.

McEwan (1934)   McEwan, C. W. *The Oriental Origin of Hellenistic Kingship.* Univ. Chicago Oriental Institute, Studies in Ancient Oriental Civilization, 13. Chicago.

McGiffert (1890)   A. C. McGiffert. "Prolegomena and Notes to the

Church History of Eusebius." In *A Select Library of Nicene and Post-Nicene Fathers of the Christian Church,* ed. P. Schaff and H. Wace, ser. 2, 1: 1–403. New York.

McLynn (1994)   N. McLynn. *Ambrose of Milan: Church and Court in a Christian Capital.* Berkeley.

Meigne (1975)   M. Meigne. "Concile ou collection d'Elvire?" *RHE* 70: 361–87.

Meredith (1980)   A. Meredith. "Porphyry and Julian against the Christians." *ANRW* 2, 23, 2: 1119–49.

Meyers & Sanders (1982)   B. F. Meyers & E. P. Sanders, eds. *Self-Definition in the Graeco-Roman World.* Jewish and Christian Self-Definition, vol. 3. London.

Meynell (1990)   H. A. Meynell, ed. *Grace, Politics, and Desire: Essays on Augustine.* Calgary.

Mill (1977)   J. S. Mill. "On Liberty" (1859). In *Collected Works of John Stuart Mill,* ed. J. M. Robson, 33 vols., 18: 213–310. Toronto.

Millar (1971)   F. Millar. "Paul of Samosata, Zenobia, and Aurelian: The Church, Local Culture, and Political Allegiance in Third Century Syria." *JRS* 61: 1–17.

Millar (1972)   F. Millar. "The Imperial Cult and the Persecutions." In *Le culte des souverains dans l'Empire romain,* ed. W. den Boer, Fond. Hardt, Entretiens, vol. 19, 143–65. Geneva.

Millar (1977)   F. Millar. *The Emperor in the Roman World (31 B.C.–A.D. 337)* Ithaca, N.Y.

Millar (1984a)   F. Millar. "The Political Character of the Classical Roman Republic, 200–151 B.C." *JRS* 74: 1–19.

Millar (1984b)   F. Millar. "State and Subject: The Impact of Monarchy." In Millar & Segal (1984), 37–60.

Millar (1998)   F. Millar. *The Crowd in Rome in the Late Republic.* Thomas Spencer Jerome Lectures, 22. Ann Arbor, Mich.

Millar & Segal (1984)   F. Millar & E. Segal, eds. *Caesar Augustus: Seven Aspects.* Oxford.

Miller (1994)	P. C. Miller. *Dreams in Late Antiquity: Studies in the Imagination of a Culture.* Princeton.
Momigliano (1963a)	A. Momigliano, ed. *The Conflict between Paganism and Christianity in the Fourth Century.* Oxford.
Momigliano (1963b)	A. Momigliano. "Pagan and Christian Historiography in the Fourth Century A.D." In Momigliano (1963a), 79–99.
Momigliano (1990)	A. Momigliano. "The Origins of Ecclesiastical Historiography." In idem, *The Classical Foundations of Modern Historiography,* 132–56. Berkeley.
Mommsen (1894)	T. Mommsen. "Firmicus Maternus." *Hermes* 29: 468–72.
Montgomery (1968)	H. Montgomery. "Konstantin, Paulus und das Lichtkreuz." *Symbolae Osloenses* 43: 84–109.
Mosca (1939)	G. Mosca. *The Ruling Class: Elementi di Scienza Politica.* Ed. A. Livingston, tr. H. D. Kahn. New York.
Müller-Rettig (1990)	B. Müller-Rettig. *Der Panegyricus des Jahres 310 auf Konstantin den Grossen.* Übersetzung und historisch-philologischer Kommentar. Palingenesia 31. Stuttgart.
Needleman & Baker (1979)	J. Needleman & G. Baker, eds. *Understanding the New Religions.* New York.
Neri (1971)	D. Neri. *Il S. Sepolcro riprodotto in Occidente.* Jerusalem.
Nicholson (1994)	O. Nicholson. "The 'Pagan Churches' of Maximinus Daia and Julian the Apostate." *JEH* 45: 1–10.
Nicolet (1991)	C. Nicolet. *Space, Geography, and Politics in the Early Roman Empire.* Ann Arbor, Mich.
Nilsson (1945)	M. P. Nilsson. "Pagan Divine Service in Late Antiquity." *HTR* 38: 63–9.
Nixon (1992)	R. M. Nixon. *Seize the Moment: America's Challenge in a One-Superpower World.* New York.
Nixon (1993)	C. E. V. Nixon. "Constantinus Oriens Imperator: Propaganda and Panegyric. On Reading Panegyric 7 (307)." *Historia* 42: 229–46.
Nixon & Rodgers (1994)	C. E. V. Nixon & B. Rodgers. *In Praise of Later Roman Emperors: The Panegyrici Latini.* Berkeley.

Works Cited

Nock (1930) A. D. Nock. "A Diis Electa: A Chapter in the Religious History of the Third Century." *HTR* 23: 251–74.

Nock (1933) A. D. Nock. *Conversion: The Old and the New in Religion from Alexander the Great to Augustine of Hippo.* Oxford.

Nock (1947) A. D. Nock. "The Emperor's Divine *Comes.*" *JRS* 37: 102–16.

Nock (1951) A. D. Nock. "Soter and Euergetes." In *The Joy of Study,* ed. S. Johnson, 127–48. New York.

Nock & Festugière (1954) A. D. Nock & A.-J. Festugière, eds. *Corpus Hermeticum.* 4 vols. Paris, 1954–60.

North (1992) J. North. "The Development of Religious Pluralism." In *The Jews among Pagans and Christians in the Roman Empire,* ed. Judith Lieu, T. Rajak, & J. North, 174–93. London.

Nulle (1959) S. H. Nulle. "Julian and the Men of Letters." *CJ* 54: 257–66.

Nulle (1961) S. H. Nulle. "Julian Redivivus." *Centennial Review* 5: 320–38.

Odahl (1995) C. Odahl. "The Christian Basilicas of Constantinian Rome." *Ancient World* 26: 1–26.

O'Donnell (1977) J. J. O'Donnell. "Paganus." *Classical Folia* 31: 163–69.

Orgels (1948) P. Orgels. "La première vision de Constantin (310) et le temple d'Apollon à Nîmes." *Academie Royale des Sciences, des Lettres et des Beaux Arts, Brussels, Classe des Lettres et des Sciences morales et politiques, Bulletin* 5, ser. 34: 176–208.

Orlandi (1975) T. Orlandi. "Sull' Apologia secunda (contra Arianos) di Atanasio di Alessandria." *Augustinianum* 15: 49–79.

Padovese (1992) L. Padovese. "Intolleranza e libertà religiosa nel IV secolo: alcune considerazioni." *Laurentianum* 33: 579–90.

Parkes (1964) J. Parkes. "Jews and Christians in the Constantinian Empire." In Dugmore & Duggan (1964), 1: 69–79.

Paschoud (1971) F. Paschoud. "Zosime 2,29 et la version païenne de la conversion de Constantin." *Historia* 20: 334–53.

Paschoud (1988)	F. Paschoud. "La Storia Augusta come testimonianza e riflesso della crisi d'identità degli ultimi intellettuali pagani in Occidente." In Bonamente & Nestori (1988), 155–68.
Paschoud (1990)	F. Paschoud. "L'intolérance chrétienne vue et jugée par les païens." *Cristianesimo nella storia* 11: 545–78.
Peeters (1944)	P. Peeters. "Comment S. Athanase s'enfuit de Tyr en 335." *Academie Royal des Sciences, des Lettres, et des Beaux-Arts de Belgique,* cl. let. sci. mor. pol. Bulletin, ser. 5, 30: 131–77.
Peeters (1945)	P. Peeters. "L'épilogue du Synode de Tyr en 335." *Analecta Bollandiana* 63: 131–44.
Pelikan (1985)	J. Pelikan. *Jesus through the Centuries: His Place in the History of Culture.* New York.
Penella (1990)	R. Penella. *Greek Philosophers and Sophists in the Fourth Century A. D.: Studies in Eunapius of Sardis.* ARCA Classical and Medieval Texts, Papers and Monographs, 28. Leeds.
Penella (1993)	R. Penella. "Julian the Persecutor in Fifth Century Church Historians." *Ancient World* 24: 31–43.
Peterson (1935)	E. Peterson. *Der Monotheismus als politisches Problem: ein Beitrag zur Geschichte der politischen Theologie im Imperium Romanum.* Leipzig.
Pettegree (1996)	A. Pettegree. "The Politics of Toleration in the Free Netherlands, 1572–1620." In Grell & Scribner (1996), 182–98.
Pezzela (1967)	S. Pezzela. "Massenzio e la politica religiosa di Costantino." *Studi e materiali di Storia delle Religioni* 38: 434–50.
Pharr (1952)	C. Pharr et al. *The Theodosian Code and Novels and the Sirmondian Constitutions.* Princeton.
Pierce (1989)	P. Pierce. "The Arch of Constantine: Propaganda and Ideology in Late Roman Art." *Art History* 12: 387–418.
Pietri (1976)	Charles Pietri. *Roma Christiana: Recherches sur l'église de Rome, son organization, sa politique, son idéologie, de Miltiade à Sixte III (311–440).* 2 vols. Bibl. des écoles françaises d'Athènes et de Rome, 224. Rome.

Piganiol (1932)   A. Piganiol. *L'Empereur Constantin*. Paris.

Pincherle (1929)   A. Pincherle. "La politica ecclesiastica di Massenzio." *Studi Italiani di filologia classica* 7: 131–43.

Pohlkamp (1988)   W. Pohlkamp. "Privilegium ecclesiae Romanae pontifici contulit: Zur Vorgeschichte der Konstantinischen Schenkung." In *Fälschungen in Mittelalter. Internationaler Kongress der Monumenta Germaniae Historica, München, 16.–19. September 1986.* 2: Gefälschte Rechtstexte—Der bestrafte Fälscher, 413–90. Hannover.

Pohlkamp (1992)   W. Pohlkamp. "Textfassungen, literarische Formen und geschichtliche Funktionen der römischen Silvester-Akten." *Francia* 19: 115–96.

Pohlsander (1984)   H. Pohlsander. "Crispus: Brilliant Career and Tragic End." *Historia* 33: 79–106.

Portmann (1990)   W. Portmann. "Zu den motiven der diokletianischen Christenverfolgung." *Historia* 39: 212–48.

Potter (1994)   D. Potter. *Prophets and Emperors: Human and Divine Authority from Augustus to Theodosius.* Cambridge, Mass.

Previale (1949–50)   L. Previale. "Teoria e prassi del panegirico Bizantino." *Emerita* 17: 72–105; 18: 340–66.

Price (1980)   S. R. F. Price. "Between Man and God: Sacrifice in the Roman Imperial Cult." *JRS* 70: 28–43.

Price (1984)   S. R. F. Price. *Rituals and Power: The Roman Imperial Cult in Asia Minor.* Cambridge.

Price (1987)   S. R. F. Price. "The Future of Dreams: From Freud to Artemidorus." *Past and Present,* no. 28: 8–31.

Pritchard (1969)   J. Pritchard, ed. *Ancient Near Eastern Texts Relating to the Old Testament.* 3d ed. Princeton.

Quasten (1950)   J. Quasten. *Patrology.* 3 vols. Utrecht.

Raaflaub & Toher (1990)   K. Raaflaub & M. Toher, eds. *Between Republic and Empire: Interpretations of Augustus and His Principate.* Berkeley.

Rabello (1970)   A. M. Rabello. "I privilegi dei chieriche sotto Costantino." *Labeo* 16: 384–92.

Rambo (1993)   L. R. Rambo. *Understanding Religious Conversion.* New Haven.

Ramsay (1925)   A. M. Ramsay. "The Speed of the Roman Imperial Post." *JRS* 15: 60–74.

Rapp (1998)   C. Rapp. "Imperial Ideology in the Making: Eusebius of Caesarea on Constantine as 'Bishop.'" *JTS,* n.s., 49: 685–95.

Razavi & Ambuel   M. Razavi & D. Ambuel, eds. *Philosophy, Religion, and*
(1997)   *the Question of Intolerance.* Albany, N.Y.

Remer (1998)   G. Remer. "Ha-Me'iri's Theory of Religious Toleration." In Laursen & Nederman (1998), 71–91.

Richardson (1890)   E. C. Richardson. "Prolegomena and Notes to the Life of Constantine by Eusebius." In *A Select Library of Nicene and Post-Nicene Fathers of the Christian Church,* ed. P. Schaff and H. Wace, ser. 2, 1: 404–559. New York.

Richardson (1953)   C. C. Richardson, ed. *Early Christian Fathers.* Library of Christian Classics, vol. 1. Philadelphia.

Riddle (1931)   D. W. Riddle. *The Martyrs: A Study in Social Control.* Chicago.

Robbins (1989)   G. A. Robbins. "'Fifty Copies of the Sacred Writings' (VC 4:36): Entire Bibles or Gospel Books?" *Studia Patristica* 19: 91–98.

Robinson (1993)   T. Robinson. "Oracles and Their Society: Social Realities As Reflected in the Oracles of Claros and Didyma." In White (1993a), 59–77.

Rodgers (1980)   B. Rodgers. "Constantine's Pagan Vision." *Byzantion* 50: 259–78.

Rossignol (1845)   J.-P. Rossignol. *Virgile et Constantin le Grand.* vol. 1. Paris. (No subsequent volumes ever appeared.)

Roueché (1984)   C. M. Roueché. "Acclamations in the Roman Empire." *JRS* 74: 181–88.

Rousseau (1994)   P. Rousseau. *Basil of Caesarea.* Berkeley.

Rousselle (1997)   A. Rousselle. "Aspects sociaux du recrutement ecclésiastique au IVe siècle." *Mélanges d'archéologie et d'histoire: Antiquité* 89: 333–77.

Rubenson (1990)   S. Rubenson. *The Letters of St. Anthony: Origenist Theology, Monastic Tradition, and the Making of a Saint.* Bibliotheca historico-ecclesiastica Lundensis 24. Lund, Sweden.

Rubin (1970)   Jerry Rubin. *Do It: Scenarios of the Revolution.* New York.

Ruggini (1977)   L. Cracco Ruggini. "The Ecclesiastical Histories and the Pagan Historiography: Providence and Miracles." *Athenaeum,* n.s., 55: 107–26.

Saller (1982)   R. P. Saller. *Personal Patronage under the Early Empire.* Cambridge.

Salmon (1990)   J. H. M. Salmon. "Clovis and Constantine: The Uses of History in Sixteenth-Century Gallicanism." *JEH* 41: 584–605.

Salvatorelli (1928)   L. Salvatorelli. "La politica religiosa e la religiosità di Costantino." *Richerche Religiose* 4: 289–328.

Salzman (1987)   M. Salzman. "Superstitio and the Persecution of Pagans in the Codex Theodosianus." *Vigiliae Christianae* 41: 172–88.

Salzman (1990)   M. Salzman. *On Roman Time: The Codex-Calendar of 354 and the Rhythms of Urban Life in Late Antiquity.* Berkeley.

Sanders (1980)   E. P. Sanders et al., eds. *Jewish and Christian Self-Definition.* Vol. 1: *The Shaping of Christianity in the Second and Third Centuries.* London.

Schattschneider (1960)   E. Schattschneider. *The Semisovereign People: A Realist's View of Democracy in America.* New York.

Schmitz (1997)   T. Schmitz. *Bildung und Macht: Zur sozialen und politischen Funktion der zweiten Sophistik in der griechischen Welt der Kaiserzeit.* Munich.

Schoenebeck (1939)   H. von Schoenebeck. *Beiträge zur Religionspolitik des Maxentius und Constantin.* Klio Beiheft 43, n.s. 30. Leipzig.

Schwartz (1907)   E. Schwartz. "Eusebius of Caesarea." *RE* 4, 1: 1370–1439.

Schwartz (1908)   E. Schwartz. Review of J. M. Pfättisch. *Deutsche Liter-
                      aturseitung* 29: 3096–99.

Scott (1924)   W. Scott, ed. and tr. *Hermetica: The Ancient Greek and
                      Latin Writings Which Contain Religious or Philosophic
                      Teachings Ascribed to Hermes Trismegistus.* 4 vols.
                      Oxford.

Scott (1932)   S. P. Scott, ed. and tr. *The Civil Law, Including the Twelve
                      Tables, the Institutes of Gaius, the Rules of Ulpian, the
                      Opinions of Paulus, the Enactments of Justinian, and the
                      Constitutions of Leo.* 17 vols. Cincinnati.

Scribner (1996)   Bob Scribner. "Preconditions of Tolerance and Intol-
                      erance in Sixteenth-Century Germany." In Grell &
                      Scribner (1996), 32–47.

Seeck (1919)   O. Seeck. *Regesten der Kaiser und Päpste für die Jahre
                      311 bis 476 n. Chr.* Stuttgart.

Seeck (1921)   O. Seeck. *Geschichte des Untergangs der antiken Welt,*
                      4th ed. 6 vols. Stuttgart.

Segal (1990)   A. Segal. *Paul the Convert: The Apostolate and Apostasy
                      of Saul the Pharisee.* New Haven.

Selb (1967)   W. Selb. "Episcopalis audientia von der Zeit Konstan-
                      tins bis zur Nov. XXXV Valentinians III." *Zeitschrift der
                      Savigny-Stiftung für Rechtgeschichte* 97, romanistische
                      Abteilung 84: 162–217.

Seston (1936)   W. Seston. "La vision païenne de 310 et les origines du
                      chrisme constantinien." *Annuaire de l'Institut de Phi-
                      lologie et d'Histoire Orientale (Mél F. Cumont)* 4: 373–95.

Seston (1947)   W. Seston. "Constantine as a 'Bishop.'" *JRS* 37: 127–
                      31.

Shaw (1998)   T. M. Shaw. "Askesis and the Appearance of Holiness."
                      JECS 6: 485–99.

Shepherd (1967)   M. Shepherd Jr. "Liturgical Expressions of the Con-
                      stantinian Triumph." *DOP* 21: 59–78.

Shepherd (1968)   M. Shepherd Jr. "Before and After Constantine." In
                      Braner (1968), 17–28.

Shiels (1984)   W. J. Shiels, ed. *Persecution and Toleration.* Studies in
                      Church History, vol. 21. Oxford.

Sickle (1939)   C. Van Sickle. "The Changing Base of Roman Imperial Power in the Third Century A.D." *Antiquité Classique* 8: 153–70.

Simmons (1995)   M. Simmons. *Arnobius of Sicca: Religious Conflict and Competition in the Age of Diocletian.* Oxford.

Sivan (1988)   H. Sivan. "Who Was Egeria?: Piety and Pilgrimage in the Age of Gratian." *HTR* 81: 59–72.

Small (1996)   A. Small, ed. *Subject and Ruler: The Cult of the Ruling Power in Classical Antiquity.* JRA suppl. 17. Ann Arbor, Mich.

Smelser (1962)   N. Smelser. *The Theory of Collective Behavior.* New York.

Smith (1988)   H. Smith. *The Power Game: How Washington Works.* New York.

Smith (1989)   M. Smith. "Eusebius of Caesarea: Scholar and Apologist: A Study of His Religious Terminology and Its Application to the Emperor Constantine." Ph.D. diss., Univ. Calif., Santa Barbara.

Smith (1995)   R. Smith. *Julian's Gods: Religion and Philosophy in the Thought and Action of Julian the Apostate.* New York.

Smith (1997)   R. R. R. Smith, "The Public Image of Licinius I: Portrait Sculpture and Imperial Ideology in the Early Fourth Century." *JRS* 87: 170–202.

Smith, C. (1989)   C. Smith. "Christian Rhetoric in Eusebius's Panegyric at Tyre." *Vigiliae Christianae* 43: 226–47.

Spiegl (1971)   J. Spiegl. "Eine Kritik an Kaiser Konstantin in der Vita Constantini des Euseb." *Wegzeichen, Festgabe H. Biedermann,* 83–94. Würzburg.

Spira (1989)   A. Spira. "The Impact of Christianity on Ancient Rhetoric." *Studia Patristica* 18, 2: 137–53.

Stark (1987)   R. Stark. "How New Religions Succeed: A Theoretical Model." In Bromley and Hammond (1987), 11–29.

Stark (1993)   R. Stark. "Epidemics, Networks, and the Rise of Christianity." In White (1993a), 159–75.

Stark (1996)   R. Stark. *The Rise of Christianity: A Sociologist Reconsiders History.* Princeton.

Stark & Bainbridge (1985) R. Stark & W. Bainbridge. *The Future of Religion: Secularization, Revival, and Cult Formation.* Berkeley.

Ste. Croix (1954) G. E. M. de Ste. Croix. "Aspects of the 'Great' Persecution." *HTR* 47: 75–113.

Ste. Croix (1981) G. E. M. de Ste. Croix. *The Class Struggle in the Ancient Greek World: From the Archaic Age to the Arab Conquests.* Ithaca, N.Y.

Steinwenter (1946) A. Steinwenter. "NOMOS EMPSUXOS: Zur Geschichte einer politischen Theorie." *Anzeiger der Akademie der Wissenschaften in Wien,* Phil.-Hist. Kl. 83: 250–68.

Stevenson (1929) J. Stevenson. *Studies in Eusebius.* Cambridge.

Stevenson (1957) J. Stevenson. *A New Eusebius: Documents Illustrative of the History of the Church to A.D. 337.* London.

Stockton (1975) D. Stockton. "Christianos ad Leonem." In *The Ancient Historian and His Materials: Essays in Honour of C. E. Stevens,* ed. B. Levick: 199–212. Westmead.

Stoops (1993) R. F. Stoops Jr. "Christ as Patron in the Acts of Peter." In White (1993a), 143–57.

Storch (1970) R. Storch. "The Trophy and the Cross: Pagan and Christian Symbolism in the Fourth and Fifth Centuries." *Byzantion* 40: 105–117.

Straub (1939) J. Straub. *Vom Herrscherideal in der Spätantike.* Stuttgart.

Straub (1957) J. Straub. "Kaiser Konstantin als ἐπίοκοπος τῶν ἐκτός." *Studia Patristica* 2, 1: 678–95.

Straub (1967) J. Straub. "Constantine as KOINOS EPISKOPOS: Tradition and Innovation in the Representation of the First Christian Emperor's Majesty." *DOP* 21: 39–55.

Stroumsa (1993) G. Stroumsa. "Le radicalisme religièux du christianisme ancien." In *Les retours aux Ecritures: fondamentalismes presents et passés,* ed. A. Le Boulluec & E. Patlagean, Bibliothèque de l'École des hautes etudes, Section des sciences religieuses, 99: 357–82. Louvain.

Stroumsa (1994) G. Stroumsa. "Early Christianity as Radical Religion." *Israel Oriental Studies* 14: 173–93.

Suberbiola (1987) J. Suberbiola Martinez. *Nuevos concilios Hispano-*

Romanos de los siglos III y IV: La coleccion de Elvira. Malaga.

Sugars (1997)   J. M. Sugars. "Themistius' Seventh Oration: Text, Translation, and Commentary." Ph.D. diss., Univ. of California, Irvine.

Sutherland (1967)   C. H. V. Sutherland. *Diocletian and the Tetrarchy.* Roman Imperial Coinage, vol. 6. London.

Syme (1939)   R. Syme. *The Roman Revolution.* Oxford.

Syme (1971)   R. Syme. *Emperors and Biography.* Oxford.

Syme (1978)   R. Syme. "Propaganda in the Historia Augusta." *Latomus* 37: 173–92.

Szemler (1972)   G. J. Szemler. *The Priests of the Roman Republic: A Study of Interactions between Priesthoods and Magistracies.* Coll. Latomus 127. Brussels.

Tabbernee (1997)   W. Tabbernee. "Eusebius' 'Theology of Persecution': As Seen in the Various Editions of His Church History." *JECS* 5: 319–34.

Taeger (1957)   F. Taeger. *Charisma: Studien zur Geschichte des antiken Herrschenkultes.* Stuttgart.

Taft (1925)   W. H. Taft. *Our Chief Magistrate and His Powers.* New York.

Talbert (1984)   R. Talbert. *The Senate of Imperial Rome.* Princeton.

Taylor (1993)   J. E. Taylor. *Christians and the Holy Places: The Myth of Jewish-Christian Origins.* Oxford.

Teall (1967)   J. Teall. "The Age of Constantine: Change and Continuity in Administration and Economy." *DOP* 21: 13–36.

Tilley (1990)   M. A. Tilley. "Scripture as an Element of Social Control: Two Martyr Stories of Christian North Africa." *HTR* 83: 383–97.

Tocqueville (1835–40)   A. de Tocqueville. *Democracy in America.* Tr. Henry Reeve. 2 vols. London.

Toynbee & Ward-Perkins (1958)   J. Toynbee & J. Ward-Perkins. *The Shrine of St. Peter and the Vatican Excavations.* New York.

Trompf (1983)   G. W. Trompf. "The Logic of Retribution in Eusebius of Caesarea." In Croke & Emmett (1983), 132–46.

Turchetti (1991)   M. Turchetti. "Religious Concord and Political Tolerance in Sixteenth- and Seventeenth-Century France." *Sixteenth Century Journal* 22: 15–26.

Turpin (1991)   W. Turpin. "Imperial Subscriptions and the Administration of Justice." *JRS* 81: 101–18.

Usener (1905)   H. Usener. "Sol Invictus." *Rhein. Mus. für Phil.* 60: 465–91.

Vance (1997)   N. Vance. *The Victorians and Ancient Rome.* Oxford.

Van Dam (1985)   R. Van Dam. "From Paganism to Christianity at Late Antique Gaza." *Viator* 16: 1–20.

Vanderspoel (1990)   J. Vanderspoel. "The Background to Augustine's Denial of Religious Plurality." In Meynell (1990), 179–93.

Vanderspoel (1995)   J. Vanderspoel. *Themistius and the Imperial Court: Oratory, Civic Duty, and Paideia from Constantius to Theodosius.* Ann Arbor, Mich.

Vessey (1993)   M. Vessey. "The Origins of the Collection Sirmondiana: A New Look at the Evidence." In Harries & Wood (1993), 178–99.

Vincent (1913)   L.-H. Vincent. "Quelques representations antiques du Saint-Sepulchres constantinien." *Revue Biblique,* n.s., 10: 525–46.

Vivian (1994)   T. Vivian, tr. *Athanasius, Life of Antony.* Society of Coptic Church Studies, Coptic Church Review 15. Lebanon, Pa.

Voltaire (1912)   Voltaire. *Toleration and Other Essays.* Tr. Joseph McCabe. New York.

Walker (1990)   P. W. L. Walker. *Holy City, Holy Places?: Christian Attitudes to Jerusalem and the Holy Land in the Fourth Century.* Oxford.

Wallace-Hadrill   D. S. Wallace-Hadrill. *Eusebius of Caesarea.* London.
(1960)

Wallace-Hadrill   A. Wallace-Hadrill. "The Emperor and His Virtues."
(1981)   *Historia* 30: 298–323.

Wallace-Hadrill (1982)	A. Wallace-Hadrill. "*Civilis Princeps*: Between Citizen and King." *JRS* 72: 32–48.
Wallace-Hadrill (1989)	A. Wallace-Hadrill, ed. *Patronage in Ancient Society.* New York.
Wallace-Hadrill (1993)	A. Wallace-Hadrill. *Augustan Rome.* Bristol.
Wallis (1972)	R. T. Wallis. *Neoplatonism.* London.
Walsh (1986)	M. Walsh. *The Triumph of the Meek: Why Early Christianity Succeeded.* San Francisco.
Walter (1970)	C. Walter. *L'iconographie des conciles dans la tradition byzantine.* Paris, Institut français d'études byzantines.
Wardman (1982)	A. Wardman. *Religion and Statecraft among the Romans.* London.
Ward-Perkins (1966)	J. B. Ward-Perkins. "Memoria, Martyr's Tomb, and Martyr's Church." *JTS,* n.s., 17: 20–37.
Warmington (1985)	B. H. Warmington. "The Sources of Some Constantinian Documents in Eusebius' Ecclesiastical History and Life of Constantine." *Studia Patristica* 18, 1: 93–98.
Warmington (1988)	B. H. Warmington. "Did Constantine Have Religious Advisers?" *Studia Patristica* 19: 117–29.
Warmington (1998)	B. H. Warmington. "Eusebius of Caesarea and the Governance of Constantine." In Hillard (1998), 2: 266–79.
Webb (1981)	D. M. Webb. "The Truth about Constantine: History, Hagiography, and Confusion." In *Religion and Humanism,* ed. K. Robbins, Studies in Church History 17: 85–102. Oxford.
Wheelock (1990)	A. K. Wheelock et al. *Anthony van Dyck.* Washington, D.C.
White (1993a)	M. L. White, ed. *Social Networks in the Early Christian Environment: Issues and Methods for Social History.* Semeia 56.
White (1993b)	M. L. White. "Social Networks: Theoretical Orientation and Historical Applications." In White (1993a), 23–36.

White (1993c) M. L. White. "Finding the Ties That Bind: Issues from Social Description." In White (1993a), 3–22.

Wiemer (1994) H.-U. Wiemer. "Libanius on Constantine." *Classical Quarterly* 44: 511–24.

Wiles (1962) M. F. Wiles. "In Defense of Arius." *JTS*, n.s., 13: 339–47.

Wiles (1996) M. F. Wiles. *Archetypal Heresy: Arianism through the Centuries*. Oxford.

Wilhelm (1986) R. Wilhelm. "Apollo, Sol, and Caesar: Triumvirate of Order." *Augustan Age* 5: 60–75.

Wilken (1979) R. L. Wilken. "Pagan Criticism of Christianity: Greek Religion and Christian Faith." In *Early Christian Literature and the Classical Intellectual Tradition . . . In Honor of R. M. Grant,* ed. idem & W. Schoedele, Theol. Hist. 53: 117–34. Paris.

Wilken (1983) R. L. Wilken. *John Chrysostom and the Jews: Rhetoric and Reality in the Late Fourth Century.* Berkeley.

Wilken (1992a) R. L. Wilken. "Eusebius and the Christian Holy Land." In Attridge & Hata (1992), 736–60.

Wilken (1992b) R. L. Wilken. *The Land Called Holy: Palestine in Christian History and Thought.* New Haven.

Williams (1951) G. H. Williams. "Christology and Church-State Relations in the Fourth Century." *Church History* 20, 3: 3–33; cont'd 20, 4: 3–25.

Williams (1985) S. Williams. *Diocletian and the Roman Recovery.* New York.

Williams (1987) R. Williams. *Arius.* London.

Williams (1989a) R. Williams, ed. *The Making of Orthodoxy: Essays in Honour of Henry Chadwick.* Cambridge.

Williams (1989b) R. Williams. "Does It Make Sense to Speak of Pre-Nicene Orthodoxy?" In Williams (1989a), 1–23.

Williams (1998) D. H. Williams. "Constantine, Nicaea, and the 'Fall' of the Church." In Ayres & Jones (1998), 117–36.

Wilpert (1903)   J. Wilpert. *Die Malereien der Katakomben Roms.* Freiburg im Breisgau.

Wilpert (1924)   J. Wilpert. *Die römischen Mosaiken und Malereien der kirchlichen Bauten vom IV. bis. XIII. Jahrhundert.* 3. Aufl. Freiburg im Breisgau.

Wilson (1987)   B. Wilson. "Factors in the Failure of the New Religious Movements." In Bromley & Hammond (1987), 30–45.

Winkelmann (1961)   F. Winkelmann. "Konstantins Religionspolitik und ihre Motive im Urteil der literarischen Quellen des 4. und 5. Jhrdts." *Acta Antiqua* 9: 239–56.

Winkelmann (1962)   F. Winkelmann. "Zur Geschichte des Authentizitätsproblems der Vita Constantini." *Klio* 40: 187–243.

Winkelmann (1975)   F. Winkelmann, ed. *Über das Leben des Kaisers Konstantins. Eusebius Werke,* I, 1. Berlin.

Winkelmann (1978)   F. Winkelmann. "Das hagiographische Bild Konstantins I. in mittelbyzantinischer Zeit." In *Beiträge zur byzantinische Geschichte im IX.–XI. Jht. Akten des Colloquiums . . . Liblice, 20–23 Sept 1977,* ed. V. Vavrinek, 179–203. Prague.

Wiseman (1981)   T. P. Wiseman. "Practice and Theory in Roman Historiography." *History,* 2d ser., 66: 375–93.

Wolfe (1948)   B. Wolfe. *Three Who Made a Revolution: A Biographical History.* New York.

Woods (1992)   D. Woods. "Two Notes on the Great Persecution." *JTS,* n.s., 43: 128–34.

Woods (1997)   D. Woods. "Where Did Constantine I Die?" *JTS,* n.s., 48: 531–35.

Woods (1998)   D. Woods. "On the Death of the Empress Fausta." *Greece & Rome* 45 (April): 70–86.

Woollcott (1922)   A. Woollcott. *Shouts and Murmurs: Echoes of a Thousand and One First Nights.* New York.

Wortley (1992)   J. Wortley. "The Spirit of Rivalry in Early Christian Monachism." *GRBS* 33: 383–404.

Yarnold (1993)   E. J. Yarnold. "The Baptism of Constantine." *Studia Patristica* 26: 95–101.

Young (1983)   F. Young. *From Nicaea to Chalcedon: A Guide to the Literature and Its Background.* Philadelphia.

Zanker (1988)   P. Zanker. *The Power of Images in the Age of Augustus.* Tr. Alan Shapiro. Ann Arbor, Mich.

Index

ANCIENT SOCIETY AND HISTORY

The series Ancient Society and History offers books, relatively brief in compass, on selected topics in the history of ancient Greece and Rome, broadly conceived, with a special emphasis on comparative and other nontraditional approaches and methods. The series, which includes both works of synthesis and works of original scholarship, is aimed at the widest possible range of specialist and non-specialist readers.

Library of Congress Cataloging-in-Publication Data

Drake, H. A. (Harold Allen), 1942–
    Constantine and the bishops : the politics of intolerance / H. A.
Drake.
        p.   cm. — (Ancient society and history)
    Includes bibliographical references and index.
    ISBN 0-8018-6218-3 (alk. paper)
    1. Constantine I, Emperor of Rome, d. 337—Religion.
    2. Athanasius, Saint, Patriarch of Alexandria, d. 373—Relations
with Constantine I.   3. Church history—Primitive and early church,
ca. 30–600—Political aspects.   4. Paganism—Rome.   5. Tolerance—
Rome.   6. Religion and state—Rome.   I. Title.   II. Series.
DG315.D72   2000
270.2′092—dc21   99-31865
                                                                              CIP